Conversations

on Art

and Performance

PAJ BOOKS

Bonnie Marranca

Gautam Dasgupta

Series Editors

Conversations

on Art

and Performance

Edited by Bonnie Marranca
and Gautam Dasgupta

A PAJ BOOK
The Johns Hopkins University Press
Baltimore and London

© 1999 The Johns Hopkins University Press
All rights reserved. Published 1999
Printed in the United States of America
on acid-free paper
9 8 7 6 5 4 3 2 1

The Johns Hopkins University Press
2715 North Charles Street
Baltimore, Maryland 21218-4363
www.press.jhu.edu

Library of Congress Cataloging-in-Publication Data
will be found at the end of this book.
A catalog record for this book is available
from the British Library.
ISBN 0-8018-5924-7
ISBN 0-8018-5925-5 (pbk.)

All of the conversations have been reprinted from
Performing Arts Journal (1976–98), except "Performance
and the Body" (Carolee Schneemann), "Personal
History" (Rachel Rosenthal), "Acting and Nonacting"
(Ruth Maleczech et al.), and "United States" (Laurie
Anderson), which originally appeared in another PAJ
publication, *Performance Art*, renamed *LIVE* (1979–82).

Note: All headnotes written by Bonnie Marranca: BGM;
all headnotes written by Gautam Dasgupta: GD.

To the memory of Ross Wetzsteon (1932–98),
Village Voice editor and critic,
for his enduring commitment
to the experimental arts in New York

Contents

Preface: Aural History | ix

ART AND ITS AUDIENCE

Art and Consciousness *Susan Sontag* | 2

Art and the Imagery of Extinction *Robert Jay Lifton* | 10

Theatre in America *Harold Clurman, Stanley Kauffmann* | 26

The Play of Thought *Herbert Blau* | 44

The Politics of Reception *Johannes Birringer, Bonnie Marranca, Gerald Rabkin* | 76

Radicalizing the Classics *Julian Beck, Judith Malina* | 102

Art in the Culture *John Cage, Richard Foreman, Richard Kostelanetz* | 114

The Modernism/Postmodernism Debate *Hilton Kramer* | 128

Criticism, Culture, and Performance *Edward Said* | 148

Interpretation and the Work of Art *Umberto Eco, Robert Wilson* | 170

WRITERS AND COMPOSERS

The Theatre of History *Charles L. Mee* | 182

Composing for the Opera *Philip Glass* | 194

Figure of Speech *Mac Wellman* | 206

Poet in the Theatre *John Ashbery* | 216

The American Playwright *Gautam Dasgupta, Michael Earley, Bonnie Marranca* | 230

Playwrights Making Movies *John Guare, David Mamet, Wallace Shawn, Steve Tesich, Michael Weller* | 248

Music and Theatre *Richard Peaslee, Stanley Silverman* | 274

The Playwright as Director *Maria Irene Fornes* | 288

Theatre and the Ridiculous *Charles Ludlam* | 296

Bodies of Work

The Politics of Representation *Elinor Fuchs, Bonnie Marranca, Gerald Rabkin* | 310

Performance and the Body *Carolee Schneemann* | 330

Personal History *Rachel Rosenthal* | 338

Making Dances *Trisha Brown, Douglas Dunn* | 344

The Mind of Dance *Kenneth King* | 352

Liminal Performance *Gary Hill* | 360

Environmental Theatre *Jerry Rojo* | 384

Acting and Nonacting *Laurie Anderson, Scott Burton, Elizabeth LeCompte, Ruth Maleczech, Michael Smith* | 394

Reminiscences of a Dance Critic *Edwin Denby* | 410

A Lifetime of Dance *Bessie Schoenberg* | 420

La MaMa and the American Theatre *Ellen Stewart* | 432

The Search for a Universal Grammar *Joseph Chaikin* | 442

Interculturalism and Performance *Lee Breuer* | 452

Working with Puppets *Bruce D. Schwartz, Theodora Skipitares, Julie Taymor* | 460

United States *Laurie Anderson* | 472

Performance Strategies *Richard Elovich, Karen Finley, Ishmael Houston-Jones, John Kelly* | 480

The Real Charles Atlas *Charles Atlas* | 492

Preface: *Aural History*

ALL OF THE SELECTIONS in *Conversations on Art and Performance* originally appeared either in the pages of *Performing Arts Journal,* which began in 1976, or in *Performance Art* magazine (later called *LIVE*), published by PAJ from 1979–1982. This volume serves then not only as a publishing history of *PAJ*, founded by Gautam Dasgupta and me twenty-two years ago, but also as a history of the "downtown" arts scene in New York, starting from the mid-seventies and continuing to the closing years of the twentieth century. The performers, playwrights, filmmakers, composers, critics, and scholars whose contrapuntal voices distinguish its timbre of ideas have generated together as an arts community the intellectual energy around which the important art and cultural issues of our time circulate. There is a special reason for this: virtually all of them made, if not began, their careers in New York, where they were obliged over the years to acknowledge and participate in the city's ongoing artistic ferment and critical scrutiny.

The historical eras that frame their dialogue are the period between the two world wars, the postwar period of experimentation extending through the seventies, and arts activity at the edge of the millennium. This continuity of styles and movements shapes both artistic practice and the commentary on it across art forms, generations, and cultures, easing the articulation of thoughts that have the most urgency for artists, critics, the public, and arts institutions. New York has had historical links to European modernism, which is the reference point for several generations of American artists and intellectuals who converse here, whether in terms of its impact on them or their attempts to break away from it. Germany and France, in particular, and Russia, have been prominent, not only for their extraordinary contributions in performance and the visual arts but also due to the pervasiveness of exiles and emigrants from these countries who settled in the U.S. to teach or work, many staying on after the war. Japan, as the artists' own words attest, has been a major source of inspiration, aesthetic and philosophical, outside the Western tradition, affecting all avant-garde art experiments, especially performance, in the last half century.

What is most surprising, even more so to be applauded, is the large number of participants in this volume who are still active and influential in their chosen fields, some of them speaking from a point early on in their careers, others at mid-career, still others looking back. Many of their topics of concern anticipated contemporary thought in ways that now seem prophetic, and subjects that were once the provenance of art in recent years have come to the forefront of American social thought and cultural policy. Though the twentieth century is marked by great artistic output and innovation, the spheres of influence spoken of are easily contained, for in so many of these conversations the artists and thinkers referred to as touchstones of ideas and ideals are repeated over and over: in theatre—Ibsen, Strindberg, Chekhov, Stanislavsky, Pirandello, Stein, Brecht, Beckett, Artaud, Genet, Grotowski, Brook, Williams, Shepard; in visual art—expressionism, surrealism, Duchamp, Picasso, Pollock; in music—Mozart, Wagner, Stravinsky, Weill, Boulez, Cage; in dance—Balanchine, Graham, Cunningham, Judson Dance Theatre; in philosophy—Marx, Freud, Wittgenstein, Foucault; in letters—Thoreau, Rousseau, Yeats, Pound, Eliot, Barthes. And always, the Greeks and Shakespeare.

In any given period serving as a context for discussion, a marked consensus flows around what is important to speak of, and why. Remarkably, and for the most part, traditionalists and avant-gardists claim the same artistic heritage. What emerges are the intellectual rigor and high standards, and commitment to the search for new artistic and critical languages, of these speakers reflected in their demands on themselves, on artworks, and the public. A persistent theme coursing through the volume is the devolution of critical commentary into a form of publicity or its subservience to ideology, mindful of the consequences of this situation on art and its audiences.

The antidote to either of these conditions is the example of how much artists learn from each other and how essential aesthetic values and their own work processes are to them. In every sense, the historical continuum their chosen art form inhabits still retains its significance. If the Western canon has been under assault in the university and in arts institutions, the artists themselves unashamedly declare allegiance to surprisingly stable canons. For all the theory pouring out of universities and impacting academic criticism and journalistic opinion, the artists and intellectuals inspired by their constant exposure to art largely disregard it, educating themselves, as always, in artworks. What is the nature of the performance act? Where does language reside? Performers are still struggling to understand the ecstasy of presence, writers desperately want to live inside words, and everyone is concerned with the varieties of Time.

What is it that they speak of? In the early years of *Performing Arts Journal,* major preoccupations were consciousness and process, the potentiality of performance space, invention and experimentation, the divorce of literary and theatrical culture and the alienation of theatre from intellectual life, the decline of playwriting and the stultification of regional theatres, the discomfort with the notion of the "theatrical" in art and theatre worlds, the rise of performance art and art as entertainment. There were plenty of inquiries: What is the nature of performance space? How does one see? Why is acting not the same as performing? Is art an image or an object? Over the years the conversations turned from space to text and narrative to fragment, from the modernist heritage to postmodernism, from group to solo, from art forms to arts funding, from the situation of the object to subject positions, from process to pedagogy, from art to culture. Power, representation, transgression, violence, ritual, gender, race, autobiography, censorship, and the critiques of representation, the image, and the canon were now subjects that filled the new dictionaries of ideas, received or otherwise.

At the center of thought: the palpable body, the mediated voice. When is a man a woman? When is the body a text? The emphasis shifted from experience to interpretation, from art to theory, from the personal to the political, from high culture to pop, from invention to anger. Increasingly, performance space came to be regarded as public space, and the individual as social construct. The body, once celebrated as the site of pleasure and freedom, was now analyzed as a repository of disease, pain, death, and contested being, all of them powerful themes which raise disturbing epistemological questions about the ever-expanding lyric of performance and aging avant-garde.

Representations of the body reveal all the recent upheavals in attitude towards myth, history, culture, and political systems. In the last two decades, sweeping social movements, a changing economy, AIDS and other health controversies, the threat of cold or nuclear war, ecological crises, technological advancement, and the globalization of all manner of human activity in a post-communist world have left no one unperturbed. We have seen the English language, and American media and ways of doing business, come to dominate world-wide communication and exchange. Decade by decade American models of scholarship and education, popular culture and art movements, are being assimilated into other cultures, willingly or not. Performance has become a major subject of study in the West as it is increasingly absorbed in the analysis of culture and, at the individual level, redefined as a medium of self-empowerment.

Yet, still a new field of serious study, performance lacks a coherent history, one more capable of synthesizing the century of theatre and visual arts achievement, instead of each subject propagating its own history of performance. The more than two-decades' evolution of *Performing Arts Journal* from primarily a theatre publication to one that now covers video, installations, photography, architecture, and museum/gallery exhibits, embodied in its recent modification of title to *PAJ: A Journal of Performance and Art*, reflects our growing alliance with the visual arts. Likewise, the new PAJ Books series, entitled Art + Performance, further solidifies the effort to develop a more complex and comprehensive view of performance history.

What these conversations underscore is the ongoing struggle to dissolve the boundaries of artistic forms and forms of criticism, in recognition of the fact that throughout the entire twentieth century the ideas and experiments of writers, directors, painters, dancers, musicians, designers, photographers, and filmmakers were enlivened by their collaborations and explorations of different media in relation to each other and to the arts, themselves, and grounded in an art-historical consciousness of forms and preoccupations. In our own time, the relationship of art and theatre has been thwarted by the specialization and separation of their histories and scholarship, beginning in the university and spreading outward in the professional world to mostly separate publications, critics, venues, curators, festivals, and funding sources. Not surprisingly, if one of the ongoing themes in this volume is the education of the artist, the elaboration of distinctions in performance/art/theatre demands substantial attention.

One of the most significant changes that occurred between the mid-seventies era in which *PAJ* was founded and the climate of today is the displacement of critical activity from its organic development out of the experience of art to its isolation in academia, a turn of events which has had a still-to-be-fully-understood impact on discourse in the arts. For, if previously contemporary criticism grew in relation to artworks, themselves, the vast majority of writing on the arts now being published is removed from actual art practice and the world of artistic experience, and frequently circumscribed by irrelevant theories. One can chart the awareness of this change in thought and vocabulary within the arts community over the last two decades in these pages which frame *PAJ*'s own orientation toward the primacy of the artwork. It is revealing to see that many of the trends in contemporary thought are actually at odds with the expressed world of artists, summarizing contrary positions. If the critique of humanism and the enlightenment has been well underway for some time, nevertheless, the comments of artists reflect a longing for universal and cross-cultural aesthetic languages.

Nowhere is the separation between art and much of the extra-artistic commentary on it, appearing now in numerous cultural forums, more insistent than in those passages that illuminate the force of inner necessity that compels artists to search for an authenticity rooted in emotional need. This tendency moves away from the current emphasis on the social foundation of each individual act and towards the role of contingency, chance, and technical problem solving. Another antinomy is the sheer attachment of artists to the object and materiality of their creations, which resists preemption by critical systems. Even though theory has come to play so dominant a role in the discussion and teaching of the arts and humanities today, there is a widespread disenchantment with the hyperactive politicization of art and culture, a tiredness with the predictability of most critical writing, and a growing desire for the freedom to value a work of art for itself alone. What is apparent in these pages is the tension and ambiguity in the range of responses from the generally apolitical or outright politically resistant to the more self-consciously political, which by now has affected both artists and critics.

Often overlooked in contemporary culture is precisely that condition the voices in this volume so eloquently speak to: the role of art as a spiritual discipline. There is a fundamental duality of purpose and expectation in the public perception of art which has moved away from acceptance of the privatization of experience to viewing the artist as an organizer of social reality. But, artists are also interested in privacy, solitude, spiritual life, quiet, intimacy, even as they engage in the symbolization of experience. What should a work do? How shall I make it? Simple questions, but bound to the profound quest that moves the will towards genuine artistic life. And, what cannot be overstated is the very real conflict between the desire of artists to make work that reflects their attachment to the world, even to making visionary works, at the same time that many of them have abandoned the moral imperative of previous art making. Today, aesthetic, formal, religious, social, and moral values are fiercely undermined. But, what do we value in art any longer? For some, the answer is to consider all life as art, while others speak of the irrelevance of art. Which is it that we want more of—life or art?

The idea of what makes an artist has been so transformed in the twentieth century, especially in the American educational system, that it has come to be meaningless, precipitated by an inevitable collapse of artistic and critical standards. A certain amount of demythologizing of art and artists is necessary, but to ignore the special grace of artistic vision is to trivialize the entire realm of human endeavor. Among the themes these conversations highlight are the newness of the place of the arts in twentieth-century America, the history of non–mainstream art's dependence on Europe for financial and critical support, and the uneasiness artists have with their own status in society. Not to be overlooked is the enormous difficulty, for the serious artist, of pursuing a life in art, in a society which perennially calls into question its validity as a quality of conscience and consciousness.

Who cannot smile and yet wince hearing John Cage tell of running his finger through the pages of a phone book, determined, at age fifty, to find a publisher for his music? And is it really so long ago that an immigrant named Bessie Schoenberg marched downtown to her bank in Eugene, Oregon, to demand five hundred dollars to go to New York and become a dancer? As if to corroborate the optimism of creating an art that was to be new and American, there are plenty of unpublished New York stories of the hardships of contemporary writers and dancers proofreading all night in law firms to support their work, with accomplished artists long past middle age devoting the greater part of their energy to fundraising or touring to raise revenues, or working abroad to support their creative life at home. Little more than two decades ago Philip Glass was driving a cab the day after *Einstein on the Beach* closed at the Metropolitan Opera house.

In the generosity of their regard, these conversations variously inflect the essential philosophic and poetic themes to contemplate the nature of human acts: how we see and do, and to what ends. Where does the ineffable sense of work and art, and the work of art, reside? Here we may discover in the economy of adverbs what kind of a people, and continent of marvel, we are. Whether our sentences bespoke truth. Could we find joy in the things of our world? Was the "I" a capital letter?

Bonnie Marranca
April 1998
New York City

ART AND ITS AUDIENCE

Susan Sontag

FOR MORE THAN THREE DECADES Susan Sontag has been a prominent and controversial commentator on the arts. She is a passionate spectator of theatre, opera, dance, and film, who in recent years has turned her attention increasingly to writing fiction. But, Sontag's love of performance carries over into her fictional worlds, with her new novel in progress, *In America*, based on the life of the Polish actress Helena Modjeska, who moved to America in the last century, and an earlier book, *The Volcano Lover*, featuring *Tosca* as operatic motif. In several volumes, including *Against Interpretation*, *Styles of Radical Will*, and *Selected Writings of Antonin Artaud*, which she edited and introduced, Sontag has written about performance issues, reflecting on Happenings, camp, drama, film, photography, dance, and popular culture. Refusing the term "critic," she contends simply, "I had ideas, and I attached them to works of art that I admired."

Sontag demonstrates an extensive theatrical knowledge, which is unusual among American intellectuals who are notorious for ignoring the performing arts in favor of literature. One of the themes she addresses is the activity of consciousness in relation to the temporal demands of theatre and to aesthetic values. At the time of her conversation with the editors of *Performing Arts Journal*, consciousness and perception were major preoccupations of artists and audiences. Sontag argues that consciousness has a structure and thematics, and cannot be considered abstract: "We're not being honest about our experience if we ignore the iconography of consciousness." Emotions have historical dimensions, just as ideas do.

The moral urgency and rigorous standards of Sontag's modernist commitment, obvious even as she acknowledges the contemporary disenchantment with modernism and high culture, challenge any reading of her influential essays as "postmodern" manifestos. Sontag reveals herself to be an ardent seeker of knowledge who affirms both the adversarial power and sensual pleasures of art, which she does not find incompatible in the least with her faith in its will to truth. BGM

Conversation with Bonnie Marranca
and Gautam Dasgupta, 1978

Art and Consciousness

PAJ: What performances in the past few years have you felt were worthwhile experiences?

Susan Sontag: Lucian Pintilie's *Turandot.* Robert Anton's puppet theatre. Merce Cunningham. Peter Brook's *The Ik.* Beckett's Berlin staging of *Waiting for Godot.* Plisetskaya doing Ravel's *Bolero.* Watergate. Franz Salieri's *La Grand Eugene* (the original Paris production, not the one that went on tour). Strehler's production of *The Cherry Orchard.* The invented Act Three of the Met's recent production of *Lulu.* Maria Irene Fornes's staging of her play, *Fefu and Her Friends* . . . Shall I go on?

PAJ: Why haven't you written about these events?

SS: I'm writing other things. Mostly fiction.

PAJ: Don't you want to go on writing criticism?

SS: I don't consider that I ever was a critic. I had ideas, and I attached them to works of art that I admired. Now I attach them to other things.

PAJ: How do you view the current critical scene?

SS: You mean monitoring productions and giving out grades—the kind of consumer reporting that decides whether something is good or not good, well performed or not well performed?

PAJ: If that is what people are satisfied with, isn't it due to the lack of a new critical vocabulary with which to treat the new theatre?

SS: I don't expect ideas from critics. They come from poets and painters and novelists and even playwrights—doing a stint of writing about the theatre. And from directors who found their own theatres.

PAJ: But the current experimental theatre is such a radical break from our theatrical past, not part of a developing American tradition. No one seems to know quite how to deal with it.

SS: I think the problem is that the more than sixty-year-old international tradition of modernism has bequeathed us a surfeit of critical perspectives—Constructivism, futurism, Brecht, Artaud, Grotowski, et al. And that we give an open-ended but increasingly limited credence to them all. It's not lack of familiarity with experimental theatre that explains the critical vacuum. It's the mounting disenchantment—partly justified, partly shallow and philistine—with modernism. And a widespread boredom with high culture itself.

PAJ: You mentioned Artaud and Grotowski. Their theories—which go back to the origins of theatre in ritual and ceremony—seem to be a negation of everything that's transpired in Western culture. Isn't that a regression? And doesn't their kind of theatre remove one from the immediacy of the moment?

ss: There's no opposition between the archaic and the immediate.

paj: I see such theatre as a form of hermeticism, a withdrawal into a world that we have no contact with whatsoever.

ss: Well, I've no objection to art that is hermetic. (Some art *should* be hermetic, I think.) But, far from being hermetic, the theatre influenced by Artaud and by Grotowski is very much about immediate, present experience. The difference is that both Artaud and Grotowski believed in the reality of evil—the reality treated superficially, or denied by so-called realistic theatre.

paj: Why do you emphasize evil?

ss: First of all, because it exists. And because an awareness of the reality of evil is the best defense against artistic trivialization and vulgarity.

paj: The modern attack on "dialogue" or realistic theatre seems to have taken two directions. One, represented by Artaud and Grotowski, explores feelings. The other, represented by Foreman, is more interested in exploring the thinking process and modes of perception.

ss: Perception in and for itself?

paj: Yes. In order to perceive *better*.

ss: Perceive *what* better? Doesn't the material offered for perception have to be trivial, precisely so that the audience can't be distracted by it and can concentrate on the process of perceiving? If you are invited to consider the relationship between a chair and a grapefruit—that is, what's on the stage is a chair and a grapefruit and a string connecting them—then you will indeed perceive something about how they are alike and how they differ. But it's no more than an interesting perceptual problem (and that largely because it's a problem one does not ordinarily consider).

paj: You don't think being interesting is enough?

ss: I used to think so. But I don't anymore. You know, that notion has a history—a rather brief one. To apply the word "interesting" to a work of art was an invention of the Romantic writers of the late eighteenth and early nineteenth centuries, and one that seemed very peculiar at first. (Hegel, for example, thought it was *not* a compliment to say that something was "interesting.") The notion of "the interesting" is approximately as old as the notion of "the boring." Indeed, it seems to me that "the interesting" presupposes "the boring," and vice versa. One of the proudest claims of the modernist theatre is that it is antipsychological. But "the interesting" and "the boring" are psychological categories, nothing more. They are feelings, assumed to be of limited duration, and to be capable of mutating into each other—categories of the solipsistic, narcissistic worldview. (They replace "the beautiful" and "the ugly," which are attributes—hypostasized, quasi-objective, assumed to be permanent.) An "interesting" object has an arresting quality: it seizes our attention, we take cognizance of it, and then let it go. An "interesting" experience is one that has no lasting effect. The notion of "the interesting" arises when art is no longer conceived of as connected with truth. (When truth comes to be reserved for science, for so-called rational inquiry.) In continuing to consider something to be valuable—valuable enough—because it is interesting, we perpetuate a Romantic attitude that needs reexamining.

PAJ: Foreman's theatre is about thinking, about the-being-consciously-aware at the theatre event of the working of the mind in the theatre. I can't think of another kind of theatre where one feels so consciously in the present. It's Foreman's attempt to actively engage the audience that is important.

SS: I don't agree that consciousness-as-such is Foreman's subject. Or, if it could be—and I don't think consciousness-as-such is really a subject at all—that it could be very engaging.

PAJ: What about Beckett?

SS: Beckett is dealing with emotions, however abstractly, and there is a progress from one emotion to the next that feels inevitable. Not only are his plays narrative but, as Joe Chaikin once observed, Beckett has actually discovered a new dramatic subject. Normally people on the stage reflect on the macrostructure of action. What am I going to do this year? Tomorrow? Tonight? They ask: Am I going mad? Will I ever get to Moscow? Should I leave my husband? Do I have to murder my uncle? My mother? These are the sorts of large projects that have traditionally concerned a play's leading characters. Beckett is the first writer to dramatize the microstructure of action. What am I going to do one minute from now? In the next second? Weep? Take out my comb? Stand up? Sigh? Sit? Be silent? Tell a joke? Understand something? His plays are built on reflections leading to decisions, which impart to his dramas a real narrative push. Lessing was right about the irreducible difference between spatial and temporal arts. A play—or a novel, or a film—can be nonnarrative in the sense that it need not tell a story. But it has to be linear or sequential, I think. A succession of images, or of aphorisms, is not enough to give a play the linear cohesiveness proper to the temporal arts.

PAJ: Do you feel the same way about Peter Handke's works—his *Sprech-*

stücke, particularly—which resemble Foreman's plays in the lack of dialogue, in the attempt at consciousness-raising, in the dialectical relationship of the stage and the audience?

SS: No, because Handke's plays are about specific ideas or problems (not about consciousness or perception as such), dramatized in a sequential form. The ideas matter dramatically.

PAJ: In Foreman's recent *Rhoda in Potatoland*, there are many quotations—from Breton's *Nadja*, from Wittgenstein, et cetera—allusions to paintings, and so forth. How can the contemporary artist cope with the radical strides made in art in this century without alluding to them in his work?

SS: Modernist self-consciousness can take many forms. Painters like to quote other painters. But one can't imagine Beckett quoting anybody or making allusions to predecessors and models—as Wittgenstein didn't. The demands of purity and the demands of piety may be, ultimately, incompatible.

PAJ: Consciousness is the principal subject of modern art. Is that in some way a dangerous tradition?

SS: It seems to me that its biggest limitation is the value placed on consciousness conceived of as a wholly *private* activity. Modernist art has given the central place to asocial, private fantasy and, in effect, denied the notion that some intentions are more valid than others . . . It's hardly surprising that so many modernist artists have been fascinated by the diseases of consciousness—that an art committed to solipsism would recapitulate the gestures of the *pathology* of solipsism. If you start from an asocial notion of perception or consciousness, you must inevitably end up with the poetry of mental illness and mental deficiency. With autistic silence. With the autistic's use of language: compulsive repetition and variation. With an obsession with circles. With an abstract or distended notion of time.

PAJ: Are you thinking of the work of Robert Wilson?

SS: Of Wilson, for one. More generally, of the long faux-naïf tradition in modernist art, one of whose great figures is Gertrude Stein. (What *Four Saints in Three Acts* started, *Letter to Queen Victoria* and *Einstein on the Beach* continue . . .). But the symptomology of mental deficiency recurs in most of the really seductive productions I've seen recently: Pintilie's *Turandot*, *The Ik*, Carmelo Bene's *Faust* fantasy, Patrice Chereau's production of Marivaux's *La Dispute* . . .

PAJ: Twelve years ago, in "One Culture and the New Sensibility," you advanced the argument that the function of art is to extend and educate consciousness. You seem now to have moved away from the ideas expressed in that essay.

SS: I don't disagree with what I wrote then. But to assert that art is an exploration of consciousness is vacuous, unless one understands that consciousness has a structure, a thematics, a history. The choice of materials is never accidental or extraneous.

PAJ: Is that what you were arguing in your essay in the *New York Review of Books* (February 6, 1975) on Leni Riefenstahl and fascist aesthetics?

SS: Yes, that's one assumption behind the essay. It seemed to me all too easy to say that Riefenstahl's work is beautiful. The question is: What kind of beauty? In the service of what ideas, what forms of consciousness, what emotions? Not only ideas but emotions—joy, fear, whatever—have a history. There is such a thing as fascist emotions, a fascist aesthetic impulse.

PAJ: How do you feel about Adrienne Rich's attack in the *New York Review of Books* (March 20, 1975) on your Riefenstahl piece for its "unwillingness" to discuss Riefenstahl as a product of a patriarchal society? Do you feel put upon by feminists who demand that you take another "line" in your writing?

SS: Since I'm a feminist too, the situation can hardly be described as a difficulty between me and "them." As for Rich's argument, I said what I thought about that in my reply (in the same issue of the *NYR*) to her letter—that it's not as if Nazi Germany were a patriarchal society and other societies aren't. What society is *not* patriarchal? Riefenstahl's work is explained by Nazism, not by the attitudes of Nazis toward women.

PAJ: Yet many people see Riefenstahl's work as purely aesthetic, beautiful films.

SS: There is no such thing as an "aesthetic" work of art—as there is no such thing as the engagement or exploration of consciousness as such. Neither consciousness nor the aesthetic is something abstract. We're not being honest about our experience if we ignore the iconography of consciousness. You can't look at the Rembrandt self-portraits and see them just as an arrangement of forms, as studies in brown. There's a face there.

PAJ: Isn't this way of looking at art radically different from the one you espoused in "Against Interpretation"?

SS: No. I never argued that all art should be looked at *abstractly;* I argued for the intellectual importance of its being experienced *sensuously.* "Against Interpretation" was a polemic against one reductive way of accounting for art, much more common a decade ago: treating a work as if it were equivalent to the account that could be given of its "meaning." This practice seemed to me misguided—first of all, because a great deal of art doesn't mean very much, in any nontautological sense of meaning. (Of course, a work may not have a "meaning" and still contain "referents" outside itself, to the world.) And because it weakens and corrupts our direct appreciation of a work's "thingness." Instead of relying so much on questions about what elements in a work of art mean, I thought we could rely more on questions about how they function—concretely, sensuously, and formally—in the work.

PAJ: I categorically refuse not to see meaning in a work. Otherwise it doesn't pay for me to go to see something. I have to approach the problem that is put before me and make it worthwhile for my own experiences.

SS: I categorically refuse to ask art to "pay for me." Nor does it have to touch me personally, as people say. Isn't pleasure "worthwhile"? Among other things, art is an instrument of pleasure—and one doesn't have *that* much pleasure in life. And pleasure can be quite impersonal. And complex.

PAJ: Are you positing a hierarchy of art—the kind that gives pleasure and the kind that makes you think? Are they mutually exclusive?

SS: Hardly—since thinking is one kind of pleasure, both solemn and playful. But I don't want to minimize the fact that the role of pleasure in art raises all sorts of serious questions. I find it impossible to keep moral feelings out of my desire for pleasure. That is, part of my *experience* of pleasure is that there are facile pleasures, as there are facile ideas. Since art is a form of flattery, I find myself also responding to the quality of an artist's refusal. The history of art is not only part of the history of pleasure. It is also a series of renunciations.

PAJ: Why should art have to renounce anything?

SS: Because every leading idea—every leading style—needs a corrective. As Oscar Wilde said, "A truth in art is that whose contrary is also true." And a truth *about* art is one whose contrary is also true.

PAJ: What do you hope for when you go to the theatre?

SS: Passion. Intelligence. Intensity. Lyricism. Theatre—and poetry and music—supply a lyricism not to be found in life.

PAJ: Why not?

SS: Because life is too long. For life to be like *Tristan and Isolde,* the average human life should last two months instead of seventy years.

PAJ: Is intensity the same as pleasure?

SS: It's better. Sexier, more profound. As you see, I'm an incorrigible puritan.

PAJ: You seem to be excluding humor.

SS: I'm not. But I get restless when the treatment of the emotions in art takes second place—it does in so much of modernist theatre—to the dramaturgy of surprise, to a negative desire, the desire to avoid the expected.

PAJ: Are you suggesting that surprise is not a worthy element in the performing arts?

ss: After a century and a half of surprises in the arts—during which time the ante has been upped steadily, so that people are harder and harder to surprise—it seems to have gotten much less satisfying. Most instances of outrage or shock now are gags.

PAJ: You have written in one essay that "the history of art is a series of successful transgressions." If, as you say, the ante of shock and surprise is always being upped, what is left to transgress?

ss: The idea of transgression, perhaps . . . Transgression presupposes successful notions of order. But transgressions have been so successful that the idea of transgression has become normative for the arts—which is a self-contradiction. Modern art wished to be—maybe even was, for a brief time—in an intractable, adversary relation to the established high culture. Now it is identical with high culture, supported by a vast bureaucracy of museums, universities, and state and private foundations. And the reason for this success story is that there is a close fit between many of the values promoted by modernism and the larger values of our capitalist consumer society. This makes it difficult, to say the least, to continue thinking of modernist art as adversary art. And that's part of what lies behind the disenchantment with modernism I spoke of earlier.

PAJ: You seem discouraged by this situation.

ss: Yes and no. Rebellion does not seem to me a value in itself, as—say— truth is. There's no inherent value in transgression. As there is no inherent value to being interesting. My loyalty is not to the transgression but to the truth behind it. That the forms of life in this society, having become increasingly permissive, corrupt, vulgar, and disgusting, thereby deprive artists of the taboos against which they can, comfortably, heroically, rebel—that seems far less dismaying than the fact that this society itself is based on lies, on untruths, on hallucination.

PAJ: What should artists do now?

ss: In a society that works and enriches itself by means of organized hallucination, be less devoted to creating new forms of hallucination. And more devoted to piercing through the hallucinations that nowadays pass for reality.

Robert Jay Lifton

WHEN THIS DISCUSSION WITH Robert Jay Lifton took place, polls showed that most Americans expected a nuclear war in the near future. While nuclear warheads were aimed at Europe, American and Soviet officials played a tense game of one-upmanship with studied rhetorical and military gestures, creating transcontinental fear and protest that reached a fevered pitch. Lifton, a psychiatrist and social critic, who now heads the Center for Peace and Social Justice at John Jay College of the City University of New York, was heavily involved in the antinuclear movement and coauthoring a new book, *Indefensible Weapons*, on the shift in consciousness produced by the nuclear threat. He has also been active in Physicians for Social Responsibility and International Physicians for the Prevention of Nuclear War.

Here, Lifton turns his attention to the preoccupation with death, disease, and violence in contemporary art whose forms of radical discontinuity are rooted in the collapse of traditional symbols and the imagery of the end of the world. Expanding the ideas in his then-recent *The Broken Connection*, and already echoing themes of *The Protean Self*, which he would write more than a decade later, Lifton contrasts the psychologies of more Freudian modern dramatic characters and the contemporary sense of self. He draws on examples as varied as Ibsen, Strindberg, Chekhov, Beckett, and Woody Allen to celebrate the resymbolizing power of art and the use of humor, which turns the imagery of death into life-generating images. Likewise, he emphasizes the importance of understanding violence in art. What kind of theatre does Lifton envision to represent the threat of extinction while still affirming human continuity? For him it is a post-Beckettian theatre, one "that can imagine the end of the world and create beyond that."   BGM

Conversation with Bonnie Marranca, 1982

Art and the Imagery of Extinction

Bonnie Marranca: Can you outline a particular kind of character, in film or theatre, who offers a psychological profile of a person living under the threat of nuclear war and possible extinction?

Robert J. Lifton: I don't think the theatre can be expected to have caught up with a "character of extinction," if there is such a character. The terrible problem for art is that an artist is asked to create a narrative or a set of symbols around our own collective and total demise. We resist the narrative, understandably, and it's a tough one to enter, artistically.

In my work I take three dimensions that you can roughly connect with postmodernism, or with our contemporary situation. The first is the breakdown of traditional symbols and of modern parallels or developments of those symbols; the second is the mass media revolution; and the third is imagery of extinction or threat of extinction. This last is the most difficult for art to confront, and I don't know if it's really been represented yet. But maybe the way art has begun to confront it in the theatre and elsewhere has been through increasingly radical discontinuity.

BGM: Do you mean in terms of narrative?

RJL: Yes, in narrative that hardly exists or is circular or recurrent rather than continuous or linear; in terms of characters who feel cut off from a past or future. If you're cut off from a future, your past is threatened also.

BGM: I don't know if I could suggest the particular kind of character because it's always difficult to figure which came first and what, in effect, people are reacting to. But I think there are some manifestations of new feelings and responses in the theatre. For example, take a piece like *Satyagraha*, the opera that Philip Glass and Connie De Jong created, also the ACT company from Buffalo under Joseph Dunn, and some of Meredith Monk's work. I think these are examples of a new expressionism or a holistic approach to theatre. Some of the expressionistic work we're seeing now could be a different kind of spiritualism. And it's not the same as German expressionism.

RJL: Well, I wrote a piece a few years ago called "Survivor as Creator" in which I took up three writers: Camus, Vonnegut, and Grass. Each saw himself as a survivor, and creatively, a survivor has to imagine that death encounter in order to create past it, to stay in it and use it, yet move beyond it. There the artist and the writer parallel and anticipate some of the thinking and politics necessary to stem the nuclear threat. You must

11

imagine what the end of the world is, as Jonathan Schell tries to do in his book *The Fate of the Earth,* in order to prevent it.

For me, then, the problem is to get a handle on this, and the psychological handle is death and the continuity of life and the larger symbolization of human connectedness, or the "symbolization of immortality." So the theatre has the task of expressing, symbolizing, and representing how, in the face of or threat of extinction, one imagines human continuity. Perhaps that spiritual theatre or expressive theatre you mention is one way of imagining it.

BGM: Or turning away from it . . .

RJL: Something in terms of feeling is happening that's important—after the decades of numbing that followed World War II, the numbing is beginning to break down. That's got to affect the theatre, too. It's a breakdown of the kind of collective arrangement, collusion, and "not-feeling"—especially not feeling what happens at the other end of the weapon, and especially what might happen to us. People are afraid. When I talk to audiences now, kids at colleges are frightened, sometimes at secondary schools, and ordinary audiences. The polls show that most Americans fear and even expect a nuclear war in the not-too-distant future. That's new. There's a movement now toward awareness or a shift in consciousness that's quite hopeful.

BGM: One of the things you mention in *The Life of the Self* is a human hunger for an evolutionary leap, that it will produce a new kind of art. Do you see a manifestation of this new art?

RJL: Not really; now I question what I wrote. Yes, there's an appropriate moment where an evolutionary leap would be parallel to the technological leap, and perhaps that evolutionary leap would be parallel also to this incredible demand on artists and on all of us that we imagine the end of the world. People have been thinking of the end of the world for a long time. Every kind of millennial imagery and major religion represents the end of the world in some way, but there's a distinction between that millenarian imagery where it fits into a system of belief and structure, and millenarian imagery that has to do with the nuclear holocaust. In Christian religion, God will punish all sinners and there'll be a judgment day, after which everything will begin again. Not so, now, when it's a matter of doing ourselves in with our own tools in an absolutely meaningless way.

For an artist, that kind of end of the world is a very demanding artistic requirement, so we can't expect artists to suddenly move into an evolutionary leap any more than anyone else can. Incidentally, Alvarez in his book on suicide claims that recent increased incidence of suicide among artists—and he means writers and painters and artists broadly defined—has to do with reaching a point where it's impossible to find meaning or words that express life's continuity in the face of extinction. He draws on my Hiroshima work to make this argument. Therefore artists shout more loudly or more desperately but can't get through with the words or the images they need, and that's why they become desperate.

BGM: But isn't there another side of the issue—more and more people wanting to be artists? I don't mean necessarily that the average person wants to drop his or her career to become a painter or a writer. But you do find people—and I find them often outside of the city—taking up painting or creative writing, and it's become a major involvement. It's a much more philosophical impulse than, say, a leisure-time activity.

RJL: If meaning is harder and harder to come by, and the ordinary symbolic structures are crumbling, they're burdensome rather than liberating. One can feel the increasing appeal of art because art is constantly trying to resymbolize, express symbols; and probably art does thrive, or at least increase its energy, where there is a threat to the existing structure. For instance, there was the extraordinary resurgence of German literature, film, and theatre after World War II.

The problem is what artists do when becoming artists, and maybe it's only a certain extremely brave and talented vanguard that really moved toward this kind of abyss, or challenged it, and then faced the kinds of issues that Alvarez writes about, or that I write about too. Or, there's a sense in which there's absolutely nothing you or I or any artist encounters in everyday life or art that's totally caused by nuclear weapons or the threat of extinction, because we still have our work and our struggles with our love lives, our children and our parents and our marriages and friends. On the other hand, there is nothing in our lives that is not affected by the threat of extinction. I guess it's that double life we all live in in which the artist has to create. And I think that's quite possible.

BGM: In the seventies there were a lot of plays around the subjects of cancer and death, plays such as *The Shadow Box, Whose Life Is It Anyway?*, and *Wings*. We've also seen simultaneously disaster films and an exceptional amount of violence. Would you say that while these things are not about the nuclear power issue, they are manifestations of paranoia about destruction and death?

RJL: Absolutely. As soon as you have the threat of imagery of extinction, death and life are out of kilter, and that's why I called my most recent book *The Broken Connection:* the connection between the two is radically threatened. That feeds back into what Vonnegut calls "plain old death."

We're creatures of our own history and so we're influenced in what we think and study about. This is true in all of the arts, with a great focus on death in the sixties and seventies, and the nuclear threat creates or contributes to that preoccupation with death.

America has been notable in repressing death and maybe reaching the most radical form of denial of death that any culture has ever "achieved." So there's a kind of rebound reaction here along with the nuclear threat and some other influences, with a great sense in America that it's now discovered death. Twenty years ago nobody in America ever talked about death because as a young culture we're not supposed to die. It's Europeans and Asians who die. All of a sudden Americans are talking about nothing but death, it's the way Americans embrace things. But with that—again that's the seeming trivialization of the mass media—something happens, some kind of struggle with death and with pain that has been taking place in America is expressed. The plays you mentioned reflected that. They can go just so far, though, can't they?

BGM: Because they drift into sentimentality. They create a vogue for certain kinds of death plays or cancer plays and young playwrights follow the lead—and then there is a rash of plays on these topics. I'm more interested in the shape of "character" and how that can change. For example, at the turn of the century, and in the twenties and thirties, there was a certain type of character, the hysterical woman. You see this in Artaud, in Witkiewicz, Strindberg, Musil, to name a few. Now that kind of Freudian character doesn't exist. Except for some remnants, say, in Tennessee Williams and others. I want to pin you down and see if you can create a model of the contemporary character.

RJL: The hysterical character you're talking about began to disappear twenty or thirty years ago. To have an hysterical character you need a whole life pattern, a full individual. Even if that woman or man has gone a little berserk, it's still a life that's relatively intact and has a beginning and a middle and an end, or a sequence. We don't have that now. Freud believed in reason and in cause and effect, and in a linear sequence to lives, and of course we still live around those principles. But here I think art does move ahead of everyday life, and has, in contemporary theatre and films.

There's a kind of transition between Freud and proteanism, shape-shifting, multiple selves without a linear process, that's more characteristic of a contemporary character. And in between somewhere as a transitional or connecting figure is the character of identity struggle. You find them in Miller and Williams, for example, some of the American playwrights who are transitional, Freudian in their influence, but they're also a little post-Freudian in no longer portraying straight neurosis. Strindberg is straight neurosis with hysteria or whatever, but with Williams and Miller it's a lot about identity and confusion and who one is. That isn't the question Freud asked. That's the question Erik Erikson asked. Freud asked, "What does one do with one's instinctual drives, and how does one tame them and become human or live a human life?" Erikson asks, "How does one maintain a sense of sameness over incredibly shifting environments and themes and influences?" That's the question Williams and Miller and a lot of other playwrights are asking. The protean or postmodern question is, perhaps, "How does one maintain a sense of life—continuity in the face of the threat of extinction, and in the face of the breakdown of all the symbols by which our lives are organized?"

BGM: Didn't absurdism dramatize those feelings in the postwar period, with playwrights like Beckett, Adamov, and Ionesco?

RJL: Beckett is very much asking the question of identity, but he does it beyond identity; he's very much in the realm of extinction. Beckett has his characters so constricted to accentuate by contrast the richness of life. I take from Beckett not a positive message—that would be putting it too strongly—but a great imaginative vision that is very much touched by extinction, but is a little bit beyond it. Beckett is the best example still of a theatre that does something with extinction. He's the only one I can think of who can really talk about having a profound sense of the imagery of extinction or death in life, yet preserving that notion of continuity. You mentioned Ionesco. He certainly explores and plays with some of these issues; he's a little more concrete. He talks and writes in his journals about the threat to life continuity, but he doesn't transmute them as powerfully as Beckett, and his plays are more limited or cerebral. Maybe that's why when we read and see Beckett, he does something for us that nobody else does, because he has really immersed himself in this ultimate image of extinction and come up from it.

BGM: In an interview we published with Susan Sontag in the late seventies, she mentioned something Joe Chaikin had said about Beckett, which is that the problem for Beckett is what to do the next minute. It's a profound, concise statement. That's not the problem in Ibsen, if you know what I mean.

RJL: Ibsen assumed that a life would be led and that it would reach its conclusion, that there would be old age unless there was some kind of tragedy.

BGM: But we begin to see Beckett's vision in Chekhov, whose sentimental side is, unfortunately, what is stressed in most productions, and yet he dramatizes broken conversation, society falling apart, inertia.

RJL: With Chekhov, yes, society is falling apart and his relationship to time takes a new direction. Chekhov is not worried about what happens the next moment. He's worried about what you do now in your life when all the fundamental structures no longer pertain. Part of the power of Chekhov is that along with the symbols and values breaking down there's an odd timelessness created because there are no meaningful actions to interrupt the flow of time. Chekhov's characters try desperately to carry out meaningful actions, but they never quite succeed. I don't know of another playwright who gives us that odd suspension of time, or time-lessness, because something that is supposed to happen never does and never can happen because people are not hooked into time in a meaning-ful way.

BGM: The question of time is interesting. During the sixties, a lot of the ex-perimentation in theatre had to do with space. I felt it coming that at some point in the past five years or so there would be a switch to time and to narration. In fact, with the rise of autobiography and more inter-est in writing as a craft, the theatre is moving again toward narration and use of writers, toward dealing with time. I think we've gone through our experimental theatre period when there was an attempt to control the environment or space.

RJL: If there is a return in the theatre to the writer and the experience of time, it might partly parallel the return in painting to the figure, but if it's to be at all powerful it's got to do that along with retaining considerable doubt and absurdity or worse, some of the influence of extinction. One thing that is crucial to this, both predating but reinforced by the threat of extinction, is the use of absurdity, and then more intense developments of absurdity in the form of extreme mockery.

BGM: As opposed to satire, or do you mean the grotesque?

RJL: The grotesque has always been with us, and that has to do with the threat of death and the threat of unacceptable death. Maybe the gro-tesque is especially a modern genre, but it's still not new. Irony requires a strong sense of self because it must reflect on itself in order to be ironic. Absurdity slips off that a little bit, and a lot of theatre and modern art, particularly contemporary art, has to do with a kind of absurdity that I think has to do with death. Mockery is absurdity with a lot of doubt about the self. When you mock something, you take a look at someone else's self or claim to a self and do something with it. You're not clear about your own self, you're not self-observing in the way that genuine irony is. If there's to be a return to more formal elements of the theatre, it has to have some of that edge of mockery, absurdity, doubt about the flow of time along with a reinstatement of it.

BGM: There's been a resurgence in comedy, not only in the theatre world, but also in the art world. There have been a lot of stand-up comedy people, a renewed interest in the clown performer, and the New Museum recently had a show on humor in art. It's often more like television comedy, only a bit more arch. Nevertheless, it's comedy, and comedy is classically considered a form about self-survival or about limited achievement, as opposed to tragedy, which is about unlimited goals. When you think about popular, contemporary playwrights you think of someone like Christopher Durang, who's mocking Catholicism and bourgeois family life. Or, in film, you think about someone like Woody Allen, whose work exemplifies the humor of disjointed, contemporary characters on the edge. Would you agree?

RJL: Yes. Woody Allen is a good example. He is constantly self-absorbed, he's worried about his body and what it does or doesn't look like and what it will or won't do, and his precious little sense of self in this world in which the self takes such a beating. But underneath that, what gives Allen power is the more primal fear of coming apart, disintegrating. And the way of evoking humor, quite wonderfully at times, humor and connection, because he does, I think, rather touchingly, portray love. *Annie Hall* is a good example in which the contemporary sense in all of us of falling apart is embodied by Allen, and he moves into and through it, and beyond into a self-mocking rendition of it. The self-mockery is central—obviously, it's Jewishness universalized—and then beyond into something like love. *Annie Hall* does say something about love; if not permanently or enduringly or perfectly, love is still possible in the face of this threat of disintegration.

BGM: Do you watch much television?

RJL: My television is limited to special programs, sports and news, and occasional pornography. From what I've seen I guess there's a lot more death and an extremity in comedy-situational dramas and soap operas. Soap operas are a lot more serious and have a lot of death, mourning, fear, neurosis, and trouble in them. They're struggling with a mass cultural rendition of what we've been talking about, and that's difficult.

In discussions about violence on television, I find myself a little reserved. Most television violence is very exploitative, horrible, and harmful psychologically. The trouble is that people need some kind of rendition of violence in order to register and reflect the threats as well as the inner violence they're feeling, in order to avoid recourse to actual violence.

BGM: In *The Broken Connection* you quote Franz Fanon, who talked about the "shared violence" that a culture goes through providing "therapeutic knowledge." What you're saying is that an audience, or American audiences who watch television, need to go through this violence to express what they cannot do in reality. Do you mean psychologically or physically?

RJL: Well, psychologically, and creatively, perhaps, touching on the actuality of violence. It's a problem of art, though, because nobody would want to prohibit any rendition of violence in any art form. The problem is it's really bad art, so the violence becomes exploitative and I think violence is the issue around which good art and bad art make such a profound difference.

BGM: Did you see The Wooster Group's *Route 1 & 9?* It's a brilliant piece, and the only one in years that really divided an audience. It's about nihilism and images of death and life, and social violence . . . You've written on The Living Theatre—do you think their work is useful violence?

RJL: I think it has been. I guess something like The Living Theatre finds a métier, works in it, then loses it. In those years it had something to say about violence—the late sixties—and it did connect violence in our lives with some kind of transmuting process of the theatre. The moralistic approach to the question of violence flattens it, and reduces it to a simple cultural good and evil, and misses the whole point.

A good example of the border of this in film is the *Dr. Strangelove* theme. It's very literal, it's about nuclear weapons, but consider the end of that film, where the captain goes roaring down with the bomb, straddling it like a horse and yodeling in a great expression of triumph. It's a brilliant mockery of the whole nuclear madness; on the other hand, there is more than a suggestion of a kind of ultimate nuclear high—going down with the bomb. And that's attractive to some people.

BGM: Isn't this what you refer to as "nuclearism"?

RJL: Yes, and in the new book that Richard Falk and I are just finishing, *Indefensible Weapons,* I have a whole section on what I call "nuclear fundamentalism." I take this up again as an ultimate nuclear high, but nuclearism is the ultimate fundamentalism in regard to the weapon. There are a lot of people seeking high states through fundamentalist religious or political movements and I think they have a fairly direct relationship to nuclear threat.

BGM: In Stanley Diamond's book *In Search of the Primitive,* he talks about the problem of violence in contemporary culture, that unlike in tribal times we don't have rituals to exorcise this lingering need for violence.

RJL: Violence in my kind of theory—I develop this in *The Broken Connection*—all violence probably, and this is the irony of violence, is in the service of more life. "More life" is a phrase used by Ernest Becker. There's a search for vitality around the expression of violence. For instance, in the initiation rites, which can be quite violent, with scarification or other expressions of violence to the body, violence is in the service of a death and rebirth ritual, initiation. That channels tremendous energy around anger, rage, fear, and their transmutation into some sort of adult constructive work or pastime, like hunting, or whatever adults do in a particular society, and adult rules and rituals around which the society is built. The theatre doesn't have sufficient power in our culture to be an initiation rite, but I think people can experience through powerful theatre something parallel to that.

BGM: In the past fifteen years or so there's been a strong movement toward what Richard Schechner and Victor Turner, among others, refer to as "interculturalism"—it brings social anthropology into theatre, creating a kind of global theatre field in which all communication is seen as one kind of social drama or another. There's been a lot of talk in all this about shamanism, ritual, healing, and other rites. I think there's a significant need among many theatre people in the world to turn away from theatre in the conventional sense while at the same time viewing all human activity as a theatrical paradigm.

RJL: That has parallels with what I would call an experiential mode. When it is strong it looks for premodern truths and premodern sources of psychological power. Also, this gets complicated because, take the figure of the shaman, and shamanism, it's a key figure both for premodern human power and power over death, which is what a shaman had as a precursor of the physician and as a kind of priest. The shaman is a figure of life power, power over death. He or she is a kind of ideal figure to go back to because shamans touch on magic and that life/death axis. I find myself now confronting the negative side of shamanism—my work with Nazi doctors and the shamanistic legacy is what the Nazis called on in a murderous way to enlist doctors in the killing process—and probably some of the interest of the theatre in anthropology and shamanistic ritual has to include its murderous capacity or the murderous or more negative use of magic, though the premodern shaman could never begin to approach the modern physician enlisted by Hitler.

I think that when the future is threatened one reaches backward, and rightly so. I speak of the mode of restoration that can be a form of re-action or a reactionary mode. Reactionary—if you try to restore a past of perfect harmony that never was, something like the Moral Majority. On the other hand, you do need elements of restoration. You've got to look back and see what the shaman really was like and then combine this with very contemporary motifs where you feel some fundamental threat to human continuity, so it makes sense.

BGM: Often what they're doing really goes way beyond art; it's more a way of life, really, and it seems almost religious. What Grotowski is doing is also beyond any expression of art. The reports of his rituals in the woods or his theatre of sources sound a lot like what I remember in the six-ties—"T" groups and retreats and group encounters. What is problem-atic about some of these manifestations is the authoritarian male figure involved in all of this—the guru aspect.

RJL: That reminds me, there are certain elements of the late sixties and early seventies that had a tyrannical authoritarian component and expressed that totalistic component in the name of liberation. It usually had to do with a demand to liberate the body, and there would be certain rituals and arrangements of the group that were immediately and totally legis-lated by the leader. I have an aversion to that—how can I describe it?—an allergy to any kind of totalism. What we're also talking about is a sev-ering of the experiments of the self from what we consider theatre, from the discipline of creative performance, from the discipline of creating an experience that can be shared by an audience and that has some relation-ship to a tradition.

BGM: Since you mention it, there is a trend to do performances without spectators. Alan Kaprow has done this kind of work in California, and this is what Grotowski is doing now, and sometimes Barba. It's an attrac-tive idea to a lot of people. This boundary between the spectator and the performer is largely breaking down, and who knows where it's going to go. My feeling is that those people interested in linking cultural anthro-pology to theatre, while often meaning well, assume too many univer-salities for the audience and the artist. I question the feelings and the as-sumptions they have about the theatrical experience. There is something too ordered in the anthropological view of the community, and contem-porary society is not like that.

RJL: One can have a kind of retrospective wisdom. It's hard to make a judg-ment of how much that tradition is being struggled against and how much it's been abandoned, and it is a kind of critic's own personal judg-ment about it. I would sense that the anthropological theatre has lots of possibilities, but it just depends on what one is doing, and it has a kind of responsibility to the tradition of the theatre even, and especially, as it breaks off from it. You can make your most extraordinary innovation by being grounded to some degree in your tradition.

BGM: Can you apply the notion of being "grounded in tradition" to the -ability of today's artists to successfully use the imagery of death that's all around us, to turn it into life-generating imagery?

RJL: Yes. I think that people need discipline—you can't impose classical authority on them anymore because even mentorship and discipleship, or learning and teaching, have different dimensions now. But one needs rigorous teaching and learning, still. You can't be grounded in the theatre or in any other art form without a period of real study. It requires a disciplined exposure toward what is known and what has been learned over decades and centuries in the theatre. Then, when you have that—as a sensitive writer, director, or performer in the theatre—you can connect that grounding and relate it to life/death issues that are imposed on us. Grounding can give one the strength and courage and innovative potential to immerse oneself in a terrifying imagery of extinction and death-haunted issues that we have to face.

BGM: What kind of theatre, then, do you envision that faces these issues?

RJL: A theatre with elements of a struggle back toward and forward from ritual. A theatre that struggles with nothingness and beyond and that has to be post-Beckett. It's hard to be influenced by Beckett without being drowned by him. A theatre that is concerned with death but not narrowly and not necessarily concretely, but with what death symbolizes, and with different forms and dimensions of death and its grotesquerie but that transcends it. A theatre that can imagine the end of the world and create beyond that.

BGM: A theatre, then, that can imagine the end of the world but that also believes in tomorrow.

RJL: Exactly. Therefore it's a theatre of faith. It can be a religious faith or a kind of secular faith—it has to be for many of us—but you require faith and faith is something that always goes beyond evidence but not totally without evidence in the idea of a human future. But, in order for the faith to be powerful, it has to really immerse itself into precisely what threatens the human future, but it's got to do that in its own way and that way is hard to come by.

BGM: Do you think that because theatre is built on the notion of representation that it has a special power to help an audience go through a catharsis—to go through that way in the experience of the performers?

RJL: For instance, JoAnne Akalaitis's *Dead End Kids* is a relatively more concrete work about the nuclear and radiation issue. It's the most successful play on that issue because it uses a lot of contemporary imagination, very protean in spirit, it's death-haunted but mocking while joyous and humorous, with a lot of gallows humor, which to me is a great plus. Humor is liberating, deepening, pedagogic in the best sense—a theatre without humor at all is worthless. The more threatening and serious things get, the more humor that's needed. There are different kinds of humor, and of course it's the quality of the humor that's important. If you only stay in the death immersion without the humor you're in some degree perhaps getting pornographic.

BGM: Joe Chaikin always seems able to combine death and humor in his work. But he is out of fashion now with audiences who are more used to highly imagistic or technological work. The thing he provides that no one else involved in group work does is the evocation of real emotion, and he's always been able to do that. That's the problem some people have with Chaikin. They're not used to seeing genuine sentiment anymore.

RJL: Yes, he seemed to be in his earlier work, and probably is now, too, on the edge. The issue of emotion becomes very important. Another way of putting it is, emotion is a form and you need formed feeling in the theatre. Experiments in the late sixties, seventies, and some today, too, have difficulty giving form to feeling and therefore giving it depth, and feeling becomes all too forgettable, or transient. Perhaps a man like Beckett is committed because his way as an artist one can take as a commitment to the world. That means stepping over a line in which one relates one's life to dealing with the world in some important way, as opposed to simply stepping back from it. And that may be an issue for the theatre from now into the future, I don't know.

BGM: I think it's a kind of Sartre-like drama, which you talked about, a special kind of theatre of commitment, of ethics.

RJL: But now the Sartre-like question has to be altered. Yes, it's a similar question but it's already a different time, because it's infused with extinction, which gives it a kind of mixture of terror and amorphousness, and a greater imaginative requirement. It gives it a more wild and extreme dimension. The theatre can't shy away from that, either, but it's that grounding that may give it the freedom to be wild or extreme.

BGM: But, dealing specifically with death imagery, it's beyond humor, it's beyond the comic wildness say of an Innaurato or a Durang, but actually dealing with death and felt emotions, getting back really to a classical drama.

RJL: It may be possible that one can embody the nature of nuclear threat in other metaphors. The limitless symbolizing capacities of the human mind are the same source of either dooming us or saving us. It's that same gray matter that constantly re-creates and symbolizes and it's very hard to imagine how to subsume human extinction to some kind of artistic or theatrical metaphor. The art generally suffers, and the theatre suffers in the effort, as you know. It needn't literally be a death-haunted play about nuclear weapons or about actual death and destructiveness.

BGM: There has been a school of theatre, an extreme kind of realism primarily by French and German writers, the "theatre of everyday life." Perhaps even in some cases with those kinds of plays the attention to detail is more of an involvement in the life process.

RJL: Yes, it could be, and it's the power of realism of a certain kind. And any worthwhile so-called realism or focus on everyday life has to be touched by madness and the imagery of our time.

BGM: It will be interesting to see if we go back into a period more like absurdism or like the period between the Wars when there was the greatest experimentation, and perhaps some of the strongest questioning of representation in the theatre. The most recent movements have been realism, back to naturalism—but a kind of flat, stylized naturalism without the heavy psychology. Kroetz, Botho Strauss, David Storey, some of the early Edward Bond is like this. It hasn't been a movement that's influential here because Americans are more into the psychological factor of character, and less formalistic and artificial dramatic techniques of stylization. Part of that has to do with the lack of class consciousness, I think.

RJL: If the realism is too bound to a kind of old-fashioned version of realism then the theatre is holding on tightly against the threatening images. But art can't follow rules, it has to be antihistorical, and in my terms some of this realism would be moving back into a restorationist mode almost with a vengeance, almost with a caricature, and it may have to abandon that. Something will be learned in the process.

BGM: At a time, now, when people are moving more and more toward art because that kind of experience fills some kind of void in their lives, I think the culture is moving toward seeing itself as spectacle, in terms of seeing its citizens as performers in a way. The media has caused this to a certain extent, but I think it's also a human development. Maybe now we can begin to discover again what it means to go into the theatre and go through certain experiences as a culture, which is what live actors should do to live audiences.

RJL: I think so, too. An awful lot of people are now "imagining the real," in

Buber's phrase. The "real" is the threat of nuclear holocaust in the most extreme way. It's a terribly demanding and difficult thing to imagine. But with more and more people forced into making that imaginative effort and never fully organized in an orderly way, that means more and more people are open to art in the best sense, art that has the courage to do something like that.

The fact that this numbing could break down is what I take to be a significant beginning shift in consciousness. It's what I call a movement from a fragmentary awareness to a struggle for formed awareness. The struggle has two sides: one, cognizance of actual danger, being wary; and the other, awareness in the way that theatre and artists and visionaries have always understood it, the sense of special insight or vision. There's a struggle for awareness on both of these levels that's more widespread in the culture now, and that I think enhances the possibility of a theatre that can say something. Because the theatre becomes part of this awareness, this dreadful but possible moment in our culture, it can also have an audience to join in that process.

Harold Clurman, Stanley Kauffmann

TWO GRAND MEN of the theatre, Harold Clurman and Stanley Kauffmann, bring their wit and wisdom, and fifty years of theatregoing, to this interchange of views on the American theatre and its audience. Admittedly, when they began careers in the theatre Broadway was the only theatre that mattered, and there were well over two hundred new works produced a year, whereas now the theatre is drastically changed, and not only due to its decentralization. One of the early dialogues conducted by the editors of *Performing Arts Journal*, it covers a broad range of troubling issues that include the collapse of Broadway, the burgeoning off- and off-off-Broadway scene and its problems of quality, and the status quo nature of regional theatre. What comes through in eloquent detail is their love of acting and actors who, even in the precarious conditions of a country that has no real repertory theatre, provide moments of shared pleasures. These men pull no punches: they were shaped by an intellectual culture in which critics wrote criticism, not publicity.

Both Clurman, now deceased, who was then writing theatre reviews for *The Nation*, and Kauffmann, whose criticism was appearing in *The New Republic*, where he continues to write on film, agree that the contemporary theatre is fragmented in its audiences and underfunded as a nonprofit art, its best talent unchallenged. Kauffmann's words of two decades ago now seem prophetic: "It may be that we're in for a long period in the theatre where we're going to have—not as the equivalent of but as a replacement for genius—committed activity, committed pursuit of ideals rather than actual accomplishment." For his part, Clurman, who was one of the founders in the thirties of The Group Theatre, still echoes the vision of his early fervent years in linking the spiritual state of society and the quality of its artistic expression: "We cannot make theatre out of theatre only. We make it out of life."   BGM

Conversation moderated by Bonnie Marranca
and Gautam Dasgupta, 1978

Theatre in America

PAJ: Let's start with the current state of the theatre; in terms of the American past, that is.

Harold Clurman: I think that the best period of the American theatre was in the twenties. When you have playwrights like O'Neill, Sam Behrman, Maxwell Anderson, and George Kelly, and very good musicals—Gershwin and so forth—and many people coming from abroad—the Moscow Art Theatre and Habimah—you have an active theatre. Some of the plays that were then very important, popular, or valuable are of course much less so today. But there was a richness of product.

And also the actors, many of whom became moving picture actors—Spencer Tracy, Clark Gable—were all present. And we had rather better critics. George Jean Nathan I don't think was a very great critic but he was a stimulating one, and Stark Young was certainly good, and Atkinson, while he had severe limitations, was a very honest and respectable person. The Broadway theatre is no longer a place for serious drama. I think that on the whole it is a place for musical comedy and plays from England, and not necessarily the best plays from England.

Off-off-Broadway you have a very spotty situation. Some promising young people and experiments that are not to be scorned, but are on the whole immature. But the tendency for the popular press is to exalt them and therefore to mislead the people who are conducting these things and to mislead the public. So you get things about which a nice word might be said made into very, very important events. You have young playwrights like Mamet, who's talented, and they're praised beyond all credibility. That's very bad for them because they think this will go on. We have playwrights like Odets and Williams who were greeted enthusiastically but when they got to slow up and then got to be a little less exciting they began to be shamefully scorned.

PAJ: How do you feel about the European situation?

HC: It's hard to know. I've been to Poland and to Germany, and in both places the quality of production is very good. Except that the director and the scene designer have taken over at the expense of playwriting. Sometimes you're dazzled by what you see and you say, What did I get out of this? There's a very talented man in Berlin, by the name of Peter Stein, though I only saw one of his productions, *Summerfolk.* Handke is very much touted by my colleague Mr. Gilman and others. The theatre in

France seems to me utterly dead at the moment. I very rarely see anything on the level of Sartre, Camus, or on the Beckett, Ionesco, Genet level.

I think the best plays—not necessarily very fine plays—but the best general output today is in England. The English are responding to their situation. In other words, they're disgusted, angry, bitter, they all try to cover it up with humor and make a joke of themselves, but at least it's *a response*. What is of the first importance in considering any theatre is the degree to which it responds to the situation in which it is placed.

Stanley Kauffmann: I would like to flesh out bits of what's been said. It happens that it's just fifty years that I've been going to the theatre. I don't think there is any question that Broadway was an infinitely more interesting place fifty years ago. The 1927-28 season was the high point numerically. There were 234 productions. Long ago the number sank below 100, and has never got anywhere near it since. O'Neill got the Pulitzer Prize in that 1927-28 season for *Strange Interlude*. *Showboat* had its premiere. The Broadway range was much greater in those days than now—not just the quantity but the qualitative range. For a very simple reason. Broadway was the whole New York theatre—more or less. Therefore, if a play was to have any kind of production in New York, which meant in effect in America, it had to be done on Broadway. The situation has changed in the fifty intervening years, and changed most rapidly fairly recently—beginning about fifteen years ago. Nowadays it's perfectly obvious that Broadway is only one locus in New York. This city doesn't own the whole American theatre the way it used to, figuratively, but we can still say that New York is, in terms of theatrical energy, easily as active, in sum, as it was fifty years ago.

There are 160 theatres that are numbered in the off-off-Broadway Alliance. We're talking about energy now, dedication and commitment. And this leads to a kind of cultural paradox. We are in a city that teems with various kinds of theatrical vitality. And still we ask each other, as was asked us at the beginning of this conversation, "What do you think of the theatre?" in really a kind of almost despairing tone, or at least an unexcited tone, which I share.

So we have at the moment a city—one of the world capitals of theatre—in which activity is immense and in which quality is a recurringly desperate question. It may be that we're in for a long period in the theatre where we're going to have—not as the equivalent of but as the replacement for genius—committed activity, committed pursuit of ideals rather than actual accomplishment.

HC: I agree fundamentally. I think that I—we both—neglected to mention that some of the plays that are interesting on Broadway come from small theatres outside of New York. Beginning with *The Great White Hope*, which started in Washington. A number of things from Long Wharf and other places outside New York where they can undertake things, first of all, at less expense. So what we have is a deadness at the center which is Broadway, and a certain amount of life at the periphery. That life on the periphery is very important because, while I'm also a New Yorker and have worked in the theatre as a professional so to speak for fifty-three years, this is a very deplorable thing about the situation here. But it's not really deplorable at all, but encouraging, for people to realize that New York is not the center of our universe. That there's no reason why San Francisco or any other place should not also contribute, perhaps valuably.

SK: What happens in most of the theatres throughout the country, however, and I don't say this with any glee, is more or less imitative of New York still. There are very few theatres around this country that are generative in themselves. Either in terms of new plays or of new approaches to the theatre. Some of them are what's called experimental. But the majority of the first-line resident theatres take their guiding genius from what happens in other theatre capitals, primarily New York, in terms of plays and style.

No New Orleans writer of consequence now thinks of writing for a New Orleans theatre. What has to be accomplished underneath the structural change, which, thank heaven, has occurred in this country in the past thirty years with the establishment of theatres around the country, is a return culturally to a condition that existed 100 to 150 years ago, a local audience with pride and taste and ambition. And that means, too, local criticism of consequence. If you are an actor or a director or a playwright working at a resident theatre, you starve after a while for recognition you can respect. I certainly don't mean that the New York critical corps is a body of Lessings and Hazlitts. But in the sheer vulgar currency of fame and energy, New York audiences and critics are still the most vital.

PAJ: Let's talk about the problem of funding for the arts. Who should be funded? Private versus public support. The country seems to be at an impasse on this subject.

HC: I don't want to talk about it because to me it's futile at the moment. The government is doing more than it ever did before, but it's not doing anywhere near enough. And you can't have a national theatre in this country at the moment because if there's going to be a national theatre, there have to be four different national theatres because the country is too big. But where would we have it—Washington? The Texans would say, Why should we pay? I think that that whole idea of funding theatres from established governmental sources is based on a European idea—on European thought—where countries are much smaller. In Germany every town over twenty-five thousand people has its own theatre and its own independent productions. We can't do that. The possibilities for really big money are not present. If anything is to be done, it must be done through cities and through states rather than on a national level.

SK: I think it's exactly true that these ideas come from Europe. But they haven't come forcefully enough. There's a paradox in this. This country is, always was, a democracy. The idea of subsidy that prevails in Europe and elsewhere was originally an aristocratic idea. It's been taken over by many socialist and many democratic countries that have an aristocratic tradition behind them. It doesn't shock anyone in Germany that huge subsidies go to theatres and opera houses. I don't remember the figures offhand, but the Hamburg Opera gets more than the entire national allotment for the theatre in this country. That doesn't strike them as out of the ordinary because the grand duke so-and-so was doing it three hundred years ago and now they're proud to have it taken over by republican hands. The once-aristocratic system now belongs to the people.

HC: Poor England—destroyed England—has got this terrific National Theatre building. And terrific activity. We are not rich enough in this country to afford those things. We're a poor country!

SK: It's all in the state of mind. This country was founded on self-reliance, but as applied to the arts that's a blind principle. It assumes that if you open a grocery store on the corner, work hard and deal fairly, and are a decent fellow, you will succeed. And if you open a theatre and behave the same way, the same thing will happen. In point of fact, the better your theatre is, the less likely it is to make money. The fact that business and art are not analogous has taken about 250 years in this country—from before the country was founded—to crack through.

HC: Besides, Truman said most artists are a bunch of bums.

SK: Nixon said they are Jews and radicals.

HC: This is a true story, by the way: Mr. Koussevitsky of Boston, speaking to Coolidge, asked him why they didn't pay for the arts in this country, for culture. Coolidge said, Why should we spend money for culture? We can buy all we want from France.

SK: But it goes on—this problem of subsidy—which is terribly grave, particularly for people in the performing arts these days. There is a further analogy that is harmful. If you work in a TV factory, your salary responds to the market for television, but if you work in a theatre, especially a nonprofit theatre, your salary has no such huge commercial impetus to respond to. Yet you must buy your food in the same supermarket as the TV man, pay equivalent rent, et cetera. So the theatre is put in what you might call a golden vise. In the theatre, the ballet, all kinds of music, the situation is ghastly, ghastly. And it's the kind of situation which, if it's allowed to harrow down to the roots of art institutions, may destroy things past recovery.

PAJ: Let's go back to a point mentioned earlier: we can't have a national theatre here, but we can and do have city theatres, "state" theatres. And yet they cannot be compared to the national theatres in Europe in terms of accomplishments.

HC: I think something could be done, but it should be done in those states by the people who are interested. In other words, they have to have some kind of civic pride. You know, Margo Jones did a very good thing in Texas. She went to the rich people and she said, You're very wealthy people. Do you mean to say New Yorkers can afford a theatre and we can't? In other words, in towns they should work. But they shouldn't work so that they could come to New York, but they should do the necessary things in their towns. No matter how bad the situation we must fight for something else. We must keep reminding the people that what we are doing is inadequate for what should be done. And we must fight even in the greatest despair.

PAJ: There are contradictions in what both of you have said. On the one hand, you are saying, fine let the pocket theatres thrive, and on the other, that New York is the locus. It is finally where all lines have to meet.

HC: That's not a contradiction, because as Stanley also pointed out, these small theatres are based on a New York idea. That is, they are not generating new things like the small theatres in Germany, where they generate new productions, new ideas, new directors. They don't aim at Berlin or wherever the center is. They are self-sustaining.

SK: You're talking to the point of a national theatre and that raises expectations that I'm not sure that this country can ever fulfill. Here's my definition of a true national theatre, derived from European examples: a permanent company playing in a repertory that consists to a considerable degree of the great dramatic literature of *that* country. Now the prime handicap here is that there is only a handful of truly great American plays. So that sooner or later, any American artistic director who runs such a theatre—if he deals honestly and doesn't want to blow up out of all relativity things that don't really belong on the scale of the names you and I could cite by the dozen—has to make the bulk of his repertory foreign.

Even that would be fine and necessary from another point of view. If we're not going to have any theatres comparable to, let's say, the Comédie Française, then we ought to have in New York—in many cities—what one might call a museum theatre, a theatre that is absolutely essential and is sadly lacking anywhere in this country. A theatre that does for the great dramatic literature what, for example, the Metropolitan Opera tries to do for great operatic literature, what the Philharmonic does for great symphonic literature. In other words, give everyone in his lifetime at least some chance to see and hear great works. Such a museum theatre is generally derided nowadays, by young theatre people particularly. Derided, I think, because it's outside their competence rather than because of conviction. I think it is culturally imperative as one part of the theatrical spectrum. The reasons that mitigate against it are obviously expense, and obviously, too, the difficulty of keeping anything like a permanent company.

PAJ: It is astounding that with all the money poured into theatres and the amount of people studying theatre that there is such a lack of really creative talent. There aren't many artistic directors who are very creative, there aren't many good directors anymore, or playwrights. Why do we have diminishing returns when so much is going into building?

SK: There's not necessarily a connection between the first part of that statement and the second. That is, education doesn't create talent. Maybe we put false expectations on education in the theatre. That is by no means an argument against it because the more that people know, the more likely it is that things can happen. It hasn't happened in a period of a mere twenty or thirty years, which is really what we're talking about.

But one important thing must not be overlooked when we say glibly that we have no great writers. Fifty years ago, almost all the playwriting energy went into Broadway, and we had a lot of prolific writers who had usually one play a year on Broadway. There is, I think, even more playwriting energy nowadays. You know the names, both of you, better than I do. Very few of them dream—as O'Neill dreamed—of going to Broadway. They dream of getting their plays done as they want them done. Here is one thing that must, I think, be said loud and clear about contemporary playwriting: on the whole it is much more serious, liberated, free, and personal than it was fifty years ago. I'm talking about the general level; the peaks don't exist yet. I can think of one or two exceptions. I always want to make an exception of Sam Shepard.

HC: I don't have much to add to what Stanley has said on this score. I'm so disappointed very often in the work of the young playwrights. Not that they aren't sincere and making efforts that are very original. I think Shepard is very talented but he never quite "brings it off" completely; here and there he does. I liked *Curse of the Starving Class* a lot. I feel there is a sort of mystic essence in his work that's important, but he's not always articulate about it.

A lot of the others are still amateurs. They haven't worked hard enough. That's because they're often praised too highly sometimes. They're told everything is fine—experimental. Actually many of these people are half-baked, both in their ideas and their techniques. They are sopping with energy and desire, but they haven't learned how to think well and enough. They are greeted by a lot of slapdash criticism.

I have just written a book on Ibsen in which I point out that he worked many years writing very faulty plays, although there was talent in every one of them. But he fought and he worked and he learned; he really dug in. These other people don't. One of the reasons is that they're American. I don't mean that Americans are an inferior people, but the whole effort is to make everybody seem important, to produce stars—if not in the *New York Times*, then a star in the *Soho Weekly News* or some other place. You have to achieve quickly, you have to be a director in three years, you have to be an actor in four years. And everybody's a great actor and everybody's a great playwright. Our entire culture tends in this direction. This is what's happening to David Mamet and it's ridiculous. I'm for him. I thought *American Buffalo* was a very promising play. But what's happening is that the plays he wrote before that, like *A Life in the Theatre*, are considered wonderful plays. They're juvenilia.

PAJ: It seems that theatre criticism is what we should discuss now.

HC: It's the most damaging thing, not because most critics don't agree with Stanley or me; sometimes we don't agree with each other. But very few critics tell their readers that a play doesn't have to be a masterpiece to be worthwhile . . . We must have standards. High standards. But we don't have to have standards to kill the work of young people who are not first-class. But when we say Sam Shepard is definitely a promising young writer—there's something in his heart, something in his technique—we ought to suggest: go to see it even if you don't like it. They used to say that about modern music and people understood. You didn't have to love Schoenberg. You say this may be difficult, but listen to it. It's important.

These are the things that should be said over and over and over again. But until we have them repeated, most journalistic criticism will remain destructive, because the newspapers are the audience's chief reference in theatregoing. As a director and as a producer, every time I did a play that had good notices people came the next morning with a paper in their hands. The minute we got a weak notice nobody was there. By the way, the critic's responsibility is not to the newspaper, but to the theatre itself and to the artists who work in it. Excuse my vehemence, but I feel strongly about this.

Still, the main problem is not our criticism; it reflects a larger problem. The whole attitude toward the theatre in our country is a diseased one. We all seem to be on the lookout for the greatest show, the greatest actor. I have an idea for the *New York Times* or the *Post*. Let them say, "This is the greatest show on the left side of Forty-fifth Street this week." The publicity/advertisement complex in this country is spoiling and sickening the whole goddamned country from top to bottom. That's how I feel about our beautiful land, for which I harbor so much hope.

SK: I have a clipping at home of a movie ad—a terrible picture. They found one thing to quote: they said, "One of the better movies of the week." The only thing that cheers me up about the state of theatre criticism which, I agree with you, is the core of a lot of the trouble, is that it's *never* been any good. We think reverently of the great critics of the past, but if you read their contemporaries . . . In terms of power there is really only one critic in this country. It's the most powerful critic's job in the world in any art.

HC: I felt like writing to the *New York Times*: "My dear friends, since you have a foreign correspondent as your critic I suggest that I become the critic of finances. I have no knowledge of arithmetic, but I write well."

SK: And you like money.

HC: Why not, why not?

SK: I agree with you that playwrights suffer—I mean really suffer terribly—from overpraise. One thing happens as a result of this, which did not happen in the old Broadway days. You find a playwright writing his sixth, eighth, twelfth play for off-Broadway, off-off-Broadway, with the same faults—curable faults—that he had in his first play. You find talent wasted because of critical pampering and because of the very reaction against the Broadway regimen. There's hope that this may be changing now because the profession of the dramaturg, another European institution, is coming into some standing in this country.

Now, nothing is a solution, but the idea that there should be someone on the staff of a theatre, one of whose chief functions it is to be interested in not just finding good plays, but the art and development of playwriting, to find talent, is a great step forward. There's been this conduit atmosphere—mostly in OOB—in the past twelve to twenty years: if it exists on paper and has some promise of warmth and talent and poetry, let's put it on. And the twelfth play by that author, which is in the same state, is put on too. I will name one theatre—La MaMa, run by a wonderful woman, Ellen Stewart—which has operated on the assumption that it's better to do something that shows some talent than not. And in the long run—and we're getting to be in the long run now after about twenty years—we come to the situation where people ask, "Where are the new playwrights?" What has happened out of all this? Part of what has happened is no discipline, no discipline proceeding from no knowledge.

HC: I think one of the things that we may fall into error about is that we're too self-generating in talking about the theatre. The state of society—the whole of our civilization—has a lot to do with why we're not having better playwrights at the present time. It is a phenomenon in France, in Germany to some extent, and certainly in Russia. There is something about the world that we're not facing sufficiently. The conditions—mental, moral, spiritual. This is upsetting to discipline and to patience, which are all necessary for the creation of art. We cannot make theatre out of theatre only. We make theatre out of life.

SK: There are theatres that try to deal with various aspects of society and of modern consciousness in America.

HC: I don't mean that. I'm not talking about the theatre itself, of course. We as critics, we as dramaturgs, we as people contemplating theatre are saying, If only we get different critics or different this or that, everything will be okay. No, the world has to be changed. If not changed, better understood.

SK: I think we would agree that if the level of spirit and intellect of American society could be raised 50 percent tomorrow, the theatre would automatically improve. But we can't exactly control that.

HC: Obviously, but we should keep on remembering that. I say to the kids who want to be actors, et cetera, Fine, fine. But you've got to start reading the newspapers more carefully . . . and read novels, not novels that were written yesterday or those that received great notices in the *New York Times*. I remember one day in class I said, "You know, you should all by now have read Dickens, Dostoyevsky, Thomas Hardy, Flaubert, Balzac," and after I made a list of such standard names there was a big howl of laughter. And I said, "What the hell are you laughing about?" When I was twenty-five I had read those things and now that I'm somewhat over twenty-five I want to re-read them. I went to art exhibitions and I went to the Metropolitan Museum and I followed modern music. What happens is that now everybody has gotten into his little groove and acts as if that little groove were the whole story. We acquire standards by imbibing the best of our culture.

SK: The curious thing about the theatre—to pick up a point of yours—and its relation to society is that obviously it's the product of the society in which it exists. But the best theatre is always prodding the society at the same time. It's always trying to make it a little disturbed, at least, if not better, than it was. And I'm not talking, by any means, of political theatre. Very little political theatre has been successful, artistically, in terms of vision. But theatre people finally can't do more than what they can do within their professions.

HC: I would like to say that the only way to help today is to blow up all the theatres on Broadway.

SK: I once asked students in a critical seminar to write on what they thought of Broadway, and a very young playwright said Broadway is a place where, if you're lucky you get a job in a play and you go there eight times a week and you do the same part for three years. This, he said, is called the Theatre of Cruelty.

PAJ: We've covered a lot of ground concerning artists and institutions. Now let's move to the changing tastes of audiences.

SK: That's an interesting point. Let's talk about New York audiences. The audience of fifty years ago was by and large a middle-class audience—with a certain view of itself as the apex of Western history. Middle-class values were considered the summum bonum and, although there were radicals who disagreed, no one took them very seriously. The bulk of the audience today—Broadway and much of off-Broadway (at the Public Theater, for example)—is still middle-class. I don't think there is any discernible difference between the audience that goes to *A Chorus Line* uptown and that which went to it downtown. But they have different attitudes today toward themselves and toward their middle-classness. There is more of a sense of guilt about being middle-class because of events that have happened in the intervening fifty years, because of the ferociousness of the attacks on them, and because, as against their forebears, they are in the majority college graduates and have at least different kinds of pretenses, if not different basic ideals.

So there's a kind of openness to innovation that the previous middle-class audience didn't have. There's also an openness to kinds of sexual behavior, to sexual language, that would have been unthinkable, not fifty but fifteen years ago. And another change in the middle-class audience is that now it contains a good number of black people, which it certainly did not contain before. And that's been reflected in Broadway productions of plays by and for blacks. Another chief component of the present-day audience in New York, which did not exist before, is the audience that goes to off-off-Broadway, which I think is centrally different from the uptown audience, even the off-Broadway audience. People who go to see Richard Foreman's theatre do not conceivably go to see *Annie*.

PAJ: Or Foreman's *Threepenny Opera* uptown at Lincoln Center or *Stages* on Broadway.

SK: And they don't go in any great numbers to see John Guare's plays. To use an old-fashioned word, they are "bohemians" and they represent a special theatre audience in this city—the most cogent and recognizable, as a matter of fact. There's a defect in that audience, as there is in almost every virtue, in that they become a coterie audience, they're almost conspiratorial to keep their theatre sort of amateurish. Anything that is unpolished is good. They've made an aesthetics out of amateurism. But we must also note that there are many OOB theatres that have an organizing principle—for certain kinds of plays, a certain kind of directorial approach, or an ethnic or social basis. The feminist theatre has come up in the past five or six years, as have several avowedly homosexual theatres. All these theatres represent elements in the New York social fabric, but they wouldn't have been so clearly represented fifty years ago.

Just one last note about change which is not entirely tangential. When I was going to Broadway, up until certainly the time of the Second World War, going to the place itself, the physical place had great attraction and glamour. It glittered. What Broadway meant to the world, it meant to me.

HC: Absolutely true.

SK: There was excitement. Even if you said to yourself, "Oh, I'm above all this," you loved it. You *loved* it. You loved going to a smart, glittering musical. You loved seeing the latest George S. Kaufman play.

PAJ: Was it true of the twenties, thirties, and forties audiences that the musicals had one audience and the straight play another?

SK: Not in any really distinctive sense. There were people who didn't like the plays that the Theatre Guild did because they thought they were too heavy, and people who would only go to musicals and comedies, but it wasn't a severe class distinction, just a matter of taste. But the point I want to make is that now there are three theatres in New York—Broadway, off-Broadway, and off-off-Broadway. You know when you're seeing an OOB show.

HC: I almost killed myself at Foreman's theatre. I call it the Theatre of Jeopardy.

PAJ: Foreman had a big laugh once when a woman asked him where the lobby of the theatre was.

HC: My point is that in the sixties the artists—mostly painters—founded a community. Now audiences are divided into small groups. There was the OOB playwright who said he did not want to see his work done on Broadway.

SK: It's silly to have to be fooling around with these acronyms but the OB playwright who existed before the OOB playwright became firmly centered off-Broadway, moved uptown then if he could and if he was invited to. I think what we're getting at is that the OB play is now more transferable. It may be written with the same OB intent but it's more transferable.

PAJ: David Mamet and Albert Innaurato fall into this category, but they are hardly off-Broadway playwrights, in the experimental sense.

SK: That's what I mean.

PAJ: There is another problematic point regarding playwrights. Today we have playwrights who come out of some of the best universities in the country, where they are exposed to great dramatic literature, and yet who are incapable of writing anything more than television-level work.

SK: I understand your point but what you're really doing is criticizing an educational system for not creating talent.

HC: We're not Europeans. That's my quarrel with Stanley, or sometimes with Brustein and Bentley when they say O'Neill isn't good. They place him against Ibsen and Strindberg—but they had a long head start. We have to accept a man like O'Neill who is not as great as the others because our whole theatre began in 1920.

SK: When I say things like this in film criticism I'm always accused of being an inverse provincial. It nevertheless works out to the fact that this is an inheritor country, a scion country of culture that's made its own distinctive contributions but did not originate much in any art.

HC: Except in musical comedy.

SK: There's an argument on that, too. But that fact, which is a historical not judgmental one in the theatre, has produced a tradition toward the theatre in European writers that's very different from here. Point one: most European plays are written by men and women who are more than playwrights. Very, very few of the greatest plays have been written by people who wrote only plays. Theatre was part of the instrumentality of culture. It's a lie that novelists can't write plays. That's only true of English-language novelists. The theatre has always seemed for the elite European writer—and I mean that with respect, not pejoratively—as an avenue open to him for one kind of idea, one kind of poem, a dramatic rather than lyrical poem.

Point two: Europeans operate out of a more homogeneous culture and see themselves as immersed in the tensions, the polarities, of an organism, more than Americans. Why have there been so many good Southern writers in this century? Because they are the most homogeneously "culture-conscious" of Americans. Harold spoke about the English playwrights. The English believe, they say so, that they're more diverse than Americans, within an organism. And because they are more, in a sense, compact or contained they're more acutely aware of their differences. The early Edward Bond plays—in my opinion his best—are very keenly aware of what it's like to suffer in the country, à la Thomas Hardy. That's something for which we have no exact equivalent in the contemporary American theatre . . . I think two or three of the German-Austrian playwrights are among the best now writing.

HC: Peter Handke.

SK: Handke, Wolfgang Bauer, Kroetz. American plays are trying to sense this—let's call it community hunger—by the transmogrification of pop culture. Sam Shepard does this, particularly in his rock plays. But it is not quite the same thing. I don't know if there's anything to be done about this except for the country to live a little longer. I'm just trying to understand in my own mind why more interesting writing is coming from England and Germany than we're getting today in the United States. . . . This is not a general American phenomenon; it's an American *theatrical* phenomenon. There is very fine American poetry being written now. There are some fine American novels being written. And there are good painters and architects. I think the problem of playwriting has deep roots in American attitudes toward the theatre. As Harold said before, in terms of theatre *seriousness*, this is a very young country.

HC: A society has to stay together longer to have good plays. The Israelis say, "Why don't we have great plays? After all, we're a very bright people." I say, "You're new." They say, "What do you mean—we're two thousand years old." The Jews may be that old but it's a new country. You cannot have it that quickly. Theatre has to do with the social collective that has been established, and living together for a long time.

PAJ: The topic of playwriting has taken a good deal of our interest. Acting is a subject we haven't yet covered in this discussion.

HC: I'll tell you what I think about actors. They don't get enough work. They're amateurs. Why? Not because they lack talent. Al Pacino and Dustin Hoffman are talented. They don't act. Henry Irving played two hundred roles before he came to London. How many parts has Colleen Dewhurst played? Our stars don't act, and when they do they play one part all the time.

SK: One of the things Harold says is absolutely true, seen differently. The amount of activity is inseparable from the state of the theatre. I think one of the problems with acting today is that there is so much of it. There is everything that goes on in the theatre, everything that goes on in films, television, and commercials. And what has become the obsessive criterion of all this activity? —*how much it does not look like acting . . .* This criterion has to do with photography, it has to do with American film, it has to do with the kinds of writing that we like. Embarrassment with large gestures. It has to do with art as a buffer against emotions and experience. These things are militating against much serious activity in this country. When you see a young man come along like Stacy Keach, whom I saw in very early appearances at the Yale Rep and in *Macbird*, you see a talent. But it's chewed up, not so much by commercialism or the fact that there is no good theatre to step into, but because all he can sell is *not being an actor.*

PAJ: Both of you have had the opportunity over the years to watch the careers of actors in many great roles. And both of you have had the opportunity to write on performance. When we were writing for the *Soho Weekly News* there was hardly a performance one could write about in terms of acting style. Many of us feel cheated out of the chance to watch good actors develop over the years.

HC: That's what I'm saying. They don't play the parts.

SK: There have not been many auspicious careers opening in the past fifteen years. When I think of an actor who has grown in the past ten or fifteen years, I think of two principally: James Earl Jones and Geraldine Fitzgerald. A kind of inertia settles in with people who could grow. Marlon Brando, whom Harold directed early in his career on Broadway, has settled into a life of rich self-loathing in Hollywood because he's not doing what he could have done. Or younger magnificently talented actors like Paul Newman and George C. Scott. They are men who have achieved a kind of power in our commercial theatre where they could do whatever they choose to do, and they choose to do nothing—except an occasional film that appeals to them or a revival. Scott is a wonderful actor but he has no sense of career in the way we are using the term. The last actor I can think of in that position in the English-speaking theatre who insisted on having a career, what he considered to be an aesthetically honorable career, was Olivier.

HC: So did Alfred Lunt, although he didn't get to do enough classics. He saw himself in a film and said, "I'm not so hot," and stopped.

PAJ: Where does the teaching of acting fit in?

HC: I teach master classes. That doesn't mean that the people in the classes are masters. It means they are supposed to have mastered the basic techniques. I said in a lecture in Russia once: "America is lousy with talent." America has as much talent as anywhere in the world. But the stranglehold of the cultural system allows actors to play only one kind of role. They want to get to Broadway, to television. But talent's not enough to make it. You have to have discipline. You have to have guts. People don't have that feeling today; it's gone. There's no struggle.

PAJ: We know there have been great actors in the past. Were the directors quantitatively better?

HC: The good directors were Stanislavsky and others. The greatest director whose work I ever saw was Meyerhold. The actors didn't want to work for him after a while; he became too much the controlling factor. He had two good actors and they both left. Grotowski had one good actor and now he's mostly occupied teaching the Grotowski technique. Today we have directors who have a feeling about acting. The actors have to help them.

SK: Harold made a good point by bringing up the name of Meyerhold. He represents something that's happened with the directing in this century, which is that the director has taken over from the actor.

HC: By the way, Reinhardt was a much better director of actors than Meyerhold, but Meyerhold was an even greater director. I think the greatest directors were Meyerhold, Stanislavsky in the sense that he built a great theatre, Brecht, and Grotowski are or were very important. But they were not necessarily the best for actors. Reinhardt was very useful to actors and Stanislavsky was marvelous.

SK: But that depends on whether you mean representational acting or not.

HC: But look, people off-off-Broadway can do acrobatics and the like. They do it well or badly, but that's not acting. Meyerhold, for example, insisted most of all on physical and vocal virtuosity. If they were good actors, they made something of his biomechanics. Our actors' deficiencies are not the directors' fault. The fault is the actor's lack of work opportunities. I think human beings nowadays are being whittled down by society to half size anyway.

SK: The best first performance I've seen in my lifetime since O'Neill was a play by Athol Fugard—*Boesman and Lena*. And that did present opportunities for wonderful representational performers. Ruby Dee is one of the fine unacknowledged actresses of our time. But in her case that's not only an acting problem but a race problem. We have in the representational mode a very fine director of actors with almost no ambition— Mike Nichols. He knows how to direct actors. And what does he direct them in? I don't have to answer that question.

On the other hand, Foreman, who is, I think, within strict limitations an interesting artist, is not remotely interested in representational acting. And it would be a mistake to say that it's a fault in Foreman not to be producing theatre in the Stanislavsky vein. If he is going to have any benefit for us at all he has to be what he is.

HC: I have seen wonderful nonrepresentational actors in the Meyerhold theatre. All these experimentalists are complete amateurs compared to Meyerhold and the Moscow Art Theatre. By the way, they had body work ten times better than anything I've ever seen, they had better training in their schools. So, this whole business about the realistic and the nonrepresentational is nonsense. All this is based on one thing: the person who is really well trained. They didn't have amateurs like Schechner and to some extent Foreman. The German actors today can do things representationally. Peter Stein's mostly representational.

PAJ: But the German actors respect Stein and are willing to be trained in the representational mode. They are willing to be trained to be good actors.

HC: We don't have directors who have their own theatre. Nichols, who's very successful, doesn't have his own theatre. I had my own theatre for ten years, with Strasberg and Crawford, and we were doing representational plays to some extent. But I'm sure if we had one now, we would have expanded our methods and techniques because we were anxious to move with the times.

SK: Let me say one more thing on this subject. I think that directors make their theatre. And the only directors I can think of in New York, or in the country—in the past fifteen years—who have generated enough enthusiasm to have people follow them, have been nonrepresentational directors.

PAJ: You've both painted a despairing picture of contemporary theatre. What can we hope for in the coming years?

HC: I don't despair, I never despair. I complain, shout, fight, work, propagandize—through lectures, acting classes, reviews, articles, books. In brief, create the kind of world—in the theatre at least—I believe in. That's all any *one* of us can do. I hope many others will do the same.

SK: Trouble. Money trouble. Social trouble, which automatically means trouble in the theatre. But one thing that good theatre education has been doing, the education that you're impatient with for not producing masters, is to produce—let's call it—a certain disgust. At least some of the people who come out of good theatre education are disgusted with a trick-dog theatre that sits up when a bored audience snaps its fingers. These people want to do something more with their lives. We can't look forward to geniuses—that's like pinning hopes on miracles. We can reasonably look forward to honor and commitment in the exercise of talent, in the face of a cloudy situation getting cloudier. It's even not impossible that the audience—I mean wherever there are theatres in this country—will get again that sense of possessiveness toward their theatres that once made the theatre truly decentralized in this country. And there's one other thing—part of all this and in my mind not one whit less important. There's good reason to hope for some improvement in the level of theatre criticism.

Herbert Blau

WHEN HERBERT BLAU BEGAN his life in the theatre, moved by the ideals of the *théâtre populaire*, what mattered to him was theatre's role in the creation of civic culture. But, after confronting the municipal reality of San Francisco in the fifties, where he had founded The Actor's Workshop to introduce important European playwrights to a newly decentralized audience, and then finding himself unable to project a national platform at Lincoln Center when he became its codirector during the upheavals of the Vietnam War, Blau abandoned his dream of making theatre central to American social debate.

In more recent decades, after starting his KRAKEN company and becoming a distinguished educator, Blau has turned his restless dialectical intellect from the activities of producer and director to a contemplation of the nature of theatrical experience. Elaborating on themes that preoccupy him in *The Audience* and *To All Appearances,* once again Blau explores his fascination with the taboo of seeing and being seen and the instability of appearances that theatre investigates. How does the theatrical act materialize, and when does one know it? For Blau, whose touchstones remain the Greeks, Shakespeare, and the modern repertoire, the audience is what happens, the theatrical event becoming what prompts thought. "I'm known to myself more acutely in art than I am known to myself outside it," he offers.

As he moves between the social engagement of Brecht and the absolute void of Beckett, one satisfying his need for history, the other for poetry, Blau finds in the actor's body a spiritual discipline approaching the state of pure mind, theatre itself suspended, Platonically, above the material world yet rooted in corporeal reality. What kind of performance will satisfy the postmodern strategies and high modernist disposition of the melancholy Blau? It sounds perfectly sublime: "I've always wanted to create a theatre that would be like Picasso's sculptured 'Death's Head.' So dense it would be almost like a black hole, the gravity so great it would warp back into itself and come out the other side." BGM

Conversation with Bonnie Marranca
and Gautam Dasgupta, 1992

The Play of Thought

Bonnie Marranca: Let me begin by reading something to you from *The Im-possible Theater,* which may be a good place for us to start. In that book, you said, "The chief thing for us to do is to start creating real alternatives in popular theatre to the community theatres and the shopping cen-ters which reflect, not the spiritual power, but the moral stupor of our cultural explosion. I am thinking of regional centers, widely recruited audiences, in collaboration with scholars, churches, unions, industry, workshops, critiques, lectures, tours, youth conferences—a full public life growing around a substantial repertoire." It's almost twenty-eight years now since you wrote that, in what was declared a manifesto. I'd like to set that in the context of where you are today, because obviously you've gone through many changes in your long career in the theatre. This was a vision of theatre rooted in Vilar and Copeau and the Little Theatre movement in America that was still possible to dream of in the sixties. Is that dream possible any longer?

Herbert Blau: No, I don't really think so. There are actually two dreams folded in each other in that statement. One was the notion of a local energy, making the scene wherever you happened to be, part of which was realized in the sixties. The other was attached to what still seems to me the major dream of this century, a dream with scale. I'd associate that with the movement of *théâtre populaire* in Europe, of which the Ber-liner Ensemble became the emblematic theatre. Jean Vilar and Roger Planchon were the major practitioners in France, Joan Littlewood in En-gland. All represent what we thought we were, or might become, when I was in San Francisco with The Actor's Workshop. But the overall dream, the one with scale, was the marriage of socialism and surrealism, which remained the impelling promise of the century, as it was, say, on the bar-ricades in Paris in 1968. When I came back from Europe, where I went in the late fifties because there was next to nothing to be learned in the United States—it was this vision that I tried to bring back to San Fran-cisco: a theatre of some activist dimension, with an audience composed of workers, intellectuals, and students. I hadn't seen anything like that occurring in American theatre at the time.

Gautam Dasgupta: Was it because of the political situation in which Europe found itself after the two devastating wars that the dream could not be transplanted to this side of the ocean?

HB: You have to back up half a century in order to see what we're always contending with. When I started working in the theatre, what dominated everything outside of New York was the notion of "Tributary Theatre." The old, yellow-covered *Theatre Arts* magazine enunciated the idea, but the word "tributary" was always used in a double sense. On the one hand, New York was the fountainhead and source of all power in the theatre, with minor channels and rivulets of possibility leaking out into the provinces. Then there was the second sense of the term: everything outside of New York would be "paying tribute" to New York. I'm speaking now of the late forties and early fifties.

The problem was compounded by the fact that theatre has always been a secondary or tertiary art in this country. If culture in the United States was secondary to begin with, theatre was a shadow of that secondary culture, a shadow's shadow. I'm not sure that we will ever be able to change the fact that people don't grow up in any sort of tangible relationship to theatre practice.

BGM: But it seems to me that you had, at least at the start of The Actor's Workshop, very broad ideals for what theatre could be: reflecting the life of the mind of society. Your ideals of the theatre expressed in the manifesto and the writings on The Actor's Workshop reflect the belief that theatre encompassed civic participation. So the public would witness itself in a spectacle *as a public*. It seems to me that what you were getting at then, and which no one thinks about now, is theatregoing as a form of citizenship.

HB: Oh, yeah. I think that distinction is quite true. And that's a distinction you also tried to make in your essay, "Thinking about Interculturalism" in the recent PAJ book *Interculturalism and Performance*. I think that you were also right there in making reference to Hannah Arendt. Her view of the city is a really quite different view of civic space than that which prevails in the theatre as we know it. On the other hand, we have different cities. Our cities are deteriorating before our eyes. If they were always psychically polluted, as in *Oedipus*, they're quite specifically polluted now, dangerous and forbidding in ways that they weren't at that time, not in San Francisco. That was an accommodating city then, almost pristine, with a realizable space of possibility. At least that's the way we looked at it. Still, there are a couple of things that should be qualified. There are certain subtexts all the way through *The Impossible Theater*. As vociferous a book as it may have been—because it was a manifesto— there were also things that were partially repressed, having to do with the attitudes of people *in* the theatre toward its evolution as a theatre with designs on the city. There was not only considerable resistance to its more adventurous repertoire, but also a certain jaundice, a sense of our (my) being pretentious in talking about the theatre as a social or political force, a significant civic space. If most of the actors were gradually won over, then there were other resistances.

We were aspiring to be a civic theatre, but the civic administration of San Francisco never really helped us out, and it wasn't until we got good reviews in New York that the audience in San Francisco paid any serious attention to us. It wasn't until we were invited to go to Lincoln Center that there was an immense civic uproar about the potential loss of The Actor's Workshop. By the time we left San Francisco we had anywhere from three to five theatres playing simultaneously in miscellaneous spaces, but we never had an adequate theatre, not even remotely like a European state theatre. The city, from time to time, would promise to do something for us, but never did. No sooner were we invited to go to New York than the city immediately promised to build us a theatre. We told the city to go to hell, and left. The status of a theatre in this country, as you know, is simply a function of what's said in the newspapers. And that's true, by the way, not only of what we used to think of as commercial theatre, but it's equally true of experimental theatre.

BGM: So actually, Hannah Arendt's idea of the public realm has been perverted into the publicity realm.

HB: The publicity realm, the media realm—it's the mediascape that we're actually talking about.

BGM: But, you know, a strong thread going through all of your work, and it certainly starts in *The Impossible Theater*, is the spiritual dimension, which really connects your ideals so much to modernism. I feel very strongly about the fact that postmodernism in its critique of modernism has obliterated and distorted and written out this spiritual dimension that is behind so much of modernism. Even your so-called dream of socialism and surrealism has to do very much with this spiritual essence. Maybe we'll come back to this, though I feel you're more of a materialist than, say, someone who's apt to fall into the spiritual realm, even though you might be attracted to that. But it's the more messianic quality of the work that links it to modernism. I have the feeling from reading the work that you regarded—and maybe still do—theatre as a sacred institution.

HB: I suppose I've always had a feeling for the sacred, though I'm not religious. I tend to resist amorphous and vague notions of the spiritual. But I do believe in energies and powers. And I have a very strong feeling for what, say, Milton suggests when he talks about princedoms and dominations and powers and authorities. I really do feel that there are constituted energies in the universe, and that they embody themselves from time to time. Sometimes I see these in what are now thought of suspiciously as canonical texts, and in the virtuosity and the intelligence of particular artists. And I've always felt that the theatre, which we think of as a carnal form, a form that's essentially embodied, acquires this power not so much from the simple material presence of the human body performing, but even more materially from power of mind. That's its real authority. A book that I recently published, *The Audience*, concludes with an image that combines the idea of authority, virtuosity, discipline, and power in a kind of suspension of the material world, *above* the material world, something like a Divine Idea. That's the image of Philipe Petit walking on a tightrope between the twin towers of the World Trade Center. There you have a pure existentialist act that is contingent upon extraordinary physical prowess. It's what one comes to understand through a spiritual discipline or the most admirable accomplishment in sports: that when the body is perfected to a certain limit, it almost becomes something like pure mind. As Vince Lombardi used to say, at that point it's all *mental*.

GD: You sound Neoplatonic.

HB: True, and not unlike what Artaud talks about in *The Theatre and Its Double*, when he describes a painting called *The Daughters of Lot*, in which hieratic figures are walking across a deep crevasse, as if above the material world, very much like Platonic ideas.

BGM: But what intrigues me about some of the themes you bring up, and this seems to be a strong one in *The Audience*, is looking at the audience as constituted as a body of thought and desire—that *the audience is what happens*. That's an interesting notion about perception. It's not the play that happens, but the audience that happens. You take the emphasis from the play or the production onstage or the event to the mind of the audience. And also, I think, you go further than that by talking about the thing not happening until it is thought. So you get into the whole area that Gertrude Stein wrote so eloquently about: the difference between seeing and hearing, or how one understands what is going on in the theatrical performance—how you know what you know.

HB: What you're describing now comes out of a considerable shift in the object of attention. There's a significant difference between trying to make *theatre*, and trying to make *a* theatre with a large number of people, a tangible public institution, whether it achieves widespread public acceptance or not. I spent the early part of my career working (with my partner Jules Irving) to form a company, to get plays on, to be able to pay the actors, to raise money, and to run a repertoire, at the same time thinking about (I'll bracket the word) the "nature" of theatre, what it should be or might be. The distance, however, between the work done in San Francisco and the work that I did later with the KRAKEN group was considerable. In that work I was exceedingly attentive to, consumed with, the *idea* of theatre itself: Where did it come from? Or was it always already there? I mean: *in the beginning*, if there was a beginning. It's at that subjunctive point that theatre intersects with theory, the emergence of a specular consciousness dwelling on an origin, either refusing to accept the notion of a beginning, a source, or developing some tracelike relationship to the inauguration of a possibility, a prospect, so that the memory of what you're seeking virtually creates it. What were the impulses of the theatrical act? How were these constituted? And how could we know when they materialized? Let me put it this way: when I began to theorize the work with KRAKEN, from which all my theoretical writing has been derived, I realized the degree to which I had been fascinated by the activity of consciousness itself as the primal scene of theatre. That activity, reciprocated, is also what creates the audience. The audience does not exist until it is *thought*. Nor does the theatre exist until it is precipitated from whatever it is it was *not*. What I've been increasingly interested in is a sort of ontological inquiry that addresses the old question of "what is theatre?" but in terms of its materialization from whatever it is it was not.

BGM: It's really the Pirandellian question . . . speaking of which, tonight is the Halloween parade in Greenwich Village.

HB: Yes. It's the Pirandellian question.

BGM: But I want to point out one thing. You do agree that thinking is not the same as consciousness.

HB: No. You make an issue of thinking and, as you know, I wrote a book called *Blooded Thought*. I've always felt that Wallace Stevens' phrase—"an abstraction blooded as a man by thought"—is a fine description of what most charges, initiates, incites a theatre space. In recent years, what has incited my thought (in-site) is the most minimal prospect of theatre. For example: the moment that *I*—my "self" precipitated at this table, *right now*—I look at you and you look at me. Whatever we were doing before *this* moment was occurring without consciousness of a relationship that has now been theatricalized. The theatricalizing occurs simply by looking, with that inflection of consciousness we now call "the gaze." I'm very conscious that you're there, you're very conscious that I'm there, and Gautam is conscious that we have this relationship—different now than just before—and is observing us both, and we can now, of course, implicate Gautam, he *has* been implicated, in this precipitation of theatre. How does the theatrical moment materialize, as if from nothing, its most minimal sensation—that's what I've been trying to theorize in recent years.

BGM: But then you turn it into a taboo.

HB: Well . . .

BGM: I mean, in some sense, you speak of theatre being about the taboo of watching. You give it a spin into psychoanalysis.

HB: Well, it was interesting to me, when I first called attention to the watching, that you slightly withdrew.

BGM: I've never liked being watched.

HB: Well, that's why one has to propose the possibility that there's an operative taboo in the look. Which is to say, we are referring to issues of voyeurism and exhibitionism. At one and the same time, we in some sense want to be observed, we want to be recognized; and then there's something in us that fundamentally resists it. Maybe even fears it.

I had this experience not long ago with my daughter—well, it was when she was still a baby in the crib. I remember it quite distinctly—the first moment when I felt that she withdrew from my gaze. There I was looking at her with a kind of devotion or love, but that time, in the purity of my regard, there seemed to be a withdrawal. She simply turned away, gazing, from my gaze. Beckett actually talks about this as the "nesting stare," as if the infant were looking back to a purer state, something other than the possession implicit in the gaze.

GD: Similar, in a sense, to the symbolist aesthetic of bridging the chasm between the spectator and the stage, the perceiver and that which is perceived. He who is spectated upon seeks ardently to enter a state in which he is a spectator, in the process dissolving the very distinction that gives birth to the idea of theatre.

HB: It seems to me that there are certain almost archetypal moments, even within the canonical drama, that address precisely this issue. And I'm not talking here about the kind of thing that's involved in reception theory. I'm rather indifferent to that sort of treatment of the audience. As you know, *The Audience* hardly addresses at all the audiences I have known. And I have known over the years a lot of audiences. We're all really aware that at some time tonight (or when night comes where they are) people will be gathering in spaces all over the world. That's not, however, the audience I'm really talking about in the book.

But let me see if I can explain, by drawing on a couple of things referred to in the book. It may be some sort of poetic accident, or poetic justice of history, that in the only extant trilogy among all the Greek tragedies, the *Oresteia*, the first character to appear is called The Watchman. Try to reconstruct in your mind the festival of Dionysus at a theatre in Athens, with eighteen thousand people observing at dawn this character who seems to appear as if from barbaric darkness, as if he's awaking into the Platonic tradition of the Western Enlightenment itself. He is waiting, as you remember, for the light to come across the mountaintops from Troy, as if, as I say, he were awaking into the dream of civilization itself as it's been constructed by the West. That character, designated The Watchman, is watching and being watched.

Remember: he situates himself in the universe, below all "the grand processionals of all the stars of night." He operates at one and the same time in and out of the play, so to speak.

Within the dramaturgy there's a kind of paranoia: he's worried about what Clytemnestra might do if he says too much, but yet he has to speak so that the play can get underway, to provide the others watching with exposition, to let us know what's happening *within* the play. What's always interested me especially is a line toward the end of his speech (however it's translated), when he says, after setting up the ambiguous conditions under which the play will proceed: "I speak to those who understand, but if they fail, I have forgotten everything." What is the audience? *Those who understand.* Now there the issue of taboo and the issue of the sacred and the issue of perception and the reversal of theatre, its inverted doubleness, seem to operate all at once. He speaks to those who understand, which implies that even before the play begins, you already know. Except that you don't know that you know. So what would constitute a deal that would permit you to know what you already know?

BGM: Well, I can understand why you chose that, because of your way of thinking about theatre as remembrance and as memory. But it's also interesting that in *The Audience* you turn around the terms of the notion of audience—the auditory—by expressing your interest in the audience as a figure of speech. Could you elaborate on that?

HB: I think that comes about at the other end of the play, with the arrival of Athena, that bisexual rhetorical figure. But let me shift to another context: "Who's there?" That's the opening line of *Hamlet*. Already there's an ontological reversal: the wrong guys, as you recall, say it. And the response is, "Nay, stand and unfold yourself." Now there you have a case in which the text, which seems to be in command of expression, is so to speak addressing the untexted, those *out there*. And saying, You're going to get nothing from me unless you speak up. Right? "Stand and unfold yourself." Which is to say, at some level the audience has to identify itself by a kind of counteraddress. It has to be recognized and it has to respond. The beginning of *Hamlet*—you see it in Pirandello too—is the prototype of those moments in the drama that seem to break the sound barrier between the perceiver and the perceived. It ups the ante on perception itself, making the demand, requiring the spectator in some sense to *speak*.

With the *Oresteia*, we may be conscious in the beginning of the taboo that inhibits speech: I speak to those who understand, but if they fail, I don't remember anything. What's remembered, however, is not exactly easy to understand. Which is why it seems to open up the entire history of interpretation. As you make your way through the *Oresteia*, you may look to the Chorus for guidance, only to find it exceedingly conscious of the play of appearances and the impermeability, even the opacity, of ap-pearance. Or *dis*-appearance, like "the oar-blade's fading footprint." They keep asking the gods to "grant meaning" to the appearances. They ad-dress Zeus, or whatever name he might have, because it's not even clear what names should be used for the indeterminable powers who may be watching, presiding over these things. But whoever it is, whatever power it is, is petitioned for meaning.

Now, for me, that is the great mission of theatre: to grant meaning to appearances, the appearances in which we commonly live, the feeling that we have about whatever constitutes reality, that we're always in the immanence of theatre, that we may be perceiving at any moment—even among the three of us now—merely the appearances of what should be transparencies. Which is to say, you ought to be what you appear to be. But at some limit of our knowledge of each other, there is always the sen-sation that somehow we're not seeing it, or each other, truly. Through the entire history of the canonical drama, we appear to be dealing with some essential rupture that even love can't heal, a fundamental wound that prevents us somehow from being precisely what we are, and to be perceived as what we are.

GD: Doesn't this rupture come about because of language? In some sense what you're asking for is the purity of theatre, that point at which theatre truly precipitates into pure theatre, into the idea of theatre. That obvi-ously happens in a soliloquy. I mean, when someone retires, becomes entirely separate, draws the curtain, what he is essentially saying is: Lis-ten, I deny spectatorship. Or else it happens in a play such as *Oedipus*, where he chooses to blind himself. At that point, Oedipus does become pure theatre, because then he can't reciprocate your gaze, he can't engage in a certain duplicity with his audience. That's entirely introverted, as it were, through his blindness. The entire world only exists in his mind. It doesn't exist as exteriority. So what you're asking for then is that theatre as we know it, to meet the demands that you wish to place on theatre, will have to deny certain basic characteristics of the form in which one enters into a relational duplicitous system of discourse. So one has to deny language, one has to deny the gaze. Are you talking about some sort of a closet drama of the mind?

HB: I'm not necessarily talking at this point about a construct of theatre that I would like to see occur. I'm simply trying to understand my experience of theatre and my reading of plays, regardless of what any of us might *want* the theatre to be. It's as if the theatre, the social institution, has its own closet drama, leaving us with this question: Why is it that the theatre is—in every culture that I have known—troubled by the nature of theatre? The canonical drama of the West seems to me to be pervaded by a ludic resistance to the idea of theatre itself. When we went through the period, in the sixties, when the texts were disappearing, it's as if the drama was phasing itself out historically, almost scared to death by its essential content. Its essential content was that we live in a world of appearances and we're not known to each other. All the great plays in one way or another are concerned with that, as well as the incapacity of perception itself. Look at what's happening in a play like *Troilus and Cressida:* when Troilus, for example, is watching Cressida being seduced by or seducing Diomedes, the appalling effect on Troilus is such that even the extraordinarily acute capacities of Shakespeare's language can't exactly describe the demoralizing difference between the Cressida that was and the Cressida that he sees before him, the seeing itself being part of the problem, to which there appears to be no solution.

BGM: What strikes me in thinking about your work is how utterly Freudian it is. You write so much about theatre and the primal scene, and repression as an activity of perception—the impossibility of viewing theatre as anything but repression. In that respect, you seem to be going between the two poles of Norman O. Brown, whom I was glad to see you brought into the discussion of the audience in your recent book, and the schizo-culture theory of Deleuze and Guattari. I'm not certain where you stand, because you seem not to be able to go all the way with Brown into the spiritual transformation that he speaks about.

HB: In reference to the tantrism at the end, mysticism.

BGM: Into the "om." But on the other hand, there's an intriguing term that he uses in *Love's Body* in which he calls for an end to repression—"body mysticism." I think we're seeing more of this now, more than thirty years since Brown wrote about it. There seems to be a body mysticism in French continental theory—and it all circles around Artaud.

HB: In *The Eye of Prey* there is an essay in which I try to explain how that comes about. If you look at what generally passes under the rubric of deconstruction, and take the major figures that came to our attention during the seventies—Derrida, Foucault, Barthes, Deleuze, and Lacan—you can ask the same question about them that Freud once asked about women: What do they *want*? Well, essentially I think they want what students wanted in the sixties in this country. As I try to explain in *The Eye of Prey*, when the countercultural movement receded here and began to go underground in its most volatile form, say in the image of the Weathermen, totally underground, by that time it had already gone abroad with acid rock, blue jeans, pop culture. A lot of the tendencies of the sixties—the "polymorphous perverse" tendencies of the period, the addiction to body language, valorization of the body, the feeling that the body had a fundamental truth that was an unrecognized truth—had already gone to Europe. There, as opposed to what happened in America, it immediately entered the high intellectual structures of European thought, was intensely theorized, and came back to America doubly sublimated: reified in theory, repressed in behavior—and then was taught in the schools.

What does this theory fundamentally want? It wants alternative institutions, it wants a return of the repressed. It wants to deal with what seems to me a major issue in the conception of a public space and, thus, a civic theatre: the degree to which a culture can make allowance for what has at some level to be repressed if we're to have a culture at all. I am speaking of primary narcissism. There are somewhat different versions of it in the libidinal economy of Lyotard or the desiring machines of Deleuze, a pure libidinal play of surfaces in which there would be, in some sense, pure expenditure, no risk, no cost. We would be able in that economy to recover all the libidinal energy that has been traumatized and arrested, and reinvest it in the body. It would become wholly available to us, and we would be a kind of purified body in Brown's most extreme sense, love's body. All of that was the more utopian promise of French theory, French Freud, but such ideas also circulated, in quite other terms, including Brown's, through the counterculture of the sixties.

GD: Still, this is obviously something that also happened much earlier on in France. You're saying it started here, but in some sense it starts with de Sade and Rousseau. So, then, are you against the idea of, or the practice of, theatre because it is the consequence of conscious thought as opposed to pure presence? Does the nature/culture debate—if we can rename the two cultures debate—concern you very much?

HB: Certainly the nature/culture debate is a way of formulating the question of "where does it come from?" And "what comes first?" As you know, most theatre departments and most theatre history books to this day will say that theatre is derived from ritual. And the implication is a kind of a priori: ritual comes first, theatre comes second. But it may be the other way around.

GD: But some would say that theatre begins with play, that theatre is predicated on the very idea of play, play itself is really its literal energies, and therefore there is a certain purity of play.

HB: Yes, I've written various essays about the idea of play which, along with the body, was also valorized during the sixties and has persisted as a highly charged, coded term within recent critical theory. But I've also written an essay in *Blooded Thought*, which you published, called "The Remission of Play." I meant remission in a double sense: there's a point at which you want to say, "Now look, stop playing. Everybody stop playing around." There is also a sense in which you want to *redirect* the energy of play. Beckett understood that play is deadly. The idea has always been latent in the theatre. Let me explain by going back to the issue of the body. In the play of presence and absence, the body is obviously central, though we may have a sense of its presence even when the body is absent. Beckett understood this too in that little piece he called *Breath*. A human presence in a vacated space. Insofar as the theatre materializes around the human body, there is this one simple, elemental, undeniable fact: he or she who is performing there—and this is what differentiates the theatre from any other form we know—is dying in front of your eyes. Right there. Now it seems to me that everything else in the theatre, its entire apparatus of revelation and disguise, develops around that idea. All of the theatre's conventions are designed either to intensify your awareness of it or to deflect it, or to cover up your anxiety by appearing to celebrate it.

BGM: What you seem to be doing is embracing the concept of repression, or death in life, which is actually precisely the thing that Norman O. Brown was talking about, that it would make us freer if we got rid of this death anxiety. You seem to be embracing it almost as a way of perceiving theatre.

HB: I'm not necessarily embracing it—although perhaps I am. That may be also a matter of temperament. But what I think I'm addressing is the evidence of my experience of theatre. I say, Look, what are the things that I respond to in theatre? What are the things that I've seen? Or read?

Or even heard about the theatre? Or what has happened—after all, I've spent almost thirty-eight years rehearsing theatre—sitting there in the dark, watching people do things up there on the stage in this strange, phantasmic form in which we have, as we commonly say, a play of appearance. Or we create illusions, or we create realities of illusion, or the illusions of reality, and all the mutations and crisscrossings of those two ideas.

I read texts, I go to plays, I try to think seriously about them. But if I take them seriously, it's hard to divest myself of the idea that repression is not only operative in human experience, it's possibly unavoidable. I can think of no social order that's not contingent upon it. And the unconscious, as Freud told us, is constituted by repression. One of the most moving things in all of Freud came at the end of a long clinical career when he wrote, almost against his wishes—after all, he wanted to heal, cure, relieve people of repression—*Civilization and Its Discontents*. It ends like a tragedy. After trying with all his genius to think his way around it, he had to concede, finally, that repression may be the price we have to pay for civilization.

Now, the big dream of the sixties was the undoing of repression. That was an essential part of its participatory mystique, a recurrent mystique, still alive—at least residually—in the anthropological or ethnopoetic approach to performance, and to the analysis of multiculturalism and interculturalism. I still think it may be a very energizing mystique at certain historical moments. Yet there's an affinity in all that to the wish-fulfilling fantasy that we're going to be redeemed by collectivity, whether in the festival or the carnival or what-have-you, which will liberate us from repression and restore to us the arrested libidinal energy. Freud is saying, this is a great dream, but it's not going to happen. Not if we're going to have a civilization, or maybe even stay alive.

BGM: You call yourself a postmodernist and yet you don't accept one of the cardinal principles . . .

HB: I don't call myself a postmodernist. I never called myself a postmodernist. I wouldn't dream of that . . .

BGM: That's right, you're dreaming of surrealism. Well, let's say you choose postmodern strategies or postmodern subject matter. Personally, I think you're a lapsed modernist.

HB: As a matter of fact, I think I am a lapsed modernist. But *The Eye of Prey*'s subtitle is *Subversions of the Postmodern*, again with a double meaning: subversive *of*, and a sub*version*. In either case, quite clearly, in my theatre work, in my interests outside the theatre, in my collaborations with various artists, I've always been engaged with experimental forms.

BGM: But the point I wanted to make is that your skepticism—and I share this, too—with the whole idea of *communitas*, in a sense goes against one of the main features of what is considered postmodernism, which is the erasure of the boundary between the spectacle and the spectator. And one of the things that you do valorize is a preference for the solitariness, the aloneness of the performer and the audience member. Yet throughout your writings you take issue with Strasberg's "private moment" and what that's degenerated into for the performer.

HB: I have ambivalent feelings about Strasberg's particular notion of the private moment. We know it led to certain excesses in practice in the theatre. On the other hand, the notion of the private moment, as when Gautam was talking about the soliloquy a moment ago, has always had great appeal to me. The work I did with KRAKEN was both specifically directed to the allure, the temptation of solipsism, and to its danger. Stanislavsky's notion of "public solitude" has also been very meaningful to me. So, too, Brecht's notion of the "splendid isolation of the actor" and the "splendid isolation of the spectator."

BGM: What I had in mind when I called you a "lapsed modernist" . . .

HB: I'm not even lapsed. ·

GD: Not done yet. Ah, to begin again.

BGM: I think it's so clear in your writings—the attraction to a rigorous intellectual attitude toward an artwork, the sense of contemplation of a tableau, epic structure, the separation of the audience and event. You really are, in some sense, connected to the Brechtian-Diderot Enlightenment project, moving toward the notion of a philosophical theatre.

HB: And also from the beginning I've had a kind of Yeatsian feeling for what's most difficult. I've never really entirely bought the idea that complex ideas can be simply said. In other words, I think complexity warrants complexity. Brecht himself wobbles on this issue: sometimes he speaks one way, so that, as he says, the ass will understand. But then you begin to understand with Brecht that there are asses and asses. Sometimes he is very complex indeed, and when you read through, say, *The Short Organum*, the best parts are the parts that are virtually opaque. It very often strikes me that people are most interesting at the point in which they don't quite understand what they're saying. That, for me, is the great appeal of Artaud. Artaud is most interesting at the exfoliating or fibrillating nerve ends of thought, where you have the feeling that thought is escaping thought. I mean, don't you have that feeling when you write sometimes, like you're really on the edge of something and you know that your best idea is just escaping you?

BGM: Of course, sometimes you put things in an essay that you know you haven't quite figured out or you hope you might not get caught for.

HB: But you know that very often, there, you are on the edge of something. I used to say of my writing or when I was working in the theatre, "You know, I can't understand why anyone else in the world but me would be interested in this." There, of course, is the danger of the solipsistic as well. It's not that I didn't care that anybody else was interested, but I couldn't imagine why anybody would get so obsessed with this particular issue at that limit of thought, so attached to it as I was, I may not have understood at the moment why it was of great importance to me, but I knew it was. It felt that way when I was doing theatre, and now I do my best writing and my best thinking, I think, at the moment where thought escapes me.

How did this come about? I'm not sure, though it's by now a matter of principle, or obsession, becoming style. About the time I went into the theatre, one of the writers I was reading with some intensity—for a paper I had to write—was Henry James. You know how students go to the library, they look up the author and he may have written twenty or thirty books, right, but there are only three or four on the shelf, so I happened to pick up *The Golden Bowl*. They used to speak of early James, middle James, and darkest James, and there I was with *The Golden Bowl*, the darkest. I couldn't figure out what that book was doing. But it was to me immensely fascinating. And among the things that made it fascinating were the long interlocutory, parenthetical, diversionary, deferred sentences in which I had the feeling—which I may not have been able to articulate, but I can now—that to say it another way would be not to say *it* at all, or to say it in an unfaceted way, without sufficient nuance or qualification, as if the only way to say it were to say it all at once, like *spatially.* Even when I'm speaking to you right now, I can't say all the things that I want to say, temporally, one word after another, except inadequately. It's like I want to push all that I want to say, all that I want to understand myself, *in saying it,* up onto one plane at once so that you can see it all at once. And it seems to me that Jamesian language, with all its ellipses and interventions, was something like that. It always had to qualify itself, it always had to say something else, it always had to interject something. And it was a mode of thought that constituted itself by a kind of maximum density.

BGM: James is the person between you and another critic that I admire. I've always thought that your work is to the theatre what William Gass is to literary criticism. And you're both linked by the Jamesian line. I think that the two of you elaborate a particular kind of sentence.

GD: Of course, in some sense, your philosophical commitment vis-à-vis the theatre also displays a certain antitheatricalism on your part. That stems a lot from Yvor Winters, who was also one of your teachers, doesn't it?

HB: It's really hard to siphon that in or siphon it out, which is to say, there may be some truth in that. Winters, of course, had an antitheatrical prejudice, which I didn't entirely understand when I was working with him. He thought my going into the theatre was a waste of time, and given some aspects of theatre practice I sometimes felt that way myself. The only thing that Winters and Ezra Pound ever really agreed upon was that the theatre is "a form of third-rate intensity." I can't speak for all directors, but I have certainly known some, and we've all read about others, who at critical points in their careers really understood that, at some level, to do theatre you have to also hate it. There are ontological grounds for that, as I've been suggesting. And the nature of the profession, especially here in America, doesn't help. Speaking of appearances or duplicity, preparing a face to meet the faces that you meet. You know the issue that's defined by the Greek name for the actor: hypocrisy. Still, the ontological question is complicated: Why does one act? It's a rather perverse notion when an actor says, "Well I act because I want to know myself." Why would anybody want to know himself by becoming something other than himself? Or herself? The issue is further complicated today with the insistence on controlling representation by means of masquerade.

Eric Bentley asked many years ago, "What is theatre?"—and in *The Impossible Theater* I commented on that. I said I meant the word "impossible" in every conceivable sense, from the visionary to the material. Artaud's theatre is impossible, so was Gordon Craig's. But I also meant the word as when you say it with your teeth clenched: "It's *impossible!*" Like people who are contemptible, the organism is awful, you can't raise money for it, the audience stinks, the city won't support it, everything that surrounds it . . .

GD: Let me ask you now about the nature of artifice. Because what you are saying, obviously, appertains not just to theatre, but to all art. Whether it's fiction, poetry, painting, film—art is involved in both the transcendental quest, the ontological sense of purity, and, at the same time, it is negated by that very quest, by the very procedure that it has to employ to approximate its goals. If that's the case, then what is art? And why do we need it? If we're not willing to accept the artifice of art, not willing to accept its liabilities, then why are we drawn to art for sustenance, or for spiritual growth?

HB: Over the years, I've had varying responses, if not answers, to that question. But the question about theatre has often been—a big issue in the art world during the period of minimalism and conceptualism—*is* it art?

GD: That may well have to do with a historical inability to see the theatre as being comprised of anything other than words. Once language itself is discredited as the sole means of attaining ontological purity, and if theatre is seen as predicated on language only, then theatre has little to defend itself on that score. As the medium becomes less dependent on words, and more visual in nature, the question of theatre's ontological essence does become relevant and problematical at the same time. Look at Wittgenstein, for instance, who seeks refuge from the ambiguity of language in the world of the visual, in his particular case, film.

HB: Film as a sort of maternal embrace. Art has never represented anything like that for me. Art is what happens when I think better of myself. To the degree that there's any purity in that, it accounts for the discrepancy between what I am and what I'd like to be. I can at some level, even when I fail in art, respect myself there more than I can in reality. Which is to say, I'm known to myself more acutely in art than I am known to myself outside it. This is not all egocentric. Art for me has always been the means by which I become more available to myself, and thus more responsible. Insofar as there was anything messianic, what Bonnie talked about earlier, that I wrote in *The Impossible Theater*, I was in the theatre to save the world. The world, of course, doesn't always want to be saved.

BGM: If what you say you understand from art—the kind of knowledge you perceive or is put on you from your experience of art—what do you find, or what are you looking for, in criticism, then, as an enterprise?

HB: See, I don't think I write criticism.

BGM: Okay, let's say writing then.

HB: Very much the same kind of thing that I used to look for when I was doing theatre. Yet I'm quite well aware of the material difference. When the work that I was doing with the KRAKEN group ended, as I say in *Take Up the Bodies*, what I was trying to do in that book was to transfer the energies of the theatrical inquiry, insofar as they were translatable, to the page. As it happened, I wrote that book at a time when performance was the honorific term in criticism itself. People began to think of writing as a kind of performative activity. So in some sense it was more legitimized, ideologically, if not in practice.

Now, I'm interested in ideology, but I've never had an ideological program, nor what they now call in critical theory a "subject position" that is easily definable. You know that from reading me. What I'm really interested in might be defined by something like "catastrophe theory," those threshold moments when something transforms without our perceiving it. One of the things I'm dealing with, moreover, in the book I just finished—on ideology and performance—is the limiting conditions of any set of ideas, as if there were a statute of limitations on the best of ideas. Surely there is on the worst, but then they may be testifying to some historical necessity. I may find contemptible what Jesse Helms represents or what Ronald Reagan represented, or the Moral Majority, but when a phenomenon like that manifests itself in a culture, like the emergence now of David Duke, a person of liberal or leftist disposition has to think it through. Simply to mock it, dismiss it, or cite it as a clear and present danger is not enough, for it's also an index of unrecognized need and desire. All aversion registered, the bigots and know-nothings denounced, there may still be something else at stake.

But when we shift to the radical voices that are, to begin with, more like our own, there is another present danger that may not be so clear. So when I write, what I'm trying to understand is those limiting conditions in the activity of thought where something that I may have thought myself becomes other than what it appeared to be. The harder thing to deal with is the thing we believe that in the course of history goes wrong, or exhausts itself. We know that there have been all kinds of liberating ideas in this century, good ideas, powerful ideas, the most admirable idealisms that at some limit of their emancipatory function warp and become lethal. It was why, when I came to Lincoln Center, the first play I chose was *Danton's Death*.

GD: Your interest in implicating yourself in these moments of rupture or slippage in terms of various epistemologies that are at work in any given time suggests to me that you, as a writer and thinker, situate yourself on a bed of shifting sands. But if that is your authorial agenda, as it were, then how does that measure up to this very Platonic stability, in some sense, of form that is unchanging?

HB: These two things operate at once. Let me see if I can address that in terms of theatre, as I do in *Take Up the Bodies*. Theatre is a temporal form. It passes. Shakespeare addressed that in Prospero's notion of the insubstantial pageant fading. All drama addresses that. The East addresses it in another way: the One and the Many, the Many changing paths. One can celebrate that, one can lament it, one can create dithyrambic odes about it. But it's the very temporality of the form that is alluring, and exasperating, and at some critical limit the source of the desperation that is dramatized in the greatest works of theatre. It ends, it passes, it disappears, it's not there, while we dream of an Eternal Return. Of what? Whatever "it" is. It's sort of like a director saying, "Do it again." Even when I used to say to the actor, "Do it again," there was always the second thought: "What 'it' are we talking about? And do we really want *it?*" For that would be merely repetition. "It all, it all," says the woman in Beckett's *Footfalls,* which also implies the repetition you don't quite want to repeat. So do it again, but not *that.*

Here, then, you have this temporal form, this impossible form: everything passes, it slips, it changes, it's an insubstantial pageant. I've always wanted to create a theatre that would be, as I say in *Take Up the Bodies,* like Picasso's sculptured "Death's Head." So dense it would be almost like a black hole, the gravity so great it would warp back into itself and come out the other side. And yet, it would be like that sculpture, impacted, dense, or as if set in stone. I've always wanted to create a theatre that had such mass and spatial power, such density in its passing that it would be virtually absolute. Like Plato's Cave, always questionable, but simply *there.*

Let me move this onto the plane of speech, which also disappears. We did a piece some years ago, which was in fact derived from the *Oresteia.* It was called *Seeds of Atreus.* Whatever it is that we did or didn't do, the KRAKEN group was probably more committed to speech, and to text, than most groups of that nonverbal or antiverbal period. Almost from the beginning, in our very methodology, there was a kind of superabundance of language. So it was with *Seeds of Atreus* as it developed, a massive textuality. We also did things that were very intricate chorally, very complicated. Across forty feet of space, the actors would be speaking at exceedingly high speed, dropping or raising pitch, splitting syllables. But it was meant to be intelligible, the words legible, at high velocity or in pulsating masses of sound. When the murder of Agamemnon took place, Clytemnestra putting the net over him in the bath, there was a choral effect in which the language, massed, seemed to be coming at the audience like ax blows. There was, as I'm suggesting, a torrent of language, but I remember saying to the actors at the end of one rehearsal of these very intricate masses of words: "You know, if we do this thing right"—this is the modernist coming out—"this should sound as if we have only spoken one word." One word.

Now, as I say, I'm not religious, and I have only very shaky affinities with the sacred, but that's sort of like the word within a Word unable to speak a word of T. S. Eliot's poem. Which is swallowed in darkness. A word which is the revelatory Word, the sacramental Word. There, you might say, are my affinities with Winters, too. When I first began to be interested in literature, I was fundamentally interested in poetry. And those were the days in which we thought of poetry as sacramental, we really treasured words. I still fundamentally feel that about language. While I engage in a postmodern project that has to do with slippery signifiers and all that, I still feel with the high modernists that the invention of language was one of the great achievements of civilization. Words have powers, they release power. As Emerson said, they're forms of fossil poetry, they contain ancient wisdom. They are what keeps us in history. The signifiers may slip, but you want them to slip responsibly, with precision next to godliness.

BGM: Since we're talking about writing and the word, one of the things I feel is going on in your work, as part of its philosophical dimension, is that there is a certain sense of the performance of the text and the actor as writer. In this constant decentering of yourself, the representing of many different positions, you set up a cast of voices. It seems that for you writing is a kind of acoustic mask. There are a series of acoustic masks that are voices. In the beginning, when you wrote *The Impossible Theater*, you had a great vision of who an audience was. You could see an audience. But now it's as if the work echoes the Beckettian voice: "Who's there?" You're writing now for an audience you don't know of, for a theatre that perhaps might not exist; or perhaps the one you want doesn't have an audience.

HB: Beckett was one of the voices that had a major influence on my own ideas in the theatre, and the growth of The Actor's Workshop. At that time, two major presences were on the scene, along with Genet: Beckett and Brecht. And if there was a line of inquiry in our theatre, it was defined by the Brecht-Beckett dialectic. There was that part of me that was committed to the notion of popular theatre, public theatre, political theatre—what we talked about earlier. But at the level of temperament, taste, it was the Beckettian mode that always had for me the deepest appeal. From the very beginning there was a kind of contradiction in it, a disturbing but seductive contradiction. Beckett once said to me, "I'm writing into the void." There's nobody there. So then they always ask, "Why do you do it?"

GD: I always thought the overwhelming theatrical episode in your life, if I can read into your life for a moment, was when your daughter Jessamyn was born. I still recall vividly an essay in which you wrote about seeing someone who didn't want to be there. Someone who was forced, for all intents and purposes, from one void into another void, at least for that moment.

HB: You're talking about "The Bloody Show and the Eye of Prey." I don't know. That may be true. Of course, I've had three other children. Certainly it was a moment, Jessamyn's birth, at which I was able to define, as if it were an epiphany, what I was already thinking about. After the bloody show, when we went to the hospital, it looked as if it was going to happen very quickly, that Kathy wouldn't labor much. The doctor thought it would take three or four hours at the most. But then, as Kathy said, she didn't *want* to push down. Jessamyn wouldn't come out, and they eventually had to put on those big cusps of surgical steel, the forceps—"the grave-digger puts on the forceps." No question, Beckett has been ubiquitous in my thinking. When you were talking before about the solipsistic image of Oedipus, the sealed-off eyes, it occurred to me that the emblematic character between the modern and the postmodern is Hamm. "There's something dripping in my head." Don't you always feel that? And if it would only cease. Thoughts going around like mad. Who wants to think like that when a child is born . . . Well, about writing into the void: Why? Why do people climb Everest? Because it's there, right? I write for the void because the void is there.

BGM: Your formative years in the theatre were shaped by such major figures as Brecht, Beckett, Genet, Pirandello. Today there is no group of playwrights of the same intellectual order to articulate the idea of theatre. Certainly we can take the notion of performance to write about, or theatricality, or society as spectacle. But if you look at recent decades, or project to the near future, there's not the same kind of engagement with dramatic literature that you experienced early in your career. Imagine art criticism without important paintings to speak of. Ironically, we now have in the United States the most highly intellectual theatre criticism of any time in the twentieth century.

HB: I think that there are more substantial young people writing about theatre today than there were when I was first working in the theatre. When Bob Corrigan started *The [Tulane] Drama Review*, trying to set new standards for the theatre, and keep it up to date, there were very few people who could write for it in this country. The first articles that I ever published, even before *The Drama Review*, were in the *Educational Theatre Journal*. And then for about twelve years I refused to write for it, because it was so vapid. There was really no discourse at all. Whatever one thinks of the newer theory, or the writing that's now being done on issues of performance or spectacle, it's also led to the fact that more intelligent people are writing about the drama too. There are good young scholars writing about British drama or feminist playwrights or the butch-femme aesthetic over at the WOW Cafe. Where it will lead I don't know.

Meanwhile, the social institution has to be reassessed. Look: there are over 250 regional theatres in the country now. When we were out in San Francisco, there were less than a handful, struggling to come into existence. Until the Ford Foundation came on the scene, at the end of the fifties, I didn't know very much about the Arena Theatre or the Alley Theatre or the Seattle Repertory Theatre, nor did they know much about The Actor's Workshop. We were the first four theatres that Ford gave any money to, and before that—people forget this—there was simply no money on the scene: no grants to apply for, no NEA, nothing. Now we do have the regional theatre network, for better or worse. It's subject to boards and bottom lines, of course, and without the intellectual matrix that exists in other countries. In France, for instance, there was a powerful institutionalized framework out of which, through the ideological struggles of the sixties, the Maisons de la Culture could develop. Major writers, artists, intellectuals care about the theatre; Sartre and Camus wrote for it, Duras today; Chéreau collaborates with Boulez. That's not true here. Our best artists and writers couldn't, for the most part, care less about the theatre.

Then there's also the power of the Comédie Française, the national theatre against which everything is defined. The dynamic in the French theatre has been, traditionally, that somebody out of the underground rises to the attack: "The Comédie?—*merde!* Desecrate it, blow it up!" Ten years later, that person ends up directing it. We still don't have anything like that going on here. Lee Breuer should have had a theatre by this time. Richard Foreman should have had a theatre by this time. All right, now JoAnne [Akalaitis] is running the Public. She's obviously an intelligent woman, and it may be that it will set some sort of pattern, so that in time people with innovative capacities will take over one or another of our regional theatres. We hoped that would be the model when, in the sixties, we went to Lincoln Center in New York, which we thought might be the focus of a national theatre. One could say that was simply a desire for power, even a self-betrayal, since I had been the most polemical voice on behalf of decentralization of theatre in America. In *Take Up the Bodies* I tried to explain or rationalize that move, and I won't elaborate here. But right in the middle of the Vietnam War, there we were with the biggest public soapbox in the country. We really had some access to power, we thought it might be exemplary. Well, it didn't work then, and the idea of a national theatre was always an untenable notion, the merest vanity now.

Meanwhile the theatre will still suffer competitive abrasions from the media. Plus the fact that younger people aren't interested. My very best students—as you know, I don't teach in a theatre department—have next to no interest in the theatre. The form doesn't really compel them. They are interested, however, when you talk about things like body art, or *Twin Peaks*, on which they can write brilliantly.

GD: But doesn't that itself augur for the demise, in some sense, of the canonical line of theatre? Whether it's conceptual or body art, and performance, or even this minimalist prospect of theatre you were talking about before, that you, as a writer and thinker, value so highly.

HB: I've always had a feeling for scale. I've always oscillated. From that minimalist thing to what I talked about years ago as "risking the baroque." In fact, I don't think you can talk seriously about the idea of a civic theatre unless you address the issue of scale. That was not an issue for me, however, with the KRAKEN group. That work was in part a sort of historical necessity; in part, a psychological necessity. Which is to say, when I left Lincoln Center, in 1968, I was trying to rethink what I wanted to do with the rest of my life. It was right in the middle of a period when there was this intense critique of all our social institutions. It seemed to me interesting to say, Well, yeah, let's address the problem of developing a collective form, articulating theatre value not by a single vision, but in a participatory process. That was in the spirit of the times, but I still think it may be the most valuable experimental project in the theatre—as it seemed then, too, in education. I had worked over the years with various superb, well-known actors, but it was apparent that this had to be done with younger, probably untrained people whom I'd have to train myself.

That was the major reason I went to Cal Arts, but one of the things that attracted me was the opportunity—everybody wanted it at the time—to rethink education from the ground up. Now, at Cal Arts we were trying to address almost every problem on the public agenda, but most immediately the old problem of what an artist *should* learn, other than what an artist wants to *do*. What should an artist study other than the making of art? We took that on in the conception of the School of Critical Studies, where the focus was not so much on criticism—there was that, too—but on what was *critical* at the time, critical to know and think about. It was also a matter of interest and need. We said, Look, students today are concerned with the Vietnam War, drugs, the opening of new sexual possibilities, alternative lifestyles, et cetera. So we tried to get first-rate scholars, orthodox and unorthodox, to engage them on these issues. Classes were conceived, pedagogically and performatively, in response to interests. Now you can only do that, obviously, with very motivated students to whom you can virtually say, Create your own curriculum. There were dead ends and excesses, sure, but I don't anticipate in my lifetime I'll ever encounter anything as productive as the two or three years I was at Cal Arts, just in terms of sheer creative energy in an environment where one could learn what one wanted to learn.

BGM: Do you think that schools now are equipped to accommodate the incredible amount of new knowledge that's available to us, to bring into each of our subjects?

HB: No. Schools are not addressing that, except maybe in multicultural terms. Also, the time scheme of learning inhibits the ready acquisition of knowledge.

BGM: To move briefly from pedagogy, say, to ideology, when we were in Berlin last year together, it was just a few months after the fall of the Berlin Wall and the collapse of communism in Eastern Europe, and you were in the process of writing, or perhaps finishing, the book on ideology. How has this historical turn of events, plus your now-divided time between the United States and Paris, influenced the direction that the latter part of the ideology book took?

HB: I rewrote quite a lot. When I was in Paris, I thought I would finish the book in a month. All this stuff was taking place in Eastern Europe, the Gulf War came, I had to rethink parts of it. Not because I was committed to the ideology that seemed to be failing, but because what was happening simply verified what I wrote. That is, ideologies had caused immense disaster during the twentieth century, and yet our institutions required, still, ideological analysis. Then there was the paradox of an insurgence of ideological thought in our universities, and in the arts, when ideologies were on the ropes all over the world. As for myself, I'd learned a lot from Marx, though I'm not a Marxist. I grew up in a neighborhood in Brooklyn where there were a lot of socialists, and I had that in my background. I should add, by the way, that my interest in Marx has to do also with the way he writes. Not quite like Henry James, but closer than you'd think, with a nineteenth-century rhetoric at the selvage of thought, a kind of threshold at which he can't quite keep track of the ideas. There are aspects of *Capital* that are simply opaque. That's when I find him most interesting. My book is called *To All Appearances: Ideology and Per-*

formance. I say in the preface that when the book appears to be about ideology it's really about performance, and when it appears to be about performance it's really about ideology.

Actually, you can blame that wobbling effect on Marx. He didn't really define ideology all that extensively, not like fetishism or surplus value. Now, it's possible to speak about ideology in a doctrinal sense. It's possible to speak of it in terms of certain displacements of value, or in the metaphors of displacement by means of which Freud defines the unconscious. The image of ideology most germane to the book is Marx's notion of the camera obscura, and the inversion of value that comes about as a reflection of social relations that are already inverted. What we're dealing with, then, is a double inversion. All of this—as in Althusser, who was influenced by Lacan—returns to Marx's view of ideology as phantoms in the brain. Which is to say, ideology as theatre. All that one might say about ideology, aside from the doctrinal, seems to me to describe the theatrical. A reality that is constituted by appearances, like the phantom, now you see it now you don't.

GD: Let me ask you, Herb, since you're so immersed in this quicksand of shifting perspectives—theatricalist, ideological, et cetera: Do you sense that there is a certain danger in pursuing a line of philosophical thought that can lead to a virtual dismantling of the social fabric of a nation or of a culture? It seems as if something has to be said for stability. Eternal verities can always be put under a question mark, but to implicate this kind of interpretive dance as the basis for understanding the world, do you at all see this as a dangerous enterprise?

HB: Oh, yeah, absolutely. I acknowledge that the temptation of the solipsistic is an aspect of it. On the other hand, if you look through all the books I've written, you'll see that there's a threshold at which I'll say that, if I'm committed to anything, it is to that in the theatre which resists its being totally theatre. Which refuses in some way to give itself over simply to slippage. That, in fact, is the value of art, the artifice that resists. That's the Brechtian part of me, I suppose, the desire to construct an image in the shape of history, even if it be an image of maximum slippage.

GD: Is that not the very pivot on which the postmodernist enterprise turns, the desire or need to construct, knowing full well in advance that what is being constructed partakes willfully of ideological and/or historical ambiguity and cultural relativism?

HB: As I said earlier, when I used the subtitle, *Subversions of the Postmodern,* I had a certain duplicity or doubleness in mind. Which is to say, my writings have a certain sympathy, or identification, with the tendencies of postmodern or poststructuralist thought—the two are not always the same—and at the same time I'm subverting it. *The Audience, Take Up the Bodies, The Eye of Prey,* are fundamentally a critique of the extremities of poststructuralist thought. But it's a critique as if from the inside.

BGM: I think you're describing yourself as a Laudisi: it is so, if you think it is. A kind of *raisonneur* figure.

HB: No, that's a little different, although Laudisi could be played very close to what I'm describing. Which is to say, the right kinds of subversion occur from within. Let's get it straight: when critical theory came on the scene, as an aspect of postmodern thought, there was every reason for it. There was a critical necessity. As I suggested before, however, there's a threshold to any emancipatory dispensation of thought. Various aspects of postmodern critique have reached that threshold, are merely spinning wheels. In other respects, though, it's changing direction, going back over neglected terrain. Actually, certain rejected ideas are being refocused in that critique, including issues of authority, order, and ethics. There were issues that had to be opened up. They were urgent: questions of race, sexuality, class inequity, the canon, multiculturalism. Other things were displaced, phenomenologically bracketed. Now they're coming back, as the repressed always does. What's distressing, of course, is the repression that occurs on behalf of liberation.

GD: You're talking about the right subversions of identity. Who is to know if the enterprise you are engaged in is right? You're just telling me so. In the work itself, you are of course always placing that within a destabilizing context.

HB: Yes, *exactly* so. But it's as if I'm trying to create in writing a theatrical version of what, in fact, needs to be felt and perceived, so that you can know if you're going to take issue with it, and what in fact you're taking issue with. It's like the problem that you have with students who, for example, describe postmodern effects, and have a lot of sympathy for postmodern tendencies. I keep telling them, You keep describing it, but few of you are willing to take the risks of what, in fact, you're admiring. You write the same old square essays that you've always written, like every other essay, just like the essays that I used to see on old academic subjects. You're now writing these about postmodernism, although what you're describing implies that you shouldn't be doing what you're doing. Now, I realize that the other kind of writing suffers at some limit from what my old teacher, Yvor Winters, would call the fallacy of imitative form. But I still think that there's a critical and important difference between warding off something and understanding it by moving in its rhythm. Still, what is to say that you should take my word for this?

GD: Yes. Do you believe in truth?

HB: I don't believe in truth. Let me correct that. I may even believe in *absolute* truth, as Milton talks about it, for example, when he speaks of Psyche trying to cull the seeds. In other words, one is engaged in a limitless project of trying to ascertain what it is. I may believe in its absoluteness, but I'm not in any way entirely confident that I'm going to be able to see that. The issue, however, seems to me not so much one of truth, but as it might be understood in conventional dramaturgy, a matter of credibility and authenticity. Both of which, particularly authenticity, are very much discredited by new critical theory, with its ethos of suspicion. How do we know anything, then, with any reliability? All intelligence fails. The issue in writing is to make it as credible as possible, with intelligence as the measure, *before* it fails.

GD: I understand what you're saying, that one has to be inside the rhythm. But at the same time, there has to be a sense of apartness, something that Brecht was trying to get at. At some point, you've got to get outside the rhythm, you've got to be inauthentic. To be credible, at some point, you have to counterpoint that with the incredulous. If there is no way of understanding, of always destabilizing both the credible and the incredulous, the authentic and the inauthentic, if they all start partaking of this game of shifting signifiers, then it's impossible to truly stand apart from it. Is there a way of standing apart? It's like the Archimedes thing—I forget exactly what he said—give me a lever and I can move the world. That obviously suggests that there has to be a certain fixity and a certain permanence in this relationship between the world and the observer.

HB: Let me use the lever to make a distinction. There is an immense difference between the game of signifiers and the reality of slippage. Which is to say, as I look at the world it slips. It's not anything I want for the world. I want permanence. I honestly value it. I value continuity. I care about people being credible. I treasure authenticity, or at least what appears to be authenticity. And for me, the measure of any friend is whether you can trust that person in a crisis. Take another criterion of the postmodern: the fetishism of play. As I've said, I never overvalue play. The discourse on play has never really interested me. Nor the forms of theatre, during the sixties, that made a big thing of play. That was a difference I had with Richard [Schechner] during those years. Relative to that scene, I'm a formalist. Bonnie is quite right when she says I'm a modernist, though as I think it over I'm not quite sure whether lapsed or prelapsarian. I spoke before, like Yeats or Eliot, of the fascination of what's most difficult. That isn't play. Still, intelligence curves, and there were things happening in the sixties, within the ethos of play, that captured attention, even mine, like the Halloween parade downstairs. Look, the sixties hardly need defending, so far as it was a period that questioned inauthentic power, by making things livelier as well.

BGM: At the end of *Life After Death*, Norman O. Brown talks about the fact that the greatest social problem facing us is when political leaders realize that people want happiness, not power. That's interesting.

HB: People are willing to give up a lot of power if they can live a reasonably decent life. They're perfectly prepared to let others do the job of running things. It takes nothing away from the accomplishments of feminism to observe that many women today, even with the awareness of other options, are willing to relinquish a lot of patriarchal authority in order to preserve the family. It's one of the reasons why the abortion issue is as complicated as it is. As for censorship, that's far more complicated in a pluralistic society—where even your worst enemies have the vote—than you'd gather from *The Village Voice*. I think the art community to this day is really pretty sappy in its attitudes about what went on in the NEA with the Mapplethorpe thing. That issue was, once the iron was in the fire, relatively simple: you either have the NEA or you don't, and it's always been pretty anomalous to expect the extremist forms of dissidence to be endowed. That some of the know-nothings make this the basis of their argument doesn't reduce the anomaly, which is a historical matter—a legacy of the avant-garde, unhappily not so dispossessed, with or without grants, as it once was.

It would be nice to think the government would finance the most advanced research in the arts, as in the sciences, but that analogy fails as well, since it's a lot harder to see where and how the sciences are obscene, outrageous, subversive, though they may very well be. The NEA is peanuts compared to the huge public subsidies abroad for theatres or artists that we respect, but let's face it, Peter Stein and Patrice Chéreau, or even Peymann—who was fired at Stuttgart for running a benefit performance for the Baader-Meinhof group—are conducting their critique of the social order that supports them within institutional structures that are like public utilities. There's no question of money for that, it's there. Even Manfred Rommel, the Mayor of Stuttgart, who protected Peymann before, couldn't protect him when he stepped over the line. Peymann is now at the Burg Theater in Vienna, where he's getting a lot of flak for his dissidence, and he may or may not survive. The institution will. If our institutions, the orchestras, ballets, and regional theatres, get the lion's share, that's only to be expected. What we still can't expect, however, is that we'll have anybody of Peymann's distinction, or Stein's, running our regional theatres. That bothers me more than whether or not Karen Finley was denied a grant. As for Frohnmayer, he was just about what one might have expected in that job, a decent man who wobbled, as one will in the whirlwind that hit him right away, his instincts being—when confronted with an impossible politics—to keep the bloody thing alive. Do you think if he hadn't buckled the budget would have been approved?

BGM: Yes, the arts community easily got involved around a sexy issue rather than long-term cultural policy and the real politics of arts funding. Speaking of the NEA controversy and some of the issues that haven't been aired out, but just glossed over in the censorship debate, maybe the next big threshold, and the kind of issue that should be addressed, is the politics of multiculturalism. With regard to theatre, it is an implicit attack, I think, on the avant-garde and formalism, as opposed to the notion of people's theatre, or populism. Political correctness can be just as censorious as official culture.

HB: This issue would take us back to the Brecht-Lukács debates, though Brecht's populism was a formalism, and Lukács's realism was in the big leagues, in the spirit of Balzac and Tolstoy, requiring the highest consciousness. There was, of course, a populist strain in the avant-garde, more or less strained by confusion of classes, those out to shock the bourgeoisie not exactly card-carrying members of the proletariat. Where they tried to become that, in the early days of the Soviet Union, there was reason to believe that formalism could become a populism, as in the suprematism of Malevich or the cubo-futurism of Popova or the constructivism of Meyerhold. Even Trotsky's critique of futurism assumes that art under the revolution will be a matter of the highest intelligence. The new populism is nothing like that, whatever other justifications there may be for multiculturalism in the theatre or the arts or education.

One needn't put it down as a new tribalism to be disturbed, nevertheless, by an ideology of difference rejecting the melting pot and sustaining ethnic identities, if not divisions. You both make good distinctions in the essays you wrote for the interculturalism book, particularly in shifting attention from the Far East back to Europe, reminding us that you have to be careful of thinking the Eurocentric when Europe itself is so ethnically divided. Yet there are lessons for us in Eastern Europe. Again, it's a matter of historicizing, or keeping a temporal dimension in mind, the limited longevity of any value. In this country, for the time being, ethnicity may be good; elsewhere, in the dissevered Soviet Union, in Yugoslavia, ethnicity may be regressive, reactionary, even barbarous—even when certain of its claims are legitimate. The thing about differences is that we want it and we don't want it.

People's theatre? Popular theatre? The idea I had in mind when I returned from Europe in 1960—with the practice of Vilar, Planchon, the Berliner Ensemble as exemplary—is a far cry from what passes for such theatre today. Which doesn't mean it shouldn't pass. There is certainly historical justification at the Mexican border for the work done by Guillermo Gómez-Peña. Move it to BAM, as he did recently, and that's quite another matter. I was brought up not far from there, down Atlantic Avenue into the heart of darkness, and if you could get the people who now live in Ocean Hill-Brownsville to come to BAM, you'd have a working proposition.

BGM: One of the difficulties with the discourse on multiculturalism is its tendency toward ghettoization, and its attack on European culture. A true recognition of the diversity of cultures would lead one to a more far-ranging cosmopolitanism. It's easy to make proclamations about global consciousness, but rather difficult to cultivate worldliness. But, to follow up your last point, what concerns me is the widespread withdrawal of support by funding sources, critics, artists, and institutions for work that does not in some way deal with a circumscribed politics of victimhood or the marginal. One strategy of postmodernism is to make modernism seem conservative because formalist, as opposed to postmodernism, which is deemed pluralistic. It's a specious version of the high/low culture debate.

HB: The pluralism of art is not the pluralism of politics, particularly when the low culture of the right comes into the picture, and even the populists get on their high horse about the inalienable rights of art. By the way, the attack on formalism in the art world, which started in the sixties, persists until this day with an intensity to which there is nothing comparable in the theatre. Read the journals, *Artforum* or *October,* they're still clobbering Clement Greenberg. But who, really, would theatre people clobber of comparable status? And what was there in the American theatre that, as the aesthetic site of domination and power, the target of attack, would have had anything like the substance of abstract expressionism?

But the problem with the critique of modernism, particularly by younger people to whom it is now a reflex, is that the object being deconstructed is not sufficiently rich, invested with its *historical* power, what it *earned* from history. The modernist object is accorded all the critical substance of an empty sign, its essential radicalism ignored on the grounds that it's essentialist. I find with my students that they're putting down works they've hardly read or never seen. It's like the conferences they used to have, "Beyond Freud," or like one I attended several years back, "Beyond Beckett." Beyond *what???* What does it mean to go beyond work that is itself so complicated and ambiguous that it is virtually inexhaustible?

BGM: Yes, I find the same tendency in the university, and among artists and critics: a desire to be identified as postmodern, while having no clear sense of the philosophical, aesthetic, and political issues that created the idea of modernism. In theatre this debate is exacerbated by the fact that postmodernism elaborated a critique of modernism with no input from the history of theatre, but rather architecture and literature. For example, postmodern claims centered in issues of purity, of pastiche, of popular culture, of textuality, of representation, as they are used to distinguish it from modernism, were articulated decades ago in modern and avant-garde theatre practice. Any number of influential theatre minds call into question the definition of postmodernism — for a start, Jarry, Yeats, Pirandello, Cocteau, Stein, Marinetti, Meyerhold, Brecht. In addition, what has been overlooked is that modernism in the performing arts — music, dance, theatre — drew heavily on folk motifs and popular entertainments, frequently mixing the classic with the most contemporary.

GD: Be that as it may, the term "postmodern" is here to stay, its varied inflections employed for ideological purposes by theorists of the left and the right alike. On the sociopolitical front, however, postmodernism and its attributes have been tied to a "progressive" agenda, as defined by conservatives during and since the Reagan presidency, while its cultural implications have been viewed as anathema. Liberal thinkers, who concede the first point to the conservatives, nonetheless find the second disturbing and problematical. If in the first grouping, I would place someone such as Fukuyama, in the second group the figure of Habermas looms large. What I am trying to get at is whether postmodernism signals a triumph of conservative thinking in our time.

HB: If I follow you, and you're making, say, multiculturalism an aspect of postmodernism, then I'm not sure it has been embraced by conservatives on the political level. No doubt, most conservatives will concede the rights of women and minorities, but actions here speak louder than words, and even the words indicate that they don't like monkeying around with the curriculum, say, to assure alternative readings of history with an altered reading list. Your question separates politics and culture, but it's an insupportable separation now, which is why the currency in theory of the term "cultural politics." As for postmodernism, it's a pretty big umbrella, but it may be better to distribute its sins in the plural: there are various postmodernisms like various feminisms, et cetera.

GD: What it finally all boils down to is appearances, I guess.

BGM: Trick or treat. Let's watch the parade—it's starting.

GD: We never know what is appearance and what is reality. Or at least, to all appearances we don't.

HB: I wouldn't swear by it, but so it seems. The words are slipping again, or somebody's playing around. For the time being, even with this relatively genial setting, music from the parade, I'm saying things and I'm wondering . . . the words are slipping. The words fly up, the body remains below, always bereft, always feeling there's some kind of inadequacy to what I just said. At that moment, yes, it's nothing but appearance. Still, I assume that if you were in trouble and you called my name, I would recognize it.

Johannes Birringer, Bonnie Marranca, Gerald Rabkin

THE CONTROVERSIAL 1985–86 New York theatre season was enlivened by the appearance of several performance works and stagings of new plays that not only signaled an interest in classics, myth, and dramatic narrative but fiercely proclaimed the psychosexual politics, stage language, and artistic values that were beginning to define contemporary theatre. In this probing exchange of ideas, Bonnie Marranca, *Performing Arts Journal* contributing editor Gerald Rabkin, and Johannes Birringer, who later wrote *Theory, Theatre, Postmodernism*, occasion one of *PAJ*'s periodic overviews of the current theatre scene. Their point of departure is Wallace Shawn's *Aunt Dan and Lemon*, whose affable reactionaries and pro-Nazi sympathizers challenge liberal principles, which were also under assault in Reagan-era conservatism. The subject of victims and victimization was seen from another angle during the same season in news of the scandal created by the Frankfurt production of Rainer Werner Fassbinder's *Garbage, the City and Death*, which brutally depicted the social mechanisms of corruption, anti-Semitism, and guilt.

If Shawn and Fassbinder, albeit with very different politics, undermined the belief in moral consensus—in the theatre and in society—Kathy Acker's *The Birth of the Poet*, staged by Richard Foreman for the Brooklyn Academy of Music Next Wave Festival, shocked audiences by its radical disengagement from theatrical and linguistic norms. Both Acker and Pina Bausch, whose dance company also performed at BAM, brought to the stage highly charged sexual images and the temptation of voyeurism. Richard Schechner instigated similar dialectics in *The Prometheus Project*, whereas Sam Shepard revealed a more conventional psychic terrain in *A Lie of the Mind*.

These new works raise complicated questions about the production and reception of disturbing imagery in the theatre, explored here in the context of gender, the performing body, social taboo, and technological mediation. These subjects were to come to the forefront of artworks and criticism by the mid-eighties, demonstrating how much theatrical vocabulary had moved from the phenomenological interests of a decade earlier to the cultural politics of today.

BGM

Conversation moderated by Bonnie Marranca, 1986

The Politics of Reception

Bonnie Marranca: The recent theatre season was characterized by a number
of productions that, while exploiting taboos, raised issues to which contemporary audiences are responding more and more, in all forms of art.
Among these issues I would include the question of representation, particularly in relation to race and gender; an exploration of liberalism as a
political philosophy; and uses of technology in performance. It seems to
me that we might begin with any one of these topics.

Gerald Rabkin: I assume by the failure of liberalism you are referring to Wally
Shawn's *Aunt Dan and Lemon.* That is an interesting question, particularly
if you read the appendix to the published version. Here Shawn makes
explicit his working by negative example through the quasi—and not so
quasi—fascist mentalities of his central characters and the positive need
for liberal values: the recognition of the individual human being within
a liberal framework is the only guard against the acceptance of the monstrous assumptions Aunt Dan and Lemon "logically" develop. But we see
the failure of liberalism by the marginality of Lemon's mother, the one
liberal voice.

BGM: She clearly has no response in the play. That's obviously deliberate,
and in some ways makes the play less interesting. There is no dialectic;
it's completely one-sided from the point of view of reactionary politics.
It seems to me a little bit dangerous about the play, and it's part of the
ethos of the appendix as well—this danger of not distinguishing between
things in our world. In *Aunt Dan and Lemon* there is no differentiation between the kinds of killings that are spoken about. There must be a difference between killing criminals, Indians, Jews, and cockroaches. Lemon's
point of view is faulty in that all kinds of killing are equated—you simply
can't link killing cockroaches and Nazi philosophy.

GR: I agree that there are certain moral premises, historical premises, that
are problematic in the play. The very choice of Kissinger as Dan's idol
is deliberately provocative: he hardly tops the list of radical/liberal demons, even taking into account his involvement with the overthrow of
the Allende government. But the moral issue is ultimately larger: unless
one accepts a totally pacifist position, you come down to the old question of necessary violence. Shawn deliberately fudges the question here.

BGM: Shawn's point of view doesn't necessarily attach itself to a fully developed philosophy, and the person representing the liberal point of view

is completely inarticulate. Shawn makes the point that we have a certain freedom because other people in the world don't, that our freedom is dependent on their oppression. Aunt Dan's philosophy suggests to her that Kissinger takes responsibility for his action, while journalists and other detractors enjoying the freedom in American society simply criticize him.

GR: There is an element of truth in much of this critique, and that is why the play is so disturbing. It's very easy to attack the villain, the Other. Here Shawn recognizes the undeniable logic of Dan and Lemon's reasoning. But he's also saying there are crucial leaps that are irrational, and negate morality—a twisted process by which the ordinary, somewhat "decent individual" is forced inexorably into the position of monster. That is the valuable part of the play.

I accept your judgment that the minute you begin to probe the overall intellectual structure of the play it begins to unravel. It does *not* distinguish between the act of necessary self-defense and the act of wantonness. Is every violent act immoral? Well, the fight against Hitler produced violent reactions that few of us would condemn as immoral. Shawn puts his finger on a certain kind of logic and sensibility that leads to the inconceivable. He catches that in the logic of the two major characters and that is why his focus is on them and *not* on the liberal response to evil.

BGM: What you're outlining also bothered me as an argument in the play. It's not exactly clear in terms of morality whether Shawn is distinguishing between a person of action and a person reflecting on acts. In other words, Dan's argument is that a person attains a certain stature through action. It's somewhat faulty because action and reflection represent two different realms of society and they're both necessary. Dan's argument rests on the fact that Kissinger was a man of action and the rest of us, the rest of the liberals, talk and criticize.

GR: You're right. We vicariously identify with the hero, the one who *acts*. That point, however, was ambiguously presented by the two casts at the Public Theater: How *literally* are we to take Dan's adventures? The physical presences of Linda Hunt and Pamela Reed created different emotional profiles in the play. Hunt is powerful but idiosyncratic physically: her reported affairs with Mindy and her professor seemed vicarious within the context of her physical presence. Reed's physical and emotional profile was such that you could believe her. It's ambiguous in the text to what extent Aunt Dan acts on her "amoral" premises, which lead to the immoral. The amoral for Shawn is the world of sexuality, and the world of the bedroom is connected to the world of politics. It's an audacious play in that

Shawn deliberately avoids narrative and psychological elements except subtextually and focuses the play on the rhetoric. These long set speeches are disturbing because on one level he succeeds in what he wanted to do: to force the audience to accept a certain kind of complicity. Aunt Dan, on one level, is a crazy, eccentric Auntie Mame who says all these wild and crazy things that are fantastically attractive to sweet, neurasthenic, sickly Lemon. If the mother were strengthened as a figure, and the liberal alternative presented more strongly, then it would be clearly "them" against "us." We'll instantly identify with the liberal alternative. Shawn succeeds in finding a less conventional attack. I would love to get a reaction to this from your European perspective, Johannes.

Johannes Birringer: I think the play is avoiding the complexities of the issues by positing the arguments in a monological way, completely withholding any critical point of view within the play. This strategy, which one might call insidious or irresponsible, collapses everything into a kind of seductive surface where eccentricity comes to look innocent, and innocence eccentric. If the play assumes the audience's complicity, as you have argued, it does so because there is no "liberal alternative" that wouldn't look hypocritical. Shawn's American liberalism admits frankly that it is susceptible to "slightly" inappropriate analogies, and the play becomes dangerously predictable in the sense in which it presents a kind of pragmatized amoralism.

GR: Did you sense an identification with that amoralism?

JB: The performance trivializes the issue by making us understand one continuous irony in the play, namely, the monstrous views put forth by two relatively nice women, who seem so innocent in what they're saying although it is outrageous. That quality of outrage gets lost once you see that the play only works in this one mode. I felt really disappointed by the presentation of the issue of Nazism and Kissinger's involvement in the American war machine.

What I would raise as a question since we're talking about the politics of performance is, Can the theater, especially in this country, deal with that question in a public forum, and what are its means? The play shows the difficulties of actually dealing with political questions, especially since a counterpoint or critique was not given in the play itself. I don't know whether it was expected from the audience.

Maybe I can make that comparison to the situation in Frankfurt and the recent controversy over the production of Fassbinder's *Garbage, the City and Death*. It also dealt with the touchy subject of how to address total immorality and total perversion of human values in the past and in a present *influenced* by that past. In Frankfurt, members of the Jewish community prevented the play from being shown. Now, in New York, when I saw *Aunt Dan and Lemon* there was a total passivity in the audience, which in one sense was striking and in another, totally expected, because the play cannot really achieve what it wants to achieve, namely, to create a critical dialogue, or an analysis of the guilt of silent complicity.

GR: But clearly the cultural contexts are so different. Fassbinder's play, whatever one's vision of it and of the political action taken against it, must be viewed within its unique historical circumstances, just as Shawn's play comes out of a culture that was never physically brutalized.

BGM: Paradoxically, Shawn is criticizing the liberal point of view in the play, while relying on a liberal audience to identify with it in the broadest, most old-fashioned sense. To say, which he does in the appendix, that there's a little bit of Hitler's ghost in all of us is a real cliché. It's a spurious point to be constantly told in American dramas about Nazis that we're all Nazis. The critique of Nazism and its philosophy has to go beyond this liberal point of view that there's a little bit of the Nazi in all of us.

JB: It's the problem of an antiliberal humanist play written by a liberal humanist who really doesn't know how to formulate the problem in different ways and whose irony depends on a naive belief in a moral consensus. Shawn's idea of moral corruptibility or complacency, at the same time, seems tied to a history of American political commonplaces that is unaware of its own ideology of innocence or "compassion," as Lemon calls it (the kind of "compassion" that makes the Reagan administration support "freedom fighters" in Central America and elsewhere).

GR: I find it no small achievement that Shawn tried within the sense of his culture and the values he shares with the culture to see how monstrous inhumanism can emerge out of individuals who are not themselves monsters and inhuman.

BGM: But the dynamics show that that is precisely the weakness of the liberal humanist critique, because Shawn is caught up in the same dynamic he's criticizing. Let me mention one other point: Irene Fornes mentioned something interesting with regard to this play. She was disturbed by the fact that he gave the reactionary speeches to women. She thought that Shawn, since he was an actor in the play, was hiding behind another character rather than giving these speeches to his own character. What if Wally Shawn were Lemon? Is it a way a playwright hides an unpopular point of view? It's more difficult for a playwright to come right out and say something in a very direct way than it is to couch it in irony or metaphor, giving the speeches to others. That's why his appendix is also so ambiguous. What is Shawn actually saying about morality? On the one hand, applauding a turning away from morality, how it traps us in guilt; on the other hand, in the last paragraph he's saying, "Well, the world isn't all evil."

GR: He would probably acknowledge that this is the dilemma of the liberal in the present day, in that no clear alternatives seem to be viable. As a consequence, one has to try to understand.

Let's return to the Fassbinder play, where similar questions are raised in a radically different context. Let's, for the moment, defer the social implications of the protests against it to focus on the play itself. It is a very, very powerful play, there's no denying that. But it is also a profoundly ambiguous play in that its explicit politics on slum landlordism and property—its inception was real-estate speculation and political corruption in Frankfurt after the war—are constantly at war with an intense sense of the impossibility of the human condition.

Obviously, Fassbinder identifies, as Brecht does, with the outcasts, the marginals, as a means of critiquing capitalist society at large. But also as in Brecht, there is a tension between social critique and an existential pessimism about the human condition. In Fassbinder the balance is further skewed by a scream of angst that recognizes *every* character in the play as simultaneously victim and victimizer. There are *no* alternative positive models that suggest the possibility of change, and the play as a political critique is totally overwhelmed by a vision of thanatopia. If there is an anti-Brechtian act of identification at work in this Brechtian play, it's certainly Fassbinder's with Roma B, who asks for her own death and is granted it.

JB: I think it is written from an entirely different perspective, the perspective of suffering due to the perceived impossibility of changing the oppression and exploitation of human beings in particular social and political conditions. For Fassbinder the condition of minorities did not change in postwar Germany. That experience of suffering is totally lacking in *Aunt Dan and Lemon*, where the two leading female characters are looking from the outside on something they explain in ludicrously perverse ways. Think of Roma B in Fassbinder's play: she can't get out of the position of being exploited, and she finds understanding and affection from precisely the one character, a rich Jew involved in real-estate manipulation, who became the protagonist in the Frankfurt controversy.

BGM: You said that the Rich Jew is the protagonist. I might add that Fassbinder's German publisher has requested that in future editions of the volume, we change "The Rich Jew" to "A, the Rich Jew" in the cast list. I suppose that means he won't be a type. Do you think that the Rich Jew is the main character in the play, and if so, why?

JB: Yes, I would argue that in terms of the representation of social contradictions in the play. It is written of course from within the German situation of remembering guilt and not being able to get out of the self-entrapment of that guilt.

In Fassbinder's perspective it is a way of capitalizing on existing corruption and human degradation produced by the system, where Jewishness becomes almost a metaphor for a complex of guilt, oppression, and self-oppression. In other words, both the characters who are non-Jewish as well as the Rich Jew are part of the same system, which instrumentalizes guilt and the mechanisms that lead to the production of evil.

GR: Fassbinder has always worked with traditions of provocation, in this play primarily overt sexuality and obscenity, the intensity of its violent imagery and sadomasochism. The act of labeling a character "Rich Jew" is to some extent comparable to what The Wooster Group did in using blackface in *Route 1 & 9:* a similar act of provocation against the subject of the unspeakable.

Though I abhor the tradition of censorship, I cannot accept an absolute standard of total freedom of expression regardless of social context. History, German history in particular, shows us that there may be times limits have to be drawn. Whether in the present German context this was the place to draw the line I am not sure. But bad boy Fassbinder will say the unsayable, denying the cordon sanitaire created around certain subject matter by German guilt about the tradition of anti-Semitism.

What Fassbinder says is that each human being will use what he or she has to victimize others; in this case the Jew uses German guilt and his connections with the Establishment as a means of maintaining his economic power. On the other hand, he is also a sympathetically ambiguous character who sees with a depth and perception that other characters do not.

BGM: Let me raise an alternative point. I think that the play is more virulently antiwoman. Obviously, that doesn't have the same kind of political imagery or impact in Germany as the representation of a Jew does. But if you look at the imagery of the play, it is more violently antiwoman, as much of Fassbinder's work is. For example, the play takes place on the moon, which is a female image. Also the image of the city is a spider; if you extend that imagery, the female spider devours the male in the act of copulation. The whole urban image is around the notion of this spider-like web of filth and corruption. Also, Roma is hated by both her father and her mother, she's abused physically by Franz, and Oscar is openly antiwoman. The female image is the image for pollution in this play, not the Jew.

GR: But Fassbinder, in his own sexual ambivalence, more often than not *identifies* with female victimization at the same time that he portrays a world in which the female—but not only the female—is brutalized. Shall we extend this question to similar images of victimization in male-female relations in Pina Bausch, whose appearances at the Brooklyn Academy's Next Wave Festival were obviously one of the highlights of the fall? There are many who have reacted negatively to the intensity of Bausch's symbols of victimization, feeling that she goes beyond the traditional feminist critique to indulge and indeed exploit the victimization of women. How do you react to that, Bonnie?

BGM: I see her work as an elaboration and an extension of much of the Judson aesthetic, except what is different about it is the exploration of male and female social and sexual relations. Her theatre is perhaps more important for German theatre than it is for American. What's important about it for German theatre is the influence and move toward spectacle in a theatre that has a very strong literary tradition.

But from its feminist point of view her work is really quite extraordinarily different in the context of dance. Her dancers are choreographed as obscene, awkward, ugly women. So it's a direct attack on the notion of the beautiful female dancing body. Also within the context of feminist theory, Bausch reverses the notion of "the gaze." She refuses to let the female be the object gazed upon and instead turns around the entire dance ensemble to gaze at the audience. It's a rather simple flip of the equation, but within the context of her work it's developed politically, in the use of the body in performance and in terms of the imagery. One of her strong pieces, *Kontakthof,* which is very Brechtian, also uses this fertile tradition that Fassbinder draws on. But in both situations there is a sense, which you don't have in *Aunt Dan and Lemon,* of a very strong social *Gestus*. The entire world created in the German pieces—Bausch and Fassbinder—has a political, social, aesthetic philosophy that is integrated, even though there might be contradictions within it. Now some people say that if a man did what Bausch does he would be criticized for being sexist. That's interesting and perhaps partly true: maybe only a woman could get away with this kind of choreography. How do you feel about that?

GR: You're quite right that there is a tremendous energy in both Fassbinder and Bausch, and in the other figures, like Reinhild Hoffmann and Suzanne Linke, who appeared at the Next Wave Festival, a reconnection with Weimar energy. It's a unique historical situation of having to leap back beyond the Nazi period to reestablish strong links with the past. Bausch's evening of Brecht-Weill, *Don't Be Afraid* and *The Seven Deadly Sins*, was enormously effective in establishing a sense of continuity—within her own concerns, with her own subtexts—with the Weimar tradition.

But there are contradictions in Bausch's work that I'm trying to resolve: tensions between form and formlessness, between gimmickry and stunning visual innovation, between intensity and repetitiveness in her fundamental obsession with the battle of the sexes. My feeling, and I know others don't agree, is that when there is a strong coherent structure at work, as in *Kontakthof* or *Cafe Müller*—and despite her sometimes surrender to theatrical effect—her work is powerful and important.

But to get back to your point of the continuation of the Judson aesthetic, some dance critics dislike her work because they feel that it denies the body by using it in ways that destroy its capacity for making formal aesthetic gestures.

BGM: Bausch and Fassbinder are doing the same thing, in one sense. They're addressing taboos in language: Fassbinder's dealing with literary language and imagery, and Bausch with taboos in body language. Brecht is the ideal mechanism for this kind of aesthetic because of the sense of *Gestus* in which the body represents an entire political world. As far as my own interest in Bausch's work, it remains at this formal, feminist theoretical level, which is interesting at this point in dance. It doesn't seem to be coincidental that we should have now a dance theatre that deals with sexuality, representation, and social relations between men and women.

JB: I disagree with the notion that both in Fassbinder's play and in Pina Bausch's work there is a recognizable exploitation or use of antiwoman or antiman or anti-Semitic positions. We're not at all dealing with essentialist or racist categories in their work, but rather with the mechanism, perhaps I should say the violence of the mechanism, in which femaleness or Jewishness or maleness appear (i.e., come to be represented). Pina Bausch's work is quite clear in the association between maleness and machismo and the kind of sexist attitudes we identify with male aggression. But it's demonstrated as part of the ideological and social construction of behavior, the "training" of roles that become second nature. Through the Brechtian model it can be shown, in the way certain patterns of behavior are written into the body and the way victimization surfaces in those patterns of behavior. It's not a matter of exploitation but a matter of *dem-*

onstrating it to an extent that it becomes almost unbearable, especially in America, where, as you say, it's unacceptable to show the ugliness entrenched in social behavior.

BGM: I don't think it's a particularly American attitude. Let me just go back a second. I didn't say that she was exploitative. Neither do I think of Fassbinder that way. I do not consider *Garbage, the City and Death* as an anti-Semitic play.

GR: To label it an anti-Semitic play is not the same as to say that it is a deliberate provocation in its utilizing of traditional anti-Semitic elements. We have to recognize that Fassbinder consciously utilizes elements of the anti-Semitic tradition because figures on a stage are exemplary. It's naive to assume that someone with Fassbinder's intelligence didn't know what he was doing.

BGM: That's what people said about The Wooster Group, too—that they're an avant-garde group, how could they be racist? Now we've come to the base of how to consider representation. We're back to the Platonic argument that because representation in performance is twice removed from reality it seems inadequate as a clear political philosophy.

GR: We also come in conflict with the intentionalist question. Let's extend this into the Foreman-Acker collaboration, *The Birth of the Poet*. If we were just presented with *Garbage, the City and Death*, and if we had no knowledge of who Pina Bausch is, would our apprehension of their work be transformed? What would our interpretation of Kathy Acker's text be if we discovered that it was a man who wrote it instead of a woman?

BGM: People have said the same thing about that play as they did about Bausch: if a man did that, it would be considered sexist. We're dealing with the same thing in terms of the image of Jew in German literature. Historically, certain imagery is potent, and there's just no way to get around that.

GR: The contextual element cannot be eliminated. Representation doesn't exist in a void; it exists within the series of apprehensions that a reader or an audience brings to it. Anyone who sets up a totally formalist aesthetic is not really facing this reality.

BGM: This gets back to what we started out with—the issue of liberal humanism. We seem to be in a period where there are several hot issues: we're thinking about cultural images, the politics of representation, sexuality, and, hopefully, not overpoliticizing art. More and more we are dealing with taboos of different kinds of imagery that we didn't see on the stage fifteen years ago. If you think of the ways we talked and wrote about Richard Foreman in the seventies, it's almost astounding that nobody wrote about his use of the body. Now it's inconceivable to think about Foreman's work without dealing with it in terms of sexuality.

GR: Let's talk about *The Birth of the Poet,* because this is a very interesting and problematic work, one of the few works in recent memory in the American theatre that has created the kind of scandal Fassbinder's play represents in Germany. Even the very "hip" Next Wave audience was booing, hissing, walking out in droves. Without discussing the sociology of that at the moment, we have to admit we saw a disturbing, malformed kind of event. In my view, the text Kathy Acker produced could not have received a less informed production. The Cunningham-Cage model that prevails in so many Next Wave productions—each element going off on its own independently—is exactly *not* the kind of model that can deal with a text as supercharged and as powerful as *The Birth of the Poet.*

BGM: Is that because it was theatre, or do you think the model works better for dance?

GR: The model is most successful in work that assumes a kind of Brechtian distance, work that is cool, in which elements can establish a dialectical relation. Here you have a text that is so hot, so eruptive, that any kind of balance becomes almost impossible unless there really is a strong theatrical welding of all production elements. But it seems to me that Kathy Acker is on to something that connects with the themes we've been talking about. Let me read one passage from the typescript of the text: "The implosion of the world of unbearable passion is the destruction of human meaning. The only possible world for humans now is the realm of ornament, pure nonrepresentation. All languages are finally ornaments or nonrepresentation is the word of God but even God the Father being a religious centralization must be abandoned before we who are abandoned, who are politically powerless can speak." It's these elements that led Erika Munk to defend the play from a feminist point of view, saying that it represented women's throwing their desire back in the face of male phallocratic power. It led Elinor Fuchs to say in conversation that she felt this play signaled the eruption of nonrepresentation in theatre, a breakthrough that implodes language as power.

BGM: Interestingly, it's dealing with the same issues as Fassbinder's play—death, pollution, racial issues, and sex, in an urban environment.

GR: One finds that in reading the text, not from the BAM production. Yet even as a written text the play is so contradictory, so ambivalent, so ultimately incoherent as to negate the effectiveness of its undeniable power. I don't find here what I do in Fassbinder's play, a critical intelligence that knows what it's doing, shaping and controlling its provocative events and images. The play is a garbled scream of rage and pain in which I find a complicity with, as well as an attack upon, victimization. It asserts that language is nonrepresentational but is intensely aware of the power of the representation of obscenity. The text is schizophrenic: meaning is always partially created by the reader or spectator; but in this case you have to work overtime.

JB: It is a total self-contradiction in the premise that language or action in the theatre could be nonrepresentational or could implode in the sense that she's implying. In Bausch's work you can see clearly through what is represented: the connection between sexual conflict and political conflict and the relations of power. In *The Birth of the Poet* the whole question of ornamentation really diluted that and played into a postmodern interest in surfaces, incoherence and indeterminacy of surfaces that is rather regressive.

The production was very incoherent, especially in the interplay among the staging, libretto, and stage design by David Salle, which made no sense at all and seemed to conflict with the taboo breaking and deliberate obscenity of the text.

BGM: That play is such a direct link to Foreman's own work. I have the feeling that—looking back at his Rhoda cycle—if Rhoda wrote, she would be writing like Kathy Acker. Acker is doing some of the same things as Pina Bausch: a woman who's dealing with obscenity. Certainly no woman has ever used language like this on the stage, and that is deliberately provocative. Some works have a topicality in a certain historical period— Acker, like Bausch, is dealing with the representation of the female body, not only linguistically but also physically as a body, and she's denying the tradition of the beautiful female body as the object of contemplation, of the sublime, of the aesthetic. Again, it's getting away from the idea of the gaze, which has become a dominant rhetorical point, if you could call it that, of feminist theory. That is directly connected to how we see spectacle.

Aside from that, we've accepted this kind of literary tradition—if I can separate the performance from the text for a moment—with Pasolini, Burroughs, Céline. She is working within and playing with that very male tradition of philosophical eroticism and obscenity. These factors are startling regardless of the ultimate satisfaction of the text as a closed form.

GR: I don't disagree, but why should many who look at works by men that advance new images of the female be surprised by the fact that a male is going to have a male gaze? The other problem suggested by Kathy Acker is the danger of ghettoization, sometimes operative at the time of the rise of the black aesthetic. Does the fact that Kathy Acker as a *woman* utilizes this language negate the inadequacies and difficulties within the text itself? There is a danger in that. Ultimately, while recognizing contextual diversity, we still need to work with some standards of universality that allow us to make aesthetic judgments, standards that go beyond the biographical and biological.

BGM: Let's go back to the point of universality. That is the same thing as saying that a work is complete, and whether one's point of view is reactionary, or deconstructionist, or humanist, or formalist, the work remains the same. There is a difference between work that is created in different historical periods, by men or women, or marginal groups. What's interesting in Acker's work is that, like a number of different kinds of new work—Heiner Müller's, for example—in our time we're seeing the history of sexuality connected to the history of the world. Now, I'm not making extravagant claims for her work, but simply pointing out elements that for me in 1986 are interesting to think about, regardless of the lack of success of the production.

GR: I suppose it's a question of difference of perception. I fear the tendency to evaluate the social significance of the artistic act rather than the actual aesthetic result. I didn't mean to advance a universalist aesthetic theory; but it's still necessary to recognize that we *do* have aesthetic models that we apply within our own contextual realities.

BGM: I'm a little surprised at your reaction because of your longtime interest in the Theatre of the Ridiculous tradition. I see *The Birth of the Poet* connected to that and a step beyond it. Twenty years ago the Theatre of the Ridiculous dealt with many of the same taboos, if you think of early Tavel or Vaccaro. Don't you see this as part of the Ridiculous tradition?

GR: Yes, in its time the Ridiculous Theatre very definitely challenged traditional models of representation, but I don't think every work of the Ridiculous tradition demanded equal aesthetic respect.

BGM: I'm not thinking about this production in terms of success. I simply wanted to suggest the idea that the Ridiculous has turned into the punk aesthetic.

GR: To that extent, the Ridiculous was a politically revolutionary movement that has been subsumed by all kinds of other changes, in pop and high culture.

JB: I think we should ask the question whether we are currently in a phase of rethinking representation. The biggest problem was that even if Kathy Acker's text was coming from a new voice—we're also talking about the increasing work now done by women artists—did it materialize in the production? That is to say, since Richard Foreman was directing it, what happened to the libretto? Why were there so many quotations of surrealist staging techniques, and why in a sense was the staging going backward?

GR: There were problems of sensibility, judgment, and autonomy. The problems that surfaced in the production were also found in other work Foreman has done this past season in staging texts other than his own. In the case of Vàclav Havel's *Largo Desolato*, perhaps someone said, "Well, Richard's world is a world of paranoia, often a world of fear, a world in which buzzers interrupt," and this seemed a perfect kind of metaphor to impose on the Havel text.

The evidence of both the Acker and Havel productions is that the playwright's and the director's sensibilities did not really mesh, and as a consequence both productions went off in contradictory, unsatisfying directions.

JB: The superficially paranoic staging for Havel does not really come to grips with the play itself, because that play is dealing with the utter normality of the terror in Czechoslovakia, which is a different matter. The premise of *The Birth of the Poet* was that we are at a point *after* the catastrophe, after the explosion, so to speak. Set in New York after the nuclear blast, the play showed that something has happened by that time, namely, that we have lost a certain meaningfulness.

GR: Let us note that there *is* a connection of this theme to Richard's perceptions as expressed in his works from *Egyptology* onward through *Miss Universal Happiness* to *Africanus Instructus*, a movement from the purely phenomenological, intermixed with his own vision of the body/mind dichotomy, to the quasi-political. Images of terrorists, revolution, and the Third World have increasingly intruded in his work, as well as an element of social apocalypse, a common theme in many of the works we've been considering. It's certainly in the Acker text and in Schechner's *The Prometheus Project*, which, interestingly enough, have the exact same structure and admixture of sexual violence and nuclear holocaust.

In the case of the Havel play, I absolutely agree with you, Johannes, the absurdism of reality—the paranoic, the hysterical, the hallucinatory—are all part of the fabric of everyday life. Terror is interiorized. To exteriorize it into gestures and Rhoda-like crouches and walking the walls is to ask for the exact kind of reaction that it got—laughter, which *defuses* terror.

JB: Do you think that the whole question of the language might be an important one, if we think, for example, of the ten or so years of a theatre of images? Think of Wilson and that kind of theatre, which virtually excluded the use of textual language. We're now seeing an increasing interest in using language, in revising myths and representations. For example, Schechner was deliberately going back to revise a myth by conjoining the Prometheus myth and the Io myth.

GR: That is exactly one of the problems that both Foreman and Wilson face as they move more in the direction of dramatic text: they have to face something they never faced before—the performer as actor. In creating their theatrical vocabularies they developed a very specific kind of technique in which acting was negated, in which amateurism, the ordinary individual's deadpan reading of lines, was substituted. Now all of a sudden they're dealing with dramatic texts, in the case of Wilson's *Golden Windows*, perhaps not a coherent narrative text but still much more verbal than anything he had tackled to that point.

BGM: One thing in regard to *Golden Windows* that was interesting to see was the use of David Warrilow. Suddenly his performance, and our knowledge of him as a performer, brought Wilson's text into the world of Beckett, and this was a revelation. However, Wilson mixed nonactors and actors, so it wasn't totally carried through. I feel that his work would benefit by using real actors, and I understand from people who saw *Golden Windows* in Munich that the result created a very different effect because of the use of well-known actors.

JB: That raises the question whether we can really speak of a return of the actor if Wilson employs technology to the extent that the text is distributed through amplification and an audio system, in spite of the presence of the actor. Often I have trouble connecting the voice with the body of the performer, and that creates a different sense of what happens.

GR: Certainly in both *Golden Windows* and *Alcestis* the multiseparated voices were used, but, nonetheless, there still were actors speaking live dialogue. It was interesting to note the intersection of the various texts in *Golden Windows*—the visual text with the shifting perspective of the house, the aural text of the separated voices coming on the sound track, plus the verbal text that was emanating from the actors. But if you look at the verbal text, you see that it functions in much the same way in *Golden Windows* that it has in other Wilson pieces.

Wilson and Foreman have always used language to deliberately cut loose its signifiers. But now, all of a sudden, in the presence of the performers we begin to feel the desire to impose a kind of signification on what is spoken. The failure of *Golden Windows* was a failure of the dramatic text because the language does not function in a way consonant with the whole chamber structure as expressed visually and aurally. The very banality of the language, which Wilson has always played with, in this case becomes an obtrusive element working counter to the integration of the multiple texts in the piece.

BGM: I feel Wilson could be an extraordinary artist and that we would see the real connection between Craig and Appia and the theatre of images in our own time if he could work with writing as writing, if he could devote time to thinking about the text in an all-encompassing sense of his performance work.

GR: *Alcestis* was very interesting in that regard because the main body of it was a coherent if not absolutely faithful reading of the Euripides play. Even in the prologue by Heiner Müller, interpersed through the main body of the play proper, and in the Kyogen epilogue there was a coherent structure of signification. Nonetheless one felt, How are we to read those actors' performances? Wilson himself did not seem to know how to deal with actors as actors—whether to deal with them in his traditional way as presences, part of the landscape, or to engage them within the context of a narrative.

JB: One of the biggest provocations in the German productions of Wilson's work in Munich and Cologne was that he used very well-known character actors, who were turned into carriers of nonsensical, banal, everyday speech. That shocked people a lot because they could not identify emotionally with what was said. The question is whether we can go back to actually using actors in that kind of work, which seems so much more interested in the scenography of the performance as a whole.

GR: Obviously, the actor has always been the primary figure of representational theatre, whereas the radical experimentation of the past twenty years has, at least partially, reduced him or her to a performer who is one part of the total scenic representation: neither visuals, aurals, nor actors are privileged. If Foreman and Wilson are going to use the actor in more traditional ways, then they are going to have to rethink the meaning of acting and performance.

BGM: In the past few years we've seen a return to myth, to the proscenium, to the actor, and to classics and texts. Clearly we're in a kind of transitional period.

GR: The reemergence of mythology is an interesting question, as Johannes was saying before.

JB: It means a return to narrative, doesn't it? If you deal with myth that presents problems, you need to confront the *construction* of the myth.

GR: Particularly in *Alcestis* you felt that what was missing was what Lee Breuer was able to find in *The Gospel at Colonus*—some modern receptacle for the tragic "spirit," whatever it may be. Breuer found it by connecting with the vital black gospel tradition. But in *Alcestis*, here was a classic myth with no new objective correlative, and that weakened the mythic dimension. Let's extend the discussion to Schechner's *Prometheus*. Schechner had the same aims as Kathy Acker: to intersect nuclear holocaust, sexual violence, and victimization. The problem for me was an overly schematic use of the myth and its modern equivalences, which dissipated the energy coming from the imagery and the performance. I'm sure we will respond to the work from our different male and female gazes. The part that worked for me from the point of view of performance was the Annie Sprinkle pornography-show segment, except for its very end, when there's the obvious point of stopping—one, two, three—and glaring at the audience as if to say, "What *are* you looking at, you people?" You could see that coming. Nonetheless, it created the kind of disturbance that on one level Kathy Acker was able to set in motion—at least for males, because pornography is a male genre and most males have had experience with it at some time in their lives. So observing pornography, *not* in the enclosed worlds of all-male bonding, but within the context of an art occasion with women present, was genuinely unsettling, more provocative than sitting back and saying, "Yes, I agree with you; yes, victimization and rape and sexual violence are terrible."

BGM: Schechner operates on the same assumption that Shawn does, which is the Aristotelian humanistic tradition of audience identification, that certain point of view that we're all the same, that we all have a little bit of the pornographer or Hitler in us. On the other hand, Kathy Acker was working totally in an antihumanist tradition. She does not operate under the same assumptions.

The problem with the Annie Sprinkle porno section is that it isn't very compelling to have a female stripper, which is a kind of cliché, undressing and talking to an audience that is then supposed to feel that they're voyeurs because they let this happen very passively. What surprised me was the way she could move among the audience, get men to touch parts of her body or put their heads in her breasts.

GR: That was a bravura gesture. I disagree—I felt embarrassed the night I saw it.

BGM: But you know, that makes me think that men must be very comfortable with the female body, that even this stranger could come up in the audience and get any kind of reaction. The representation of women onstage or in film is always done from the point of view of male psychology. The men in the audience obviously were quite comfortable with this poetic perception of her body. I think it would be far more provocative if it were a male there and to see if the same thing would happen, whether men could touch other men. Whether they could perhaps get the women to have the same physical response.

GR: I agree with you that he used a male erotic model here. It's just that *my* male reading of the show sensed a general male embarrassment that nonetheless led, like stag fraternity-house circumstances, to a certain kind of macho pose of knowledgeability.

BGM: Did you hear of anyone refusing to participate in her seduction?

JB: Everyone was quite willing the night I was there.

BGM: I didn't hear of any controversy. I would have been curious to see if women staged a protest or if men refused to engage her. Schechner was dealing only with clichés, he did not deal with the representation of women or pornography in any way that contradicted or criticized the cultural production of imagery.

JB: Maybe it wasn't thought through, although he actually used the positioning of the striptease in direct relationship to the positioning of an audience vis-à-vis aestheticized images of destruction. In the first section, he showed in very fast movement hundreds of images—slide projections—that were taken after the bomb was dropped on Hiroshima. I saw this as an attack on the idea that you can actually watch these images, from an aesthetic distance, and feel secure. In other words, to let Annie Sprinkle walk out into the audience had something to do with physical rupture: we could no longer sit back and gaze at pornography or "beautiful," slow-motion imagery of Hiroshima. This is the kind of slow-motion, anesthetized situation we have in Wilson, when for four hours you see extraordinarily stunning images that go past your eyes. Schechner tried to break down that aesthetic flow.

BGM: I think his work was devoid of strong political content for the opposite reasons that Bausch's and Acker's works were much more compelling in the use of images or sexuality.

GR: He's coming from where he's coming from, and it's his gaze, and within the context of what he devised he tried to create some kind of bridge from this underground world that *does* exist and to have it enter the world of other images of destruction.

BGM: What I find problematical is the same attitude that's problematical in Schechner's writing: after he exposes these so-called everyday performance situations, there is no critique of them; it's a purely descriptive act that accepts performance at face value.

GR: You don't think there was a critique within the performance context?

BGM: Then we're assuming that the critique is always coming from the audience. Perhaps we assume too much. Is it necessary to assume that when things are not politically clear in a performance the audience must make the judgment? I suppose I'm more drawn now to work that seems to have a very connected and clear politics of form, a morality of form, rather than opaque or weak narrative structures that leave the issues of values to the spectator.

JB: It has to do with what Roland Barthes has called the "responsibility of forms" that an artist uses. It is precisely because Wilson has no political or historical consciousness that his recent work seems stuck in the visually beautiful but mystifying landscapes that he builds, in the same way in which Sam Shepard repeats his obsession with the empty mythos of the American family.

GR: Schechner is a heterosexual male and has a heterosexual male gaze. The kind of critique that you want to see is a critique that will come from women who are the recipients of that gaze. Nonetheless, I think there is something to be said for the exposure of the gaze and the investigation of it as a beginning.

BGM: I wouldn't deny that at all. I think it's Schechner's most intellectual piece, and he certainly showed a great leap into using more of his own theoretical work and other ideas about performance and technology. I'm simply critical about the pornography aspect and the issue of voyeurism. Back to Johannes's point about Shepard. Audiences and critics have made the assumption that he's criticizing male mythology. What if we were to ask if Shepard is a reactionary? People have said of *Aunt Dan and Lemon* that Shawn's play is reactionary, that he's a reactionary; they've said that Fassbinder's anti-Semitic. But no one has raised the issue with Shepard. Is he a redneck or is he a reactionary? Nobody has dealt with the issue, which is a central issue of the play, that a husband has beaten his wife— he didn't just step on her toe—and she's brain-damaged.

GR: I don't go to a work of art, Bonnie, for ideological correctness. That's not what I want in my perception of it.

BGM: I'm not proposing that. I'm simply saying that you should look at the politics of a work.

GR: But you seem to be imposing the requirement of a correct political position, a political grid that you place on the work of art. It is obvious that if certain works manifest values that one finds totally abhorrent, then that is going to drastically affect one's investigation of it.

The question that you raise in reference to *A Lie of the Mind*, the question of brain damage, is not a disturbing question to me, because I don't read it, first of all, within the context of a realistic play in which a sympathetic character one identifies with commits some kind of heinous act that is then, by whatever means, morally justified. I don't see that model operative at all in this play. I see a play in which *all* the characters are brain-damaged, battered travesties of the pioneer spirit. I see a play that in all its imagery—particularly in its final image of the fire in the snow perceived across half a nation—says, Don't take this too literally.

BGM: I'm not posing any model, I'm simply posing questions. It is strange that in all the reviews I've read—written, incidentally, by men—they have concentrated on the father-son relationship, and several reviewers picked out the image of blowing the ashes from the father's cremated body in the little tin. No one has dealt with an issue that seems to me to be important in the play, which is the relationship of the husband and wife and the issue of wife beating. Second, if you look at the last scene of the play, in my view it was staged with the husband downstage, virtually center, in a very sympathetic position physically. Sympathy went toward this man rather than dealing with the issue of violence. Now, I'm not saying that Shepard *has* to do that, but if we transfer our thoughts about Fassbinder and whether this play is anti-Semitic or whether he is, and whether *Route 1 & 9* is racist, why don't we think about Shepard's work and its philosophical view? I'm not posing a corrective or saying that he should have a program, but we assume certain things about artists because they're a little bit experimental, and perhaps we shouldn't.

GR: Everybody's noted, you have yourself noted in essays about Shepard, that he has always had a problematic relationship to women in his plays, which have for the most part dealt with a world of male bonding. Particularly in his early plays women have *very* insignificant roles. But it is certainly also true that since *Fool for Love* there has been some attempt to deal with male-female relations in a way that Shepard has not done in the past, and it's even more strongly so in *A Lie of the Mind*. We definitely find in that play a continuity from *Fool for Love* in that the interrelations of the family and its mutual cannibalization are contrasted with some indistinct vision of possible redemption through love. Now, admittedly, this is a redemption that is built on the character of a man who has beaten his wife practically to death. Obviously, the element of subjectivity we all bring to various works prevents me from responding as intensely as you, Bonnie, to the images of wife beating and victimization that you cannot eradicate from your reading of the rest of the play.

BGM: I think you're reducing my entire comment to a women's issue. It's very clear that we see different things, we see different things even as men or women, but no one here is talking about censorship. However, I am suggesting we look at a work in larger, more demanding ways rather than being overly attached to the notion of artistic effort.

I always look at work formally—but what is the morality of this form, the system of values it outlines? The critical response to *A Lie of the Mind* is more interesting for what is not spoken of. What are the taboos in terms of the work? What are the assumptions?

JB: Maybe within the world that Shepard creates there is a politics of sentimentality that doesn't confront the final collapse of moral values, but dreams about final redemption. I'm sure most people prefer the dream, and that's why they don't really react to the sexual frustration and the content of violence when it is directed against Jake's wife.

GR: But I don't think Shepard denies it; he faces it. He is honest to that extent. He doesn't try to mitigate it; it's a submerged violence he makes overt.

BGM: I agree, he's a very honest artist. To mention Fornes again, she made an interesting comment one time in *PAJ* which is that she found in response to audience discussion of her plays that men in the audience responded to only the male characters and women responded to both male and female characters. Just to be provocative, I raise the issue again: If there's such a discrepancy between the way we see things, what is the nature of our looking?

GR: The issues you raise, particularly in connection with all the other issues, are enormously significant, and we have to pursue them.

BGM: I simply think that whoever people are is in their writing. I don't see a separation anymore between, say, the world of the play and the world of the author. Now, I'm not speaking of autobiographical elements, but of philosophies, vision, and human values. Pirandello's fascism was in his work, as Chekhov's humanism was in his structure of writing.

GR: But why should we expect otherwise? I find it almost impossible to read Celine because of the virulence of his anti-Semitism; it is impossible for me to consider Wagner from a totally aesthetic point of view. One has to acknowledge that from the start. That doesn't mean to some extent we can't stand back—it would be foolish to say that Wagner is an insignificant artist. Nonetheless, insofar as we're functioning critically and trying to relate our aesthetic judgments to larger moral, ethical, and political judgments, we have to acknowledge the premises from which we're coming and examine them.

JB: Would you say, then, that it's possible to argue there is a logic of the material itself, that there are limitations to the kind of material Shepard treats, going back again and again into the American family and obsessed males in their relationships with their fathers and battered women? That is a limitation I don't see, for example, in a piece that was written, so to speak, from the outside about America as a dreamland. I'm referring now to *Dreamland Burns* by the Squat Theatre. It opens up the problematic in a very different way: a group that has just arrived here looks at what is happening to them.

GR: Yes, there are similarities in apocalyptic imagery between *A Lie of the Mind* and *Dreamland Burns*. Think of Squat's development since they arrived on these shores ten years ago. *Pig Child Fire* was overtly a work of the European avant-garde, very Artaudian, deliberately provocative and similar in certain strategies to the work of Kantor. But gradually there is a thematic transition in their work. The most fascinating element in their early work was the strategic use of their Twenty-third Street Theatre to create a theatre of the street, where everything that was happening outside was visible to the audience inside. This device lost its provocation in successive pieces but nonetheless remained effective. Thematically, their work was interesting because of its enormous ambivalence toward the American experience. As a band of Hungarian hippies who were kicked out of their country as subversive, obviously they relished the enormous freedom now available to them. On the other hand, immersion in a plethora of media imagery, in the wildness and violence that is the dark side of the freedom of the West, set up a fascinating tension in their work. On one hand, they reveled in their new freedom; on the other, they were overwhelmed with technology, media—America as a huge baby with television eyes in their piece *Mr. Dead and Mrs. Free.*

The interesting thing about *Dreamland Burns* for Squat is the transition it represents in their work, in a sense coming out of the movie *Stranger Than Paradise,* with Eszter Balint, Stefan's daughter, all of a sudden emerging as Squat's very own homegrown movie star who is an American! She fits and yet she doesn't fit *as* an American, and *Dreamland Burns* is their most American piece, the least apocalyptic despite its apocalyptic title and elements: its opening fire, its shower of objects dropping down, collapsing, but by the standards of the earlier pieces— where shish kebob skewers were being stabbed into groins and people gave blow jobs and were shot—what struck me was how the coolness of postmodern America has filtered in without totally transforming their sensibility. Through the figure of Eszter as the new urban woman the hippie clan that escaped from Hungary has entered its second generation.

JB: But it shows a coolness and ironic thrust toward images of America produced by the American "consciousness industry" that are at the opposite end of the sentimental gesture of the miraculous fire in the snow—the concluding image of *A Lie of the Mind,* which connects the two families.

GR: Shepard likes to end with these ambiguous images, but I don't think it's a completely sentimental image, Johannes. It breaks the realistic convention: the mother in California burns the house, the other mother in Montana sees it. It both universalizes the fact of destruction and suggests the possibility of redemption, the miracle of resurrection. On one level this play is a Western: the California people are the homesteaders and the Montana people are the cattlemen, the hunters. Shepard plays, as always, with mythic American forms, even affirmations: the patriotic ritual of folding the flag, the kiss after all these years. But he also points out that the fire in the snow casts severe doubt on a possible rekindling of the American spirit. The brain damage is something that cannot be overcome. That's the ambiguity in Shepard—the lies of the mind—one can hope that they can be overcome, but ultimately they can't. At least one can hope for the miracle.

BGM: Except that his wife is now a kind of Blanche duBois and totally demented.

GR: But there is a kind of recovery within a structure that is comic as well as mythic.

JB: But it's a very strange comic sense. It's as though the wife who is almost beaten to death recovers only to be seen to be married again, to the brother of the one who has beat her.

GR: I think we have to see that for all these losers, no one is going to escape.

BGM: And to see it in the context of all that we've been talking about. In every single case, in almost all the plays we're talking about, we're dealing with female characters who are coming to represent these points of view, starting with the reactionary point of view in *Aunt Dan and Lemon.* The interesting thing is, we still come down to the point that the female body is the scene of this politic, whatever it is. Bausch and Acker, whose sense of sexuality is very different, have confronted this issue. In the work of Shepard and Schechner we are simply given the same old tired images and psychology.

GR: Nonetheless, I think that within the legacy of the limitations created by one's gender, people like Schechner and Shepard are trying to, shall we say, deepen their gaze—perhaps from your point of view insufficiently, but I think honestly.

BGM: If you recall, ten or fifteen years ago the way people wrote or spoke about work was much more formalistic or structural. We've seen in recent years a real return to issues of representation and the body, how technology is used, the politics of taste . . . I think that we've moved from that highly formalistic phase when we were trying to establish a new stage language for theatre, and now we're moving much more as the theatre itself is, to narrative, to interest in writing and all different kinds of textuality.

GR: Let us move from what you said to the subject of to what extent the development of technology has altered the way representation is achieved on the stage. At present, there's an intense recognition of the conflict between the physical "presence" of the actor and his or her mechanically reproduced screen or video image; an example is *Dreamland Burns*. All of a sudden you realize in that work that a number of figures speaking to you are molded mannequins, with moving faces projected on their sculpted faces. Their utter immobility strikes you, and you recognize that you're dealing with a deceptive image, which is interacting with and problematizing the representation of live actors. We found the same issue explored in *Deep Sleep* by John Jesurun at La MaMa.

JB: The immobilization of the body was for me very strong in the way in which Wilson uses the human body as a figure in the larger architectural landscapes he creates, contrary to the privileging of the body, let's say, in dance or in some of the pieces we've discussed. It seems that there might be an important strand in the experimental arts, in the work of John Jesurun or the recent Squat piece, where the whole question of technological reproduction or imaging and the emplacement of bodies as projections can no longer be comfortably assumed in the theatre, where real bodies or objects used to be considered more real than their images. I think Jesurun in particular addressed the crucial question of postmodern culture: What is the reality of reality? We have trouble knowing on which side we are—whether we are in the screen projected or on this side of the screen. Jesurun's piece was rather striking in making that the focus point of the performance, that struggle *not* to become a projection.

GR: What bothers me in a lot of the current mixed-media pieces is their absence of a sense of history, their intimation that the mere juxtaposition of different technologies is an act of great aesthetic daring, when in fact one can go back sixty years to the era of Meyerhold and Piscator and find the same kind of technological experimentation. In Piscator's famous *Good Soldier Schweik* production, screen-drawn Georg Grosz caricatures became animated on the stage. Film, almost from its outset, has played with its form self-reflexively. And one need hardly note that the problematic intersection of aesthetic and social reality is something that has been observed since Pirandello. So I'm bothered by the assumption that some technological quantum leap has just occurred.

JB: But our historical conditions are radically different from those of the early avant-garde. I don't think it's a matter of self-reflexivity any longer. We live in a culture oversaturated with mass-produced images, technological practices, prefabricated consumption — our bodies fragmented in so many different pieces of reified techniques. I see this as an almost total depletion of human reality.

GR: I would like to find in the new works that use diverse technologies a recognition of the way in which technology has changed. But in *Deep Sleep* I'm confronted by a technique of discontinuity and disjunction that has been used by experimental theatrical artists since the era of the Dadaists and surrealists. How indeed *is* new technology altering perceptions? Once I had grasped, in the first few seconds, the familiar metaphor of *Deep Sleep*, its levels of performance, narrative text, and technological interaction were insufficient to hold my attention.

BGM: One of the things that's become clear throughout the discussion is a kind of anxiousness to move on. To move beyond the forms that are disseminating now in theatre and to be more aware of the links between experiments in the twentieth century, knowing what we know historically and seeing ourselves poised in an era where people are being influenced thematically by new configurations in the world and new technologies. It seems we're at some sort of cutting edge.

I think what will happen in this country is that we'll move away from formalism to more critical forms. The rest of the century will be a kind of critique of modernism and modernist form, positing new ways of perceiving the human being in the world.

GR: The tradition of the new is such that we constantly insist that, as in Lewis Carroll, they run as fast as they can to stay in the same place. If someone like Kantor comes along with a new piece, *Let the Artists Die*, which uses the same vocabulary and themes of his previous works, we say, "We've seen this already. We don't need this anymore." If, on the other hand, as in the recent work of Foreman and Wilson, there's an attempt to move into new territory, we, including ourselves here today, say, "Wait a minute. They don't know how to deal with actors, there's a problem of sensibility, stick to what you can do." So as we as critics uphold the standards that are meaningful to us in trying to make informed and knowledgeable judgments about the work we see, we should never forget the burden of the tradition of the new as artists try to move off into unexplored worlds, and allow them the opportunity to fail.

JB: It is possible to see how the current conditions of our culture will determine the kinds of material or "immaterial" realities artists deal with.
What we don't know is the extent to which we are already "beyond" the
history and the forms of modernism, or beyond history, as they say in
Europe. We don't know to what extent mass-produced images have already invaded our imaginary, evacuating all individual ethical substance
or psychical interiority. We need to confront this invasion in order to
continue to be able to differentiate, to make distinctions—in a political
sense—between ethical and ideological questions raised by art. The danger of the problem of implosion we spoke of earlier in respect to *The Birth
of the Poet* is that all of this becomes a closed circuit, as in Laurie Anderson's work (cf. *Home of the Brave*, live performance art having finally
moved directly onto the screen), where you cannot possibly make any
distinctions among aesthetic, technological, and social reality anymore
because it has become meaningless. The whole question of the construction of sexual difference and of political violence seems to be something
the theatre will have to deal with in the future, as long as we still have
theatre.

Julian Beck, Judith Malina

WHAT HAS ALWAYS CHARACTERIZED The Living Theatre, America's most long-lived avant-garde group, founded by Julian Beck and Judith Malina in 1947, is a clarity of vision and purpose at the service of both radical politics and art through decades of performing modern European or contemporary American drama, classics, and collective creations. Some years after the path-breaking works that made them famous, such as *The Connection, Paradise Now,* and *Mysteries and Smaller Pieces,* and a decade after the trip to Brazil, where they were jailed, at the time of this conversation with long-time associate Mark Hall Amitin, The Living Theatre had moved to Rome, creating since the mid-seventies, as part of *The Legacy of Cain* cycle, two dozen plays that were performed in factories, hospitals, schools, and the streets of Europe, often with students and workers. The move to Italy was motivated by the presence there of the most libertarian Marxist movement on the Continent and a vibrant counterculture. The piercing intellect of Beck, who died in 1985, comes through in his comments on the choice of *Prometheus* as a response to the historical problem of revolutionary impulses dissolving in repressive political structures, when the conflict between "the anarchist impulse and the communist-authoritarian impulse is mirrored also in the struggle between the Apollonian and the Eleusinian forces."

Against the background of growing unease with the world situation, and Solidarity strikes then in Poland, Malina is remarkably candid in her criticism of the group's *Antigone,* contrasting the original production and its current revival: "What we see today is a play for nonviolence where what we saw thirteen years ago was a play for revolution." The Living Theatre, a powerful voice in the postwar American arts and controversial catalyst for the transformation of political theatre in the sixties and seventies here and abroad, has continued to engage social issues and forge ties with cultural and workers' communities. Today, a half century later, its total commitment and utopian vision mark an ever-receding revolutionary moment in American theatre and society.   BGM

Conversation with Mark Hall Amitin, 1981

Radicalizing the Classics

Mark Hall Amitin: Why did you choose Rome as the city where you would base yourself at this time, rather than, say, Berlin or Paris? What is it about Rome that creates such a special situation enabling you and your work to really flourish?

Julian Beck: In 1965 we found in Italy that there was a very open climate for discussion and the study of social and political alternatives. It was a question with which the entire country had concerned itself. When we went back to Europe in 1975, we went with the question of whether it would be possible to work there and also whether it would be wisest to concentrate our work there in the hope that it might be useful in a movement for social and cultural change. We felt that, one, there was a growing libertarian-anarchist movement and, two, there was a growing Marxist movement. It seemed also to be the most libertarian of the various Marxist movements in Europe and there was a relatively strong youth and counterculture movement.

We've always had a very friendly working relationship with the Italian theatre world, and when we returned in 1975 there were sufficient offers of work, particularly from people in Torino who found a large orphanage for us to live in and supported us for four months while we worked on a new version of *The Destruction of the Money Tower.* During that period we made many contacts in the Italian anarchist movement and among other Italian political and cultural activists. It seemed to us a territory in which we wanted to stay.

MHA: Unfortunately, there has been very little information about the new productions you've made in the past two years. Perhaps you could elaborate on the creation of *Prometheus.*

JB: Let me first give some background. We have been working in these past five years doing a considerable amount of work outside the usual theatre architecture: plays in schools, in factories, in psychiatric hospitals, and in the plazas, streets, and alleys. We have played 125 cities during this time, many of them again and again and for periods ranging from a few days to a few months. We returned to Italy in 1975 with three plays in our repertoire that were basically new: *The Destruction of the Money Tower, Seven Meditations on Political Sado-Masochism,* and *Six Public Acts.* We spent the first year adapting these plays to specific aspects of Italian culture, and then spent time observing and trying to figure out what our next step was going to be.

Our next step, we decided, was to be the creation of a series of street theatre plays on a variety of themes that could be performed by a variety of groups—anarchists, students, women, and factory employees—and to try to create a repertoire that would be adaptable to various geographical and architectural circumstances. We spent the next year or two in the elaboration of some twenty-five plays ranging from flashes to plays lasting a half hour.

We then began to consider the idea of creating a large work for a theatrical circumstance that would address itself to the political reality and political ideas being discussed in Italy, a work that would be able to support a lot of the street theatre work that we wanted to do. We centered on the theme of Prometheus because it seemed to deal with the validity of government itself. With *Prometheus* we wanted to address ourselves to the very critical question of the state in our time as an influence on human character and social circumstances. The struggle between a Prometheus who tries to liberate humankind and the authoritarian force of a Zeus who tries to subjugate or destroy humankind seems appropriate to the occasion.

It seemed a good ancient mirror of the current problem in which the revolutionary impulses of people dissolve in the authoritarian structures of government. We created a *Prometheus* in which the first act is an elaboration of that myth and the myths surrounding Prometheus. In the second act we see the growth and development of those myths as they have influenced our culture and emerged in *the* epic revolutionary struggle of our time in the Soviet Union: the 1917–18 Revolution. We transpose the myth of Prometheus and project it on the struggle between the libertarian forces and ideals involved in that revolution and the old culture— the old patriarchal masculine repressive culture—and how it reemerged in the effort on the part of the Bolsheviks to impose certain ideas and certain forms of organization on the Russian people. This seems to be an important thing in view of the fact that so many of the discussions that we have in Italy are with more or less convinced Marxists.

MHA: Could you explain how you go about creating a form for acting out the myths of Prometheus, and does it relate to *Frankenstein*, when the Greek myths were acted out inside the mind of the monster?

JB: The relationship in the dramatic structure is not the same. In *Frankenstein* we saw the Greek myth being part of the culture and the cultural input of the creature later develops, for various reasons, from a very pure essence into a very perverse and violent creature, we understand that the great myths in some way contributed to that character. In *Prometheus*, the whole mythology is laid out in the beginning and the impulse is to make it seductive, and given the quality of the dream, to create a ground or atmosphere in which the imagination of the spectator could begin to drift and feel free.

In the second act, all of the characters from the first act reappear, many of them in several guises, the intention being to indicate the sources of the revolutionary impulse of the Russian revolutionaries, of Lenin, and of the Russian anarchists Emma Goldman and Alexander Berkman who, as Russian émigrés sent back to Russia when they were deported from the United States, arrive in Russia after the Revolution (having been jailed in the United States during the Revolution) with the hope that on a large scale their dreams would be realized.

We see the gradual transformation of the revolutionary impulses of Lenin and of the Party into the opposite of their intentions as more and more of the old culture reasserts itself. Here we have tried to represent the tragedy of the Russian Revolution as a revolution that carried with it all of the old culture, at the same time trying to establish a new and different social organization and economic circumstances. Consequently, we have a scene in which the storming of the Winter Palace is staged under the direction of Lenin (played by myself), who recruits from the audience fifty to one hundred participants to play a number of roles. Among them, the insurgent Red Army, Trotsky and the Party, the Tolstoians, the terrorists, and the women who represent and mirror their own participation and transformation.

I think that ultimately what all those recruited from the audience must feel is not so much acting or participating but being manipulated. The objective is to bring people to a clear understanding of what it means to act and what it means to be led. The contrast and the conflict between the anarchist impulse and the communist-authoritarian impulse is mirrored also in the struggle between the Apollonian and the Eleusinian forces, and the inability on the part of the patriarchal culture to dissolve into a feeling of renewal, and to permit the erotic nature to express itself. Because there is a refusal to allow the erotic nature full expression, there is resulting repression and crippling, a rigidification and an anger, a frustration, a hatred, and a boredom that can only emerge as violence. This same thing happens in capitalist and socialist societies, both of which are authoritarian in nature, and it is this which we are trying to say in the second act.

In the third act we carry this step forward and we say that this authoritarianism is based on the principle of punishment, and, as Prometheus was initially punished by Zeus, so this punishment continues on every level of our society in its cruelest terms. It is manifested in the prisons, so we go there with the public to mediate our myth at the prison.

MHA: Judith, would you like to talk about your view of *Masse Mensch* and why you've chosen to work with that particular text?

Judith Malina: Whenever we choose a text, it represents the outcome of a long period of gestation and consideration. We're almost too serious about this. In each new production we make certain before we embark that it is important for us that this be the next step. We do see all the work, right back to 1947, as a continuing opus in which each event, each production, each stylistic change, and each new form is a part of a unified history. I think this is probably apparent to a lot of people who have observed the changes that have occurred in the company, occurred in response to history, in rejection of trend, acceptance of trend, and the creation of trend. Our effort, at all times, is to be sensitive to those for whom and to whom we speak.

Masse Mensch is a play I first read when I was at The Dramatic Workshop. It was a play Erwin Piscator had produced in 1921. That period had a certain eerie resemblance to our situation now, and it seemed the right moment to do a play that I've wanted to do for thirty-five years. It is a play that has always been an ideal for me because the central figure is a woman who is anarchistic, pacifistic, and politically committed, and seems to bear on her shoulders all our most desirable and noble traits, at the same time burdened with a terrible guilt and confusion of values, which I think has, in 1980, paralyzed our whole philosophical social structure.

I think the I Ching would say this is a period of standstill. That isn't a bad reading because it's a situation that can't endure. It's a stasis that must come to an end, in which the end is always implicit; a temporary situation. One that comes for us, like for Ernst Toller, when he wrote *Masse Mensch* [*Man and the Masses*] out of a period following a revolutionary upsurge, a period of great fervor. One in which a whole segment of society believed that we were about to change the world into a good, just, and kindly place. The people who believed that found themselves after this upsurge in a world still filled with the same forms of inflicted suffering as before, some worse, some slightly changed, some, maybe, alleviated, but still the present reality of every day is of suffering caused by human cruelty and thoughtlessness.

At that moment there comes this great question: Why did it happen like that? In 1919 Toller and a spearhead group of intellectuals including Gustav Landaeur and Eric Mühsam gathered together in a fervent intellectual political atmosphere and created—actually succeeding at the time of ferment that followed the Russian Revolution—a "Soviet" based on libertarian principles, as the governing body of Bavaria. But it lasted a very, very short time. It was founded on the highest ideals and ended in a horrible bloodbath.

Toller, who participated actively in both the central committee of the governing body and in the string of events that followed, was arrested when the Revolution failed and spent five years in a military prison. In this motionless place, Toller asked himself whether he was guilty of having caused this bloodshed. He was looking back trying to look forward and found that the looking is hampered by the fact that we are all burdened with our past. Today this manifests itself on the popular level in a kind of banal interest in nostalgia, and on a social, political, and philosophical level it manifests itself in this stasis of having to stop and reexamine what has happened.

The woman who represents Toller's position in the play is much more the pacifist than Toller was and that's why he drew her as a woman. I want to emphasize that.

We who like to career around the audience have created the prison made of a series of folding gates that Julian juxtaposed with a sort of a vast empty forest recalling Adolphe Appia. I don't know if he intended that, but it's green and represents, somehow, the real world against which all this horror is played out. We've created a rather small space, limited by the actions inside our imprisoned world. Imprisoned with this thought of the burden of our past and our terrific yearning for the future, which drives all the characters in the play; they're hung up by these impediments of mind, conditioning, culture, language. Everything! Everything that holds us back is depicted in this play. It's an insight at this moment when we need one, about what in the past is holding us back from our future.

I think it's a futuristic play. When you're in prison you only think about that future time of freedom. Every prisoner is committed to freedom and in some way Toller expressed that. Our epoch is the completion of that cycle.

MHA: Would you talk about the expressionist style of the work and your interpretation of the play?

JB: Expressionism becomes interesting at this particular point because it combines a very inner artistic experience with the exterior social and political world. The artist designates the effect and moment at which those two elements come together. It emphasizes neither one nor the other, but both are present undeniably, the "inner trip" and the exterior political trip. And, for this reason I think it fascinated us.

Judith and myself come out of a period in which the visual art at our beginnings was called "abstract expressionism," and it *was* expressionism—the inner impulse, the inner vision, the individualism of the artist without any clear specific reference. Jackson Pollock once said to me, "Whenever I make a line I'm always drawing something." However, he also said that he was painting a city, but, he was inside the city and he was also painting the city which was within him.

We emphasized the exterior trip during the mid-seventies when our work was concentrated on a kind of Meyerholdian biomechanic, in an attempt to show the effect on the body and on our physical relationship with each other of the exterior forces of society. Now there is a need to tell the story from the individual's point, but we want that moment of clash when the two elements come together: What do you see when you see red? What do you see when hydrogen and oxygen come together and form water? In this play we have tried, through the use of style, to show that moment and to repeatedly show that cataclysmic second. The play is a series of seconds and I don't think there's a second of the play that is not rather carefully detailed. There is not a moment in which one does not hear the angst, the cry, and does not feel the eye and sense the spirit. These elements are constantly present in a world that creates the angst, a world that is terrible but relentlessly beautiful. Then the question is, How can we have that beauty without experiencing that angst?

MHA: When you first read the text of *Masse Mensch* did you find it necessary to alter it very much to the terms of your interpretation?

JM: There are a few lines but no more than the normal cuts in trying to form and shape it.

JB: At first the language seemed problematic. It is Toller's attempt to use only a very fundamental vocabulary to discuss things in a very fundamental manner and bring us nothing extraneous. Toller created persistent philosophical dialogue and character through the way people spoke and by what they were saying. As we worked on the play we began to find that it was more and more an essential element in the art of the play. I think the language gets on the spectators' nerves in a very Artaudian manner and in that sense, it is cruel. It is always bone-bare and tears away at feelings by being relentlessly crude and direct. What we found at the beginning was problematic; but eventually in and of itself it seems to have a frightening life on the stage.

MHA: Also a part of your repertoire is a revival of *Antigone* (your translation of Brecht's version of Holderlin's adaptation of Sophocles' created in 1967). The cast is different, with the exception of Julian playing Creon and Judith that of Antigone. My question is, Why after working for thirty years always doing new work, you've chosen to do a revival of this particular play?

JB: In some ways that isn't altogether historically true. We did do Pirandello's *Tonight We Improvise* in 1955 and redid it again in 1959. Certain works like *The Connection* have gone out and come back into the repertoire.

But *Antigone* is an analysis of the nature of nonviolent protest and the play deals with the pitting of violence against nonviolence and raises a question in the same way as *Masse Mensch* of how you create protest against an authoritarian figure or government or circumstance without the cities falling. We think that this issue had to be discussed, and *Antigone* precedes *Masse Mensch* in sequence in our repertoire and seems important to bring this issue back. In terms of the political discussion of our time and The Living Theatre's contribution to it we think that it would be better now to bring back into this dialogue the voices of Brecht and Toller rather than again filling in the space of argument with that of The Living Theatre's in reposing our own discussion. Too often the listeners in the theatre don't comprehend the connections between what we are saying and other writers.

JM: I think what the audiences perceived in Italy, where we have played *Antigone* recently and sometimes even in the same cities where we played it thirteen years ago, is something very different than what they're hearing and seeing now. Although there are only a few changes of emphasis stirring out of what we feel, essentially there's very little theatrical change. The effect of the play is different because it comes at a different period in our history and at a different period in the reconditioning of the spectator.

Here, as there was in the case of the character Sonia of *Masse Mensch*, I feel a certain guilt about it. I feel there was a response to *Antigone* that was open to its revolutionary arousal, while on the other hand, and here's where the guilt lies, there was not an equivalent or even weightier commitment to the nonviolent aspects of the action. When the nonviolence isn't very deep, though it may be mouthed in the sense that everyone can say, "We want peace," and we surely know that the most warlike of people often say, "We want peace," when that commitment isn't a true commitment in a crisis and under the pressure of history, there will always be a bloodbath. Antigone raised up a fervor that can only be, as Brecht has her say, "an example." But that example is put into perspective by the fact that she's killed.

Theatrical utopianism is a great desire that we've plunged ourselves into, but *Antigone* is a sad play, a tragedy, for that reason. What we see today is a play for nonviolence where what we saw thirteen years ago was a play for revolution—now it's certainly a plea for both. The question is, Which is the firm support of the other?

The concept of revolution in a situation in which nonviolence is not very clear is intrinsically a violent one. In the tragedy of the fall of the city, for which Brecht took the paradigm of Berlin, but for us has to be the menace of ecological and nuclear horror and disaster, the whole question of the fall and of social upheaval *is* the central question. It's advanced in the sense that we're thirteen years older and wiser and I think what people are seeing is a much deeper level of the play that has already had so many playwrights: Sophocles, Hölderlin, Brecht, and The Living Theatre's interpretation. It's a whole palimpsest of cultures that we are dealing with and the presence and condition of the spectator is imprinted on this palimpsest and different things come out at different times. At this moment what people are hearing is much closer to what we meant all along, than what they heard in 1966.

MHA: The Living Theatre has always been devoted to nonviolent struggle within the Marxist goals for socialist change in the world. Coupled with these goals and that struggle has been a particular aesthetic guided by the ideas of such theatrical geniuses as Brecht, Artaud, and Meyerhold. Would you say that these ideas have remained cemented into the framework of The Living Theatre's work or are there also some newer influences?

JM: I don't think there's anything that Julian and I know that hasn't in some way flowed through the work of The Living Theatre. I wouldn't think so much "cemented" into it because we're thinking about it all the time. Sitting around in our meetings, rehearsals, and encounters with our group, in our conversations, we're debating it all the time. I think we keep changing. I don't think it's ever the same in one period as another, so that's why I think the image of "cemented" is too static for what happens. I think we're influenced all the time by all: by Piscator or Meyerhold or Valeska Gert or Charlie Chaplin. All those things are flowing through it all the time—Brecht and Shelley and Bakunin—and we're trying to enrich it. John Cage calls it to "thicken the plot . . . thicken the soup," by making our consciousness of the interconnection of concepts and people and the order of things ever denser, closer, more real, and more human. Trying to understand what these great contributors to our work means is an unending discourse.

Right now we're reading a lot of Michel Foucault and he seems very relevant and useful. We go through periods in which the influence is the expressionists that came to the fore when we were studying what happened during 1919, and suddenly there was the whole flow of our experiences with Erwin Piscator.

You asked the other day about the influence of the Oriental theatre in our work, so I made one of my funny little charts of the very many sources beginning with Erwin Piscator's *Circle of Chalk* production to the Sun Theatre [in Chinatown] performing under the Manhattan Bridge to the influence of Ezra Pound, the influence through Kenneth Rexroth's Oriental forms through our work with Teiji Ito's and Paul Goodman's Noh plays. The list is very long of influences working on us, and it's given back through our plays.

MHA: I know that during the past five years you have taken your work throughout Europe to Spain, Portugal, France, Germany, Italy, Denmark, and, recently, Greece and I wondered if you'd like to comment at all on the variable between the responses from culture to culture to the work and life of The Living Theatre. Throughout the history of The Living Theatre there has always been an excitement in exploring uncharted territory both in an aesthetic and metaphysical way in addition to taking the Theatre to new territories. Despite the year in Brazil there have been few forays into repressive countries or "socialist republics," but presently you are scheduled to go to Poland for the first time. How do you think the present political upheaval will affect your work?

JB: It is not by choice we have not played countries in the socialist bloc. For example, our effort to work in Brazil was a very specific project and program. For many years before we began touring, we of course worked steadily in New York. Then we went, as we used to say, "wherever the wind blew," wherever there was an engagement, wherever the people wanted us. Then, in 1970, when we did go to Brazil, we began to concentrate on working in specific locations in an attempt to create a theatre for the circumstances and people that we found there. Consequently, when we went first to Brazil, we were then returned to the United States, not by choice. After some years in preparation, we went and worked specifically in Pittsburgh. Then, after ten months in Pittsburgh, went on to Europe and decided, yes, it would be reasonable to work in Italy.

Although we have worked steadily in Italy for five years, we have done a lot of touring outside of Italy. Had we received any engagement to go to any other country we would have. In the 1960s we twice visited Yugoslavia, once making a tour to several small towns, including their mining and steel area.

We know under the crust something is bubbling and something is moving and there are tremors and volcanoes going off more and more in our time. It may simply be a symbolic expression of what is happening underneath. We are ready to "blow our tops." This is everywhere, not only in black communities in the United States. It exists not only among the poor and working people. This phenomenon exists in every strata of society everywhere on this planet, in the socialist and nonsocialist countries.

This is a natural drive on the part of humankind to develop and change and throw off anything that wears the mask or has the effect of being repressive in order to breathe more freely and live more fully. I think that is what is going on in Poland. Like every strike in the world it is an indication that the conditions for work are no good and they must change. And, when working people are struggling as they are compelled to by the society it becomes increasingly more difficult to live. One can then expect the lid to blow off, and for working people to express themselves by the only means they have. The apparent disposal is through a strike, there are manifestations, and protests. This is the way of saying, "No, I don't want to do it anymore!"

In Poland there has been a flowering movement in the theatre comprising many groups, many individual directors, actors, designers, and writers over the past twenty years, and perhaps the most significant one in Europe. This movement represents a kind of counterculture and representatives of this movement have, after many years of trying, finally succeeded in getting our approval to come to Poland with *Antigone*. This after the play had been screened by their cultural ministry.

MHA: How do you resolve the continuing question—that constant conflict—of whether you will make art or social change? Do you truly feel you are able to strike a balance between these two devotions?

JB: We try to enter into another world of perception than the world we are in every day. One of our problems is to bring about a unification of these two, but we rely on art as a vehicle not only of experience but of change.

Because art is a vehicle of change, it changes: it changes our perceptions, our state of consciousness; it transports. And in this way, art, as a vehicle of change, is anarchic. We've found that on the street it conflicts with all of the other things that are craving attention, because they are the necessities of daily life.

The problem is very different from that which one assembles in a ritual manner, that is, taking a certain part of your life and saying, "I am now going to take this time of my life, this hour, and give myself over to experience in order to be transported and to go freely to another place." All of the social problems are indicated by this factor. These problems within our society are clear. Nevertheless, we use our art to sharpen the mind, to create a mode of expressing all of the danger and all of the current circumstances of our lives.

John Cage, Richard Foreman, Richard Kostelanetz

Composer John Cage, playwright-director Richard Foreman, and writer Richard Kostelanetz discuss the complexities of the relationship between artwork and viewer, and the process of artistic creation itself. The idea of memory is central to their thoughts. How important is it to remember a work that one experiences? How does one become an observant audience member? What kind of work makes one mentally active? Foreman, a recent recipient of a MacArthur Fellowship, who founded his Ontological-Hysteric Theater in 1968, already shows his uneasiness with the accepted notion that art can be a transforming and comprehensible experience or, as Kostelanetz contends, one of expansion and enhancement.

The modernist prerogatives of the privatization of experience, purity of process, and displacement of the literary in nontraditional theatre frame this commentary on the nature of performance knowledge and the task of the artist as a conduit of world experience. If Foreman is interested in making performance seem less like "performance art" by injecting more "nonperformance" elements into it—his attitude reflecting the detheatricalization of theatre and refusal of art that has dominated a century of avant-garde experiments—Cage views the situation from another perspective. It is not a question of doing away with art, but letting art invade all of life, he suggests.

One insistent question regards the "muchness" or "lessness" of art. What is involved in creating a work in which nothing appears to take place when, in fact, a great deal is happening that influences both performer and audience? For Cage, who died in 1992, and whose own work involved an extraordinary embrace of both the quietude of Thoreau and the maximalist language of James Joyce, it is not simply an issue of more or less that is essential in a work, but how creation affects the artist. He considered it as a process of mind, not art, citing one of his well-known philosophical premises, derived from Coomaraswamy: "What is the purpose of making music? To sober and quiet the mind, thus making it susceptible to divine influence." BGM

Conversation moderated by Bonnie Marranca
and Gautam Dasgupta, 1979

Art in the Culture

John Cage: Perhaps we should begin by asking which arts are the performing arts?

Richard Kostelanetz: To me the performing arts occur when some people gather together to make an event for other people. An event has a durational character—a beginning and an end—and exists in time. Now, performing arts aren't necessarily live. They can include videotapes, audiotapes, film, and musical concerts.

JC: It could also enter the field of graphic arts as in the making of an Indian sand painting. Robert Rauschenberg made painting in the course of dance performances by Merce Cunningham.

RK: But then only the "making" is a performance. The painting itself, the sand painting, or the Rauschenberg, is visual art.

Richard Foreman: What interested me, when I was interested in the performing arts, was the attempt to redeem the performing arts by making them less "performance art," more a way of injecting nonperformance and the sort of activity that artists did when they did *not* perform, injecting those kinds of activity and processes into public events. I have a lot of prejudice against the whole notion of performing arts because I happen not to trust anything having to do with audiences.

RK: I share some of your biases. I've worked in many arts, and one I've never worked in is live performance. The whole notion of doing so does not particularly attract me. Why? Because there's an awful lot of preparation and expense involved in something that will have a comparatively short life. Second, there's a kind of hysteria—and that's more true in commercial than experimental theatre—that follows from the author preparing the work for a kind of "boom or bust" economic situation. This hysteria leads to pandering and compromise. Finally, in making live theatre one needs to work with a large number of people over a sustained period of time. Unless these people are perfect collaborators, this situation gets one into an authoritarian cast of mind, which I'd rather not find in myself. On the other hand, I myself am very interested in other performance mediums like videotape, audiotape, and film, in part, because they get around these problems of live performance. Why do you do live performances, Richard?

RF: Well, I suspect that I'm on the verge of not doing much more of it because of all the objections that you've just delineated. When I started doing performances many years ago at the Cinemathèque, one of the first things that I tried to do was to evolve a theatrical form that would *not* need that much preparation. When I was younger I used to think it was a great existential gesture to kill oneself for five months and then have it be over after two hundred people had seen it. It would exist as a fleeting, important memory in perhaps only thirty minds. But I no longer find that very exciting.

Now I've gotten into film, having just completed my first, and it seems to me to be a radically different process. Mostly, I suppose, because it is not so much a matter of preparation for performance. I guess that my definition of a performing art would have to involve a period of preparation followed by a period of performance. It doesn't necessarily apply to what John has done.

RK: John, as we know, is a master of performance that depends on minimal preparation! His events succeed because he knows how to give out just enough instructions to make them happen, but don't need a lot of rehearsals to make them go.

JC: But I did that in order to avoid all the problems the both of you are talking about.

RF: I think that John does occurrence art rather than performance art.

RK: A vivid instance of the kind of thing John does just struck me. Do you remember, John, the Theatre and Engineering Festival of 1966? You were one of several artists. The others all slaved very hard, preparing and rehearsing, and you arrived a couple of days before, gave people instructions that got them to work. And it was a great success.

JC: Yes, but there was a very serious problem there—total disorganization on the technological level by the scientists involved. At the very last minute a computerized control board was brought in, requiring a total rewiring of what had already been carefully prepared. We were all sitting around in huddles, splicing wires almost twenty four hours a day preparing for those performances! So the first performance of that festival was actually a rehearsal.

RK: But then your piece also allowed for the possibility of such failure in detail.

JC: Yes, but it wasn't done correctly. I had arranged carefully to have twelve telephones dialed directly to twelve sound sources outside the hall, like the myna bird cage at the Bronx Zoo. And I dialed all these numbers carefully and put the receivers aside. But then the people from Bell Labs, when they saw all these telephones off the hook, hung them up. And it was impossible to call these numbers again because they were then busy on the other end. So in that first performance none of those sounds were heard. It finally worked because there were many other sounds, too.

RK: But your genius was to create a performance so abundant with aural material that it could tolerate omissions and errors . . .

JC: I think that we can give up the notion that I have any genius. Instead, we could simply speak of the nature of silence. If the mind is silent, and is willing to accept what happens, there are some very receptive happenings. So there is actually nothing to fear.

RK: Excuse me, John, I don't believe that. The work reflects your calculating cleverness.

JC: What I'm saying is that if there hadn't been as many sounds as there are, there would still be other sounds.

PAJ: Is this laid-back quality you've been talking about, this willingness to let things happen, indicative of a purely American perception in the arts?

RK: I've written a good deal about this topic. To me the "Americanness" of American theatre exists in the performance theatre, where the performer controls the entire production rather than realizing a script or being at the service of a script. Certainly John and Richard's theatre has worked in that way. You see this performance tradition in nineteenth-century American theatre, too. Later, you find people like Edmund Wilson writing surveys of the theatre in the twenties where he says that the literary theatre isn't half as interesting as Minsky's Follies. H. L. Mencken said something similar. I remember a forties survey by Eric Bentley in which he said that none of the theatre he saw was nearly as interesting as Martha Graham. Or was it José Limón? It seems to me that we have always known this about American theatre but never fully recognized it. Instead, the effort has been to say that we had a European literary theatre epitomized by O'Neill and later, to a certain extent, by Williams and Albee. Nonetheless, the best American theatre, for me, has been and is now a performance theatre.

RF: Yes, but that was certainly a Parisian tradition also—artists always talking about the circus and the music hall . . .

JC: And that there is an event theatre, too. For me the work of Antonin Artaud was very important. In *The Theatre and Its Double* he speaks of something quite different from a literary theatre. In literary theatre the text is pervasive and everything else is made to serve the text. Artaud pointed out, in contradiction, that every element in the theatre is its own center, so to speak. That is, a cry, a color, a word, or anything else is *the* most important thing onstage when it happens. So the notion of center stage is removed from the center of the stage and put everywhere. And the same thing with time. Would you agree with those ideas?

RF: At this point I don't know. After performing many years I find myself dissatisfied. The part of Artaud's theorizing that I find most moving are his frustrated attempts to try to write. It has something to do with the effort of his brain or mental process to steer its way through the world. I remember Gertrude Stein's remark to young writers: "Be careful. All we're seeing in your writing is the strain of the process." Increasingly, as the years go by, I'm only interested in seeing that strain. I have more and more become interested only in some kind of mental phenomenon, or phenomenon breakdown, that is very much like hitting your head against a wall. It's there in Artaud in a way.

Just last week I was reading René Girard, a French writer whose books are starting to be better known in this country, and I was noticing that all my life what has been the most thrilling experience for me—what I used to call an aesthetic experience—is reading a difficult text. In reading a difficult text like Girard's I noticed I was skimming along, waiting for something to strike my interest. Then, at a certain moment, I said, "Wait a minute! This isn't enough. I have to *make an effort.*" Once having made that effort, I experienced a kind of epiphany, a kind of psychological response, I think. That was delightful. And it's that, or something akin to that, which I look forward to more and more.

RK: But in your theatre, Richard, the text is often about this kind of difficult language perception but the staging is not. And I wonder in looking back at your work whether the staging stays with me far longer than the text. And I'm a fairly verbal, if not literate, person. I wonder if that's a general impression everyone has.

RF: Yes, I think that's relevant. And I'd probably respond in the same way. But I think my staging—because it's better, more moving, and more effective—is not as effective in terms of what I think I should be doing. Because I think what you are saying, and what we're all saying, is akin to saying: "Wow, that advertising agency really was successful in making the image of the Marlboro Man stay in my mind for the next three months." I'm not so sure that's any kind of achievement. A couple of years ago somebody criticized my theatre by saying, "Well, you know, Foreman's plays are very exciting and interesting while you're there, but then the next day they've sort of evaporated." But I'm not so sure that it wouldn't be better to create events that focused a certain kind of attention so that the next day you couldn't remember what the hell happened to you. You the spectator would be forced to say, I can't remember that play, I can't remember that work of art, I can't remember how it worked. The rest of your life would have to be dedicated to trying to discover how it worked, how to make it, how to do it. I'm not so sure how useful it is to have all those wonderful evocative memories of works of art.

RK: That's a very challenging statement, because I always thought that the essence of success in art was to put something permanently into people's heads.

RF: I wonder. It seems to me that the things that have changed my life most have been works of art that have been upsetting and awakening in a proper sort of way so that I felt I had to struggle and spend the next ten years trying to figure out why I had liked them.

JC: There would be another possibility. And that would be a work of art which you wouldn't understand, but which would have the effect of changing your mind not by filling it with the desire to understand the work, but changing it in such a way that you see all of the experience differently.

RK: But that's the contrary of what Richard is saying, because such work would have an effect, even if subliminally. He's talking about a really radical notion. And from what he's saying it seems to me it would be hard to tell a good work of art from a bad one.

RF: Who cares, except critics?

RK: It seems to me that you're courting insignificance to a large degree.

RF: Isn't that, perhaps, the final message of modern art? It seems to me that modern art has been an attempt to do away with art. A laudable attempt.

RK: To do away with art and yet *still* be art, which is a paradox. And in doing away with art you create something so radical it's unforgettable and it changes your experience of other art.

JC: Yes, it's really not to do away with art but to really invade all of life with art. When I was young I noticed the difference in some modern things. Say, the difference between a Pollock, on the one hand, and a Richard Lippold on the other. One could see those tendencies in modern art such as symmetry and also the absence of a center of interest. And I think those two things, instead of being opposed, became identical in my mind. For the simple reason that when you looked at a symmetrical work of art you couldn't be interested. You had to become active as an observer if you were going to continue looking at it. In the case of Pollock there is no center. So you are obliged to wander, homeless, over the whole thing or pass away from it. I think that in theatre there is not just this tendency that we've been talking about with events and Happenings, but another theatre that corresponds to the highly focused. I wonder if it wouldn't be better in theory. Where the subject is so harped on that it becomes uninteresting. And where the listener in the theatre has to do something in order to pass the time by becoming active in some way.

RF: But, of course, that has been the strategy of so much avant-garde art since the war. It's evident in film, particularly in the so-called French structuralist films. I'm frustrated because I spent ten years in New York being terribly influenced and saved, I feel, by this art that forced you to be active in your perception of it. And I wondered if art wasn't simply becoming my drug. I started to feel guilty about being interested in art and needing those pieces to make me mentally active.

JC: But if you move in the direction that you're talking about, toward a theatre that both is and is *not* performance, where the elements that are not performance enter into the performance, then it could move off into your observations of everyday life. So I don't know why you should feel this absence.

RF: We've been talking about the major things that have happened in performing arts since the war and I think it's clear that we've delineated one tendency. But there is a countertendency in modern art and that is the tendency to help people redeem their own garbage. To take failure, awkwardness, ugliness, whatever we have been told is the garbage that we've produced, and find ways to realize that this garbage is the only available energy.

RK: I've described it as exploiting one's incompetence. In John's case it was no feeling for harmony. So John made music some other way. In your case, Richard, we could say that you could not succeed in writing a slick play, and so you made something special out of your incompetence.

RF: All I would say is that these two processes in art are very closely related. Looking at it from one perspective it seems like a pure and formal art. But from the perspective of garbage it looks romantic and baroque.

RK: Another idea I've always had about recent art deals with the amount of activities within the frame. Some of your pieces, Richard, move very much toward "moreness." Some of John's theatrical pieces of the late sixties moved very much toward "moreness" and more recently toward "lessness," as was the case in *Empty Words*.

PAJ: There seems to be a great deal of boredom nowadays with theatre and the performance scene. How do you account for that? Is "more" less?

RK: As someone who went to graduate school in intellectual history I've thought a lot about periodization. There were two cultural boom periods in recent American history: 1946 to 1952, and 1959 to, roughly, 1968. During both those periods there was an incredible amount of innovative and excellent activity. We are simply *not* in one of those boom periods now.

JC: In terms of my own work I felt most active in 1952, the year I made the "Silence" piece and finished the *Music of Changes.* If I listed all the things I did in 1952 I would be surprised to recall how many there were. All sorts of things happened. And I again have the feeling that at the present moment I'm just as active in as many different directions as I was then. For instance, I'm developing a new idea—at least it seems to me to be new. The word that describes it for me is "contingency." It means acting in such a way that not necessarily anything happens. But that if you didn't act, if you didn't perform, nothing would happen at all. I'll give you an example. In a piece of music called *Inlets,* which I made for the dance by Merce Cunningham, I used conch shells filled with water. When the shells are tipped they sometimes gurgle and sometimes don't. They're impossible to control. This is an act of contingency—you don't know what will happen. Now if between the cause of an effect and the effect itself—the effect being a performance—there are junctions which are flexible and which you are ignorant about, then when you activate the removed cause and travel through this junction to the effect you don't necessarily do anything.

RK: It's interesting to me because this seems very close to Richard's hypothesis of theatre in which nothing memorable happens.

JC: Does what I've said interest you or leave you cold?

RF: No, it interests me, as all of this work interests me as a model of a scientific process. You're really creating a brain model on one level.

JC: I've noticed that as a performer in such a process I've described, the performer identifies himself with the audience. Because as a performer he's not certain of his actions. He's perfectly attentive, interested, and curious as an observer.

RF: Something is clarified for me here. Hasn't Western man, and Western science for that matter, been engaged in this process of trying to cut the ground from beneath our feet? Western science has been engaged in trying to figure out, in a technical sense, how we work and explain what's going on. Now we are finding out that the explanation is in the process of dissolving us. And I'm wondering now if my questions about art and my wondering if art isn't trying to decide that also, isn't part of that same project—dissolve whatever we call man.

RK: I don't think modern art is a negative operation, it's not a question of dissolving but rather one of expanding and enhancing.

RF: I guess in the final analysis I don't agree.

RK: What amuses me about our conversation, Richard, is that you're so negative about what you're doing, whereas John and I are so enthusiastic about what we're doing.

JC: And, I might add, about what you're doing, too! I haven't seen a lot of your theatre but what I have seen I've enjoyed. And now that I'm deeply involved with Joyce I think that I would rush to the opportunity to experience your work again. When you used the terms "baroque" and "muchness" before you're obviously in the world of Joyce, aren't you?

RF: Yes.

RK: You and I, John, work very much on building on what we did. And go in other directions because of what we did in the past. Richard's talking as if he's really dissatisfied with what he has done.

RF: I'm not dissatisfied with what I've done because I feel it's as good as anything anyone else has done. I'm dissatisfied with what I am because I know that I'm not as good as my plays. To me that's the issue.

JC: There's a remark of Thoreau that I think needs to be quoted now. He said, "It's not important what form the sculptor gives the stone. It's important what sculpting does to the sculptor."

RF: Yes, that's my position.

RK: I take the opposite position. What we're doing as artists and writers is making things that are superior in perception and intelligence to us: what we do usually extracts from us a cost not only in money but psychic health.

JC: Since the forties I have thought that wasn't true. So when I read Thoreau's statement I was delighted. The same thing is echoed in that line you're so familiar with: "What is the purpose of making music? To sober and quiet the mind, thus making it susceptible to divine influence." Which is another way of saying music is of no importance whatsoever. What is important is the mind of the musician. We're dealing with mind not art. At one time, in the field of music at least, there was a lot of talk about audience participation. And what we've been talking about, if not audience participation, is audience activity.

RK: But audience often has to do with muchness and lessness as well. You're giving them a different amount of input from what they've had before. I think that's entwined with excellence.

JC: Is there a theatre now that has an activity on the part of the audience that's more visible to other members of the audience?

RK: Such as theatre in a revival church?

JC: Yes. But that's characteristic, too, of ritual, isn't it? Does that kind of thing involve you?

RF: As I've said many times, reading is the only thing that interests me. For a long time I was trying to figure out a theatre event that would somehow be akin to what I felt I was experiencing when I was reading. I don't think I ever really succeeded.

JC: A great deal of my recent work has to do with finished works from the past like the *Journal* of Thoreau, Joyce's *Finnegans Wake*, the *Socrate* of Erik Satie, or the eighteenth-century hymns that I used during the Bicentennial. In other words, making art from art. And I think many people are doing that.

RF: Oh, yes. I'm very fond of Ronald Johnson's piece *Radios* based on *Paradise Lost*, which is essentially an erasure piece where he has erased about 80 percent of the text. But what he left makes a wonderful poem.

RK: I'm now engaged in taking some of my own earlier works and both recycling and reducing them. In a current project I'm taking an earlier book of mine and trying to extract the essential sentences, piecing them together visually.

RF: You know, actually, that's a very appealing strategy. And we've all done it at various times.

RK: Extracting yourself?

RF: It's not a question of extracting. When I began making theatre I was at Yale studying playwriting. We were taught by John Gassner that one doesn't write plays, one rewrites them. And I would take great pleasure in sitting there going through draft after draft. At a certain point I realized that essentially what I was doing was hearing a voice reading the plays back to me. And the voice was my mother's voice reading bedtime stories to me and my sister. I knew that to be a playwright you had to sound like Arthur Miller; you couldn't sound like Richard Foreman's mother! So I would rewrite my plays trying to eliminate that tone of voice. Then, at a certain point, after seeing the movies of Jack Smith and others, I said, No, you have to be heroic. Like Jonas Mekas is teaching us, you've got to accept your own voice, your own inflection, your own tonality. What I write down now I will not rewrite, I will not polish, I will not try to make sound slick. Then when I staged it I kept it as is, but I had tapes going, doubling all the words, repeating the words, really hiding it. The doubling that was going on was a kind of reprocessing of the material. And I'm wondering to what extent that reprocessing is again a failure to accept what simply comes out. We're all, on a certain level, dissatisfied with what we do, embarrassed and have problems with what we do. How much of our activity is simply just trying to cut a slightly different figure in the world?

JC: I was expressing this idea of going forward with the human spirit the other evening and this artist friend of mine denied that, insisting that each of us has to relive for himself the whole mystery of the human race. I think we can take advantage of things that have already been experienced, tried, and tested. And then we should be able to go on to some other level of activity . . . And again, the absence of any activity is already a world full of activity. Sound, for example, is going on all the time as you can hear at this moment. That is constantly changing. And it can have the effect of doing all that needs to be done. And it's such a complex situation that I don't see that you can ever have the feeling of having finished.

PAJ: Take Richard Foreman for instance. Isn't it true that his success could only have been possible in a period like the present one?

RF: Oh, absolutely. I probably would have been forced into other fields. I feel that I ended up making theatre through contingent circumstances. Here's what happened. I was a shy kid who could not relate to other kids. I found that theatre was a way to make your own little world in which you could pretend that you were relating to other people. Then when I began making theatre I began to realize that all the other people making theatre weren't the best and brightest in the culture. So I began to discover that in the other arts things were going on that were a hell of a lot more interesting. So I could, at that point, have gotten out of the theatre. There's always been a war in me between what I consider the bad half of me—the part that went into making theatre—and the good, vigorous half that wanted to do something else. And yes, I don't think that I could have made the kind of theatre I have done in any other period of American culture.

PAJ: Yet you condemn the country for being at such a low cultural ebb?

RF: I feel that I have always been able to exploit the situation very cleverly. I think I have been able to *choose* a cultural moment when the energy is at a low ebb and have the feeling that there is nobody else you can turn to right now. I don't think that a lot of the people who are interested in my theatre would be around if there were a lot of other things they could also see.

PAJ: But the fact remains that the entire avant-garde has been able to find a larger audience now than at any other period in history.

RK: The proof of that fact is that none of us are employed in any other field at the current time. Each of us is living off his art.

RF: So what does that mean? That happened, I think, partially because the federal government, through funding, decided to buy us all off after the sixties.

PAJ: On the question of funding, has it been helpful, detrimental, or both?

RF: Often it's been necessary because of the size of the pieces. When I'm making one of my plays there are generally twelve actors and four or six people helping me with the scenery. Then there is equipment and administration. So in all about twenty-five people. But I create my work in very exploitative circumstances. I use performers, for instance, who don't depend on me for their livelihood, so I pay them very little. And I decided to do that ten years ago when I began. I felt that the only way I could make the art that I wanted to make was to find a way to apportion the money in such a way that would serve my needs. That's another one of the reasons why I think I'm stopping, because I feel I'm exploiting people.

JC: Merce Cunningham, through Lewis Lloyd, made a great effort—and succeeded in part—to provide livelihoods for the people who worked with him. But it had a horrendous effect on fund-raising. Because such a large amount of money goes into each piece, no sooner did they finish one when you had to start raising funds for another.

RF: Well, if I'm going to continue making art I'd rather do it in film, which is what I'm doing now. Because at least the result of all my efforts won't be gone after four thousand people have seen it. To me that's a bit obscene.

PAJ: Has the growth of experimental theatre in this country been made possible largely through public funding?

RK: I'd say in my case that it has to do with the growth of academic institutions. John and I do a lot of touring, for universities are willing to pay us several hundred or even a thousand dollars just to show up. At that level we're beneficiaries of the sixties culture boom. And mind you, this happens even though most people in universities might disapprove of what we do. But as long as enough people like what you do, you have enough funding sources to support yourself. Also, people who are not well known are not as well patronized by even the noncommercial culture agencies. And it has a lot to do with the media.

I'd like to mention one thing that fascinates me. Merce Cunningham brought this to my attention. During the forties there was only one showcase for choreographers in New York. And if you were cut out, as Merce was, it was quite detrimental. Now there are so many showcases. And I think a major cultural fact now is a quantitative one—that there are twice as many people writing serious literature today, three times as many doing serious music, four times the number of people doing theatre, and five times the number doing dance. It's incredible how many people are doing art in New York today. I find it amazing that anything of quality surfaces and stands out. The competition, in terms of numbers, is just that more severe.

RF: In very practical terms, here's another side of the same problem. Although maybe twenty experimental theatre companies have grown up, there is only one newspaper on which they depend for reviews—the *New York Times*. In my lifetime I can remember when there were seven or eight papers in New York. Now that's a very practical consideration because one of the major ways you get funding is to get noticed by that one newspaper.

JC: When I first tried to get my music published I failed. And I didn't try again for two or three years. Finally, in the course of writing the music for Jackson MacLow's play that was done by The Living Theatre, *The Marrying Maiden*, I just decided to put my pen down and not write any more music until I got it published. Anyway, I ran my finger down the list of publishers in the phone directory and I was determined to keep at it until I solved the problem. The very first one I hit was C. F. Peters. And when I called Mr. Hindriksen there, he was overjoyed and gave me a signed contract when we met. I was fifty years old at the time.

RK: It seems to me that one still gets known from doing very distinguished work. There's also an advantage to getting known outside your initial trade. All of us have gotten a certain amount of recognition from the visual arts world. This gives you more presence in your original trade than you might otherwise have, and it can also make you an issue as well. To me, art works like this: you do what you do and show it to your friends and they tell their friends about it. It's like circles within circles, radiating outward. If you can persuade those in your trade, you have a base of support. And unless you have a base, an intimate circle, you become solely a creature of publicity and promotion.

Also, what I think has happened is that recognition in the visual arts world has a certain currency. It may be limited, it may be detrimental. I'm sure that musicians hold it against John that visual artists like his work. To an enormous degree his concerts were known as art events. And I know that Richard's initial audiences, several years ago, were the same as John and Merce's in having the crème de la crème of the visual arts world.

RF: For some time now we have been talking about performance artists who owe their early backing to what is called the visual arts scene in New York. And that means a world that is tied to people with money. But plenty of people in that world who *don't* have money come and see our performances, too. But somehow in the background there is a more aristocratic notion that relates to elitist notions as opposed to theatres that come from more popular and commercial sources. Also, it's not so much a question of patronage and money. It creates a different kind of expectation so that the artist, even if it's a delusion, proceeds to work with a different dream in mind. And that dream is counter to the typical American one of making it such as I might have had in mind in terms of the popular theatre. I just saw this other possibility and learned that somehow you could survive.

PAJ: How about the European arts scene as contrasted with art activity in America today?

JC: I think that Europe at the moment, and particularly Paris, is very lively.

RF: What I find interesting in Paris is the continuing high level of theoretical and critical activity. In contrast, though, here in "primitive" America more interesting art is being produced than in "civilized" and "sophisticated" France.

PAJ: People also talk about the "theoretical" in Europe as opposed to the "experiential" here.

RF: That's always been my problem in dealing with the theatre. How do you define the two terms? For me, all kinds of passion that I have people would say are theoretical. But the theoretical occupies my brain, my body, and my entire physiology at certain hours of the day. And those hours of the day belong to my experience. So I don't know about that distinction.

RK: I would have to agree with your objection. I don't know where theory ends and experience begins, especially since theorizing is a heavy part of my experience.

RF: The last issue of the French publication *Tel Quel* talked about America and this idea of the experiential. But in America it's not experience, it's the body. How do the French, who are still very Cartesian, escape? They escape into popular music that is basically very sentimental. Americans, who aren't intellectual at all and who are very puritanical, escape with the help of music that is essentially body music. I think it's clear that the French are just looking to us for what they lack, which is a certain refreshing vulgarity of the body. To them it's something exotic. And they're also praising American works for something having to do with sex in a revolutionary way.

Hilton Kramer

FOR HILTON KRAMER, the former *New York Times* art critic and now editor of the influential neo-conservative monthly *The New Criterion*, one of the most contested issues in the debates surrounding postmodernism and its critique of modernism is the abandonment of the primacy of the artwork in favor of the critic or spectator. What Kramer disdains is the celebration of personality and politics over the formal vocabulary of a work of art and criticism that is addressed only to critical systems. For him, art is not a "purely political construct," and the role of the critic is still that best set forth by Eliot as the elucidation of art and the correction of taste.

Kramer, who regards the arena of modernism as pluralistic and complex, draws distinctions between "mainstream" modernism and "guerrilla" modernism and between the aesthetics of modernism and the rhetoric of modernism, with the postmodern as more of a challenge to the latter. If Duchamp paved the way for the dissolution of modernism into conceptual art, it is the more pervasive politicization of contemporary art, in which he sees parallels of the prescriptive Popular Front leftism of the thirties, that disturbs Kramer's own belief in artistic values and standards. He makes a forceful statement in arguing that the turning point in American culture was in the forties, which not only signaled the shift from Marx to Freud and Jung, but the subsequent turn inward for inspiration. Artists were absorbed by formal concerns rather than by external criteria and attention to subject matter.

In its sweep of focus, this colloquy strongly reflects the arguments on art and the audience, the function of criticism, and on education and the canon, that defined the American cultural landscape of the mid- and late eighties, when intellectual life was polarized around the issue of what constitutes a proper sense of history, whether of art, of literature, or of civilization. Likewise, the encroachment of popular culture as pastiche in serious art and its increasing place in the university, blurring the boundaries of high and low culture, elicited widespread discussions, in art, on the nature of representation, and in education, on the curriculum. BGM

Conversation with Gautam Dasgupta, Herbert Blau,
and Gerald Rabkin, 1986

The Modernism/Postmodernism Debate

Gautam Dasgupta: Ever since your tenure as an art critic for the *New York Times*, and now as editor of *The New Criterion*, you have aligned yourself with the modernist temperament. Over the past decade and a half, you have increasingly situated yourself at the crossroads of modernism and contemporary art practice, commonly referred to as postmodernism. You have also been critical of forces you believe undermine the achievements and high tenets of classical modernism. Could you chart for us the areas of contention, as you see them, operating in today's cultural landscape?

Hilton Kramer: Among the important areas of contention are, I think, the following: where there has been a strong modernist tradition, that is, strong in the sense of producing a great many works that are now recognized masterworks, the area of contention is to be found precisely where the standards governing that tradition have been most directly challenged by a variety of forces, perhaps the most prominent of which generally goes under the heading "postmodernism." In those areas of the arts where there has been a less robust modernist achievement, particularly say in the last quarter century or the period since the fifties, in music, for example, I don't think postmodernism looms as so much of an issue because there is in a sense nothing to combat.

However, as soon as one attempts to discuss the conflicts between, say, the modernist tradition and the postmodernist challenges to it, one has to recognize that the term "postmodernism" means a great many different things to a great many different people, in different fields. As far as I'm aware, the term actually has its origin more or less in two fields, architecture and dance. At least those are the two areas in which I first became conscious that there were artistic movements stirring that were pleased to regard themselves as postmodern. In dance, where I suppose it began with the Judson Church performances, the notion of postmodern dance seemed to me to become less and less viable because the continuities with modernism seemed so direct, that is, it was more a challenge to the rhetoric of modernism than to the aesthetic of modernism.

The challenge has been most open and flagrant and in many respects victorious in architecture, where there was a concerted effort—one might even say a conspiracy—to devalue and deconstruct the reputations of modernist masters and substitute a kind of pastiche, or I suppose we could call it an architecture of appropriation and parody, in its place. In certain other fields, particularly in criticism and in some of the literature that is allied with criticism, postmodernism also acquired a political, which is to say a radical, component as well, so that certain Marxists or deconstructionists tend to regard themselves as practicing a kind of postmodernist mode of criticism. In any case, I think that is perhaps enough to give you some sense of the perspective I bring to this issue.

Herbert Blau: Today modernism itself is being reconstituted theoretically and reinvestigated, and in that discourse there's a complication in the relationship of modernism and the avant-garde that seems to me to be germane to the distinction between modernism and postmodernism. The supposition is that there was always a repressed content in modernism that is now emerging in what people speak about as postmodernism.

HK: Well, I've long held the position that modernism was itself a much more complicated and pluralistic enterprise than any of its sectarian champions was ever willing to acknowledge. In the essay that I wrote as the introduction to *The Age of the Avant-garde*, I attempted to set up the terms by which that pluralism could be understood. I talked, for example, about what I called the modernists who were acutely conscious of tradition and of wanting to extend tradition, to revitalize it, and who conceived of themselves as following in a certain line of a tradition.

In poetry, it would obviously be Eliot and Pound; in music, Stravinsky and Schoenberg; in painting, Picasso and Matisse. It distinguished what I think of as mainstream modernism from what I described, only half-facetiously, as guerrilla modernism, represented specifically by futurism, Dada, certain elements in surrealism, and the beginning of which I specifically identified as coming from Jarry's *Ubu Roi.* I think there has been throughout the history of modernism in its most vital periods a certain dialectic between mainstream modernism and guerrilla modernism.

But one of the problems of this whole discussion is that there are so few reliable accounts of the artists involved. For example, take a figure like Schwitters, who until very recently certainly—and one hopes that the recent show at the Museum of Modern Art will change that—has always been regarded as a quintessential Dadaist, that is, a man who attempted to destroy the rhetoric of high art by making collages out of tram tickets, tobacco wrappings, and so on. You could say that Schwitters was in a sense a mainstream modernist masquerading as a guerrilla modernist. I think we cannot really understand the true nature of the modernist tradition without understanding that it's made up of these different elements, and there are many more nuances involved in distinguishing those elements than I've cited here.

But nonetheless I think there is a real break in some fields between modernism, no matter how it's construed, and postmodernism. The real break comes with a figure like Duchamp, whom I don't really think of as a modernist, from about the time of the First World War on. As soon as Duchamp abandoned art, he ceased to be a modernist and he became something else which we didn't for a long time have a word for. I think the real term for it is nihilism—that is, a kind of nihilism with a wink and a smile, nihilism with a sense of humor, nihilism with a sense of irony. But once Duchamp really abandoned the idea of making art to take up the role of judging it and mocking it, he opened the door for a great deal of what we now call postmodernism.

Gerald Rabkin: There has been since the advent of critical theory attempts to define an essential modernism. The question you raise is a very fundamental one because "post" implies "after," but modernism has always located itself as something distinct from contemporary. Now if we are beginning to create a paradigm of postmodernism that can go back as you've stated, on one hand to Jarry at the end of the nineteenth century, and Duchamp some decades later, I'm wondering if perhaps we're not constantly in hot water because we're interpenetrating a synchronic model, a model of modernism, and postmodernism, a diachronic model that cuts across time.

HK: I did not mean to suggest that I consider Jarry a postmodernist. No, I consider him among what I call the guerrilla modernists, but nonetheless I think his work is firmly contained within the sensibility of the modernist idea. Duchamp was also a modernist up until the time he stopped making art, which suggests to me that one of the elements we're trying to identify out of this sense that something has happened is not only the making of art but an attitude toward the making of art. In my view, as a practicing artist Duchamp was thoroughly second-rate, always an imitator until he came to "found" objects, and there too that's a mode of imitation in itself where it's only the idea, not the thing made, that constitutes the statement. And once you have got to the point where you recognize that in what has happened an attitude toward the making of art has priority over the actual making of art, then I think you are beginning to make some headway into answering what it is that's happened.

HB: Much of your position is located in the modernist ethos, yet in your criticism of other art critics like Greenberg you distinguish your own position on the basis of some kind of fundamental or rudimentary human exchange that he doesn't allow for. Yet there is an aspect of what we're now naming postmodernism that directs itself particularly to this aspect, in some sense siphons it off from art making. It says that of all the things one might privilege in art perhaps this fundamental exchange among human beings is in some sense more important than the object, which is after all adjudicated differently through long periods of time.

HK: Certainly I've had a running quarrel with Clem Greenberg for many years on these issues, but the nature of the quarrel is this: whereas Greenberg wants to reduce all of modernism to what I think he'll legitimately describe as formalism, for me that is only one element in the whole organism of modernism. But I agree with Greenberg that it was the achievement of modernism to produce a certain kind of art, not a certain kind of personality.

The achievements of the modernists are in that sense objective and not contingent upon the attitudes people have toward the object. That there's an ontology to the object that survives that is quite independent of the uses to which it is put or the attitudes that one holds toward it.

The real difference between that attitude toward modernism and what I take to be a postmodernist attitude is that a modernist would not be of the opinion that he had, so to speak, reinvented the object every time he experienced it. That is, that it was the artist who made the object, not the critic and not the spectator.

I go back to the way modernism was conceived and presented institutionally when I was a student. To the Museum of Modern Art, modernism was not found to be located only in, say, abstract art. In the first anthologies of modern poetry, it wasn't just Eliot and Marianne Moore and Stevens. Robert Frost was in there too, and Robert Frost *is* a modern poet. He probably would have died to be called modernist, but in some sense he was. His whole attitude toward his medium, his whole attitude toward his subject, everything makes him a modernist.

I think one of the dangers is this impulse to reduce modernism to something less than it has been all along. We all have our different chronologies of modernism. In art I start with Courbet since I think of realism as being the first quintessentially modern style. In painting it certainly concluded a decisive phase in its development in the fifties with abstract expressionism, what I call "the last of the unpopular styles." From the early sixties on with the advent of pop art, which was the first of the popular styles—and it's not just a play on words—the first of the new movements in art that became an instantaneous success with the public, you're in another historical period. It's not that modernism has been supplanted or destroyed but something else now occupies the scene along with it, something that owes its very existence to modernism but is no longer modernism in itself.

GD: Could you speak to these polarities of high and popular culture and how they figure traditionally in this broader spectrum of the modernist/postmodernist debate?

HK: Everything I have been referring to in our discussion so far I think of as belonging to the realm of high culture, high art. I don't think that popular culture or mass culture, as the Marxists like to call it, really lends itself to these distinctions. It would be very hard for me to isolate an object of popular culture and identify it as being modern or modernist. Is Irving Berlin a modernist as distinguished from Elvis Presley, as distinguished from the Beatles? It would be absurd to apply those categories, so what I've been discussing belongs entirely to the realm of high art.

However, from virtually the very beginning of the modern period, almost every practitioner of high art or high culture in various fields has drawn a certain amount of inspiration, or has used as a foil of some kind certain elements from the popular culture of his period or the recent past. That seems to me just to be a fact of cultural life. What I find alarming generally in discussions of high culture in relation to popular culture, particularly in the academy and certain government agencies and foundations, certain parts of the media, is the imperative to erase all distinctions between high culture and popular culture. The recent attempt by the NEA to create a single category of musical theatre rather than make a distinction between opera and musical comedies is a very alarming sign. It suggests that somebody either does not understand an absolutely crucial artistic distinction or understands it and wants to destroy it. Then there is this other tendency in the academy, which is primarily a political tendency to—as the jargon has it—"deprivilegize" high culture by substituting the objects of popular culture for study and for serious attention.

GR: Isn't part of the problem in the borderlines? Take the examples of *Porgy and Bess* and *Mahagonny* in a commercial theatre venue. The erosion of lines between high and popular art came about not because critics have forced this but because artistic phenomena themselves have eroded them.

HB: Here's a specific case: someone in the postmodern camp that you don't disapprove of—say, Julian Schnabel, of whose work you have some positive views though you find problematic other aspects of his work. It seems to me—and I'm not defending him because I have reservations about his work—that the thing that really distresses you about him is connected to what you were dismissing earlier on as that smiling nihilism of Duchamp. Art after all has certain cultural continuities. Sometimes things abrade into each other, sometimes they are vaguely developmental, sometimes recycled images, sometimes rethought. What you get with somebody like Schnabel can't properly be understood without the fact of dissolution of high modernism into conceptual art, and then a restitution of the object after that historical phase.

HK: Something *has* happened with Schnabel, but I think it has to do with the lateness of the line that he's pursuing. I cannot see that he really introduces a new attitude or a new period. What I think is the principal problem in Schnabel is that he creates the expectation that the imagery in his work will play a major, if not a dominant, role in our experience of it, whereas in fact in our experience of it, it is not the content of the images that matter, but simply the presence of images. That distinguishes him quite emphatically from an early expressionist like Kirchner or Nolde, for whom the very *nature* of the image was crucial to the creation of the objects. *Nudes in a Sun-drenched Landscape* for Kirchner signified in a sense the whole symbolic crux of what the painting was and what the painting was supposed to achieve, whereas in Schnabel it doesn't particularly matter whether he puts St. Sebastian in or a movie star or whatever.

GR: In your writings on postmodernism you make the essential attack upon the facetiousness, banality, triviality, nonseriousness of however we define the postmodern. The opposition here is a moral opposition, that is, that somehow there was in modernism, I think the phrase you used was high moral purpose and moral grandeur. All modernism did not achieve this grandeur. I wonder if you could address yourself to this question. It seems to me a problematic criterion in the attempt to locate this moral seriousness. Where does it reside? Does it reside in the artist's intention? In the artist having a strong personal heroic vision as in many of the figures you evoked earlier? Or does it reside in the work itself? Does it transform through history?

HK: I would say yes, I do believe the work is there and that it is not stable. Now what are the elements that determine its relative stability or instability? For me those are mainly of a creative nature. For example, take an artist I believe satisfied my criteria of having a noble as well as a high moral purpose: Mondrian. He looks one way to us if we approach him by way of the whole Miesian architectural tradition because there's obviously an affinity between Miesian structure and Mondrian's aesthetic. It looks one way if we see it in those terms than it does, say, if we approach it by way of the Mondrian dress. Fifteen to twenty years ago, there was the Mondrian dress. It was a hot item on Seventh Avenue for about two seasons—a white dress with yellow rectangles and blue rectangles and black grids, which I think we can agree is a pure trivialization of a great formal concept. The quintessential postmodern take on Mondrian would be a painter who was, as they say, appropriating Mondrian's imagery for the purposes of both mocking it and deconstructing it. Now in the process of appropriating that imagery, what is occurring is the removal of the image from the idea because the only thing that can be appropriated really is the image, and so Mondrian has to be transformed into something less than he is in order to be appropriated.

HB: In the New Critical era a lot of attention was given to the question of how morality and/or politics got into art. In the back of whatever quarrel is taking place in your work there is obviously the experience of the Stalinist battles of the postwar period and even before that. You say at one point that there was a vanquishing of the last residue of the Stalinist ethos in the art scene here, but at the same time you are talking about art as art. So the question is, How does art vanquish anything politically, how does it manage to do this, how does it vanquish a Stalinist ethos if in fact there isn't some kind of political component in the art?

HK: The forties in this country, since I regard that as the turning point in the whole history of American culture, provides us with some clues. I'm not sure you could actually say that you get rid of ideology without any other ideology coming in because one of the things that happened in American painting, between let's say the Moscow trials and 1945, was a switch in inspiration from Marx to Freud or Marx to Freud and Jung. Now there's obviously an ideology either implicit or explicit in Freud and Jung as much as there is in Marx, but it's a shift from drawing inspiration from external criteria to attempting to draw inspiration from internal criteria, that is, a turning inward and to some degree also a turning away from a sense of obligation to deal with a certain kind of subject matter in order to deal with a certain kind of form. You find the same thing very much in terms of American music from the socially inspired Americana works of the thirties to more abstract compositions of the forties and fifties. You find very much the same thing in the ballet and so on. For me, it's not so much a matter of a perfect escape from ideology as it is an escape from an ideology that is destructive of artistic values.

GR: To some extent the judgment really is of a particular kind of morality. You seem to imply a distinction between ideological constructs that are useful, helpful, and reductive, mainly because they turn the individual toward some kind of internal vision, as opposed to that which, moves the individual as part of a political apparatus that dictates other imperatives.

HB: You have located in your writings, and you've affirmed here today, a very crucial distinction: Certainly at the very core of your article which begins *The Revenge of the Philistines* is the insistence pretty much on one principle, despite the plurality of modernism that has produced a plurality of postmodernisms. the facetiousness, the banality, the trivialization of that which you characterize as the postmodern, as opposed to the moral grandeur and high moral purpose of modernism. Now throughout the rest of the volume you continually deplore this trivialization and yet you also attack the politicization of art and the forcing upon art of certain political imperatives, which are indeed also moral imperatives.

HK: In the best of all worlds, which none of us is likely to inhabit, art would be free to pursue its purest goals. But since we live in an imperfect universe and we know that there are a great many pressures that oblige artists to engage in compromises with those pure pursuits, it's a question of making judgments about which of those pressures are conducive to greater artistic achievement and which are really destructive of artistic achievement at all.

If I may just go back again to the forties, I'd put the question this way: What did figures as totally different from each other as, say, Jackson Pollock, Lionel Trilling, and George Balanchine have in common in the forties? Certainly one of the things that made what they achieved in the forties possible was that each in his way rejected the whole Stalinist ethos in art and culture. Whatever it was, and each did quite a different thing as a result of that rejection, it was that they did it individually. That whole ethos of social consciousness—which I would describe as false consciousness—came out of the Popular Front of the thirties. That really had to be categorically rejected by all three before they could proceed to achieve what they achieved.

HB: But you seem to imply that there has been a return to that.

HK: I think something akin to that Stalinist ethos began to be generated again out of the political culture and out of politics into the artistic culture as a result of the sixties and the counterculture, the New Left and all the things that are familiar to us from the sixties on.

GD: When various people talk about you and *The New Criterion,* they always seem to preface either your name or the title of your publication with the term "neo-conservative" or "conservative." Would you respond to that comment? Is it a misconception on the part of the reading public that you're engaged in some sort of a political agenda?

HK: I certainly do not deny that my own political views sort of answer the general description of neo-conservative and that we've been very concerned in *The New Criterion* to both oppose and explain the kinds of politicization of the arts that have come from the left. On the other hand, there is no neo-conservative position on the arts except I suppose insofar as we represent, you might say, in practice more than in theory. Now if I try to think of the work that has been praised in *TNC* and it could range from, let's see, Aaron Copland to early Robert Lowell to Alfred Barr, Malcolm Morley, *Sunday in the Park with George*, I don't know that you could, by drawing a line from one point to another, establish that we have an artistic line that could be described as neo-conservative.

It's inevitable that any attempt to isolate and identify the politicization of the arts and of cultural questions generally, is going to lend itself to the charge that we are only attempting to substitute our modes of politicization for those we are opposed to. But I don't think that is actually strictly the case.

We set off from a situation which was the given that there was an *overwhelming*—as we say it—politicization from the left of all cultural and artistic questions, the making of reputations, the very content of criticism. I observed it for years at the *Times*—not that the *Times* is a left-wing paper, but it employs a great many liberal writers, reporters, journalists, critics, and so on who don't regard themselves as political because for them what they believe is, you might say, a reflection of the pure state of nature. That is the way I think most liberals see the world. They don't regard themselves or their views as being overly politicized. They look on what they believe as normal, sane belief, just a reflection of what's right in the world. So to take an extreme example, if you believe in abortion on request you tend not to think of that as a political decision because it represents just the normal enlightened view you believe most people to have, whereas it's only a position against abortion that's regarded as political and extreme.

GR: That is exactly the point—the state of nature question that you raise. You seem to assume that the great masterpieces of the world are unchallengeably there, that the canon has existed for all time.

HK: I don't believe that for a moment. Anybody who is serious about criticism, who's acquainted with the history of criticism, can't believe it.

GD: How do you view the role of the critic in contemporary art practice, in terms of his response to innovation and the tradition of modernism? How do you view the role of criticism in *The New Criterion*?

HK: I think the role of the critic is now what it has been at its best for as long as we've had criticism—which is to say for about two centuries. I think Eliot said it best: he said criticism has two functions, one being the elucidation of works of art, and the other what he called the correction of taste. Now I take the correction of taste to imply something rather larger than is commonly associated with the concept of taste, which tends to be thought about in purely solipsistic terms. He was talking about what he did when he wrote about Donne and it was very much what Ruskin was doing when he wrote about Turner and Roger Fry when he wrote about Cézanne and Greenberg when he wrote about Pollock.

I think there are fundamentally two basic ways for a critic to function in relation to the new art of his own time. One is to be a sectarian critic, and in my opinion some of the best criticism comes out of that. Certainly Greenberg was very much a sectarian critic in relation to the New York School, as say Fry was when he wrote about Cézanne and Matisse. The other alternative is to be an aesthetically nonaligned critic, which is the way I see myself. That is, I've never felt that I attached myself to any particular movement because perhaps I could see what was good and bad or strong and weak or achieved and failed in all kinds of art. Both kinds of criticism are necessary and at their best are both important but I think we understand criticism much better if we understand that those are the two basic modalities of criticism. Harold Clurman certainly started out as a sectarian in my sense, but I think as he developed as a critic, though maybe not as a director, he became much more of an eclectic or a nonaligned critic.

In *The New Criterion* we try to find room for both types. I think probably we've published more what I call aesthetically nonaligned criticism because those are the people who tend to find their way to us and frankly at the present moment I think write better than many others.

GR: At the end of *The Revenge of the Philistines* essay you stated that there may be an end to an era in art criticism just as there was a generation ago in literary criticism. And yet the sort of common assumption that I read among partisans of all camps, pro and con, approvers and denigrators, is that we *are* in an age of criticism, in which criticism overwhelms the "creative."

HK: The kind of criticism that we're overwhelmed by now, as I read it, is criticism that has absolutely nothing to do with art. We're talking about structuralist, poststructuralist, deconstructionist criticism and a lot of the politically inspired sociological criticism.

GR: But certainly artistic questions are raised.

HK: I would have to say not many; that's a body of criticism addressed almost entirely to criticism itself.

HB: There's an important thing that you do in your essay on Arshile Gorky, which is to restore some attentiveness to what had been flushed out of criticism by formalism, which is to say content. In that essay you impugn Harold Rosenberg and certain people, but the same thing can be said of the highest formalists. But once you do that, don't you, to follow up Gerry's question, have to entertain again the question of what does it mean to say that this does and does not have to do with art?

HK: For example, a critic like Fredric Jameson I don't think is really addressing himself to what artists or writers do as artists and writers. I mean, he's trying to get a new critical context for criticism. The relation in which he stands to contemporary artistic practice is virtually nonexistent, as I see it.

HB: It's interesting that you choose Jameson, because he's elucidating critical systems, but it's not true, say, of Roland Barthes or Jean-François Lyotard, who've written extensively about any number of artists, or Derrida or Foucault.

HK: What contemporaneous literary or artistic practice does Derrida address himself to?

HB: What I'm saying is that they have shifted maybe the locus of the kind of questions one asks about art, although Barthes and certainly Lyotard talked about formalist questions. But even putting aside what I think are minor incursions on their work, nonetheless, they've asked very different questions—canonical questions, how one makes judgments, what ascertains the grounds on which one makes judgments.

HK: That's what I mean by this criticism—it is criticism addressing itself to critical questions.

GR: Say you're a director of a play and you have a problem of interpretation. You have to put it on, you have to cast it, you have to produce it. Now your attitude toward what you're going to do is going to come very directly back to some of these theoretical questions, such as this question of intentionality that we've been throwing around. What do I view as my job as a director: Is it to realize the intention, or my perceived intention, of that text, which may have been written five hundred, four hundred, three hundred years ago, or even yesterday? Or is it perhaps my job to read it in a certain way that can communicate within the strategies that I have available to me artistically to a contemporary audience? The theoretical question of how you judge the intentionality of the work you are interpreting is a reading no different from a critical reading and is certainly going to affect very crucially the sense of what you do as a director or as a playwright.

HK: I wouldn't say that intentionality there was the key issue. I would imagine it would be more a problem of grasping the structure of the play, of understanding also what it was that drew you to that play to begin with because it's not too likely that what drew you to the play was the problematics of it. Then of course how you do it is going to be determined I would guess, having no experience in these matters, more by the nature of the resources available than by, say, the interpretation you're going to make of it. If you want to do *Hamlet,* and you don't have a single actor who can speak the verse—

GR: —the very idea of what constitutes "speaking the verse" is transformed.

HB: When Gautam asked the question before as to what responsibility does the critic have to innovative or new tendencies in the arts, going back to what you said almost at the beginning about Duchamp and the question of intentionality—it seems to me the real splitting point in the modernism/postmodern issue has to do with the performative, which of course as you know has crossed over from the theatre into practically all other disciplines, never mind the arts. How do you stand—how do you deal with an art that is in fact now to some extent committed to performative consciousness if not actually to performance itself, both on the part of the maker and the perceiver? That's a new phenomenon obviously that art criticism has to deal with.

The tendency that moves up from Duchamp and Cage is that the art gesture is essentially a performative gesture. So I was asking how you stand, say, in regard to Michael Fried's argument at the time when he recoiled against the theatricalization of art.

HK: I didn't agree with Fried in his objection because I think you would have to outlaw too much art in order to make that premise viable. Nevelson, for example—I think of those first exhibitions when she presented her work in a tremendously theatrical way or what we would now call environments. And it was not only intended to have that theatrical or performative aspect, but there was something in the presentation that communicated something that was essential about the art. Any attempt there to make a distinction between the work and the way it was presented turned out not to be a viable distinction because one's experience of each individual object turned out to be the same experience on a smaller scale than the whole exhibition was on a larger scale. I think, on the one hand, it's very important for the critic to make that distinction between the work and its presentation; on the other hand, I think lots of room has to be left for works that do have that theatrical quality that Fried was concerned to expel.

GD: To pursue that idea of the theatrical a little further, isn't it true though that one of your basic reasons for being drawn so much to modernism is that it values the individual spirit and the unique and original spirit of the artist? On the other side, those who are now making extravagant claims for postmodernism—Jameson among them—demystify the idea of originality. Postmodernism is linked to pluralism and collective creation. Where do you put an art like theatre, which is not an individual art—it's collaborative and collective to begin with. Is it necessarily within the canons of modernism then a lesser form?

HK: One never thought of it as being either lesser or outside. In fact, it was always assumed at its best to be the place where it sort of all came together. I think the problem for some of us—to just speak for myself—in discussing theatre in relation to the whole issue of postmodernism is that theatre occupies a position of such marginality artistically that it doesn't seem to any longer broach these issues in a significant way. I think I can honestly say that except for the people who write about theatre professionally, I don't know of a single writer for whom the theatre is a matter of central artistic importance in his experience.

GD: Yet the interesting thing in this context and I think you mention this in your book as well, is that the art world has an audience that constantly wants innovation and is prepared to accept it, whereas the opera audience or the theatre audience or the music audience does not want anything new. There are people around whom this modernism/postmodernism debate circles, for example in Richard Foreman's last production, *The Birth of the Poet*, David Salle created the set. Robert Wilson's work deals very much with the issue of appropriation, which means something different in terms of speech and language in theatre than it does in terms of imagery in painting. There is a very strong literary tradition in German-language theatre that has to do precisely with the question of appropriation in language. It's difficult sometimes to situate the argument because it does mean different things in painting and theatre.

HK: That's true but I can't really address that issue.

GD: Could you address yourself to Robert Wilson?

HK: Wilson is primarily a pictorial artist and a movement artist, that is, he combines the pictorial with the choreographic. Not altogether but for the most part what the words actually are is mostly beside the point— they could be these words or those words.

GD: But he's appropriated texts from television and radio. Would he be a serious modernist artist for you or for people who would be interested in modernist fiction or other forms of literature and painting? If not, why not? Why has the art world not dealt with people like Wilson? A lot of painters don't go see his work. The performance artists were very antitheatrical, the Happenings people too. It seems like there's a long tradition of antitheatricality within the art world.

HK: I think there probably is a tradition of antitheatricality in the art world although when *Waiting for Godot* was first done in '56, virtually every painter in New York went to see it, and it was by far the most talked about thing in the art world for several years.

GR: A lot of artists are interested in Wilson and—

HK: —and his drawings have been shown at the Museum of Modern Art, where he fits into this modern/postmodern configuration. It is an interesting question—I haven't really pondered it.

GD: Postmodernism as an "ism" has already embraced a lot of contemporary practice in theatre despite the fact that within the theatre history of this country there has not been a modernist tradition.

HB: I think the distinction needs to be made at the level of the way the art world has been drawn to what I call the performative, or to theatricality and an interest in theatre. You were talking earlier about Eliot. It's again related if not to the issue of intentionality which Gerry's been pressing then to the issue of content. Remember Eliot himself did plays, although when he thought about theatre or theatricality, he preferred the ballet. He probably had something in mind like what eventually materialized in Balanchine, which was like a certain kind of purist ballet that extruded at least the appearances of ordinary experience, common experience, popular experience, public culture. I remember him even saying that he preferred the Mass—

HK: —or the music hall.

HB: —both of which had a certain kind of purity to them. But I think that still probably exists in the modernism/postmodernism debate. The one thing that formalist modernists have a problem coming to terms with— particularly of my own generation, which is essentially modernist—are the dirty traces of theatricality that is disruptive, disjunctive, collaborative, intrusive. It has to deal with the unaccountable spectator and ups the ante on the demands of the uncontrollable, which is I think a really important aspect. It certainly does relate to the performance of the critic. How does the critic deal with that?

In other words, how do you see the relationship between high culture and low culture today? We know that modernism has a relationship to that. All the early modernists were interested in popular forms to revitalize whatever form they were working in—Brecht in the theatre, Picasso. But now popular culture isn't the question. It isn't a question of going to

Bohemia to seek out popular culture; popular culture is here. How one deals with that new immanence seems to me to be a large part of the problem.

HK: I think the kinds of answers one is going to bring to that question are going to depend very much on where one is coming from. When I go to see a show of video art and it's filled with—so I'm informed—sardonic references to things shown on television every night the whole thing is an absolute blank to me because I don't look at television. All the allusions, all the appropriations are totally lost on me, I've absolutely no idea what they're referring to. As a theoretical proposition I have to confess that I have doubts about where an art that is so deeply indebted to something so meretricious for its données is going to be going, but that's a theoretical doubt. I wouldn't base a critical essay on that doubt and that's one of the two main reasons why I virtually never wrote about video even when I was a critic for the *Times*.

GR: The technology of the photograph changed the reality of the history of painting and wouldn't you think similarly that the advent of new technologies would inevitably change the nature of the art in our time?

HK: Of course, but I think there is a difference between the way painters as different as they are from each other, Alex Katz or Chuck Close, are indebted to the movie close-up on the one hand, and the commercial billboard on the other, for the way they use a great overscale face in a painting. There's a difference between that, because basically what they're deriving from their sources is a formal idea.

GD: We've been speaking a great deal about artists, critics, and the world of art. Could you talk about the teaching of the humanities and the arts?

HK: That is a large question. My own view is that those years have to be looked on as an opportunity—you'll smile when I say this—as Matthew Arnold said, "for the student to become acquainted with the best that has been thought, and felt, and said in the history of Western culture." If we're talking about the arts and humanities, I think it should primarily be an education in Western culture because I don't think any serious student can begin to have a grasp of any other cultural tradition unless he has a pretty firm grasp on his own.

HB: Is this true now that 10 percent of, say, the students in California schools are Japanese or Chinese?

HK: Yes, but they're in California. They're not in Japan. They're growing up as Americans. I think it's very important to know, to master the ground on which you stand before you try to master anything else.

HB: Even with the continental tilt?

HK: Even more so. I also think the emphasis should be exclusively on the masterworks of high culture and not on popular culture because there is no way you can keep a student from becoming involved in the popular culture of his time. You're not going to shut him off from that, but he's not going to come to Shakespeare or *Paradise Lost* in the street and if you don't put those great masterworks—or give him an opportunity to put those within his possession in the sanctuary period—then it's going to be lost, in most cases, forever.

GR: When I was a graduate student, all study in English literature ended with Carlyle because the exact same argument was used—Joyce, Yeats, Eliot, Hemingway are modern people, students will read them themselves. That changed within the space of a very few years. I think we can all agree about the wilder excesses of the sixties, but I think all we are saying is that these questions are *not* state of nature questions about what a work of art is, what the canon is, how you interpret it, what the line is . . .

HK: I think maybe the real difference between us is the nature of the critical revisions that occur. To take the most obvious example, when Eliot wrote about the metaphysical poets, put them into the mainstream of English poetry, and established them as a kind of ancestry to twentieth-century poetry, it was the kind of twentieth-century poetry he wanted to write and he was encouraging to be written. That I think is a rather different basis for, as you say, revising the canon than the papers one hears at the MLA meetings in which the canon is talked about as a purely political construct.

HB: It *was* a political construct. I did my dissertation on Eliot: it was absolutely a political construct for him.

HK: Are you saying it was a purely political construct or that there was a political component?

HB: I don't think anybody would say it's *purely* political, but they would say there is a political construct. After all at the time he declared himself a classicist in poetry, an Anglican in religion, and a royalist in politics, so the canonical issue was posed by Eliot himself. One of the things that is consonant with postmodern revisionist tendencies, and recanonization tendencies, is in fact what was indeed necessary in response to this other Eliotic dominance of literary thought for a long period of time, a revaluation of Romanticism. There were a lot of poems by Shelley and Keats that were disdained, mocked at the time I was a graduate student. But I would certainly make this claim. Eliot, Joyce—all the high modernists— were very much aware of the canonical problem, regardless of what was in and what was out. They knew that knowledge was proliferating with *immense* profusion and that there was no way to adequately accommodate it. I would say *The Wasteland* or *Finnegans Wake* or works of that kind and certain modernist paintings as well show the presence of multiple aspects of reality, and there was a new configuration of knowledge, in some sense a humanist curricula of instruction. They were telling us the way the curriculum is now composed is intolerable and impossible. That there had to be some sort of new synchronic way of thinking.

HK: What you're saying is that there was really no way of retaining the historical sense.

HB: No. I'm saying that there are very different views. One of the things that operates in the graduate schools—and I think a good conservative, whether neo- or any other kind should be very much aware of this—is that whether in art history or literary history or theatre history, everybody's saying the students have no sense of history. Well, in fact, the teachers have no sense of history, by which I mean they have no concept of history. They'll say, Well you ought to study this period, this period, this period. We do that in my department and I teach in an English department. My colleagues who keep insisting on developing a sense of history don't know that they have no concept of history, whether a Marxist concept or a metahistorical concept. They have never thought about what constitutes history.

HK: That is I think a real cultural tragedy. My own first acquaintance with that attitude came when I taught at Bennington in the early sixties, so we can't blame it all entirely on what happened in the later sixties. I actually had juniors and seniors in my class who heard for the first time in their lives of the Revolution of 1848 and the Commune in my lectures on Courbet. Yet I was called in after several weeks by the president of Bennington and told that a delegation of students had come to him to complain that they had not come to Bennington to study the work of some old nineteenth-century realist.

GR: The position that is reflected in articles like Norman Kantor's in *The New Criterion* last year is that somehow the cancer started in the sixties and has particularly been virulent in all the deconstructive/poststructuralist strategies attacking the humanist tradition. I think what we've been saying to some extent denies that. When I was a graduate student there was an assumption that one thing followed another and that somehow there was just an a priori state of nature in what constituted the classics. Now part of the reaction against New Criticism was the fact that it so absolutely eliminated considerations of all sorts of biographical, historical, extraliterary questions. I think we could argue that the impulse, of much, not all, of the poststructuralist impulse, in all its diversity, is a historical impulse in that it forces you to ask historical questions: What is the nature of history? What is the nature of modes of production? How is discourse generated? This represents a reintroduction of history to a situation that had been denuded of its reality.

GD: Are you at all disturbed by the reactionary agenda of so many of the classic literary models—Eliot and Pound and Yeats?

HK: Of course I'm disturbed, for the same reason I'm disturbed by Picasso doing propaganda paintings for the French Communist Party. Of course it's disturbing that some of our greatest artists have been profoundly antidemocratic, but you have to include Picasso along with Eliot. Céline was a monster, as indeed Pound was, but that's the problem of holding two things in one's mind at the same time. It's profoundly disturbing, but to reduce their work to their political position I think is really the beginning of the destruction of culture. I'm not attempting to evaluate artists according to their political position. What I am attempting to do on occasion is discuss the way politics have as I see it really deformed the art. If an artist puts politics into his work and makes them central to it, then I think it's the responsibility of criticism to discuss what those politics do to the work.

GR: In this context of criticism, perhaps we should end with the quote of Henry James from your essay on Tom Wolfe in *The Revenge of the Philistines*. "Art lives upon discussion, upon experiment, upon curiosity, upon variety of attempt, upon the exchange of views and the comparison of standpoints . . . discussion, suggestion, formulation, these things are fertilizing when they are frank and sincere."

Edward Said

ANOTHER SIDE OF EDWARD SAID, the cultural critic, Columbia University professor, and polemical author of *Orientalism* and *Culture and Imperialism*, comes through in this conversation: the man of deep musical feeling. An accomplished pianist and impassioned music lover who was writing a music column for *The Nation* at the time, Said acknowledges the influence of musical form, namely, polyphony, on his literary criticism. What attracts him to it is the contrapuntal play of multiple voices in a style of composition that chooses variation over domination of structure and complexity over simple reconciliation of themes. He admires Messiaen for his creation of music that inhabits time rather than overwhelming it, and Glenn Gould, who makes the activity of performance his subject. Drawing a parallel with his own interest in comparative literature, Said situates his ideas about music's capacity for multiple identities and voices within the same terms as narrative in the novel, an example of what he calls a "typology" of culture practices. Many of Said's thoughtful explorations of music, musicians, and audiences appear in his Wellek Library Lectures, collected under the title *Musical Elaborations*.

Said speaks to these New York critics and teachers of theatre of different canons and their relation to performance, such as the stifling dominance of the Italian repertoire and the conventional staging at the Metropolitan Opera, the importance of rethinking the classics in new productions of opera and theatre, and the dwindling tradition of the masterwork in the dramatic tradition. On the question of the literary canon, he affirms the importance of assimilating into it new tributaries. Elsewhere, he laments the separation of musical culture and literary culture, and the uncritical audience for the performing arts. Using Gramsci's analysis of culture as a reference point, he views the expression of dissatisfaction with inadequate reproductions of the masterpieces as an important task of arts criticism. Said's comments reflect his abiding interest in the study of processes as a model for understanding the contemporary world that would integrate the separate realms of politics, history, and aesthetics, and historicize the circumstances of production in cultures.   BGM

Conversation with Bonnie Marranca, Marc Robinson,
and Una Chaudhuri, 1990

Criticism, Culture, and Performance

Bonnie Marranca: Since you write on music performance, tell us how you feel about this activity in your life, and how it is perceived by others in the literary world.

Edward Said: I think the isolation of musical culture from what is called literary culture is almost total. What used to be assumed to be a kind of passing knowledge or literacy on the part of literary people with regard to music is now nonexistent. I think there are a few desultory efforts to be interested in the rock culture and pop music, that whole mass culture phenomenon, on the part of literary intellectuals. But the world that I'm interested in, the music of classical performance and opera and the so-called high-culture dramas that have persisted largely from the nineteenth century, is almost totally mysterious to literary people. I think they regard what I do as a kind of lark. I've demonstrated my seriousness by giving a series of lectures last spring, the Wellek Lectures at the University of California at Irvine, which are normally very heavy-duty literary theory lectures. I gave them on what I call musical elaborations, of which the first lecture of three was on performance.

It was called "Performance as an Extreme Occasion." I was also interested in the role of music in the creation of social space. In the third lecture I talked about music and solitude and melody, which are subjects that interest me a great deal. But I don't think one can really worry about music seriously without some active participation in musical life. My own background is that of a pianist. I studied piano quite seriously when I was an undergraduate at Princeton and with teachers at Juilliard. So I think what interests me in the whole phenomenon is not so much the reviewing aspect. I prefer trying to deal with the problem of the composer and the problem of performance as separate but interrelated issues.

BGM: Your music criticism seems to be different from your literary criticism. Not only is the subject matter different, but it doesn't seem to be as—let me see if I can choose the right word, because I don't mean it in any kind of pejorative sense—it's lighter, it's not as dense and politically engaged. Of course, it doesn't always lend itself to that, depending on the subject matter. On the other hand, the piece that you did on Verdi's *Aida* is a model for a new kind of theatre history. But it seems to me that there is something you allow yourself to do in music criticism that is not there in your literary criticism.

ES: What I'm moved by in music criticism are things that I'm interested in and like. I am really first motivated by pleasure. And it has to be sustained over a long period of time. I don't write reviews; I think that's a debased form, to write a kind of scorecard, morning-after kind of thing about performance. So what I like to do is to go to many more performances than I would ever write about and then over a period of time, certain things crystallize out of my mind as I reflect on them and think about them and the music I'll play over. In the end, what I really find abides are the things that I care about. I don't know what those are until after a period of time has elapsed. It's a different type of occasional writing from the kind that I do in literary criticism, where I'm involved in much longer terms of debates. Whereas in this I don't really engage with too much in music criticism, because most of it is to me totally uninteresting. There are a couple of interesting music critics around. Not the journalistic ones. Andrew Porter in the *New Yorker* I think is challenging and quite brilliant at times. And then there are people who write from the extreme right wing, like Samuel Lipman, who writes for *The New Criterion*, and Edward Rothstein, who writes for the *New Republic*, who are very intelligent music critics. And that's about it. The rest is really a desert; people who write about music in a nonmusicological way are quite rare.

On the other hand, I have had lots of response from young musicologists, who write me about some of the issues that come up. For example, I wrote a piece about feminism in music and the problem of that. And I've written about the problems of political power and representation over the years in some of the things I've done for *The Nation*. But my main overriding concern is a record of a certain kind of enjoyment, which I think can be given literary form, without drawing attention to itself as a kind of tour de force. "Lighter" is the word you used; I would call it glib and superficial.

Una Chaudhuri: Do you think that performance, as a category, has something to do with the difference?

ES: Tremendously. That's what I'm really interested in. I think the thing that got me started was Glenn Gould. It was really the first extended piece that I wrote which appeared the year he died, or the year after he died—'82 or '83—in *Vanity Fair*. I'd long been fascinated with him. And I also was very interested in the phenomenon of Toscanini. Just because it seemed to me that both of them seemed to be musicians whose work, in a certain sense, was *about* performance. There was no attempt to pretend they were doing something else, but they had sort of fixated on the notion of performance and carried it to such an extreme degree that it compelled attention on its own, and it attracted attention to the artificiality of performance. And to the conventions of it, and to the strange—in the case of Toscanini—well, Bonnie, you write about it, too, in your essay on performance versus singing—the difference between performers who heighten the occasion and those who turn it into a kind of extension of the drawing room or social occasion. So performance is very interesting because then there's the other problem, that you don't have either in theatre, the visual and/or literary arts, in that the performance of music is so momentary—it's over!—I mean, you can't go back to it, anyway, really. And so there's a kind of sporting element that I'm trying to capture. I talked about it once with Arthur Danto, who said, for example, if you read his pieces, they're all about going back to an exhibition, leaving aside what he says and what his attitudes and his ideas are about art. I can't do that. So I have to go back, really, to my recollection. And my attempts, in my own mind, to restate it or experience it in another context.

Marc Robinson: On the whole idea of performance, let me draw you out a bit on opera performance, especially the staging of it. For so many people in the theatre, the whole world of opera is a foggy, dead zone that most of us don't go to because the theatricality of it is so conservative. But now many of the experimental directors are going back to opera—Robert Wilson, Peter Sellars, Andrei Serban—and trying to revive it from a theatre background. Where do you see opera performance going?

ES: Well, it's a tremendously interesting subject that excites me in many different ways. I think for the most part there is a deadness at the heart of opera performance, largely because of institutions like the Met, which for one reason or another—some of the reasons are perfectly obvious— has been dominated by what I call Italian *verismo* opera, and strengthened in this ridiculous kind of thing by the revival, that began in the sixties, of the bel canto tradition. The result of this is that a kind of hegemony has formed between the blue chip opera companies like the Met, and this repertory, and has frozen out a large amount of really extraordinary music. It has hardened performance style into a ridiculous conventionalism that has now become the norm. It infects everybody, even the greatest singers. It is certainly true of Pavarotti, sort of on the right; and on the left, Jessye Norman. You see what I'm trying to say? It's narcotized audiences. The thing I cannot understand is how people can sit through operas at the Met.

MR: I remember when you reviewed the Schoenberg opera *Erwartung* and were so disappointed. Didn't you say something about how it would be much more rewarding just to stay at home and stage it in your mind?

ES: Exactly. Or watch it as a concert performance with Jessye Norman. It's the story of a woman who's going mad. And she's looking for her betrothed. The text is written—texts in operas are very interesting—by a Viennese medical student. The text is not of great literary value, but it's about hysteria and it bears an interesting relation, Adorno says, to Freud's case studies. So it is a minute, seismographic dissolution of a consciousness. Now here is this wonderful singer who hasn't got a clue what it's about, much too large in size to represent neurasthenia and hysteria and all this kind of stuff. As the opera progresses she goes deeper and deeper into the forest, losing her mind and looking for her fiancé. And then it's discovered she really might be a patient in a mental institution who's run away. And right in the middle of the set—right in the middle of the stage—is this enormous grand piano. What is a grand piano doing in the middle of a forest? So I opined that the reason she was going mad was that she couldn't figure out what to do with the grand piano. Which produces a kind of—I mean, you could say—it's a kind of perverse version of the opera. It's a glorious misinterpretation of the opera. That's not what's intended; it was supposed to be a deeply serious kind of thing, and it just didn't work. That's what the Met does, and I don't understand how it continues to do that.

MR: Maybe the consequence of that is there are certain works of music-theatre that simply shouldn't be staged. You always hear that with dramatic literature, there are certain "unstageable" texts—an awful lot of Shakespeare . . .

ES: Yes, that's certainly true, but a lot of those derive from performances where the unstageability of the piece can be made evident, you know, like a late Ibsen play, *When We Dead Awaken*. It has a lot to do with musical performance as well as opera . . . That is to say, how do these—this is a sort of Gramscian phrase—how do these hegemonic canons get formed? I mean, for example, the exclusion of French opera is really quite extraordinary. There is a wonderful tradition of French music and French drama—music-drama—that just doesn't find its way onto the American stages. Think of Rameau; think of Berlioz; think of most of Rossini, aside from *The Barber of Seville*. I mean, Rossini was a French opera writer. Berlioz: you never see him. Bizet is the author of ten operas, of which *Carmen* gets fitful performances—*Carmen* is one of the great masterpieces—but precisely because it's kind of an anti-French and anti-German opera, in a way. Then there's Massenet and Fauré. Why this *verismo* and then a little smattering of Wagner—Wagner sort of turned into Italian . . .

BGM: I think the last time we spoke we talked a little bit about the Philip Glass operas, about whether you had seen *Einstein on the Beach, Akhnaten,* or *Satyagraha.* Are you interested in the contemporary repertoire?

ES: I am. I've heard those and I've seen videos of them—one or two of Glass's things. It's not a musical aesthetic that moves me tremendously. It doesn't seem to me to exploit to the maximum what is available there.

BGM: What about as critical material, in the sense of writing about or looking at the *Akhnaten* opera . . . Even in terms of political themes I would have thought they'd attract your attention.

ES: That's true. It's just . . . I don't know. I can't explain it. As I say, I work with fairly strong likes and dislikes, pleasures and so on . . . I don't derive the kind of interest from Glass that I would have found, say, in other contemporary composers, like Henze. I think Henze is a more interesting writer of opera.

BGM: I was interested to read in a recent interview—one of the things you mentioned in talking about your writing—how the concepts of polyphonic voice and chorus interest you. Could you elaborate on that in terms of your own critical writing?

ES: These are things it takes a while to fetch out of one's own interests and predilections. I seem to have always been interested in the phenomenon of polyphony of one sort or another. Musically, I'm very interested in contrapuntal writing, contrapuntal forms. The kind of complexity that is available, aesthetically, to the whole range from consonant to dissonant, the tying together of multiple voices in a kind of disciplined whole, is something that I find tremendously appealing.

BGM: How do you extend it to your own essays?

ES: I extend it, for example, in an essay I did on exile, basing it on personal experience. If you're an exile—which I feel myself, in many ways, to have been—you always bear within yourself a recollection of what you've left behind and what you can remember, and you play it against the current experience. So there's necessarily that sense of counterpoint. And by counterpoint I mean things that can't be reduced to homophony. That can't be reduced to a kind of simple reconciliation. My interest in comparative literature is based on the same notion. I think the one thing that I find, I guess, the most—I wouldn't say repellent, but I would say antagonistic—for me is identity. The notion of a *single* identity. And so multiple identity, the polyphony of many voices playing off against each other, without, as I say, the need to reconcile them, just to hold them together, is what my work is all about. More than one culture, more than one awareness, both in its negative and its positive modes, its basic instinct.

UC: Do you think there are certain cultures and cultural practices that are more encouraging of polyphony?

ES: Absolutely. For example, in music, one of the things I've been very interested in—and it occupies the last part of the three sections of my book on music, which will appear next year, is a kind of opposition between forms that are based on development and domination. Like sonata. Sonata form is based on statement, rigorous development, recapitulation. And a lot of things go with that: the symphony, for example, I'm staying within the Western, classical world; certain kinds of opera are based on this, versus forms that are based on what I would call developing variations, in which conflict and domination and the overcoming of tension through forced reconciliation is not the issue. There the issue is to prolong, like in a theme and variation, in fugal forms. In polyphony, like in my own tradition, the work of Um Kulthum. She was the most famous classical Arab singer of the twentieth century. Her forms are based on an inhabiting of time, not trying to dominate it. It's a special relationship with temporality. Or the music of Messiaen, for example, the great French avant-garde composer who I think is divine. You see the dichotomy of that. On the one hand, domination/development; on the other, a kind of proliferation through variation and polyphonic relationship. Those are the culture practices that I think one could use as a typology of *other* culture practices: they're based on the whole idea of community, overlapping versus coercive domination and enlightenment—the narratives of enlightenment and achievement that are to be found in novels.

UC: I'm very interested in what you say about this idea of inhabiting the time of performance, instead of dominating it.

ES: Trying to ride it. It's a phrase that comes out of Gerard Manley Hopkins, who has a very strange relationship with time in his poetry, especially the last part of his first great poem, *The Wreck of the Deutschland*. There's this whole thing where the question of whether you try to resist the time and erect the structure, or you try to ride time and live inside the time.

UC: I think of theatre performance as such, as somehow demanding that the time be inhabited. That is, it makes its own demands, even in the masterful performer, who may try to dominate it, but may not succeed.

ES: Yes. There really is a difference in musical performance between people who are involved in remaking the music and inhabiting it in that way, as opposed to just dispatching it with efficiency and tremendous technical skill.

MR: It is also very much in the nature of the exile. I mean, there's a sense that you're either living in the past or living in an ideal future, and the present is such a dangerous equivocal realm where you can't place yourself, and yet you're forced to.

ES: What's interesting about it is, of course, that you get a sense of its provisionality. That's what I like about it. There's no attempt made to pretend that it's the natural way to do it. It's giving up in a temporal sort of way to that moment.

MR: Such a balancing act too. Both in terms of time, but also in terms of the exile's relationship to the world. On the one hand, you have the wonderful worldliness or the ability to partake of so many regions. And on the other hand, the enforced isolation. How does one balance between those two?

ES: I don't know. I don't think there's a formula for it. I think one can call it a kind of ceaseless, but unresolved, trafficking between those situations.

MR: The whole idea of private space connects to that and might be a topic to pursue. I'm very moved by your idea of the secular intellectual, the secular artist, partaking of the public world in a real, strong way. And yet all the changes that are going on now in Eastern Europe started me thinking about alternatives to that point of view. There was an anecdote about East German playwright Heiner Müller—he had always been in opposition to the government—who was asked by somebody from Western Europe, "Aren't you excited now that the chains are off, you're able to write your plays that really do take on the political situation, take on the government, what have you . . ." And he said, "No, actually, freedom now means freedom to read Proust, to stay at home in my library." That seems to signal a rediscovery of private space, a retreat from what used to be an enforced secularity.

ES: Privacy for me is very jealously guarded, because so out of my control is the public dimension of the world I live in, which has to do with a peculiar sensitivity and intransigence of the Palestinian situation. And thinking about it for the past fifteen or twenty years has been very difficult for me to guard. Partly the music has been very much that way, because it's a nonverbal idiom. I've been involved in the thick of these battles over what one says, what one can say, and all that kind of stuff. The public has been so much with me it's been impossible for me to retreat into the private. Although, obviously, we all do have a kind of intimate private life. But it's not recoverable for me in any easy way. In the past couple of years—partly because I'm getting older—I've been deeply resentful of how much, quite against my will and intention and any plan that I might have had, public life has usurped so much of my time and effort. By that, I don't mean only politics. I mean teaching, writing, the whole sense of having an audience—sometimes completely unpredictable and against my will. So that inwardness is a very, very rare commodity. I'm not sure that my case is a special case. I think it may be true of more people than we suspect.

UC: Do you think that somehow a certain kind of engaged intellectual is being made to carry more cultural burden than ever before?

ES: Well, I feel it. I can't speak for others. I find it very hard to speak for others, because I'm in a strange position. I mean, I don't have as much time for reflection. And that's why, for me, the musical experience has been so important. Because it's something that isn't changed and inflected in quite the ways that some of the other things I've been doing have been. I just feel that for the public intellectual it can be extremely debilitating. It's almost paranoid: something you say can be twisted into a thousand different forms or only one different form that can have untold consequences. And in my case, also, I have many quite different and totally impermeable audiences. I write a monthly column in Arabic for one of the largest weeklies in the Arab world. And then the constituencies you have, necessarily, in the world of European languages is also very different. So it's extremely draining, just to try to keep up with it, much less to contribute.

MR: I wonder if we're going to see some of the models of the intellectual artist change, as is the case already in Eastern Europe, with many who are now retreating from that public role—seeing it as a burden, and now evolving into a secluded hermeticism. A lot of the artists there want to rediscover beauty.

ES: I understand that perfectly. What we live in, in a way, is what Eliot called a wilderness of mirrors—endless multiplication, without tremendous significance, but just a spinning on. And you just want to say, Enough. I don't want too much to do with that. And therefore, one of the things that I find myself thinking about, not only privacy that as we talked about earlier is virtually impossible, but also looking at performance exactly like Gould, who understood this problem, and because of that, therefore, was able to focus and specialize and control what he did to the extent that it wasn't a limitless spinning out. There was this kind of—now this hasn't been written enough about or noted about Gould enough—massive effort on his part from the moment he thought about a work to practicing, preparing, and then performing it, and then recording it. He is one of the unique examples of somebody who was a public performer, whose attempt was to enrich the art of performance by, at the same time, controlling it. There is something, of course, quite cold and deadening about it, at the same time. But on the other hand, it's an interesting model to think about. Not many people do that. Most people tend to be profligate and they want more multiplication. There is a sense in which he wanted that, but he wanted to control it as much as possible. Perhaps because he feared that being on the stage had already showed him what was likely to happen: that he would just become a creature of this public space.

MR: Genet might be another example, a man who was always preserving the private realm.

ES: Exactly.

MR: In *Prisoner of Love*, he was able to understand what went on in the Middle East because of his own experience of outsiderhood.

UC: And also in the plays as well.

BGM: Beckett, too.

ES: But what you feel in Genet and Gould you don't feel in Beckett, that is, that there's a flirting with danger. I've never felt that about Beckett. Who can't admire him—but on the other hand, there is a kind of safety in Beckett's work that you don't find in Genet. In Genet you feel the incredible risk involved in all of his drama.

UC: It's also a provocation, isn't it?

BGM: One of the things that strikes me about Beckett is that he's so great a writer and so overpowers theatricality that it's not necessary ever to see him performed. But Genet gains by being in the theatre . . . We've been talking about the private moment and the Eastern European situation, the sense of aloneness and solitude that somehow seems to be demanded after so strong a public life.

The death of Beckett set many people wondering about just what will come after Beckett, of course. And in some ways it seems it's the end of the universal playwright and the international dramatic repertoire. Also, because culture has become so public and so much a part of spectacle, and where there's so little emphasis on the private moment, it seems to me that drama, which is such a private, reflective, intimate form anyway, is falling further and further down in the hierarchy of forms experienced by serious people who would ordinarily have gone to theatre, those who read serious novels and go to the opera. People like Havel and Fugard became known not necessarily because they are great playwrights. They got into the international repertoire because of their politics and their symbolic value. It seems more and more that drama will be a kind of local knowledge. And in the theatre we see the ascendancy of spectacle, of performance, rather than drama. International performers like, say, Laurie Anderson or Wilson, make things that can travel in culture.

ES: Or Peter Brook . . . But even Laurie Anderson, and Brook in particular—what underlies them, also, paradoxically is a kind of modesty of means. It's not like a traveling opera. It has, in fact, a kind of easily packed baggage, which you can transport from country to country and do with a small repertory, the same pieces. But I think one thing that you didn't mention about drama—that in the Palestinian situation, for example, which is the only one I can speak about with any assurance—is that the drama has a testimonial value, which is different from symbolic, when you talk about symbolic. That is to say—take Joseph Papp canceling that Palestinian play, *The Story of Kufur Shamma*, last summer. It wasn't because of the content of the play, it was Palestinians talking about their experience. That was what was threatening. And that's why he had to cancel it. So on that level it is local knowledge, but a local knowledge that is frequently engaged in translocal issues. Things that are of interest to other places. I suppose the burden placed on the playwright and the performer is somehow to translate this local situation into an idiom that is contiguous to and touches other situations.

BGM: In that way, I suppose, drama can travel. But so much of it now, when you compare the theatre of the past four, five, or six decades—what used to be considered international and of interest to an international audience—no longer appears on Broadway. For example, when was the last, say, German or Hungarian or French play on Broadway? In this sense the international repertoire is shrinking.

ES: Although, I'll tell you, Bonnie, I was in Delphi last summer giving a talk at an international conference on Greek tragedy. I talked about Wagner, I believe. Every night there was a performance of a play in the theatre at Delphi. And I was there for two performances, the second of which was extraordinary, the performance by Wajda's troupe of a Polish-language *Antigone* . . .

MR: I saw it in Poland.

ES: You saw it in Poland. Well, I saw it in Delphi. And the audience was entirely Greek . . . modern Greeks, obviously. It was overwhelming. It seemed to me to have there a peculiar mix of things. It was the "OK cultural festival," it was the antique representation of self that was acceptable to the powers-that-be, because it's sponsored by the Greek government which is in a great crisis at the moment. It was an occasion for the local folk. OK, all that. But in addition, it was for me a very powerful theatrical experience. I don't know which performance you saw, because there were several versions. When did you see it?

MR: In Krakow in '85. It was a very bad time, politically, for Poland.

ES: Were there transformations of the chorus?

MR: Yes. The chorus changed throughout the play—moving from bureaucrats, maybe Parliament members, to protesting students to, finally, shipyard workers, like those from Gdansk who started Solidarity. In a Polish theatre, it becomes extremely powerful. Actually, it's an event that makes me question or at least want to take issue with your idea, Bonnie, about the universality of a play.

ES: No, I think what she's talking about—which I'm interested in—the great master theatrical talent that produces, I have to keep using the word over and over again, a masterwork of the sort that created the nineteenth-century repertory theatre, that continues into the late symbolic tragedies of Ibsen and Strindberg, and then moves into Brecht and then Beckett. There's a pedigree here that you're alluding to: people who dominate the stage. The model is one of domination. I don't regret its end, to be perfectly honest with you, because of a lot of what goes with it. In the same way that you could say, well what about the great—think of this—what about the great Austro-Germanic symphonic tradition that begins with Haydn, goes through Mozart, Beethoven, Schumann, Brahms, I suppose Wagner's in there a little bit, Mahler, Bruckner, Schoenberg . . . and then what? Nothing. It ends. And you get these local nationalists, you know, Bartok. I mean, it took place, but we can live without it. It can be respected and memorialized in various ways, but I'm not so sure of that, given the damage to other surrounding clumps it overshadows and dominates. It produces a certain canon or canonicity.

MR: Yeah, and aren't we all trashing the canon!

ES: Not trashing. It isn't the be-all-and-end-all, is what I'm saying.

BGM: I understand your point of view about attacking universality, of course, but the issue is that in drama there's almost nothing else. There are plenty of musical traditions to follow. There are plenty of great novels that are breaking out of the mode and being enjoyed by wide groups and nationalities.

ES: Yes, that's true.

BGM: But with drama, the whole thing collapses, because if there's no international repertoire, then it's a gradual decreasing of the form itself. And what's left are just the best-sellers, the topical plays that somehow travel, and then the classics. But maybe two of Ibsen, or a few of Brecht. What I'm saying is the other traditions are so much richer, and the repertoires are so wide, but if you begin to have a form that worldwide audiences lose interest in—in terms of the new—then I think it's a problem for the form, and that that's different than, say, the situation in music.

MR: But isn't that a Romantic idea, that of an international work of art?

BGM: But it still exists in art. If you look at paintings from many, many countries, a lot of them look the same, and there are good and bad works. I see nothing wrong with large groups of people in different cultures around the world appreciating the same work. That always happens in terms of fiction, for example.

ES: The way you describe it, it certainly sounds special and peculiar to the drama. But why is it?

BGM: One of the things I hinted at before is that what we are seeing now are international spectacles found in several cultural festivals, works by Brook or Laurie Anderson, whose recent piece can be just as accessible in Japan or Western Europe or Brazil, or someplace else. Often we're seeing a kind of internationalization of performance. When I use the word "performance," I mean something different from the theatre. It's not textbound, it doesn't deal with a play. Performance work is often highly technological, and reflects a certain transfer of pop imagery and music.

ES: Recognizable and commodified styles.

BGM: Exactly. And they are understood by people all over the world now, because of the international youth culture. And that has unseated drama somewhat . . .

ES: And also because of film and television and all the apparatus of the culture industry.

BGM: So that the great theatres now tend to remain in their own countries and build their repertoires on the classics, redo them, and are rejuvenated by new people. But we don't see this travel in theatre that we're seeing in video or visual arts, or fiction, or "performance" as a genre in itself.

ES: And, of course, in music you find it in the cult of the traveling maestro or the celebrated pianist or the important diva and tenor, and so on and so forth.

MR: Maybe theatre is less suited to this kind of travel because of the holdover of the idea that a play should somehow address the issues of the people in front of it, the audiences. It's the most socially connected of the arts, of course. And I would think people would be reluctant to give up that possibility of engagement that the theatre provides, in a much more immediate way than art, music, or TV.

UC: There's another way of looking at this. There has always been this dimension of locality in the theatre, this connection to a specific time and place. And it's always been special to the drama. Now, for all its power technology is not going to promote a better means of a direct collaboration with people than the theatre event. So that this "local knowledge" characteristic may be what will save the theatre, and give it its future.

ES: But she mourns it. I think you really do have a nostalgia for the great figures. Or the great forms. It's a kind of Lukácsian, early Lukács—you know, *The Soul and Form* . . . a kind of Lukácsian forlornness and melancholy, which is there. I think you're right. I'm not saying you're wrong.

BGM: To tell you the truth, I'm more interested in the idea of performance than I am in drama, with a very few exceptions. Of course, as a publisher, knowing what it's like to sell books worldwide, on a very practical basis I find a loss of interest in drama.

ES: What does that mean? You've lost interest in the drama and you watch the performance. In other words, it would matter more to you that Vanessa Redgrave was acting in a play, rather than that the play was, say, *Macbeth,* or something like that. Is that what you mean by performance?

BGM: No. I mean something else. I've lost interest in conventionalized stagings of drama. In that case, I would rather sit home with a play and not see it. Though I take a larger interest in performances such as Wilson's work, and some avant-garde performance.

UC: That's really a question of quality, isn't it?

BGM: Yes.

ES: See, the other part of it is, and I think it's very important for people like us, who are interested in these issues and questions, not simply to celebrate the avant-garde—that is to say, the novel, or the exciting and unusual that come along in the cases of Peter Sellars or Wilson—but also, to stimulate greater dissatisfaction and anger on the part of audiences who now sit sheepishly through unacceptably boring reproductions of masterpieces. That's the part that I find the most puzzling of all. Why is it that the level of critical sensibility has sunk so low? The threshold for pain is so high, that people can sit through abysmal "conventional" reproductions of classical masterpieces in the theatre or in opera or in music. Rather than experience something quite new in a contemporary work or a dangerous or innovative restaging of a classical work. I don't understand that. Do you understand it?

BGM: Well, certainly part of it, but not all of it, is that the commentary is so bad in the papers of note—that's one major issue.

ES: Well, there it becomes an important thing to talk about. This is where some of Gramsci's analysis of culture is very important, where you can look at the papers of note and the people who write commentary as sort of organic intellectuals for theatre interests. In other words, they are advance guard, in the military sense—advance guard organizers of opinion and manufacturers of consent for important interests in the theatre, whose role is to colonize and narcotize and lobotomize audiences into accepting certain kinds of conventions as the norm. I think that's an important part of one's work: to raise dissatisfaction at this time.

BGM: You know, the other thing is that, unlike the art audience, for example, which always wants to see something new, the theatre audience and music audience basically want to see the greatest hits in familiar settings. And so the audiences are fundamentally different, even though they might be the same people.

MR: But sometimes that struggling with those greatest hits can be very fruitful, and writers are doing it all the time. Hofmannsthal will deal with the *Electra* story as handed down and absorb it into a creation of his own. Heiner Müller will write *Hamletmachine* in order to kill *Hamlet*.

ES: Or, in some cases, to keep adapting to the changing conditions of performance imposed by the patrons.

MR: It seems like there are two ways for contemporary artists to deal with the classic tradition, and the canon. One is just to keep pushing it aside and write or compose new work. And then the other one—Heiner Müller, Hofmannsthal—is to try to absorb it and then remake it somehow, to kind of neutralize it, recharge it in a subversive way.

ES: I'm of the second opinion. In all of the discussions that have been going on in literary studies about the canon, and the whole question of the Western tradition, it seems to me that one of the great fallacies, in my view, has been the one that suggests that you, first of all, show how the canon is the result of a conspiracy—a sort of white male cabal—of people who, for example, turned Hawthorne into one of the great cult figures of American literature and prevented a whole host of, for example, more popular women writers of the time, or regional writers, and so on . . . Therefore, what is enjoined upon holders of this view is you push aside Hawthorne and you start reading these other people. But that is to supplant one canon with another, which, it seems to me, really reinforces the whole idea of canon and, of course, all of the authority that goes with it. That's number one. Number two—half of this is my education and half of this is my age and predilection—I'm interested in the canon. I'm very conservative in the sense that I think that there is something to be said, at least on the level of preference and pleasure, for aspects of work that has persisted and endured and has acquired and accreted to it a huge mass of differing interpretations, ranging from hatred to reverence. It's something that I find enriching as a part of knowledge. So I'm not as willing as a lot of people to scuttle it. My view is to assimilate to canons these other contrapuntal lines.

You could take the extreme view of Benjamin: every document of civilization is also a document of barbarity. You can show—and I've tried to show it in this book that I've been writing on culture and imperialism for ten years—that the great monuments (well, I did it in the *Aida* case) the great monuments of culture are not any less monuments for their, in the extreme version, complicity with rather sordid aspects of the world. Or, in the less extreme case, for their participation, their engagement in social, historical processes. I find that interesting. I'm less willing to toss them overboard and say, "Let's focus on the new." I mean, I find the idea of novelty in and of itself doesn't supply me with quite enough nourishment.

MR: The whole canon becomes an incredibly sharp weapon for a non-Western writer, too. Somebody like Soyinka can take *The Balcony*, or *The Bacchae*, or *Threepenny Opera* and rewrite them as parables of colonialism.

ES: And not only that, but in the best instances—I think more interesting than Soyinka is the work of the Sudanese novelist Tayeb Salih. He's written several novels, but his masterpiece is a novel called *The Season of Migration to the North*—it came out in the late sixties—that is quite consciously a work that is reacting to, writing back to, Conrad's *Heart of Darkness*. This is a story, not of a white man who comes to Africa, but a black man who goes to Europe. And the result is, on one level, of course, a reaction to Conrad. In other words, this is a postcolonial fable of what happens when a black man goes to London and wreaks havoc on a whole series of English women. There's a kind of sexual fable. But if you look at it more deeply, it not only contains within it the history of decolonization and reaction to Western imperialism, but it also, in my opinion, deepens the tragedy by showing that this man's reactive revenge, which to many readers in the Third World, in the Arab and African world, is a just revenge. But Salih does it fresh because it's futile, pathetic, and ultimately tragic. Because it reinforces the cycle of isolation as insufficiency of the politics of identity. It is not enough to just be a black wreaking havoc on a white; there's another world that you have to live in. And in that sense, it's a much richer and more interesting work than Conrad, because it dramatizes the limitations of Conrad. And I'm second to none in my admiration for Conrad, but this is a quite amazing type of thing which is in the novel, which is quite powerful in its own sense—it's in Arabic, not in English—depends on the Conrad novel, but is independent of it at the same time. It's quite fascinating.

MR: And that may be a solution, as it were, to the whole problem of locality of a work of art. Because what you are describing can be both a very potent work in a local context, but it's also an intercultural work.

ES: Absolutely. And that's where I finally disagree with Bonnie's idea. In the implied contrast between the local and the universal, I think the local is more interesting than the universal. It depends where you look at it from. If you look at it from the point of view of the colonized world, as Fanon says, the universal is always achieved at the expense of the native. I'll give you a perfect example—look at the case of Camus. Camus is the writer who, practically more than anyone in modern French culture, represents universality. A more careful reading of the work shows that in every instance of his major fiction, and even the collections of stories, most of them are set in Algeria. Yet, they are not *of* Algeria. They're always parables of the German occupation of France. You look even more carefully at that and you look for the point of view of Algerian independence, which was achieved after Camus' death in '62—and of course, Genet answers to this, because Genet was involved in the same issue in *The Screens*. If you look at that and you see what Camus was doing throughout his work was using the cultural discourse of the French Lycée—which gives rise to universalism and the human condition and the resistance to Nazism and fascism and all the rest of it—as a way of blocking the emergence of an independent Algeria . . . It seems to me, *there* is the importance of local knowledge which you bring to bear on this text. And put it back in its situation and locale. And there it doesn't become any less interesting, it becomes more interesting, precisely because of the discrepancy between its universal reach and scope on the one hand, and reputation; and on the other, its rather more complicit local circumstances. But maybe we're making too much of it . . .

BGM: I think in some sense we're talking about different things. Because literature and the general secular intellectual life lead a more ongoing life in terms of debate and internal politics than drama does. I simply wanted to point out, if drama was no longer going to add in some sense to an international repertoire, and we were only going to have a local drama, which I value also, then that means something entirely different. For example, in drama we don't really have secular theatre intellectuals in the sense that literature does. Almost all discourse and dialogue and debate on theatre issues is either in the reviewing mechanisms of the popular papers, which don't have any kind of interesting debate going on internally, or in marginalized journals like our own, or in the academic world. So that theatre issues are not brought to bear on general cultural-political issues in the same way that other subjects are treated now, in science or in literature. So I think that this kind of loss is more serious for theatre than it would be in the novel.

ES: I think you're absolutely right, and I think—yes, I see your point. That's a much larger way of putting it.

UC: In the light of what you're saying about the burden on the public intellectual, and how you get caught up in this machine of duplications and spinning out of ideas, it may be a kind of blessing or gift for the theatre to be local or private in that sense. To have it occupy a space where it can do its intercultural practice and experimental thinking without too many public pressures . . . About the canon—this idea of not just throwing over one canon and putting another one in its place—it really seems that what's missing in that approach is that many people are not looking at how these things are taught and how they're presented. They're really only looking at what is taught.

ES: Yes, exactly, although "what" is important, also. The exclusion of certain "whats" is very interesting.

UC: But it's almost as if one doesn't want to give up something deeper, which is certain models of evaluating texts . . .

ES: I call them models of veneration, and that's what they are.

UC: That veneration is transferred to something else, and it leaves you in the same abject position vis-à-vis the text or the artwork or whatever.

ES: Well, it is one of the constitutive problems of academic debate in general, but it's basically unanchored in real engagement with the real world. It's largely theoretical. So the "what," on the one level, is equally important. It's a claim to certain kinds of authority and turf and so on. But the "how," you know, the "how" becomes relatively weightless, in a certain sense; it becomes one method among others. I'll give you an example of what I'm trying to say. Look at the result of all the massive infusion that American literary, and I suppose, cultural studies in general, have received through "theory" in the past thirty years: structuralism, poststructuralism, deconstruction, semiotics, Marxism, feminism, all of it. Effectively they're all weightless, I mean they all represent academic choices and a lot of them are not related to the circumstances that originally gave rise to them. For example, Third World studies in the university are a very different thing from Soyinka or Salih in their own immediately postcolonial situation trying to write a narrative of the experience. You know how sometimes a critic like Ngugi talking about decolonizing the mind is one thing for somebody who's been in prisons, lived through the whole problems of neo-imperialism, the problems of the native language versus English, et cetera. They're very different things than somebody deciding, well, I'm going to specialize in decolonization or the discourse of colonialism. So that's a very great problem.

UC: The academy is actively rendering them weightless . . .

ES: In a certain sense you can't completely do away with that, because the university is a kind of utopian place. To a certain extent, these things should happen. Perhaps the disparity between the really powerful and urgent originary circumstances of a cultural method, and its later transmutation as a theoretical choice in the university, is too great.

UC: Do you think it should remain utopian? Maybe that's part of the problem, that this is a model that has outgrown its usefulness.

ES: I think that's where we are right now. We're watching a very interesting transformation. Most students, I think, the good students here, my students—and I know this from direct contact with them—are really no longer interested in theory. They're really interested in these historical, cultural contests that have characterized the history of the late twentieth century. Between racism and imperialism, colonialism, various forms of authority, various types of liberation and independence as they are reflected in culture, in aesthetic forms, in discourses, and so on. So that's where I go. The problem is how you relate that to social change; at a time when it seems everything is now moving away from the contests that determined the history of the twentieth century hitherto—the contests between socialism and capitalism, and so on. So it's a very troubling moment. I think the important thing is to be exploratory.

BGM: You know, in fact, in the little piece in *The Guardian* that you wrote, you mention that you felt somehow the history of philosophy and politics, and general drift of intellectual life, was really almost inadequate to deal with the new situations.

ES: I think it is. I think it certainly is.

BGM: What directions might this view of the arts and sciences coming together somehow in some new understanding take? Where would you like to take it in your work?

ES: Without getting too specific and detailed, I think that if you take a general thing that you've been interested in, interculturalism, I think that's obviously where it's going. That is to say, various types of integration between formerly disparate or different realms, like politics, history, and aesthetics. But rather than just leaving it at that, it seems to me that new kinds of formations seem to be particularly interesting and important. One would be relationships of interdependence and overlapping. We've had a tendency, you see, to think of experiences in national terms. We say there's the Polish experience, there's the French experience, there's the Haitian experience, there's the Brazilian experience. It seems to me that that's pretty much over, where one could give a certain amount of fidelity and attention to basic national identities. What's interesting is the way the national identities have historically, in fact—and the present moment facilitates that—interacted and depended on each other. I mean the relationship between Brazil and North America is very, very dramatic now in the situation of the rainforests. The relationship between North Africa and the European metropolis is very dramatic now, because of the presence of a large number of Muslim immigrants in France.

What you begin to realize is the universality, therefore, not of stabilities, which have been the prevailing norm in cultural studies, but of migrations: these massive transversals of one realm into another. That seems to me an entirely new subject matter. Refugee studies versus the studies of stable cultural institutions that have characterized the paradigms of the social sciences and the humanities of the past. That would be one major thing. Another would be the study of what I call integrations and interdependence versus the studies dominated by nationalities and national traditions. The conflict between emergent transnational forces like Islam, which is a subcontinental presence, it's an Arab presence, it's now a European presence. There's a total reconfiguration of the cultural scene, it seems to me, that can only be understood, in my opinion, historically. You could see elements of it already in the conflict between Europe and the Orient, for example, which I talked about twelve or thirteen years ago.

BGM: Do you have any thoughts on interculturalism as it relates to performance or any of the other kinds of things you might want to take to your work, besides the *Aida* model of doing theatre history?

ES: Not at this stage, no, because I'm so mired in *contested* regions between cultures. I'm very much, I'm afraid, marked by that. In other words, I'm really a creature whose current interest is very much controlled by the conflict between the culture in which I was born and the culture in which I live at present. Which is really quite a strange phenomenon. It's not just that they're different, you know, but there's a war going on and I'm involved on both sides of that. So it's very difficult for me to talk about interculturalism, which would suggest a kind of sanity and calm reflectiveness.

BGM: Do you think of interculturalism as a kind of Orientalism?

ES: Well, it can be. Yes, absolutely. Because I think there's a whole range of what is acceptable and what is not acceptable. We haven't gotten to that stage yet, I don't think, of being able to talk about it in an uninflected way, in a way that doesn't bear the scars of contests between the North and the South, or the East and the West. I mean, the geographical configuration of the world is still very strongly inscribed, at least in my vision of things.

MR: Drawing out of what's just been said, it seems that there's good interculturalism and bad interculturalism. But after I read *Orientalism*, a great paralysis set in.

ES: Sorry about that.

MR: Every time I consider or reflect on another culture, I feel my "power" position coming into relief. But is the alternative to that power just a greater distance or isolationism? I don't want that.

ES: No, no, no. I don't think it's possible. You know, I think one of the great flaws of *Orientalism* is the sense that it may have communicated that there is no alternative to that, which is a sort of hands-off sort of thing. That's not what I would imply. And I think, at the very end I say something like that. That there is a kind of "already given," you know, a sort of messiness and involvement of everyone with everyone else. It's just that I would like to think that the inequalities, as between, say, a native informant and a white ethnographic eye, wasn't so great. I don't know how to talk about this without seeming to congratulate myself, but it was interesting, to me at any rate, that *Orientalism*—partly because I think that it was already in the air—seemed to have released a lot of quite interesting work that went way beyond it. It instigated a certain kind of self-consciousness about cultural artifacts that had been considered to be impervious to this kind of analysis. And the irony is it didn't make them less interesting, it made them more interesting. So I think the history of Orientalism—I don't mean the book, I mean the problem—is really the history of human— how shall I put it?—human meddling, without which we can't live.

Look, any time you globalize, let's say East versus West, you can come up with convincing formulas that always suggest the triumph of the West. That's why Naipaul is successful. I mean, that's the basis for the Naipaul appeal. He says the world is made up of people who invent telephones and those who use them. Where are the people who use telephones? We don't know that. See, you can always fall into that trap; the trap that C. L. R. James never fell into, because he said if you're a white man you can say you have Beethoven, and the black man's not supposed to listen to Beethoven, he's supposed to listen to Calypso. That's a trap you can't fall into. You've got to be able to make the distinctions and use what you want and think of it as part of the possession of all mankind or humankind. I don't know how to get to that point without waging the struggle on some very local and clearly circumscribed level.

So on one level it seems to me that there's a need for historical understanding of various contests. That's why I don't believe in "literary studies." I don't believe in the study of English literature by itself. It should be looked at with West Indian literature, with American literature, with French literature, with African literature, with Indian—you understand what I'm saying? The deep historicization of the circumstances of production of culture and along with that, an acute understanding of the extent to which every cultural document contains within it a history of a contest of rulers and ruled, of leader and led. And third, that what we require is a deep understanding of where we would like to go.

Umberto Eco, Robert Wilson

WHEN HE IS ASKED with which of the characters in his internationally cele-brated novel *In the Name of the Rose* he identifies, Italian author Umberto Eco replies, "With the adverbs, obviously." In a meeting with theatre and opera di-rector Robert Wilson, on the occasion of his exhibition of furniture/sculpture works and videos at the Centre Georges Pompidou in Paris where he was also preparing a production of *The Magic Flute,* the playful Eco questions the American artist on the nature of interpretation and the artwork. Is art free of ideology? What is an open work? The ensuing remarks contrast the Euro-pean intellectual tendency to see the making of art as an encoding of specific social themes and the American intuitive stance that resists any imposition of an artist's views on the work. Wilson is adamant in his formalist approach, while also offering fascinating insights into his choice of materials to repre-sent different temporal senses of a work, particularly in his design of the chairs for *A Letter for Queen Victoria* and *The Life and Times of Joseph Stalin,* two early pieces. Likewise, when Eco contrasts the geometry of his furniture with the *informel* style of his art, Wilson is quite revealing: "The drawings are like diaries for me . . . They are much more emotional, very personal and very private; I create them alone."

In the past two decades Wilson, whose productions now mainly originate in Europe, has directed many of the European theatre and opera classics, in addition to new plays, literary adaptations, and music-theatre works. When Eco asks how he upholds his approach as "nonliterary theatre" while at the same time choosing subjects such as Freud (*The Life and Times of Sigmund Freud*) and Einstein (*Einstein on the Beach*), who have a narrative existence prior to art, Wilson has a thoughtful response. He is doing what Euripides, Racine, and Molière did when they wrote about the gods of their time, cre-ating new stories around these mythic characters from the communal ideas they evoke. Charmed, Eco pronounces this intersection of myth and history "in the mainstream."   BGM

Conversation with Umberto Eco and Robert Wilson, 1993

Interpretation and the Work of Art

Umberto Eco: It's always silly to ask an author, "What did you mean by this or that?" It also happens to me and I answer, "If I meant something more, I would have written it." It can be more silly with you because it's notorious that when you are asked something like that, you say, "Well, I did it because it's beautiful!" So I won't ask you about the meaning of your works, but rather about your feelings before and during some of them.

Today I saw the *maquette* of this exhibition. As a first impression, I saw there a city that I can focus from different perspectives. I don't know if you are familiar with David Lynch's book *A View from the Road,* on the American city designed so as to be viewed from the highway. When I think about your work—what I loved most was *Einstein on the Beach*— I have the suspicion that you start doing something thinking of a city, of somebody who moves into a city, who can drop one thing and look at something else, who changes his own perspective, who is allowed to refuse to consider something today, in order to reconsider it tomorrow. It seems that you foresee an audience able to complete your work. I have written a book, *The Open Work,* in which the same ideas were used for literature.

Robert Wilson: Yes, I think it's a good analogy to compare it to a city. I am looking out my office window now and I see a contemporary building. Next to it is a building from the eighteenth century and over there is a building under construction. I see not only the Parisian present but also traces of its past and premonitions of its future.

I look above and I see clouds changing. An airplane crosses. On the street I see a man walking and a car passing. All of these events happen simultaneously and at different speeds. The exhibition is a little bit like that, full of various spatial and temporal layers. The space is like a battery with different energies. It is a space that is full of time; I would not say timeless, but a space for memories.

One of the layers in this exhibition is the videos. These videos are very different in nature, rhythm, color, texture, and structure than the rest of the room. The room is rather severe in terms of its materials (steel, lead, copper, and black-and-white lacquer) and colors (gray, black, and brown). Amidst these cold materials, the video is something very bright, very colorful, very light, and often quite humorous. They are the counterpoint to the rest of the exhibit. They are like punctuation in

Kabuki theatre; you see a character moving very slowly for a long passage and suddenly there are very fast movements. Likewise, the videos in the exhibition are a punctuation of the space, an interval that supports the continuous line. The videos are about close-ups and things that move fast and have bright colors.

UE: I understand the difference between the exhibition space and the movies, but my analogy would cover the whole of your exhibition and maybe of your activity. Each of your works seems to me like a video, where one can select different images by maneuvering a sort of remote control. From another point of view, when I think of *Einstein on the Beach*—where it was possible both to look at *all* the frames at the same time or to select your area of interest—I feel tempted by another analogy (maybe I am exaggerating with analogies): it seems to me that in computer terms your way of working is not a serial, but a parallel one.

RW: Yes, I think so. I believe that we think like remote control. One of the first plays that I wrote, *A Letter for Queen Victoria*, and several other pieces I did after that, *I Was Sitting On My Patio This Guy Appeared I Thought I Was Hallucinating*, were very much along the idea of a remote control. I grew up in a small town in Texas and as I was growing up my father never allowed us to watch TV. I went away to a university and when I came back I was surprised to see my father was watching TV constantly. He would sit with a remote control and watch all the channels at once. He would watch a bit of this, a bit of that, and this fascinated me. My early plays were very much like that. They consisted of numerous little pieces that had to be put together by the viewer, just as if one were watching a channel that had a thousand programs and one could constantly switch between them. This exhibition is similar. One can free-associate all these parts in multiple ways. There are no definitive ways to link up the various images, sounds, and other pieces of information. There is an infinite number of possibilities. It is a space in which we hear and see and experience, and then we make associations.

UC: Since you want to make a "nonliterary theatre," a nonstory theatre, why do you choose, as a starting point, names (Freud, Curie, Einstein) who bring with them a story as a background? Don't you see a conflict between a refusal of a story and the preexisting story of those persons and, therefore, the expectations of the audience?

RW: No, I don't see a conflict. Men of the theatre like Euripides, Racine, and Molière frequently wrote about the gods of their time. I think that figures like Sigmund Freud, Joseph Stalin, Queen Victoria, and Albert Einstein are the gods of our time. They are mythic figures, and the person on the street has some knowledge of them before he or she enters the theatre or the museum space. We in the theatre do not have to tell a story because the audience comes with a story already in mind. Based on this communally shared information, we can create a theatrical event. An artist re-creates history, not like a historian, but as a poet. The artist takes the communal ideas and associations that surround the various gods of his or her time and plays with them, inventing another story for these mythic characters.

UE: Well, the spectator is free to choose his own itinerary in your story. I agree that you are making "open" structures inviting people to collaborate, but (this is a very malicious question that concerns some of my present preoccupations) would there be a certain way of responding to your painting, to your theatre, a certain way of interpreting it, of using it, that you would refuse, by saying, "Oh no, there is an ultimate point beyond which you cannot go"? Suppose I say, "Oh, you know, that reminds me of Versailles, I find it very Molièresque." The American-Italian-French Constitutions allow me to make this interpretation, but do you have the right to be dissatisfied with such a reaction, or not?

RW: No, I don't have the right. My responsibility as an artist is to create, not to interpret. This is true of my work both in the visual arts and in the theatre. I am working right now on *The Magic Flute* and I tell this to the singers all the time. This is very confusing for them because they are accustomed to thinking that they must interpret their roles and play in a naturalistic manner with psychological reasons for everything. I think interpretation is for the public, not for the performer or the director or the author. We create a work for the public and we must allow them the freedom to make their own interpretations and draw their own conclusions.

UE: But you are at this moment interpreting the text of Mozart, and then somebody else would interpret your interpretation of the text of Mozart.

RW: I do not think I am interpreting, but anyway, go ahead.

UE: No. Why? I think that directing a symphony of Beethoven is a way of interpreting it, because you can stress a given rhythmic passage in order to direct in a given way the attention of your audience. I use "interpretation" in a very wide sense.

RW: In that sense, there is, of course, my interpretation of doing it.

UE: Okay. Mozart was a Freemason and he believed naively in those very vague, sentimental, moral principles exposed in *The Magic Flute*. In the same way, in *Don Giovanni*, he wanted to say that the Commendatore was an evil character destined to hell. So, Mozart took a position. *Your* interpretation, your way of staging Mozart, can stress certain elements of the libretto or of the musical score, to focus more or less the attention of your audience on the moral issues of Mozart. There are moral issues in Mozart! What do you do in this case?

RW: First, I don't agree with your premise. I don't believe that Mozart understood what he wrote. I don't think that Shakespeare understood what he wrote. It's something that one can think about and reflect on, but not completely understand. The works are larger than the man. I directed *King Lear* last year. It is not possible to fully comprehend *King Lear*. It is cosmic. I am the kind of artist who does not want to pretend to understand what he is doing because I think that is a lie. If I said that I understood a work, I would be limiting myself. I would overlook the many interpretative possibilities that are in each great work of art by choosing only one perspective when I claim to understand it.

I can read *King Lear* one night in a certain way and read it completely different the next. It's the same with *The Magic Flute*. On one hand, the story seems very simple, but on the other hand, it is very complex. It is something that one wants to reflect on. If we know why we do something, there is no need to do it. That is why both *King Lear* and *The Magic Flute* are great works of art. That is why they live through time and why we go back and rediscover them. They become avant-garde as we rediscover them.

UE: Yes, but you can do something in order to encourage the people to read Mozart on the surface level as a simple structure, or to encourage them to read it as a complex story. That is already an assumption of interpretative responsibility. And when you think, "I *want* them to see that it's very complex," then you make a decision. The meaning is unprejudiced, but the attention you stimulate depends on a decision on your part.

RW: Yes, I think that's true. The danger is that you should not believe anything too much. This is why I prefer formalism in presenting a work because it creates more distance, more mental space. If I aggressively say, "I WANT TO KILL YOU!" that is one thing. But if I say, "I want to kill you," and I am smiling, it is much more terrifying. I think it is the same way in directing Mozart. The singers can be very serious, but somehow they must also know that there are other things going on. The mystery has to be deep in the surface, but the surface itself must be accessible.

We make a work in the theatre or in the museum so that the surface is simple and accessible to everyone—to a person from Africa or China or to that man on the street we saw earlier today. Everybody should be able to walk into the museum and get something from the exhibition. The same is true in the theatre. The surface remains simple but beneath that it can be very complex. The surface must be about one thing, but underneath it can be about many things.

UE: Apparently, it's a marginal question but it has something to do with the same problem: let me say roughly that usually your furniture is very geometric. Let's say it reminds me of Mackintosh or Mies van der Rohe. Except the "Stalin Chair," which is *terrestrial*, made with a sort of underworld material, like lava. Why? Is that a way of interpreting the character?

RW: Yes, I think so. I had two chairs built in lead for Queen Victoria (*A Letter for Queen Victoria*). They are very severe. The chairs have right angles and car lights with large electrical cords protruding from the backside. They sit facing each other. They are very simple. I shouldn't tell my own ideas and associations about these works because I do not want to impose my ideas on others, but for me, these two severe chairs are like Victorian time. For Stalin, a twentieth-century figure, I built two draped, organic lead chairs. Stalin had two identical apartments. Everything was the same: the same furniture, the same stoves, everything down to the smallest detail. In each of these apartments there were two armchairs that were always draped with fabric.

I associate the blast of an atomic bomb and its mushroom cloud with these chairs. I think that one of the greatest discoveries of our century was the splitting of the atom. It is the splitting of the mind. The splitting of the atom takes place in our mind. I liked using this free, organic form for Stalin and the very severe use of this same lead material for Queen Victoria. To me, the two types of chairs represent two very different uses of material and somehow relate to two very different times, namely, the nineteenth and the twentieth centuries.

UE: You said a few minutes ago that in order to keep the interpretation unprejudiced, you choose formalism. But now you are telling me that choice of a form expressed an ideological position. Thus formalism is not the denial of interpretative engagement. It *is* an ideology, and you know it, evidently, because you said it!

RW: Rules are made to be broken! You should not believe anything too much. You must always contradict yourself! When you turn left, think that you are turning right!

UE: How did Walt Whitman say it? Do I contradict myself? Well, I do contradict myself! But, apropos of contradiction, I don't know everything of your painting, but I have the impression that while in furniture you are very geometrical (let's say Mondrian-like), in painting you are *informel*. It seems that there are two radically different choices. It is due to the different matter, or is it your split personality, or something else?

RW: The drawings are like diaries for me. I can go back and look at a drawing that I did many years ago and say, Oh! that is when Nixon was resigning as president, or this is when I fell in love with someone, or this is when such and such happened. I can read the lines and they evoke memories. Martha Graham once said that in her work she was charting the graph of her heart. In some ways, my drawings are like that. They are different than my work for the stage or my furniture pieces. They are much more emotional, very personal, and very private; I create them alone. In the theatre, I work with many people in collaboration and when I create a piece of furniture, I work with craftsmen and other people. The drawings are something completely personal, coming from my hands and fingers.

UE: Recently I met Günter Grass in Italy. He was exhibiting his drawings. Very beautiful. And curiously enough, he said, "I would prefer to be remembered as a painter rather than as a writer." I don't know whether he was sincere or not. What would you answer if you had to choose, to be remembered for your drawings or for your structures; for your two-dimensional activity or for your three-dimensional activity, or for your four-dimensional activity, like theatre?

RW: I think that it is all part of one body of work. I would like to be remembered for my work in each field.

UE: In which way was your work influenced by your initial activity with Soleri?

RW: I apprenticed with Soleri in the early sixties. At that time, I was more interested in the ideas behind his architectural designs than in the individual designs themselves. I was fascinated by the scope of his thinking. He was a dreamer. He was designing cities that were underwater, spanning the water, and in the sky. I was finishing school at the time, and my classmates were designing office buildings for their theses. I could not do that, it didn't interest me at all. Soleri was a man making architectural designs by drawing in the sand with a stick. He didn't know what it was going to be—a game room or an auditorium or whatever—he would simply start drawing. That is how he would plan buildings. It was amazing to see an architect work like that. It really impressed me. It was the same with Einstein—Einstein was also a dreamer. At the time I was finishing school, I was quite confused, and these men were a confirmation for me, because I was also a dreamer. For my thesis, I designed an apple with a crystal cube in the center. This crystal cube was meant to be a window to the world. It could reflect the whole universe.

I worked once in a hospital with paraplegics, quadraplegics, and people with iron lungs. It was a hospital on an island in the middle of the East River in New York, where the patients were geographically isolated in addition to being paralyzed. They didn't have Junior League Women or volunteer people come into the hospital because it was very difficult to reach. The patients were people living on welfare. When I worked there, we raised money in order to bring television into the hospital wards. It was fantastic because we opened a window to the outside world for these people who had been isolated for so long. They could watch what was happening in China or Africa—even go to the moon with the televised space launchings. The television functioned as a window to the world for these people.

I think the Centre Pompidou is also a sort of window to the world. It is in the center of Paris and it is a center in itself. It is the cube inside the apple that reflects the whole world. It is a place where people congregate, where they can gather together to observe and be observed, a space that people can move freely in and out of. It's the number one tourist attraction in Paris, and it is a museum! It is not a morgue or a place that is just collecting works by artists. Artists can go to the museum to create work. I just created my videos in the sound studios there. The medieval city had the cathedral as its core. It was not only a place of worship but also the center of cultural and urban life. I think the Centre Pompidou is similar.

UE: And sometimes the events taking place outside, on the square, are more interesting than those taking place inside.

RW: That is certainly true. It is exciting not only for what happens inside the building but also because of the people who gather around it. Another interesting thing about the Centre Pompidou is that it has extensions throughout the city. It once sponsored a work of mine that did not even happen in the museum, but in a theatre outside the Centre. Art can radiate out of the museum and reach the whole city. In that sense it is a true center. That is what we need in cities today.

UE: So you see that the analogy of the city is still returning. This conversation probably will be read by people before entering your exhibition. There will be very smart visitors who will recognize the chair of Einstein or of Freud. But there will be normal people who can have different attitudes toward your pieces of furniture. First: Oh! I *wish* to sit in this chair. Second: Obviously, I cannot sit in this chair, this is the Platonic idea of a chair. Third: It is a torture chair, a *machine celibataire*, like in Duchamp or in Kafka's *The Penal Colony*. Or fourth: It is a Brechtian action to defamiliarize me with the chair, you know, I look at it in a new way, Wilson has succeeded in what the Russian formalists called the *priem ostrannenjia* or, "the device of making it strange." You are not obliged to select a single kind of reaction, maybe you are sympathetic to all of them . . .

RW: There are many different ways you can look at them. First of all, many of the pieces were previously seen in the context of a theatre piece. Now they are seen in a museum and arranged in a certain way. They are in a completely different context. They are like molecules that break apart and recombine. They change through the deconstruction process.

I think that the chairs are sculptures. They are pieces that you can sit on or be seen sitting on or imagine someone else sitting on. They take on personalities of their own, evoke associations and thoughts.

UE: But why is a given chair compared with Giacometti and another one with someone else?

RW: I think that it is my concern with form. I design a chair with as much careful attention as when I create a play. All the details relate to form, line, time, and space. It is interesting that you previously mentioned Kafka and the theme of torture. There was once a form of Mongolian torture that is a little bit like my chairs and this exhibition. A man was buried up to his neck in the desert sand. His hair was completely shaved and his head tightly covered with an animal hide. In the intense heat of the desert with his head covered, the hair would not grow out but inward into the brain. The result for the man was a loss of memory. Maybe in some strange way, this exhibition is also about the loss of memory. When I was creating *Death Destruction & Detroit II*, I kept thinking about a room that would create an experience of loss of memory. That piece was actually based on Kafka. Perhaps this exhibition is such a space.

UE: Walking through a new city always implies a loss of memory. A city is a place in which you walk without being able to draw its map. Very seldom do you know the map in advance. I think you like your visitors to walk—in time or in space—through your works, losing memories of certain parts, then recollecting something, or dropping something else. In the middle of *Einstein on the Beach* I went out to the corridor to smoke a cigarette and then I went back in. I am the kind of person who likes to enter the movies not at the beginning but at the middle because, as I say, movies are like life. I entered my life when Julius Caesar was already assassinated but I reconstructed everything pretty well. You like this way of visiting places and stories, I suppose. You could think of one of your plays like a ring, perhaps like a Moebius ring.

RW: There was a song that Dionne Warwick sang in the film *The Valley of the Dolls* which had the constant refrain, "I got to get off, I got to get off this merry-go-round." The song kept repeating all the way through the piece. It could have gone on forever. I was especially concerned with this theme of eternal recurrence in my early plays. I created plays that were twenty-four hours long or even one that lasted seven continuous days. I even thought there could be a theatre with a play that ran continuously, so that you could go for your lunch break for fifteen minutes or for the afternoon the way you go to the park to sit and watch clouds changing or people walking. There would be no beginning, middle, or end like in Shakespeare, but simply one continuous line.

UE: To enter a theatre and to stay there from beginning to end is a very recent idea. Think of the Greek theatre—four tragedies plus a satyr play, and people eating and chatting in the meanwhile—or Mozart's operas, with people making love in their loge with the *rideau* closed. Well, I think theatre is more that than Ibsen. You are in the mainstream.

WRITERS AND COMPOSERS

Charles L. Mee

HISTORY AND THEATRE have been the two constant poles within which Charles L. Mee has situated his dramatic works. Some of his readers have known him to be a chronicler of American history and postwar politics in *The Genius of the People* and *Meeting at Potsdam;* others have known him primarily as a playwright of texts in which history jostles with contemporary politics to create a trenchant mirror of the times. In recent years, Mee has devoted himself exclusively to writing for the stage, and although he has not abandoned his passion for history, his newer plays—*Orestes* and *The Trojan Women,* among others—are rewritings of classical Greek dramas as seen through the prism of American politics and culture. They appear in PAJ's new volume of Mee's drama entitled *History Plays.*

In this interview with *Village Voice* theatre critic Alisa Solomon, which took place at the end of the Reagan era, Mee presents a powerful case on behalf of the centrality of social and political history in the making of drama. It is a history, however, that has more in common with the new historicisms—the bottom-up view—inaugurated by scholars such as Braudel, Ladurie, and Darnton, than with traditional historians. His dramatic precedents clearly lie in the line that stretches from Georg Büchner through Bertolt Brecht to Heiner Müller, where the common practice of rendering historical subject matter in chronological and simplistic terms is abandoned in favor of complex and episodic readings.

Predictably, Mee, whose belief in the social function of art serves as the indispensable foundation for all his plays, condemns much of contemporary theatre for its emphasis on individuality and excessive psychologizing: "It sets a frame of discourse in which you cannot have historical perspective, and therefore makes it impossible to arrive at political understanding." Arguing for a theatre that lends meaning to the participatory processes of democracy, Mee also proposes new narrative and theatrical strategies that range from intricate textual interweavings of fragmentary episodes to a farrago of performative styles. Only through such extreme interventions, he concedes, can theatre cast off its authoritarian linear style and more accurately reflect the turbulent emotions and complex lives of audiences.   GD

Conversation with Alisa Solomon, 1988

The Theatre of History

Alisa Solomon: I want to begin by talking about the treatment of history as a subject in the late eighties in America, and the different forms it takes. Writing both historical theatre pieces and dramatic history books, you've often treated the same subject matter in disparate ways. For instance, you've recently published a book on the Constitutional Convention and you also have a play called *The Constitutional Convention, The Sequel.* What's their relationship?

Charles L. Mee: The book is called *The Genius of the People.* It's a narrative history of the Constitutional Convention during the summer of 1787. I let the delegates speak for themselves, using the dialogue that was preserved in the notes that Madison made from the convention. The book is meant to provide the setting and the context so that you can understand what those arguments are about, and then draw out of that a general argument which is that this is the story not so much of a few great men making history, but of a few representative people who are created by history as much as they create it. The history by which they are created is the six hundred years of English history generally, and that is a set of political beliefs and instincts that's really in the bones of the people who were in America at that time.

During the convention a delegate would sometimes say to one of the others, "Well, you may wish you could establish a House of Lords in this country, but this would not suit the genius of the people," by which was meant the spirit of the people—so that's where the title comes from. It means a certain developing democratic spirit, and beneath it, the understanding that everyone in a society is safest, in their lives and the sanctity of their beings, when political power is most thoroughly dispersed throughout the society. They were forced to fall back on this principle because they themselves really were not a homogeneous body of people. They were all male and white, but some were slave owners, some were large plantation owners, some were small farmers, some depended on international trade, some on the openness of the frontier. No one wanted any one group to be able to dominate that government, so they were forced constantly in their arguments to the dispersion of power. That then puts into the fundamental design of the Constitution a momentum toward true democracy from which the country can never escape unless it throws out the Constitution itself.

AS: Some of the themes you describe here—the idea that history is not created by a few great men, but that they are as much products of the historical moment; your insistence on, even preoccupation with, the process
of democracy—are elements of your play, *The Constitutional Convention*,
even though it takes a wildly different approach and form. How are they
connected?

CLM: While I was working on the books, thinking about constitutions and
conventions and rules and laws, I was thinking about these same things
in a more general and modern way. The play is about conventions and
rules of all kinds: social rules, rules of politeness, rules between partners
in sadomasochistic relationships. The play is meant to make you think of
the many rules you live by, most of them unconscious, and the way those
rules constrict our freedoms. Rules of what is done and what isn't done,
what is acceptable behavior and what is rude behavior—all become techniques of political control. At the same time, there's a disintegration of
those rules so that we end up today with a society in which it's not quite
true that there are no rules. It may rather be that there are too many rules
that are in conflict with one another. On the one hand, that creates chaos,
and on the other, liberation. It is the strain of living under both chaos
and liberation that is such an enormous, stressful burden for people.

AS: It seems you've built that chaos and liberation—which you also get with
the final image of the piece, a man running, either toward something he
can't wait to get to, or away from something terrifying—into the very
structure of the play with the insertion of performance art bits, and your
choice of music.

CLM: The performance art pieces seem to me like facets of the modern
world. They're hard to accommodate or make coherent, but somehow
they all exist. The world is all these pieces that don't go together. So they
just slam in there. They come from the wings, perform, and then leave,
and you just have to deal with it, make something out of it, or figure out it
does belong or doesn't belong, follows from what went before or doesn't
follow. Just like life.

The piece is meant to have music by John Zorn, which to me is the
greatest liberated music we have today. When I saw him at BAM, he had
fifty people onstage—electric guitarists, drummers, people with Chinese
instruments and African instruments, a vocalist yelling and screaming
and carrying on. Zorn conducted in a way, cueing somebody in to do
their thing, then another to do their thing, and so on. And it's this wild,
hair-raising, cacaphonous mess that finally leaves you feeling completely
exhilarated and joyful. It's chaotic, but in this wonderful way, and that's

really the promise of liberation. So I guess the play takes people through all this and tries not to conclude for them whether they should be more frightened by the chaos or thrilled by the liberation.

AS: In one case, then, you're writing about the way consensus is arrived at, and in another, how it disintegrates, but both works are interested in a kind of disjunction. While the book takes a straight narrative form, the play, though full of little parallel narratives characters might recount, is completely nondiscursive. How is it that writing about history for the stage or in a prose account suggests one form or another, or makes a formal approach more available or likely?

CLM: The truth is I feel schizophrenic. I was trying to write *The Genius of the People* for a certain audience and trying to present an argument in a way that seemed sort of sober and sound. That audience is middle America. The book was published by Harper and Row and picked up by the Book-of-the-Month Club. Perhaps there is a certain way to write for that audience. When I write a play, though, I don't think about the audience at all. I think of pleasing myself. I don't feel any constraints or need to be reliable or responsible. The narrative form of history is constraining; it's artificial. In a theatre piece, you can go anywhere you want; you can shift perspective. The books that I've written have almost been long preparations for writing plays. *The War to End War* came out of my having written a book about the Versailles peace conference of 1919. It also comes out of the feeling that I never got it right in the book because that nineteenth-century Newtonian cause-effect construction of narrative is a lie about how history happens.

AS: Using that language—Newtonian, cause-effect, nineteenth century—you could be talking about naturalistic theatre. In a way, you are. Your history books set the stage, introduce the characters, and then they speak, working out conflicts within an established situation. You can almost see little prosceniums around them. You could even say that your books were your naturalistic plays. Does that have to do with the nature of historical narrative itself?

CLM: Maybe it's just because I started writing plays in a very particular way—with no hope of having them produced. Years ago I wrote plays and wanted to become the greatest American playwright. Then that didn't work and I quit writing for the theatre for twenty years. One day I was throwing away a novel I'd worked on for an entire year that had been stillborn, and then I thought, there are a couple of little things that I don't want to forget. And so I sat down at the typewriter just to make notes of these things and they took the form of a trilogy of one-act plays.

That's just how they came out. I figured I'd put it in the drawer, and that would be the end of it. All the plays I've written since have come out of that same instinct: I'm going to write this for myself so that I like it. I'm fifty years old. I'm too old to care about being a success anymore.

AS: And yet you have sent the plays around and came close to having a production of *The Investigation Into the Murder in El Salvador* at the Public Theater this year.

CLM: The Public held onto the play for three years, saying they were going to do it, and I shouldn't take it anywhere else. JoAnne Akalaitis was going to direct it. Then they dropped it. They might be interested again, but the only way I would give a piece to Joe Papp would be if he gave me $250,000 up front, which I would refund after he opened the piece, and if it didn't open, I'd use the money to produce it elsewhere. Now the play's in the hands of Lewis Allen, who produced *Annie* on Broadway—so he knows how to produce large, expensive shows and has interesting taste. He's also worked with Peter Brook, Truffaut, and Peter Sellars. He's trying to find a way to produce all four pieces of mine under the general title *The American Century.* His hope is to get some done at individual theatres and then bring them all together at some festival, perhaps L.A. The fact is, there aren't that many theatres that could do these plays—the Guthrie maybe, the A.R.T. (Brustein is interested if he can get Robert Wilson to direct), La Jolla, perhaps the Goodman. They're expensive. And they need directors like JoAnne or Wilson or Robert Woodruff, who's also interested.

AS: In addition to the size and expense, is there something about the way you treat history and politics that most of our theatres just don't know how to deal with? Are they so locked into a conventional way of dealing with such topics, if they deal with them at all? Do people not want to, or perhaps not know how to, talk about history in a complex way, and might that be a function of the continued dominance of psychological naturalism?

CLM: What we really mean by history is the historical condition—politics, economics, society, and the interaction of those things, and how they shape individual and collective lives. But most of our theatre excludes that understanding of history, so it actually makes us stupid and ignorant of the conditions under which we live because it focuses on psychological interactions. It sets a frame of discourse in which you cannot have historical perspective, and therefore makes it impossible to arrive at political understanding. In a political play written according to the rules of psychological naturalism, it's possible for you to achieve political passion, but not political understanding. As soon as you say two plus two, you've entered mathematical discourse and within that frame, you can't make an aesthetic observation. It's the same with psychological realism. Once you've entered that frame of discourse, there are certain modes of understanding that are excluded. Once you decide that the basic truth about human relationships is psychology, you can no longer understand anything else. You can be led up to the gate where you see just beyond it is another world, another understanding. But you can only stand there and be angry or self-pitying or hopeful or despairing. You can have all sorts of emotional reactions, but you can't have political understanding.

AS: So how can the theatre give you political understanding?

CLM: True political theatre would take human relationships as a part of a larger set of relationships. It wouldn't exclude the private world as trivial or meaningless, but see it as part of a continuum that goes from private to public. All relationships play off against each other, affect one another, shape one another. Instead of traditional political plays where issues are confronted head on by characters who take different sides, which seems simple-minded to me, or psychological realism, which takes the status quo as a given, imagine a play written simply with a different set of assumptions. How would that play look? Write a play, say, that simply *assumes* capitalism is an exploitative economic system rather than tries to prove it.

I also have to say that psychological realism is just too pokey for people in the twentieth century. We're too smart for it. Think of television. You're watching these guys on "Miami Vice" and there's a commercial break and suddenly you're in Paris with an automobile, and then you switch to the Arctic where you're smoking cigarettes, and then you're back in some other narrative line and you have to decide whether that commercial for Pepsi Cola really does or doesn't bear on the national psychology that helped elect Ronald Reagan. So you're taking in information that is sometimes relevant, sometimes irrelevant, and all the time you're following six or eight narrative lines simultaneously. We do that and call it relaxing. Whereas you walk into the theatre and most plays give you a single narrative line for two-and-a-half hours. It's just not interesting enough, and it's definitely not real, not the way things are occurring today.

Now I don't want to get too ahistorical here. When naturalism developed it was shocking and revolutionary, a great step in the democratization of the theatre. It argued that the everyday life of ordinary people was worth paying attention to in the theatre. But what has happened politically is that it stopped at the middle class. It's astounding that there is no recent great naturalistic play about the homeless, or about the truly dispossessed. It's the duty of naturalism to explore their lives as three-dimensional characters.

AS: Instead, though, such characters are only treated as symbolic and sentimental. If the audience is bourgeois and the whole mechanism of naturalism is identification, that's all you can possibly get. It's all about assuring the audience that they aren't that bad off so it's safe to feel sympathetic in the theatre. It seems to be a particularly American failure of the form.

CLM: At the same time the dispossessed aren't being truly represented. There still exists the idea that history is created by a few great men. I don't think that all theatre needs to be informed by the new history or deal out of that sensibility, but I do think it should start from the understanding that history is created from the bottom up, not from the top down.

AS: I was just reading about Gertrude Himmelfarb's new book [*The New History and the Old*] that trashes the new history. There were a couple of things she says that interested me in terms of what's happening, or could be happening, in the theatre. She says that one result of the new history, which overemphasizes sociology or economics or psychology or Marxist determinism, all to the exclusion of politics, is that the sense of a narrative in history gets lost. She complains that people don't have a sense anymore of one event leading to another, or of a continuity of narrative movement. You could apply this directly to recent experimental theatre and come up with an ordinary postmodern analysis about the breakdown of linear connection. I think that has particular bearing on history's relationship to theatrical form. We've moved quite far from Brecht's epic structure in your plays.

CLM: I think they are related. That things don't have narratives shouldn't be seen as a criticism, because the world doesn't have a narrative anymore. The notion that history should have a narrative derives from the notion of a Newtonian universe where you have a certain set of causes and effects to be discovered. Gertrude Himmelfarb and Jacques Barzun probably think that they will turn out to be rational, ordered, structured. But if you're dealing with a world where those orders and structures are disintegrating or being purposefully destroyed, then you won't have an old-fashioned narrative. Indeed, to understand the world of the past you are often better off dispensing with the artifice of narrative and working with the artifices of such new historians as Braudel, Le Roy Ladurie, Peter Laslett, Robert Darnton, and Carlo Ginzburg. I remember something Jonathan Marks once said about Robert Wilson's work: most traditional plays take a body of material and the job of the playwright is to carve a channel through that material so the audience can follow through it and experience the material. Whereas Robert Wilson takes you into something more like a river delta where there are many rivulets running to the sea and you choose which rivulet you want to follow, and all choices are equally valid. This structure strikes me as being more democratic.

AS: Why call that democratic?

CLM: Traditionally a playwright is godlike and organizes the audience's view of the universe. It's authoritarian; it's given to you and you take it or leave it, and you have to take it because you're sitting there and the doors are closed. All these old narrative structures are in some fundamental way authoritarian. Part of the struggle in the arts is to figure out a way for a person sitting alone in a room to come up with a structure that allows other people to take part in the making of the experience.

AS: I think it's exaggerated to call that authoritarian and something else democratic. Certainly a play itself determines, demonstrates, and teaches the audience through its style how it's to be taken as it's going along. But there is always some kind of collaboration of the imagination in it, and always some kind of guidance. At the same time, for the sake of argument at least, you could say that the principle of democracy that you equate with participation does take place in naturalistic theatre, at least insofar as participation in democracy happens by virtue of representation.

CLM: Rousseau said once you vote you've given away democracy. But you're right. I'm saying extreme things. As long as there is an individual who sits down and puts words together that will set up a situation and set the terms of the discourse the audience will engage in, there's no way to escape some sort of leading, guiding role. But there is a big difference between opening up options to people that they may or may not choose to follow and deciding there is only one way through the material. I think that is what most playwriting since Ibsen does—that's the modern theatre.

AS: True enough, perhaps, but you seem to be defining democracy in a dangerously broad way. You're equating it with a kind of groundless relativism that says all options are equally valid. I hate to say it, but it makes me think of Allan Bloom's hateful book, *The Closing of the American Mind.*

In his critique of liberalism, which blames the sixties for everything that's wrong in America and in education, he argues that a relativism of values, the supposition that any point of view is as good as any other, has caused the demise of the Republic. While his conclusions are completely reactionary, I recognize a lot of his observations, especially about undergraduates, because I teach at Baruch College. It's true they have little sense of history, and that often they back off from arguing through an issue with the simple dismissive summation, "Well, you're entitled to your opinion and I'm entitled to mine," as if that's all that ever needs to be conceded, or even examined. And they apply this not only to politics, but to literature. It's so ingrained that they have a very difficult time trying to grasp the notion that it's possible to go astray in a reading, say, of a poem. And I don't mean this in any sophisticated Derridean sense.

CLM: Intellectually, we're entering an age in which people are going to be so much smarter than they've ever been, so much more sophisticated, subtler, complex, and suppler in the way they consider things that it will take Allan Bloom's head off. And the reason for this is that we've dropped a lot of old structures, authorities, and hierarchies, and we're moving into a realm of incredible intellectual freedom, experiment, and adventure. It has made it harder to keep a cohesive and coherent society to train workers—and that's really what you're talking about at Baruch, not educating thinkers. When the traditional educational hierarchies disintegrate, it makes it much harder to train job holders to perform nine-to-five jobs because they share in the general cultural disintegration. But it makes it easier for artists, thinkers, political theorists, economists, and others to arrive at extraordinary new ideas.

AS: I'll buy that people know more than ever, but in some ways they also know less, especially about history. Going back to Himmelfarb, one thing she blames this on is the New History's tendency to make different elements of the culture equivalent in importance. She disparagingly quotes the radical cultural historian Warren Susman, who says that to understand the thirties it may be more important to understand Mickey Mouse than FDR. Again, this seems to describe a lot of new work in the theatre where pop icons are used, and have almost taken over as a way of evoking a period. Your plays use such icons and images of historical personages to evoke, I think, a cultural attitude which you could say is itself as much a character as any of the people onstage. I wonder when such figures are used if an audience can even recognize them. Would an audience know FDR onstage?

CLM: Maybe not. But I don't think I'd have recognized Warren Harding on-stage when I was in college. I graduated in 1960 and Harding was president in 1920—that's forty years' difference. The statement that it's more important to know Mickey Mouse than FDR is on one level obviously a yahoo statement. But if you understood Donald Duck as it's been written about in Marxist analysis, you might understand more than if you just knew that FDR was president and made an inaugural address and was nice and smoked cigarettes. Who cares? This is meaningless information. So it's possible if you thoroughly understand a symbol of popular culture to understand something very profound.

AS: What about the historical figures in your plays? Can you say something, then, about how these figures function? They seem different, for instance, from Robert Wilson's use of characters, such as Stalin or Frederick the Great, who are not really personages but vague reminders of something.

CLM: The way I see them is as representative of certain attitudes, social and historical positions, and political ideas. The movement of my four plays goes from *War to End War*, which includes historical characters who are fairly representative, to the El Salvador piece, where characters descend from the ruling class to upper-middle-class civilians, and then to the next piece, which is the *Constitutional Convention*, to the final piece, *Imperialists at Club Cave Canem*, and by the time you're there, you've gotten to the middle- or lower-middle-class people who are hanging out in the East Village. So you've gone from the leadership class to ordinary people in the course of these four pieces. The people at the end think about daily life but are totally politically and historically unconscious, whereas one can't say that about Wilson and Clemenceau. Yet these are three-dimensional characters. It's just that unlike the characters you see in naturalistic plays, these are characters who have been taken and smashed on the floor like drinking glasses, and then a few shards of that glass are picked up and put onstage.

AS: Would you include *Nixon in China* as a piece that's looking at history just through its major figures? Do you think it deals with history at all?

CLM: I think it's dealing with history in a marvelous way, but in a completely different way. I loved that piece. It was so staggeringly, elaborately, expensively banal. Two great world leaders meet and do *nothing*. And they make boring speeches at each other. This incredible historic opportunity occurs and passes without a dent being made on the reality or consciousness of the world. As *Boris Godunov* is a great nineteenth-century opera where some incredible figure bestrides the world and blood flows and the earth is shaken, here you have everything to make an opera just like that and instead you have blandness upon blandness.

AS: Maybe this goes back to our disagreement about authoritarianism as a way to describe the artist's role. But what I took to be an absence of point of view in *Nixon*, you took to be its very subject. That's such a tricky question, especially when you're talking about politics. Robert Wilson is the greatest example of this problematics. To pick up on your image from before, do you think his *CIVIL warS* offers rivulets that have some sort of historical or political significance or strike off any specific associations in those directions?

CLM: I'm not sure whether Wilson has either a historical or a political mind, or whether he uses history as history. In a way I think he uses history just to get his pieces a large space to play in.

AS: I worry about the postmodern way history has become an image heap for the theatre, especially for a lot of younger theatre artists. There's this idea that there is a sea of icons and you can pick one from here, one from there and it will be something called evocative. In your pieces you seem to use symbols with a sense of precision, but also in a kind of haphazard way because there's so much disjointed information coming at you at once. In *War to End War*, for instance, there are politicians, nuclear physicists, a Dada dance performance, people from the Third World.

CLM: Yes. I'm trying to throw in images and music and other events to invite people to let their minds roam over the material—not only the material that's onstage, but the material that these other things will make them think about. In *War to End War* all those images invite an audience to consider the nature of war, why people go to war. It doesn't try to lead them to a conclusion about that, but to consider to what extent it is rooted in human nature or psychology, in economics, and in inevitable scientific progress. People have to find their own way through and arrive at their own conclusions. This is a democratic process, a participatory process. The pieces are suggesting that this is the process we have to follow politically.

AS: You sound like Brecht—you're saying your plays are a rehearsal for the audience, that theatre is a place for them to practice a certain kind of thinking about the world, in this case, the democratic process.

CLM: Yes. And what I mean by democracy is people coming together as equal citizens to deal with the issues that concern them, and without any set of previous authoritarian agreements.

AS: As much as I just compared you to Brecht, there's also a Chekhovian, sort of *Cherry Orchard* sensibility to your plays, a feeling of an old order dying out as the new century approaches.

CLM: I think this society's days are numbered, and that's ultimately the historical condition of the country. But it's my society, so I feel a little bit nostalgic. This is my family. This is my childhood. It's going, it's just going.

Philip Glass

ALTHOUGH PHILIP GLASS was well known to new music aficionados for his loft concerts in New York in the early seventies and to habitués of the theatrical avant-garde for his musical scores for Mabou Mines productions, it wasn't until 1976 that he came to greater public attention with *Einstein on the Beach,* an opera on which he collaborated with director Robert Wilson. Until then, Glass was primarily a composer of instrumental works shaped by his exposure to the rhythmic intricacies of Indian music while working with the Indian sitarist Ravi Shankar. Performed mostly by himself or by The Philip Glass Ensemble, these early compositions, including *Music in Twelve Parts* and *Another Look at Harmony,* were considered in the context of minimalism, although Glass's lush sounds and rhythmic complexities seem to belie such attribution. He was grouped together with composers Steve Reich, Terry Riley, and La Monte Young as creators of a new sound. Increasingly, Glass's filmic compositions, starting with *Koyaanisqatsi* in 1982, have earned him a wider public as an avatar of trance or New Age music. His work on Martin Scorsese's epic 1997 film *Kundun,* for which Glass received an Oscar nomination for "Best Original Score," links his unique harmonic style to the spiritual dimension of Tibetan music.

Although he claims to have gotten into opera accidentally, Glass went on to create other works after *Einstein,* including *Satyagraha, Akhnaten,* and *The Voyage,* the latter commissioned by the Metropolitan Opera in New York in 1992. As he points out to John Howell, at the time a frequent contributor to *Performing Arts Journal,* the operas mark a decisive break with the historical tradition of operatic writing, which is based on literary sources; his grew out of a background in the non-narrative, image-based theatre of the sixties and seventies. Realizing that his radical approach could pose a problem to singers accustomed to traditional ways of working, Glass enumerates the various strategies he employed to make them receptive to his challenge. Here he elaborates on his attraction to historic or mythic figures like Gandhi and abstract ideas like nonviolence as subjects for his operas, in addition to his penchant for esoteric languages, such as Sanskrit in *Satyagraha* or solfège and numbers in *Einstein,* as the basis of his libretti. GD

Conversation with John Howell, 1981

Composing for the Opera

John Howell: Why do you think very few composers have worked in both opera and concert music at the same time?

Philip Glass: Is that true? There's Mozart, Beethoven did one opera, Dvorak wrote about nine . . .

JH: Handel, Britten too, but the list is very short. I know you've written vocal music since the beginning of your composing career.

PG: I wrote a lot of vocal music when I was just out of music school. Within the first two years after I left Juilliard, I wrote some twenty choral pieces, so I was pretty well prepared when I began writing *Satyagraha.* Of course, I had written that big choral piece for the Carnegie Hall concert in 1978, *Another Look at Harmony, Part 4,* and there was a lot of choral music in *Einstein on the Beach.* So I've done a lot of vocal music but it's not that well known because most people associate me with Ensemble music.

JH: When I met you, you were making up pieces for *The Saint and the Football Players,* and had already written music for *The Red Horse Animation* and for *Music for Voices,* all for Mabou Mines. So I thought of you as a vocal composer as well because you didn't seem to make any distinctions between vocal and instrumental music composition.

PG: Writing for voices is kind of a specialty, it takes a long time to learn how to do it. There's a lot to be learned about the voice and I'm still learning. *Satyagraha* is the most vocal piece that I've done in the sense that the voices really stand out as voices and are not used instrumentally. With the Ensemble, the voices are used in an instrumental way, but by *Dance 5,* the voice has separated from the Ensemble. That happened partly because I began to work more and more with people who had legitimate vocal training.

JH: You used to avoid those people.

PG: Yes. For the most part, singers work within a very limited range of music and sing in a certain style that is not appropriate for my music. With the *Einstein on the Beach* music, I was working with nonsingers and I got out of them what I wanted, but there were real limitations in what they could do. Since *Satyagraha* was commissioned by an opera house, I was given trained singers, and at that point I addressed myself to the problems and possibilities of real vocal writing. Then what I tried to do was to convey the style of singing I wanted in the opera, and I was more or less successful. Doug Perry has a beautiful, clear tenor and I can find nothing wrong with the way he sings. With some of the others, it was a problem to get them to adapt to the kind of very extended singing that was required. For example, I didn't want heavy vibrato or warbling onstage.

JH: Does all of that come under the heading of bel canto?

PG: Generally speaking it derives from bel canto although my knowledge of opera history and tradition is pretty sketchy.

JH: In your vocal work for Mabou Mines, you asked for a reasonable voice and good timing, not training.

PG: But in the preparation of those pieces, they had to undergo rudimentary vocal training. We did a lot of singing to get the actors to be able to sing at all. I did that with the *Einstein* people too; we began every session with vocal exercises. There were some professional singers in that company and we had a vocal coach, Gene Ricard, for the others. So we did prepare their voices even if they were untrained. It's very hard to take someone who has no vocal training and have them sing for any length of time on the same pitch. They just don't know how to breathe, and being able to sing with someone else, to be able to tune the notes—that's all part of basic training. With people who regularly work in an opera tradition, which is the case with the Brooklyn cast, those aren't problems at all. But there are other problems, like conveying a unique style and convincing them that it's a legitimate pursuit.

JH: So you're trying to redirect operatic vocal technique?

PG: It's not the technique but the mentality that's a problem. It's when a singer says, "How do I know who I am if I'm not saying it in words?" "How do I create my character if I don't have literal actions?" For singers, creating character is an important part of what they do, and operatic acting is unlike any other kind of acting in theatre. So there are special problems in the music itself, then other problems in the presentation of character on the stage; how do they create that character if the text or scene doesn't relate to who they are?

JH: You mean relate directly and literally, don't you?

PG: Yeah. Here we're using the *Bhagavad-Gita*, which is an allegorical Indian religious text, and it serves as a commentary on the action, like a subtext. So the cues for the singers' characters have to come directly from the stage action. I also told them that since we were dealing with historical persons they could find out who those persons were. There are writings about them, photographs, descriptions. They weren't imaginary people but real ones.

JH: So you ran up against the tradition of operatic acting as well as of operatic vocal technique. Many contemporary composers would probably ignore or attack those conventions. Yet here you are with two operas to your credit.

PG: I got into opera by accident. I backed into it by working with Robert Wilson. We did *Einstein* which, whether or not it was an opera, could only be done in an opera house. I didn't really care what people called it, we performed in opera houses, opera people came to see it and one of these people was Hans De Roo of the Netherlands Opera. He was not convinced by *Einstein,* but he was certainly intrigued enough to ask me if I would like to write "a real opera." I said sure, I had an idea for an opera, and that's how I got commissioned to do *Satyagraha.* But had that not happened, it's doubtful that I would have written another opera. Because of the success of *Einstein* and the obvious theatricality of it both in Bob's work and mine, De Roo was willing to take a chance. Of course it's a big gamble for him. He commissioned a piece from a man who had never written "a real opera" before, he committed himself to a major world premiere and a big expenditure of their annual production money, so I give De Roo a lot of credit. There are a lot of problems with opera and I can see a lot of reasons why people wouldn't want to do it at all. For one thing, the tradition is so moribund, who would want to get involved with it? When you walk into an opera house, you're walking back a hundred years, and you're dealing with people who are quite happy back there. Most of the repertory comes from the nineteenth century and that's what they want to do: Verdi, Donizetti, maybe a token modern piece like Menotti. Because of singing this confined Italian literature, people learn roles and they go through their career, doing this or that part for different companies. Many singers aren't willing to take on the challenge of creating a new character. All this is more true in America than in Europe, where there's more of a tradition of contemporary opera. There's another obstacle: Who wants to write an opera which at best opera companies are reluctant to stage? There aren't too many people who will write an opera and put it in their drawer hoping someone will do it. So then you get into this Catch-22! How do you get commissioned to write an opera if you haven't written one?

JH: The *Satyagraha* gamble paid off, didn't it?

PG: I never doubted that it would, but you try and convince somebody before doing it and that's a different game. A lot of people have great ideas, it's getting someone to do them that's the problem. From the beginning, Hans was interested and intrigued, and committed himself to a production very quickly after our first conversations. I think that he's happy with the way it turned out. It takes people with that kind of courage to do new opera, and in America I can't think of anyone like that in a major opera house at the moment. There are people who will produce work but they're not opera people, like Harvey Lichtenstein at Brooklyn Academy of Music, and David Midland up at Artpark, and there may be others.

JH: Did you have the same kind of problems with the orchestra that you did with the singers?

PG: Oh yes, we had quite a few problems. First, I had written a lot of orchestral music, I think the last piece when I was twenty-five. By then, I had written a violin concerto, two or three symphony-type pieces, pieces for strings. When I began writing for the Ensemble, which I did because no one would play my music, there was simply no one to play the orchestra music so I didn't write any for eleven or twelve years. Not until *Satyagraha* did I have the opportunity. In fact, I think that Hans wasn't even sure that I could. If you heard my music between '65 and '79, you wouldn't know I could write for an orchestra because I didn't write any orchestra music. At any rate, I produced the *Satyagraha* score, and we had quite a go-around about that. Bruce Ferden, our conductor in Holland, had quite a time persuading the orchestra to do the music at all. They almost couldn't rehearse the last act, people just refused and walked out of the pit. Even in Stuttgart where we had a much better orchestra I remember one rehearsal in which the clarinetist tied a handkerchief to his clarinet and waved it. Now the Buffalo orchestra which we had at Artpark played with almost what you could call enthusiasm. Because it was an American orchestra I think it was more recognizable to them in an idiomatic way.

JH: What do musicians object to in your music?

PG: The way it's written. The kind of continuity that's required throws them. They sight read the score and think it's impossible where, in fact, what you do is to trade off parts: people take breaths at different times and they just arrange to do that. There's a way of splitting the music up among the people so that I can get the continuity the music requires and not kill the players to get it. Of course I was aware of that when I wrote the music, but when musicians look at the score for the first time they say, "What's this?"

JH: On tape, the orchestra sounds like your "sound."

PG: That's an interesting point. When I was younger I asked myself, "What can I make the orchestra do?" This time I thought, "What can I make the orchestra do to sound like my music?" As a twenty-five-year-old composer I was trying to discover the orchestra, to find out what it was able to do. At thirty-nine I had already created a sound image that was so clear

that the question was how to bend the orchestra to produce that image.
In a simplistic way, I tried to make the orchestra sound like the Ensemble.

JH: I think you succeeded.

PG: I think so too. For example, you almost never hear an instrument by
itself. If you hear a clarinet you're hearing a clarinet and a flute. All the
timbres are mixed. I wasn't interested in solo writing but in the mixed
timbres that I had become accustomed to working with in the Ensemble.
That whole style of orchestration can be called, by modern standards,
either very reactionary or very radical, depending on which point of view
you want to take. It's definitely not post-Ravel, post-Rimsky-Korsakov
orchestration in which you listen to the brilliance of the instruments. My
intention was to make the orchestra disappear into the music to create an
overall sound. When you look at the score, it looks wrong, it doesn't look
like an orchestration is supposed to look, but when you hear it, you hear
a sound that you haven't heard before, which is what's interesting for me.

JH: If you've heard the Ensemble, you've heard something like it.

PG: That's right. People familiar with the Ensemble music will recognize
the sound.

JH: It surprised me that the voices sounded so good in that kind of orchestration.

PG: There's no problem with hearing the voices, they come through very
well. There's always the problem of balance when you're mixing voices
with instruments, but that can largely be solved by a very astute conductor. In fact conductors often have the burden of that problem. If
Christopher Keene, our conductor at Brooklyn, hears that a voice is being
covered, he knows how to balance things from the pit. On the whole, I
find that I had not created unsolvable problems in the *Satyagraha* music.
I had created some moments that needed sensitive conducting, but you
hear the voices quite well.

JH: Earlier you said you didn't know much about opera, but *Satyagraha*
corresponds to some operatic traditions. For example, there's "opera
seria," a three-act opera on a serious subject which was an innovation in
eighteenth-century Italy, and Wagnerian *Gesamtkunstwerk, leitmotiv,* continuous orchestral music, and mythic subject matter, all used or alluded
to in *Satyagraha.*

PG: That's been pointed out to me, that there are historical operatic periods
that this opera corresponds to, but it isn't my intention to revive any antique forms. At some point in my music studies years ago, I had to study
that stuff, but at the time I was studying composition and was not interested in opera, so my survey of the opera literature was very cursory.

JH: Some of those operatic features are hardly definitive since it's not un-usual, for example, for drama to have three acts.

PG: It's also been pointed out [by Andrew Porter, *New Yorker*, August 17, 1981] that there are strong resemblances to the structural principles of Monteverdi's operas. But by now there's so much history that you're bound to sound like somebody here and there. I never set out to cre-ate a totally original form and it doesn't surprise me that I unwittingly come close to music done years ago. After all, theatre is theatre and there are only so many ways you can put something onstage. Certain formulas come up again and again. For example, three acts seems a comfortable form for this material, so why not use it?

JH: Are there more parallels between *Satyagraha* and older operas than with newer, twentieth-century ones?

PG: Certainly contemporary opera has not been a big success although there's been a lot written. The operas we hear the most are Benjamin Britten's and, recently, Berg's at the Met.

JH: What about their Brecht-Weill *Mahagonny?*

PG: That's a conceit of the Met to do that. I'm not saying the work doesn't belong there, but I don't think that Brecht and Weill ever intended it to be there. That the Met puts it on has more to do with how they like to think of themselves than what the authors intended. I think there's a kind of exploitation involved, and it's being done at the expense of works that might more legitimately be there.

JH: What do you think of Britten operas?

PG: I don't like them very much. He writes in the grand tradition.

JH: What about Berg?

PG: I'm not sure that those operas are so successful, certainly *Lulu* wasn't for me. *Wozzeck* seems to work better, it's actually a pretty opera. In 1959 I thought it was a very radical work, charged with emotion and daring ideas. By 1979, I thought of it as a very lyrical work, very pretty, and a bit inconsequential. That's a minority view of Berg, since most other com-posers consider him the major operatic composer of our day. I certainly don't.

JH: You don't even think *Lulu* is pretty?

PG: I just don't like it, and I'm not the only one.

JH: Who do you think is the audience for all these recent *Lulu* productions?

PG: I wonder if that wasn't just some publisher pushing it off on the world, if there weren't some heavy financial interests involved in the promotion of that opera. I have dark suspicions about all those *Lulu* productions be-cause it's just not an appealing work. Arguably, it's an important work, but it depends on who's doing the arguing. So those Berg operas aren't an issue in contemporary opera for me, nor are the Britten operas because I don't feel that they're fully contemporary in any way.

JH: Does that have anything to do with your theatre background?

PG: It's important to remember that my background in theatre is non-narrative theatre. My first contact with new theatre was The Living Theatre in 1957, and after that came The Performance Group, Meredith Monk, Robert Wilson, Richard Foreman, Joseph Chaikin, and Mabou Mines, all theatre that rarely began with a literary source. When I began doing operas, it never occurred to me to take a play and set it to music although that's how operas are written. I never did that because my theatre tradition is the nonliterary tradition by my friends and associates which is all around me and my work in New York.

JH: When you worked with Bob Wilson, his theatre and your music shared an aesthetic point of view.

PG: They are extremely close, and *Satyagraha* was a development of that way of working. Almost all opera composers start with the play and set it to music. With *Satyagraha* I worked with a writer, Constance DeJong, but we worked on scenes and the action together, getting an overall shape for the opera, and also we worked with the designer Robert Israel, who had a large say in the dramatic shape of the opera. So we worked as a team on what we called the book.

JH: How did you decide what the singers sing?

PG: The lyrics were adapted from the *Bhagavad-Gita* by DeJong, whose job it was to find the passages that were relevant to the scene we were looking at and to work with me on what seemed appropriate. Also we discussed how much we could expect people to memorize because memorizing a language you don't know is much more difficult. So even though I worked with a writer, there was never any question of starting with a finished literary object and setting it.

JH: Yet you've written the score itself within certain operatic traditions.

PG: I made a point of writing duets, trios, quintets. There's a lot of operatic stuff in there, but it doesn't sound the same in *Satyagraha*. There are reasons to do that; for example, singers are trained to sing together and good ensemble singing sounds good, and I availed myself of those conventions when they suited my needs.

JH: *Satyagraha*'s language is Sanskrit, a cliché for an esoteric language, and I would think that current opera audiences often don't know the language of the opera they're listening to, but did you ever think of doing it in English?

PG: Real opera buffs will not accept that argument. They say, "Of course we know what they're singing, and if you don't, you're some kind of buffoon." My motivation for separating language into two components, sound and meaning, which is a conscious separation on our part, is that I felt to hear the words sung demystified the experience. I prefer to have the meaning and the sense of the drama conveyed by images and sound. I felt that putting the words on the images and sound overliteralized the experience and made it less interesting. For example, in one scene in *Satyagraha* the characters burn their registration cards: they hold up the cards, walk over to a black pot, and throw them in. Now they're singing a language we don't understand, Sanskrit, but I picked a language that is a vocal language, one of the main languages of the vocal literature of South India, and it has a beautiful sound. Now what if, when they walk over and put their cards in the pot they sing, "We are now putting our cards in the pot"?

JH: Couldn't they have said something less literal, maybe more abstract, and said it in English?

PG: Well, I had another experience that convinced me not to do that. I saw Britten's *Billy Budd* in English about two years ago and I understood maybe 40 percent of what people sang. Most of the time I was in an agony trying to understand the other 60 percent. It definitely limited my ability to experience the opera. You can relax in *Satyagraha* since you don't have to understand the words.

JH: Language is just one level in any opera.

PG: DeJong, Israel, and myself consider that *Satyagraha* exists on three levels: one, the idea that the main gist is conveyed by images and music; two, that if someone was interested in knowing what was being sung, the text was provided in the program; third, there's a whole historical social context in which the opera exists, and the book produced by Standard Editions was meant to supply that kind of information. It's up to listeners to decide to what extent they want to listen. The idea of untying language from meaning is perhaps a novel idea, maybe even a subversive one for opera, but it's one that's given me a lot of freedom in the way I work. Also, it's one that comes from my experience in nonliterary theatre. With Mabou Mines, for example, it's not necessary to understand every word, and often language works as sound along with image rather than as meaning.

JH: So your problem with trained singers is compounded by a staging that gives them as few clues as Sanskrit.

PG: The nonliterary theatre doesn't exist for opera people, they don't even know it happened. By the end of the production in Holland, though, our company had all gotten well involved in the piece in the way I had intended. So this mode of presenting characters onstage seems to be a learnable experience.

JH: I know you've had a personal interest in India for a long time, but why present Gandhi as an opera subject?

PG: I'd been to India several times and I couldn't help but find out who Gandhi was: he's on the money, his picture is in every post office, the style of dress that he identified with himself is common among a certain generation of Indians. I came on Gandhi in the natural course of going to India. Of course he's not merely an Indian national but an important figure in world history, so I don't think it's a particularly Indian opera.

JH: What about the use of the *Bhagavad-Gita?*

PG: That was Gandhi's favorite book, the one he measured his actions against and referred to constantly, so that became a natural choice, it's not an imposition of mine.

JH: You've also chosen to present what is, for most people, a relatively un-known part of his life, which is his work in South Africa, a very topical Anglo-Third World subject.

PG: That's part of the opera's interest. Those years in South Africa were when Gandhi created himself. He went there as an English lawyer, a barrister, in a pinstripe suit, and he comes out looking like the Gandhi we know. After that, all the events that unfolded in India were inevi-table given the character who left South Africa in 1914, but they certainly weren't from the character who left India in 1893. There was no way of knowing that the man who left then would come back and change that part of the world and really change the world for most of us.

JH: Gandhi in South Africa has to be a blank subject for maybe 99 percent of your audience.

PG: I suppose so, and it's particularly interesting because of contemporary events in South Africa. In fact, Gandhi's place in South African history is almost forgotten whereas his main adversary, General Smuts, is one of the national heroes of the country. And the events of South Africa in the late nineteenth century have repeated themselves in a much more devas-tating way in recent years.

JH: The Dutch were in South Africa, too.

PG: I asked De Roo how he felt about a Dutch opera company commission-ing a piece about this situation in South Africa between the Dutch and the Indian community, and he said that the contemporary Dutch don't feel that much connection to the Boers. But I've talked to other people who have relatives in South Africa who've said that wasn't exactly true. So showing this story in Holland was quite a curious twist, a kind of ironic and lucky accident in a way because perhaps it made *Satyagraha* more relevant to them somehow.

JH: *Satyagraha*'s subject is a near-legendary person and a very idealistic idea, nonviolence. How did you choose material which fit that concept?

PG: The intention is certainly toward an epic form. I was conscious of it, and that goes well with my music which, because of its non-narrative flow, tends to hint or allude to some kind of nonordinary experiences. To turn the music to the uses of mythic or epic theatre seems particularly appropriate. I didn't have to alter my aesthetic very radically in any way to take on this epic operatic form.

JH: Do you think of *Satyagraha* as political music, related in any way to a Brecht-Weill tradition in opera?

PG: No, that was a very conscious decision to politicize art. I'm not saying that isn't interesting, but it's not the intention of *Satyagraha*. I didn't set out to write a political opera or a period piece. I got interested in a person who lived at a particular time and who was involved in a certain kind of political activity, but it was not the primary intention of the opera to delineate that political idea or that historical period. Those facts happen to come along with who Gandhi was.

Mac Wellman

After starting out as a poet, Mac Wellman emerged in the eighties as one of a group of playwrights, including Jeff Jones, Eric Overmyer, and Len Jenkin, committed to revitalizing American drama with an impassioned emphasis on language. Proceeding from a firm belief that language and its usage have been woefully debased in our times, he has taken on the standards of Mencken and Bierce, two of his acknowledged literary predecessors, in the fight to reclaim for the American vernacular its unique vitalism and innocence. In this conversation with Marc Robinson, who has written on Wellman in his PAJ volume *The Other American Drama*, the playwright talks of ironically subverting the primacy of "written" language and upholding the virtues of what he terms "bad writing," claiming further that "as soon as you stop writing in the official style, you multiply your aesthetic choices." These choices, familiar to most Wellman readers, range from quirky neologisms and syllogisms to freewheeling satire and parody.

Given his heavy reliance on wordplay and nonrealistic dramaturgy, Wellman's plays have been performed throughout the United States, mainly in theatres devoted to experimental work. And though he has often had to face up to the charge that his plays are, for the most part, engaged in literary pyrotechnics, he sees himself as one who engages "language as gesture," adding that "theatre writing is a kinetic, physical thing . . . there's a physical direction to a sentence or a word, even a physical *feeling*" that goes out into the world. Indeed, Wellman rarely turns away from confronting contemporary issues as the subject of his plays, even as they draw upon his inimitable linguistic resourcefulness. He did come to national prominence, after all, with *7 Blowjobs*, a sarcastic portrait of the government's attempts at artistic censorship. He has written two novels, most recently *Annie Salem*; several of his plays from the past few years have been collected in a PAJ volume entitled *The Bad Infinity*. Wellman remains a fervent champion of a younger generation of playwrights, and his continuing interest in radical styles of dramaturgy resulted in *Theatre of Wonders*, one of two play anthologies by contemporary dramatists edited by him.   GD

Conversation with Marc Robinson, 1992

Figure of Speech

Marc Robinson: We should probably start with the reason we're sitting here tonight: the publication of *Terminal Hip.* Could you talk a bit about the genesis of this play?

Mac Wellman: Terminal Hip is actually the second part of a project called *Cellophane,* which I began about six years ago. It came out of my interest in basic issues of writing and speech. As you know, a good deal of postmodern theory has to do with a reversal of the traditional priority of speech over writing. This comes as quite a surprise for most Americans, because people like Whitman and Emerson have told us that writing is a kind of cancer on speech, and that if you want to find the "authentic" you have to go back to speech. Everybody who's tuned into American poetry has regarded speech as the highest thing, even though none of us really can know what speech is. I began to look at H. L. Mencken and other people who actually studied American traditional speech and realized you could write with it. You could use all the tools that the writerly postmodern people applied to their own sense of language. But the more I began to study out-of-favor American speech, I began to understand how the American language got to be the way it is now.

MR: What aspects of American language fascinated you most?

MW: I'd come across a phrase in Mencken, "If I hadda been"—which is bad language. There was another one—"if I mighta could." It's the kind of stuff that you'd hate if you thought about writing well every waking moment. These horrible statements are things you try to get out of your system. You just look at them and they make your skin crawl. But then I'd put them together, these two phrases—"If I hadda been I mighta could." I thought, How wonderful, this is something you cannot say in any European language I know, or even in English.

I read three volumes of Mencken's *The American Language.* I looked at other books on dialect speech, which are all considered trash by the postmodernists, because they hate speech. But I began to think, Well, what happens if I treat this stuff as raw material?

As soon as language goes out of fashion, two things happen to it. For one thing, the meaning becomes richer. A word or a phrase has all sorts of associations, many of which are unpleasant. But it also rolls off the tongue. Old expressions, jazz-age stuff, anything that's been said by hundreds of thousands of people for over twenty years is far more speakable than anything you can ever write. It's like old wood: it has a texture and a grain to it. That is something that I've never been interested in until recently because I had always wanted to challenge actors, to make constructions that were impossible to say, which I realized I have a talent for.

So I discovered that you can take things that are a little bit dated, and break them into pieces, and put them back together in such a way that they're not dated anymore. They're actually enormously powerful oral systems that had this traditional strength and power that was "mythic." You could also put them together in a way that *was* postmodern—that involved all those very sharp dislocations of meaning—and you could say everything you wanted to about the current culture.

When I was working on the *Cellophane* texts (*Cellophane* and *Terminal Hip*), I wrote one page a day for two-and-a-half years, until I had this big stack of legal pads. I was attempting to make poetry that was *not* for the stage, that was just for me. I was also attempting to write badly, because you get so stuck all the time trying to write well. You get caught up with a degenerate notion of style. There is no place, certainly, for a really *radical* style. You know, we were always taught to believe that anything that was theatrical, that had large emotions, had no ideas in it. When I began writing I wanted to argue with that notion. I began to appreciate ideas directly.

MR: Was it something in your research of American speech that led you to set aside standard dramatic exchange in *Terminal Hip?* The play doesn't seem simply to lack dialogue. The writing is aggressively *anti*dialogue.

MW: I'm not really antidialogue. But it's harder to be very focused on ideas if you're worried about character, which involves breaking speech down into two or three parts, and then having to worry about the consistency of characters. Actually, I wrote my first plays as monologues, and then I broke them down into different characters. I did that to make the dialogue more disjointed. But that's something I haven't done in ten or fifteen years.

I finished the *Cellophane* text in August of 1986—as poetry. I woke up one morning soon after that and wondered what would happen if I gave this text to actors. I did it at New Dramatists: I went in there with the Bible, Walt Whitman, Blake. I had six or eight actors; Jeff Jones was my dramaturg; and I said, I want to make this into a play. Jeff had been working on his quotation plays, so he pushed me in the direction of chopping it all up and making it into a quotation play. I was trying to come up with characters; the actors were beating themselves against the wall, trying to make my text into dialogue, but it wouldn't budge because it was not *written* to do that. It was written in one-page chunks. I learned an important principle: you cannot violate the nature of the writing. If something is written as a monologue, it's going to be a monologue.

MR: Tell me more about what bad writing is. It's not just bad grammar, obviously, or inappropriate vocabulary. Does it have something to do with subject matter? Or the writer's attitude?

MW: It does. Inevitably, if you start mismatching pronouns, getting your tenses wrong, writing sentences that are too long or too short, you will begin to say things that suggest a subversive political reality.

MR: After scoffing at traditional rules so steadily, do you now find that this impudence has become a rule in itself, a trap? Do you now have to find a way to break this new rule?

MW: Yes, sure. In a sense (at least in the context of "bad" writing), what you have to say is more interesting when you're learning the language than when you've mastered it. When you've mastered it, you can use the language system to exclude meaning, which I think is what most professional writing is about. It's very narrow. A lot of journalism is often about closing off avenues of expression or interpretation. What we accept as correct prose is very limiting. Anyone who's a professional writer knows it's a pain in the ass to write. The most liberal style manual is terribly confining and overrated in our mandarin culture. But, you know, I don't think language is the most important thing.

MR: That's a surprise, coming from you!

MW: People tell me all the time that I'm only about language, but I'm not! I'm just trying to make a language that comes close to what I feel and think. A statement like "if I hadda been I mighta could" is an enormously complex metaphysical statement. It's not just bad language; it's saying something that's real, that's possible; that's only contradictory in terms of *good* language. But it's something I know: I feel like that every day. Most bad language describes a spiritual condition that is not grammatical, but it is *real*. I'm more interested in the world than language. I'm more interested in syntax than grammar.

MR: Why's that? Why favor syntax over grammar?

MW: Syntax is the flow of meaning through language. Grammar is the set of shackles that gets imposed on meaning. Don't get me wrong: I also like good language. I like Proust, Henry James.

MR: What about those who say that your work is merely the product of automatic writing? Gertrude Stein, you know, often heard these things from critics, and she always protested that, no, every word was agonized over. Do you have to defend yourself against the same accusation?

MW: I haven't had to yet, but some people do think that it's easier to write this way. As soon as you stop writing in the official style, you multiply your aesthetic choices. I'm fortunate in that I have an ear for this sort of thing. I have a tendency toward malapropism. I want to go with the wrong word and see where it takes me. I can always find the right one; they have computer programs to correct style now.

MR: Do you do a lot of revision?

MW: My texts all go through multiple drafts before anyone sees them, so obviously I'm not against rewriting. But I do have a problem with re-vision as it is practiced in the theatre—that is, the endless reworking of text that happens during the near-panic of rehearsal. Most revisions for theatre works end up being bad. I think theatre writing is a kinetic, physical thing—the faster you write it, the better it is, most of the time. Usually, when you attempt to rewrite for the theatre, your play becomes more long-winded. You try to explain and justify things; the play gets less interesting. I'd rather write a lot and cut. Or start a new play. It's very hard to reenter the world of that moment of creation, because it's not just a language moment; it's a physical one as well. You're not just imagining the world.

MR: In *Terminal Hip*, I saw you playing a lot with the various languages of our day—the languages of the politician, the evangelist, the huckster, the professor, the Dale Carnegie figure run amok.

MW: Yes, that's true. The play was also me talking to me.

MR: How so?

MW: It's me saying, Well, you think you're so smart! It's very private. But then again, I didn't know I was going to make *Terminal Hip* into a perfor-mance. It began, in a sense, as a self-accusation, a dialogue with myself. A dialogue of self and soul, as Yeats would say. I interrogated myself. "Is that what you think you're doing? This is what I think of you." I was dealing with my own notions of what it means to be a person who does my sort of work. I didn't mean it to be cultural critique at all, except in-sofar as I'm a member of this culture. I don't think I accuse anybody of anything worse than I've committed or imagined I've committed myself.

MR: The title certainly leads one to see the play as satire.

MW: Yes. The title comes from a poem of mine—a mock epic—a terrible satire of the East Village and all the pretentiousness that I found there. A lot of the scathing attack of downtown New York fell away, but I kept the title anyway.

MR: You directed the first production of *Terminal Hip*. How did you ap-proach the play? What did you talk about with your collaborators?

MW: I'd never directed before. So what I did came from instinct. Some techniques I borrowed from the arsenal of other directors. Robert Wilson, for instance, always makes sketches of what he wants his show to look like. So I had everybody who was working on *Terminal Hip*, including myself, go home one night and draw pictures of what we thought the play should look like. We all came back with these horrible stick figures—except Steve Mellor, who first performed the play. He's a very good artist. He drew the set as you see it now. We then went through the text meticulously—that's something Des McAnuff does with Shakespeare—so that Steve knew what it meant.

MR: I remember Eric Overmyer's essay on you in *Theater* magazine, in which he talked about being disappointed with most productions of your plays. He laid some blame with the actors, who often play at being coy or detached. Is there an approach to Wellman texts that is particularly appropriate? Are there acting styles to be avoided?

MW: I know what he's talking about, although I think that's mainly true of productions a few years back. I don't think it's such a problem now, because I know more about how to explain things to actors. Mainly what you have to do is treat the language as natural—not naturalistic—but natural within the context. I'm much more interested in actors' voices now than I was before. Not that I'm so interested in the Method or anything. But you can explain the text in such a way that will suggest helpful things about the world of *this* language. You also have to find the right kind of actors. Some people connect with it, some people don't.

MR: Maybe now's the time to ask the Obscurity question. One constant comment about your work, from certain quarters, is that you confuse for confusion's sake. Even an admirer like Overmyer will write that you pursue "an ideology of obfuscation." Are those fair assessments?

MW: I do pursue a kind of experimental agenda with the writing. I hope in time that people will read my texts as carefully as they read any other dramatic literature. I don't think I'm a difficult writer at all, but I have not gotten a close reading of my texts, particularly of the ones that are supposed to be obscure.

MR: It seems that in *Terminal Hip* indeterminacy is built into the text. The function of "X," for instance: "X" can really mean whatever you want it to. In your play *Bad Penny* you write that "X" is "the nothingness of the unknown, the nothingness of infinity." Could that mean that "X" is also a place for our acts of interpretation?

MW: Yes, I think so. All I'm trying to do is make a space where language can be taken seriously and have a little space. We live in a sea of explanations, and I'm trying to get beyond that. The impulse to explain, and make everything rational and clear, is wonderful up to a point, but then it becomes suffocation.

MR: In one of your essays you talked about "language as gesture." That sounded very tantalizing, but I've never really known what you meant.

MW: I meant that there's a physical direction to a sentence or a word, even a physical *feeling*. Up until the twentieth century, prosody—the poetic standard of what constitutes a poem—has been a numerical thing. Ezra Pound has said that a beautiful line of poetry should have a shape—like a vase, for instance. That idea breaks with conventional prosody. I feel that way, too. We don't pay enough attention to the physical aspects of language. Particularly in the theatre, words should be objects flying around the room.

MR: Somewhere else you had said that language as gesture is both "near and hard to grasp." Is this idea related to your distrust of paraphraseable plays?

MW: Yes. There's a poem of Hölderlin's called *Patmos*. The first line is "God is near and hard to grasp." Hard to grasp. We think we know what language is, what it can do. I don't think we know anything about it. You know, I often get the feeling that the whole world is about to blow itself up because we're not listening to language anymore. We have cleaned up language so much that we don't pay attention to the aberrant things that language does.

MR: Speaking of politics, let me ask you a bit about political theatre, the subject of your essay last year in *American Theatre*. You were calling for indirection in politically minded plays, it seems—an end to didacticism. Yet your recent play, *Sincerity Forever*, is thoroughly political, and it quite clearly corresponds to a contemporary situation—the morality debates that overtook Capitol Hill last year. The play isn't didactic, but it certainly isn't indirect. Have I spied a contradiction?

MW: I changed. I'm now getting very interested in religion. This whole thing with Helms made me think about what should be the place of religion in an organized society, a secular society. The world is looking for meaning, but I don't think it lies in Western religions. Certainly that's what *Cellophane* and *Terminal Hip* are about—my desperate search for meaning.

MR: When I was reading the long interview with Vàclav Havel, *Disturbing the Peace*, I came across a wonderful question that I want to put to you. The interviewer asked what Havel did when he "exhausted the initial impulse that compelled him to write in the first place." The interviewer felt that such moments of helplessness were very important. A writer has to decide whether to experiment with a new identity or to go over the old concerns again, looking for different ways to answer the same impulse. Is that moment of exhaustion something that you've also experienced?

MW: That's actually the point when I began to write things like *Cellophane* and *Sincerity Forever*. I think, initially, a dramatist writes from his own life. And you exhaust that material fairly early. Then you have this problem of not knowing what to write about. And in my case, what I've done is attempt a move to other scales. The notion of scales is from chaos theory, and it means that you can examine the physical shape of a process by jumping from one scale to another—from macro to micro. I think the study of self-similarity from scale to scale—fractal studies it's called—has great relevance to current theory and practice of dramatic form.

MR: Over the past couple of years, a sudden and considerable success has come to you after being just a coterie playwright. Does all that attention have its costs?

MW: I never thought it would happen. I'm still surprised by the attention. I don't know what it means. I know I have to formulate a new set of practical ideals—working goals—because I never thought I'd get this far.

MR: What are those new ideals?

MW: I talked about this with another playwright, Connie Congdon, who is also quite shocked by the fact that anybody wants to do *her* work at this point. We've been talking with the director Jim Simpson and some other people about starting a national theatre. I'm not sure it will happen because I'm not a great organizer. But it's a focus for discussion. The theatre won't have a company, nor a building. It will be based with people all over the country who could initiate projects. If you wanted to do a show in a real theatre building, you could do it. But if you wanted to do something in Mississippi in a field, you could do that, too. I'd love to make something national that didn't have to do with intransigent, careerist institutional theatres. I just hate the whole strange system of putting theatres all over the place that all do the same play.

I've gotten some attention, and that's been nice, and I'm really grateful for it. But mainly it was contingency, and there are a lot of people who've worked just as hard as I have who, for one reason or another, haven't caught on. It's just an accident that it happened to me.

I got into teaching at the point when I had given up and said, "Fuck it. I'm a loser and nothing's ever going to happen. And I don't care anymore." And at that point everything started to turn around. I no longer cared about my career, and I became fearless, because I didn't have any-thing, so nobody could take anything away from me. I'm not going to become the next big playwright in this country. I'd love to see my work done, but it's too strange ever really to catch on, I know. I keep trying to write like Chekhov and it just comes out wrong!

John Ashbery

JOHN ASHBERY'S STATURE as one of America's eminent poets was firmly secured in 1975 with the publication of *Self-Portrait in a Convex Mirror,* which won both the Pulitzer Prize and the National Book Award for Poetry. What is less well known is that as a student at Harvard in the fifties, he aspired to play-writing, an ambition not unlike that of other poets of the era. It was a time, however, when there was a budding movement of poets' and artists' theatres, most of them anxious to duplicate the energies of European institutions and art movements associated with modernism—primarily, expressionism in the arts and surrealism in writing. It is in that context that Ashbery, together with fellow poets James Merrill, Barbara Guest, Paul Goodman, Frank O'Hara, and Kenneth Koch, to name a few, found themselves writing for these small the-atres at the same time that they were collaborating with artists such as Jane Freilicher, Roy Lichtenstein, Larry Rivers, and Red Grooms in many of the stagings. A theatre particularly receptive to poets was The Living Theatre, which not only produced Ashbery's *The Heroes,* but, as Ashbery makes abun-dantly clear, was open to new developments in writing.

Ashbery's career as a playwright was short-lived, and he soon gained greater fame as a poet and art critic. Nonetheless, his statements below at-test to an ongoing interest in drama and in its interplay of voices. "I suppose there is a suppressed orator in every poet who occasionally wants to get out and hear himself haranguing on the stage." In talking to critic and translator Roger Oliver about his ambiguous love for the theatre, Ashbery also touches upon the nature of the theatrical in his poetry and the legacy bequeathed to him by modernist practitioners of the theatre, from Pirandello, Vitrac, and Roussel, oddly enough, to Scribe, Sardou, and Labiche. Today, when it would be rare for any playwright to suggest a historical continuity with any of these names, Ashbery's inclusiveness carries with it a poignancy that signals a final break with the traditions of early modernism. He also paints a robust por-trait of a lost moment in American culture when theatres and audiences were open to the experimental urges of contemporary poets and artists.   GD

Conversation with Roger Oliver, 1979

Poet in the Theatre

Roger Oliver: When did you begin writing plays?

John Ashbery: I wrote a short verse play when I was a student at Harvard called *Everyman,* which was actually performed by the Poets' Theatre in Cambridge—not while I was a student, but shortly after I graduated. As a child I used to attempt to write plays and I had at that time ambitions to become, not only a playwright, but a director, I think, so that I could boss people around and have them do what I wanted to—recite my lines and so on—but this actually was just a fantasy and I don't think any of those childhood efforts survived. I don't think I made any further attempts to write plays in verse, after *Everyman,* which coincided with the renewal of interest in verse theatre—Christopher Fry and Eliot's *Cocktail Party* were of that period. I didn't feel that contemporary verse worked very well on the stage even as I was attempting to write a verse play myself. Then there are other very short little experimental plays, most of which were not published. The ones I liked the best are the three that are in the volume, and of course they're all in prose.

RO: The earliest of those is *The Heroes,* which you wrote in 1950. Had you already published poetry at that time?

JA: Very little. I'd had a couple of things in small literary magazines, including the Harvard *Advocate,* which I was an editor of, but that's all.

RO: Is there anything in particular that attracted you and still possibly attracts you to the dramatic form?

JA: Yes, I am very attracted to it, but I'm not entirely sure why. I do not have a great interest in the theatre. I do not go to plays very often or read them. The theatre is not a suppressed passion of mine, something I wish I'd gone into. Nevertheless, I have enjoyed writing plays, and I think this is because I tend to think in different voices, none of which ever seem to be my own. Perhaps I am able to write more easily when I imagine what another person might be thinking or saying than if I were to imagine what I might be thinking or saying. I think that in my poetry one can become aware of a number of different voices carrying on a dialogue or conversation in the poem even though it's not indicated, of course, as it is in a play. This I think kind of naturally led me to attempt writing dialogue.

RO: In previous interviews you've voiced dissatisfaction with your plays, even saying you didn't want them to be reprinted. What made you change your mind?

JA: Well, I'm not dissatisfied with them as long as it's realized that these were written during the fifties, and I think what I meant when I said that was that I wouldn't feel happy about them being published by the same publisher that publishes my poetry (which is now Viking Press) because people would then be tempted to see them as a new development even though the dates were given. But the fact that they came out with a small press and no particular publicity or anything was okay with me. I'd like to have them around for people who are interested to be able to look at, but again, these are old things that I feel quite distant from, although fond of, at the same time. I wouldn't object in the least if they were performed. In fact, *The Heroes* was given a staged reading three or four years ago in Houston at Rice University, which I was present at.

RO: Are there other plays?

JA: No, except for the short verse plays I mentioned, which went into the fifties, there aren't any. There was a short play about two pages called *To the Mill* which was published in some obscure publication—I think it was a one-time literary review called *Hasty Papers,* which was published by Alfred Leslie, the painter. *The Compromise* was also first published in that. Richard Howard describes *To the Mill* in an essay on my poetry as being somewhat anticipatory of later avant-garde theatre in New York, although it actually, I think, came out of what was even then a kind of avant-garde theatre movement.

RO: I want to ask about that movement. The plays of Frank O'Hara have just been published, including one with a poem dedicated to you. Were many American poets of the fifties interested in the theatre, talking about it, working together toward a new kind of theatre?

JA: I'm not sure about that. I know that in Cambridge there were a number of people, just because the Poets' Theatre there gave one an opportunity to write for the stage and see one's work performed. But elsewhere there weren't very many examples of this. The poets who had things done at the Poets' Theatre included O'Hara, and of course William Alfred; Lyon Phelps was another person, and I think James Schuyler had some short plays performed there. There wasn't really much of any place that I know of where there was an interest in poets writing for the theatre, and therefore, I suppose, very little interest on the part of the poets themselves in writing for the theatre.

RO: Do you think there is a significant relationship between poetry and drama? Most poets seem to try the dramatic form at one time or another. Is there a particular reason for this?

JA: I don't know. I suppose there is a suppressed orator in every poet who occasionally wants to get out and hear himself haranguing on the stage. And I suppose everybody has the example of Shakespeare to try to measure up to. I don't really know why they are interested in it. In my own case I don't think of it as an activity related to writing poetry. I feel it's somewhat different—in fact, that's why I like it; it engages another part of my mind.

RO: You don't think of yourself as a poet writing plays when you're in fact working on a play?

JA: Well, no, but I don't usually think of myself as a poet.

RO: *The Heroes* was first done by The Living Theatre. Was it written for them?

JA: No. It was written perhaps not before they came into existence, but before I knew about them.

RO: How did they come to produce it?

JA: I was acting in one of their productions. It was Picasso's play, *Desire Caught by the Tail*, in which both Frank O'Hara and I had small roles. In fact, I meant to tell you, I acted in high school productions and at that time was fancying myself as an actor. I forget exactly how I got to know Julian Beck and Judith Malina. It may very well have been through Paul Goodman, whom I knew at that time. At some point during the run of the play, which went on for several months, I mentioned to them that I had a play and they consented to look at it and liked it and performed it as a curtain-raiser for *Ubu*, but they were closed by the fire department after only two or three performances.

RO: Did it have anything to do with the play itself?

JA: I think it probably did. This was 1952, when two men dancing together on the stage could easily be considered scandalous, and this was compounded by *Ubu*, which of course starts with a four-letter word that we hear all through the play, and everyone thought that this fire inspection was a way of closing down the theatre because the plays were considered unsavory.

RO: Could you talk a little bit about the way The Living Theatre worked—how they produced your play and the kind of work they were doing at that time?

JA: Well, as you know, that is a terribly long time ago and I don't really remember that much about it. If I had known I was going to amount to something, I would have taken notes as well as a lot of precautions. Since I didn't my memories are very sketchy. At that time The Living Theatre was much more conventionally literary in what they put on and at the same time, I think, very open to new developments. When they read my play they immediately liked it and wanted to perform it. They were also doing plays by Paul Goodman and other people who were contemporary, as well as their own interpretation of certain plays that were classics and others that were known but were relatively obscure.

The first thing I ever saw them do was a play by Gertrude Stein called *Doctor Faustus Lights the Lights*, which I remember as one of the most beautiful things I've ever seen on the stage. They didn't always achieve that perfection, but they were usually pretty interesting. Other beautiful things they did, really on a shoestring—barely any costumes, sets, or anything, in the loft they moved into on West Ninety-Ninth Street—were Pirandello's *Tonight We Improvise* and *The Ghost Sonata* of Strindberg. Both of those were terrific. Less successful to me was Paul Goodman's play *Faustina*. They also produced a staged version of Auden's *The Age of Anxiety*, again not very successful, but certainly interesting.

RO: Would you say the productions themselves were experimental or that it was more the novelty of the material?

JA: They seemed experimental at the time and probably were, in relation to other experimental theatre, if there was any, and I'm not sure that there was. Now I think they might seem relatively conventional.

RO: *The Heroes* was also done a year or two later by the Artists' Theatre. Was the production very different?

JA: Well, there was a very beautiful Légeresque set designed by the painter Nell Blaine. I think she also designed the costumes, and it had a very nice look. In fact, this theatre was an attempt to bring poets and artists together in a sort of collaboration. My play, for instance, was done on a program with three other plays by poets, each one of which had a different set by a different artist who was associated with John Myers' gallery, Tibor de Nagy Gallery. He was sort of the artistic director of the theatre with Herbert Machiz, the director. As far as the acting and so on goes, it's very hard for me to remember what it was like or whether there was a great difference. I don't think there was. Both were fairly straightforward.

RO: How long was the Artists' Theatre in existence?

JA: I think about three or four years, but I could be wrong about that. I left New York in the mid-fifties and lived in France for a number of years, and I'm not too familiar with the subsequent developments after I left.

RO: In the performances you saw, was the collaboration between poets and artists a successful one?

JA: I thought it was in my case. As I recall I didn't really confer with Nell

Blaine at all about what her designs were going to be like. I knew her work and was pleased that she was doing them and was very pleased with the result. I remember a very beautiful set done by Jane Freilicher for another of the plays on the program, which was a play called *The Lady's Choice* by Barbara Guest. The others I simply don't remember. I know one of the plays was *The Bait* by James Merrill, but I can't remember what it looked like. Later on they did Frank O'Hara's play *Try, Try* with a set by Larry Rivers, which worked pretty well.

RO: Was *The Compromise* your next play?

JA: Well, I didn't write that until about five years later. I went through a period of writer's block shortly after I wrote *The Heroes*. During that time I didn't write anything, poetry or plays, and I think that in a more adventurous climate where I felt that I could have written for a theatre that would perform the plays, I might have gone on to write some more, but that didn't seem very likely at that time. So I just drifted back into writing poetry, always the idea that I would like to write plays if I had the time and the possibility of having them performed, but I wasn't particularly interested at that time in writing a closet drama that would never get put on the stage, and which I don't approve of anyway.

RO: And even though there had been the two productions of *The Heroes*, you didn't think there were very many opportunities?

JA: Yes, both of them seemed like lucky accidents that weren't likely to be repeated.

RO: You've said of your poetry that you don't think of it as coming from nowhere, that it extends certain traditions. In the three plays you seem particularly aware of theatrical conventions and traditions, and much of the humor in the plays comes from the parody or juxtaposition of various old forms. Was this something you were definitely thinking about when you wrote the plays?

JA: Well, I've always been very sensitive to the devices of the theatre—the ways of getting people on and off stage, the ways of arranging things that we're conscious of even when we're being taken in. Very often this is more exciting for me than what actually happens in the play—the part we're supposed to pay attention to. That certainly was the kind of apparatus or convention in the theatre that I was interested in, and it occurred to me that the experimental theatre, which is often very boring, even when it's very moving, needn't necessarily be that way. A lot of things could be happening on the stage. Doors could be slamming and people going on and off, and it wasn't really necessary in writing an avant-garde play to have somebody sitting on the floor mumbling throughout the entire evening. As I said, I don't know why, but I respond very much to the artifice of the theatre.

RO: Both *The Compromise* and *The Philosopher* seem to borrow not only from the conventions of the stage and the theatre, but from film conventions as well.

JA: Yes. Well, I think that the theatrical conventions that I allude to in these plays actually came to me via movies rather than plays. As I told you, I've never been much of a theatregoer. There was a time when I went to the movies a great deal. I don't much anymore, but I used to haunt old film societies. In both of those cases there were films that directly suggested the plays. I got the idea for *The Compromise* after watching a silent Rin-Tin-Tin movie called *Where the North Begins*, made in 1923, and what I did in the play was to take more or less the plot of that, omitting the dog, of course, who was the main event in the movie, and just using the plot that had been constructed around his talents. Then I also preserved a few of the titles from the movie. I've always been very intrigued by the titles of silent movies, which are so corny and yet do exactly what they're supposed to do. Particularly the films of D. W. Griffith, which I always enjoy seeing, largely for the titles themselves.

RO: Which film suggested *The Philosopher*?

JA: That came from a number of films, I think. One obvious one was Paul Leni's film, *The Cat and the Canary*. I never saw the Bob Hope-Paulette Goddard version of it, but I did see the silent one, and of course this is the same plot that occurs in a number of mysteries—the heirs being invited to the house to hear the will read. There was another one that I saw on TV at the time called *Who Killed Aunt Maggie?* I believe it was a forties "B" picture. The character of the philosopher in the movie was probably suggested by the man in *Pandora and the Flying Dutchman*, the sort of esthete, smarty-pants philosopher who's always giving out dubious epigrams and aphorisms.

RO: Is there any particular reason why you chop off *The Philosopher* right at the point where the mystery is getting most complicated? Were you not really interested in developing it beyond that?

JA: Well, no. I was, in fact, and that was just supposed to be the first act. I'm revealing all my secrets to you now. In fact, I went on to write some more of it, and my idea was that in the latter part I would have the same people but they would be completely different characters talking in a much more serious way—the play would suddenly cease being a farce and become a sort of Ingmar Bergman drama with these same people left over from the B-movie farce with which the play began. I did that, but wasn't very happy with the part of the second act that I'd written and sort of laid it aside. Then at some later point it seemed to me that possibly it was enough just the way it was; having set a lot of complicated machinery in motion, to sort of follow it to the point where it finally ran down would seem absurd. The thing that interested me most was getting these little machines to start performing, and I figured, Well, now they can be forgotten about; as far as I'm concerned, I've done what I wanted to do. I don't know if this is sour grapes or what, but anyhow that's how the play now stands.

RO: Getting back to *The Heroes*, were you at all thinking of the kind of Neo-Greek plays that were being written at that time by people like Sartre and Eliot and Giraudoux?

JA: Yes, I was, I'm sure. I'd seen a number of them—Cocteau's *The Infernal Machine* and Anouilh's *Antigone* are other examples of a genre that was very popular in the thirties and continued to be so after the war. The immediate inspiration of that play was the short novella by Gide called *Thésée*, or Theseus. I read it shortly before writing the play, and, as so often happens, was unaware of the Gide work while I was writing. It was only some time later that I noticed the very strong resemblances between the two.

RO: In fact, in *The Heroes* you have Theseus describe the minotaur as a great fake that did not "make the slightest effort to convince me of its reality, not a pretense. But there it was, a stupid, unambitious piece of stage machinery." I think it's very interesting that in your most recent book of poems, *Houseboat Days*, there's a very similar image in a poem called "The Wrong Kind of Insurance": "Yes, friends, these clouds pulled along on invisible ropes are, as you have guessed, merely stage machinery, And the funny thing is it knows we know About it and still wants us to go on believing In what it so unskillfully imitates and wants To be loved not for that but for itself . . ." These are works that are written over twenty years apart. Do you see the world in theatrical terms, particularly in terms of stage machinery that is obviously false but wants us to believe in it anyway?

JA: I guess I do since you just presented me with the evidence. In fact, you are very clever to have come across those two uses of the words "stage machinery." I can't think of any other place where I have used the term. The idea is, of course, very similar: the stage machinery wanting to be loved for what it is rather than for what it so unskillfully imitates is a statement of how I felt about it from the beginning. I do see this and there are many examples of allusions to the theatre in my poetry. One that you may not know is in *Three Poems*. In fact, there are quite a few there, and particularly at the end of the last poem in which the poem is a kind of performance and at the end of it the curtain comes down and the audience leaves and goes home to sleep. These do keep popping up in my work and I don't exactly know why because the theatre as it exists is not something that particularly attracts me, but I tend very often to fall into these metaphors of things concerning the theatre—stages, actors, public. I don't know why.

RO: Earlier you spoke of The Living Theatre production of *Tonight We Improvise*, and certainly you use a very Pirandellian device at the end of *The Compromise* when you as playwright walk out and say that you haven't been able to decide how to finish the play—which lover to have the heroine go off with. Have you been influenced by Pirandello?

JA: Well, as I recall, I wrote the play shortly after seeing The Living Theatre's production of that play. I'm not sure that I had ever seen a play by Pirandello before. I had read some and knew what "Pirandellian" meant without its affecting me, and was affected by it on the stage to the point that I started being Pirandellian without probably realizing it—the way influence worked as I told you in the case of Gide. I do remember being tremendously excited by that play and that production, and it undoubtedly corresponded to something within me. I mentioned before that I find it easier to imagine the speeches of imaginary characters than my own speech, or at any rate my own speech tends to be channeled into the personae of others. Perhaps that was one reason why the play moved me.

RO: You've mentioned in another interview a dramatic work in progress that you characterize as very long and totally unstructured and free-associating. In fact, you read part of it last year. Is it similar to the plays that have been published, or is it something totally different?

JA: It's very different. First of all, I don't want to talk too much about it because it's a work in progress and writers usually don't like to talk about their works in progress.

RO: How long have you been working on it?

JA: I started it about five years ago and I haven't really worked on it in the past three years, but I think of it very much as something I want to finish when I have time. It's not entirely unstructured since it begins in a fairly conventional way, but the characters keep stepping out of character as they do in my earlier plays, in fact, but here much more wildly I would say. It becomes increasingly dreamlike as it goes along. It starts out like a rather conventional *piéce à thése* of the early twentieth century, maybe

Ibsen or even someone more like Brieux, but it's as though the actors had all dropped acid at the beginning of the play and it gets increasingly out of hand as it goes along. So far I've only written the first act of the play, which is about a hundred typewritten pages.

RO: Do you think you would have more of an incentive to complete it if there were the possibility of a production, if there were a kind of theatre that was open to this kind of work?

JA: I think now there might very well be such a theatre, so I'm not lacking the incentive to finish it, it's just a question of finding the time to do it and continuing to write poetry. I've discovered that having this play in the works caused me to write more poetry than usual, because when I sat down to work on the play my usual reluctance to work got shifted and I would end up writing a poem instead, whereas before, without the incentive or the duty perhaps of the play to finish, I might not have written anything at all. So I found it a rather useful device for writing something else.

RO: Is there any particular reason why you have decided to start another play after not having written one for quite a while?

JA: It might have had something to do with my seeing a number of the Robert Wilson plays on the stage and realizing that there was a place for this kind of grandiose, surrealist kind of spectacle. I think the kind of *folie des grandeurs* in his earlier work influenced me, or at any rate showed a possible way of continuing to write for the theatre and interest myself at the same time.

RO: He's now working with Philip Glass and writing what he calls operas, and I noticed somewhere that you are working with Elliot Carter on a piece for singer and orchestra. Have you ever contemplated writing some kind of piece of musical theatre, or could music be used in this play that you're writing now?

JA: Quite a lot of music does occur in the play. I've given very specific indications about what it is. The Carter piece is not actually a collaboration and I'm not entirely sure yet what Elliot Carter's using. I know he's using one poem I'd already written before we started working, which is called "Syringa." It's a poem about Orpheus, and I think the Carter work was going to be entitled Orpheus or something with Orpheus in the title. It hasn't been an actual collaboration in the sense of my providing him with a text to work on. He selected the work himself and I think may be using that poem and perhaps fragments of other poems of mine.

RO: You give frequent readings of poetry. Do you see any connection between these readings and theatre?

JA: I try not to. I do it just because everybody else does it and we all get paid for it. It's the only way poets have really of making money. This current fad for poetry readings began in the fifties with the Beat poets, who made their poetry readings a kind of performance. I perhaps go to the opposite extreme of making my poetry readings completely untheatrical and undramatic and flat just because I don't like the feeling that the work I'm reading could conceivably be improved by dramatizing it, for instance. I think that's what will prevent me from ever actually becoming a playwright because I don't want to give up my autonomy to the extent where I could work with a director. But I don't have any great commitment to poetry reading. Perhaps I do have a sort of suppressed theatrical person inside of me, but this has nothing to do, I think, with poetry reading. One just does it.

RO: So there's no sense in which you're either trying to interpret or perform your poems; you're just basically trying to present them, to read them?

JA: Yes. I'm trying to bring out the various voices and to read them in a way that lets the text itself be apparent to the audience without dramatizing it. I have noticed occasionally that I've written something in a poem that is obviously meant to be spoken to an audience, but I try to extirpate these things as much as possible since I don't particularly believe poetry should be heard and declaimed. I myself am much happier reading poetry to myself and not hearing it aloud, though I'm in the minority.

RO: Would it then follow that you don't think the reading of poetry by actors really adds anything, perhaps even detracts from the experience of the poems?

JA: I think it does. I don't think I've ever heard a successful reading of poetry by an actor. Once in Paris at the Biennale they had poetry readings by various actors. I think one of my poems was read by the actor Daniel Gélin, a popular French movie actor of the fifties, and it seemed to have absolutely nothing to do with the poem.

RO: Did you go to much theatre while you were in Paris?

JA: Yes, I did quite a bit, although I've told you I don't go the theatre very much. I used to go the Comédie Française a lot and also to the boulevard plays more than to the experimental ones. I particularly liked Feydeau and always went whenever any of his plays were revived, the same for Labiche. I've also been quite interested in the well-made play, and occasionally those are revived in Paris. I saw a play by Sardou once and I've read the plays of Scribe.

RO: That's interesting, because it certainly ties in with your view of theatre as stage machinery. There's a wonderful line in "Pyrography" where you write: "The page of dusk turns like a creaking revolving stage in Warren, Ohio." That seems to go along with Scribe and Sardou, but even Feydeau, where the plays almost become a world of stage machinery brought to life.

JA: Another French playwright whose work I find very interesting, and in fact, might be one of the few writers who besides myself has been interested in integrating a surrealist kind of poetry with the traditions of conventional theatre is Roger Vitrac, whose play *Victor* is probably the best known. That was revived once in Paris when I was there. There's another play called *Le Sabre de mon père*, which is a kind of surrealist imitation of Labiche's *The Italian Straw Hat*. And one which takes place on the 14th of July in 1914 and is about the doings of a bunch of crazy and demented bourgeois characters living in an apartment house in Paris.

RO: You wrote *The Philosopher* while you were in Paris?

JA: Yes, I think that it was in 1959.

RO: Was there any particular external stimulus from being in Paris that made you decide to write a play and to write that particular play?

JA: While I was living in Paris I was thinking a great deal about America most of the time. You probably know the well-known Gertrude Stein remark to the effect that one can be American more easily in France than one can in America; one has the proper perspective. Actually, I've forgotten to mention the plays of Raymond Roussel, and at that time when I was living in Paris it was my intention to do a dissertation about Roussel, and I did collect a lot of material and wrote three articles, including one on his plays, but I never wrote the dissertation. His plays undoubtedly influenced me. The two that were published begin again in a very conventional way—start out like popular French boulevard plays of the nineteen hundreds and after about two or three pages suddenly have the characters telling each other complicated anecdotes describing various curiosities or strange sights they've seen. The action is completely suspended after about the third page and is finally resolved on the last page when the sort of dramatic situation that was set up at the very beginning achieves a miraculous resolution. But all the time in between has mainly been taken up with these people telling each other these senseless stories that go on and on. At the time, just before I began writing *The Philosopher*, I was particularly interested in Roussel's theatre.

RO: It sounds like you're attracted to the theatre in spite of yourself, that there is this pull, this attraction that you can suppress for a while and then it lures you back.

JA: I probably would go to the theatre more if it were easier to get tickets to the good plays and if one didn't have to go into a strange dark place to sit with a lot of strangers in the dark and not be able to leave when one wanted to. If it could be brought here to me I would probably spend a great deal of time watching it. I'm both lazy and timid, so I don't go very often.

RO: You're attracted more to the theatrical than you are to the actual theatre itself?

JA: Probably. Yes.

Gautam Dasgupta, Michael Earley, Bonnie Marranca

BY THE LATE SEVENTIES disillusionment about the future of playwriting in America had set in, brought about by a realization that the impetus that had generated the dramatic inventiveness of modern European drama and the sixties theatre was fast dissipating. Many of the best theatrical minds were working in nonliterary avant-garde theatre as interest had shifted more toward performance than drama. Likewise, the splintering of theatre into feminist, gay, and experimental work reflected the fragmentation of American society. In addition, the decentralization of theatre away from New York had resulted in a diffusion of energies with plays being done in isolated pockets all across the country, thwarting any sustained theatrical focus and debate. It is against this problematic landscape that the following dialogue took place, just three years after the founding of *Performing Arts Journal*, between its editors, Bonnie Marranca and Gautam Dasgupta, and its associate editor at the time, Michael Earley.

The fate of the playwright had particular relevance in the day-to-day professional careers of Earley and Marranca, both literary advisors then at the McCarter and the American Place Theatre, respectively. Marranca and Dasgupta were at work on their study of the post-Albee generation of American dramatists, *American Playwrights: A Critical Survey*. A few years earlier Marranca had described the recent avant-garde as a "Theatre of Images." Their remarks on excessively self-absorbed plays, the absence of innovative directors, the detrimental influence of media hype, and the alienation of theatre culture from intellectual life articulate the issues that still dominate discussions about plays and productions. If anything, the situation seems to have gotten worse, with even less commitment, financial or artistic, to high-quality work and greater acceptance of the status quo, though there has been renewed interest in narrative and the dramatic form. GD

Conversation with Gautam Dasgupta, Michael Earley,
Bonnie Marranca, 1979

The American Playwright

Michael Earley: I'd like to continue some of the points that Stanley Kauff-mann and Harold Clurman made in the dialogue we published in *PAJ* in 1978 about the level of American playwriting at the moment. It seems to me it's in a rather problematical state. Although we have a number of fairly good young American playwrights writing now, here we are at the end of the seventies and no really outstanding body of work has evolved during the past ten years.

Bonnie Marranca: Some weeks ago Robert Brustein wrote in the *Times* that the American playwright, like much of American society, is being split off into a lot of different groups. For example, gay theatre, experimental theatre, feminist theatre, political theatre. What's happened is that even though this might be a reflection that now you have different people having a voice in American drama and American society, you have con-sequently no one who really speaks *for* that society, or for a generation. Sam Shepard in a sense can speak for the counterculture, but he's already thirty-five and he can't keep writing about science fiction and cowboys and rock music as he approaches middle age. His drama is still youth-ful in its perspective. Even playwrights like Williams, Miller, and Albee, who in the past have been counted on to do some of this work, have had no major plays in recent years.

Gautam Dasgupta: It has to do with the loss of the humanist tradition. With postwar playwrights, the problem here was the same as that which arose in Europe: lack of identity, loss of humanitarian values, et cetera. The interesting thing is that in America, even though a lot of the recent plays are absurdist, they're not absurdist in the European sense, where there is a philosophical and moral basis to it. Here, in the first half of this century, an era of individualism, there was a growing sense of pride. You were not only making it for yourself, you were making it for a country. And then suddenly in the fifties, with America's economic boom, it wasn't a sense of country that was important. Individualism became autonomous, not a social fact. And so there was a falling back into one's own experience, the world one knew as an individual. For the artist, the world became very circumscribed at that point. And unfortunately that is what happened to most American playwrights who today are in their thirties and forties. Their world is centered around their selves, and consequently their work has few repercussions outside that world.

ME: Since the fifties in other American art forms, such as painting, music, poetry, fiction, and film, you can really identify—even up to the present—various schools. You can see novelists and poets practicing similar traditions, using similar forms, even using similar themes. Yet it's very hard to make the same connections in American playwriting. Perhaps the vision of the individual writers is simply much too personal. In the other arts, traditions are constantly being invented, kept alive, and eventually reacted against. You don't have that in American literary theatre. We have it in some smaller, cohesive schools such as The Living Theatre, The Open Theater, Theatre of the Ridiculous. With the exception of David Rabe, for example, there has been no strong reaction to the Vietnam War.

BGM: Except that you have, in the theatre of the sixties, a lot of political theatre pieces and street theatre, the San Francisco Mime Troupe, The Living Theatre, and Peter Schumann . . . In the experimental theatre branch, there is seemingly much more of a tradition. For example, these people are continually rethinking ideas of Brecht, Artaud, Meyerhold and extending them further. True, they're not drawing so much from an American tradition, except the traditions of painting, sculpture, dance, and poetry. But most of the experimental writers who are producing avant-garde texts—Richard Foreman, Robert Wilson, Lee Breuer, to name a few—are not really drawing on American drama, except for the influence of Gertrude Stein.

ME: They're drawing on these other art forms where there is an identifiable style, center of interest, and thematic and formal concerns.

BGM: Right. But on the other hand, I think that what has been happening in recent years is that we're seeing more content—along with the formal experimentation in the avant-garde. Especially in the use of autobiography. There is the notion of the self as text, as in the work of Breuer and Foreman, and, in a very conceptualized way, the use of the actor, the actor's body, and his own raw material, as in the work of Spalding Gray. Particularly in the past ten years, writing by blacks, gays, and women has drawn on personal experiences; but they don't really relate to a larger world. One thing that's always been missing in our drama is a lack of an expansive vision. Sometimes Shepard reflects this, and that is what makes his work stand out.

ME: It always amazes me how American playwrights tend to weaken rather than grow stronger with time, including Albee and Williams, with the possible exception of O'Neill.

GD: I think that with most of the contemporary playwrights the question has to do with the ability to experience life in all its diverse manifestations and to intensify that experience on stage. The ability to feel and experience life in different dramatic modes has been greatly eroded. Plays must deal with strongly felt emotions (be they of a realistic or formalistic orientation), and that capacity to feel is no longer there. I find this, say, in Richard Nelson's plays, and in the works of older playwrights like John Guare and Robert Patrick. Their plays constitute nondramatic narrative at best; they *tell* us a story rather than *enact* one. Also, what most of these playwrights have to offer is usually a long-winded exploration of personal myths and concerns that, more often than not, determine all the situations and relationships that comprise these plays. Characters are objectified only in so far as they reflect, in varying degrees, the playwright's own obsessions.

Playwrights are more concerned with relating a story or depicting a milieu, howsoever radical the narrative form may be. There is a reactionary element at work in the writings of experimental playwrights of the off-off days. Although the structure is radical, the scenes that make up the play are way too realistic. Rather, the impulse is to depict a milieu realistically, howsoever absurd the situation. Jean-Claude van Itallie, Shepard, and William Hauptman are the only exceptions I can think of, playwrights who create conceptually unified pieces for the theatre.

ME: What I find interesting vis-à-vis American drama is how American poetry and prose fiction have developed new strategies for dealing with what are new problems. American playwrights, on the other hand, seem so wedded to a kind of romantic realism that leaves them shallow in terms of confronting harsher realities.

GD: Yes and no, because contemporary attempts at creating new dramatic forms in recent playwriting have been quite inventive. Judging from theatre in the rest of the world, off-off-Broadway is radical by comparison. I agree with you that realism is predominant, but it is not so much a realism or naturalism in terms of genre, as in Zola. It's a naturalism only in terms of telling a story; that is, the reliance on either storytelling or evoking a milieu or realistically dissecting a character's emotional life.

BGM: One of the points I want to get back to is the descriptive nature of American drama. I noticed from all the reading I do at the American Place Theatre as literary advisor, that that tends to be the greatest problem: writers describe reality rather than analyze it. I think it also has partly to do with the American mentality being much more empirical rather than analytical. So we don't have much of a drama of ideas, we have generally family dramas, or situation comedies drawn mostly from television. Usually, a playwright's first play is about his father, or leaving home, or wanting to be a writer. Now women are writing about their mothers, their children, their husbands—dealing with these subjects in a manner that was until recently taboo.

Another point I want to mention about the playwrights of the sixties is that while I agree it was a high point in American drama in terms of experiments with narration, character, transformations, et cetera, the problem with many of these people who are still writing, some of them in middle age, is that they haven't advanced. In this context you can mention almost any one of the inventive playwrights of that period— Paul Foster, Amiri Baraka, Ronald Tavel, Rochelle Owens, Jack Gelber, Michael McClure, Megan Terry, Leonard Melfi—the list is almost endless, we can fill in the names. There are very few people who are doing better work now. Shepard and Maria Irene Fornes are two exceptions.

ME: But I'm wondering if the problem has something to do with the whole American theatre and not just playwriting. It seems to me that our greatest playwrights developed in connection with specific theatres, which themselves were opening a new vision. O'Neill had Provincetown, Odets had The Group Theatre. Even David Belasco had the luxury of a controlled theatrical environment. Shepard now has the Magic Theatre in San Francisco. His best recent work is coming from there. The overwhelming problem of getting your play produced and having a stable environment in which your work grows causes the art to suffer. Since it's a collaborative art, if you don't have the people to work with you're left incomplete as an artist. Megan Terry and van Itallie had The Open Theater, Lanford Wilson has the Circle Rep, and that element of stability can really account for something.

BGM: In one sense, a lot of the people who did produce plays off-off-Broadway at La MaMa and Caffe Cino, at Genesis and Judson, just put the plays on and didn't give the writers much direction. You see people making the same mistakes now, after twenty or thirty plays, that could have been cleared up over a dozen years ago. It becomes very depressing when a writer is approaching middle age, when the work should be mature, structurally better, and more demanding, and it's deteriorating instead because these people are writing with the mentality of people in their mid-twenties.

ME: There was a kind of transference of energy, too, which I think we should mention. Those plays were very energetic. They may not have been structurally sound or mature in many respects, but there was a dynamic quality to them that would repeat itself in other works.

GD: Yes, but before you mentioned that O'Neill had Provincetown, et cetera, and coteries are very good for developing a playwright. But at the same time they can be detrimental in that a playwright may then find himself writing for a coterie *audience* that wants him to continue writing in the same style. Bob Patrick at the Caffe Cino is a striking example of this.

ME: But that was a high point . . .

GD: It was a high point because of the radical forms of the plays. All the playwrights we are talking about—Patrick, Wilson, et cetera—they've all written at least *one* very good play. More often than not, that play came early in their careers. A new form is always exciting and worthy of attention. But also, various factors, including reaction to Broadway fare, gave rise to coterie audiences and "club" plays. Lack of money, space, et cetera, also determined a playwriting style that, although inventive, created a new audience who came to expect a dramatic idiom that was soon forced on their favorite playwrights. Again, with the formation of a coterie, it was the first time that these playwrights had ever received any notice. Newspaper criticism then, as now, was hardly of any consequence. Even newspapers, particularly the *Voice*, were out to attain antiestablishment status, and so they too became part of the coterie audience, mostly acting like claques and sycophants. And, of course, the concept of controversy is nonexistent in this country. Even if a newspaper gives something a bad review, unless it's a commercial play, it rarely matters. The audience is a given, a ready-made.

ME: Now it seems to matter quite a bit, especially since funding agencies follow the reviews so closely. It matters in terms of future productions, for instance.

GD: But not in the coterie theatres.

ME: True. Also, of course, if the playwright comes out of a theatre that will develop him—David Mamet with the St. Nicholas Theatre in Chicago, David Rabe with the Public Theatre.

GD: Furthermore, this notion about the coterie and the fact that plays weren't carefully put together has to do with the whole anti-intellectual tradition in America—with original, uncontaminated artistic impulse and the authenticity of emotion. "Sincerity" is a key word in American society. Revising your work is not only seen as imposition or a kind of censorship, but as antithetical to the concept of emotional purity.

ME: In relation to American playwriting would you say then that the writer lacks discipline as a result? Because, to a large degree, as Bonnie mentioned earlier, writers have really been allowed to go their own way.

GD: Yeah, but I think that the writers believe they're doing their best. For all we know, the playwrights we are discussing are by no means, and have little intention of being, profound. A writer has to be told that he is not necessarily the best judge of his work. The task belongs to critics and dramaturgs, and the latter, as you two well know, only serve as play-readers in the American context. Artistic directors are the people who work, if time permits, with authors, and they are only interested in serving the play as best they can onstage. For the artistic director, the play is a commodity to be marketed in the most appealing manner. And while artists cannot most certainly be said to be revered in this country, there is a romantic attachment to the notion of the artist and his vision. That what he has to offer is virtually a godsend.

BGM: One thing about criticism in that early period is that there were people like Michael Smith and Ross Wetzsteon writing from a supporter/advocacy point of view. Going back fifteen years, what was done in American drama was a complete break from the Odets, Williams, Miller tradition in terms of the construction of the text and experiments with character, even the notion of performer. If you look at a play like *Tom Paine* or *Viet Rock*, in their time they were very radical formally. The politics weren't terribly radical—like most American politics. The plays, I don't think, grew from great political feelings, from political ideology. They grew from very deep personal feelings about something wrong with American society. But the structures are extremely inventive as concepts and offered a new notion of space, time, character, and situation. During the past fifteen years, there has been no critic to emerge with a theory of drama to intelligently analyze these experiments.

ME: To go along with that—there really is no one great book of American theatre criticism. Criticism in every other American art form is distinguishable in some way. Most Americans who write well about the theatre tend to write about European theatre. You have a condition at the moment where no one is really taking American playwriting to task intelligently and dissecting it in some way—finding out what the problems are and suggesting solutions. I think it's a failure, in part, of American academic institutions and critical institutions—you have basically, in America, theatre reviewers who aren't really critics. On the other hand, look at Europe. Critics of Brecht were intimately involved with Brecht. Critics of Artaud were intimately involved with Artaud. Who is seriously attuned to current plays the way Joseph Wood Krutch was attuned to O'Neill?

BGM: Take the situation of *Curse of the Starving Class* and now *Buried Child*. None of the reviewers make much of an attempt to see these works in relation to Shepard's career. The notion of a career almost doesn't exist because each play is taken on face value for itself as if it came out of nowhere. There's no real connection with anything that's happened either last year or five years or fifteen years before that. And it's very damaging because a lot of people around the country who don't see these plays take this criticism at face value. Then it gets reported in history books—people are now doing chapters on off-off-Broadway—and you get mistakes and misconstrued ideas.

ME: You read a European critic like Walter Benjamin on Brecht, someone who was intimately involved with that whole notion Brecht was getting at, and you have this extraordinary sense of illumination, not only of the writer himself, but of the theatrical context in which he wrote. You have nothing like that in America at all in terms of theatre criticism. I guess Eric Bentley came closest.

BGM: One of the things is that the best minds in America—the best literary minds—don't even give a second look to American drama, because it really offers nothing to them. There are skimpy ideas in the drama, and for the most part it derives from popular culture, or from television, and it doesn't offer the same kind of brilliance and cosmological views as fiction or poetry does. There are no American playwrights writing today who compare with the best fiction writers or poets.

GD: A lot of this has to do with the emphasis on style in American theatre. Every playwright now has a style, or better yet, a gimmick. In a sense, it is very difficult to say that of the classic playwrights. Take Ibsen, for example. He was writing in the realistic tradition, but it was not putting the same people in a different context. Each of the characters has a unique personality that one can study, apply to the times or to oneself. The problem here is that so much of the playwriting emphasizes style and, unfortunately, most of the playwrights do not have the range or knowledge of the variety of human life that can, within a given style, make all of their works uniquely different.

Character, to take one element, has no depth or uniqueness to it. Not that character per se is essential to drama. The absurdists did away with it, but it was replaced by a philosophy. In American playwriting, the notion of character did not shift gears as radically as the play's structure. With the plays of Guare, Wilson, and even with the so-called absurd playwrights like Albee and Kopit, I always get the sense that here is a normal character who is just acting strange in a ridiculous situation. What is missing is an organic cohesion between the form and the realization of the characters.

BGM: One person who is an exception to this is Fornes, who turned after many years of non-naturalistic playwriting to a very naturalistic form in *Fefu and Her Friends*. And Shepard seems to have moved into a whole new area since *Curse of the Starving Class*.

GD: The interesting thing with Fornes and with Shepard is their ability to objectify experience in a mature and vitally significant way. That doesn't mean that one has to write serious plays. It has to do with the playwright's capacity to comprehend the essential nature and underlying current of life in relation to a participating consciousness. Also to come to terms with the subject, nature, and the historical evolution of consciousness. One must also be able to understand the nature of metaphor and irony—two essential critical and aesthetic functions—which are not used often enough by playwrights. There are many exciting things about the literary theatre in America, particularly in its fanciful use of language (David Mamet, for example), but what it lacks is a probing consciousness.

BGM: While it is not true of the more conventional playwrights, I think the avant-garde theatre of the past ten years has made consciousness its subject. There is more of an epistemological concern among avant-gardists. Incidentally, though this branch of theatre is generally thought of in terms of performance only, it has produced the most provocative texts; the ideas and theories contributing to them often come from dance and painting and other arts. These artists seem to live in a world that is much wider and broader than themselves—the more expansive consciousness you are talking about.

ME: American playwrights, who have never created a drama of ideas, often seem to be writing for actors and directors—also a tradition that is not wholly literary.

BGM: And then there is the problem of finding good directors. Very few do much more than simply move people around onstage. A lot of contemporary plays of the past fifteen years would look much better on the stage if people knew how to direct them. Most of these plays are really lost to the dramatic repertoire now. They're not published and rarely revived in the professional theatre because everyone is looking for a new hit. Also, I don't think the playwrights wrote these plays with the belief that they would last. There are very few non-mainstream plays of a decade ago that could be done again as anything more than curiosity texts, because the approach and style just doesn't transcend the period.

ME: And directors are more interested in getting the work out of the actor, not the playwright. Playwrights rewrite a line or two of dialogue, they don't recast forms and ideas. Those of us who work in theatre see this happen all the time.

BGM: For one thing if you get your work done in a regional theatre or on Broadway, you only have a few weeks of rehearsal. Most plays that come into any theatre go on the stage with very little rewrites because everything revolves around getting the production going and making sure there are good casts.

GD: The American playwright really sees his work as craft more than anything else. It's a typically American phenomenon—the work ethic that is associated with labor. And the two best things about American plays are the uses of language and visuals (the latter with regard to Bonnie's concept of "Theatre of Images")—which is natural, given both the antiliterary (that is, verbal) thrust in this country and its predominantly visually oriented culture.

BGM: Since you mentioned language I just wanted to add that without a doubt one strong contribution of contemporary American playwriting is the use of the American vernacular. It's a terribly exciting, energetic use of language. Also, it has a certain lack of formality that most drama of other cultures don't have. American drama is very nonliterary. Whereas, say, for example, British drama is very literary. American drama is much more off-handed, casual, much more liberated in all manner of approaches. There is no doubt that that's a major development in the use of nonliterary stage language. Some of Shepard's work is astounding, for example, *Tooth of Crime*, in which he creates a whole new stage language. And the avant-garde texts—a drama of no dialogue!

ME: Getting back to the idea of the transformation play, what seems to be so important about those plays is how they evolved in collaboration. Everyone seemed to be thinking about the text and trying to make it work better—actor, director, playwright. I'm thinking about van Itallie's pieces with The Open Theater, and Megan Terry's. Mabou Mines' pieces, too, even though Breuer may have written them. Still, I think there is a certain element of collaboration in which all of the people together keep focusing on the text, and making it work, at the same time they are trying to make the production work.

BGM: I think that the one great problem in dealing with the avant-garde is the almost total emphasis on performance and the fact that nobody is analyzing texts. There is a tremendous amount of work to be done, on the part of critics, in analyzing these texts because there is very definitely a thematics there; it's not just raw consciousness. You can analyze these texts in terms of dramatic literary tradition: metaphor and symbol, rhetoric, theme, and so on.

ME: If we saw a flock of American critics exerting the same amount of effort on the plays of Foreman as they have on the plays of Samuel Beckett, we'd have in our midst, I think, a great American artist!

BGM: Avant-garde artists, at least some I know, wish that people would deal with their texts. Audiences are very sophisticated now about performance ideas but not about radical dramaturgy.

GD: Conversely, let's hope that with productions of off-off-Broadway plays, we now begin to see an emphasis on style in production.

ME: It's happening with Shepard. Only in the productions that Robert Woodruff has done recently do we really get a sense of Shepard as a truly original voice.

GD: And then along come critics who are not used to theatrical style. Bill Hauptman's production of *Domino Courts* at the American Place Theatre is a case in point. An elegant production of a fine play was viciously denounced by Clive Barnes. It's a critic's absolute inability to deal with style.

ME: It's a question of solidity. They're not looking for subtlety.

BGM: Take a person like Walter Kerr who, whatever his tradition, is a person who thinks about drama, however conventionally. When he discussed *Curse of the Starving Class* he didn't even deal with it in any kind of serious way, and spent more time in the same review on a lesser play by Thomas Babe because it was easier, conventional drama. Kerr made no attempt to situate Shepard in a context. I think part of the problem is the attitude of the literary establishment and the academic establishment. These people have never quite made the break from a literary notion of theatre to a more performance-oriented, nonliterary notion of theatre. They're still dealing with very traditional notions of character, history, fate, dramatic action, and structure and they don't really know how to deal—how to even enter into a dialogue—with an experimental work.

ME: In the academic environment, on the other hand, if you were to teach a course, or take a course, in American theatre you would probably stop in the fifties. You wouldn't advance any further than Albee.

BGM: One of the reasons is that a lot of these texts aren't available. Publishers rarely publish plays anymore unless the play gets a Pulitzer Prize, or the Drama Critics Circle Award, or maybe a Tony. So that you have a situation where the only contemporary drama being published is Shange's *For Colored Girls*, David Mamet's work, *The Gin Game* and *The*

Shadow Box. There hasn't been one recent anthology of contemporary plays. There is another factor too, which is that it is extremely difficult to write about the theatre unless you are in New York and going to it constantly. This limits most of the country. Certainly you can't be a critic of the American theatre without following it over a period of years and being there every weekend watching performances. You can't develop a performance theory without seeing performances. And then if you're outside of New York—with texts not being published—how can you develop ideas about a writer?

With contemporary drama, many of the people who are interested in it haven't even been in New York very long, so they can't possibly have a sense of history. There is a sort of crisis in developing critics for performance theory because though there might be people who are very informed about Foreman and Wilson and Mabou Mines and The Performance Group, they may not have been in New York during the Happenings. So no one can quite put together a movement from Happenings to Fluxus to contemporary avant-garde theatre performance to performance art. There are no theatre critics who have the necessary art background, and art critics know even less about theatrical theory. Almost nothing exists in the way of substantial tapes or films or books on contemporary performance. That's another reason why archives and documentation and criticism have to begin to exist in the performance areas, so that people can begin to develop a history about it. That avant-garde performance may have a history possibly dating back to the Bauhaus, or constructivism, or to Brecht, or to painting or to dance theory.

ME: That's what makes art criticism so good. You get the impression that Meyer Schapiro on modern art wouldn't be nearly as good if he couldn't keep going back and looking at those works again and again. Or that Andrew Sarris wouldn't be nearly as interesting on film if he couldn't go to retrospectives constantly and keep re-viewing American film and reevaluating his stance. But you never see American theatre critics even think about reevaluating their stand in the light of what they're seeing now as opposed to what they saw ten, fifteen, twenty, even thirty years ago.

BGM: People don't think of studying the theatre like poetry and fiction. Theatre has no real respectability as literature.

ME: It has respectability in terms of acting and directing. But certainly not in terms of literature.

BGM: Going back to what Gautam was talking about—developing critics who can talk about style, performance, texts—structuralists, semiologists, sociologists, and anthropologists who write about theatre don't usually enlighten us because they don't really understand theatre beyond what the basic graduate student understands. I find reading these people very disappointing at times because they think they're making major statements on the way the theatrical idiom functions, and they're not.

GD: But, American plays, playwriting, and production in general would benefit from bringing in the techniques or at least a knowledge of other disciplines. Chaikin and Schechner/anthropology; Foreman/philosophy; Breuer and Wilson/fine arts. It's about time that literary playwrights—off-Broadway and off-off-Broadway—saw the benefit of an interdisciplinary approach. It's true that off-off-Broadway playwrights got a lot out of popular entertainments. No one has really discussed that thematics. But a lot of them got a lot of mileage by refunctioning forms taken from musical comedy, vaudeville routines, et cetera. Today, the overriding influence is of television. Which is both good and bad. Some playwrights have been able to do it moderately well—I'm thinking of someone like Guare. Others have ended up writing pseudo-intellectual television fare. It's a hybrid that could be termed "experimental sitcom family dramas." And America is a society that is built on the principle of comedy. You fall down, you get up, and you move on—from one situation to the next. Hence this stranglehold of the TV sitcom.

BGM: I think that you will find tragedy in European drama because the notion of fate and history is much stronger since they've had constant wars. In America, not having that kind of a history, not having war here, naturally I think we'd be drawn to comedy: we don't see fate as unalterable. You see constant change or progression and that's the movement of comedy. I think American playwrights are incapable of writing a tragic play because they don't believe in the ideals of tragedy.

ME: Well, I think Rabe tried to, and he tried to do something like O'Neill—to go back to a tragic tradition, build a play according to certain mythical themes.

BGM: Yes, but *Sticks and Bones*, which is a war play, encompasses the structure of television commercials. So even within his approach to tragedy he reverts to a traditionally less serious form . . . The other point I wanted to make is that most of the playwrights can't follow the logic of the form they set up in the play. That's a drawback with Shepard. He's so powerful theatrically and has enormous potential in terms of what he's doing within a realistic context, making it much leaner, and really reinterpreting realism—I think any person who writes after Shepard in the mode of realism has to contend with his achievements already—and also what he's done with the notion of actualization, with the characters actually making themselves up on the spot. But his plays go off in all directions because he can't shape the energy he lets loose in them.

GD: Another thing, speaking of the interdisciplinary approach to theatre, is the notion of myth, of a collective mythos. The sort of mythopoeic element that one finds in Shepard suffers badly in other American plays. I suspect a lot of this has to do with the fact of poetry and that America is such a romantic country, going back to Thoreau and Emerson. Artists, primarily playwrights, have found a common denominator in the poetic spirit—whether it be in creating some sort of striking dialogue or some sort of visual aura. The plays are more akin to poetry. The mythopoeic impulse is paramount. Maybe bad poetry, but at times pretty good poetry. Overall, I think that the guiding force has always been poetry. And by emphasizing that more than anything else, dramatic structure, the drama of a play, as opposed to the poetry of a play, suffered a lot.

BGM: One of the difficulties that poets have, take someone like McClure, is that they fall so in love with their own language that their plays begin to dissipate because of the excesses of the language, the repetition of sounds. Rochelle Owens, who is a good playwright, also suffers from this in her work. Falling in love with the language and taking off from there, from the sound values of the poetry and the rhymes, and forgetting where she is in terms of the line of the play.

GD: I'm astonished reading so many American plays that every play has a poem in it, has passages inevitably set to music. To me that's a very interesting indication of where so much of the impulse is coming from.

ME: Do you think it might be not so much poetry as American musical theatre?

GD: Yes, that's part of it, too. Interestingly, look at the theatricalization of jazz, poetry, and rock. The problem is that the poetic or musical element appears only as divertissement, as another independent element not totally integrated into the dramatic form. Also, the poetic in these plays is a half-baked idea of poetry. For many of these playwrights, poetry only means expressing your innermost beliefs. And then nearly every character in a play is imbued with those beliefs, as if a quantitative explosion of the poetic thrust will balance out a lack of structure. Look at some of the long plays of Lanford Wilson.

ME: You know, so many American playwrights have succeeded best in the one-act play. Someone like Israel Horovitz, for example, writes very good one-acts. When he moved to the full-length trilogy that he wrote a few years ago, it was not nearly as successful as his short pieces.

BGM: Of course Shepard is an outstanding example of someone whose full-length plays often fall to pieces by the second act . . . *Curse of the Starving Class, Mad Dog Blues, Angel City.*

ME: It just takes that ability to focus and to clarify dramatically. The great achievement of Pinter, it seems to me, is that he was able to individualize characters. He created private idioms for them, and when he brought them together onstage they clashed and drama was created. You often don't get that essential conflict in so many American plays.

BGM: I'm not sure I'm willing to go all the way with the idea that drama has to have conflict. This again might be something to reinterpret in terms of a contemporary consciousness.

ME: But I'm talking about a clash between private idioms, which is different from essential conflict.

BGM: I don't think American drama by the non-mainstream people is very much a drama of conflict.

ME: It's what we should call a drama of incident. *American Buffalo* is a play about situations.

GD: Yes, but *American Buffalo* is a good example of this. But the trouble with so many of the others is that there are many situations in the plays, and so many of them just seem to be excuses. To either provide some exhilarating moments, some dialogue, some flashy comments, and the like. But in the overall structure those situations are snippets of life.

BGM: To go along with the idea of situations and to extend my idea that ours is not a drama of dramatic conflict—I think that American drama is extremely action-oriented. For this reason, it's not particularly character-oriented, or conflict-oriented, which requires a lot of reflection. It's a drama that constantly keeps moving. People worry all the time—when you talk to people who are reading plays in a conventional way—about keeping the drama moving all the time.

ME: Maybe we should move on to some general comments about what the structure of the American theatre has done to playwriting. The notion of the hit, which includes success and money. Theatres seem to be using writers up—consuming them. Theatres have to constantly attract audiences, constantly keep their subscriptions up, so they in turn can receive more funding. That creates a crisis of a different sort for the playwright.

BGM: First of all, it's probably easier now than ever before for playwrights to get their work done. Because there are so many more theatres and they're all looking for new American plays—not only the new American play, but the Great American play. The Actors Theatre of Louisville has a Great American play contest. Foundations are probably overfunding theatres to produce only American plays. Then you have all theatres around the country competing to find the new young fashionable playwright and then sending him to Broadway.

ME: And then he in turn gets attracted to films and television, where the big dollars are. He leaves the stage quite early. That happened in the twenties and thirties too, of course—but they tended to go back to the stage occasionally. Now I think the American writer is consumed by other media so quickly that there really is a crisis for the young American playwright.

BGM: Last year in the newspapers there were numerous articles discussing the great discoveries like Innaurato, Durang, and Mamet. This year there are no articles like that in the papers. There's no new wunderkind.

GD: Well, the economics are such that most of the adventurous theatres must rely on federal and state support, which in turn pushes them into producing American plays. Although that's good in a sense, it is unfortunate for reasons of their not being able to develop a comprehensive repertoire. If a company could develop freely a foreign, classical, and mixed repertoire, not only playwrights but the entire theatre community would benefit as a whole. After all, how many of us here have had the opportunity of seeing the great classics done well, or done at all?

BGM: There's something else also—forgetting for the moment the notion of people not being able to see classics. They don't even see an American dramatic repertoire. There's absolutely no connection made between what's done now and what's been done in the past. If you take a case like Germany, you see each generation of playwrights reworking the provocative ideas of the past. You can trace a direct line from Büchner to Brecht to Peter Weiss to Handke, and its exciting to think who's going to come after Handke, to recharge this Brechtian line. But American playwrights work in a complete void; there's no sense of tradition, where they're coming out of, where they're going, what are the links. They're here today and gone tomorrow, and all the theatres and critics and even the foundations propagate this whole consumer notion of the playwright, based entirely on his function in a consumer society.

GD: I think the whole ideology of trying to look for the Great American play in this fiscal year is stupid. The way the endowment and private foundations are set up—relying so much on reviews—a company simply can't possibly take risks. You have to do a play that will get you a lot of subscribers and a good press.

ME: That happens in all the arts, in film certainly. There's a darling director this year, and the next year he or she turns out a bad film, and no producer will handle them again.

BGM: There is no sense of playwrights having an audience. They have to almost re-create everything new for the first time, with each play. That may be one reason why there is no experimentation in current playwriting.

ME: Well, we know that the foundations and the government are supporting populism in the arts. They're looking for a commodity that will appeal to the broadest range of society.

BGM: Any one of the new playwrights who have had any popular success have gone immediately to Broadway. If you remember, in the sixties the younger playwrights had a sense of being "downtown" people who wrote plays that never would have made it to Broadway, nor did they want them to. These more experimental playwrights will more than likely never get to Broadway.

ME: There again we have that process of acceleration of culture. The culture using its artists in a way that is really prohibitive to creating art. In the case of the younger playwrights it might have something to do with the so-called new conservatism. They're not liberal or radical in the sense that playwrights were in the sixties. They've grown up in an age that has restraints on it, and as writers, they recognize those restraints. And the chances, too, of getting to Broadway or to the big regional theatres is much greater than it ever was.

GD: True. This lure of a professional production—and why shouldn't a playwright go after it?—has totally demoralized the original entrepreneurship that was associated with off-off-Broadway. Today, a truly experimental playwright has two options. Give his play to a small theatre with little resources, and perhaps jeopardize his chances of a revival, since everyone is looking for a new play to do. Or else leave it to accumulate dust in his drawer.

In terms of contemporary playwriting, not the avant-garde, one should not look for every generation to come up with a great playwright. One shouldn't have inordinately high goals, because it's never happened in the history of the theatre. When it does happen, then you have someone to measure your own work against, and that in turn generates a healthy theatrical environment. Hopefully, Shepard will become that model some day. I have hopes for someone like Bill Hauptman. Mamet, perhaps too early to say. In the avant-garde, I too have immense hopes for Spalding and Liz, and Stuart Sherman.

ME: All of this new playwriting activity and heavy financial support has only been with us for the past five years. It may very well produce writers, critics, and maybe even directors of true quality. So I'm not totally pes-

simistic about what the current atmosphere is, and what it might in fact
become.

BGM: I can feel myself going both ways. I can't deny the fact that everyone
I talk to is so disappointed at the state of the theatre. Many people are
even thinking of not going to plays anymore or are just constantly disappointed by bad plays, bad productions, bad criticism, quirky kind of
funding. So it seems that the only real place to look for any kind of rigorous thought is the avant-garde theatre, which is also in its own way
coming to the end of an era. Foreman is leaving theatre for film, Wilson
is now working in Europe, Mabou Mines is splintering into factions. Except for Spalding Gray and Elizabeth LeCompte, whose work is the best
new work now, there are no provocative newcomers in the theatre. In a
way they bridge the gap between the theatre and performance art, the
latter being the most exciting area of performance theory now—the area
of more conceptual performance.

My hope rests with the experimental sector because it reflects a tradition, a theoretical foundation, and a willingness to explore new areas
of perception. Of the young playwrights, the people whom I think are
talented are Richard Nelson, Bill Hauptman, and Richard Lees—three
people, who are not generally known but are emerging writers. But
maybe I shouldn't overembellish the situation.

ME: Yes, and put them under the pressures we've been talking about.

John Guare, David Mamet, Wallace Shawn, Steve Tesich, Michael Weller

EVER SINCE THE GLORY DAYS of cinema, Hollywood studios have relied on the dramatic skills of playwrights to add prestige and literary cachet to their screenplays. The five playwrights here who carried on in that tradition launched their careers and national reputations in New York's off-Broadway theatres, except Mamet, who first came to prominence in Chicago. At the time of these conversations, the off-Broadway scene was waning and, as a result, many playwrights turned toward Hollywood either to willingly confront new artistic challenges or to reap the benefits of a more remunerative line of work. In all instances, as the playwrights suggest, they were not so much wooed by Hollywood studios as they were invited to collaborate with specific directors (Malle, Forman, Yates, Rafelson) familiar with their stage works and under whose tutelage they developed as screenwriters.

The baneful effects associated with working in a high-stakes environment dedicated largely to commercial interests and popular appeal do not seem to have had deleterious consequences for any one of the playwrights. Whether adapting novels (Tesich, Mamet, Weller), writing original screenplays (Guare, Shawn), or working from plays of their contemporaries, they all speak eloquently to the differences between various genres and how their experiences as dramatists either helped or impeded their writing for the screen. Years of working with stage actors give them unique insights into the differences in work habits and approaches to characterization that distinguish film and stage acting. Interestingly, they also talk of how an apprenticeship in film in turn affected their playwriting skills after returning to the theatre. Today, when more and more stage actors and directors are gravitating toward film, be they independent or studio features, the prescient remark of Tesich, who died in 1996—"I think actually that you can be much more daring in films today than in theatre. I find that quite incredible"—has taken on added meaning.   GD

Conversations with Michael Earley, 1981

Playwrights Making Movies

Steve Tesich

Michael Earley: You've had four film projects now back to back. Has screenwriting been your main concentration for the past three years?

Steve Tesich: Yes, except for *Division Street*. That came after *Breaking Away*.

ME: Have you worked on other plays since that one?

ST: No, I really haven't felt the impulse. I just follow my cycles. I'm working on a novel right now. That's been the primary thing for the past six or seven months.

ME: How long did it take you to prepare *The World According to Garp?*

ST: The first draft took about six or eight weeks. I work very fast when I sense how to do it. And all I do is write. Off and on we've been working on slight revisions with the director, George Roy Hill, and the cast, and certain elements got strengthened, certain story points got clarified better. But the central vision remained as written the first time around.

ME: It's a hard novel to adapt for film, isn't it?

ST: It certainly is. It's a large, hefty movie. A lot of things had to be left out, and a lot of things had to be added that weren't in there. Because if you see a vision of how a movie should be done, then you remove certain things that are in the book. You have to have a focus that can't be the focus of the book because you don't have eight hours of screen time.

ME: Did you choose to isolate one narrative line in the novel to the exclusion of others?

ST: I don't make clear-cut decisions like that. I just go instinctively on what it feels like it should be. I definitely strengthened certain lines that were minimal in the novel, making them much bigger. But they were there to begin with. So the spirit of the film is the spirit of the book. It's just that I would say certain elements and characters are not there, certain others who were not in the book appear in the film. Because I don't think you can have a good adaptation if you treat the source as a Bible, where you can't feel inspired by it. I'm a writer myself and I'm just glad I can be inspired by it. But I never really thought of doing an adaptation until I read *Garp*.

ME: Did you work with John Irving at all?

ST: No. It had to be done independently. He's a wonderful novelist, but I just don't honestly feel that he could have helped. I didn't really talk about anything with anybody anyway until I'd written it, because a lot of people can talk wonderful screenplays and it just kind of diffuses things when you're gabbing instead of writing. I like to write and get it done. I submitted the script to John as a courtesy, and we then did a reading with the cast. Anything he wanted to say at that point was certainly welcome, but not when I'm writing.

ME: So you don't even work with a director at that stage?

ST: No. I finish it first. They read it then and we have something to talk about. I didn't want to hear how they would have written it because they're not writers. The thing that I've written becomes the focus of our discussions.

ME: Do you find that when you do an adaptation like this, which is different from the original work you're accustomed to, you have to change your style in terms of language and point of view?

ST: Not at all. The central character was somehow close to me so I thought I was writing about myself. In fact, the dumbest thing you can do is start fiddling with your style. Supposedly, the reason they wanted you to do that project in the first place is *because* of your style. My point of view is my own, no matter if I write on my own or focus on someone else's work. It's different from anything I've written, but then *Eyewitness* is different from *Breaking Away*. And that's really something I love to do as I get older—look at things differently.

ME: Are your concerns as a playwright different from those as a screenwriter? Do you separate these two aspects and do you see a difference in each medium?

ST: Essentially, I think of myself as a writer and not as a playwright, and so it's not like suddenly I have to have another discipline. Or I have to somehow kill the playwright in me to do the screenplay. It's just that you take advantage of what's available. What's available in a film is a whole world of images, a whole world of nuances that the characters can portray with a look, with a single word. You can focus in a way that you can't in theatre. You can't build a stage character out of a glance or little gestures; language and bigger actions tend to build character onstage.

ME: Can you write those things into a screenplay, or does the director do that?

ST: I write everything, much to the displeasure of some directors—certain images that I feel are crucial and must go on screen. Because without them each moment would not make sense. So everything is written in. Everything that is shot may come out different, because any good director will add things of his own. But the core of imagery is there in the screenplay. I'm very visual, so to cut myself off from that in the writing would be ludicrous. It's part of my speech. I don't differentiate between imagery and speech in film because they both communicate.

ME: There are moments in *Eyewitness* that go on for a long time without any dialogue and it reads to the eye almost like a novel.

ST: Well, I really like the idea of letting that world enter without dialogue. It's a new world that we don't normally observe and I think it gets the mind of the audience going. Once the mind is employed, it requires paying attention on the part of the audience. You could not do that in theatre.

ME: What is the difference in theatre? What do you have to do there? Do you have to maintain a different kind of interest?

ST: I see it as a realm where ideas dominate. I like theatre in which big ideas have their forum. You can use language that you can't in film. You can use a certain kind of eloquence that in film sounds very artificial. People who say things well in film sound realistic. In theatre characters can battle ideas and you will follow it, if it's well done. But in film, somehow, unless it's Bergman or someone like him, we usually won't accept that. But basically I think I'm much more traditional in theatre. A theatre of the past rather than the theatre that is there now, which I don't seem to care for.

ME: When you say the "past," is there anything specific that you have in mind? *Division Street*, for instance, is a very classical farce.

ST: Right. Well, the past to me goes back to comedy of the thirties and forties, and then it goes back to Chekhov. And there's a lot of theatre today that is really almost an extension of television—if it's to succeed in a big way in New York. If you take that television form and fiddle with it slightly, that seems to have the easiest access. And that is very irritating to me.

ME: What are the irritating elements?

ST: It's the obviousness, the certain kind of predigested quality where things are stated rather than arrived at. The problem is stated, the solution is given, all step by step. And nothing of substance is at stake. I feel for some reason that the theatre is a form where things of substance should be discussed. We have so-called entertainment all around us. An area should be left where substantial topics have a place.

ME: Do you see the same motive operating in most feature films?

ST: I think actually that you can be much more daring in films today than in theatre. I find that quite incredible.

ME: Bracketing the films on one hand, and the plays on the other, what was your experience with television? Were you story editor on the *Breaking Away* series?

ST: I would read the scripts and comment on the story lines. I saw wonderful cooperation with the people involved. We had seven episodes and really liked five a lot. The show made me happy—I thought it was pretty damn good.

ME: What do you think happened to the series? Was it the time slot?

ST: In television, unfortunately, they put you in a time period—teenage kids are not home at 7:00 Saturday night. So the audience you're aiming at just isn't there. The second thing is that there was absolutely zero promotion for the show. The third thing is that this not an instant hit kind of show. It doesn't have the biggest tits in the world, it doesn't have anything that is striking . . . I wouldn't do anything in television unless it were more to begin with.

ME: You've been fortunate perhaps, but not everyone else has been.

ST: I just feel that I've been able to be much freer and have a certain degree of success in film without censoring, without trying to do anything but what I want, and it seems to work. In theatre, the things I want or think theatre should be don't seem to coincide with, let's say, what the critics think theatre is. Either I'm at fault or the way I do things, or they're at fault in not allowing whatever's up there to exist. They make decisions very early in a play. I also think film critics are better, probably because there are more of them, and not just three or four who can determine whether a film will run or won't run. In New York three or four critics can kill a wonderful play, or they can make a rotten play run a while.

ME: You've had the good fortune in film to work with good directors. Have you been as fortunate in theatre?

ST: I think overall probably not. There have been two or three exceptions, where the work has been done marvelously and where I couldn't think of anything to criticize—*Baba Goya*, three one-act plays at the American Place Theatre. I think Tom Moore did a wonderful job with *Division Street*. I think there were other things that just didn't work. Now perhaps the reason they didn't work wasn't always the director's fault, because I was there too. So if it doesn't work, you can't turn around and say, "Boy, my director let me down." But as far as films are concerned, I really have been unusually lucky to have had Peter Yates, Arthur Penn, and now George Roy Hill.

ME: What is the quality of the collaboration between the screenwriter and the director, as opposed to the stage director and playwright?

ST: It hasn't been any different for me. Essentially, what you do is have to trust in each other. Nobody's there to undermine the other person. There are only two people on a movie who know what the movie is—and hopefully that's the director and the writer. Therefore, it would be absurd for them to be at odds. Now it helps that I probably knew all these directors before I started working with them.

ME: Have your screenplays and stage plays undergone any radical changes in production?

ST: I would say plays more than screenplays. First of all it takes longer in film and you get more time to work at it. Also more things are questioned in a screenplay because everything is more expensive. You have to get to things quicker because of schedules. So you question everything more thoroughly than you do in the theatre.

ME: The chaos of theatre must make the work take directions you hoped it wouldn't take.

ST: Well, you're not aware of it at the time. Chaos creates its own kind of emergency when you're exhausted and rushed.

ME: In your films you seem to be showing that movies can be a writer's medium as well as a director's. *Eyewitness*, for instance, has a lot of scenes that seem dramatic, scenes in which we get a chance to explore characters. *Breaking Away* had a lot of the same techniques.

ST: Well, the whole thing is to write a film where those things are inseparable. In my films, unless you have a sense of the characters, the plot won't function. I don't want to write films where lines are interchangeable. There isn't a plot in the world that will function without characters. We won't watch or listen to any story unless we care for the people or understand them. Now, a director who feels uneasy with that will not do my screenplays.

ME: Has the problem come up?

ST: No, I'm now talking hypothetically because it never has been a point of contention. I assume the director likes what he's read and wants to do it. Both Peter Yates and I wanted to do a thriller, but we wanted to do it differently. We had all kinds of things not normally in a movie like that.

ME: Did that become a challenge in *Eyewitness?*

ST: Well, to take one instance, at the height of tension, the father comes in and you have to hear about his problems with his wife. But that's how life is. Life isn't neat plots. None of us lives in plots where we go step by step. So I really base my screenplays on what my life feels like. Unexpected events. I like to stay honest in my writing and portray life as it is.

ME: When you compare *Eyewitness* with a Hitchcock, he would have wanted it more step by step, more formulaic in terms of plot.

ST: Yes, but it worked brilliantly for him because he believed in it. He saw that world and was honest about it. I couldn't be honest about it because I don't believe it, even though I adore his work. I have to believe because my experience is the only thing I have. Then you have no regrets.

ME: Has writing screenplays changed the manner and form of your plays?

ST: I don't know because I haven't gone back to theatre, and won't for at least a year or two. I hope it does because I love to be affected and changed. I don't want to be the same person. I suppose it will affect me in terms of really getting rid of the theatrical language, and relying more on plodding humanity speaking its mind, rather than quotations. But that's bullshit until you sit down and do it. My novel writing has affected my narrative forms greatly. I can visualize now and single out things better. I think anything can be a film if the right person writes it.

ME: You started off with three original screenplays, which is wonderful for a writer. Most screenwriters seem to do more adaptations at first.

ST: You can't blame studios or producers for that. Nobody is stopping a writer from sitting down and writing a script. A lot of writers in film have the attitude that they're not going to write anything until they're paid. The idea of just sitting down and writing a screenplay the way I've done is really alien to a lot of writers. I wouldn't say I've been "fortunate." I had to sit down and decide to do it whether or not I was going to be paid. And I will continue to do that. I'd written five screenplays before *Breaking Away* that were never made. You're a writer—that's what you do. You're not a merchandiser. A lot of writers lose sight of that. They rely on others to give them the impetus to write.

ME: Obviously the success of *Breaking Away* and the Academy Award must have helped with the next two films.

ST: It's helped a lot. I was writing *Four Friends* while *Breaking Away* was being shot. Then I stopped to write *Eyewitness*. Now I have to be hard on myself. Where once people were too critical, now, if they don't understand something, they think, "Well, maybe Steve knows something we don't . . ."

ME: Has the success you've had in film made it easier to get plays produced now than, say, five years ago?

ST: I suspect I wouldn't have difficulty with a play of mine getting strong consideration. But that's guesswork. It would be easy to get involved in a lot of things—people call me with offers. They want me to do musicals. That I think is a result of the films, because a lot of people haven't seen my plays. When *Division Street* opened, I had had six plays done, and some of the New York critics wrote that the Hollywood writer was now writing theatre. At that time I had only written *Breaking Away* but because it had won the Academy Award, it made them get all surly—how dare I write a play. They just skipped the play, though the theatre was where I began. . . .

Wallace Shawn

Michael Earley: How did *My Dinner with André* evolve? Had you written film scripts before?

Wallace Shawn: No. I never had. André and I were planning to collaborate on something. The general idea was that I would write it and he would direct it—a play or something. He had directed my play, *Our Late Night,* with The Manhattan Project. That was the first play of mine that was ever done. We wanted to work together again. We talked about all these different projects and this idea was obviously a film idea because it's absolutely wonderful to look at people's faces on film and hear them talking. It's not very enjoyable in the theatre because all you see is a little dot unless you're sitting in the front row. And my opinion would have been that in no way could you have stood watching this as a play. As it turns out Louis Malle thought it would be a good idea to do it in the theatre to solidify the performances. It turned out that it was fine—people survived.

ME: Whose idea was it, yours or André's?

WS: My version of how the whole thing came about is that I had the germ of the idea but then we immediately began discussing what sort of an idea it would be. I think I had the idea where we'd have the conversation and really be ourselves. We met for about three or four months a couple of times every week, with a tape recorder, and just talked about anything that occurred to us—in no order. His life, my life. It took me a year to come up with a script, working with the million pages of transcript.

ME: At that point what were you looking for—a structure?

WS: The actual script has nothing to do with any conversation we've ever had, though it's almost entirely made out of conversations. When André says something in the script, he really did say that to me. But each half of a sentence is attached to another half of a sentence from months later. It's a confection. It looks like André and me, but it isn't really us—we're characters. One of the points that André and I discussed at great length is that it should be a conversation interesting to anyone. In the movie the pretense is that we hadn't seen each other for five years . . . Well, that wasn't true at all. And there was no dinner that we ever had. On the other hand, when André says, "I went to the Sahara desert and rode on a camel," it's true. All of the surprising stories he tells about his life are true.

ME: Is it like the kinds of things that Spalding Gray does when he constructs pieces around incidents from his life?

WS: His work is what it is—frankly autobiographical. Mine is a very formal piece. It's meant to stand totally on its own as fiction. In other words, it should work even if you did not know there were really two people corresponding to these two. We don't step outside of ourselves. What I've seen of Spalding Gray is that he actually says, "I'm Spalding Gray, and now I'm going to show you certain scenes that are based on my life."

ME: How did Louis Malle come into the project?

WS: We wanted somebody who had an incredibly good sense of humor. On the other hand, we didn't want somebody with a totally cold sense of humor who would do it as a satire on us, although we are both absurd figures in a certain way. We wanted someone with a great psychological understanding and sense of drama . . . Louis Malle seemed the obvious choice.

ME: When did you begin work on the project?

WS: We made the film in or about 1980. We all worked in the cutting of it but Louis was the guiding force. We cut as we rehearsed; it wasn't theoretical. In the summer we rehearsed on tape and watched ourselves.

ME: Why did you think it would make a good film rather than, say, a video project?

WS: I think it would be fine for television, but it's more exciting on the big screen. It's rather dramatic. It's not a sort of relaxed interview between André and me, not like a talk show.

ME: Has the project changed your writing in any way? Are you contemplating more movies?

WS: This was totally different from anything that I've ever written or that André has ever worked on. But it's a jinx to talk about such things. If you compare this with any of my plays, you will see that it explores areas of life that have been totally unexplored in them. It was for me a great revelation.

ME: As a writer, what are you trying to do in theatre and in film? How do these experiences differ emotionally for an audience?

WS: It's very hard to make a very powerful emotional scene between people working in movies, whereas in the theatre it's much easier. If you have someone sobbing on stage for the audience it's usually quite moving even if the play or acting is bad. At least you're in the presence of this sobbing human being and your feelings are easily aroused.

ME: People are very moved by movies. A friend of mine went to see *Gone with the Wind* the other night and said that a third of the audience was crying by the end of the movie. People felt very bad at the end of *Tess*, too.

WS: In life we go through great emotional experiences every day. We don't show them, but we feel them. If there were a camera close enough to you, it would see them. So a movie is much more like life because you can show the way people's emotions really register, which is very subtle. In a play you have to have people say things or they have to really show their feelings. I've only recently begun to be able to stand watching a play from far away in the theatre or to think of writing a play that would work if you were quite far away.

We did *Marie and Bruce* in a three-hundred-seat theatre, which is the largest theatre that I had ever experienced because I'm strictly from the underground world of the theatre. To see that you could do certain things that would actually work even if you were sitting in the back row of the theatre was very fascinating to me. But, in my experience, I've enjoyed sitting in the front row, and in a sense writing for the front row because I don't really like theatrical acting. I like movie acting.

ME: How would you describe movie acting?

WS: I like completely naturalistic acting. Of course, sometimes in the theatre you're dealing with material that is rooted in the unconscious and a naturalistic portrayal of those scripts can be quite bizarre. I've written some myself, but I don't like anything that I feel is being projected out to me. I'm alienated by that. I like to feel that the people onstage are just behaving in the privacy of their own home—and I happen to be there. There are certain exceptions. For instance, I enjoyed Raul Julia's performance in Wilford Leach's production of *Taming of the Shrew* as much as anything I've ever seen. I loved his performance and it was very theatrical. It was nothing like anything you could do in a movie. But he was acting with the two thousand people in the audience in mind—not pretending he was in the privacy of his bedroom.

In the theatre you have to use a little dialogue to convey what's going on, but in movies you can get away without it. In a play you can follow the relationships between people over the course of fifteen minutes in a way that you never could in a movie. I find that very exciting.

There's in a way a kind of naked examination of a person in the theatre that can't happen in a movie because the characters are there for a long time, and you just keep looking at them. They're trapped up there on the stage and you can follow their fate in an unrelenting way. In a movie you're cutting away from them, and also the movie shows you what to look at. In theatre, the audience decides what to look at. You can see things develop in an undistracting way—the shots and the scenery are not constantly changing.

ME: What you seem to be saying in a certain sense is that playwriting is a lot harder than movie writing, which may be more fun because you can get yourself out of things more easily. In playwriting you write yourself problems that you have to confront directly. They don't go away.

WS: You could perfectly well have a movie that's an hour and a half long about a couple and might never notice that the couple never had a conversation during the course of the movie, or only confronted each other for fifteen seconds. Now, in a play that evasion would be very obvious. But there are so many things that can make a movie interesting—the scenery, the way a person's face is photographed, the costumes. The theatre is so austere in comparison.

ME: How did Malle shoot *My Dinner with André?*

WS: He shot it in the most austere way he possibly could have. There is a scene in which I go to the restaurant that contains a lot of action but that only lasts seven minutes. But once we meet and sit down at the table, you don't see anybody but the waiter, André, and me until the end.

ME: How did it come to be staged just in England? Were you there already?

WS: No. Malle thought we should do it for an audience. We didn't want anyone we knew to see it. The first performance that we did was in a theatre called Upstate Films in Rhinebeck, New York. We had a tiny audience.

ME: Would it have made a difference had the audience been there as you were filming? Would you have found values in the script that could be translated into film by doing it in front of an audience?

WS: Doing it all the way through with the kind of incredible concentration that you have in front of an audience is almost impossible to re-create in rehearsal. We did learn a lot about the shape of the piece doing it with an audience. I find it impossible to ignore the audience and not perform to some extent. If an audience seems bored and wants to move along the performance a little bit faster, it's very hard not to move faster. A stage actor should be aware of the audience, and you do perform differently for each audience.

ME: What style were you looking for in the film?

WS: It was obvious from square one that the style we wanted in the movie was of the utmost naturalism—totally believable. All acting is supposed to be as if for the first time. If this movie had not been, it would have been a disaster. It's terribly hard to perform in the theatre for more than a couple of performances without beginning to have a few habits. We did not dare to do it more than we did in London. The main reason we didn't is that we were terrified we'd be giving a stage performance in the movie.

ME: Was it up to Malle to help you stage the performances?

WS: Oh, he staged the whole thing.

ME: One of the things you must have learned is a new kind of intimacy. I've seen you in things such as the very theatrical play *Chinchilla* and André has always been a theatrical director. The sense of intimacy, you said, is important to your plays.

WS: Of course this play has a script. Some of my earlier plays are in the unconscious half of the time. *My Dinner with André* is on the conscious level. It was like having eight years of experience as a film actor doing the work we did. It wasn't like a regular film where you're acting for fifteen minutes out of a day—we were sitting there for ten hours at the table every day. The actual filming took three weeks, but we had been rehearsing for a few months before that. If our goal in life were to be film actors, no one could pay for the training André and I received. It is much more intimate than what was done in London. People who saw it there said they saw it as a philosophical dialogue. The movie is totally personal.

ME: Did he get you away from stage actor tendencies?

WS: He took us away from any attempt to be ourselves. Initially, our impulse would have been to be exactly like the way we really are. From the audience's point of view that's totally irrelevant. In the film we're acting these roles as if we were two actors who got these scripts in the mail.

David Mamet

Michael Earley: Is *The Postman Always Rings Twice* the first film you've written?

David Mamet: I wrote a couple of adaptations of my own plays for film, none of which have been done though.

ME: Why is that?

DM: Well, I don't think they were very good. My beginning to really write for film had to do with Bob Rafelson, who directed *Postman*. He took a lot of time teaching me how to write a screenplay. Ulu Grossbard once said the better the play the worse the movie it's going to make. That may be true. What you work on lovingly in one medium doesn't always translate well into another.

ME: What was the collaboration with Rafelson like?

DM: He's a wonderful teacher. He instilled a magnificent amount of confidence in me. The operative thing from his standpoint was I know you can do it. We worked for several months together just talking it out. Often we just talked about screenplays in general. He tried not to be prescriptive, which was a big help, and eventually we began to be more specific about the general form he wanted the screenplay to take, and then I went away and wrote a draft, and then another draft. I was on the set almost half the time and did a fair amount of work there. The actual film was very close to the first draft of the script and I sat in on the pre- and post-production as well. It was more as a student than as a collaborator, but he made me feel like a collaborator. He said to me at the beginning, "Listen, I'm going to adopt you. I'm going to teach you how to write a screenplay and direct a movie."

ME: What has the experience done for you? Do you want to work in film more or make a film yourself?

DM: I wouldn't mind it sometime. But I am happy to get back to the theatre for a while. The money in film is very seductive. Also the fact that you're an employee. Plus you begin thinking, Well, I've got to do another movie, then another. I didn't though and I'm glad. But it's different than playwriting. Arthur Miller said, "You've got to do both or you'll lose the touch." A lot of the same skills are involved, especially writing dialogue. It's very different in a movie than in plays. In a movie you're trying to show what the characters did and in a play they're trying to convey what they want. The only tool they have in a play is what they're trying to say. What might be wretched playwriting—describing what a character does—may be good screenwriting.

ME: What about the quality of the dialogue?

DM: Well, the purpose is different and each has to be effective in its own way. But I like writing for the stage more. You can be much more lyrical. That wouldn't work on the screen—we'd say why are people saying that, because we can see what they're doing. We can see in a cut what their interests are, or what the director is trying to tell us about them.

ME: When you were writing *Postman* did you at any point find yourself writing a play?

DM: No. I kept the scenes very short, very choppy. I was rather amazed myself. In fact, Rafelson said, "If you see a lot of dialogue, then it's a bad screenplay," and it probably is. If anybody wants to know about the difference between writing for film and the stage, they should read Fitzgerald's *The Last Tycoon*. There's a beautiful scene between Thalberg and a playwright who's just come to Hollywood. Fitzgerald also said that the only difference between a secretary and screenwriter in Hollywood is that they call the screenwriter "mister." I was treated very well, but still you are an employee.

ME: Were you ever interfered with?

DM: Not a bit. But that was basically due to Rafelson. It's something he demands in his movies.

ME: What's the difference between working with a director for film and stage?

DM: A theatre director is there to serve the play. The playwright in the theatre is king. But in a film you are working for the director. He's king. The closest thing to playwriting is film editing, because the real art is in the cutting room, where the raw material is made into something. It's like running paper through a typewriter when you have down scenes and dialogue and refine it into something. It's all in the juxtaposition of cutting.

ME: What about working with actors on film and onstage?

DM: The task of the stage director is to bring out the meaning of the play through the performance of the actor. Most contemporary film directors don't know that because they come from a different tradition, a different generation, not a theatre generation. They are interested in beautiful pictures. For instance, the best way to teach playwriting is to teach acting, to make writers really understand what can happen onstage.

ME: Did Rafelson talk about a screenplay in terms of the camera's needs?

DM: No, he never talked about the camera or angles. He said to just describe what the audience should see. There should be great clarity and simplicity. In a way it's very much like writing jokes. It's visual play, completely narrative, only touching on the essentials. It's storytelling boiled down to its most essential elements. It's keeping only those things you absolutely must know in order for you to get the punch line. If you put in anything extra, you lose interest.

ME: Has the experience changed your method of working on a play?

DM: Yes, it did. It took away some of the onus of working on a plot. It's very difficult for me to write a plot. That's really the art of playwriting, I think.

ME: Do you feel your plays don't have plots?

DM: No, they have plots. But most of my plays have been episodic—*Sexual Perversity, Duck Variations, A Life in the Theatre*—and they are easier to do. But the real challenge is to write a play structured along traditional, Aristotelian lines. It's what makes a potentially good play much better. I think poetry was much better when it had to rhyme. Now there's a lot of wretched poetry because everybody's a poet. But to stick to those unities takes much more than just talent. It takes a lot of hard work. I think my best plays stick to them, like *The Woods* and *American Buffalo*. And my children's plays are strictly classically structured, because "what happens next" is crucial to kids. And that's the question in movies. The minute the audience stops wondering, forget it. We're really coming out of the "beautiful photography" period in movies. We've seen the disappearance of plot in movies and charm in acting. *Days of Heaven*, for instance, is all about photography. But now we are going back to a traditional kind of movie making where plot is once again essential.

ME: What about the James M. Cain material? How did you respond to that?

DM: He's a wonderful writer. He makes Hemingway look like a sissy. It's like taking a Dreiser novel, boiling it down to eighty pages, and what you end up with is Cain.

ME: Do you feel more allegiance to the stage? Is screenwriting now just another part of the craft?

DM: Screenwriting I can do. I get offered a lot of screenplays but I've only accepted two. It's fun, it's a change, and it offers a lot of money. But playwriting is really what I want to do. It takes a lot of solitude and leisure. But I'm just coming back to writing a play after a couple of years. Now I'm writing a few different plays.

ME: We seem to have the habit of using up our playwrights so quickly in this country.

DM: There's a great crop of new playwrights. Richard Nelson is a perfect example—incredible talent. His stuff is as good as anything that's been written in the past twenty years. Another great talent is Wallace Shawn. People don't yet know how good he is. But the stuff that's really good is not the kind of material that lives up to people's expectations. It shocks and affronts. So we have the kind of things that have been done on Broadway for the past ten years. Our fears and desires seem to be so great that we can't acknowledge that they exist. We want to be placated.

ME: Has the work in film changed your approach to plays?

DM: It gave me a lot of self-confidence. I had quite a few years of a kind of lassitude and writer's block after my later plays were badly received, especially after early successes like *American Buffalo*. So writing a screenplay was a refreshing break from the theatre. After nine openings of new plays in five years I began to feel a physical revulsion every time I entered a theatre. I feel very refreshed now.

John Guare

Michael Earley: Was *Taking Off* your only other experience in film prior to *Atlantic City?*

John Guare: I did a screenplay of *House of Blue Leaves* but it was never made. Carlo Ponti couldn't get it together without Sophia Loren. So with the money I made from *Atlantic City*, I brought the rights back to *House of Blue Leaves*. I did a screenplay of *Landscape of the Body* for Sam Spiegel—a terrific old producer. Working with him was a wonderful experience. He had this hallucinatory sense of narrative. I did the screenplay and it was just depressing. Spiegel said, "You've done everything I asked you to do except that it's so depressing the only place we could open this picture would be Jonestown." Then I was asked to do a version of *Rich and Famous*, which is about a bunch of kids in drama school, and then *Fame* came out so that killed that.

ME: The ones you've mentioned are adaptations of your own work. What about an original screenplay, like *Atlantic City?* Was the concept yours to begin with?

JG: Yes. What happened was Louis Malle, the director, had seen *Landscape* and we met during that. He was in a bit of a panic because in Canada, about five or six years ago, they gave 100 percent tax write-offs to encourage private investors in films. So people came to Louis with a project that had not worked out. Louis was in despair because they had all this money (somewhere near $3 million) and nothing to film. So he asked if I had any ideas for a film.

I had been reading a great deal about Atlantic City. A friend (Tony Ray) of my parents was managing this big dying hotel that was being torn down to make way for gambling in Atlantic City (this friend now runs Resorts International). So I kept hearing a lot about it—it was in the papers every day. Although I had been there once when I was twelve years old, it just seemed to be a terrific kind of filmic environment, a terrific place to go into and capture in some way. Louis and I went down one day and Tony Ray showed us around. What was extraordinary about it was that we had a story almost immediately. Two things that the producers demanded was a role for a "bankable" male star and a role for Susan Sarandon.

Atlantic City is so theatrical. Our first image was of the boardwalk, which was going to be like Boulevard du Temple in *Children of Paradise*. There were so many rules to be followed if you came from out of town to be part of this kingdom. And all the people that were being displaced. It was material that I felt I could be very much at home with. I had written a play, *To Wally and Tony We Leave a Credenza*, which was the first play I had done in New York, about an old couple being evicted from a house being demolished. And that plan was very much at home in the potential of this material. And so Louis went to France and ten days later I went over with a story. A month later the screenplay was finished.

ME: It took just a month?

JG: Yes. The terrific thing about it was that it *had* to happen quickly. So we put all our interests into it. We had no time for meetings or discussions. There was no committee work. The wonderful thing about the time factor was that it kept the producers out of our lives. And it became a very close collaboration between Louis and me.

ME: Did the screenplay undergo a lot of change after that initial draft?

JG: No, but I would make adjustments throughout the filming because I was on the set all the time. And we would watch the rushes every night with the editor, Suzanne Baron, who's edited most of Louis's films. Louis and I would go to the next location with the cameraman the next day and act out the scene, and make adjustments as needed. It was a very theatrical experience—like working on a play.

ME: I noticed that the whole style of the film has the feeling of a play.

JG: What I admire about Louis is that he really wanted to protect the theatrical aspect of Atlantic City. So each scene was shot, not as a master shot, but as a very long take. The scene in the bedroom where Susan is painting, that's one long scene with very complicated camera moves. Louis wanted each scene to have a long, fluid line.

ME: Does Malle have a background as a theatre director?

JG: At Spoleto he's done opera (*Rosenkavalier*). Last winter at the Royal Court in London he did Wallace Shawn's *My Dinner with André*, which he then filmed. Wait till you see that: two people seated at a table for two hours and that's it.

ME: As a playwright you like to write extended monologues for your characters. How did you adjust that tendency when writing for the screen?

JG: Well, there are sections where each character has his or her monologue. The main thing was that since I knew I could have the scene with Burt Lancaster walking down the boardwalk, I looked for writing moments. But I just realized I would have to keep it short. I didn't want to write things that would have to be cut. There are lots of speeches throughout, for a film, that is.

ME: It must have been terrific fun for you as a writer who in so many of your plays finds a special joy in films and has your characters talk about movies. They themselves seem to want to break out of the frame of the stage. You use the techniques of quick cuts and dissolves in action or quick shifts in lighting on stage. Do you find one medium more to your liking than the other?

JG: I never thought about it until I realized that *Atlantic City* is about this yearning for the stage.

ME: Is it a big readjustment to move to film after theatre?

JG: Well, I felt no difference in writing for film than in writing for the stage. The only thing I knew was that when you write for the theatre, the words have to set the scene. They have to let us know where we are, and so that's why it is trimmed down to essentials. On screen the camera would take care of details and there's no sense having the words competing with the visuals. So the words were all concentrating on the character rather than having to describe the scene. I don't like much scenery in plays. I'd rather the words created the set.

ME: Is there any difference for you working with a film director than with a stage director?

JG: Working on a film is more like working on a musical than on a straight play. One change affects an enormous number of people. Also, a musical has to travel through so many spaces, it has so many short scenes. The music gives the weight, in the way that the camera gives the density to a film. There's more intimacy in a play when there's just you and the actors.

ME: Did you work with the actors at all on the film?

JG: I would say that in some instances I would bring the next scene to the actors. Actually, I went right through the entire process with the editor.

ME: How does your own sense of writing for the stage transfer to writing for film? Has it undergone any kind of change? One thing I noticed about both your plays and the film is the instant transformations that happen.

JG: No. There's no change of hats. The year that I worked for Spiegel taught me something about narration. He'd say to me, "I like this moment right here. But how are you going to pay for this twenty minutes from now? That will affect this, this, and this. This could go this way or that way." Working with him made me think that rather than just settling for a terrific moment I ought to think about how that moment would bleed through the entire event.

ME: One of the things I noticed in the film is the richness and finesse in even the smallest character, which seems to me the unmistakable mark of a dramatist who knows that he has a certain allegiance to his character.

JG: Well, we just wanted to make sure that everyone in it would have an arc, no matter how small the action.

ME: What part does character play in structuring a script?

JG: For me the characters are what dictates the structure and one is always trying to find new doors, new corners to play in, new spaces. And it's for the first time in the past couple of years I've come to realize how I can earn the structure rather than mimicking someone else's structure. One is always trying to find new ways of using that structure to release character, but not just to move into naturalism, rather to find new ways to use it.

ME: When you say "earn structure," what do you mean?

JG: I love things that are really beautifully made. But I think it's quite possible in theatre or film to use the well-made structure. And it is easy for me to mimic another structure. But how do you find something that is beautifully crafted without echoing someone else's form? That's what I mean by earning a form—when you can find a form that will contain that life without letting it spill over into all idle sidetracks.

ME: It strikes me that you come out of a school that could be called the well-made fantasy, which allows a structure to be dictated by the direction in which you're taking your character.

JG: I don't think it's fantasy, though, because that implies a kind of whimsy. My plays are about people's dreams—what they would like themselves to grow up to be. And it seems the plays are about filling up that space. But when you are working on people's dreams, in order to communicate that dream to an audience, there does have to be some sort of container around it so it doesn't become filled with all private references that mean something only to the dreamer. And I believe it's structure that links the audience to the stage event. So when I was talking about earning structure, I was talking about earning our limits rather than having limits imposed on us.

ME: Having made a film set in Atlantic City, do you have any special feeling for the place as a structure of experience?

JG: In Caesar's Palace in Las Vegas there is a lake in the casino, and in the lake there's Cleopatra's barge . . . there are girls in little togas serving you drinks. In that same place in the casino in Atlantic City there is a coffee-shop. That's what's amazing. What I loved about Atlantic City is that there is no fantasy. They have no time for it. They are not interested at all in creating any kind of never-never world. They just build and build and build—and it's all falling apart as they build. The place is on fire—people just wanting to get their money and get out. So there is no Coney Island slowness, no chance for reflection. There was no chance for Chekhov in this one, no place to stop for remembrance.

Michael Weller

Michael Earley: How did the *Hair* script come about?

Michael Weller: Just by accident. I was broke and the producers were in trouble looking for a writer. Peter Shaffer was the one who organized it. He called and said he heard they needed a writer and that the producers were doing his film of *Equus*. He said, "Why don't you go meet about it?" I said, "Who wants to do *Hair?*" He said, "No, no, it'll be a lot of dough and you'll be free to do your plays for a couple of years." Then I found out that Milos Forman was doing it and that was great. I had always thought of films as something to do if I really ran out of ideas, and that if I really couldn't write plays anymore I could do films.

ME: When you actually started filming *Hair* did you work closely with Forman on a day-to-day basis?

MW: I was always on the set and did a lot of time in the editing room as well. I made suggestions if something looked worth it. And there were times when Forman let me direct little sequences if they just needed a reaction shot or cutaway.

ME: Is it unusual for a screenwriter to be that involved?

MW: In American films it is, but I wonder if that's true in European film-making, where it's approached much more as a collaborative art, in the sense of its being an art, not a product of commerce. Here I think there's a kind of divisive feeling between the writer and the rest of the production crew. He's not wanted on the set. When I did *Hair*, at the beginning there was a little bit of suspicion; it was virtually the same problem on *Ragtime*. But then you become one of the gang and can pester people, find out technical things you want to know, and learn a great deal.

ME: How much change did the screenplay for *Hair* undergo during the shooting?

MW: The writing of it was done with Milos every day for five or six hours. Then, it's never really finished. We hand in a script because you have to get the production plans approved. But you just keep on evolving it all the way through, even in the editing room.

ME: Was it the same situation with *Ragtime?*

MW: I knew there had been a bunch of attempts at the script but I didn't want to see anybody else's crack at it. Often you develop an overreaction to the former attempts, which might have some good stuff in them.

ME: Was it also a day-by-day process where the script evolved slowly, rather than being set from the beginning?

MW: Yeah. But it went much more quickly because we were used to each other and I could see certain psychological traps Forman gets into and can avoid them now. In *Hair* I remember there was a period of two-and-a-half months where we could not get anywhere—we'd meet every day and we couldn't break through the situation in the middle of the script. So we sat every day, swapped stories, had a beer, and watched TV. Then finally we started to move on it. But on *Ragtime* we just sort of blasted along.

ME: Yet it seems as if *Ragtime* would have been the more epic project than *Hair*.

MW: In *Hair* you virtually have to make it up—the songs and some character names. With *Ragtime* you mainly have to select and compress.

ME: Did *Ragtime* go through a long evolutionary process during the shooting?

MW: Not radically, mostly cutting. With *Hair* we improvised things after we knew who the actors were, but with *Ragtime* we struck close to the script.

ME: Did Doctorow get approval of the *Ragtime* script? Did you work with him?

MW: I didn't work *with* him but when we were done with a draft we'd sit and he'd make suggestions and if they seemed like good ideas they'd go in; if they weren't achievable in film then you couldn't use it.

ME: When you worked on the films, were you also able to work on plays? Or do you like to do just one project at a time?

MW: I like to do one project at a time, but I did rewrite a play (*Dwarfman*) while we worked on *Ragtime*.

ME: Are there different processes involved in the writing for the different media? Did you have to adjust in any way?

MW: Well, I wasn't writing *Ragtime* at the time of rewriting my play. But by then the real problem in *Dwarfman*—getting a certain tone and style of speech—had been ingrained in my head and I could plug it in pretty quickly. So, I could pretty easily disengage at the end of the day and step into a new kind of rhetoric.

ME: What about the rhetoric of the stage as opposed to the rhetoric of the film?

MW: It's very, very different but I still haven't been able to define it. I do know that in a play, even the plays I write that may seem very naturalistic, the language is very calculated so that I can achieve rhetoric when I need it. I had to find a way to make you think you're just overhearing things, which is not at all the case. It's very carefully worked out. So when I'm ready to go on a binge and I have to fly a little in the language, it'll come out. In *Dwarfman* there's much more high rhetoric.

ME: Where do you see the place of rhetoric in terms of film?

MW: You can't do it. Films are like documentaries in that if you photograph something everyone knows that whatever you're seeing was really there. And if it couldn't have been there you wonder immediately how they did that. It's not like you suspend disbelief as in a play, and you buy the game that the production is playing with you. You know literally if you're photographing something, it happened. That means whatever comes out of the character's mouth has to be literal. If you see a face and it's talking unlike any human you've ever seen, it sounds funny. The words should be at the same level of reality that the photographs are.

I find the most satisfying film to be documentary, and the most satisfying an actual playing of a scene improvised. If it's improvised with the proper external observation, not that clumpy emotional observation where you get into the "truth" of things, but where the surfaces are exactly right and the camera can just wander in and look at how people do things. That's my favorite kind of film.

ME: Do you find writing plays a more satisfying experience for you as a writer?

MW: Oh yeah. I don't consider doing films "writing." I consider it more like assisting Milos in putting a script together . . . If nobody paid me I just wouldn't write an original screenplay. I don't get off on it because there's too much corporate machinery between your idea and what finally reaches the audience. And if it's done wrong once, it's not going to be done again. A play can have a bad production but then you can hope that it'll have a good production. The only solution is to direct your own stuff. I'm going to try that.

ME: Have you been asked to direct a film?

MW: That's the next thing I'm going to do after *Dwarfman*. That's just to see if I like it.

ME: Will the screenplay be like your films?

MW: If I'm doing it I guess it'll be like me. I think it'll be a very improvisational film—no actors. I'm going to try to write the scenes so that what's happening is so inevitable and so real you can kind of clip it together.

ME: When you work with someone like Forman in film, or Schneider in theatre, are there certain differences in the medium that you play off of? What is the sense of collaboration in each case?

MW: They're both good collaborators. The difference is such that when it's a theatre piece the director is really serving my aims. Alan will come to me and say, "What do you need here? What do you want to do here?" In a film Milos won't say that because he knows exactly what he wants.

ME: So the theatre director is serving you and helping you make the play even better.

MW: If the director's good, or if he seems to get my work, the way Alan does. I haven't had many directors who've been good that way with the text.

Most directors in America haven't really read the literature. They know a few modern texts that have come their way. But their sense of what to refer to when a play's structure is in trouble just isn't there.

ME: We've been talking about collaboration with directors, but what about stage and film actors? Have you noticed anything about their capabilities—what you can expect from them or what you have to write for them, in terms of creating a character?

MW: I don't think the distinction would come to me in that way. There are people who are just real interesting on film—I don't know what it is. They have a kind of mystery to them—you always wonder what is going on. I can sense it now. And not that many actors have it. A lot of actors who are fairly well known don't have it for me, so I guess that quality is not really objective.

Stage actors are different. They have to have the same fascination, and there are actors who can do both equally well. But they usually become movie actors too soon and too exclusively, at exactly the point where their equipment has to be honed really hard if they want to make the leap into being real leading actors. They lose all of their smarts about how to build the performance over an evening if they've done film for a couple of years and haven't gone back onstage. They've just lost that canniness but they won't lose the animal thing on stage that makes them watchable. It's like you're only seeing five-eighths of an actor.

ME: Do you find that there are certain things you can't expect from a screen actor that you can expect from a stage actor? Consistency, for example. One actor has to be onstage in a concentrated period of time, the other creating character over weeks or months of shooting.

MW: I don't think about that at all. You just write the story and don't ever worry about how to film it. It becomes an entity unto itself, with its own logic. When it's done you start to go—oh, wait a minute. That happens in plays, too. Although my instinct for plays, because I've done them a lot, is usually pretty good about where a play has to go. Usually, what you try to do in a play is write a role that's increasingly rewarding to play.

A performance is a loosening up of an actor's fear, in a way. It happens that they thaw out during a play. If an actor is starting out, psychologically, down the tunnel of a two-hour performance, and he doesn't have a big juicy scene to play late in the play, he'll go nuts. It follows the arc of a play's logic anyway.

ME: Do you do the same thing in a screenplay?

MW: Yeah, except, of course, the screen actor doesn't go through that process. He comes to the set in the morning and they say, Okay, stand over there and in this scene you blink your eyes. It's going to be in the editing room that you put together the performance and you choose which moments you want. In fact, sometimes we write long scenes and we know we're not going to use all of them, but we want to have all those points for the actor to traverse in the scene so we can cut out just the ones that were played wonderfully.

ME: You've said you worked in the editing room on post-production of both films. Does it give you a certain amount of power to know that you can actually structure a performance?

MW: It doesn't give me any because I don't do the structuring. What it gives me is the sense of why it was filmed a certain way. I'm just really a student in the cutting room. I don't think I really fully understood the strategy of shooting a scene until I had seen the editing of it—what freedoms you supplied yourself with by filming in certain ways. With *Ragtime*, by keeping a shot journal of the whole film, I was able to realize the strategies.

ME: Let's turn to the question of adaptation. *Hair* was originally a play and *Ragtime* a novel. Do you find any special problems with adapting another author's work? In the case of *Ragtime*, for example, did you have to really like the book before you could take on the project?

MW: It would be dumb to stick yourself for months with something you're not going to like. This is a good time in my career so I don't have to take on things that I hate. But you shouldn't forget that for some years you're going to have to do things you don't like, when you're in an eclipse, or whatever.

ME: Were you ever approached about making any of your own plays into screenplays?

MW: *Loose Ends*, which I did a version of as a screenplay, and another play called *Now There's Just the Three of Us*, and *Moonchildren*. I'm not real keen on that. Once I've solved something as a play, to do it all over again is like copying out a book in longhand—unless you have a real exciting director who has his own ideas for the film.

ME: Now that you've had experience in both media, have you felt constrained by the film system more than the stage?

MW: There are people who've worked very hard to enter the film business, they've struggled and had to make deals. I suppose that's the normal trajectory a professional career in films would take. I was a playwright sitting home writing my plays, and someone came along and said, write *Hair* . . . Then they came along and said, do *Ragtime*, and I said okay. My attitude was, and always will be in a way, if I've got a pen and paper, they've got no power over me.

I think the film world is very childish. It's all really like kids in a store—they're grabbing everything on the counter. That's fine as long as I don't have to deal with it. Fortunately, I'm not setting out to do film work. It may be different when I do my film—I'm probably going to end up struggling with production. But I know the ways of it all now and I find it a bit of a joke anyway. If it doesn't work out, I'll just go back to writing plays.

Richard Peaslee, Stanley Silverman

DURING THE SIXTIES and early seventies, a new direction was charted in musical theatre that challenged the tradition of the Broadway musical. In England, Joan Littlewood's *Oh, What a Lovely War!* set music and text as separate but equal entities in the service of a serious dramatic idea. In America, a similar approach was adopted by Richard Peaslee and Stanley Silverman, two composers who collaborated with playwrights and directors of the experimental theatre, much as in an earlier era Kurt Weill had joined forces with Bertolt Brecht.

Peaslee's involvement with music-theatre, a term specific to this type of collaboration, began with his introduction to Peter Brook, for whom he wrote, among many others, the famously popular score of *Marat/Sade*. The Brook connection led to his acquaintance with Joseph Chaikin, for whose Open Theater Peaslee composed music for such landmark pieces as *Terminal* and Jean-Claude van Itallie's *The Serpent.* For some years after, the three continued to work as a team on many productions. Silverman came to be associated early on with the work of Richard Foreman, creating with him a number of significant music-theatre pieces of underground renown, including *Elephant Steps, Dr. Selavy's Magic Theater,* and *Hotel for Criminals* at the Lenox Arts Center, a producing organization that encouraged such collaboration. He also served as musical director for the acclaimed 1976 Lincoln Center production of *Threepenny Opera* under Foreman's direction, bringing back Weill's original orchestration to the staging of this play. Silverman served as orchestrator and arranger of the musical and choral sections of Paul Simon's 1998 Broadway debut *The Capeman.*

Coming out of traditional musical training, both Peaslee and Silverman, in this dialogue that appeared in the first issue of *Performing Arts Journal,* find much in the practice of process-based and improvisational experimental theatre to reinvigorate their own craft. The overall theatricalization of American culture in the sixties was making its presence felt in the new music, and it was only a matter of time before other composers, among them Philip Glass, John Adams, and John Corrigliano, would reach out to theatre and opera. GD

Conversation moderated by Bonnie Marranca
and Gautam Dasgupta, 1976

Music and Theatre

Stanley Silverman: I'd like to address myself to the issue of the tremendous place the new theatre has had in the general cultural scene. In the sixties—at the time of the second coming of expressionism in music as exemplified by Boulez, Stockhausen, and Berio—music was incredibly vital and at the forefront. It was a rebirth after the war—the post-Webern generation. Theatre had always been in those days either commercial or interesting off-Broadway or offshoots. It definitely was a time for music. Now, I find we live in a time when the theatre has taken the forefront of the artistic stage, so to speak. And that the new writers and directors such as Chaikin, Gregory, Foreman, Schechner have really emerged as a powerful force in the arts not only in this country but in Europe as well.

Richard Peaslee: I think that's very true. And it also manifests itself in contemporary music, which now has a real bent toward theatricality. Stockhausen working with Béjart, Berio getting more and more theatrical. Jack Druckman introducing a lot of theatre into his concert pieces. On the subject of new music versus new theatre what really interested me when I first started working in the theatre was the fact that there was an audience coming in night after night whereas in contemporary music you put on your concert, and you were lucky if you got forty or fifty people for that one night. It is a real attraction for a composer to work in a medium where you have a larger audience.

ss: A subtle but perhaps more ferocious point is the fact that the new theatre has a much more real kind of self-trust, the belief that no matter what comes out, even if it comes out in its most banal form, could be dealt with and art made out of it—as opposed to imposing technique from without. That kind of trust in basic materials is something that had been lacking in music, which had gone almost entirely the other way—it became almost exclusively about technical accomplishment, numerics, charts—or the about-face from that—throwing the dice, chance. So that when one went to a new theatre piece it was very gamey, very real, very kind of frightening, a direct type of experience. I felt that the new music that used music exclusively, and the new music that used theatre, such as Berio and Druckman, were hiding behind almost an old-fashioned expressionism. In other words, basically the gestures of *Pierrot Lunaire,* 1912. The new simplicity, the directness—I can't quite label it—had superseded this in the avant-garde theatre and I found that refreshing.

RP: That's a very good point because there's a great deal of intuitive work in the theatre that does not exist in music. I know it's the way Chaikin works. I don't think he can explain why he's doing what most of the time—it's just a matter that it works or it doesn't work.

SS: I think that way of working is liberating, especially for a composer. You trust yourself and see what you can put together. It's not like "where one is at that's art," but it's "given a certain level of input" in the composer. But what about the case where consumer pressures enter into it?

RP: I was just thinking about the pressure I felt in the last two weeks seeing an audience sitting out there [*Boccaccio*] paying eleven or thirteen dollars a seat. You can't fool around, you can't in any way be self-indulgent. You have to please them every moment. In a way it's a good discipline, there's nothing to hide behind. Either it works that night or you're dead. It's not always productive as far as experimentation goes.

SS: Did you feel pressure from the audience or was it in collaboration with the producer?

RP: We had a production in Washington that worked very well with the audience. And yet, we didn't have nearly the resources that we had available in New York. So, I think a lot of it is just the system, the pressures, the whole money thing, and also people's reputations and all that. It becomes a very tight situation as you probably know from your many years at Lincoln Center.

SS: It was easier at Lincoln Center because you could hide behind the classics. I've written music on Broadway for plays and invariably every piece is judged by nonmusical people. I'm very impressed by the fact that Gilbert and Sullivan were responsible equally with D'Oyly Carte for the box-office receipts. And that when they wrote a flop they would pay dearly and either keep it floating or get a new show in there right away. I thought it counted for a great deal in Gilbert and Sullivan and I felt that way about Brecht and Weill. You can't think about these people solely in experimental terms—they had tremendous success in their time. This is the kind of thing that Richard [Foreman] and I talk about regarding our work. We'd like to present them in an arena where they'll run and be quite successful.

To get back to the question of bringing a show in from out of town, it's a very intricate issue. It really has to do with the whole spatial conception of where a piece belongs. In other words, when you're doing a piece for the first time in a space the piece becomes a part of it. And it's not just a matter of: "Now let's bring it to New York."

RP: It was a great luxury with both *Marat/Sade* and *A Midsummer Night's*

Dream to package them in England—get all the bugs out over there—and bring them into New York. We did all our work over in England under circumstances much less hysterical, less pressured. Brought it in and people could take it for what it was. I'm not saying it was idyllic over in England because there were a lot of fights there, too, and tough decisions made that didn't always make us very happy.

ss: I know that in those pieces you had the kind of time to evolve scores in rehearsals.

RP: Peter Brook always asked for eight weeks of rehearsal. So a great deal of the scoring was done then. What happened with *Boccaccio* was after we'd done it in Washington we decided that we'd better rewrite the whole thing. Even though it was a nice show down there we thought that New York was a different situation. So we did a tremendous amount of work on it but we're still trying to figure out what went awry. I think the main thing is having someone in authority who, in the last two weeks, can take over and everyone respects and goes with because when you get down to the wire it's not a democratic practice. Collaboration has to exist for most of the time but at the end the director really has to take over and put it across.

Brook and Chaikin are both very intuitive directors. Brook is a little more mystical or mysterious—a little aloof. When I first met Chaikin it was through Brook. He'd come to London to do a little work on a show called *US*. He was describing his workshop in New York and he said in a kind of modest way: "Our situation—The Open Theater—it's not like Brook where you have one guy with all these great ideas—we have to work out things together."

ss: All the people we've mentioned are directors; we haven't really talked about writers. Even Richard Foreman who started as a writer is also now known as a director. I still have that old nineteenth-century hang-up of working with writers. I do choose usually to work with writers that can direct. I just find it easier—it's closer to the initial impulse. My interest in Richard started originally as a writer.

RP: How did you two connect up?

ss: I got this Fromm Commission to write a theatre piece. I saw Richard and asked to see some of his plays. He was just breaking from his Arthur Miller-Ionesco conventional role. He showed me one play, one he had just started—in very short, sparse language—kind of influenced by Gertrude Stein and it looked a little bit like that Cocteau piece I like very much, *The Marriage on the Eiffel Tower*. It looked like a translation of one of these strange surreal plays of the twenties and thirties. I use the word "translation" because it was that far removed. I was, and still am, a great Cocteau buff. I thought, Fabulous—this is the kind of thing I want to do. So he then wrote *Elephant Steps*. We were looking for a director and Richard said, "If we can't find anyone, I'll do it." And that was his directing debut.

Then in rehearsal both Richard and I made certain kinds of performance discoveries. He got to write first, I would then compose; he would then work against his writing as a director and I would orchestrate. It's not just a matter of writing the piano thing. It's sort of sitting, looking at the thing, and seeing either a dopey, funny, or quirky energy emerge and orchestrate against the music I've written so that a very sweet little ballad sometimes would orchestrate in big, huffy, heavy, ferocious counterlines. The same with tempi—I never really commit a piece to tempo in the writing until I see it. But it's hard for me to write in a rehearsal situation.

RP: I know that feeling because "workshop" is sort of a bad word in some ways. For musicians it often means sitting around and watching actors work out. It's just not the way musicians work—they come in, they sit down, look at their notes, and get on with it. Actors work in a different way. But I don't know if you've found that a certain amount of that workshop thing is essential. When we first started working on *Fable* I had no idea what kind of music to write and we made a couple of false starts but it was immediately apparent that the music was in the wrong style when we sang it with the piece. So the only way it was possible to develop a style for the piece was to hang around rehearsals and see what the actors were up to.

SS: This is something I think about in relation to you very often. Have you ever thought of doing a really totally musicalized piece—in other words, one in which you really take the reins, not as an equal, but as a leader, so that they'd have to sit around and make it work?

RP: When I did *Songs of Love and War* I enjoyed that as much as I did anything. The problem was it wasn't a very commercial piece—I mean, it didn't go anywhere. We did this up at the Lenox Arts Center at the same time as *Dr. Selavy's Magic Theater*. Your piece sounded real theatrical—the songs could attract an audience in New York and it did. Mine never had that potential.

SS: I think that you, and another name that comes to mind, William Bolcom, are among the few that can write—for lack of a better phrase—a parallel piece. In other words, if you listen to material from *Marat/Sade* or *Dynamite Tonight* as a song cycle, each is totally commanding in shape as a musical piece. That's terrific. I'm working on *Threepenny Opera* with

Richard and I guess one of the great shocks for the audience will be to finally see that huge play that goes with it because I don't think it's done much. They usually use the Blitzstein version, which is quite chopped down.

RP: I didn't know you were working on *Threepenny Opera*.

SS: I'm music directing and conducting and we're doing a new but kind of authoritative reminder of what the original piece was. The new version is by Ralph Manheim and John Willett. Anybody that knows the old Blitzstein version is going to be immediately shaken by the new translation. There are many differences in the songs. There's no doubt that the text is brilliantly handled. What I'm doing with the Manheim and Willett lyrics which are very good is—and I did this once in *Galileo*—take the original German plus the authorized one we were using and found that the key to making it *not* sound like a translation was not so much touching up the lyrics but—forgive me, Lotte Lenya—touching up the music a little. When I say touching up I mean very simply that I find the German very downbeat, suspension-oriented. Everything happens right at the leg of the bar lines. You could almost fix every phrase simply by having an upbeat . . . you don't tamper with the pitches so much as where the rhythms and stresses would fall. Hopefully—and I know this sounds strange—the process should bring you back to Kurt Weill.

RP: It's happened to me time and time again when working with a lyricist who is told to change the lyric. So he changes it and it kind of still fits, but it's just not right anymore. So often he knows where the accents are and everything, but it's more than that. It's a fact that setting words is a very important part of composition. Sometimes composer's ideas can't be second-guessed, even by the guy who wrote the lyrics originally.

SS: Going back to *Threepenny Opera*, the rights situation in this capitalistic society of ours is always amazing. Because of it, Mr. Weill's orchestrations had to fight their way to this country. That is one reason we haven't heard the original. However, we're working that out and would endeavor to use Kurt Weill's original orchestration—a first for an American audience, naturally.

RP: Like a Moussorgsky.

SS: I think it was done in the thirties when *Threepenny* came over but it didn't do too well. Another thing I'm doing . . . I'm adding a tuba. I'm also using—as a matter of fact I'm going to play it myself—the original guitar scoring, which calls for banjo, bass guitar with a low C, and Hawaiian guitar, which is never done. It's in the Pabst film, so I assume it was done originally. In the soldier's song and one of Polly's love songs there's this incredibly marvelous Hawaiian guitar obligato. I'm also going to use a very young band and try to emphasize the whole Chicago jazz aspect and really get swinging. Not just theatre players, but musical comedy type players.

RP: There's much too much reverence for Brecht over here as far as his productions are concerned. The old Berliner Ensemble was very, very theatrical and used a lot of glitz.

SS: He's either treated not seriously or too seriously. I have to endorse Stefan Brecht's choice of Richard Foreman to direct it because that is absolutely what is needed, a combination of austerity, brilliance, and showmanship that makes up Richard's work. The most successful performances of Kurt Weill I've heard have been by people from the music world, like Gunther Schuller, Michael Tilson Thomas, Eric Leinsdorf, who did the most brilliant performance of *Threepenny Opera Suite,* and Arthur Weisberg—people who know how to play Schoenberg and Berg, who treat him like a musician, not a show writer. That's what we are going after. The final point I want to make about *Threepenny* is that this was the work of kids—two people in their twenties—which is why I'm going for a young band. We want to get the feeling that this was a kind of Beatles or Rolling Stones experience for the people who wrote it . . . Now, *Marat/Sade* has many of those incredible elements. How did you get involved writing for the theatre?

RP: I sort of happened into the theatre by accident when I was in London working with Bill Russo, who had a jazz orchestra there. Bill had scored a show for Peter Brook, who was looking for a theatre composer to work on a small experimental thing called the Theatre of Cruelty. That was the first time I worked in the theatre. Then we did a production of *The Screens* and after that came *Marat/Sade.* A lot of the same actors worked in all three productions so it was sort of an ensemble feeling that was building up in those earlier productions. It helped us enormously in doing *Marat/Sade.*

SS: How come you lived in England? How long were you there?

RP: Well, it was basically because not much was happening in New York.

SS: But, to get back to one of the earlier points—in the sixties theatre was really happening in this country.

RP: At that time I couldn't have been less interested in writing for the theatre. When I first talked to Brook about working for his production I had barely heard of him. I knew he had just done a production of *Lear* but other than that I was unaware of his work, and not that interested in getting involved in the theatre, especially in small experimental works.

Because I thought of theatre music at that time as watery, incidental stuff that goes between scenes or else Broadway, which didn't excite me. Fortunately, I found out that Brook was on an entirely different wavelength. He had been doing some of his own theatre music prior to that—tape, natural sounds. Soon we got crashing around and making a lot of *musique concrete* and things like that rather than this underscoring type music, which he didn't like either. He liked music in or out—to be striking, an important part—or not there at all. So it became very interesting working with him. The best thing about *Marat/Sade* was that there were real songs to write. *Musique concrète* is fun but ultimately it's not as satisfying as writing a real song and real music. When you can mix them all up together in the same show it's really fun.

SS: We both have been involved recently in workshop situations—with option to buy. Lyn Austin and the Lenox Arts Center have produced works that we were involved in and done them first in a kind of workshop-equity thing. A lot of works are happening this way. One of the terrific things about the new theatre is it has built its own audience where many of our friends in theatre are able to run their straight plays for three, four, or five months. The very same excitement and reviews generated by the pieces that use music are usually curtailed because of the economics of keeping the thing running. There's no easy answer except for the fact that there are probably more actors out of work who are willing to work even for the interest of the project. That is something almost unheard of with our colleagues in the music field.

RP: Your *Hotel for Criminals*—now there's a really brilliant piece of writing. But the economics of off-off-Broadway is just impossible and it could only sustain itself on Broadway and then you're into at least a couple of hundred thousand dollars to start with. And where's that money going to come from?

SS: After a while the thing about "new theatre" becomes a little boring if you can't use the orchestra. So, I had decided that I would write for nine or ten people just to show everybody "Hey, I can do this: this is what I do." I didn't mean it to be a suicidal step but there they were—nine, ten musicians every week had to be paid and fed . . . it's very hard. Of course there is a way around it. You can choose to write electronic music. But that's not an option I feel too comfortable with because of the nature of my own work. I have a tremendous indebtedness and feel for live music. One of the things I've been arguing about with the *Threepenny* people is keeping the orchestra out front.

RP: I'd love to write for dance. There you have a lot of advantages you don't have in the theatre. Nobody competing with your sound! But it's easier I think for dancers to use tape because they are so locked into movement. An actor likes to have some leeway from night to night to stretch his lines. Last spring I did a work on a production [*Legends of King Arthur* at St. Clement's] where we used tape primarily and one live instrument. A quadraphonic setup, synthesizer on tape and a harp. And the actors had to sing a couple of songs with the tape, which is okay, but it certainly is relentless. That tape goes on regardless of whether you're ready or not. There's something very mechanical about the whole process. I do think that there's something to be said, especially because of the economics of the thing, for using tape coordinated in a way with a live musician who can take the edge off a purely electronic sound.

ss: I've seen the tape thing work, especially in my own particular interests. But, I am a musician and I have a tremendous subplot thrill working with live players in a certain kind of gamesmanship and proficiency. I always think of the relationship between their energy and a successful piece. I maintain that one of the things that helped *Selavy* go over the line was the fact that besides the input and the talent of a very energetic cast we had this incredibly gifted, hand-picked band.

RP: The dilemma as far as I can see right now is that off-Broadway does not exist anymore musically. The finances are such that a three-hundred-seat house cannot support an orchestra. So, either you scrape something together off-off-Broadway or try and find musicians who will work for twelve performances on a kind of charity basis. Or else you go that whole Broadway route. *Boccaccio* was never intended for Broadway. It's just a chamber musical. It works best in a small house, in an intimate relation-ship between three or four players and a small cast. It's not the same when you have five hundred people out there. I think this is a tremen-dous problem facing anyone composing in the theatre. On the one hand, we'd like to say, "The hell with Broadway and all that schtick and pres-sure, there's got to be a better way." But, as far as I can see I haven't seen a better way yet. Broadway is the only way you can launch a piece on a wider basis around the country and get it recorded.

ss: There's definitely a need for a middle situation for music-theatre. I'm thinking of all those great smaller works like *The Marriage on the Eiffel Tower.* The mini-Met was just squaresville and made the typical choices that everybody expected. But, there's no doubt about it, what's really needed is space well-endowed to do in repertory old and new works — Monteverdi pieces, Purcell — the kinds of things that Yale announces all the time. They seem to be the only ones doing this kind of thing. The union thing is very complex, but not as complex as it seems. My own feeling is to tend to withdraw from that battle and just opt for creating works and hope that after ten or fifteen years a dozen or so works will simply pump their way into the repertoire. That they'll be thought of as a body of work that one can do.

I'm doing a chamber work now with Arthur Miller. Quite frankly I see in it no other aim but to create the repertoire. I have no particular feeling toward a first performance or how sensational it should be. It's about writing. There it will be—x pages long—and hopefully it will work in ten years like it would today.

RP: I find that it's a problem to write without a specific performance in mind. I don't write effectively unless I have a deadline or a situation I know I'm composing for.

SS: But in the theatre you don't have to work all alone. Knowing who's going to sing helps to write it. I like to cast before I write. I don't work in rehearsals unless they're way up front. I like to know even if they change because if x is busy come the opening and we have to get y at least I know that x's sound is the role . . . When I did *Hotel for Criminals* I had to know what these people would sound like in order for it to be real. The thing about you, if I may volunteer this, is that maybe the question you have to ask yourself is: Why you don't want to seize a situation totally for yourself and get people to be *not* on an equal footing with you? In a situation like *Marat/Sade* you demonstrated quite well that you can write a masterpiece, an absolute classic. I think that you are one of the few people that can put together a formidable musical shape.

RP: I think one of the problems I see is that some people are born bandleaders and some people aren't. For a couple of years I had a big band that rehearsed every week and I also started a smaller group. I just found that running an organization like that involved so much of everything except composing—phone calls, running people down, being a librarian. A lot of people can deal with that, and get other people to do things for them. But, I find I'm not very good at that. I think you're right. You face a choice as a composer—do you work for someone else or with someone else and reap those advantages of someone who is organizing everything for you? Or do you go out on your own and do exactly what you want and take on all those responsibilities? I seem to go back and forth. I admire guys like Foreman and Gregory who start their own groups. Some people are able to both carry out their artistic aims and do the organizing at the same time.

SS: Except in the case of Richard, who admittedly writes on the run. The primary obligation goes into a much more social thing than you or I are into—the rehearsal. That's one of the distinctive differences between the new theatre and the new music. Finally, the new music is a terribly private, painful type of experience whereas the new theatre is a more communal, out there effort to be worked on within the rehearsal situation.

RP: I've become very envious of directors who can walk into a rehearsal and move people around or call for a cut in the music or an addition of a few bars. In a few minutes it's all done as far as they're concerned. But you, as a composer, are up all night making those changes. That's part of the problem. Composition takes one hell of a lot of time. I don't find much time left over to organize and make phone calls . . .

You are a master of really using every conceivable type of music in a delightful way, but also having your own personality come through it . . .

SS: Very rarely do I ever use anybody else's music. What I do is fantasize in the style that I think a certain song should go. Like an old-fashioned radio show, or a movie I believe I somehow saw. I know this is very crazy, but I just absolutely go into it and that language becomes the language that I speak for that day. And it's very Luciferian—finally you get possessed by those choices. I would say—and this is certainly true of *Hotel for Criminals*—that the canvas that I do that kind of thing on is usually very austere, which is obviously why Richard Foreman is a good choice of somebody to write a text and direct it. What I do want to emphasize is that the motific material and the pitches in the most eclectic moments of my scores are usually unified. The thing I fuck with is the language, the stylistic consistency, but never the pitch. And the songs do refer to each other. Now in a piece like *Hotel for Criminals,* which is about 1912 Paris, as a subplot I decided to do a whole thing about the Russian invasion of France so that I used consciously counterlines and bass lines from various Diaghilev productions. I start the piece with a quote from the writing music of *Boris Godunov* and then write free music above it. Throughout the entire piece there are references to Stravinsky, Schoenberg, and the music of 1912 and the turnaround of the *1812 Overture.*

RP: Did you use a little bit of *Alexander Nevsky* in there?

SS: I don't think so. The one real "quote" I've done, and it's very conscious, is the first measure of *Rite of Spring* in alternation with the first measure of *Pierrot Lunaire* as an interlude. And then, finally, just making a piece out of the accents of *Rite of Spring*, taking out all the chords, and just having those off entrances that the horns make and making a separate piece out of the variations. Last year I did a piece called *Crepuscule* for the Chamber Music Society of Lincoln Center using Django Reinhardt. Fundamentally, for me it's not collage or pasteup or pastiche—it's *Haydn Variations*. If I use a tune I'll make my own variations. Yes, that has existed in my work. I remember in *Elephant Steps* there's a constant surrendering on Richard's part to Gertrude Stein and on my part to Boulez. Very often we'd encase these Gertrude Stein quotes like "Begin again" with some Boulez to indicate our most paranoid fears of being discovered as to where our influences came from. At that time, and still, one of my influences is Boulez—the whole way of putting pitches together.

RP: How did you get to know Boulez?

SS: As a guitarist. I played *Le Marteau sans Maître* in the early sixties when he first came to this country. We toured with him. I showed him my music. He's performed it and been very influential. Who did you study with?

RP: I studied at Juilliard with Persichetti, Giannini, Henry Brant, and then I studied in Paris with Nadia Boulanger for a year.

SS: You write singularly your own music. But I find that jazz comes in a lot.

RP: My original interest in music was to be a big band arranger. When I finally got around to the point where I could arrange for big bands they were on their way out. But the jazz always seems to creep back in.

SS: The jazz in *Marat/Sade* is brilliant. And one is reminded of the whole Kurt Weill way of dealing with eighteenth-century English tunes and turning them into something absolutely unusual and original.

RP: I can remember hearing Peter Brook once on the radio talking about his theories of staging. Actually we all knew they were theories after the fact. He just went out there and staged it. If it worked out, fine, and if it didn't he tried something else. I guess that's how we worked on *Marat/Sade*. We knew it was a certain period so there were those connotations in my head. There's this one song with just a blues progression—that's because it was part of my background. Certain things of your own background mix in with the demands of the situation. You try it out on the actors in a situation and sometimes it works. There's a song called the "Corday Waltz," which Charlotte Corday sings. That was not in the original Peter Weiss script, but as we were in rehearsal Brook said he thought Corday needed a song in a certain spot. So Adrian Mitchell went off and wrote some lyrics and told us they fit the "Blue Danube Waltz." I went home and wrote what I thought was a joke—a very corny waltz. Anyhow, I had to bring it in because we had to have something for rehearsal. For me it was just to kind of test the waters. I didn't take it very seriously; I knew I had to write something more sophisticated. The problem was that they bought it and it went in the show. I said, "You can't be serious." Now another instance—the refrain that states "Marat we're poor / the poor stay poor." Brook had heard the German score and seen the German production and he had something in his head for that. I'd written what I thought was right but he thought it wasn't quite right. It was an important part of the score so I kept revising it and writing new material. Finally, one day he walked into rehearsal and said he wanted to do the version I originally wrote. So, things happen in a lot of different, strange ways. There's no real system. Often songs that are written in an offhand way will work and things you've slaved over don't work at all. Right up through my most recent experience it's been hard to predict what will happen on the stage.

Maria Irene Fornes

THE 1977 PRODUCTION OF *Fefu and Her Friends*, one of the best-loved plays of the contemporary American theatre, and other works that soon followed, such as *Mud* and *The Conduct of Life*, sparked the eventual "discovery" by younger generations of Maria Irene Fornes, two decades after she began writing plays. At the time of this interview, *Fefu*, which she directed, and the recipient of one of her eight Obie Awards, was enjoying a successful run at the American Place Theatre, where many of her plays have been produced. To Bonnie Marranca, then the theatre's literary advisor, Fornes offers fascinating insights into her thinking about dramatic structure and style, contrasting the realistic play, where "one can feel the characters breathe," with the abstract play, in which "it is the play that breathes." Likewise, for her the plotless play deals with "the mechanics of the mind, some kind of spiritual survival, or process of thought" while plays dependent on plot emphasize the mechanics of social arrangements. *Fefu and Her Friends* describes a world of women both shocking and full of humor and passion in its extraordinary emotional timbre. And, as always, there is the circulation of dramatic intelligence.

One of the pleasures of *Fefu*'s environmental consciousness was the staging of the play in five different rooms of a house, with groups of audience members moving through different spaces and experiencing the scenes simultaneously and in a different order. The proximity of audience and actors allowed for an intimacy and close-up style associated more with film acting than theatrical performance. But the sense of "wholesomeness," which is so important to the play, comes from its setting in 1935 before, as Fornes explains, the popularization of Freud had made human behavior suspect through incessant interpretation. The nonjudgmental and tender quality of social interaction, which are enduring traits of her characters beginning with early plays such as *The Successful Life of 3* and the musical, *Promenade*, have made Fornes one of the most widely respected American dramatists and teachers of playwriting today.   BGM

Conversation with Bonnie Marranca, 1978

The Playwright as Director

Bonnie Marranca: Fefu and Her Friends is a departure from your other plays, which are nonrealistic, isn't it?

Maria Irene Fornes: My first work on the play actually was less realistic. The play started in 1964. That is when I wrote some of the first scene— when Fefu takes a gun and shoots at her husband out the window . . . Whether the play is realistic or less realistic has to do with the distance I have from it. I feel that the characters of *Fefu* are standing around me while other plays I see more at a distance. When I view a play far away from me, perhaps the characters become two-dimensional. They become more like drawings than flesh and blood. The question of what ends up being a realistic play has to do with the fact that one can feel the characters breathe, rather than in a more abstract play, where it is the play that breathes, not the characters.

BGM: Do you feel that each of the eight women is symbolic or representative of a female personality type or quality?

MF: I don't think so at all. Doesn't every character in every play have a different character than the next one? The fact that *Fefu* is plotless might contribute to the feeling that if the women are not related to each other, and not related to the plot, then perhaps they represent certain types. In a plot play the woman is either the mother or the sister or the girlfriend or the daughter. The purpose of the character is to serve a plot so the relationship is responding to the needs of the plot. Although *Fefu* is realistic, the relationship of the women, in that sense, is abstract. The purposes these characters are serving is different from how a character serves a plot.

BGM: How are you distinguishing between plot and plotless plays?

MF: Plot, which has generally been the basis for plays, deals with the mechanics of life in a practical sense, with the mechanics of the peculiar arrangement a society makes. For example, a plot story in Alaska might be that in winter there was more sun than usual, the protagonist is in deep distress and commits suicide. And we would say, Why is that a reason for distress? Then we find out that there is reason for distress when there is more sun because the fish don't swim close to the surface. Therefore, there is no food and there is a reason for famine. There is a reason for unhappiness, a reason to commit suicide. So that in dealing with plot we are dealing with those things that have to do with external life—the mechanics of how we manage in the world. A plotless play doesn't deal with the mechanics of the practical arrangement of life but deals with the mechanics of the mind, some kind of spiritual survival, a process of thought.

BGM: Fefu is a fascinating woman. She seems to be the center of the play, the most complex woman in it. Did the idea of the play grow out of the idea of Fefu?

MF: Fefu took over the play . . . She is the woman in the first scene that I wrote, the woman who shoots her husband as a game. The source of this play is a Mexican joke. There are two Mexicans in sombreros sitting at a bullfight and one says to the other, "Isn't she beautiful, the one in yellow?" and he points to a woman on the other side of the arena crowded with people. The other one says, "Which one?" and he takes his gun and shoots her and says, "The one that falls." In the first draft of the play Fefu explains that she started playing this game with her husband because of that joke. But in rewriting the play I took out this explanation.

The woman who plays such a game with her husband grabbed me. Fefu is complex, but I find her a very unified person. However, by conventional terms she is contradictory, she is very outrageous. Fefu is very close to me so I tend to understand her, and find her not unusual at all . . .

I said that Fefu took over the play but it's not really so. Julia is a very important voice and there are times when I feel the whole play is about her. Although Fefu has more of a mind than Julia, Julia is the mind of the play—the seer, the visionary.

BGM: You mention that you first began the play in 1964. When did you begin working on it again?

MF: About five years ago in 1972. I did a considerable amount of work then during an intensive period of two or three months. When I stopped working on it—for whatever reason—I put it away and didn't think about it again. At the beginning of 1977 I decided that I would do a play for the Theatre Strategy season. Each year I would think of doing a play, then I would become so involved in administration and not do it. I got a date to do a play but I wasn't sure which one I would do because I had another play that I was very interested in, and there were possibilities of other things I had started. I decided since I had so little time I would read what I had written of these various plays and whichever one would grab me the most I would work on. When I looked at *Fefu* my feeling toward it was so intense that I knew that was the one I should work on.

BGM: In the past several years it has usually been experimental theatre directors rather than playwrights who have worked with environmental theatre concepts. Yet you have structured *Fefu* around five different environments. How did the environmental concept evolve?

MF: When I had a date for the play to be performed I had to start looking for a place to perform it. I saw this place, the Relativity Media Lab on lower Broadway, and looked at the main performing area and thought it wasn't right. But I liked the place and the general atmosphere very much. The people who owned the place took me to different parts of the loft and said, "This room could be used for a dressing room," and I thought, This room is so nice it could be used for a room in Fefu's house. They took me to another room and said, "This you can use as a green room," and I thought, This is nice, this could be a room in Fefu's house. They took me to the office where we were to discuss terms, dates, et cetera. I thought this could be a room in Fefu's house. Then right there I thought I would like to do the play using these different rooms . . . So then I went home and continued writing the play with this new concept in mind.

BGM: Experiencing the play, moving from room to room, becomes more important than following a story. When you watch something in a normal proscenium setting you have a fixed perspective. Whereas here you are in the actual rooms, moving about a house.

MF: I think what makes it special is the fact that there are four walls. If the audience went inside a set that had only three walls, there would be a sense that this is not a room but a set. The fact that in *Fefu* you are enclosed inside the rooms with the actors is really the difference. You are aware of the four walls around you, and it is very important that the audience be on only two sides of the room. So when you look at the actors you should not see the audience behind them. Perhaps it's more a question of being a witness than—

BGM: —an average spectator. You're not really following a story or plot but are overhearing conversations in a way, witnessing a series of encounters. The audience is involved in the play in a much more experiential way than is common.

MF: I expected that the audience would feel as if they are really visiting people in their house.

BGM: In some ways *Fefu* seems Chekhovian—a kind of mood piece. Do you think so?

MF: I think so even though I didn't think of Chekhov when I wrote it. I don't know if one could analyze it technically and find similarities. What would be similarities? The way dialogue proceeds, the presentation of a section of an event? I haven't studied Chekhov. But I think in spirit it is very Chekhovian, and also, though it is realistic, *Fefu* is very abstract, as Chekhov is.

BGM: Is it a feminist play? *Fefu* shows women together onstage as they have rarely been seen before.

MF: Is it a feminist play? . . .

BGM: *Fefu* is not a militant or ideological play, but by feminist I mean it has all women as characters who do not relate to one another in terms of stereotypes. They have a certain way of being in the world, a certain perspective that is seen from the female eye.

MF: Yes, it is a feminist play. The play is about women. It's a play that deals with each one of these women with enormous tenderness and affection. I have not deliberately attempted to see these women "as women have rarely been seen before." I show the women as I see them and if it is different from the way they've been seen before, it's because that's how I see them. The play is not fighting anything, not negating anything. My intention has not been to confront anything. I felt as I wrote the play that I was surrounded by friends. I felt very happy to have such good and interesting friends.

BGM: There is a contemporary perspective in the characters. Yet, the play is set in 1935. Why?

MF: The women were created in a certain way because of an affection I have for a kind of world which I feel is closer to the thirties than any other period. Simply because it is pre-Freud, in the way that people manifested themselves with each other there was something more wholesome and trusting, in a sense. People accepted each other at face value. They were not constantly interpreting each other or themselves. Before Freud became popular and infiltrated our social and emotional lives, if a person said, "I love so-and-so," the person listening would believe the statement. Today, there is an automatic disbelieving of everything that is said, and an interpreting of it. It's implied that there's always some kind of self-deception about an emotion.

BGM: You speak about wholesomeness in the characters in the play, the acceptance of things at face value. What qualities were you looking for when you cast the play?

MF: That very quality—wholesomeness. It has to do with not being bitter, with accepting responsibility for what happens to you in life. When I was casting it was very clear to me when a person entered the room whether she belonged in the world of *Fefu*.

BGM: You also staged *Fefu*. How do you like directing your own work? Do you feel you can maintain a certain objectivity about the text?

MF: I think so. You mentioned before that it is usually directors who deal with environmental work rather than playwrights, and my first thought was that I probably first responded to the loft environment that I visited as a director. However, since I am both a director and a playwright it's difficult to separate the process of creativity which, in me, has no separation. It isn't that I first write the play and then direct it, like two different people. It's a similar process that continues. However, when I'm writing a play I'm planning what I am going to do when I direct it.

BGM: For me one of the great pleasures of *Fefu* has to do with your choice of a "natural"—almost effortless—performance style. What were you attempting in the direction of the play?

MF: In the process of auditioning there were people who read for me who were extremely talented but I thought they would shatter the play. I began to see the play almost as if it had glass walls and I felt there were people who would break the walls. A lot has been said about the style of acting and the style of production in *Fefu* and that surprised me. I told the actors that the style of acting should be film acting. That's how I saw it. Perhaps when you do film acting onstage it seems very special. Do you think it's any different from film acting?

BGM: The style of the production seems to be a kind of untheatrical naturalism—a certain flatness that appears stylized, very casual. As in film, the characters are seen in close-up, which is a big change from the way one relates to a theatre performance. Realistic plays are normally done from a fixed perspective. In *Fefu*, not only is the style of acting cinematic, the structure of the play is cinematic, too. It incorporates jump cuts when you move from a study to a bedroom to a croquet field. You don't get the beginning or end of a scene because you are going in and out of the different performing spaces.

MF: Pinter is done somewhat in this style of acting, isn't he? The timing in *Fefu* is very important. So is the texture of sound. For example, in the third scene—it moves back to the living room—if the timing is not impeccable there will be no scene. If someone else were to direct the play I think it would be very difficult to do unless it were thought of as music. For example, when the women are having a water fight there is a lot of laughter, a lot of screaming. In the scene that follows Julia talks about death. For that scene to begin, the sound of the laughter in the room has to have subsided completely. The laughter is like a substance that takes over the whole house—a laughter that comes from the kitchen to the living room almost like a body that moved around the house, then finally went back to the kitchen and subsided. And then, from total silence Cindy asks Julia a question and she begins talking about death.

In *Fefu* the style of writing in the first and third scenes is different from the style of writing in the close-up scenes in the center of the play. These scenes have a more theatrical style of writing, and though I also try to tone down the performances in them, they take on a larger life.

BGM: *Fefu* has many of the qualities of your other plays—whimsy, lightness of touch, economy of style, bittersweetness, an interest in exploring human relations. Yet it is also very different in that the characters, being realistic, are less given to dreams, myth, or ritual. How do you view *Fefu* in relation to your other work? Do you see it growing out of the earlier plays?

MF: I think *Fefu* comes straight from *Cap-a-Pie* because that play was based on the personal experiences and dreams and thoughts of the cast. Dealing so intimately with the realistic material left me with a desire to continue working in that manner. In *Aurora* there was a sense of characters going from one room to another though the scenes were not played simultaneously. I was not aware that this was happening in *Fefu* as it happened in *Aurora* until the day when I first rehearsed all the scenes together. I really don't see much difference between *Fefu* and my other plays. Any difference is a stylistic one. I think that tenderness toward the characters is what is at the core of my work and that is no different in *Fefu* than in the other plays.

BGM: Does *Fefu* tell us where your future interests in drama lie?

MF: Perhaps it does. However, a great many people have found *Fefu* to be my most important work and in doing so I feel that there is a subtle denial of my other plays. I like *Fefu* very, very much but I feel almost like a mother who's had eight children and the ninth is called the beautiful one, the intelligent one, and everybody is saying, "Aren't you glad you had this one?" You feel they are all your children. It could very well be that *Fefu* is more successful than my other plays and that it would be a clever thing for me to continue writing in this manner. I will if that is my inclination but not because I feel I have been on the wrong track previously. I don't see my work in relation to its possible impact in the world of theatre or the history of theatre. The shape that a play of mine takes has to do with my own need for a certain creative output.

Charles Ludlam

IN THE HISTORY OF American avant-garde theatre, few groups have had as much staying power as the Ridiculous Theatrical Company, founded by Charles Ludlam in 1967, and still in existence more than ten years after its founder's untimely death in 1987 from AIDS at the age of forty-four. For twenty years, Ludlam created an outstanding repertory company and starred in works that he wrote, produced, and directed. Toward the end of his life, Ludlam staged productions for the Santa Fe Opera and acted in television shows, movies, and other theatres.

Despite the identification of his work with the aesthetics of "camp," the "ridiculous," and "gay" theatre in the minds of his public, Ludlam eschewed easy reductive formulations. In a posthumous collection of essays, *Ridiculous Theatre: Scourge of Human Folly*, he argues against his theatre ever being wholly committed to narrow definitions: "I never thought of it as gay art." Nor did he consider female impersonation as anything other than his desire to explore the entire range of human feelings. Ludlam's views, which anticipate the discourse on gender and performativity that now dominate academic theatre criticism, often run counter to current sexual politics in his refusal to devalue art in favor of sociopolitical commentary.

Ludlam was a workaday artist who saw himself as part of a revered theatrical tradition. From his signature piece *Camille,* to the playful encounters with Shakespeare in *Stage Blood* and Molière in *Le Bourgeois Avant-Garde,* and to reworkings of operatic fare in *Bluebeard* and *Der Ring Gott Farblonjet,* he lay claim to that history with an undiminished admiration for masterworks. From a genuine commitment to drama and to a variety of theatrical styles, and a belief in the authenticity of characterization rooted in an actor's emotional needs, Ludlam created spectacles of wondrous amazement riddled with laughter and scatological humor. In that sense, he was very much a part of the historical avant-garde, linking his art to "lowbrow" entertainment. His was the hedonistic and maximalist counterpart to the minimal and ideological works of many of his contemporaries. GD

Conversation with Gautam Dasgupta, 1978

Theatre and the Ridiculous

Gautam Dasgupta: How would you define the term "Theatre of the Ridiculous"?

Charles Ludlam: It has to do with humor and unhinging the pretensions of serious art. It comes out of the dichotomy between academic and expressive art, and the idea of a theatre that revalues things. It takes what is considered worthless and transforms it into high art. The Ridiculous theatre was always a concept of high art that came out of an aesthetic which was so advanced it really couldn't be appreciated. It draws its authority from popular art, an art that doesn't need any justification beyond its power to provide pleasure. Sympathetic response is part of its audience.

Basically for me, and for twentieth-century art, it's always been a problem of uncovering sources; it proceeds by discoveries. In my case it was based on a rigorous reevaluation of everything. Like yesterday, I was working on a sculpture, and Bill Vehr [an actor in Ludlam's company] stood over me and corrected me every time I did something that was in good taste. It's really an exercise to try to go beyond limitations and taste, which is a very aural, subjective, and not very profound concept for art. And to admit the world in a way that hasn't been precensored. For instance, a handy definition for avant-garde art is that it's in beige-black-white-and-gray. Ridiculous theatre is in color; it's hedonistic. Different artists define it their own way, but basically it's alchemy, it's the transformation of what is in low esteem into the highest form of expression.

GD: Your early academic training in the theatre was rather traditional, wasn't it?

CL: I was a theatre major at Hofstra, and did the classics, staged and acted in them, and the rest.

GD: Was there a disillusionment with the naturalistic (or less expressive) theatre that led you to the Ridiculous style?

CL: Well, naturalistic theatre is a very recent innovation, a corrective device, and it wasn't the end of anything. It was a fashion to do things naturally. You can't really perform an unnatural act, unless you claim to have supernatural powers. So the whole idea of something being natural becomes a very oppressive concept; it's shallow. Gradually, through training with Stanislavsky teachers, I realized that they wanted me to behave in a civilized manner in a room, and not do anything extraordinary. But everything I'm interested in is extraordinary.

GD: The technique of the Ridiculous is, of course, closer to expressionistic theatre or earlier modes of highly stylized theatre.

CL: Yes, and it seems now as if I wrote my way through history. I've written plays that were trying to revalue techniques from various periods. But ultimately, that is an academic approach, and modernism isn't about being academic; it is about being primitive. And becoming primitive isn't easy when you've been overeducated, overcivilized.

Another fact is that all modernism was born in the theatre. Every painting technique, everything we associate with modernism—for instance, Jackson Pollock's "scene-painting" techniques; and Salvador Dali's dreamscapes is like looking at a cyclorama, a barren landscape. Everything about naturalism is, in a sense, a distortion, because they (Zola, et al.) were reacting against the theatre of Sarah Bernhardt and others, and it made a mass movement. But finally it became too selective: it set out to prove a point, and proving a point is working from a preconception, and that is academic. Concept and execution is academic; going crazy and committing an atrocity is more modern. In the case of the Ridiculous, it is the only avant-garde movement that is not academic. It is not creating an academy out of former gestures and looks. If you look at today's avant-garde, it has an unmistakable look, and it moves more and more toward a vocabulary. It makes the art respectable, but it doesn't give us anywhere to go.

GD: But isn't it fair to say that within the Ridiculous movement your theatre seems to be more polished, less "mad" than, say, the works of Jack Smith, Jeff Weiss, and John Vaccaro? It is less anarchic.

CL: Well, in the Ridiculous theatre there was a highly competitive feeling among the practitioners, which did not encourage anybody new to do anything extraordinary. And in a way I'm very divorced from the work of the others. Since there's an element of almost demented competition among the various branches of the Ridiculous, which I think is way out of proportion and totally inappropriate, I had basically to go on and create the entire genre myself. As far as my work is concerned, I work in greater continuity—I've written, produced, directed, and acted in more works in the past ten years than the others. We were a group that continued to evolve in techniques, etc., and we built on our foundation. With the others there is the tendency to start everything from scratch, or else the individualism is so great, they can't work with anyone else. That attitude is good for research, the private attitude, but in terms of running a theatre it requires some sacrifice—not merely to exploit the moment, but to develop people, be loyal to them, and that's why our theatre got more polished.

GD: Isn't there a danger of this stylistic refinement itself turning academic?

CL: Sure, but that is a question of the rigor one applies to oneself—you can do the same thing better and better, or do different things. The Japanese playwright Chikamatsu wrote on one theme, but just varied the context over and over and refined it. In my work, the panoramic quality saves it from academicism. It encompasses a much broader worldview, and I've been able to bring more material into my work. You see, there are different kinds of artists—innovators, masters, and journeymen—and some people are very good at uncovering little techniques, discovering fine points, while others, like myself, are able to organize vast amounts of material into a very solid body of work.

GD: Since you have drawn from the vast reservoir of dramatic and operatic literature, in both theme [*Hamlet* in *Stage Blood*, *Camille*, *Bluebeard*, and *Der Ring Gott Farblonjet* (Wagner's *Ring*)] and technique [Jacobean, epic, etc.], what makes these works of the Ridiculous different from, say, lampoon, parody, or satire?

CL: I think it's a question of depth and complexity. *Camille* could be taken as parody, but I perhaps have an ambiguous attitude toward these works in that while they are produced in a certain vein and in my own aesthetics, the thing to do is to examine the Ridiculous as if my work didn't exist, and then see what my work made of it. From my own point of view, there wouldn't be any Ridiculous if it weren't for me. There is a large extent of pain in my kind of Ridiculous. And there is a problem with pain. Aristotle defines ridiculous as the laugh of the ugly that does not give rise to pain. But pain has a lot to do with the significance of the work in our minds. How lightly does it go by? How easy is it to take? To what extent are you asked to suffer, the way you are asked to suffer in opera or a piano concerto? In my work there is both inner and outer direction. And the depth of involvement changes it from a mere spoof to something that transcends it. *Camille*, on the one hand, *is Camille*, it's a totally legitimate interpretation of the original, and I think the amount of personal anguish, how much of yourself are you going to reveal in it, is what makes it more powerful than just a spoof.

GD: Does this tension between the inner and the outer apply to the other actors of your company? Are roles handed out in the belief that such tensions will make themselves manifest?

CL: Yes. Another thing we are not talking about is that the theatre is a madly complex art form. It is not personal, and to make it personal one has to alter it or simplify it to some extent. Some people can control it, but it takes a lot of years. My early plays are more anarchic than any plays produced in this genre; my newer works are more classical. My early works had some classicism in them, but people couldn't perceive it then. It's not that they didn't understand the plays then, but that they didn't or couldn't see what went into creating them. And that's enough to drive anybody crazy: the distance between what you're experiencing while creating it and what the audience feels. Another thing is that today humor is in very low esteem. Today, the whole idea of humorous art is prostituted to such an extent that it can't be taken "seriously," that there can't be "serious humor." Now the whole idea of seriousness is awful to me—it sounds like something imposed from without. It doesn't really imply gravity or profundity; it implies decorum, behaving yourself, and that's what I don't like about it.

GD: So, essentially you're talking about an earthy, scatological, Rabelaisian sensibility.

CL: But what about the unbelievably sublime writing or acting that occurs? If you have shit in the play, and also have sublimity, you have a total panoramic view, like Dante (in his *Inferno*) or Shakespeare. Other artists want to slant the world one way. Now, I love belles lettres—Ronald Firbank, for instance, a sublime writer, so perfect in creating a small world—but other artists are bigger in a way, they encompass more, they encompass opposites. It's okay to say the plays are scatological, sure, but at the same time they do rise to heights of bliss and sublimity at moments for various reasons. You can't have highs without lows. The thing I'm against is appropriate and inappropriate material in art—it's shallow.

GD: Does it ever bother you to have to rummage through the repository of past art to come up with materials for your plays? This notion of cultural imperialism, of "quotation art" . . .

CL: Picasso said that no artist is a bastard. We all have forebears; we build on history, and rework it at times.

GD: But in the Ridiculous style there does seem to be an infantile regression at work, a pervasive and morbid sense of nostalgia for the movies of old, particularly Maria Montez movies. Could contemporary social and political events be dealt with in this genre?

CL: I don't see why art that has a history and a tradition is regressive. The danger is not so much regression; the danger is the morbid effect of repeating yourself, and that's where modernism—our contemporaries are Johnny-one-notes; each has a look (as in advertising) that he or she works for—comes in. Paintings begin to look alike in most galleries. They cater to people's need for the mass-produced, the reassurance you have when you go to a grocery store and you see a brand name. All of a painter's works today are supposed to look alike. This to me is insane tyranny; it is absolutely sterile, and that is more of a crisis to me than the problem of diversity, or what a friend of mine calls "virtuoso maximalism," the antidote that will supplant minimalism. Also, I don't want the savor of the art taken away, the actual enjoyment and appetite one has for creating something from something else, from something varied.

GD: Let's move back to the Montez films . . .

CL: With Maria Montez, as with pornography or anything held in low esteem, it's really a cultural prejudice; it's not inherently low. Those films were meant for children, and not that that's fine, but they were meant to be comedies and she gave her all. She gave the films a conviction, which was a fabulous quality to impose on something that most people wouldn't care for. The thing those movies have that today's movies don't have is actors sort of winking at you from behind their masks telling you they don't mean it. Not protecting themselves, not afraid to look foolish, not afraid to be thought mad. If actors then could seem to be possessed by their roles, they could justify any kind of theatrics, because the conviction of motivation was there to fill it out, this bigger form. Not everyone has that much life to fill a bigger form, and those who do become great performers. Now in naturalism there is always the tendency to be less than you are, to be more specific and less, and that was always a terrible danger. It certainly didn't work for me. I am able to do very lively, different roles.

GD: Your productions are indeed comic and lively, but some women find them deliberately caustic and painful in the way their gender is treated onstage.

CL: I think that's a misconception. I think women have traditionally been considered sacred, in a way, and that's something that had to go out the window if women were to become people. Women fare very well in my plays—they come out on top—but what people are disturbed by is female impersonation. They don't realize or understand its inner motive. They see something that is humorous; they don't understand what it means to play a woman. There's an incredible cultural taboo against it, particularly in Anglo-American culture. It takes a lot of courage to open yourself up to those feelings. Obviously, in a Ridiculous play everything is ridiculous, but the women in my company feel that they get a fair shake. And it's not so much as being against women as being skeptical of them and not taking a kind of blanket sentimental attitude toward them. Just the idea that women are equal to men doesn't mean anything; specific women have to be compared to specific men, and even then how can you compare two people? Even the idea of liberating women makes no sense to great women; it only appeals to women who have accepted rather conventional and erroneous ideas about their own existence because of economic factors and the like.

GD: Why is it that in New York most of the Ridiculous theatre has been created by homosexuals?

CL: Well, it isn't entirely male homosexuality though. Homosexuality is not a sexist phenomenon—so it's not homosexuals against women. And in the theatre there's always been a high percentage of homosexuals because, for one thing, to pursue a life in the theatre it's better not to have a family. Gay people have always found a refuge in the arts, and the Ridiculous theatre is notable for admitting it. The people in it—and it is a very sophisticated theatre, culturally—never dream of hiding anything about themselves that they feel is honest and true and the best part of themselves. NOTHING is concealed in the Ridiculous.

Also, I think a company that was all-male or -female would immediately lower the level of artistic consciousness. It would turn into a social club, become political. Second, proselytizing lifestyles is a Brechtian thing—in the tradition of advertising and propaganda work—which doesn't have anything to do with the absolutely rigorous individualism that goes into our work. I think women are essential in Ridiculous theatre; if they weren't, it would be a partial view of the world.

GD: Why did you play the part of Camille and not give it to an actress in the company?

CL: I always wanted to play Camille. It had a lot to do with my feelings about love, and the nature of love in one of its highest expressions. Is love, in fact, self-sacrifice, or is there another way of expressing love? In my company we all encourage each other to do the roles we feel we must do. And sometimes people think it's sexism if you're in drag, but that's incredibly shallow.

GD: Do you think your plays could be performed by other groups without the overlay of the Ridiculous style?

CL: Sure, and they're done all the time, although I've never seen them.

GD: Of course, outside of the nature of the Ridiculous aesthetic, what makes your productions so overpowering is the emphasis placed on acting, the performer . . .

CL: Yes, that's exactly right. We always review the art of acting. Of the

three branches that broke up—John [Vaccaro], Ronnie [Tavel], and I—
John went and created a director's theatre, Ronnie a playwright's theatre
in that he continues to write, and we created an actor's theatre, an acting
troupe. In the long run, you can't get to the roots of conviction in a director's or playwright's point of view that you can get when the actors mean
it. It takes years to develop that kind of understanding actors bring to
your work, and that is what finally gives the work a base, a depth. Now of
course each actor has his or her own style, but yet it's unified. Roles are
constructed, they are not just arbitrarily given out, with careful planning
as to what impression the role will create.

GD: Is the method of creation collaborative in nature?

CL: The script is up to me. I doubt if the process is unconventional, but a
lot of groundwork is already taken for granted since we've been together
so long. Also, unlike the avant-garde, I don't feel the need to have a body
of theory to back up my work. I'm too much in the process of becoming
something else all the time to do that. I'm constantly devouring things,
so that no one approach ever quite becomes true for me for very long.

GD: Like the ventriloquist act [*The Ventriloquist's Wife*], another facet of the
actor, the mask, another approach to the theatre . . .

CL: With Punch and Judy, and now with Walter Ego . . . I'm interested in
the mask, what it can do—very objective. I was always interested in puppets, and then at one point it all came together and I knew I was going to
turn ventriloquism to a higher and new purpose. It was a breakthrough
for me, not the ventriloquism as such, but because it opened the door for
something in the theatre that I had hit upon earlier in my work—why
certain moments were more Ludlam, more my own. For one thing, it's
opened up cinema for me. I had always kept a list of possible movie scenarios with my puppets, and I always saw cinema as a kind of puppetry.

GD: Does the name Walter Ego suggest the ultimate exposé—Ludlam and
his alter ego on stage—that you think is a criterion for the Ridiculous
theatre?

CL: Right, and also the fact that I recede a bit (the play belongs to Walter) gives me a nice perspective. See, the thing is you don't want to do
the same thing forever, but you do. It's just little discoveries that keep
you going. I really think of myself as an inventor who invents theatrical pieces. I don't think of myself as writing a play and then arranging a
performance. I think my plays will probably become part of a standard
repertoire because they were invented *in* the theatre.

GD: For a genre that is so stylized and expressive, your plays are a delight to
read outside the context of performance.

CL: That's because they were born in the theatre. And also because of a sense of narrative. *The Ventriloquist's Wife* is, in a sense, pure theatricality. I was creating a piece for cabaret, and so I analyzed all that was the essence of cabaret entertainment, what made something work. I then realized that these things were essentially variety turns, and so I deliberately created a narrative out of them for maximum effect.

GD: To create a narrative is one thing, but to hang a Ridiculous-styled production on the scaffolding of some other earlier play becomes problematic. Say with *Camille,* your strict adherence to its narrative line makes one wonder if your treatment is deliberately parodic, or is it a new interpretation, or whatever.

CL: I don't think they are parodies actually. There is an *element* of parody, for parody is a way of reusing old things. But in order to do parody right, you have to do it as well as the original. That gives you the authority to make fun of it. Basically, I'm using these materials not to make fun of them, but because I think they are valuable.

GD: But is that serious intention clear in the mere fact of your choosing to do them?

CL: Well, the ambiguity of intention is probably just something in me. I don't know me or my work, and I don't want to know. It's revealed to me in flashes—the Dionysian element, if you will, whatever it is that creates it. It isn't a preconception; I don't set out to prove a theory. *Corn* came close to it, where I set out to make a point about eating food along the way, but the irrational, or better yet the intuitive element, must be the guide for me. You can't make a mistake with intuition. And as one matures artistically, one's instinct improves automatically. My plays are not parodic, but they *are* meant to be funny and humorous. There are perhaps subliminal effects that the plays have. I feel I do set up situations where the audience accepts A, B, and C, and then they are forced to accept D. It's gestalt, and, in a way, I change the culture by the way I force people to think their way through something. They went through the experience and they can't go back.

GD: Is it in that sense of subliminal change that Susan Sontag and Stefan Brecht have claimed that this sort of theatre is political?

CL: Yes, I think it is political, but what is political is perhaps misunderstood. Politics is about spheres of influence, and in that sense it is political. If a man plays Camille, for instance, you begin to think it's horrible, but in the end you are either moved or won over. You believe in the character beyond the gender of the actor, and no one who has experienced that can go back. In such cases, this theatre is political in the highest sense of influence. But as far as pushing for political upheaval goes, it's not true to the nature of art. Art is not meant to tear society down; it is meant to enhance it.

GD: Is that why you (and the Ridiculous movement in general) very rarely deal with contemporary social events?

CL: We have dealt with contemporary events, like the play on cryogenics, on euthanasia [*Hot Ice*] . . .

GD: But that's futuristic . . .

CL: Yeah, but *Camille* is a profoundly feminist work. Drag is something people today are prejudiced against, because women are considered inferior beings. A woman putting on pants, on the other hand, has moved up. So to defiantly do that and say women are worthwhile creatures, and that I'll put my whole soul and being into creating this woman and give her everything I have, including my emotions (and the most taboo thing is to experience feminine emotions), and to take myself seriously in the face of ridicule, that's it. That is the highest turn of the statement. It's different than wanting to make women more like men. It allows audiences to experience the universality of emotion, rather than believe that women are one species and men another, and what one feels the other never does. Even the women's movement is based on conflict and anger; my *Camille* is synthesis, an altogether different tactic. So you see, we do deal with contemporary phenomena. The historical thing is a pretext. The *Ring* has to do with power.

GD: Looked at in these terms, even the piece you did for the Paul Taylor Dance Company [*Aphrodisiamania*] seems to break down sex barriers. And also, based as it was on the Italian *commedia*, it seemed a logical direction for you as head of an "acting troupe" to move into.

CL: I've been doing a lot of research on Italian comedy over the years. There are two ways of doing it. You can approach it as a sentimental thing, where you are trying to re-create a sense of what had gone on before, or you use those discoveries in a collision of techniques which create a new thing that means more to us. The thing about the *commedia* is that it is all resolved at the end—marriage is a happy ending, and no one feels that way now. That's one of the problems for modern comedy, to restore harmony at the end when so many values have been toppled down. So asymmetrical and irregular works have to be produced in order even to begin to evoke reality. But I'm more interested in the collisions of aesthetics.

A friend of mine said that the nineteenth century got it right—artists perfected art—while modernism is the history of getting it wrong. All the techniques of modernism—reduction, distortion, and so forth—are lend-ing themselves to the inductive analysis of reality, of getting it wrong. When people describe a style of theatre, they are describing how it isn't like reality basically. They never talk about how it evokes reality, which is something we can't explain. I think my theatre is the most *real*, the most natural, but it isn't *realism*, it isn't *naturalism*. It's evoking reality by showing us what isn't real. If a man can put on makeup, false eyelashes and mascara, all the artifices of being woman, then obviously all those things are not part of being a woman. So something is created in that negative space, and that's where the mystery of reality is evoked. In naturalistic production, and even though I'm sophisticated enough to see what they're doing, I ask myself as an objective Martian looking at it: How much of it is intended? The moment they begin to use theatrical conventions, and there's no escaping that in the theatre, I ask myself how much of it do they want me to take as real. Whereas in Noh theatre so much more is evoked, even to the extent of bringing convincing ghosts onstage. So that's part of theatre convention, when certain issues are settled and agreed upon, and only then can you get to more profound matters.

GD: At this point in the twentieth century, however, it seems that we've become totally immune to the collision of antithetical elements, parodies of conventions, shock, etc. How much more can we take?

CL: I'm talking about the notion of something perfected. See, once the idea of theatrical event and its convention is accepted for what it is and with relish, then everything is open to one. For example, certain women have tried to play Camille in modern times and failed because they were asking to be taken seriously. They were asking to be mistaken for the character in an everyday kind of way. So the audience thought they were being tricked. But if it's played in a manner that does not call for you to be a fool, that it's being created by, for, and of the theatre, then they are able to appreciate and accept a much broader amount of material. There is this theory in our century that any particular art form comes more and more into its own, as itself, its true nature. That paint is paint, paint is not a tree. The same is true of theatre, and the more the theatre comes to this self-realization of itself, the higher it becomes and the freer the subject matter. A political theatre can't do any topic because it hasn't come to terms with what theatre *is*. That's where the confusion arises—is it political or not, is it true or not? It doesn't interest me if it's true or not, it is just there. Even my ideas, I just try them on for size, to see if they work or not. Also, I don't care whether they're aesthetic or artistic because anything aesthetic or artistic is true only in so far as we've seen it before and have come to recognize it that way. But if we've never seen it that way before, it's only then that it gets to be interesting. When standards and values are no longer applicable.

GD: Wouldn't that be difficult to sustain in theatrical production?

CL: Yes, and one of my recent crises is that all my earlier works were based on an impossible conception to be fulfilled, and in the failure we found the aesthetic margin. How could it not be perfect? The end of that for me was Wagner's *Ring*, where I chose something impossible to do in one evening and succeeded. So now that aesthetic of failure cannot operate for me anymore. Whereas in the earlier *Turds in Hell*, the concept was to synthesize *Satyricon*—and three other plots to evoke actual demons and to stage a black mass—and it couldn't be done. The resulting mess and debris was the work of art.

I was always good at creating extremely original material by failing. Once you reach a point of succeeding, there is a danger because you realize you have become simply perfect, merely perfect. No progress anymore, and that's the frontier of consciousness. For me right now my works can no longer be destruct art, an art of failing. So then I realized I could go on expanding endlessly. My work pulsates that way—from expansiveness, epic-like, panorama to concentric, precise work. And now I'm on to a new phase. The adventure of creating a work in the aspect that has to be foremost—and that's the scary and the exciting part. The irrational and one's right to madness, that's the key. There has to be an element of danger, of risk, for the art to advance.

GD: You see the theatre as therapeutic, don't you?

CL: It may be the illness . . . Ha! Ha!

Bodies of Work

Elinor Fuchs, Bonnie Marranca, Gerald Rabkin

WHAT ACCOUNTS FOR the disregard of historical, stylistic, and cultural focus in theatre—the "postmodern aesthetic" or a misunderstanding of artistic process? Does the ambiguous politics of drama reflect the complications of the post-communist world and the rise of conservatism or a lack of deep commitment to a set of political values? Is the sense of a loss of shared community generously enough compensated for in the new identity alignments of the theatre world? Drawing on their decades of theatregoing experience and knowledgeability as members of the New York press, Elinor Fuchs, whose writings are collected in *The Death of Character*, joins Gerald Rabkin and Bonnie Marranca, *PAJ* writers and former critics of the now defunct *Soho Weekly News*, to confront these anxious questions, their varying perspectives emphasizing today's lack of consensus on artistic quality and purpose.

This frank exchange of views centers on the 1990–91 productions of major nonprofit theatre institutions: the Public Theater, Lincoln Center, Brooklyn Academy of Music, and the American Repertory Theatre, whose offerings—by John Guare, Wallace Shawn, David Greenspan, Tony Kushner, JoAnne Akalaitis, Split Britches, Robert Wilson—underline the difficulties, personal and institutional, of artists coming to terms with issues of power, privilege, and class in a transforming political climate, and limited artistic resources and cultural support in a shrinking artistic milieu.

If the widespread cross-gender, multiethnic, and otherwise nontraditional casting of roles and the current sexual and cultural politics have brought new themes to the stage, nevertheless, the theatre is now indistinguishable from television and popular culture rather than acting as a forum for public dialogue, and the avant-garde is defined more by its ghettoization than as any focal point of new thinking. Only six years after its follow-up to the *PAJ* dialogue, "The Politics of Reception," this survey of contemporary work reflects the growing sense of impoverishment and fragmentation of American theatre in the last decade of the twentieth century.   BGM

Conversation moderated by Bonnie Marranca, 1991

The Politics of Representation

Gerald Rabkin: When we did the last *PAJ* discussion on the controversial sea-son of '85–'86, we found a number of productions that addressed issues central to the condition of America in the mid-eighties. Now, as we look at this rather impoverished past season, it's difficult to find the same de-gree of energy that we saw then.

We began last time by discussing Wally Shawn's provocative play at the Public Theater, *Aunt Dan and Lemon,* in which he did the unthink-able: refuse to condemn his pro-Nazi protagonist. It was a strategy delib-erately intended to disturb the liberal audience's moral complacency. Well, here we are in 1991, six years later, and another politically resonant Shawn play is at the Public. So perhaps a place for us to start is *The Fever,* and to speculate on the kind of journey that Wally Shawn has undergone in the interim.

Let me just say this: if you look back at the very beginning of the eighties, at the Louis Malle film he made then—*My Dinner with André*—you'll notice that it was André Gregory, rather than Wally, who articu-lates the moral outrage that is at the heart of *The Fever.* When you get to *Aunt Dan and Lemon,* there is movement toward André's engaged posi-tion, but it's not articulated nearly as intensely as in *The Fever.*

Bonnie Marranca: You're right about that. Early on, Wally was concerned with waking up each day, getting out of his apartment, having the ameni-ties of life; getting through a day in New York seemed to be enough for him. But if you look back, not at the play, but at his essay published at the end of the *Aunt Dan and Lemon* text, there are many similarities between it and *The Fever.* In fact, he even mentions having a fever in a similar con-text in that essay. A lot of the themes are quite the same: seeing himself in relation to a maid, and wondering what her life is in comparison to his; the desire for comfort and sensuality. In some sense, Wally is still grap-pling with existential crisis in the bildungsroman genre. Wally speaks so much about childhood in *The Fever* and in the appendix to *Aunt Dan* that it seems he is having difficulty in giving up the world of childhood for the world of manhood, in which choices aren't so clear and neither are the securities. He can't deal with this loss of innocence.

Elinor Fuchs: I think it's important that in both works we have a central char-acter who is really ill and in a crisis, in a fever; or in some long-term illness as *Aunt Dan and Lemon.* But I marked another kind of progress, in the sense of journey, which speaks to a lot of other things we've seen this season. In *Aunt Dan and Lemon* the most corrupt characters are all women. For all of the painful and ironic self-consciousness that Wally tried to bring to *Aunt Dan and Lemon,* I really think he missed the fact, while making it clear, somehow, to the audience that lesbian activity is a stage on the road to corruption. He has three female characters in this situation, maybe four. That kind of sexism he seems to be bending over backwards to avoid in *The Fever.*

GR: Yes, he does specify in the published text that the piece—as autobiographical as it seems when he performs it himself—is not meant to be gender- or age-bound. The monologue is presented in novella form, without dramatic indication of character or setting. I believe that Shawn intends for it to be performed by a young woman in L.A.

BGM: Even though *The Fever* is a piece for the voice, it was very writerly, unlike, for example, Spalding Gray's work, which is more grounded in speech than writing. Wally was able to develop a kind of Kafkaesque story that is in fact about writing, it's about the book of life that he keeps referring to. He's able to develop complex characters and voices, and structure it like a dream play of voices, but also, to develop metaphors and different narrative lines that you can't normally do in a speaking piece or a monologue. It's developed as a piece of writing. I think that's interesting, because while we're seeing many solo performances, they're not all the same. Eric Bogosian does different characters; Spalding Gray's autobiographical works are talking pieces.

GR: But I think he's very consciously working against the entertainment/ stand-up comedy aspect of so much contemporary solo performance. Nothing light-hearted here: a journey of desperation *and* of political commitment. But there's a paradox—though he acknowledges the recent death of communism, these surreal dreams often rest on Marxist assumptions: commodity fetishism, economic determinism, the systemic relationship between rich and poor, exploiter/exploited, oppressor/victim. We wonder: Why fall back on a discredited ideology?

BGM: Class-bound by his own privileged life and background, he also makes strange assumptions about the life of the poor. As if to say that only a privileged life is a sensual life and that the poor are relegated to a horrible family life. We don't know what poor he's talking about. Is he comparing himself to the poor of Latin America? Is he comparing himself to the poor here, who often have VCRs and hundred-dollar sneakers? I mean, we don't know exactly what his orientation is, there is just an outpouring of feelings . . .

EF: That's true. There's that strange section where he imagines going to dinner at his chambermaid's home. But he never imagines inviting the chambermaid to dinner. And, of course, he imagines that that's a place that he will not be able to put his body. It's not possible to imagine such a place being acceptable in the absence of privileges.

GR: But where does this lead politically? If the privileged will do *anything* to protect their privilege, if even liberals will become killers, what's the alternative? A lumpen rebellion in which we, the middle-class audience, by definition have no role? One doomed to failure or worse? There's a line in the piece about idealists always creating something worse than the problems they're attempting to solve. So, what price agony?

EF: This intensification of the contradictions is, I think, its own kind of politics and comment on the eighties. Maybe that's as far as we've come. But it's remarkable how much we're seeing it this season, and not only in this play. Look at *Six Degrees of Separation*—here again is the issue of lower class/privileged class confrontation. In George Walker's *Love and Anger,* a mainline lawyer drops out of his class through illness, and then in a crazed way as he is dying takes on a kind of ombudsman function for people who can't afford lawyers, and comes into conflict with his old class peers. And even, in a very spurious way, it's really the central effort of Martha Clarke's *Endangered Species,* with its privileged, velvet-clad young woman in her flirtations with a black slave character.

BGM: I'm still left with the feeling that I don't know whether Wally isn't sitting on both sides of the fence all these years. His piece shows a certain kind of exhaustion with the vocabulary of progressive politics. How far can we take this "We are all Nazis" of *Aunt Dan and Lemon;* or the victimizer/victim syndrome of *The Fever?* Wally is still caught in the same liberal politics. He doesn't really have a coherent political commitment. Though it's thoughtful, I don't feel *The Fever* deals significantly enough with its themes. It remains psychological and emotional. Whereas if you look at a *mea culpa* work such as Handke's *Self-Accusation,* in which "speakers" directly confront the audience for their complicity in society, it's much sharper and goes beyond the voicing of feelings to constructing a critique of those feelings, a critique of social action, and a critique of language. I think that the problem of our theatre is that it is often satisfied with just the expression of feelings. There isn't the willingness to go all the way into a subject.

GR: I don't think it fair to say that *The Fever just* expresses feelings. I do think that what you're talking about, however, *is* a problem in many new American plays. In Tony Kushner's interesting play at the Public Theater,

A Bright Room Called Day, about the inability of the German left to stop Hitler, the parallels to current leftist impotence in the face of Reaganism were incredibly and emotionally overdrawn.

The problem is the double bind the would-be radical/reformer is caught in. There's this enormous horror over the realities of the present: homelessness, poverty, racism, death squads, torture, refugees. But in a conservative era there seems to be no viable political force to identify with or to join. There seems to be no solution that hasn't proven itself hollow.

EF: I have to say something about the word "political" as we are using it here. I think that we live in a time when there are no pure politics and no pure solutions. The mixed solutions are really what are coming up, on both sides, now that the divide has caved in. What we're getting—and we see it in many different places in this theatrical season—is a politics of speaking from "my subject position," whatever it may be. You see it very much in terms of gender and sexuality, especially, say, with the work of David Greenspan, and the theatre that comes out of the gay point of view. Wally can't assert a politics that in any way denies where he came from in terms of class. So it's almost a case of the "personal is political."

GR: Why don't we follow through on some of the interconnections you made a little earlier, Ellie, between *The Fever* and *Six Degrees of Separation?* When I read the play after I saw the Lincoln Center production, I found it to be much darker than the speeded-up farce Jerry Zaks successfully presented to the very privileged class it ironically depicts. The rage for laughs mitigates the darkness, the mystery of Paul, the *Other.* We really only know him as the creation of Ouisa. Guare deliberately deepens his enigma, strenuously working to avoid sentimentalizing. In the real-life case on which the play is based, they tracked the guy down and found out all about him. He was interviewed on *Entertainment Tonight.* He proved himself much less interesting than Paul.

BGM: The situation in *Six Degrees* is the same kind of radical chic that was part of the sixties parties Tom Wolfe described. It's the perennial problem, What to do with privilege and power?

EF: Absolutely. The problem we're left with at the end of *Six Degrees* is the problem of Ouisa, the privileged wife who is terribly torn. She can't quite accept her husband's values at this point and just be relieved the young black man is in jail. She really wants, in some way, to be the mother of this young man; he pulls on her to become his mother. But she's powerless to do anything to save him and in some way to save herself. She's now beginning Wallace Shawn's journey into self-consciousness about her own privilege.

GR: Privilege is a trap, a failure of the imagination. And imagination is the only possible escape from the pain of human separation. We have to imaginatively construct the humanity of the others our social position prevents us from seeing. The art-dealer/husband's two-sided Kandinsky, which hovers and whirls over the set, is the play's governing metaphor: one side of the painting is cool and geometric, the other side wild and expressionistic. The two surfaces cannot meet. Only an imaginative act can unite them harmoniously—aesthetically, socially. But there's a self-conscious paradox in Guare's will to a harmony, a unity made impossible by the Janus-like Kandinsky itself.

BGM: I question the metaphoric use of the Kandinsky painting. Since Paul makes so much of the fact that he is a "collage" personality, making himself up from bits and pieces of chosen roles—he constructs his life as an artwork—wouldn't a Cubist painting have served as the better metaphor for a decentered self? *Six Degrees* is a very cynical play when you realize that the character who stands in for imagination and artfulness is a pathological liar with criminal tendencies, and his yearning counterpart is one of Guare's wounded women.

EF: Notice also that in *Six Degrees* you don't have a coherent political position. What you've got in both Guare's and Shawn's work is a kind of anguish.

BGM: Maybe in some way we're grappling with the idea that it doesn't seem possible now in American drama to develop a true tragic mode. We cling to hope, to excuses for things, to mixtures of victim/victimizer, so that you never have to settle clearly on either side. It seems to be part of the American aesthetic that we do not fully accept the notion of tragedy, that perhaps people or countries have tragic destinies. We should grapple with this issue, instead of saying we must be optimistic, or we must have hope, or that we are victimizers. In some sense, by universalizing these kinds of things, rather than dealing with specific local conditions, an incoherent political evasiveness prevails.

GR: Certainly one feels in contemporary art, and not only in American art, the sense of an ending of a certain movement in human history. That's what artists are trying to grapple with.

BGM: But that's another issue than the one I'm addressing. I'm simply looking at the characterological aspect of American drama. I agree with you that we are at the end of certain perspectives. But on the other hand, if we say that we are at the end of a certain kind of modernist vocabulary, one could still take the point of view that in our theatre we've hardly come to be modernist, that we're still in a premodernist vocabulary, rather than experiencing an exhaustion of it. When you think of what was done decades earlier in the century, we're way behind in terms of subject matter, political utopias, and formal experiments.

EF: I'm wondering whether you have a nostalgia for a kind of pure politics of modernism . . .

BGM: No, rather a very *impure* politics of modernism.

EF: But it's very pure in the way the dialectic works itself out, you know, in Brecht or even in Heiner Müller, compared to what seems like a mushy liberal dilemma in the plays we are discussing.

BGM: I do prefer that kind of epic dialectic, and intellectual engagement with a subject. But what I'm really declaring is a certain tiredness with simple self-expression or well-meaningness. There's a lot of self-indulgence and wanting to feel good in contemporary art.

GR: It was certainly egregious in Martha Clarke's *Endangered Species* at last year's Next Wave. An expression without real thought, simplistic oppositions between human and animal, black and white, exploited/exploiter. There was an obvious soundtrack: Adolf Hitler's Nuremberg speeches, dogs barking, bombs dropping. All of this was juxtaposed to Walt Whitman fragments that didn't elucidate the ostensible theme: the unity of all species on the planet. It was a piece—and I speak as one who responded very positively to *Garden of Earthly Delights* and *Vienna Lusthaus*—that was intellectually ungrounded, and represented all the difficulties that you are talking about.

BGM: I don't mind an artist not being able to succeed in a certain piece. What I minded more was the tremendous hype that surrounded *Endangered Species,* and that seems to be destroying so much in the American theatre culture. I also find it upsetting that in a festival situation her run was not guaranteed, that it actually had depended on ticket sales. That goes against the whole philosophy of a festival. BAM made a poor error in thinking it would run for several weeks. The producers misjudged the audience for new work. Is there, in fact, an audience for new work, or for this particular kind of vocabulary now?

EF: I would hate to make this piece the test of New York audiences' willingness to follow new work. Almost at every level, for me this is the anticase to Wally Shawn's *The Fever.* In terms of the political issues we've been discussing, there is the sense of Martha Clarke working from themes that appeal to a privileged audience. It's the same world that Wally Shawn's material is coming out of, in terms of class. Her work looks like politics attempted by one who really has not reflected deeply on politics. Black slavery is reduced to signs of whipping and lynching—an image; the holocaust is reduced to a sign.

At the center of the piece is a young, blond girl, obviously a symbol of privilege, in beautiful green velvet, riding a swing high above the others with her panties showing. We see her in a kind of masturbation fantasy on the elephant, exploiting one of our endangered species for her own pleasure. Clearly, Martha Clarke thinks that she's taking a symbol of privilege and critiquing it. But when you think about making an eleven-year-old pubescent white girl the symbol of a repressive Western culture, I think you get into trouble. There's something really misogynistic about the choice. Martha Clarke is exploiting this character sexually while simultaneously casting her as the exploiter. The whole image is seductive and exhibitionistic.

GR: Clarke desperately needs someone or something to provide her with a strong structure. When she moves off culture-specific material into generic formulations, her pieces run in every direction.

BGM: Still, it's much easier to see failure in work that is purely imagistic than in work that is literary. You know the old saying: if you keep talking you're bound to say something interesting. It's just that we are drawn more to language, to narrative, so there's a real sense of emptiness and absence when there is only unstructured imagery. Is it possible that we can excuse things in writing that we can't excuse in imagery?

GR: Maybe one of the things that we should talk about is the recent decision of Joe Papp to pass the torch to a new young generation of directors. There is an entire ideological spectrum represented in his choices.

EF: The entire season at the Public this year has also shown very clearly a turn toward history and politics in the selection of plays, styles of production, or both. These are works directed by JoAnne Akalaitis, a woman . . .

GR: George Wolfe, a black artist; David Greenspan, a gay artist; and Michael Greif, a Jew.

BGM: I'm still waiting for the first Italian to get there.

EF: That may not be nontraditional enough for Joe Papp.

GR: Surely the most provocative, if not the most successful, offerings were Greenspan's audacious version of the Chikamatsu puppet play, *Gonza the Lancer,* and his own *Dead Mother.* These productions reveal that we don't have to think of politics now in unitary terms—as the critique of an entire political system. Theatrical energy is flowing now in *particular* political directions.

EF: I was one of those who was most impressed by *Gonza the Lancer*. I found the eclectic fusion very exciting, and some of the acting was the best I've seen on any New York stage this season. The cross-gender casting was done very cannily: a young black woman in corn braids and mustache playing a warrior brother; the fiancé played by a young Oriental man. It was neither gender-specific nor gender-blind. And at the same time Greenspan mixes with this one of the most powerful scenes of sexuality I've seen on any stage—the completely heterosexual scene between Osai and Gonza. Outcasts of society, they know that they are on a flight to death. They must wait until they're killed and can die honorably. They have a desperate scene of touching, of masturbating, a coupling of despair and then rolling apart. It was so beautifully done. Even the gesture of having two little girls played by a yellow kerchief and a green glass— arguably an arch and mannered gesture—was handled with such sensitivity.

GR: I understand the logic of the taboo-shattering strategies Greenspan is employing. But as one who has closely watched the Ridiculous theatre movement since its inception in the mid-sixties, I don't find the practices you mention particularly innovative. But my real problem with Greenspan is this: my theatrical judgment rests on a balance between the appreciation of a work's theoretical frame and the skill—the craft—of its realization. Intention won't suffice. Whatever the conception—and I'm willing to accept enormous diversity in this regard—performances must engage me on the primary level of pleasure. Directorial decisions have to lead to results that are more than conceptually interesting.

BGM: I have to agree with you, Gerry. To be honest, I was surprised that Papp would let a young director make his debut at the Public with such an inexperienced production of *Gonza*. Theoretical or political correctness on the grounds of gender or multiracial casting does not justify the kind of self-indulgent, amateurish work we're seeing nowadays in theatres in New York.

GR: I think that the difference between our judgment and yours, Ellie, rests on two things: how much artistic credit we're willing to bestow on work we agree with ideologically, and how original we judge the working out of this ideology. For myself, Greenspan's level of innovation just wasn't high enough to soothe my artistic discontents. I could cite dozens of examples of cross-racial, cross-gender casting during the past two decades. Neither the Chikamatsu or his own play, in my view, explored new territory.

BGM: But you did, interestingly, allude to a certain fullness, and to structure. That's what I was addressing—the difficulty of accepting work that seems like a stylistic hodgepodge. All the gender casting is changed, historical periods are changed, genres are mixed. Of course, to a certain extent one always has to accept art as a matter of faith, particularly if you're drawn to experimental artists or art. But, I found Greenspan's approach didn't open the text, but it narrowed horizons. For example, I didn't find the use of puppetry to have the refinement that, say, Lee Breuer has shown in his work. And also, some of the acting seemed to come out of the Ridiculous aesthetic.

I think what's happening, and this was also true of *The Big Funk*, the John Patrick Shanley play at the Public, is that we're going to see more and more of a kind of Ridiculous theatre. Twenty-five years ago that theatre opened up new avenues of playing with gender, politics, sexuality. More recently, it's been revitalized by the new gay perspective. At the start of the Ridiculous there were more taboos, so it had a different kind of function. Now it is simply becoming our contemporary comedy. It's difficult to get very excited over this kind of provocation, because it's so much like television, and film—in fact, much of popular culture.

GR: I had similar difficulties with Greenspan's *Dead Mother*. It's just *too* obvious to satirize mainstream taste by having a prologue about how Public Theater subscribers are peeved at gay plays; or a scene in which characters deride an experimental play much like the one we're watching. Yes, Greenspan has a distinct theatrical voice, but an excessive, pretentiously erudite, one: everything from a Dantean trip with Alice B. Toklas to the Judgment of Paris to *Moby Dick*—all within the structure of what is essentially a sitcom farce.

EF: Oh, I wouldn't call it that, Gerry. It was more an attempt at a comedy of manners. You know, you can take eclecticism and pastiche and you can find in it an aesthetic, or you can find in it a very debased popular form. To me there is a seriousness in the way Greenspan is going about pastiche, especially in *Gonza the Lancer*. It was done in a Japanese gestural mode, and at the same time it was fifties American funk. The reaches in *Dead Mother* were incredibly wide, and I think that there was a kind of Restoration quality rather than a sitcom quality. A ghost play. *A Hamlet* play. The Alice B. Toklas scene itself is a pastiche within a pastiche. So, I feel that there was a serious effort to stretch forms, to try to work with the postmodern aesthetic of the eighties.

BGM: You know, so far we've been talking about bits and snatches of different pieces. I wonder if either of you has been absolutely wild about something, from start to finish. I think there's a tendency to be thankful for small gifts, and to become intrigued with suggestions of ideas. Still, there's nothing like the satisfaction of a fully realized production. In that sense, I don't think that this season's productions at the Public Theater were of such a high quality.

I was disappointed particularly with the acting. That's been the case with most of what I've seen this season. American theatre has always prided itself on good actors. I don't know how much the problem rests with them, or whether it's not having directors who can really stage work. But I found so much shrillness and exaggeration at the Public. It was difficult to get any coherent ensemble feeling in the productions.

GR: It's always difficult to create an ensemble feeling with actors who come together for an individual production. American Shakespeare—Akalaitis's *Henry IV* is no exception—invariably suffers in this regard.

BGM: What disturbed me about her choices in multiracial casting was the decision to cast against type, then have the actor play his own ethnic or racial type in the production. Doesn't that defeat the purpose of more racially free casting?

GR: We have to place this problem in the context of JoAnne's use of anachronism as a postmodern strategy to see events simultaneously *within* and *outside* the play's historical period. In regards to the "color-blind" casting, her aspirations are progressive. Yes, non-whites have been excluded from the Western classical tradition. Why shouldn't it be opened up to yield wider cultural perspectives? But the contradiction is that you can't do it by denying that racial characteristics mean something. So how are we to read a Japanese American, in no ways playing his culture, cast as a rebel British lord?

BGM: Yes, but he didn't really have to act "Japanese," whereas the black or Hispanic actors more clearly reflected a contemporaneity of their race or ethnic group. I found a similar problem with *The Caucasian Chalk Circle*, directed by George Wolfe who created a black Caribbean version of the play, set in Haiti. I would like to see multiracial casting go beyond racial issues, so that black directors don't just stage black versions of the works white directors do. You see, I'm framing the issue in a different way.

GR: You're right to the extent that there is a ghettoization of black directors.

BGM: But I think these theatrical practices are promoting it, too. We're not getting out of that ghettoization. We're getting deeper into it. It is not multiracial or color-blind casting in any real progressive sense, if it's still trapped by race as subject matter or race as character.

GR: My own feeling is that you can't generalize, it depends on the context.

It's not invalid to produce an all-black *Long Day's Journey into Night* in which the performers make no attempt to connect with black culture. I can accept their color as a generalized convention. But I think it more fruitful when a work is enriched by bringing to it parallel energies from a different culture. Take BAM's presentation at last year's Next Wave of the Ninagawa *Macbeth*, for example. Rooting the play in the era of samurai and warring clans made cultural *and* artistic sense. Finding native culture-specific equivalents of Shakespearean imagery—cherry blossom trees come to Dunsinane—worked beautifully. What I find hard to accept is a production of a naturalistic play, particularly a domestic one, in which white parents have two white children and one black one and nobody notices anything—as if race didn't carry its own signification.

BGM: I agree with you regarding the Ninagawa *Macbeth*, and I've seen Ariane Mnouchkine do wonderful productions, *Twelfth Night* with a Southeast Asian milieu, and a Kabuki *Richard II*. But those were conceptions in which every single fabric and texture of production is transformed, the way that Kurosawa did *Lear*. I would never think of quibbling with changing cultures. What I'm objecting to is the kind of hit-or-miss character of multiracial casting where you don't feel that it's conceptually thought out in terms of the entire production.

GR: Part of the problem was what seemed to be an arbitrary use of anachronism—beer bottles, cigarettes, motorbikes—and yet Louis Zorach looked like every traditional Falstaff you ever saw. I kept thinking, What is happening here? I remembered Ingmar Bergman's *Hamlet* of a few years ago: there was a logic, a pattern in his use of anachronism. Every time Hamlet encountered soldiers they moved up in history until, as Mad Max road warriors, they broke in with Fortinbras at the end of the play through the back wall of the stage.

EF: Well, the anachronism had a pattern in *Henry IV*, too. Unfortunately, it was the only pattern. What Akalaitis found, especially in Part One, was a clash of cultures. It was between the culture of the tavern and the culture of the court. And she made that visible by being what you call anachronistic. In other words, it was a generational divide. She stretched the generational divide, in effect, by creating different time feelings for these two worlds. But in terms of the nontraditional casting—I wish some other term could be invented for that—I wonder who she tried to cast originally, because it seemed to me that what she ended up with in that regard was really mere tokenism. To have those two women, a black woman and an Oriental woman, one in a role essentially without words, was unfortunate. I personally would rather have seen her do something much bolder. I wouldn't have objected, Bonnie, to having a white King Henry and a black Prince Hal. That would have carried the sense of anachronism, or generational stretching to a much more uncomfortable place for the audience—

BGM: —than casting an Hispanic Poins, and having him play a Hispanic type.

EF: Absolutely. As it was, she didn't have a very good Prince Hal.

BGM: I didn't think about who should be black or white. Whether it's due to a lack of rehearsal time, availability of actors in New York now, many of whom have gone to Hollywood, or lack of creative intelligence on the part of theatre artists, what we are seeing is a drop in quality of productions because of the frequent lack of a coherent cultural or aesthetic or political context.

EF: One production this season that I thought was successfully realized was *Belle Reprieve,* a send-up of *A Streetcar Named Desire,* by Split Britches and Bloolips, at La MaMa. In *Belle Reprieve,* with all the spoofing involved in the mixed genders of the butch Stanley Kowalski, the lesbian Stella, the drag queen Blanche, and a gay Mitch, there was still a dark side to the work. At one point, Peggy Shaw playing Stanley says, "You know it's no joke being butch. I manufacture myself. I'm just parts of people." And at another point there's a joke about how her mother really wants to see them play something realistic. It's Peggy again saying, "Look, we talked about this. We agreed realism works against us." What they mean is, if you're in realism then you have to line up the sex with the genders and these experiments—onstage or in life—can't take place.

GR: *Belle Reprieve* was satisfying for more than its obvious entertainment value. I think we all agree that it resonated more than most recent works that have come out of the gay ensembles. The fact of collaboration is crucial here, because, ironically, there has been a barrier between the worlds of male gays and lesbians—in more than just theatre. So this act of unity was, in a real sense, radical, a transgression. Notice the difference in the stage names—the men are called "Precious Pearl" and "Betty Born" while the women use their own names; they create themselves much less in the images of dream iconography. But it's the interaction that so fascinates— the confrontation with the extremes of so-called masculinity and femininity, particularly as defined by popular culture.

EF: It's also simultaneously undermining them and wanting you to know that it knows it's doing that. So, for instance, in playing with the Marlon Brando icon, the powerful patriarchal male, there is Peggy Shaw in her tacky men's undershirt. Suddenly she's pouring beer over her head and doing, in effect, a wet T-shirt routine. She has on no brassiere, she's got this wet T-shirt, and you're left with a kind of weird gender contradiction. She's not really playing with the icon of the male as much as she's at that moment playing with the icon of the female.

GR: But that, of course, is something that has been long done by the Ridiculous: Charles Ludlam playing Camille with his chest hair showing.

EF: But you haven't really had the same kind of conventions in a lesbian theatre. There's much more being created before us. In some ways it looks and feels more radical.

BGM: Watching the performance, I was wondering if there isn't something distinctly different in men playing women, and women playing men. It seems to me that men strive for a kind of androgynous utopia in transvestism. Women, on the other hand, tend to make a critique of maleness, and the quality of admiration is missing in their portrayal of the other sex.

GR: I felt a rootedness in the women in contrast to the artificiality of the men. Although Bloolips always had a serious agenda, beneath its music-hall frivolity, it's tended to fall easily into entertaining, with the little ukelele and the camping. On the other hand, in a number of things that I've seen at the WOW Cafe, there has often been a kind of amateur earnestness. Here each group really gave something to the other.

EF: Peggy Shaw and Lois Weaver have become the theoreticians of lesbian theatre. I have watched this over the past few years, as these performers have come again and again to the annual conference of the Women in Theatre program of the Association for Theatre in Higher Education. There's been a kind of collaboration, where they've been invited to perform, then feminist theorists explicate the productions. The performers listen with interest to them, and they take back that theory, and work with it for the next year. When you hear something like—"We talked about this. We all agreed: realism works against us."—at some level that comes out of reading Jill Dolan, Elin Diamond, and Sue-Ellen Case.

GB: Lois Weaver really connects to Stella's sexual passion for Stanley. But, of course, all that heterosexual energy is now translated into lesbian terms. It's very powerful and very erotic. It was really interesting that they finally *refuse* to play the rape scene because it's too painful. All of a sudden they stop and explain why they're refusing to stick to the narrative of *Streetcar*, why they've got to break loose from it.

EF: But the piece was not merely "theoretically correct." It's very successful because we get a kind of wholeness there which isn't a distortion of a contemporary sense of being in pieces.

BGM: Whatever it is, it *is* totally. There is a certain wholeness one looks for in works—that whatever they are they be 100 percent—

EF: —that they very consciously inhabit a gesture or a set of gestures—

GR: —then it seems an inevitability unfolds. That's where aesthetic judgment comes in to find something beyond narrative coherence.

BGM: Right, because it's not about linearity, but texture, and rhythm, and composition. There was something wonderful about seeing the Ninagawa *Macbeth* in that everybody onstage so completely inhabited the same world. That's what was so satisfying about the New York City Opera production of *Moses und Aron*, which you and I saw, Ellie. Now that was a cross-cultural production, a German-American collaboration. It existed in the double genre of music-drama, had an unfinished libretto, and was composed in atonal music. But whatever one saw onstage was so well defined, in a style that had a certain refinement and clarity to it, plus a consistently high level of performance. What I was objecting to earlier is that we are losing that sense of valuing work as art because of theatre's extreme fragmentation. I'm not sure if it isn't less an aesthetic than sloppiness.

EF: Well, of course, I take it for a postmodern aesthetic, which theatre reflects in a belated sense. Which leads me to ask, since we both saw it, How did you receive Wilson's *When We Dead Awaken*, and its knee plays with Honey Coles doing pop songs in between? How does that strike you on this spectrum between fragmentation and a sense of wholeness?

BGM: Well, I read it as more or less in a tradition of nineteenth-century theatre, where there is a play, and then a series of comic interludes. Wilson's *When We Dead Awaken* was probably the most interesting conception of Ibsen I've seen since Ingmar Bergman's *Hedda Gabler* in London, in 1970. I don't think it was completely successful, because there were too many different acting styles. I have to say, unfortunately, Wilson's work in this country is inferior to his work in Germany, for precisely the reasons I mentioned earlier. But Wilson's *When We Dead Awaken* was quite perceptive in the way he set Ibsen's play next to Albee, in the realm of domestic relations.

EF: It's the first time that the Maya-Ulfheim plot has given a countervailing force to the high plot. Wilson has a way of adding dimensions by going off on some unexpected tangent. He replicated the whole problematic of the play by having the pop culture knee plays—the blues songs and so forth—set against the high culture of Ibsen. Within the Ibsen play you have that split between the people who are going down to the forest and the people who are going up the mountain. So he's replicating this split within the play *outside* the play, with the knee plays. In his geometric stage design, too, he has very sharp lines of division running through the set. So it became very polarized, in an interesting way—less psychological, more geometrical.

GR: It's regrettable that, for the most part, Wilson has had to work abroad for the past decade. The loss for American theatre has been enormous. It would have been very interesting to watch him deal with the growing cultural diversity we've been addressing.

BGM: You know, he used black actors early on—Sheryl Sutton, for example, who's also in the Ibsen play. Wilson's one of the prime examples of fragmentation and pastiche. But again, Wilson's work, whatever it is, it is thoroughly. He has such an overriding sense of style in terms of design and use of language. Here's a good example of work that's not really unified in the old-fashioned sense, that is moving in a new direction, but work that has a sense of control and vision. This sense of an artist completely living in the world that he or she is creating, is what I frequently miss in theatre.

GR: We're not in disagreement. This is an endemic contemporary problem.

BGM: But you know, to go back to the situation of Wilson working in Europe, it's somewhat heartbreaking that a person of his stature should not have the full facilities available to him in his own country. He's fifty years old, he's worked a long time in the theatre. The amount and scope of his work—in theatre, opera, video, television—the kinds of plays he's chosen, and the people he's worked with, is formidable.

GR: And far from suffering from his uprootedness, he's grown. That's the irony. As experimental energy has diminished with dwindling resources, many of his contemporaries now seem to be going through the motions. Wilson has benefited from working with German actors who, unlike their American colleagues, don't find incompatible the traditions of realistic, classical, and experimental acting.

BGM: There's a clear sense of a culture stretching and making demands on an artist, and that's what our culture doesn't do for artists. In fact, it's terrible with older artists, because everything is always concentrated on the new plays, the new productions, the "emerging" writer. Funding follows the new. There is a lot of work that has youthful promise, but very little of maturity.

One thing I want to mention, Ellie, since we both saw it, is the Wilson exhibit in Boston. It was the first time the Museum of Fine Arts has given a show to a living artist.

EF: It must be the first time that any theatre artist has ever received the highest class imprimatur of a major museum mounting a retrospective like this.

GR: Very early on, Wilson—through entrepreneurial cunning and sheer will—broke out of the experimental ghetto into the Metropolitan Opera House and onto Broadway. Now he has internationalized his theatrical reach. As a consequence, he's one of the very few experimental artists who has been able to work on a Wagnerian scale—despite occasional frustrations.

BGM: Let's not forget, too, that many issues that we've been talking about in other works find some basis in Wilson. Very, very early on Wilson's theatre reflected themes of natural history, and his work has always shown a strong ecological consciousness. He's had cross-gender casting. He's used black actors. He's worked in other cultures. This has not been articulated or not been integrated into the discourse of theatre because of Wilson's formalism, I think.

GR: You're right.

BGM: There was a time, at least it was so in the seventies, where everyone interested in the avant-garde theatre was drawn to similar kinds of work. There was a sense of a community of people experiencing the new dance, theatre, painting, or music, as part of that scene. Now there are clear lines drawn between a certain kind of politics and a certain kind of formalism. That's been part of the critique of—to use the word—"postmodernism." And I'm afraid that we'll see this the rest of the century. I think there's a very specific rhetoric of the sixties that seems to be coming back. We are in some sense seeing a return of the counterculture theatre with the feminist and gay theatres, the more political theatres, and the ecological ones in California.

GR: Recently, I saw Richard Schechner giving a lecture on *"Dionysus in 69 and '91."* The most interesting thing was the reaction of the young people, some of whom looked like Jim Morrison. There was a hunger for the sixties. But Schechner kept saying, "Well, I can't do it anymore. I've got a new family. I'm tired. And yet, look, The Wooster Group is still going on and I'm proud about that." He said nostalgia is fruitless because it destroys action. There's a truth in that. But, on the other hand, if we look back, there *was* a community of dissent from the mid-sixties to the mid-seventies, the loss of which we can regret. And that didn't mean that all the work was the same. But there was a sense of shared community.

BGM: That's why I feel so strongly about having a new vocabulary, in reaching past the sixties and the tired rhetoric of left and right. That perhaps is behind part of what I had to say about Wally Shawn. I'd like to get beyond these kinds of political terms, because we have such a new world to deal with.

EF: I really think that what we're seeing in this season is work that tries to take that formalist vocabulary of the seventies and use it in new political ways. Those ways have to do most with the presentations of race and gender. They're not a huge universalizing politics, they're the politics of specificity, of specific communities and groups. I don't think I agree, Bonnie, that we're going to see a division to the end of the century of the formalist theatre as against the theatre of more overt political substance. Linda Mussman with her feminist *M.A.C.B.E.T.H.*, which I'm sorry got so little attention here this season, Greenspan with his cross-gendered and cross-cultural Chikamatsu, the Bloolips-Split Britches collaboration with their cross-gendered Tennessee Williams, and some of the multicultural casting we've been seeing, are in their different ways working with either a formalist stage vocabulary or the pastiche vocabulary of high culture and low culture—the postmodernist language—and they're infusing it with a certain kind of new politics.

GR: But even this political redefinition needs the collaboration of history, as in the thirties or the sixties.

BGM: I was not talking about that kind of nostalgia. I, for one, am surprised at how little influence the avant-garde of the previous generation has had in contemporary work.

EF: I think the energy you're talking about has somehow been translated back into another generation of playwrights, though the lines of influence aren't absolutely direct. Let's double back to where we started in our discussion of *The Fever*. I think a lot of people have got a kind of fever now. That theme runs through the whole Public season. Think of *A Bright Room Called Day*. And let's not forget the remarkable season at BACA that had Mac Wellman's *Sincerity Forever*, Suzan-Lori Parks' *The Last Black Man in the Whole Entire World*, Oana-Maria Hock's *The Almond Seller*. These plays reflected a political energy, discomfort, self-examination of political crises. I believe we will see a much more politicized theatre in the nineties.

BGM: That was my point: the theatre's going to be much more politicized, as opposed to dealing with a more formal vocabulary.

EF: But I think it will do it very often with formalistic means.

GR: Political in the broadest, and not the narrowest, sense. But there is a feeling of disquietude that connects us back to Wally Shawn's angst. One recalls Franz Kafka's remark to Max Brod with which Stephen Greenblatt ends his essay on the Henry plays in *Shakespearean Negotiations:* "There is subversion, no end of subversion. Only not for us."

Carolee Schneemann

"I THINK THAT BEING ABSORBED by something is what I really want. It's that self-loss," the painter, performer, filmmaker, writer Carolee Schneemann explains about herself. It is 1979, a pivotal moment in American performance history, and a dozen or so years after the ecstatic bodies of her famous Happening, *Meat Joy,* and of highly physical works by The Living Theatre, Peter Brook, Tadeusz Kantor, and the Viennese Action artists, the passion of their Artaud-inspired performances, now superseded by the technological, cool, and ironic styles of Robert Wilson, Mabou Mines, Richard Foreman, and the new dance. The expressive, spontaneous nude body has been exchanged for the costumed body of symbolic content, Schneemann tells writer and performer Robert Coe in the inaugural issue of PAJ's avant-garde magazine *Performance Art.*

For more than three decades, the pioneering feminist artist has been elaborating a history of imagery of the female body, starting with her own Kinetic Theatre performances and groundbreaking erotic film, *Fuses,* and her collection of scripts, diaries, and essays, *More Than Meat Joy,* just published when this conversation took place, up to the current videos and installations. Schneemann, whose work was shaped by the sixties ideal of group collaboration, views radical performance strategies as a form of research and performance itself as a model for new social interrelationships. She has always been controversial, at first for pushing against the taboos of culture and attempting to demystify the body and, in the past decade, for refusing conventional male-female binaries in her celebration of heterosexuality as a positive, potentially transforming cultural force, in contrast to the vociferous sexual politics of lesbian theory. Schneemann, whose body of work reflects a piercing art-historical consciousness and sensitivity to cultural values, offers a provocative insight into subtle attitudes toward the female body, operative in the reception of her work: "Some people were using cunt-wisdom against me; they were using it to be 'fascinated' and to deny its more formal values." For her, the feminist and the aesthetic are indivisible.   BGM

Conversation with Robert Coe, 1979

Performance and the Body

Robert Coe: Your last group work was *Thames Crawling* in 1970. Why did you stop working with large groups?

Carolee Schneemann: I'm not sure, but what I said in a pamphlet about *Up To and Including Her Limits* (1974-76) was that I didn't want to anymore. One of the things that happened in 1969 when I left for Europe was that I no longer wanted to be in a position of being exemplary, of being the one who saw where we all had to go. I was just going to get rid of everything, not simply a performance group but also technicians, rehearsals, schedules, specific performance times. I still don't want any of those things.

I'm feeling a lot of resistance in myself to the framework in performing art. . . . But if you look at performance art, it's got a kind of docility and yet an enormous amount of internalized fury, anger, rebellion that would potentially, in another kind of society, go to very positive social action: action that would be physical and manifest in terms of life support, cultural coherence. So much alienation and fury indicates to me a breakdown of the utilization of the self and of its integration into a real functioning unit.

RC: Most of your work seems to be about catalyzing a certain immediacy, something that can make the work usable.

CS: Up until 1973 it was crucial to me to create a situation in which people's energies could be radicalized so they could become aware of the political nexus around them. A performance work was like a trope for the organized world outside the individual. If the audience could penetrate a performance and make a collaborative determination of their mutual situation, that could become a praxis for seeing a political situation. We had to construct a set of identifications that were available enough for the majority of the audience to become active—not necessarily so they would "perform" but simply so they would work together in the environment. What would happen normally in that period is that they would absorb a sense of our sensitivity, attentiveness, and trust with one another and begin to build their own risks out of that, incorporating our work because they needed it and wanted it and because the other kind of blind, hostile, unrelational reaction wasn't possible anymore.

RC: I don't think there is much work now that's really challenging people to participate in its ethic to that extent.

CS: A lot of women's art is. But it's not trendy: the art hierarchies don't necessarily work with it. Some of it has a very specific social base.

RC: Do you feel mediated against as a woman working in the art world?

CS: That's all in *More Than Meat Joy*. Acres of it . . .

RC: Oldenburg said you had the best body in New York.

CS: And he also told me to go to Europe to be famous and successful. I didn't understand why he would say that until it was too late to do anything about it. I might have been financially successful, or would have had people backing me financially, helping things happen, which I've never had . . . It's complicated. There were friends who were helping enormously and they were often men because they were the only other artists who were in the position to effect anything.

RC: Has it ever felt difficult to separate people's sexism from their responses to your work?

CS: I've never been able to do that but I began very early on to fight for the way I meant it *not* to be separated—in really gross contradistinction to the way others might be unable to see it as integrated. For some people the feminist value of the work became the negative center, whereas for me the female value integrated in the work was the positive center, the heart and the core of it. Some people were using cunt-wisdom against me; they were using it to be "fascinated" and to deny its more formal values. It was a constant subjection from a society whose splits, fissures, and contradictions were giving me a certain kind of rage and surge to see where I wanted to push against them next.

It's the same old thing. "Your energy is so masculine but you're so feminine." "After I read about your work, I didn't know you'd be so feminine." "You seem to be able to combine femaleness and creative will." I don't know. You could never just *be*. Lesbian art and women-identified women are saying that there's a part of us that breaks away completely and says, "We can't waste time anymore. We're not going to be building in male culture anymore, it's just fatiguing. Diversionary."

RC: Your response to that kind of involvement is—

CS: —positive. But that's not my role, that's not my personal space. I identify with Anaïs Nin as someone female trying to communicate all that she felt and saw of the female to the male and the male to the female. She felt that she was actively combining with the male and had to speak about that. These are all pieces that fit together. Some people may get furious with me and say you're so heterosexual that you're really betraying issues women care about, but I don't feel that kind of antagonism.

There are only certain things we can do and you take yourself as far as you can into them.

The people who are doing other kinds of self-alterations and transformations are making their own shape. You don't have to knock one with the other. That's what male culture is always trying to do. There's the king and the queen, good and bad, winners and losers, male and female: it's all basic binary aggression.

RC: How do you shape your concern with what people make of your body, the nudity in your work? It can strike one as mythic, iconographic, absurd, erotic.

CS: The intentionality is in terms of trying to cut loose of the place where I feel a taboo affecting me or surrounding me. Because I've never had to live them out in my personal life, I've been very aware of them culturally. It's not something that I wanted to do. This has a messianic tone to it, doesn't it?

RC: How has the nature of the taboo changed since your earlier work?

CS: It's changed enormously. Every time I've done *Interior Scroll* (1975-77) the reaction from men in the audience has been most instructive and unselfconscious. One man came up after a performance and said the action had been in the nature of a religious revelation and that he has seen the vagina as the ark of the covenant. A businessman saw it as a kind of ticker tape that his whole life had somehow been on, one that falsely concentrated his sexuality in an exclusively male principle. There are still many ways that the body has to be cleared of mystification.

RC: How do you think the fact of your attractiveness has affected your work?

CS: I've had that question before. A woman journalist asked me what if I'd been short, fat, and ugly, would I have been able to get out there and work with that degree of ease? No, I don't think I could have, but that's one of the things to work toward. To get away from the standardization and idealization of the body. In my performance company I always had people of very specific varieties: short, tall, plump, skinny, perhaps a man whose arms were "too long" or "too short." But the degree of oppression has been so intensive that it's still possible for women, all women, to make a personal statement through the body. The shock is different now, more primary. It's not so explicitly sexual or sexualizing.

RC: It would be interesting to see *Meat Joy* again, with something of the potential for scandal lessened.

CS: I'm not sure the scandal would be so much lessened now, despite what has happened. Things are more synthetic now: there is more interest in camouflage of the body, or the body as an instrument that partakes of certain symbolic contents. The body is always in costume now. There's an attitude that nudity is too dramatic, too expressionistic.

RC: People see the naked body as a kind of costume, too. In general, it would seem that performance interested in positive ecstatic excess has largely disappeared. I'm thinking of The Living Theatre and Peter Brook's work in the sixties.

CS: Otto Mühl, Hermann Nitsch, Valie Export, Tadeusz Kantor. All com-out of Artaud. This branch of theatre hasn't withered. It can't wither; nicely enough, it just got chopped into other tendencies, contrasting or negating ways of reacting against those gestural principles. Artists reacting against them still incorporate more than they seem to be aware of or willing to acknowledge. But the psychological attitude is completely different. It's a funny stage, because there's all this development, refinement of techniques, and technological systems taking the vision to a very high realization: Foreman, Lee Breuer's most recent work, JoAnne Akalaitis, and Robert Wilson. These kinds of theatre combine imagistic, tactile elements originally introduced in Happenings—blown apart, thrown in, made into vivid configurations. The "collage" is not from collage sensibility anymore but that remains its origins.

The coolness, the irony, the insights aren't built out of great pleasure or great anger, something with a clear emotional key. It's much more ambiguous. The point is that there's a sociological split in radical theatrical forms now. It's economic. This generates issues with artists who want to do something extremely radical without resources.

What I was going to mention was the mesh now between punk rock and performance, which is exciting and interesting. Energy gets very high again. There are some very good women punk rock musicians, and some of them have come out of painting. It's important that we're out there making that kind of research.

RC: You see it as research?

CS: It's psychic research for the whole cultural system. That's part of what we're doing. More popular forms are being used, which is an important part of it, too.

RC: There seems to be a budding prejudice against nonperformers again in certain circles. Robert Wilson's new work, for instance, uses all professional actors from Peter Stein's company in Berlin. Being "avant-garde" is no longer an "excuse," as some people would have it, for being untrained.

CS: The younger performance artists I'm interested in, like Jill Kroesen, Laurie Anderson, and Julia Heyward, in fact make a bridge.

RC: There also seems to me to be a growing sense that spontaneity, adaptability, responsiveness to accident or limitations in a given performance situation indicates a lack of seriousness. Especially the whole movement in dance toward interior counting. People who do Child's or Dean's or DeGroat's work tell me that all that's going on inside them is counting.

CS: This is a very natural reaction to what went on before, with the randomizing and chance factors. It's like trying to use another part of the brain. It's a reemphasis that's a compensating balance, more stringent and deterministic and Apollonian. I use chance and randomizing elements to keep out on an edge of uncertainty and discovery, going into a state or a kind of overdrive, with an awareness of how to put things together and move through the unexpected, how to go with it or counter it or absorb it or be absorbed by it. I think that being absorbed by something is what I really want. It's that self-loss.

RC: When you're enchanted, things are going right.

CS: I have to go where I don't really know the outcome. I'll make dreadful risks to get there, even to the point of messing up.

RC: You've written that you see dancers as a physical palette. Do you still see performance that way?

CS: Painting is my central "language." I think in the language of painting. But my painting was influenced by other processes. I can say I'm a painter but I can't say all that that contains. I was very influenced by music and also by literature.

RC: You've also written that the body is in the eye. Is there no conflict in your mind—your eye, too—between a painter's approach to performance and your insistence on the sensual, kinetic body?

CS: Neurological function recognizes itself in terms of imagery. You don't see it in yourself, you do it. The fascination with anything that moves has to do with the primary objectification of our constant physical state. How that heightens, clarifies, intensifies, how it can move and structure itself is through the eye, where one has a chance to experience the look of what one feels.

RC: Burroughs' notorious adage is that we think in images, that language is a virus preying on a more primary mental experience.

CS: I agree that I think in images. Semiotic analysis is dead-set against it now, but that's certainly my sense of it, like my infant memories from a basinette: tactile things, color, concrete sensory information.

RC: This idea of imagery as the primary mental process radically disorganizes philosophy and demotes literature.

CS: —the august struggle to take imagery into a linguistic form and give us back imagery. It's wonderful. It's a real palindrome.

RC: What are you working on now?

CS: I have this new work, a nasty little work that takes sentimental feminism and punk art and smashes their shaved heads together.

Rachel Rosenthal

FOR NEARLY FIFTY YEARS, Rachel Rosenthal, Parisian-born and exiled by the war to America, has with fierce determination pursued a life in the arts, from an early start in the theatre, dance, and art worlds of New York to the creation of her legendary Instant Theatre workshop in Los Angeles after her move to California in 1955, eventually culminating in her unique brand of art performance for which she has been justly recognized for more than two decades. Enamored of Artaud's writings on the theatre, she favored a highly visual style, and her formal vocabulary had much in common with the works of John Cage, Merce Cunningham, Jasper Johns, and Robert Rauschenberg, friends from her New York days.

Bedeviled by the onset of osteoarthritis in her knees, she gave up the demanding schedule of the Instant Theatre after ten years, only to continue working as a visual artist and sculptor until the burgeoning feminist art movement caught up with her in the seventies. By 1975, Rosenthal was on the way to creating a series of viscerally intense performance pieces in which she fused her autobiography with a lifelong and ongoing interest in the fate of our planet and its myriad species. An ecofeminist long before such designations became popular, her performances, such as *Grand Canyon* (1978), *L.O.W. in Gaia* (1986), *Rachel's Brain* (1987), and *Pangaean Dreams* (1990), aspire to what Bonnie Marranca has perceptively named "autobiology." More than any other performing artist of our time, Rosenthal has indeed succeeded in bridging the gap between the two cultures of art and science in works that address biology, geology, chaos and complexity theories, entropy, and neurology from a biotic perspective.

Now in her seventies, Rosenthal continues to work with her newly formed Rachel Rosenthal Company, premiering works at her studio in Los Angeles and touring all over the world. Active in local and national politics, and a fervent supporter of environmental and ecological issues as well as feminist causes, she has garnered many awards nationwide. *Rachel Rosenthal*, edited by Moira Roth, has just been published as part of PAJ's new Art + Performance series. GD

Conversation with Bonnie Marranca and Gautam Dasgupta, 1979

Personal History

Performance Art: After living and working in New York and Paris, how did you end up in California?

Rachel Rosenthal: After '53, I came back to NYC and decided I wasn't going back to Paris. And that's when I became friends with Bob Rauschenberg and Jasper Johns and continued my friendship with Merce Cunningham and John Cage. I got very emotionally involved with some people in that group—it was a boiling cauldron of seething emotions—and I felt there was just no way for me in that situation. Also, I felt very energized and yet dominated by their charisma and somehow I felt that if I didn't leave this atmosphere, this group, I would never find what I had to give. Which was one of several reasons I went out to California. That was in '55.

PA: What were the beginnings of Instant Theatre?

RR: After I moved to California I started a workshop. At first it was just a simple actors' workshop. I was giving the actors exercises and improvisations—things I was thinking up. They enjoyed them so much that they stopped working on scenes and only wanted to do my ideas, exercises, and themes. One day I said, "We've found a new theatre. I think we have something very wonderful here, let's do it for an audience." And then everybody disappeared!

PA: What happened?

RR: The actors were all up-and-coming Hollywood hopefuls—people like Tab Hunter, Tony Perkins, Susan Harrison, Rod McKuen, Vic Morrow, and Judd Taylor, who is now a director. They all said their agents would never allow them to do it, it's just too crazy and way out. So I was left with just a painter, a dancer, and an actor who had been an engineering student at MIT. The four of us decided, To hell with everybody, we'll do it all by ourselves. And that's how Instant Theatre was started. It was just a little box space and there were risers and, instead of putting chairs on the risers, I had pillows. That was in '56.

PA: Who was your audience?

RR: In those days the audience was mostly poets and artists.

PA: Did people associate it with Happenings in New York?

RR: One of the problems with Instant Theatre is that we associated ourselves with theatre instead of with art. It was always affiliated with theatre because there was, at the time, to me anyway, no other affiliation possible. It suffered from that, because people's expectations of theatre were such that our theatre was considered totally off the wall. A lot of people just didn't accept it or understand it, and the artists, for some reason, stopped coming, possibly because of the affiliation with theatre.

PA: What kind of performances did you do?

RR: I'm sort of embarrassed really to tell you about what Instant Theatre was. Because it sounds very self-serving and I'm making really high claims, and there's no proof—there's no mechanical or electronic documentation, but there are a lot of eyewitnesses. It was a theatre that was the precursor of Happenings, Action Art, art performance, and Theatre of the Ridiculous.

PA: How have the history books passed your theatre by?

RR: Because we did it in California, and because I was maybe personally afraid to come out. I think that if it had come to New York it would have been very important theatre. Over there it was really buried. For a while it didn't matter to me because in those days I had very Zen ideas—it's very ephemeral, it's for now, and so on. Then later on, I was very sad because I had nothing to show and everybody was getting recognition and credit for all kinds of things that I had done long before. So I say I'm embarrassed because it really sounds like sour grapes in a way.

PA: How about now—do you find a theatre audience or an art audience for your work?

RR: Now I'm very happy that historically the two have come together, in what is now termed art performance. I do my work in galleries. I want to branch out and do things that are really between the two—between theatre and art—because I think my work is very theatrical actually.

PA: What was the theoretical basis of Instant Theatre?

RR: The whole premise of Instant Theatre was that you could create theatre spontaneously and collectively, and I assure you that it didn't come from theory. Because first of all I'm not a theoretical person, I'm an action person, and I never would have had the chutzpah to come out with such a theory if I hadn't seen it happen first. I saw it onstage. Then I started to codify my training methods in such a way that about nine months of training would enable the performer to do it.

PA: Can you describe the training approach you devised?

RR: There were two things that were important in Instant Theatre. One was the development of a free creativity in the individual, and a certain style, a certain form of work that would push them into an aesthetics which was my aesthetics really, and then also the ability to create with others, to be subservient, to the whole. In training we used a lot of movement, a lot of vocal stuff, awareness exercises. In the beginning, I even used massage. I did everything to get people loosened up, to bring things out.

PA: When you got together to do a piece, what exactly did you do?

RR: There were four ways of doing pieces. The whole company would do pieces that would last a whole act, like forty-five minutes to an hour, that were completely free and that started simply from a set. And the set was a big assemblage on the stage. The aesthetics of the period were very much an influence. They were found sets—things that we would find in back alleys or that people would give us—old chairs, old window screens, tar paper.

So we started out in this set, and the space and the mood of the set got things going. One person would start and, very much like action painting in a way, set the first touch of paint if you will on the stage and then other people would come and bring things and build a piece; the idea being that you had to be very aware, very sensitive, to what was happening, enhance what was happening, or bring collision. Surprisingly enough, these pieces had tremendous form, they always achieved their own kind of inner logic and had a beginning, middle, and end, not in a narrative way, but somehow in a formal way.

Another way was what we called a point of departure. Very often we asked the audience to give us either a word or a phrase or a mood or the name of an artist or the name of a writer or whatever, and that would be the point of departure. We also had what we called forms, and the forms were very much like in music, where you have, say, in classical music, sonata forms, symphonic forms, or whatever. They were set forms that were always different because the content would always be different. Finally, we would do structured improvs, but we would do very few of them, because, simply, there was very little time to set them.

PA: Were you influenced at all by Viola Spolin's theatre games and techniques?

RR: She came to my theatre. I was never influenced by her. She only became prominent in the beginning of the sixties and Instant Theatre was long before that. To tell you the truth my influences were really John Cage and my painter friends. I was also influenced by Artaud.

PA: What about the Black Mountain people? You were working simultaneously, or maybe a few years after them.

RR: I was influenced by Black Mountain only in a roundabout way, because I knew John Cage.

PA: There are precedents in art world performance, even going back to the

Bauhaus or Black Mountain Happenings. But in theatre, the only avant-garde group that was known at the time was of course The Living Theatre. Were you aware of them?

RR: I knew the Living very well, and, as a matter of fact, King Moody, my then husband and partner, had worked for them in New York. They asked me to come to New York to teach in their theatre. That was in '60. It just didn't seem possible then.

PA: They were still doing plays; avant-garde theatre was literary then. And improvisational theatre has always been literary in the theatre world context. So you really were doing art world stuff.

RR: Exactly. You see this is why we had so much trouble. Because people just did not understand. They enjoyed it, because it was so visual, so beautiful, but we also broke down space and time, we broke down personality components, and we used objects in a very dematerialized way. This is why I become very jaded sometimes. I see so much theatre that bores me because in the years we did Instant Theatre we did so much of that stuff in such a fabulously beautiful way. Sometimes we bombed but there was always something exciting about it because of the fact that we worked with so many different components.

PA: How did you move then from group performance to solo performance?

RR: In '66 I quit doing Instant Theatre because of trouble with my knees.

PA: How many years have you been doing solo performances?

RR: Since '75.

PA: Are your solo performances self-consciously autobiographical?

RR: The way I've been functioning with those performances has been to try very truthfully to get to the bottom of different phases of my life, so that by the time I die all my performances, end to end, will re-create my life. I've found lately that the end result of the honesty and truthfulness I try to put into re-creating my life is a total mythology. That was really an interesting discovery for me, to find out that this structure of re-creation had become a myth and runs parallel with me. It's made up of the same ingredients, and yet it is a complete fabrication.

PA: Has the women's movement and feminist politics influenced your work at all?

RR: I owe a tremendous amount to the movement. I think they brought me out. For about five years, I was totally isolated. I was doing my sculpture and living in the San Fernando Valley. I stopped Instant Theatre in '66 and I got involved with the women's movement in '71, '72, I think.

PA: Did your performance work change?

RR: It didn't change, it began. Instant Theatre was never autobiographical. I think the movement enabled me to accept myself and my life because up to then I felt that my life had been a complete waste and a mistake. I was very harsh on myself, very self-destructive, and I felt ashamed of most everything that had happened to me or that I had done. Through the women's movement, and my own growth, I was able to take a whole new appraisal of my work and change it around to work for me, instead of my being smothered. I got very involved in establishing a woman's space and in several of the galleries that were women's galleries. I started to see a great deal of women's work. At that point I started to do performances that redeemed my life by turning it into art.

PA: There are always surprises when people use very directly autobiographical material, aren't there?

RR: My main surprise, I'll tell you, has always been the response of the audience. When I prepare a piece, I always think it's just terrible, that it's going to bomb, that it's completely narcissistic, and so personal that nobody's going to accept it. Now, I know that that's how I am, so I just don't pay attention anymore, no matter how negative I get. Then I do it for an audience, and my big surprise is always their response, which is completely personally involved and with them going through a certain private catharsis of their own. With each piece, although now I'm expecting a bit more, it's still an incredible experience.

Trisha Brown, Douglas Dunn

As one of the founders of Judson Dance Theatre, Trisha Brown was at the forefront of contemporary American dance in the post-Cunningham era, forming her own company in 1970. Starting out as a dancer in works by Yvonne Rainer and Steve Paxton, by the late sixties she was creating her signature pieces, such as *Planes* and *Walking on the Wall*. These "equipment" pieces, as they were called, utilized rigging and other technical apparatus to explore alternate modes of perception of the body in motion. By the mid-seventies, her strategy had shifted away from "task"-based pieces to more structural concerns, as she affirms in this dialogue: "I start with a structure and make movement to fit my concept." An overriding emphasis on logical progression, symmetry, and counterpoint have defined Brown's dances since her *Accumulation* pieces, and they continue to be the reigning aesthetic of her work, as seen in the twenty-fifth anniversary of the Trisha Brown Company at the Brooklyn Academy of Music's Next Wave Festival in 1996.

Douglas Dunn, who began his career as a member of the Cunningham company, was, together with Brown, one of the founders in the early seventies of Grand Union, a group dedicated to improvisational dance techniques. His spare and graceful dances, solos, and group works range from pure movement to pieces employing language and theatricalized imagery. Increasingly though, as he claims here, his work, particularly with *Lazy Madge*, was leading him to question the nature of imagery and functional movement in his choreography. "I try not to have any ideas before I start working with a person. I focus on that person and not just physically: I try to generate imagery off paying attention to them." Although both Brown and Dunn are committed to a formalist vocabulary, Dunn's comments argue for a greater emphasis on the processual nature of dance and the situational context in which his dances, and his dancers, function. GD

Conversation moderated by Bonnie Marranca
and Gautam Dasgupta, 1976

Making Dances

Douglas Dunn: For *Lazy Madge* I'm working with nine dancers, one at a time, spending about eight to ten hours making about five to ten minutes of material on each person. And I am making duets for myself with several of the people. This seems to come only after I've made solo material for the person. I'm also thinking about making trios using them without me. The dancers I'm working with are people who've studied dance — and they're dancers who're all very different, have different techniques, and strikingly different personalities, which becomes very obvious when they're on the space together. I made a solo on each of two women who'd never met. They did their two solos on the space at the same time. They had a strong reaction to each another and the result was very exciting on a dog-meets-dog level as well as on a dance level. I'm trying to *not* think about all the things I used to think about — that's been my main instruction to myself for this work. Not to pay attention to most of the formal things. So I end up paying attention to simply what I have to tell a person to do and go through movement that they can remember and keep. So far there is a very strong formality to my work and it's coming out different than if I had paid attention to it.

Trisha Brown: What do you mean by formality?

DD: Everything. The time, the space, the rhythm, the movement . . . plus any general shape of the piece. I never lay out floor patterns. I try not to have any ideas before I start working with a person. I focus on that person and not just physically: I try to generate imagery off paying attention to them.

TB: So you make a solo on them.

DD: Very specifically. I don't work at all until the people come in. There is also some amount of material that I consider stylistic because it repeats. I just found myself using certain movements more than others.

TB: How do you do that?

DD: For example, the first person I worked with was Ellen Webb, and for some reason when I thought of her certain images came to mind. The second position, for one. I'm allowing imagery to come back into my work. The other formal thing that's going on in the work is that there are very, very short phrases that are almost always stopped. Each phrase is a little rhythmic invention that eventually stops. Then something else begins.

TB: Is that because you were making the piece in that size segment and stopping and teaching it to them?

345

DD: Not really. It's about having to undercut all the representational imagery that's coming in. Physical imagery—dance movement imagery as well as mime imagery. At this point I don't think of myself as someone with a personal dance style. That's irrelevant to me. What I'm dealing with is what I know about the outside world. So this piece is about that . . . I'm still relatively dedicated to being functional about getting in and out of things unless there's a specific imagistic reason not to do so. The things that I do which are specifically awkward are made to be awkward. I don't really say I want to make an image of something. I start to make steps, then think of the imagistic possibilities. So it's not as if the imagery comes first. The feeling in the image area develops later. This is new to me.

TB: I call what you're talking about a position.

DD: I'm just making a difference in the degree of attention to images in my work.

TB: I was wondering if you're allowing that a movement has more meaning than just pure physical imagery.

DD: A lot more. But I'm not asking people to perform in a way that they add to that at all. In fact, I'm making difficult movements, so that the dancers struggle with them. That's also one of the things I'm working with.

TB: What happens if they can't achieve it?

DD: Everybody can try to do something of what it is.

TB: What do you settle for?

DD: I haven't yet taken anything away from anybody because they can't do it. Watching them try to do it interests me a lot. I also see the experience of people who have that attitude for learning how to do something. That experience amazes me more and more because it's faded somewhat in me. Having this appetite to learn how to do things they can't do at first helps. They do it.

Whether they do it or not is irrelevant because there is a line of something going on that makes it feel necessary to do the next thing. Sometimes it requires something very awkward. By awkward I mean something difficult, physically or otherwise. People have an appetite for trying to do it, and as long as they have that energy, I'm going to be there. All it accepts is that people come and go. I haven't set up a schedule with nine people and said, This is what we're working on and so on. This is going to be some kind of ongoing situation until we know whether to keep going.

TB: But do you intend to have them performing all together at one time in one place?

DD: Yeah. And I tend to leave a lot of decisions undecided. I've been making these duets and I haven't been setting at all what I do. It's really that for-getting, not knowing, I guess, that is new to me. I've never been in such a dance situation. This approach is for *Lazy Madge;* this is not my approach.

TB: Right now I'm just at the beginning stage of making a new piece, *Struc-tured Pieces V.* I don't know how much of what I say will be in the piece. But I've made a section of material that is something like functional movement. Not functional movement, but a logical progression, where one movement follows another. Movement B is an obvious movement after A. C is obvious after B. No big jumps. I try not to leave anything out. There are little flashes of eccentricity along the way. This movement goes backward as well as forward. I now have two people who are doing it.

There are points in the phrase (like standing up, sitting, etc.) that are like possible intersections for other obvious moves to go in other direc-tions. I intend to make alternate phrases branching off this main phrase. They will all back up and go forward and possibly even to the right and the left. At this point two people go forward and backward in a three-minute phrase. They start out and go forward. I verbally stop them, back them up, bring them forward, put them in sync with each other . . . I try to get interesting combinations of the phrase, visually and rhythmically, by verbally manipulating them.

At this point I'd like to put this movement, and a greatly extended phrase of twenty minutes, on to at least four people and try to direct them from outside during the performance. I don't think I'll be dancing in this piece. I've been sitting more and watching my dancers work in front of me, but then I get up to do things and it's hard for me to stay warm. I was thinking about some sort of platform that could be built for me so I could stretch while I'm watching them. When they need me I could get right up. Then I thought I should put pillows on this platform. Then I saw myself sinking down into the pillows, sending messages like paper airplanes out to the dancers.

DD: It's very interesting that you should direct the new piece. When I got out of the Merce Cunningham Company and started watching pieces, one of the things I disliked was the frequent modern dance theme of the choreographer as . . . choreographer. I thought I was certainly not going to get involved in *that!* And I'm very involved in it. *Lazy Madge* is about that. It shocks me to death.

TB: Is the dancing more virtuosic?

DD: No. It's much easier to do physically.

TB: Are you thinking of a dramatic character?

DD: No. Not that strong . . . I don't want to use movement manipulations

as a source of invention. I'm involved in retrograde work . . . I'm thinking of movement in an imagistic way—images that interrupt the line of
movement.

TB: I start with a structure and make movement to fit my concept . . . I used
to always improvise, to have some sort of improvisation in my work—
which was purely dealing with my personal resources on the fly in front
of the audience. When I began dancing with the Grand Union, I didn't
have to do that anymore. There was a marked transition in my own work
from improvisation, large constructions, and language to movement.

So when I got back into making movement, I used a simple form,
which was to make one movement, repeat it several times and add 2, repeat 1 and 2 several times and add 3, then 4, et cetera. Movements were
wedged in between earlier additions, which upset the linear scheme and
caused the dance to fatten rather than lengthen—and often in a lopsided
manner. I was learning about the form by doing it. It was a messy construction job but I would never go back and correct it. *Primary Accumulation* was only one movement at a time—one, one-two, one-two-three,
et cetera. A pared-down and less emotive version although viewers were
emotionally stirred.

DD: I think your answer indicates something general, which is that there is
an interest in dance as an area to experiment with movement problems
or performance problems as possibilities—as opposed to a vehicle for expressing what you think about the world. It's like talking—through your
dancing—about the kinds of things that interest you about movement,
how you put a dance together. What is it about? Your titles suggest that
you look at dance as a formal structure. *Accumulation* as a title as opposed
to your *Pamplona Stones* points to the structural basis of the piece.

TB: *Pamplona Stones* was put together through free association, which was
a break from the more austere *Accumulation* pieces I had been doing. I
scripted it before teaching it to the other dancers. It is an imaginary dialogue based on some drawings I had made. It turned out that there was
a constant inner dramatic thread in the piece. It was referring back to
itself through words and questioning and actions. It got its name through
sounds. We were using stones as material very early in the piece and
Pamplona rhymed with stones—somewhat. One performer was Spanish
and Pamplona is a Spanish town I remembered.

DD: The question of what to call one's work is a problem. I think everybody
looks around the environment, sees how terms are being used and tries to
represent their work as clearly as possible. This was a problem with the
Grand Union. We wanted to think of ourselves as doing everything, and

just wanted to know how to say that. We didn't call ourselves "dancers" because that was too limited. We chose not to use words like "theatre" or "drama" because we didn't like the association with other theatre. We definitely wanted to be connected with an art position. We used to say "Grand Union is a collaboration of individual artists." People choose the words "dance" or "theatre" according to the elements in their work.

TB: In the sixties, a trained dancer was a person with a puffed-out ribcage who was designed to project across the footlights in a proscenium arch stage. He or she couldn't necessarily do a natural kind of movement, even a simple one. So what I looked for was a person with a natural, well-coordinated, instinctive ability to move. At that time the whole dance vocabulary was open. It was no longer selected movement or chosen gestures for telling a story within the formal vocabulary of ballet movement. All movement became available for choreographing . . . *Walking on the Wall* gave the illusion that the audience was overhead, looking down on the tops of the heads of the performers walking and standing below. It also showed what it was, the performance of a simple activity against the principles of gravity. The rigging and technical business of getting up there was in clear view.

DD: It was stylized movement in extraordinary circumstances, or ordinary movement in extraordinary circumstances.

TB: That was developing a skill for an occasion—appearing to be natural in a completely unnatural situation. The Happenings people used nonactors to do performances and that came before Judson. Also there is a certain look or personality of trained dancers of traditional schools. They train for alikeness, a certain conformity. It was interesting to have people of different personalities and postures and looks about them on the stage. I've been working with combinations of other kinds of movement than natural movement. I've been working with unnatural movement.

DD: If we talk historically, what wasn't present as available material for dances in the sixties and which later became available material was stylization. Before the sixties there was no consciousness of certain things as being dance.

TB: I think the "Twist" helped a lot in the sixties.

DD: Rock dancing was a bridge between your daily life, which was still unconscious perhaps, and part of your classroom dance life, which was not making available that possibility . . . When I came to N.Y. in 1968 and Yvonne Rainer was looking for people fresh off the farm and people who didn't know how to point their feet, I was in the front of the line. It seemed to me the most normal thing possible. I thought, Why not? I wasn't in touch with the issues of the time at all. I just enjoyed doing what I was used to doing in a much more conscious way. At the same time I was training like hell to do those things I couldn't do. When I started to make work a few years later, a broader range of movement possibilities were somehow made accessible. I feel very grateful for all of that because I don't feel at all that I have a revolutionary sensibility.

It may be true that neither critics nor audiences absorbed what happened in the sixties but I don't think I'd be doing what I'm doing now if that hadn't happened.

I've been thinking about the influences of other artists a lot lately—more than I ever have. Even wanting to begin to talk about people's work in those terms. I'm very interested in the overall energy or undertone of a work. Is there a positive or negative energy of a work? What are the generative forces of a piece of work? How is the energy being structured? I used to watch dancing like I watched people just walking on the street. Now I am more interested in the relationship of the performer to what he or she is doing.

TB: The word "energy" throws me. It's one of those words like "vibes." It has no meaning for me. Are you talking about the humanness of the people?

DD: I'm talking about emphasis. Is there a craftsman-like approach, an inspirational approach, a hard-nosed approach, a consciously avant-garde approach to the work? What is coming to the fore?

TB: I think that it comes into the category of naturalness or natural movement. Doing things in a straight way. The human way of doing something is often preferred when I give instructions to my performers to do something.

Kenneth King

AFTER WORKING BRIEFLY with filmmakers Andy Warhol, Gregory Mar-
kopoulos, and Jonas Mekas in the early sixties, Kenneth King entered the
dance world and soon made a name for himself as a second-generation Judson dancer and choreographer. As was true of many of his contemporaries,
King responded to the innovative legacy of Merce Cunningham's choreography in a complex, multilayered fashion. Unlike some of them, however, who
were more minimalist and purely physical in their compositional structures,
King from the very beginning has been wedded to texts, slide projections,
film, and thinly veiled theatricality.

The titles of some of his pieces, such as *m-o-o-n-b-r-a-i-nwithSuper-Lecture*,
Metagexis, and *cup/saucer/two dancers/radio*, reflect the range of his interests—from Joycean wordplay to Marshall McLuhanesque technospeak to the
presence of everyday objects as collage elements in the overall perception of a
dance. As his comments indicate, King is fascinated by dance as an activity of
the mind and how that mind sorts through and processes information. Many
of his dances have been inspired by philosophers and scientists who have
dealt with issues of dance, movement, the physical imperative, or transmis-
sions of energy. *High Noon* and *Battery* are terpsichorean tributes to Nietzsche
and Suzanne Langer, respectively. Marie Curie's writings serve as backdrop to
RAdeoA.C.tiv(ID)ty, which, together with *DANCE S(P)ELL* and *The Telaxic Synap-
sulator* had just been presented as part of Brooklyn Academy of Music's Next
Wave Festival at the time of this interview.

King, who is also a brilliant critic, floods the dance field with all manner of signs and codes that resemble the intricate wiring of both the human
brain and the computer. His highly analytical and fractalized choreography
draws much of its inspiration from system theories and structural linguistics,
generating a metagrammar of kinesis in the strict emphasis on movement
vocabulary. King's earliest dance experiments anticipated today's linkage of
performance and technology, and the excitement of new scientific thinking
about the brain and human creativity.   GD

Conversation with John Howell, 1978

The Mind of Dance

John Howell: It seemed like there was more dancing in your latest pieces than in previous works. Is that true? By more dancing, I also mean the kind of dancing that you're using now.

Kenneth King: What I'm so interested in in the dance field, is that there are all kinds of ways bodies make signals, or signs. A gesture erupts or a phrase suddenly swings that way, the body aligns this way. That's why I wanted to have the words going on overhead. I just thought that those impulses are not referential, but if you just had some kind of associative information to go with that, it would support both those associations and pictures from alignment. That really intrigues me.

JH: How do you go about making your pieces?

KK: I think of the overall concepts and I just deal with that in some way. In *RAdeoA.C.tiv(ID)ty,* a lot of the choreography is about deployment of the spine, what initiates or motivates that. So there's a movement stream going on and I use different tools to pull out different options as I go along. I feel I discovered something in the making of *RAdeoA.C.tiv(ID)ty* with the synapsulation movement, and I'd like to tell you where I got my clues. I got a clue from Marshall McLuhan. He talks about the interval, and that's where information either really happens, or gets processed, or where we anticipate it, or complete it. So I thought to myself, How could a dancer find out anything about the interval? And the interval of what? How one movement follows another? Or is there an interval within a long stream of movement?

Then I made some other connections. I spent two years in the early seventies reading Sartre's *Being and Nothingness.* I can't pretend that I understand it, but I kept reading. Sartre spends about 350 pages just talking about the gaze, the focus of the gaze, about being the Other, both the perception of the self and the apperceptions. I think the interval has to do with the apperceptions, the apperception of an event or an image. For example, as long as we're sensing, we're perceiving, but we have to interrupt that aperçu because the mind has gotten on the track of that information. So I was very interested in synapsulating movement.

JH: Can you explain what you mean by synapsulating?

KK: You can cite Joyce, but Joyce is so complicated, so involved with the language itself. e. e. cummings is synapsulating, he's really breaking the word apart at the typewriter. And when he did that, I think he located a tremendous energy. He didn't need references, he didn't have objective needs, he just went into the word and broke it apart and found this incredible energy. And I thought that the same thing could happen with movement. That is, a movement stream, a balletic or modern dance phrase, could be interrupted. Which is another clue, interruption. You're trying to make a dance and the phone rings. You're trying to have a rehearsal and somebody comes in late and you've got to start again. There are always these interruptions, and so how do we deal with them in the flow or the activity of everyday life, and then specifically translate it through an environment? So synapsulating movement has some correlation—I'm jumping now—with the atomic experience. So if we can break apart the energy, locate our own, release the energy of our movement, it's sort of like radiation. And it's possible to dance in a way that collapses time through compressing gestures. So a lot of the movement, especially in the solo, could look like a lot of flailing. There's both resistance and flow, there's this constant compression of space and opening up of space.

And another clue, or discovery, was a very wide transposition or interpretation of Duchamp's concept of the *delay*. What I find out about the spine is that you can put all different zones or parts of the body on delay. What does that do or mean? It means that we're playing with time. We're able to play with time because different parts of the body appear or become focused or take on shapes independently—no, not independently of one another, but at different times—by delay. So you can create time delays on your own body. Is it a concrete possibility, is it concretely actual that the body could be at several different times? I say absolutely yes, that it's possible and it can be used that way.

JH: How do you get from that kind of conceptualizing to actually making movement?

KK: I'm going about doing work every day and wondering about that. At the same time, I'm doing research. I knew I wanted to use the Curie text, I didn't exactly know why. And then, as I would read through it, it was both very obscure, very abstract, and yet, there were these concrete images, processes, and methods.

JH: And that text gave you explicit movement ideas?

KK: It gives a rhythm. What I keep exploring is something not just about the voice or movement or the body . . . I think there is a very big connection between the vocal process and the kinetic, rhythmic experience. So the Curie text is a source for generating the movement.

JH: Do you think it's analogous to using music to build a dance?

KK: Yes, I hope so. I keep reminding my dancers, there's no music, so where do you get your information? As a dancer, you should be able to dance the same experience with or without music. So, can you locate that same energy just through the text? I would say that it doesn't seem to furnish as much immediate sensual pleasure listening to the Curie text rather than music. But if you realize there's a tremendous amount of compressed complexity just in vocalizing the material, then you should be able to locate a similar energy.

This gets back to an earlier question. I was asking myself in making *RAdeoA.C.tiv(ID)ty*, What does it mean and how can a dance phrase be interrupted, or synapsulated? What does that mean? It's a kind of fragmentation of space, probably still comes from Cubism. It's a breaking apart of space and a reassemblage of space. It's a discontinuous experience in time perceptually, both to the audience and to the dancer who's doing it. We don't always know when what movement is going to follow another, and that's the excitement of it, the reason for doing it, because if you just know exactly what you're going to do . . . well, that doesn't interest me as a choreographer. And I think that surprises audiences when they realize that certain sections are much more set than others, but they can't tell which ones! And that means with the material, and the concepts of how the space is going to be organized or elaborated upon or used, especially when two or more dancers are moving in it.

JH: It looked like you had a more trained kind of dancer at the Brooklyn Academy of Music. Do you need that now?

KK: Yes, more and more I need very skilled people. I need people with ever more ballet in the legs and more modern in the torso.

JH: Is that a change for you?

KK: Yes. Well, I don't consider myself really interested that much in choreography. I feel that I'm a dance-maker and that I'm bringing something to the dance that's not choreography. I'm getting images from the theatre, I'm writing, and I'm doing a lot of work with improvisation. Still, I consider myself a classical modern dancer. That is, I do a barre and a full classical workout on the legs, Graham plus Cunningham contractions for the spine, and so on.

JH: How is it that you're so involved with dance but not choreography?

KK: I just want to bring something else to the dance experience, to come at it from a different angle. And then, something else happened in '75, when I was making the Suzanne Langer piece (*Battery*). I looked at Merce Cunningham in a new way. I didn't feel a lot of the Judson people really used him up at all. Yes, they were talking about choreographic structure and process and all that, but really, what Merce had done with the body, they hadn't touched. And then I did a turnaround, I just thought Merce's work was so important. I felt certain, I knew it by intuition, that you had to confront Merce's work. If that meant a kind of virtual imitation after all those years of whatever, then I was ready to do *that*. I really wanted to pay attention to what Merce was doing.

JH: Why Merce?

KK: There aren't a lot of models. I find it horrendous that Merce Cunningham is really the only discoverer and explorer of his generation. In this huge country, there should be six, ten, twenty Merce Cunninghams. What happened? I think there's a problem with education.

JH: So you're a teacher now with this unique idea about dance methodology. How did you communicate that to your dancers? What did you think of their understanding of it?

KK: First, I think it's still a very new experience when dancers have options to make decisions. And they're at a loss because no one's ever allowed them that possibility. The reason I do is because I feel dancers have already amassed a tremendous bank of information just by going to class every day. And that often choreographers are predisposed by knowing what they want to be realized onstage. Whereas I really try to be receptive to what the dancer brings. For example, in teaching the dancer a certain set of movements, I look for all these other possibilities around that area, the area being explored, that the dancer can make contact with. So I'm constantly trying to let the dancers make decisions. In order to do that, the dancers have to be aware of the design or concept to be able to know what the options are at certain points. I teach the dance as a puzzle. Even in a phrase, I won't always teach the phrase. I'll teach pieces of material, which forces the dancers to find their own kinds of phrased transitions. The historical turning point for me was that performance Carolyn Brown talks about in Jim Klosty's book on Merce, that performance at UCLA where the dancers could make their own decisions. The audience loved it, the dancers too, it blew their minds, but Merce said he was not in the business of making dances in that manner.

JH: Didn't he also say it was unsafe?

KK: I can understand that in terms of his aesthetic.

JH: There are a lot of things going on in your pieces, and a lot of different things, like readings of texts, music, active decor, video, and slide projections as well as dancing. Do you see a particular dance piece as a collection of things that are there and sort of proceed on their individual paths, or are they interwoven as you make the piece? I guess I'm asking how you think of a dance in terms of dramatic engineering. Obviously, they're built so that the viewer's attention is not directed and information comes from different places.

KK: Good. I try to have a very strong answer for this, because I'm always being questioned about it. I believe it's impossible to look at anything else but the dance. But I do hear from some people that they seem to see everything but the dance. So consequently, what I've done is always make two strong visual foci, so that there are two things competing for your attention within the piece. In this recent work, I've extended that so it's not just a double foci, but there are layers of perceivable experiences that come into focus and go out. In the beginning of *RAdeoA.C.tiv(ID)ty*, there's this very strong, immediate resonance between foreground and background, and in the context of the piece, the background is coming forward and the foreground is receding, and they're overlapping. So that's one kind of time-space delay. In my earlier work, I used a character or dramatic tableau to create that kind of focus, to frame or freeze one part of the stage or space while the dance continued. With this new work, it's more like layers. I suppose that's why one could get exasperated, because there's no key given exactly for what to look at.

JH: I watched the dancing itself for the most part, I think, because I looked at the center of the space more often. The video and slide screens were a peripheral frame that I checked out every now and then. I also couldn't listen to the text and watch the dancing intently enough at the same time, so I tended to hear only isolated phrases and to be aware of the drone of reading as an element of sound. But then, I was also most interested in the dancing. I saw a Richard Foreman play in Paris that was done in French, and not knowing French fluently, it was impossible for me to watch and listen at the same time.

KK: There it is, that's the connection exactly.

JH: Sometimes it feels like it's a constant and deliberately exercised choice, and then sometimes you get pushed or pulled by the work. Then, you don't always know why you're looking instead of listening, or vice versa.

KK: Tell me this: Why can't both processes happen simultaneously? Because we haven't had that kind of conditioning.

JH: I was aware of willing myself to watch the dance, even though at the start, there was that scattered feeling that comes from a lot of action with no obvious direction. I could hear the Curie text, but I couldn't attend to its meaning.

KK: There's always this string or line that you have that's not verbal or vocal, that processes, translates, negotiates. Just to perceive whatever we're perceiving, the magic invisible cement is language. That doesn't have to

mean language like the newspaper or in books. It may be language fragmented or atomized beyond its logical modes of operation. It's a kind of
language.

JH: That multiple tracking probably also fouls up your brain wiring, because
simultaneous movement and text probably involves different kinds of
perception and organization, and at a certain intensive level, that may be
a difficult process. So it's probably something biologically basic as well
as conditioning, isn't it?

KK: Yes, I feel like I'm just approaching the edge of understanding that.

Gary Hill

To MOST MUSEUMGOERS, Gary Hill belongs in the company of a privileged group of contemporary artists, including Bill Viola and Bruce Nauman, who have infused the art of video with new meaning. His reputation as a video artist was consolidated after a series of widely acclaimed solo exhibitions at sites such as the Guggenheim Museum SoHo in New York, the Stedelijk in Amsterdam, and the Centre Georges Pompidou in Paris. But as Hill adamantly points out in this animated exchange of ideas with his ongoing collaborators, he finds such categorization inimical to his artistic fundamentals. Having started out as a sculptor, he moved on to performance and video, and to their cognate, installation art, propelled by his interests in space and time, language, sound, perception, "liminal objects," and feedback and interactive processes. Although Hill is uncomfortable being tagged as a "video artist," he continues to work with the medium, claiming, "For me, working in video involves a *thinking space* that is part of working with electronic media."

Hill's early work in mixed-media and intermedia performances in the seventies and eighties led him to collaborate with artists from varied fields, but it was primarily his work with poets George Quasha and Charles Stein in the upper Hudson Valley in New York State that resulted in some of his most spectacular successes. With them, he has created sound/text performances involving video projections, but what links them above all else is their combined researches into language and the nature of the performative as it relates to thought, speech, and action. In Quasha and Stein, Hill has also found eloquent collaborator-exegetes, whose many books and catalogues on Hill's oeuvre have been issued by Station Hill Press, a publishing house founded by Quasha in 1978, and where Stein now serves as associate publisher and editor. Hill's use of texts by Wittgenstein, Maurice Blanchot, and Gregory Bateson, and his videotaping of Jacques Derrida reading from the Gnostic Gospels suggest works of high seriousness, which they are, yet the results, be they images on a video monitor, projections on a wall or on a floor, a bank of monitors, or an installation, come across as elegant sculptural figurations and subtle meditations on the act (and the art) of cognition.   GD

Conversation with George Quasha and Charles Stein, 1998

Liminal Performance

George Quasha: Your identity as artist seems complex virtually from the beginning: sculptor, sound artist (also sculptural), video artist, creator of installations involving electronics (especially video), language art ("video poetics," as we have called it), and performance art. The latter is perhaps the least well defined and therefore the most interesting ground to break in the present context. But you started out as a sculptor, working with metal. Let's begin by tracing why you turned to video.

Gary Hill: There were a number of overlapping events that took place from 1969 to 1973 when I was living in Woodstock, New York. I did a lot of sound work with my sculpture—sounds generated by the metal constructions themselves. Then I began using tape recorders working with tape loops, feedback, and other electronic sound. I had a little EMS synthesizer in a briefcase. At around the same time, and for the most part by chance, I did some recording with a portapak that I borrowed from Woodstock Community Video. The fluidity of taping and viewing in real time freed up my thinking in a very radical way. Suddenly the sculpture I had been doing for several years seemed overwhelmingly tedious and distant from this present-tense process. Video allowed the possibility to "think out loud," as if with some "other" self. It was a continuously self-renewing situation—like "reality," yet the monitoring gave it a sense of hyperreality. Here was an immediately accessible process that was a seemingly much closer parallel to thinking than basic sculpture.

The very first thing I did was to record myself as I watched myself on a monitor. Then I played *that* back on the monitor and recorded myself interacting with this prerecorded image of myself on the same monitor to combine the recorded and the "live." This really had nothing to do with making images but was rather a kind of externalized thinking pertaining to coherences between mind and body. After this initial discovery I first made a couple of tapes in which there was no editing, no effects. Then I did sort of a performance piece with a friend: we painted colored rectangles all around the town at night. After three or four nights, there were a lot of them, and we got caught and were arrested. I made a documentary about it that included individual responses and suggestions to questions as to whether we should put up more, remove them, et cetera. It was interesting how the responses correlated with property ownership and private/public space. "Decorating" the war memorial in the center of town was a lot more taboo than we had imagined.

GQ: Sculpture, sound, performance, street performance—this sequence touches a lot of bases that reappear in your work. Perhaps video, given its history of increasing portability, "takes to the streets" even more easily than theatre and performance art. Perhaps video is intrinsically performance art, particularly with the advent of the portapak, which if I'm not mistaken also marks the beginning of self-conscious "video art."

GH: Often, especially, during those early days, I would indeed "take to the streets"—just to see what I could see, so to speak. And, as you say, inevitably there was a certain self-consciousness. There was something about the extension of one's nervous system through the camera that made for the possibility of connecting to the environment in a very new way. But even when I worked with a conscious idea, with a conceptual parameter, there was always a lot left up to the "medium" and to the event itself. This usually involved feedback loops of some sort—some way of looking at oneself looking and/or performing some kind of activity. Many of my early single-channel video pieces were in a sense "system-performances" that generated their *own* time in relation to *real* time. There are really so many folds in time involving media, feedback, delay, writing, speaking, and the body. Time becomes more like a Möbius band or Klein bottle without an absolutely "real" side.

Charles Stein: So even though there is a real-time element—going into the street and recording what you see—this gets played off in relation to another sense of time that emerges in the specific piece.

GQ: Both senses of time involve "performance": street performance and in a sense studio performance. We'll be looking at the question of studio performance as we go along here, but for the moment I'm wondering about how the notion of performance functions in relation to installation. In both tape and installation work you create structures in which certain kinds of performance are released into action. The difference is that in installation work, which will perhaps be more like theatre, the structure and its resulting performances are happening in a physical space rather than on tape. Some of your installations are, from very early on, in some sense performance pieces, most obviously *War Zone* (1980), an early "interactive" piece in which the viewer/visitor in a sense "performs" the work in a way that is specific to each viewer and each viewing. That piece, with its objects whispering their own names through tiny exposed speakers that viewers had to approach, made me think of an experimental/interactive theatre set.

GH: Except for the obvious fact of a charged activated space, I'm not sure about the installation/theatre connection, at least as a generalization. There have certainly been self-conscious approaches to bridging these forms—Robert Wilson comes to mind, but in his work, however architectural its origins, there is always that "theatrical" tinge. From the other side, where the theatricality is really at a minimum, it's interesting to look at something like Vito Acconci's *Seed Bed*. The differences certainly have to do with scale and perhaps intended audience. I myself, even though at times I come dangerously close to theatricality, try not to let the work cross the line. Rather, there is always a sense of opaqueness in the way that the work is *not* calling out for an audience, or for that matter, not calling outside itself at all. Perhaps this is left over from my sculpture days, but the autonomy of the work itself is still something that I'm very aware of, at least in terms of keeping theatricality at bay.

At this point perhaps it's worth mentioning my first video installation, *Hole in the Wall* (1974), as a kind of bridge from sculpture to video that was a conceptual formal piece, installed at the time in somewhat of a political context. The work took place at the Woodstock Artists' Association, which like many other places at the time didn't accept video as an art form. It consisted of setting up a camera in front of a wall and "framing" a section of the wall through the viewfinder that is equal in size and shape to the twenty-inch black-and-white monitor, which would later be inserted there. Then, using this fixed camera, I recorded a real-time process of cutting through all the layers of the wall—muslin, wood, aluminum paper, and fiberglass—until finally the last boards were penetrated and the outside world appeared. The tape of the entire process was then repeatedly played back on the monitor, now fitted to the hole in the wall. The image on the monitor was of course on exactly the same scale as its content. Here, then, is a work in which the performance itself is seen as a video memory, shown at the site where "it" happened; and yet the object/sculpture aspect of the work modulates the performance time by its stasis, its physical presence. Is it still performing? It was certainly a political act in the art world of Woodstock.

CS: You were in fact "installing" video itself into the space of visual art! It's as if you abandon one familiar territory without crossing entirely over to another, but remain in a liminal space between.

GQ: The notion of "liminality," which I have found useful in poetic practice and in defining a "metapoetics" (circa 1969: the inquiry into the principles of open possibility in language), struck us as a necessary notion in discussing your work when we were working on *Hand Heard/liminal objects* (1995–96), and even before that in my 1988 piece ("Disturbing Unnarrative of the Perplexed Parapraxis: A Twin Text for *Disturbance*"). Indeed your attraction to the notion is expressed in your acceptance of the phrase "liminal objects" for those strange computer-generated object-entities—folded hands whose fingers pass through each other, a wheel that rolls through the pudding-like substance of a bed, et cetera. They are objects on the threshold of being something other than objects, "animated" in a sense deeper and stranger than the technical. And beyond this we quickly saw that much of your work occurs in a space that is "liminal" to one or several categories of art/thought/behavior; for instance, your work often straddles a productively unsettled space or "threshold" (Latin: *limen*) between mediums.

GH: I suppose that in thinking about my own work I use the more vernacular idea of things that exist "between." "Liminal" had a particular resonance with the computer works you mentioned, suggesting in fact many kinds of liminality and opening onto important philosophical issues. I think my involvement with this kind of issue began early on with thinking about the difference between videotape and installation works—for example, *Around & About* (1980), first a videotape, then an installation, in which a spoken monologue manipulates images, each syllable connecting to a new image. It not only speaks directly to the viewer to the point of seeming to "second guess" their responses, but also, through this image/voice linkage, draws attention to the space *outside* the monitor. One sees images "spoken" on and off the screen; the viewer's position becomes more and more complex in terms of architectural and linguistic space.

CS: So the piece is liminal not only between video and installation but between image and language as well. Both these liminal spaces seem to be developed again and again in your work. It's true for the piece that George mentioned, *War Zone*. Relations among all three elements— video, installation, and language—proliferate in a context in which each viewer is a performer. In a sense, there is no way that the piece can be taken in as a whole; rather the viewer devises his or her own itinerary through it: what you hear depends on how you approach the various "talking" objects. What you see depends on how you choose to operate the optical equipment, such as the odd binocular machine with one eye seeing into the room and the other eye viewing animated versions of the objects in the room as seen from the rabbit's point of view. These would switch left/right and even sometimes become a stereoscopic image of one or the other. Here the liminality is in the shifts between objects as animated or real, between objects and brain/eye reception, and between all of this and cognition. Even what you think is happening depends directly on your own acts of attention.

GH: It's a kind of activated field and a field at play. Objects *announce* themselves, and a living rabbit scampers through the space already littered with both visual and auditory representations, interrupting the intellect with pure, immediate intuition. The thing about *War Zone* is that even though there are infinite paths and "takes," I do see it as decodable as a whole to a large degree; but the sense of the piece comes with knowledge slowly discovered as one participates in it, so that the work can contribute to one's questions both about it and about the world at large. To a lesser degree the installation *Primarily Speaking* (1981–83) functions along similar lines. Here you have two facing rows of monitors with images flashing between them, accompanied by a text composed of ready-made phrases that are read out loud on a tape broadcast into the space. The phrases go in and out of connectivity to the images. As different viewers walk along the corridor between the monitors, they identify with the text variously regarding its relationship to the images on the monitors and to their own body. Perhaps one could say that this was a "performance for two walls"! I once received a request for a copy of the text from a man who wanted to give it to his girlfriend—it said "exactly" what he wanted to say to her. Rather strange, but it gave me confidence that I was successful in recharging idiomatic expression.

CS: Again, there is no sense in which the presentation of the material of the piece is "theatrical": whatever content an individual experiences there is not something that is being expressed in a simple fashion by "Gary Hill," either as the creator of the piece or the speaker of the verbal aspect of it. It is rather a spontaneous response of the individual who picks up on a specific set of possible combinations of image, speech, and rhythm at the moment.

GQ: And the sense of the whole of the piece, as with *War Zone*, is something that one discovers slowly as one gains in experience with it.

GH: Maybe in performance in its most theatrical sense you have to get the story *across*, even if this amounts to nothing more than expressing the character of a person. That obviously is not the case with *Primarily Speaking* or *War Zone*, but in a piece like the videotape *Why Do Things Get in a Muddle? (Come On Petunia)* (1984), which does seem to tell a story and to express the personalities of the "characters," there's a quite different raison d'être. The whole matter of character and plot just sort of implodes. The viewer isn't concerned about either character *or* plot, but rather ends up plumb in the middle of a process wherein the texture of involvement itself is the content/information of the work. The viewer becomes part of the work's unfolding. I can even imagine an audience identifying as a whole and going through something rather strange. In any case there is no theatrical projection from the "performers" out to an intended audience.

GQ: Let me recall the "embedded story" of *Why Do Things Get in a Muddle?* This involved the merging of aspects of two unrelated pieces of writing. One was a "metalogue" from the anthropologist Gregory Bateson's *Steps Towards an Ecology of Mind.* "Metalogues" for Bateson are conversations where the structure of what happens between the interlocutors repeats the content of the conversation—an instance of life imitating art at the formal level.

CS: This kind of thing happens in conversation more often than we think. For instance, perhaps this "liminal performance" is itself a metalogue.

GH: Liminally speaking, maybe.

GQ: What's striking is how *dramatic* the dialogue is in and of itself. That particular metalogue is a conversation between Bateson and his daughter. The other text was *Alice in Wonderland.* Bateson's metalogue becomes the "Alice" dialogue. At the beginning of the piece, Chuck [Charles Stein, who "performed" in it during its creation in Barrytown, New York] simply read the part of Bateson while holding the book on camera, and Kathy [Bourbonais] read the part of his daughter. But after a few minutes, things develop strangely, where Kathy turns into "Alice" and the language itself undergoes a bizarre transformation. What is actually happening is that the characters are speaking their lines and performing their actions backward, but the tape re-reversed the speech and movement so that everything seems to be happening in the right direction, only crazily distorted.

GH: The performers in fact are completely concentrated on the job at hand with all they can muster. The engagement with these tasks generates all kinds of emotive content that has nothing to do with skill in acting, and which for the most part is unknown to the actors or even actually felt by them. The viewer identifies with them as people who are going through some kind of strange trip—"through the looking glass," as it were.

CS: Certain weird emphases occur in both speech and gesture that were not even "unconscious" in the actual "take." Neither Kathy's long, sultry gazes, nor the frenzied quality of my impatience with her were actually present in the energy of the shooting situation. They seem very expressive, but expressions of what exactly? It is quite peculiar, really. I remember how while working on *Why Do Things Get in a Muddle?* we were constantly talking about the different possibilities of meaning that what we were doing supported. We had the Gregory Bateson text, *Alice in Wonderland*, the commitment to work with talking backward, and just about everything else was a matter of continuous discovery along the way. We had an intuition that reversing language, perhaps in its violence and even perversity, would be a fruitful field for exploration. But it was as if the richness of the intellectual content that I believe the piece ends up having was itself something that emerged "in process," and not at all something that *guided* the piece as its intention from without.

GH: *Why Do Things Get in a Muddle?* is a good example of how a lot of ideas begin for me as questions that arise from possibilities close at hand like one's own body or speech or the way a system is patched together. I had begun to think about the piece after experimenting with talking backward using a reversible tape recorder. That seemed possible, but I had nowhere to go with it. In fact, at first it was talking backward itself, without re-reversing the output, that seemed interesting. The ploy of performing the double reversal only came to mind after reading the "Metalogues" in the Bateson book and deciding to use one of them as a text. And then it turned out that Bateson mentions *Alice in Wonderland* so many times that what was in fact an encrustation—turning the character in the "metalogue," who actually is Bateson's daughter, into Alice—became natural. Of course the "Alice" books are filled with reversals, so there was an enormously rich area for the play of analogies and concepts, and for working with images whose import lay not in their character as images but in their logical or pseudo-logical implications. And once those ideas were in place, the work began, in the Red Hook Diner, actually.

You remember how every morning we'd go to breakfast and play this game where one of us would say a word backward and the other one would have to figure out what it was. We were in fact studying what was really involved in talking backward, which, as should be obvious, is quite different from just spelling words backward. While we practiced in this way, I was transcribing the Bateson text into a kind of phonological score —writing it out so that we would have a way to work on talking backward. As a matter of fact, this is the only piece of mine that I can think of offhand that, ironically, had to be completely scripted out; the reversed language/sound had to be worked out phonetically in detail and then scored for the rise and fall of pitches. But, even so, there were always unexpected happenings. And, as you say, there was a continuous discussion of the possibilities of meaning regarding what we were doing. Basically moving and speaking backward is something like swimming upstream.

GQ: In terms of viewer/audience, I would think the projective installation *Remarks on Color* (1994) would have had a similar relationship to performance in the sense that, here again, the qualities the audience perceives in "the character" performing in the piece are in no way things that the young girl is trying to get across.

GH: Absolutely. You see an eight-year-old child reading Wittgenstein's book of that title, struggling with pronouncing the words of a text she can't possibly understand. The piece "frames" her forty-five-minute action (facing us as a video projection on a wall) as if she's onstage, but she never looks up; she's objectified as "the reader." The whole performance has a "random" character in that it's impossible to know what she will come up with, and for her it's just a difficult and strange thing to be doing in front of a camera. It's a completely unprecedented and unrepeatable performance of the text, analogous in a way to bringing an unsuspecting person onstage in a theatre event, so that the outcome is just an actual extension of who they are in that context.

GQ: In this way it's also related to such pieces as *Disturbance (among the jars)* (1988) and *Tall Ships* (1992), which bring "real people" (nonactors/performers) into highly structured contexts, asking them to do something that is not a matter of their expertise or previously focused abilities — to perform the unknown, so that they reveal something unique to their presence there. In *Tall Ships* there are "ordinary people" who seem to walk up to you in the dark and just stand and stare — the effect of which is to make the viewer, paradoxically, feel somewhat "onstage." In *Disturbance* very sophisticated people, such as Jacques Derrida, have to read unfamiliar texts from the Gnostic Gospels (the Nag Hammadi library) — a sort of adult version of the child reading Wittgenstein. A public meditation with an unexampled sense of wonder. Indeed, the particular sense of liminal performance here consists in the apparent fact that Derrida felt free in the context of a "performance piece" to manifest himself in an unpremeditated way. He didn't have to "perform" at all; yet he was at once in an exciting way both at hazard in, and protected by, the performance context.

GH: I think that this is pretty much the space that I often attempt to work in. Many of the single-channel works were structured in such a way as to allow that unpremeditated activity on my part in producing them. I'm thinking in particular of works where I myself appear on camera. I'm not really performing as an actor performs, but rather taking part in an open system that I myself have devised. Again, in many instances they are similar to the performances in *Why Do Things Get in a Muddle?* and *Remarks on Color* and several other installations as well. For example, in the installation *CRUX* (1983–87) you see five monitors mounted on a wall suggesting the form of a crucifix. On the screens are tapes of myself: at the top, my head; horizontally to the left and right, my hands; at the bottom close together, my feet. The tapes show me moving strangely through the difficult terrain of a ruined castle on an island in the Hudson River [a few miles south of the Beacon-Newburgh Bridge are the ruins of an abandoned turn-of-the-century armory called Bannerman's Castle], and, of course, there is the symbolic suggestion of the crucified body, a kind of "Stations of the Cross" and Crucifixion all in one. But the visceral nature of my activity—walking with cameras attached to my body along with the weight of the recorders—breaks through these representations very quickly. My movement is at best awkward, and there is a distinct sense of separation from the environment around me. I'm "nailed," as it were, to a continuously changing ground and sky by the cameras, which have fixed frames focused on my extremities. What is actually happening is that I'm just trying to make it from point A to point B without falling down, and all the nuances, facial contortions, and distortions of scale between the body and the environment simply occur given the "happenstance" of the paths I take.

The relationship to performance, at least in the way we are speaking about it now, shifts in an interesting way with a work like *In Situ* (1986). Rather than setting up a frame/context in which I or someone else goes through a process, each viewer walks into a system performance: a single monitor turns on and off, revealing the collapse of the raster; electric fans in all four corners of the room also go on and off, stirring up the air, into which printed copies of images from the screen are ejected down from the ceiling on and around a chair. This chair obviously occupies *the* viewing position. It has a shrunken cushion doubling as the "shrunken" cathode ray tube that looks to be falling from its larger frame. The work physically presents ruptures between public media and private space— my first encounter with Maurice Blanchot's *Thomas the Obscure*. This was the precursor to *Incidence of Catastrophe* (1987–88).

cs: Most recently, in *Viewer* (1996), performance in a sense faces itself: the day-workers perform their own being by just standing in front of the camera, standing, that is, projected, on the gallery wall. Performance is reduced to the raw element of bare human presence on the part of the "performers" and bare presence of attention on the part of ourselves as "viewers." The viewers *perform* the act of viewing. The performers just stand and *view*.

GQ: How is this raw sense of viewing informative of "video," which is, after all, Latin for "I see"?

GH: Well, I've always downplayed the etymological root of the word "video" and its direct connection literally with seeing, because of the emphasis on image. I've even gone so far as to attack "video" as ultimately the wrong word for what I, at any rate, think I'm involved with. For me, this would hold true for the meaning of the title of *Viewer* too, even though of course it does draw on the site of seeing. It all depends on how much "I see" can be extended ontologically.

GQ: Often "to see" does have a broad ontological extension. We say "I see" to mean the mind's recognition, and of course the root of the Latin word itself is related to "wisdom," "wit," and "vision" in all its senses. There is also the connection with the Greek root of "idea" (*idein*) and the close connection between seeing and thinking in Greek thought. Visual sensation, visualization, thinking as envisioning, and insight, both psychological and spiritual, are potentially alive in the root sense of "video," so perhaps we can say that "video art"—particularly a video art that does not focus primarily on asserting images—restores the root meaning to the word. "Video art" as opposed to video as television, say, protects and recovers possibility. Certainly our choice of "Viewer" for your piece and for our book (*Viewer: Gary Hill's Projective Installations—Number 3*) was meant to do just that, by making the title "performative" of the reflexivity in the viewing situation and the liminal state of any image/object so consciously engaged.

GH: Yes, and getting further into the roots through titling the work *Site Recite* (1989) I discovered an interesting etymological twist, where "cite" in its relationship to "read aloud" and to "instigate" (e.g., "incite") goes back to something like to "make move" and eventually connects to the Greek (*kinesis*), which generates "cinematograph." In other words, speaking is directly connected to moving images. This is only a syllable within what turns out to be a very complex title, and titles that come the closest to distilling works into words have always been important to me, as you are well aware, having collaborated on several of mine—for instance, *Tale Enclosure, Hand Heard, liminal objects, Viewer, Standing Apart, Facing Faces*, and indirectly (the parenthetical part of) *Learning Curve (Still Point)*.

GQ: Over the years, however, we *have* noticed a certain impatience on your part as regards the distinction "video artist," which still tends to follow your name. Certainly there was a tactical advantage to using that term in the late seventies and early eighties, when we were applying for grants at Open Studio in Rhinebeck and Barrytown—video was young and exciting and very fundable. But you came from sculpture, were attracted to sound, and very soon to language as medium, no doubt furthered by your interaction with poets, and then moved toward performance. Certainly, it was true of the early experiments with video synthesis in Woodstock, where you were collaborating with Walter Wright and were doing mixed-media performances under the name Synergism, and later working with the electronic designer David Jones in Barrytown. All of this was inherently performative and quickly led into our actual intermedia performances at the Arnolfini Arts Center in Rhinebeck.

GH: I'm definitely not comfortable with the tag of "video artist." Once again, it foregrounds a passive sense of *image*. Virtually all my work in one way or another has something to do with putting into question the hierarchical position of the image. For me, working in video involves a *thinking space* that is part of the milieu of working with electronic media. It includes feedback processes, cybernetics, and various I/Os from and to the world, all on an equal footing with the aspect of the work that has to do with recording and processing visual images. So the term "video art," even for my work that is technically single-channel video, can be very misleading. Also, keep in mind that the art world didn't, so to speak, discover video art until Documenta 9 (1992). I think a lot of this comes out of habit and laziness but above all economics.

GQ: Okay. Let's return for a minute to an installation piece that goes far beyond the category "video" and into root issues of language, which to extend the active ground of the creative function of language I might call *metapoetic*, namely, *Disturbance*. The poets—like Bernard Heidseick, performance art master (*poésie sonore*)—for obvious reasons readily accepted our invitation to read Gnostic Gospels in front of the camera. It's interesting to speculate about why Derrida—a philosopher with no apparent connection to ancient heretical religious texts—would be willing to participate—to perform (does he "act"?). We mentioned the self-protectiveness of the art context, even when it is revealing in an uncomfortable or inconvenient way. Your sense of performance as sculpturally autonomous and not addressed to an audience is, I think, connected to issues that Derrida deals with in the process of his writing and that make it rather exciting even when one doesn't particularly "agree" with him—writing *as* performance. I've had the fantasy that he saw the connection between this opportunity to perform and his mode of "writing/thinking"

—a stage on which he could be "meditatively heretical" even to himself.

There are several fairly recent texts of Derrida that are actually lectures—I'm thinking of *Of Spirit: Heidegger and the Question* (1987), for instance, which interestingly dates it around the time of *Disturbance*. That is, the lectures/texts are writing-performances, addressed to a certain audience at a certain time on a certain issue with a certain background, yet they are driven by an internal textual dynamic. A book publishing such language-events is very much like an installation. Perhaps this liminal performance/installation quality is present in the thinkers that you are attracted to—Blanchot even more than Derrida—who seem to work in a way somehow related to how you are working. How do you see this connection between performance and writing?

GH: One might think that performance, even within the context of various self-conscious delimitations, would be closer to Derrida's ideas on grammatology, whereas editing, working with "post-performance" recorded material, might be closer to the space of writing which, by its nature, gives distance and mediation. In one sense the making of *Disturbance* was a two-part ordeal: the performance events and the editing/writing events. And the complexity of the relationship between these two stages of composition could be thought about in terms of the complexity of the relationship in Derrida's thought between speaking and writing. (Derrida thinks that speaking-performing is *already* a kind of writing.) Or perhaps, if we open up performance as we've been speaking about it, by structuring it through other media, other questions such as "What is performance time?" come into play, as well as all the ontological issues that swirl around the very questions we are asking—*then* we might begin to see performance within the domain of writing.

As you know, George, since you were there as collaborator, the production time of *Disturbance* was short indeed—about two weeks. And although we worked hard on the textual base, we didn't produce a script. I had some drawings and structural notes for the initial piece I had planned (called *Vanishing Points*), which at least gave an inkling of the images moving through a sequence of monitors. This was not much to go on, given the level of poets and performers arriving at our doorstep in a steady stream. So various on-the-spot decisions by us and the performers alike became very important, since in retrospect the collected recorded "events" would in some sense become almost "found objects," perhaps something like the Nag Hammadi manuscripts themselves (which were found preserved in ancient *jars*). I suppose a completely different final text could be made from the same raw material.

Long before this, I had similar notions about *Primarily Speaking*—that a completely different set of images could be plugged into the text, though not just *any* images. So our on-the-spot decisions became very important—decisions about the framing and the movement of the performers became deciding factors in structuring the work. Basically I had to work with what I had after everything had been recorded. During the taping, we tried to capture something from each individual performance without thinking about how everything would be woven together in the end. So the improvisational energy along with the inspiration that those heretical texts seemed to engender in the writers produced very powerful results. Given that we rarely did more than a single take, it was remarkable.

More than with the other performing writers, the pressure was on when Derrida came. It was an on-the-spot decision to have him walk back and forth full-bodied all the way through the frame each time. The fact that this made it possible, later in editing, to have him continue through the space of multiple monitors determined a major thread of the piece. (The illusion of his walking continuously from screen to screen across several monitors in a row involved reversing the image each time.) On a subtler level, since he held the text in one hand, every time he walked through and appeared on another monitor, the text would otherwise have changed hands due to the image's having become reversed. This played right into the issues of left and right that appear throughout the work and became one of the major factors in building the fundamental structure of the piece. In the end, the monitors became a fragmented sentence that he was weaving through. But it also made sense in terms of the simple act of walking, thinking, and pacing. There's an interesting connection, which I believe you expressed at the time, to Heidegger's *Conversation on a Country Path*, at least as image.

cs: This sense of language as a kind of walking—the sense that the body activates language—becomes literally the case in *Withershins* (1995), where the participant wanders through a labyrinth laid out on the ground of the installation and each step activates a phrase that is broadcast through the space of the work, so that a text is generated by the act of walking. The labyrinth becomes a kind of brain, and one becomes, as it were, one's own homunculus, walking inside the folds and passageways of one's own cranium. Or again, language itself becomes a brain. . . . We have been talking about performance in a number of different senses, and perhaps this is the moment to call attention to a meaning of the word "performative" that we have used in discussing your work elsewhere. We borrow the philosopher J. L. Austin's use of this term for utterances that literally *perform the action* of which they speak: I promise, I wish, I accuse, I name, et cetera—actions accomplished in their very saying. Such verbal actions close the gap between word and meaning, but can only do their work within the specific contexts that call them forth . . .

GQ: Performative language is always site/occasion-specific—it happens here and now.

CS: In some sense, each artistic gesture, each decision or choice, is a performative act, calling into being, or allowing to emerge into being, the particular artistic value with which it is concerned.

GH: Ultimately every word and every moment in a tape (or life for that matter) could be performative almost in and of itself in that sense. I think of La Monte Young's saying, "tuning is a function of time." Each event enters into an evolving relationship with the developing piece, spiraling around and folding in so that at any moment you might "begin" again from a different place. I mean even repeating an image or a sequence can be part of a continuous event; in working on a piece, relistening to a sequence folds a past event back into the present. One just has to be patient, believing something will emerge. But what is it that is the source of this emergence when it does happen? It happens in "the present" but the present has now gained a complexity that quite literally includes the replayed past. This really complicates the question of "real time."

GQ: Everything emerges in the present, but the present is the occasion of a "performance" that includes the replay of real-time taped sequences captured in the past. Your "every word is performative" expresses the condition of poetry—each word accomplishes its meaning immediately and concretely. In this sense poetry is not the special case of language but the emergence—the eruption—of its deepest nature. We watched your already active awareness of language possibilities grow through your relations to poets in the late seventies. Your tape *Happenstance* (1982–83), with its literal "spiraling around and folding in" of language, as you say, is as fresh today as the first day I saw it, *as* it was being made, in Barrytown. For me it belonged to the history of what I had already long been calling—thinking of Blake's nonlyric works—"poetic torsion." And frankly *Happenstance* was like a readout of a part of my own brain, because it proved something I fantasized was true, that in the deepest sense a poem is an animate force that is active in all of the mind's projections, visual/aural/tactile. Blake invented a high-tension open interaction of text and image that rendered both "mind-degradable." *Happenstance* carries that process into territory Blake would have loved. Your

sense of textuality sets the viewer-reader *inside* the experience of reading, recognizing that alert acts of reading are actually performative: the
world or content of the text is performed on the mind of the reader, or *by*
the mind of the reader, as reading takes place. But reading is also a bodily
act and a bodily performance, and a book is also a physical occasion, and
its physical properties can become part of the reading performance itself.
I think this is very much the sense of things that you evoke in *Incidence of
Catastrophe* (1987–88), which "takes place" inside the act of reading a text
by Blanchot, *Thomas the Obscure*.

GH: When I read that work, it was as if the edges of the book ceased to exist
or that the book took on enormous proportions.

CS: As of course it does for you at the end of your tape.

GH: In *Thomas* the differentiation of the space of the book from that of the
author and of the reader collapses, and this creates a state of incredible
vertigo; your position is constantly being challenged in terms of where
you fit into the narrative as a reader. All you can do is *hold* the book, *feel*
the pages, *see* the words as pure things being there, generating a cocoon
around you. That experience of reading itself belongs to the main character in the book, but it also is forced on you as you read it. It's one of the
most hallucinatory books I've ever read, not just in the images it creates
but in the play of that space. That aspect of the book really rattles me,
actually.

GQ: There's a sense that every time one comes to it, it's like a new text—you
forget what you've read. Blanchot is the most continuously forgettable
unforgettable writer I know! (Except maybe Blake!)

CS: I remember re-reading *Thomas the Obscure* a few years after experiencing
it the first time. I returned to the text with very sharp memories of certain scenes and certain passages; but when I had read it through, those
scenes had completely vanished—they just weren't there. There was, this
time, a completely different distribution of images and events—it was
quite startling.

GH: The last time I read the book—quite recently, actually—I had a similar
experience, even after my close and intense use of it in *Incidence of Catastrophe*.

GQ: What you capture in that work by emphasizing the physicality of the
book—the textures of its pages, the sounds of turning them, the resonance between those sounds and the sounds of the surf—is not just an
imaginative extrapolation from the subject matter of the book, but a direct portrayal or projection of the book itself—of that aspect of it that
is always right in your face, that means to grab hold of you and demon-

strate something of the terror and mystery of the ontology of reading. *Incidence of Catastrophe* is as much an intensive commentary on *Thomas the Obscure* as it is a work of art informed by it—a work of art that *performs* the act of reading another.

GH: The impulse to put myself in the place of the protagonist was to make that happen—because otherwise I would have just been outside, trying to *tell* you what reading that book was like. But like I say, that book really rattled me, and the whole point of *Catastrophe* was to deal with that experience.

CS: Yet, once again, that tape was not put together by following a theatrical scenario.

GH: Certainly not. I never really acted in it, per se, as I mentioned before. Most of the scenes were tableau-like. We would set them up and just *perform*. Many times we just left the camera on, recording well past the time limit we had initially decided on. Generally speaking, that was when interesting things would start to happen. I think that extending the recording time turned out to be key to actually projecting the experience of reading—the connection between real time and reading time. There are portions of *Catastrophe* where the scenes are purposefully *elongated*. Pages of the book are seen for extended periods of time, considerably longer than mere spectator time. Yet these sequences need to be there to submerge the viewer into the *time of reading*—an actual reading time that's parenthesized in the work—there had to be some actual event of reading: time spent sitting with the book, being with the book.

GQ: There's real time, performance time, and *reading* time . . .

GH: It's interesting to think in this respect about Noh drama: how in the theory of Noh there are different kinds of times—split time, reverse time, and others. I think there are four or five differentiated concepts of time.

GQ: Perhaps there is something that we could call "deep time" that runs underneath them all and makes them possible—a time that's always there and that you know you can count on; it doesn't have any structure in itself, but it allows whatever time structure is necessary to become available.

GH: It's zero time—as something like the *still point*. In surfing (I just had to get this in) this could be described as the moment in which the surfer finds a position in the "green room" (inside the curl of the wave). And that curving/breaking line is so steadily evolving that it appears to be still. Consequently, the surfer is in the perfect position "infinitely." I think when one is in the creative act, the desire is to find and stay with this kind of still point as long as possible. But it is the unavoidable breaks from it that allow the still point to reveal itself *outside* itself. Paradoxically it needs disturbance of some kind to exist so as to be what it is: the consummate tuning fork.

GQ: "At the still point of the turning world. Neither flesh nor fleshless; / Neither from not towards; at the still point, there the dance is, / But neither arrest nor movement." T. S. Eliot, *The Four Quartets: Burnt Norton,* Part II. So direct experience of the still point—whether in an activity like surfing, or in a "nonaction" activity like tai chi chuan or certain types of bodywork (in the osteopathic offshoot, craniosacral therapy, "still point" is a technical term for deep and transformative suspension of rhythmicity), or in the process of working in a specific artistic medium or between mediums, or in the actual ongoing activity of transforming the material with which one is working—the still point would be that poise of mind and hand, mind and body, where awareness and activity click in and the work is really under way. And this *still-point* experience is simultaneously the access to *deep time*—to the very time that engulfs and surrounds and underplays and nourishes and *is* the very heart of the process and the activity itself.

CS: The deep issue behind process, then, behind the creative potentialities of real time, as well as behind the complex folding of time upon itself, behind the self-referential aspects of the "performative"—is *this deep time* as the strange source or wellspring of what is truly creative in the work. This reminds me of that incredible image of the mask rising abruptly to the surface of the water in *Ura Aru* (1985–86)—as if there were a certain trust expressed in this moment, that the image, in this case the mask, has been trusted to arise, to return from the depths—that you don't always have to plan out beforehand the effects you are after, but that there is a fundamental trust in this deep time itself that you have to acknowledge, and in acknowledging, in a certain sense prepare for—but that all the planning, the contriving, the structuring is only to create occasions where a certain emergence can be allowed to happen; that given the right kind of permission, or solicited in the right manner, deep time will deliver what is needed; and I think that this is true in a great variety of ways in your work. I would say that it is what is most profound even where the issue seems to involve the relationship between language and image, and precisely where the ordinary understanding of those relationships are most challenged; that these are occasions strategically contrived so that new species of events of meaning might emerge from deep time—the time in which the work is being generated but also the time in which the work is being *viewed*. For since the image/event itself is not contrived but solicited, the moment of creation and the moment of viewing are the same.

GH: In terms of the mask I hope you are speaking figuratively because the reality of the situation was thus: throwing the mask in a small pond, hoping that it would "arrange" itself just so, and at that moment, using the end of an old broomstick to push the mask down through the water until it was all but invisible; then recording it as it surfaced in hope that it did it in "just the right way." If not, do it again . . . and again. Certainly I couldn't plan how the mask would arise in terms of all the nuances nor could I hang out by the local swimming hole waiting for an *otafuku* Japanese mask to suddenly come from the deeps! So in this sense the actual event that I wanted was thought out, knowing full well that not everything could be controlled (by a long shot). Also, if one were to imagine a Japanese person watching this activity, it would practically be a form of sacrilege!

GQ: "A line will take us hours maybe;/Yet if it does not seem a moment's thought,/Our stitching and unstitching has been naught." W. B. Yeats, "Adam's Curse."

CS: Indeed. My point was just that the meaning of the image's arising, in the context of our discussion, seems capable of such a *reading* . . . In the seventies, there was a lot of talk among poets—and I mean the poets in our scene: George, myself, Robert Kelly, and a few others—to valorize the "processual" over the "procedural" in work. And what we meant was that the life of the work came from the actual doing of it—that you felt your way along toward the emerging poem; you didn't think it up beforehand and work out a procedure that would guarantee the value of the work no matter what it turned out to be. Even "process" wasn't valued as a concept, as if anything at all could be justified because it illustrated "process" as such. But everything important came in the application of actual attention—it required a continuous alertness to the emerging possibilities with a view to realizing them, working them out, finding out what they would yield; and that this happened in the actual process of working. The work was not an *example* of its concept, but something that issued, that was projected, in the process of doing it. In that way, every poem was an improvisation, a performance—not because it was impromptu or even because it happened "live," but because the life of the activity of producing it was what made possible whatever vital qualities the work itself might show.

GQ: Perhaps we could create a useful distinction between "real time" and "actual time." Real time, following computer science, is "the time in which a physical process under computer study or control occurs"; so in video one does something like suppose a "camera time" that operates within literal clock time. *Actual time,* on the other hand, may or may not follow literal clock time—it's interruptible without loss of deeply linked intensities. Here the issue is *present time* in the sense of *being present in time*—what happens with the special intensity of the emergent and creatively unfolding *composition process itself.* It stands in relation to the temporal/auditory as *concreteness* and *particularity* do in relation to the spatial/visual. This actual-time distinction—or, paradoxically, *concrete time*—may draw out what was of interest to you in the "processual" and why you chose to apply it to video—for example, *Processual Video* (1980)—much in the sense we had had been using it for in poetics in the seventies.

GH: Whatever language I used in the early seventies—and I'm sure "process" was clearly central to it—I think it was very much along the lines of your description of the processual. There is a certain difference, though, between the processual in writing and the way I was taking it in video. Except for hard-core conceptual art and perhaps what became known as "process art," which as you say was about procedure, all the work I've done, with a few exceptions, from sculpture to sound and video emerged *in* time much in the way you speak about it. Once I became aware of your scene and aware also of the term "processual" as you were using it, I took it as a way to delineate a working space/time to yield something between an emphasis on process and on concept. Yet I'm wondering if what I hear as a certain modulated difference has to do with how the various mediums—writing and video, say—are differently informed by the same principle of emergence.

I think Heidegger's notion of *techne* is important here as suggesting that any specific technology can be transformed in its own specific way by its use in artistic work. There is a *techne* of harnessing electronic media, and in particular the complexities of multiple overlapping systems and feedback situations, that is quite distinct and offers, at times, specific opportunities for dealing with the issues and ideologies surrounding technology as such. And these issues, however much they are constantly fluctuating for me, may at times enter the fold of a work. That said, the crucial point is how to remain *in* time in relation to the *techne*—the transformation of the medium and the working through of its work-specific implications. There are types of feedback that are experienced in electronic media that don't come up in writing. Certainly the differences between writing on a computer, on a typewriter, or by hand enters into the discussion, but I think what we are searching for here is something that occurs on a deeper level.

CS: So for you the crucial issue is the possibilities of feedback that electronic media offer.

GH: I think so. And how they differ, not only from writing, but other feedback situations. I feel that feedback phenomena really dominate the whole issue of video. Actually, this seems more important than, say, the fact that a tape is made in "real time" as such, even though, of course, feedback occurs through real-time process. So the deep-time/actual-time distinction from "real time" is interesting. But the important *result* is the feedback; feedback is what gives you something different from the more ordinary ways of working with a medium. The feedback situation that arises when you are working with videotape can involve a certain cognitive element—an implication of abstract thinking that has nothing to do with, say, the way your hands work some material, that is, the ordinary sense of feedback that has to do with craft. If you focus a video camera on yourself—there you are, outside yourself.

GQ: As in *Standing Apart/Facing Faces* (1996).

GH: Right. But it is even more than that. I was thinking about this while driving today. A car is always used as a good example of cybernetic feedback—the most prosaic notion of it. You're driving a car. Your eyes see the road. You turn the wheel. The car turns. Now the *road* appears to turn because *you* have turned. There's a continuous loop. Feedback. But in the kind of space that arises in the video situation, you find yourself forced into an involvement with more abstract ideas that arise quite naturally in relation to the simple facts—ideas about identity, the nature of inner and outer, the relation between image and actuality, the meaning of presence, the role of information or real time, and so forth. And these ideas are part of your immediate, ongoing negotiation with what is actually happening, not at all at an academic or "philosophical" level, but part of the difficulty of simply existing in the situation that you have conjured up through electronic media. And once you find yourself involved in this, very unusual spaces open—spaces that can seem to hold the promise of real insight into these very difficult issues.

CS: Of course if you claim that this is happening, it all becomes quite questionable—people can say that referring to those issues is a kind of pretension, particularly if they don't enter into that kind of experience.

GH: Exactly. And at this point it really becomes a matter of belief or faith. There's nothing that's going to *prove* that you are on any said "level." You do know, say, that you're in a feedback process—there's a camera on you; there's a monitor in front of you and you're looking at it. But once you enter into what we could call "metafeedback," the space that opens up when you are simultaneously in your own body looking out and out there on a monitor or projected onto a wall being looked at—you have to make a leap—you have to commit yourself to the connection, to the fact that you believe that there's a kind of feedback that comes from this total situation that is beyond the mechanical, first-order feedback of the camera and the monitor. I think that the interest in this marks a difference between my work and that of a lot of other artists who use video feedback in one way or another.

CS: This shows up, I would say very powerfully in works like *Tall Ships* or *Viewer*, or *Hand Heard*—George and I have dealt with this question extensively in our series of books about those works. The experience of *Tall Ships*, say, has the possibility of initiating a state where something like the "common mind" of the piece manifests—where the participant enters into what you are calling the metafeedback space of a collective participation in an inquiry.

GQ: Aren't we also dealing here with something very close to biofeedback and psychofeedback? Biofeedback in some respects is the best model for discussing a whole range of processes human beings are involved with— even the crude instance of biofeedback, where you put an electrode on your head and watch a gauge that tells you when you're agitated. The feedback situation allows you to reflect on your own productive energy— what you are producing in the way of energy waves, mind waves, which exist along some kind of a spectrum of electronic impulses. One of the things that has always been attractive about video feedback is the strange way that video seems to engage the mind's sense of itself as if there were a resonance between the bioelectricity of the nervous system and the emission of electrons by the cathode-ray tube—a sense, obviously, that film doesn't excite. I don't know that I have any satisfactory notion of what it means, but it does seem to relate to the biofeedback that occurs in doing hands-on bodywork, for instance, or touch-oriented movement like Contact Improvisation or tai-chi push-hands. Perhaps we need a notion like "biointerfeed" to suggest that the feedback—the engaged "listening/signaling"—is going both ways, as it obviously is in many performance situations where the performer is modulating behavior according to audience response.

GH: I think the real difference between the kind of feedback that occurs in video and bodywork or biofeedback, on the one hand, and film, on the other, is that neither biofeedback nor video is essentially *pictorial*. The end result is not an image, even if it involves images, in a sense, along the way. One is not engaged in setting up a scenario to represent something through an image. The outcome, the output, is more a blueprint *after the fact* of what occurred in the feedback situation. That's not true of all my work, but take pieces like *Dervish* (1993–95) or *Between 1 & 0* (1993) or anything where the image is really *agitated*—the whole thing has to do with keeping you in an agitated state, to force you to remain or become aware of the process of seeing and looking and being in a certain place and becoming engaged in what it means.

GQ: An excited feedback situation.

GH: An excited feedback situation.

GQ: It moves somewhat close to a "flicker" effect at certain times. It engages you at a neurological level. Certainly you get that in *Dervish:* a strange, neurological, even *trippy* quality.

GH: *Circular Breathing* (1994), too—a continuous pulsation at the same rate. And what's interesting—and this is something I want to pursue more— is, like you say, this kind of *trippy neurological* thing that is embedded with some notion of narrative or of there being something *underneath*. In other words, it's not solely a mechanical or biochemical effect, but an opening up of another view on what a story is, what a narrative is, what images are, and what do images mean when they are next to each other flickering at such and such a rate.

GQ: The great forbidden subject—how this all works in with actual transformation, actual states of mind, the work as initiation into our "further nature," to use Charles Olson's projective term. But here we are on the threshold of another dialogue, one that leads us into the *further life* of all our genuine work. "I'm so foolish," Olson also wrote, "a song is heat!"

Jerry Rojo

ONE OF THE IMPORTANT NEW DIRECTIONS in theatrical experiments of the sixties was the move toward environmental theatre, which was influenced by Happenings, the Judson dance, popular forms, such as parades, carnivals, and sports events, and the theatricalization of culture and politics in this era. The Living Theatre had aggressively pushed beyond the boundaries of audience and event with their *Paradise Now* and, in Europe, influential artists as different as Peter Brook, Ariane Mnouchkine, and Jerzy Grotowski had created works that made the experience of space an aspect of theatrical experience. Implicit in this shift away from the conventional audience relationship to the stage, and toward group rather than private experience, was the desire for audience participation in the performance itself. Jerry Rojo, who designed many of the off-off-Broadway productions that helped redefine the idea of performance space, is most prominently known for his work with Richard Schechner and The Performance Group, especially their successful collaborations on *Dionysus in 69, Makbeth, Mother Courage and Her Children,* and *The Tooth of Crime. Theatres, Spaces, Environment,* which he co-wrote with Schechner and Brooks McNamara, details many of his design projects.

From the beginning, Rojo was drawn to architecture and building in the theatre, and to real time and real space. This direction led him to investigate how plays could be articulated in spatial metaphors. Interestingly, while some environmental theatre works of the period were based on group collaboration, many of the productions were stagings of the classics or contemporary plays. A leading innovator in the creation of a new ecology of theatre, in this interview from the first issue of *Performing Arts Journal,* Rojo is positively lyrical on the environmental approach: "What's happening here is you have a real room, a live audience, live actors who create a piece in a living way. It's a living theatre. And to exploit the living condition is aesthetically the most beautiful way of working."   BGM

Conversation with Bonnie Marranca
and Gautam Dasgupta, 1976

Environmental Theatre

PAJ: When did you first begin to think about environmental theatre?

Jerry Rojo: I was trained as a traditional designer in traditional schools—in what I call the scene-painting school of design. I guess I'm a purist in many ways. I like to find what are the elements of something, and then go after those elements. To me the theatre is accepting living time and space. When I came to the University of Connecticut in 1961 to teach I began working with Mike Gregoric, a teacher there. He and I began playing around with different things in open space work. I was interested in the Happenings movement. Then I went back to school at Tulane University to work with Richard Schechner because he was writing and teaching that kind of work there. I got turned on even more by his intensity in this kind of work. Then Richard asked me to come to New York and help him with *Dionysus in 69*. At that time, because there was so much attack coming at you from all corners, both from other theatre people, politicians, and what not, you really had to get your guns together and your definitions of the form. I began to study and understand it more and more because I was forced into a defensive position for working in this radical way.

I had an art background, a lot of art training in working three-dimensionally. That's where I think traditional designers go wrong. They're more concerned with painting, not the architectural space. I am interested in building. I love building sets of architecture and here I discovered this art form in the theatre.

PAJ: In his book *Environmental Theater* Schechner writes: "The first scenic principle is to create and use whole spaces." How do you as a designer put into practice that principle?

JR: For me there are two basic directions: one is the space that is fixed, like the Mobius Theater; another is a space that is open. Every production works in different ways. In the Manhattan Project's *Endgame*, for example, there was an open room and we dealt with that room. I felt that the audience should sit in some kind of a rotunda situation and should somehow be insulated from the performers. That's how I came up with a lighted screen. The performers in effect couldn't see the audience but the audience could see the performers very well, but not other audience members. Out of that grew a kind of carnival effect—like a merry-go-round in a way—the image of a game, endgame. The image that when you come up against a void you no longer work but play games just to kill time. So the audience pays to see this game being played and they come to a kind of merry-go-round schema by buying their tickets, getting coffee, and visiting the popcorn stand. That added to the whole image of the production. It seems to me that in each case one should try to find a spatial metaphor for the play itself.

PAJ: How is a play's content-value translated into spatial metaphor? Can you elaborate?

JR: Now I'm working on *Woyzeck* with The Shaliko Company and we've been given the Martinson Hall of the Public Theater. It is an elegant nineteenth-century room with a high ceiling, clear story light, and fluted columns. So how do we deal with that room for *Woyzeck*, which is brutal, bare, and has to do with a class system? Well, in our idea we agreed that we would play against the room. The room has an elegance, so we thought we'd come into it with a kind of violence by using steel pipes and raw timber—rough hewn timbers growing right out of these white, thin columns. The spatial metaphor is an arrowhead—a long ramp at the end of the room. The metaphor is the arrow piercing it. The major image of the play is the killing, the knifing of Marie. The arrow becomes the performing space and the audience is seated diagonally to that, creating an energy toward that centerpoint of the arrow. Here, the audience helps create the space and the metaphor for the play.

I'm most interested in cubic space—what happens diagonally, on the wall above, traversing in space. How can those spaces be divided up metaphorically? What do they mean metaphorically? Space is so precious. In a film, space is endless. If you're in a traditional theatre you have to create the illusion that space is endless whereas environmental theatre is a theatre of immediacy. You accept the room for what it is, with its spatial limitations. You don't try to distort the space. You start to exploit the reality of that space.

PAJ: How do design concepts affect audiences?

JR: In the *Makbeth* production, for instance, they were offended about having to move. There they were forced to sit at very specific spots whereas in *Dionysus* they could move freely about the space. Even though it was pretty much a center area environment, they had the freedom to move. In *Makbeth* it was a kind of regimentation. They had to go through an upstairs maze, down a spiral staircase, forced to crawl under spaces to get into the galleries. They had to go up and down ladders.

PAJ: Do you think it was manipulative?

JR: Yeah, I think possibly some were offended by being manipulated. But

that's part of the play. There again the idea of the environment helps aug-
ment the play in that sense. The audience needs to think of environment
as part of the text. And they don't or they didn't at that time; I think
more do now. I think an artist has to leave signposts and should give a
direction. I think that audiences are better prepared to do what the production wants them to do—as long as there are clearly marked paths.
At first they weren't prepared to be herded, forced to climb—why climb
a ladder when you can go up stairs? Well, ladders mean something. It
forces them to work, makes it dangerous for them. They never had to
experience danger or compactness in a literal sense before. I think performers and audiences are now more and more aware of what space and
time can do for them and what they can do in space and time.

PAJ: How far can you ask an audience to go in participating in the design of
a production?

JR: I look at theatre not as sitting in seats watching a play. When I go to a
carnival, that's theatre; when I go to a parade, that's theatre. To me theatre is a continuum of events. I don't know where one begins and the
other leaves off. A theatre artist is performing a piece that he asks me to
come to—just tell me what to do as audience and I'll do it. Do I sit in
seats and watch it? Do I wade through knee-deep in cornflakes?

Now *The Tooth of Crime* is about competition, so for an audience to
compete for a vantage point in a space is an acceptable thing to ask of
them. They don't have to compete across the city of New York—maybe
that's too much to ask of an audience. But in a room that's fifty feet by
twenty feet with only 150 to 200 people in it, the competition isn't that
keen. You're going to see, you're going to hear. Now, where do you want
to be? In the front row? Or up against the performers so you can see the
perspiration on their faces? Or farther back into a distance to see other
audiences silhouetted around a scene? Do you want to look through
holes and cubicles? People want to see things in different ways. Many
people who came sat and listened. Fine. But you had all those choices and
that became a microcosm of life in a way. *The Tooth of Crime* is, in effect,
the streets of New York. You elbow a little, you move, and you fight your
way, or you don't fight. So, I felt it was very successful from that point of
view. It really boils down to learning new ways of doing things.

PAJ: It seems that there are two contradictory elements at work in environmental theatre. While it frees space, and the audience's relation to space,
it also compels and forces the audience to move to see the production.

JR: You're right. The most exciting thing about environmental theatre is that
as a director or designer you have those options to explore. You come

to an open space and you do what you want with it. You do what the play dictates or the performance dictates. The audience has to be considered in all that. The audience becomes, in effect, scenery. They create clusters, groupings. In *Mother Courage and Her Children* there is a kind of open chaos at work. When you look at the environment and people in it you sense that you are at the front in World War I where trees have been blown to bits and holes have been gouged. Hysteria.

PAJ: How do Brecht's "alienation effects" work in The Performance Group's production of *Mother Courage?*

JR: Alienation is making something strange. If Kattrin is playing a dumb woman and at the same time leans over and says, "Please move, I have to do a scene here," what it does is create surprise, curiosity. That's what alienation means. It gets you out of the emotion of Kattrin and gets you into the intellect of the play. Not one in favor of the other. Good theatre rolls back and forth and in and out of very emotional things. That's what I call "theatrical"—in Brecht's terms "alienated," in Grotowski's "transgression."

PAJ: But environmental theatre is a dynamic process that necessarily takes you into the production rather than critically outside of it.

JR: Oh, yes!

PAJ: In that sense, it is contradictory to Brechtian aesthetics. I guess what you mean is that environmental theatre "alienates" on a different level.

JR: Well, it brings you in and out of emotion. That I think is the question here. I think *Mother Courage* is ingenious in that way. With that production for the first time I have seen what alienation *is* in the theatre. This play is so rich and ripe and ready for this kind of theatre. I think environmental theatre works because it is contradictory. In the purest sense of environmental theatre actors and performers are in a way creating a role through themselves, through their immediate place in a room. It starts there, becomes very expressionistic, very naturalistic—and I think those terms overlap—and has an immediacy to it that makes it very real and very emotional. Then, the actors' sign work—alienating devices—causes the opposite to happen.

PAJ: As an environmentalist, unlike a designer in traditional theatre, you are faced with so many choices. When you are planning a design do you work it out with just the director, or the actors, too?

JR: When an ensemble begins to work together they develop through games, transactions, and work—they're going in a certain direction. Environmentalists in a pure way can share those things with them. Different kinds of group actions will grow out of that. Those things may suggest ideas about space and these are put into a hopper, if you will. Then the director sees those things and, with the environmentalist and the actors, begins to discover new things. It's a discovery process by all the people involved, each one augmenting the other. That's if you're working off built pieces.

When you're given a play—like *The Tooth of Crime* or *Woyzeck*—then you're working with a director who has an image. You have a choice to go out and find a space to suit the play. Then, the director works with the actors. Collaborations come back and forth. The design is submitted in a very traditional way—the use of a room, the way of doing it. Where we want to put the audience in relation to the play, the images. What the actors have discovered, the way the actors want to be. For example, Joe Chaikin's actors are very physical. That lends itself to a kind of spatial way of being. How do these actors convey things? In *Fable*, they're pulling sheets and moving across space. All of that is developed in negotiation with different elements.

PAJ: Are you suggesting that *Fable* derives from environmental theatre concepts?

JR: I think the actors do, but the audience doesn't. In a way it does because they had to decide that they wanted to see this play in a certain way. The play wanted to move horizontally. Environmental theatre for me can function in a more constructivistic way, on a proscenium or on an open stage, in which case the actors then create space and time in a real way with real architecture. The actors can do this without the audience. But that's still an environmental notion—it includes the performer and the space. The concept of environmental theatre for me is the use of these elements for what they are, in an immediate way. Certain directors accent different kinds of work. Richard Foreman's work is image-oriented, nonliterary. There are surreal images that come at you, faces appearing and strange juxtapositions of people and sounds. That is environmental theatre for me. In his case it's inside the head that the world exists. Schechner's world is in that garage. He always has something to do with audiences. A very important part of this theatre is the manipulation of audience. To him the audience is alive and can do things. Push the audience to do more, to become more a participant in the event. In Chaikin's work the audience is not so important. He invests more in the actor in space and time. André Gregory, I think, is that way also. He leaves the environmentalist to arrange audiences but not to get them really into the hard aspect of production.

PAJ: In a sense, the actor becomes a scene designer, he manipulates space.

When you design you become an actor because you have to contend with space; and, in the final analysis, you also become a director.

JR: Yes. That's what I've gotten more interested in—the shapes of actors. Actors become architectural—Lee Breuer, Richard Foreman. That's why there is the superdirector in this kind of work. It's somebody who has a grand vision about the whole space, what to do with it and the actor, to control sound, space, text, everything. That becomes a natural and honest direction in environmental theatre. It's like a giant painting. As a director I began to see the possibilities of actors as architectural elements. This is not to say that I'm interested in taking away the emotion of actors. That's not the point at all. I'm interested in the physicality of the bodies in addition to the emotional content that they can bring because the physicalization—the seeing of them, instead of the hearing of them—generates a tremendous amount of emotional content.

PAJ: How do you implement these concepts in your work with the Mobius Theater project at the University of Connecticut?

JR: It is a neutral space but the arrangement is given a life by the specific production that comes into it. So that while it is a configuration of platforms, ramps, steps in the room, it has a rhythm of its own, an aesthetic value of its own. When you look at it, it looks the same all the time but as you develop a built piece in there, which is the way I work in that theatre, you discover the play. Each time we use the theatre in a different way. I find that it lends itself to actors in space because it allows them a physical extension that they can't normally have. In The Open Theater the actors, and the juxtaposition of actor to actor in the "machine games," became a basic tool. In other words, five actors in a heap created a machine à la Viola Spolin. Now, I want to add another element to that—put those actors in an architecture. Then, not only do you have the ensemble working as a machine, that machine now has architecture. If you invest in space, time, and living persons, give them that and forget all the other trappings. We work in "poor" theatre, conceptual ways. You don't spend a lot of money for each new production—all you need are people. I find that's very valuable in terms of actor and director training because they learn honest skills, the basic skills.

PAJ: To go back to your mention of "spatial metaphors"—what was the metaphor in the design of The Shaliko Company's production of *Ghosts*?

JR: It was rooms. We were very fond of that solution, that design. In effect, the audience became the walls to the rooms. In a Victorian play what you don't tell people is important—lies, deception, subtext. What's behind closed doors. That's the soul of this play—what you don't see or hear—

"ghosts" lurking around. *Ghosts* has to happen in a lot of rooms, a lot of spaces, because that's how you keep secrets from people. We had to deal with a very small room and give the sense that one conversation can happen here, another one over there. So the spacing of the audience allowed for corridors and room areas on different levels, which gave a sense of separation.

PAJ: How does an environmental theatre design play off actors?

JR: Leo Shapiro's actors are very physical. I knew that these actors were comfortable with the physical aspects of the play. So the carpeting grew out of that. There was a relationship between sensuality and the carpet—the whole Freudian undertone in the play. The softness of the carpet was important, the relationship of the characters on the floor crawling around. In negating the Victorian posturing of the play I don't think we went far enough. The leaping about the room, Oswald and his mother wrestling—those were the kinds of things that were interesting.

Also, one can take *The Tooth of Crime* in a traditional way, as a rock musical. That's the way Sam Shepard wanted it. Now, what it became was a little man's, the common man's, play. That's where Schechner's head is at. He's always putting the "people" in his plays. So, we have a Crow who is not a Mick Jagger on a trip somewhere, but he's Spalding Gray. What happens to Mick Jagger, Elvis Presley, Richard Nixon happens to Spalding Gray. You've got to give over to that as a designer.

PAJ: To return to the question of audience . . . Didn't William Shephard in *Dionysus* once stop the production by walking off with a female member of the audience? Do you think audiences can be *too* close to a production?

JR: In environmental theatre there's always going to be the element of the unknown—the living aspect—no matter how scored the production is. *Dionysus* allowed a lot of free, open time. The "Ecstasy Dance" was an open time for the audience to do something. In *Mother Courage* there is the mealtime, which is pretty well scored. The ecstasy thing in *Dionysus* depends on how much ecstasy there is in the audience—do they want to make out, to dance, do they really want to get into it? That was a more open-ended production. The production was asking the question: How much do you want to get involved? When your audience participation gets so close to where it is open-ended and you've really given them a free rein to do things, that's the chance you take. That's also what you're exploring. The minute you bring an audience to its feet, you're asking for something. I think those are exciting moments.

That was the initial fear of environmental theatre in the late sixties and even now—the fear of participation. There is an element of immediacy and involvement, the implication being that you're involved in life as opposed to escaping from it. That to me is one of the most important axioms of environmental theatre. In guerrilla theatre terms involvement is strong. We've come a long way from guerrilla theatre but I think that's where environmental theatre had a great deal of its roots. If you go back to the basic truths, what's happening here is you have a real room, a live audience, live actors who create a piece in a living way. It's a living theatre. And to exploit the living condition is aesthetically the most beautiful way of working.

PAJ: But isn't it true that the audience intrudes only in Schechner's or Shapiro's work, and not, for example, in Gregory's production of *Endgame?*

JR: I think it did in *Endgame*. They had to witness, they were put into a hotbath or steambath. When you do that to an audience you're forcing something on them. We have to be very careful about defining audience participation. It's not necessarily taking off your shoes and walking around, or ecstasy dances—that's one kind. There are other kinds of audience participation. In *Endgame* there was a tremendous amount of audience-giving to that production.

PAJ: It seems as though there is a "hot" environmental theatre and a "cold" one. In one the audience is walking around, participating perhaps, touching the actors, and in the other seating is generally fixed.

JR: I sense you're making a qualitative judgment.

PAJ: No, just a comparison.

JR: To get back to the question: What is environmental theatre? I always come back to the basic axioms or concepts. What are the things that you ask yourself about the work you're doing? What are the basic elements of it? What are the premises on which you start? The group has to discover the play because that's the most direct, honest thing. Sign work is very important. That you accept the immediacy of the time and the place is important for me. So are materials. The living audience. Now again, different groups accent different aspects of these basic principles. So there is, as you say, "hot" and "cold" environmental theatre.

PAJ: What you're essentially talking about is "two boards and a passion."

JR: There are cycles. In the Restoration period they were into expansion—material things were important. Now we are in a kind of materialist backlash. We're afraid of material things. It's contradictory—we both want them and are afraid of them. So much of our "poor" theatre concepts work with those contradictions.

PAJ: Is that why Americans have taken so well to environmental theatre? Is it a particularly American impulse?

JR: Yes, it's particularly indigenous and natural for America to get involved in this kind of work because it does question our whole material world. Also, the whole idea of action and activity is very American. We really are an activity-oriented people. We come to environmental theatre like ducks to water. Carnivals, football, love of spectacle—environmental theatre has only begun to touch on those things. We don't want to hear a play; we want to get in there and do it. Robert Wilson's and Lee Breuer's work is expanding outdoors. Theatre is going to come to a kind of football or sports event.

PAJ: Will ABC pick it up for TV?

JR: "Monday Night at the Environmental Theatre."

Laurie Anderson, Scott Burton, Elizabeth LeCompte, Ruth Maleczech, Michael Smith

THE ENERGETIC ARTS CLIMATE of the seventies fostered a performance scene full of new ideas, which were manifested in the proliferation of avant-garde theatre, dance, video, performance art, and experimental music events. The art world was becoming interested in theatricality while theatre drew closer to the visual arts. The lines between art and entertainment, autobiography and fiction, acting and performing were blurring, too. Artists such as Jack Smith and Yvonne Rainer had been influential in showing that live performance could be considered in an art context. Among the hotly debated issues of the period, which John Howell, then editor of *Performance Art* magazine drew into these interviews, were the differences between acting and performing, and theatre and performance art, complicated by the almost interchangeable usages of "art performance," "performance art," and "conceptual performance." In the eighties, "performance" would become a catchall term and the word "art" discarded.

Scott Burton, who before his death in 1989 created sculpture and furniture, also devised performances called "behavior tableaux," which focused on forms of gestural and spatial communication. He describes his work as mannequin-like or "pseudo-sculpture," the pictorial representation of an action devoid of self-expression. At the other end of the spectrum from Burton's phenomenological approach is Mabou Mines performer Ruth Maleczech, who, crediting Jerzy Grotowski with declaring that an actor didn't have to realize an author's intention for a character, reasons that once that is permissible "then a piece becomes the story of the lives of the performers." As solo performers, Laurie Anderson, disdainful of any description of her work as "autobiographical," and comedian Michael Smith, who created the character "Mike," were urged by audience response to confront questions of genre, while director Elizabeth LeCompte, speaking of The Wooster Group's *Rumstick Road*, explains her need to create a feeling of abstraction by means of physical action to distance the autobiographical narrative of Spalding Gray. Through the influence of personal material, the subject of performance would increasingly locate itself in the ambiguous crossovers of self and role, the real and the fictional, acting and nonacting. BGM

Conversations with John Howell, 1979

Acting and Nonacting

Scott Burton

John Howell: Do you think of your behavior tableaux performances as a theatre performance hybrid?

Scott Burton: Ten years ago it was fantastic that, as a work of art, art could be a live event. But within a couple of years, that in itself was no longer enough. I think one began to be bored when the time element was not manipulated. Back then, it was just fascinating that an event could be plastic art, not theatre. Not to be Greenbergian . . . but after a while people had to face up to the inherent nature of the medium, which is keeping people's attention occupied through *x* number of minutes. So I found myself very conscious of how I would have to direct time.

JH: Does that mean you adopted a dramatic structure?

SB: Not dramatic in my case, because it's just one thing then the next thing. I wouldn't want it to be dramatic. You know that Merce Cunningham said, "Climax is for those people who like New Year's Eve."

JH: So you think performance can be theatrical without being dramatic?

SB: The nature of the performance medium is inherently theatrical, even if it's not the theatre of writers, directors, and designers, which is such a schizophrenic product, usually a pseudo-collaborative effort. In my earliest performances, I used myself conceptually, but when I started using other people, I became aware of being a pseudo-director of a pseudo-theatre. My early performances were very intellectual gestures . . .

I've been sort of stagestruck all my life. I was very close to going into the real theatre at one point but the people in real theatre have mediocre minds. My mother took me to the Alabama State Fair, where I saw Gypsy Rose Lee, and I remember these strip tableaux as making deep impressions that have profoundly influenced my performance format.

JH: Why did you begin to use other people in your pieces?

SB: I think because I loved the theatre and wanted to imitate it. I wanted to deal with elements of costume, lighting, and sets, as well as directing, but in a very Walter Mitty way. That's the only way you can when you're one person. Artists' performance is an integrated form, not a schizophrenic one. One person is responsible for everything.

JH: How does that work when you include other performers?

SB: It was a breakthrough for me. I used the people like models. Like my furniture, the behavior tableaux are pseudo-sculpture. When I work with the models, I just touch their bodies and push them around.

JH: Are a lot of their poses conceptualized beforehand?

SB: I get an image in my head, then I try it on them. Then I rearrange, alter, edit, and try to clarify. But it's not schematic. I try to make the setting and costumes look like they don't exist. I try to be on the edge. It's very carefully planned but it should look like it's just that way. The tableaux are secretly completely theatrical, but I try to make it look sort of real. The costumes, for example, are carefully edited street clothes.

JH: Do you get images from the people you select as performers, as well as from your own image bank?

SB: I always use tall, slender men. For one thing, their limbs carry well at the great distance that I use. That linear clarity is the main thing. Also, the uniformity of look is very important. I try to make them look similar but not identical. Not so different that you get involved with personalities, but not so similar that they're like robots. It's not about a we're-all-machines idea.

JH: Then what makes it performance art instead of theatre, given your terms?

SB: I'm working on a new piece that's very involved in costume and narrative, which is as theatrical as I can get. In the behavior tableaux, the people are treated in some ways as automata, which must link me with De Chirico and the whole surrealist thing about mannequins. In a way, I use performers like dolls.

JH: What happens in a rehearsal?

SB: The performers are very carefully rehearsed. They have counts, moves, and cues—what they call blocking in theatre. From their point of view, it's task-oriented, but from the audience's point of view it's not. The audience sees an image or a representation or a reenaction, but the performers are trained to do it as a task.

JH: Is it difficult to keep out what you would consider extraneous material?

SB: Very hard. They can't be too good and they can't be too awkward. If they're not really in their own bodies and stumble around, their movement is not invisible and it is distracting. If they're trained performers, especially dancers, I just have to sit on them to keep their gestures where I want them. The best performer I ever had was a musician who was a performer, but not an actor or dancer. He had stage presence and consciousness, but it was his own, it wasn't a persona.

JH: So you're really muffling any projections.

SB: They can't really project except through gesture because I have so removed them. You can't tell it, but I use a whitening makeup on the eyebrows and the lips to erase the face, which my fifty to seventy-five feet viewing distance does too. So the only projection is through supple movement.

JH: Do you think of it as dance-related?

SB: I'm not involved with dance. I want to stay away from that because my work would suffer greatly by comparison. I don't want my performances to be dancerly.

JH: Do you try to teach or develop a performance attitude as to the particular tasks?

SB: No. There's no self-expression.

JH: Do you think the audience reads expression from their actions?

SB: What is to the performer a task, the audience sees as a representation of an action, an avoidance or an approach in a gesture or a display.

JH: And you don't want the performers relating to that?

SB: What the audience sees is not a task but, ideally, my representation of an action. It's pictorial rather than literal. I want the performers to just do the specific job.

JH: How do you feel about that quality in the current wave of entertainment performance?

SB: The turnaround time was so short. Performance used to be lying in the gutter on Fourteenth Street, now it's "Saturday Night Live." The old attitude toward the audience was indifference/aggression, and it wore itself out very quickly. So it seems natural to swing the other way. And, the examples of people like Foreman and Wilson, Yvonne Rainer and Merce Cunningham, the great theatre performance artists, had a great influence on this theatrical kind of art performance. Also, a lot of conceptual performance turned into body art and nothing is more boring. It was important when Acconci first did it, but it degenerated into what I call the I-do-this-you-do-that school.

JH: There are some performance precedents for theatrical works, Fluxus, for example. These events were built on whimsical timing.

SB: When I first saw Ralston Farina, I thought he was Fluxus reborn. I never saw Fluxus, but he seemed like that spirit. He was an early referent to theatre, but amateur theatre, like the kid next door who was a magician. The original performer, the primary figure for everyone from Warhol to Acconci, is Jack Smith.

JH: How do you choose your performers, and do you project on them?

SB: There is some self-projection but I'm not really aware of it. When I changed the figure from a woman to a man, it all came out. I used to use women before I began to work with behavior content, but there's something personal and projective about that kind of material.

JH: There's a subtext to what's shown?

SB: No, concrete gesture and meaning are the same thing. I work to make sure I've gotten the essential gesture that is as clear as it can be to the audience. I don't want mystery, I want them to understand the form of gestural and spatial communication that goes on between us all the time. There's no subtext because that's a narrative concept. In the behavior tableaux what I want people to become aware of is the emotional nature of the number of inches between them, or how a person uses an arm as a barrier to communication. I want to be didactic and explanatory but there's all kinds of other content which creeps in that I don't care to go into. I don't want to think about the psychological content.

JH: So you try to keep yourself out of it while you're in it?

SB: I don't believe in the artist as his or her own subject matter. First-person performance can be good but I don't think it's that great. I've done performances about the self but I consider them very minor. I'm not a personal artist, I don't believe in the validity of that stance.

JH: You prefer to be objective, almost mechanical.

SB: It's very cut and dried, almost schematic, but it's schizophrenic because I know the audience gets this other stuff from it.

JH: Then, unlike "schizophrenic" collaborative theatre, performance art is schizophrenic *solitary* theatre. But, you know there's more personal content than you've let on.

SB: I know there's a certain homosexual content which I do not put in. But somehow it comes out. The actors never do anything sexual. The audience may see something like that but it's not there.

JH: Do you think gay or straight people look harder for that?

SB: Straight people see it more. But I can't deal with that, so I just ignore it. A long time ago I did pieces with a homosexual content, and I'll do that again in a new piece that features a series of sexual self-presentations. But there's no overt sexual content in the behavior tableaux. *Group Behavior Tableaux* is about a stable peer group, then an unstable peer group, then a hierarchy with one at the top and four below, then a hierarchy with one below and four at the top. *Pair Behavior* was about strangerliness, acquaintanceship, intimacy, estrangement, alienation, aggression, and avoidance. *Individual Behavior Tableaux* is about what is called aggressive displays, threat, appeasement, and sexual displays, what one would call art poses, not for plastic but behavior reasons. I don't know who gets how much of that how often, but that's the way I think about it.

Ruth Maleczech

John Howell: As an actress, do you feel that when you perform you pretend to be someone else in a time different from the real time of the event? And is that a useful distinction between acting and nonacting in performance?

Ruth Maleczech: I always call myself a performer because I think the term "actor" or "actress" implies what you've just said. It implies the adoption of a part other than my part. But I also think that a theatrical performer is more compelled to search in areas that a performance art performer would rather avoid. That is to say, those areas that are sometimes embarrassing—psychology, emotion, feelings—and hard to deal with. It's easier to pretend that they are not material and therefore not to deal with them and make a process performance. But I don't like to define performance and performance art because I don't think there's any difference in a way. It depends on the depth to which you're willing to go to find out what's in a performance. Most performance artists content themselves with much less in-depth looking, maybe because it's not as much fun. I think performance art is more fun.

JH: What about those once-popular performances in which heavy psychological, personal material was offered in presentations that were very naive by theatrical standards?

RM: Naïveté is like a mask in performance art. It's an escape to be able to say I'm not really a performer. But it's true, you don't see that very much anymore. Now you see quite skilled performance art, equally skilled as theatrical performances, and that's why it's more interesting now because you can talk about it as a field, as an art. In a theatre of the kind I work in, what happens in performance art is very important. If you're only dealing with emotionalism and psychology, you won't make very interesting theatre. It'll look like thirties theatre; it just isn't good enough—it won't make art. So it's important what goes on in performance and in the art world in general. There's some kind of median line that has to be struck wherein the theatrical performer is performing rhythms and dynamics and the subtleties of those things in the same way as she is dealing with psychology, with words, and so on. The reason that area has been opened up to the new theatre is through performance art.

JH: Did Happenings affect theatre as you knew it?

RM: Happenings presaged what's happening now, but they didn't really develop it. They were spectacle events geared for perceptual changes. But I think it starts with a post-Judson time when Yvonne Rainer and people like that became involved in the idea of live performance as art. These gray areas that had been missing in the Happenings and that had been totally left out of the theatre began to emerge then. If you can somehow get a skilled theatrical performer to be able to think and develop along the lines of performance art, I think you end up with a better performance than without that kind of exposure. I also think a performance artist who has some background in visual art or music is a better performer than someone who is simply a stand-up talker. Where you cross-feed these ideas is where you get really good and interesting work. And there's more and more of that happening all the time now. Not so long ago the theatrical performer dealt with character and role, and the performance artist with "my" personality, and neither of those attitudes are completely true now.

JH: What other changes do you see?

RM: There are very sophisticated developments in performance art, for example, scripts and relationships to language, which didn't exist at all earlier.

JH: Mabou Mines used to perform primarily in galleries and museums, and I remember that the reactions you got from artists were praise for the visual and plastic elements, and reservations about the use of acting.

RM: Exactly, and I think that's probably still true about our work, that idea that all of this stuff could be seen better without the presence of all that feeling.

JH: I don't know if it's so true now; those distinctions seem to be breaking down. What do you call a show like Jack Smith's recent version of Ibsen's *Ghosts?*

RM: It's really hard to figure out whether he is a performance artist or a theatrical performer. I always think of him as a brilliant theatrical performer, I love his work, but I know he's not everybody's idea of theatre. The most interesting people are those you can't really categorize. While allowing for the presence of the internal workings and motivational structure of a performance, our company is always trying very hard to straddle that vague line. For example, we don't perform much in museums anymore, but almost every piece we've done has had its first performance at Paula Cooper's Gallery. We owe a lot to that world because it taught us things that kept us from being a regular theatre.

JH: And theatre as you found it when you came to New York pushed you toward that kind of influence?

RM: It wasn't interesting to play parts in other people's plays anymore. Also, it probably wasn't interesting for directors to do new interpretations of often-done plays either. Something else had to happen performance-wise, and a connection to the art world has changed not only our theatre but others as well, and it's very easy to see which theatres have been influenced and which have not. It's not just due to performance art, but to Grotowski's idea that it was no longer necessary for the actor to realize the author's intention when he wrote the part. Once that became clear, then a piece becomes the story of the lives of the performers. So the context is changing and within that changing context, you see the life of the performer. We're not really working with any material except ourselves.

JH: If performance art has contributed to this big shift in theatre, what about the performance art idea itself?

RM: Performance art doesn't seem very radical to me.

JH: Is that because it stands outside of art traditions?

RM: But isn't there a very long history of performance in art history?

JH: Yes, but I don't think that means performers know very much about it or care to. I think most performers started out as painters or sculptors and were attracted to performance because the standards and expectations were up in the air.

RM: But I still think they're under the thumb of having to make art.

JH: I think that's true for those who still perform in galleries, and who make drawings, installations, and video works as well. But I think there is another kind of performer who is only a performer, and who works outside the gallery system, usually in alternative spaces that include performance in their programs in a major way.

RM: Some of the people with whom I work and myself are starting a studio to explore these kinds of questions, because I think we're all a little confused and very happily so. It's a good confusion because a lot of good work is going to result from it. What is it that makes one narrative form not quite a theatrical performance? What element is it that allows an audience to be so objective, so passive, that is so unlike a theatrical performance there is nothing to draw it in, there is simply something being presented for the audience to see and hear? That area which is and is not performance, and which is and is not acting is the most confused and the most interesting one right now.

JH: What do you think is the essential difference between a performance artist and a performer?

RM: A performer is not on the outside of the piece showing it. The nature of a performance is performing, and to do that you need an outside eye, someone who is looking at the performing of a performance to see whether or not it matches the ideas of the performance. In other words, whether or not you can translate an idea into a moment.

JH: Do you think a lot of performance artists conceptualize pieces that they can't realize? And do you think they care to realize them?

RM: When you're a performer, you're doing it with everything you can do it with—with your body, your voice, your mind, your sense of rhythm, anything you can draw from your past, and so on. There is a whole other way to look at that which is to show an idea the performer has, to make an interesting piece about how that person's mind works, how that voice talks, and to hear what she has to say. Maybe the difference is gray, but they're not the same. A performance artist is more likely to perform her conceptual mental picture of what a performance can be because that's what she is already equipped with. That's another skill that can be developed, of course.

Michael Smith

John Howell: How do you think about "Mike," the character you've created in performance, and Michael Smith? Can you keep them apart, or do you try?

Michael Smith: I'm probably more confused about it than most people who've seen my performances and who know me. That character moves around much more slowly than I do, for example. It definitely comes from me, what "Mike" does, but there's a difference. I feel very comfortable with the character. I have a certain sort of affection for him, though not when I'm playing him because I really become "Mike" when I'm "Mike."

JH: There are some comedians who do characters, like Red Skelton or Lily Tomlin; then there are others who appear as entertainment versions of themselves, like Rodney Dangerfield who presents "himself." Do you feel closer to a comedian like Dangerfield?

MS: I feel closer to Dangerfield because I'm exaggerated, or rather in my mind I'm exaggerating, but I don't think it comes out that way. Some people, like Jackie Gleason, create caricatures, and my character isn't like that. I think "Mike" is a sort of condition, and where he is just an exaggeration of my, or somebody else's, way of being here.

JH: When you think about "Mike," do you have qualities or do things that you give to him, or do you decide that since he was such and such a person he should do this action or talk a certain way?

MS: I think he came out of a play on words. Somehow I came up with this phrase: "the blanded gentry." Then I started thinking about "Blandman." I wrote letters to a lot of people asking them what they thought blandness was. What I wanted was a script from these people, hoping they would tell me what Blandman would do . . .

My interest in comedy really comes from an interest in timing, that very slow delivery. I think "Mike" is the character who allows me to be very slow and demand a certain amount of attention. Also, I think most of my humor is visual, he doesn't say much.

JH: When "Mike" disco-danced along with the Osmonds' tape *In the Rec Room*, is that something you do or something you thought "Mike" would do and then learned?

MS: That's something I've been thinking about for years. When I first saw Donnie and Marie, I was impressed with their incredible production. I think they're insidious, but awful in an incredible way. The first time I saw them, Donnie did three types of music: he was on ice skates, he was underwater in scuba gear, then among some explosions, and there was a little bit of country, a little rock 'n' roll, all this glitter, everything kept moving, and he looked the same in everything. That's real blandness, and that's why I did that bit.

JH: When you think about timing, do you think about it as helping create that particular character, or as a technique in itself?

MS: The way the words come out, the deliberateness, says a lot about "Mike." But also, I'm getting better at the delivery. There's a certain amount of skill involved.

JH: Does "Mike's" character create a situation and then that becomes the performance, or do you think of adventures for him to have?

MS: I think in fragments really, and then put them together to get a story. But the story always comes last. I have such a hard time putting a story together that I thought a good solution would be to use the same story over and over and do different things within it.

JH: Were you ever in a real play?

MS: No. This movie I'm in is the first time I feel like I'm acting. I was a painter, and I get a lot of my ideas from the way I draw. I don't know how to draw very well, but sometimes a drawing mistake will suggest something.

JH: How have your performances changed as you do more of them?

MS: I've gotten better at dancing, at economizing, and at getting things going. I'm very interested in polish, how to keep the show going. In my first routine, I was my own technician and I incorporated a dialogue with the tape machine, which I turned on and off, into the show. But now I don't think I need to be a technician.

JH: Are there things you would like to do in a performance that you feel you need to study to do?

MS: After I learn how to do something to use it, I don't develop it anymore.

I learned juggling and baton twirling, but just the basics, enough to do them. Tap dancing is the only thing I've sort of stuck with, although I'm not very disciplined. I would like to learn some acrobatics.

JH: What about things actors study?

MS: I think I want to take some voice lessons; I could learn a lot about projections. But when I learned how to juggle, I looked at the end of the book and saw a picture of this guy juggling a tennis racket, a garbage can, and a chain. I wanted to be able to do that, but I realized it would take a really long time. I wanted to be able to go right into it at that level.

JH: Would "Mike" ever do anything that you didn't know how to do and so would have to learn?

MS: I don't think so.

JH: Do you want to make up other characters?

MS: Yes. There's this guy, somewhat along the lines of "Mike," but he's older, about forty-five, his stomach is over his belly, he wears a thick white belt. This guy is a little more active, he initiates more action than "Mike." So far I've really only got the outfit in mind. And then there's my "Baby" character, it's grotesque, he looks like a little ape. He wears a bonnet, a white diaper, and a T-shirt, and he walks and talks like a baby. He's four, and only has a one-word vocabulary: horsey.

Elizabeth LeCompte

John Howell: How do you describe what you do as the director of Spalding Gray's pieces?

Elizabeth LeCompte: What I do is organize spaces and people and make situations—really make worlds—and I make them wherever I am.

JH: Were you hired as a director?

EL: I came in as an assistant director to Richard Schechner. I was a performer for a while to explore the other side of what I liked. Then Spalding and I talked about doing a piece together, so it was a very natural evolution.

JH: Did you feel like you were learning about theatrical performance or "performance" performance, or did you think about it like that?

EL: In The Performance Group there's lots of room to develop because there's no overriding aesthetic, there's no one way of doing anything, which allowed me to develop in a way I wanted to. With Spalding, we have a very good combination of my interest in space and form and in the structure of a psychological performance, and in his interest in performing, in confessing, showing himself. Also, I think *Dionysus in 69* definitely bridged the gap between the theatre world and the art world. Structurally it was nonlinear, and it broke open a lot of ideas about theatre space. That piece should have been bridge, but I think the aspirations of the people who were involved were theatrically oriented. The performers wanted to be great actors but they had no sense of or interest in the meaning of the piece, its concept. They wanted to be told what they were to do and to do it well; the director was the person who made that concept. In performance art, and even in theatres like Mabou Mines, everyone is interested in some way in the concept of the performance, not solely in their performance within the piece. I always felt that that kind of performer had a much greater intellectual stake in the performance itself.

JH: In performance art terms it's unusual to have a director, someone who stands outside a work and helps shape it. How do you direct a performance made up of someone else's very personal material, material that seems beyond question or criticism?

EL: I'm so involved with form I could put anything into a structure. It has no personal meaning for me when, for example, Spalding hands over tapes of his grandmother talking. I'm totally involved in the form of it although I think that's a mask for the content for me. The way I'm involved in the content is through the form and the one that I choose exposes some kind of content—but I don't know what it is until I've chosen the form.

JH: So you don't judge the material or worry that such personal content might lead to a performance dead end?

EL: I don't because I don't have any stake in that. I don't have to deal with it.

(Spalding Gray walking through room): Last night I openly read from my diary to forty people and told them exactly what was happening in my life and waited for someone to comfort me. That's what I think *Sex and Death* was about, simply recounting my life. I also think I'm right at the edge of stopping performing.

JH: How does that affect the director?

EL: If Spalding stops, I just get somebody else as a performer. Not that I wouldn't want to convince him to keep going but I have to go on.

(Spalding Gray): I want to see you stop with me.

I know and I would try to stop with you because I don't see any reason for going on in the grand sense of the word but I can't help going on. For me it's a compulsion to make order out of chaos, I've spent my life doing it, and it doesn't have to do with personal material. Somewhere I'm not trying to be understood, I'm not trying to communicate to an audience. I'm just trying to make some sort of pleasurable order that will make people like me.

JH: What kind of things make a pleasurable order for you?

EL: That's impossible to explain, it's totally intuitive. Usually they're the shlockiest things—emotional, sentimental junk with no narrative, just moments. What I do then, since I am embarrassed by these moments, is to make performances with all of that emotion cut with what some people call cynicism, what other people might call coolness, just because I don't want to show too much cheap sentiment.

JH: Do your intentions ever clash with Spalding's?

EL: No, because his intention is totally removed from mine. His intention is to show himself, advertise himself, and he trusts that I'll make him beautiful or intelligent or attractive in some way to the audience. It's an act of faith. And it's an act of faith on my part, that I trust that he is those things.

JH: And he never does anything in performance that you object to?

EL: There are a couple of gestures he does that sometimes rub me wrong, that just don't satisfy my vision of him, and I'll try to stop those. Sometimes he'll balk a little about that.

JH: What about the other performers?

EL: I have disagreements with other performers sometimes, but not very often because we're all involved in an act of faith.

JH: So as performance mechanic, you're immune to issues like the controversy over the use in *Rumstick Road* of recorded tapes by people who didn't know they were being recorded, or who specifically asked that a recording of them be played publicly?

EL: No, not immune really. What Spalding played with in the subject of his material is what I played with in that very controlled visual field, the "dangerousness" of the edges of the material. By "dangerousness," I mean a certain kind of soppy romanticism and cloyingness about the illness of his mother. I walked that line all the time in the piece in the personal material and the decisions about why and what form and how to use it.

JH: Is it hard to repeat personal performances?

EL: No, all performance is physical actions. As a director, I can give the performers a physical score where they can forget that any of the material is personal and see it just as a series of actions that they must perform in front of an audience. What I do is make a score that is in essence an abstraction. Now the solo pieces are a little more difficult, but they still have a very small and tight form.

JH: Could you imagine that Spalding would come with some material you would object to?

EL: It's hard to say because that's hypothetical, and the way we work is that he says something and I'm excited about it, and I say something and he's excited about it. When that stops happening, then we'd be working in a normal collaboration. I know we don't have a normal collaboration because we would have argued a lot more. There's something else going on, something symbiotic.

Laurie Anderson

John Howell: You don't call what you do in your performances acting, and it isn't just personality either.

Laurie Anderson: I would call it talking styles. For instance, I've used about eight talking styles today, starting with a phone call about a death in the family and talking with my mother, then screaming at the lawyer in my most efficient, business-like style. A lot of audio stuff I've done has drawn on that—you could either use the filters you already have or, as I like to do, use electronic ones. The first songs I did like that were *Songs for Telephones*, half normal voice and half through a telephone filter, that voice of New York social life: "Hi, how are you, we should really get together sometime." Things people keep saying and that's the total sum of the conversation, just social jive talking that everybody does. I do it all the time. Since I work a lot with tape, I get used to hearing myself, and when I listen to myself talking with other people during the day, I realize how many styles I actually have, and it's a lot. So the extent to which I use any idea of acting is to use those different forms of voices.

JH: Also, acting sometimes meant, and probably does mean, acting out.

LA: I've been finding out a lot about acting just from moving. For years, most of my work was just standing around with my hands full of my violin. The latest piece I did (*Americans on the Move*), I considered a breakthrough because I was able to move my arm. I had a lot of gestures I wanted to put in during the snakecharmer song, gestures that were almost a sign language, beginning with a hand-waving thing, then a shrug, and so on. Also, it was a kind of two-handed duet for boom stand and microphone which came much more naturally to me than trying to think of a way to move, just because I had something and it was making sound.

JH: Do ideas come from your equipment or do you work for certain effects you've thought of?

LA: It works both ways. A lot of times I just sit around here and tape things, play with microphones, until something suggests itself. That tends to be a more organic way of going about it, although there's some thinking going on. When you get an idea and then try to do it, it almost never sounds like you think it's going to. I find it's best tŏ start with the sound to suggest what's going to happen.

JH: Do you remember the early reactions to your first performances when it seemed to be important whether your stories were true or not? Do you think of acting as pretending to be someone else, and nonacting performance as concentrated pretending to be yourself?

LA: In a way, yeah, and I've just begun to realize how much I love doing that. Part of it is just the attention, and the other part is the idea that if this experience is going to happen, it has to happen exactly now. It isn't a plan for anything else. You have to be right there and make it happen, and that's really exciting to me to have to consolidate my energy for that kind of presentation. No other part of my life is like that. You only have that one moment to make this work or not.

JH: Are there things you've thought of as material that you wouldn't perform for some reason or another?

LA: Yeah, but I can't talk about them for the same reason. I've never said anything that I felt uncomfortable saying. I'm familiar with that squirming feeling when somebody's telling something personal and you don't want to hear it. I always felt it was a mistake being labeled as an autobiographical artist. I never felt I used that kind of material as primary stuff but that it was fitted into this structure that made it something else. It was just a certain content that I felt directly connected to and used. You cannot not project yourself in some way.

JH: So you think of yourself as a character in a performance in the same way you think of yourself as a character in life?

LA: Exactly. But I've started using "you" and "they" a lot instead of the first person in performance—which is probably the main shift in the past few years. "I" is almost completely out of it at this point. I use "I" only as someone who has gotten some information but not as a prime subject, more as a sideline observer. If I use "I," it's very peripheral to the action.

JH: And what does that do for you?

LA: It makes me really free and I'm happy about that. You can get pretty narcissistic with "I" very quickly. The worst part was performances which used "I" that I had to do a number of times. I didn't like that at all.

JH: Because you would have to present something apparently personal that you didn't feel?

LA: Right. I've repeated a lot of pieces in song formats and I feel fine about that.

JH: Do you think that the "I" out of it makes *Americans on the Move* more theatrical?

LA: Probably, and more political too, more didactic. I've been using "you should" a lot. I'm attracted to the power of that statement, you can follow it with anything and it becomes immediately interesting, not just "I think" but "I think you should," and that's a different kind of assumption, a more political one.

JH: Is that directed to the audience? Do you feel different about them since you address the audience that way?

LA: I think differently about the world now, and insofar as the audience represents the world, yes.

JH: Do you feel more like a conduit for material than a focus of it now?

LA: Yes, it's much more a function of pointing to diagrams really, saying, "Look over here" and doing a sort of waving action.

JH: Do people still confuse "you" with Laurie Anderson, the performer?

LA: Not now, but it used to happen. People used to think I was their friend because they knew so much about me, or thought they did. I used to get letters that were quite personal. It was too much for me to handle, although I was enough of a voyeur to be interested. But I didn't know what to do with the information. Now the letters I get are much more factual, which I like, and full of data.

JH: You also used to wear white gowns in performance and now you wear a black outfit.

LA: I used to wear white so that I could be a film screen but more than that, to separate that sort of activity from everyday life. Very ceremonial, now that I think about it. Lately I like black a lot, I don't know why.

JH: Which can also be ceremonial.

LA: Right. Someone called me a funeral director.

JH: Do you ever think you're somebody else when you're performing?

LA: I have a vague feeling sometimes, but I don't know who it is.

Edwin Denby

EDWIN DENBY'S GRACEFUL WRITINGS on ballet and his unwavering support of George Balanchine during the thirties and forties, first in *Modern Music,* then in the *New York Herald Tribune,* stand out as exemplary exercises in the art of criticism. Frank O'Hara once said of him, "He sees and hears more clearly than anyone else I have ever known"—a trait that Denby once attributed to Balanchine. His impassioned and unabashed advocacy of dance led the *New Yorker* dance critic Arlene Croce to assert: "With other critics you can agree or disagree. With Denby you undergo a form of conversion."

Born in China in 1903, Denby spent much of his youth in Europe, where he trained as a dancer in schools influenced by Jacques Dalcroze and Mary Wigman, and performed in small troupes throughout Germany and France while continuing to work intermittently on his fiction, poetry, and libretti. As he elaborates here, his European career coincided with the forward march of modernism, and upon his return to America he became an ardent champion of modern dance, receptive to discipline, technique, and emotional rigor. What distinguishes his criticism is an eloquent poetic style and fluency with the other arts, primarily music and the fine arts, which embellish his writings. Denby's criticism, collected in a number of volumes, including the early *Looking at the Dance,* bear witness to wide-ranging artistic tastes and an unerringly precise descriptive ability that breathe renewed life into the dances on the page.

Although Denby was an avowed apologist for his charmed dancers, such as Alexandra Danilova and Alicia Markova, or his favorite choreographers, such as Balanchine, Martha Graham, and Merce Cunningham, he continued to lend support to a younger generation of dancers, including Douglas Dunn and Lucinda Childs. It was a measure of his genius and his observant eye to notice artistic innovation in the making, and to draw historical connections to the art that preceded such experiments. His passion for the new remained with him until his death in 1983.   GD

Conversation with John Howell, 1979

Reminiscences of a Dance Critic

John Howell: How did you become a dance critic?

Edwin Denby: To get free tickets. I was poor, and I particularly wanted to go to see the ballet. In the late thirties, some friends of mine had a magazine called *Modern Music,* which is now a celebrated magazine but then was known only to advanced composers such as Aaron Copland, Virgil Thomson, Paul Bowles, Marc Blitzstein. They were American composers living in Europe, studying with Nadia Boulanger, I think, and I met them in Germany.

JH: Did you meet them because you were interested in music or because you were all Americans in Europe?

ED: I had gone to a modern dance school on the outskirts of Vienna, a place called Hellerau-Luxembourg. It was an offshoot of a very famous school called Hellerau, which a Swiss musician had founded before the First World War to teach conductors how to conduct with a bodily, physical sense of rhythm. Hellerau was famous for its lyrical dancing. Diaghilev went to see it, being very interested in the fact that they taught polyrhythm, which was to hear and conduct several musical meters at the same time. And he asked them to teach Nijinsky *The Rite of Spring.* He was taught to read it, and how to feel it, I suppose one could say, although that's a difficult word. All this was before my time.

Then the war came and that school was closed. Then there was an American woman married to a German and she and her husband got an offer from the Austrian government to use a castle that had belonged to the Hapsburgs, a summer place called Luxembourg, to carry on the school. This castle was about an hour outside Vienna by train. There were several buildings there, all well-built with a number of large rooms with beautiful floors that had been kept up for many years. So this lady— who had married a man named Baer, her American name was Frissell— started and ran it.

JH: How did you hear about this school?

ED: I had been living in Vienna meaning to be a writer. It hadn't worked out very well. I had gone back to the United States one summer to see my family, and had come back, taking the train to Vienna. In those days we always traveled third class. It was wonderfully cheap and quick, and better than planes because you could see the country and talk to people. I was sitting on the train from Paris to Vienna, and a young woman came in who looked unused to traveling. She had a suitcase so heavy she couldn't lift it, and since in those days I was young and American, naturally I lifted it up and put it on the overhead rack for her. We started talking. She was going to this dancing school just outside Vienna.

I had never heard of any dancing schools at that time, this was around '24 or '25. She showed me a prospectus and it said: The pupil will learn the experience of time and space, and the relations of time and space. I naturally knew what time and space meant as words, but what one would experience in the relations of those things, that seemed to me complete nonsense. But I didn't want to tell her so. She was very French and a little gushy and she said, Will you come and visit me at the school when you are in Vienna after a while? And I said, Certainly, after a while. Then I got to Vienna and my friends had seen an advertisement for the same school and they said, You always liked dancing, why don't you go to this school? I was perplexed and thought that was a funny coincidence, but since I promised her, I supposed I ought to go.

So I did go out and watched one or two classes, which was permissible. I didn't understand at all what they were doing, but they seemed to be quite cheerful about it. They were doing modern exercises, not ballet at all. This was antiballet, anticlassic dancing. I suppose it was an offshoot of Isadora Duncan, natural dancing, what was called modern dance at that time. They were running around some rooms and doing some limbering, some gymnastics that seemed quite easy and simple. The lady in charge spoke to me. I was probably the first American interested in her work. The students were all Germans and Austrians, people from German-speaking countries, all of whom knew about modern dance in theory from Mary Wigman and the German modern dance, which was very vigorous at that time. This was the immediate post–World War I period.

JH: Were you familiar with ballet at that time?

ED: I had seen ballet once, when I was six or seven in Vienna, and I still remember the image of a man jumping and doing what's called an entrechat. It took me another forty years to learn that term. The image always remained and I always thought it was extraordinary, and it made me very happy. I did like dancing. I had seen Isadora dance in America while I was in New York, and her pupils, called the Isadorables, in Boston, while I was at Harvard. Also, I had a subscription seat to the Boston Symphony in the balcony, and in the back of this top balcony was a passageway. I found that when they were playing Wagner, I liked to sneak out of my seat and go back there and dance. Just do whatever came to me. I did that because the blast of Wagnerian noise lifts you so. I wasn't thinking of it in any theoretical sense, I was just enjoying myself. After I had been doing this secretly for four or five weeks, some other people came out and noticed, and began doing it too. I saw what they were doing and they looked so absolutely foolish, I felt embarrassed and stopped doing it.

At any rate, I went to this school outside Vienna. I did it for a week and Mrs. Baer said, Why don't you stay for a month? So I was there finally for three years and graduated. What I learned was what would be called modern dance. I'm sure everybody thought I was the most ungifted person for dance that anybody had ever seen. But I enjoyed it, and nobody minded, we were all good friends.

JH: And that was thought of as antiballet?

ED: Yes. The Diaghilev ballet came to Vienna while I was at that school and I saw a couple of performances. I got a big thrill out of the energy of the men dancers doing a very simple dance. But the complications and delicacies I didn't understand at all. I mostly understood the funny parts, and I understood the character of young Lifar and young Massine as stage personalities since I had been going to the theatre and the opera. But I didn't understand the point of the whole company and this school I attended was against that whole system of teaching, that whole way of moving. I was no radical revolutionary, you know; I just accepted what I was taught with interest. Obviously, none of the people at my school could have done what the Diaghilev people did. It did seem likely that the Diaghilev people couldn't have done what the best dancers of my school, of which I was not one, did. There was an all-girl company there that was very good and I liked their work, but I also knew it was outside of my own possibilities.

So I went to a German theatre and became a dancer. The choreographer there understood there were certain things I could do that other people couldn't and which she could use very well in her choreography. So, in this small company in a small German town, I became a professional dancer and the partner of the leading dancer. Then we danced in Berlin and got some reputation as comics doing ironic dances. They were ironic about German ideas of the eighties and nineties, and my German friends enjoyed them. I was going to go on with that as a career but with the rise of Hitler, any criticism of German culture was impossible. Our contracts were voided and there was no way of earning a living.

JH: Did you leave Germany then?

ED: I returned to the United States and had enough money to share this loft, which cost eighteen dollars a month then. Meanwhile, I'd seen lots of ballet and theatre. I was interested in dancing, so I took ballet lessons. I liked going to the ballet but it was expensive. My American friends said, Why don't you write for it? You like it and think about it, and if you write for our magazine, you might get some free tickets. So I said okay, and started in the late thirties.

JH: Having begun as a modern dancer who then became interested in ballet, where did you find yourself in the polemical wars of that time?

ED: Oh, it was very polemical. I admired Wigman's intensity, which was terrific, but I didn't really enjoy the dances. I was more awed by them. The more I got into the theatre, the more I enjoyed the fun of the dancing. Modern dance here was Martha Graham. My first contact with it was difficult and, luckily, I didn't have to write about that. That was before I was writing. Not only do one's opinions toward art change but also one's emotions. There are things you don't enjoy one time but do enjoy later, and the other way around as well. Balanchine I had seen in '33 in Paris and I thought that was the most wonderful thing I had seen in my life. It was a strange combination of wit and joy and intelligence and tragedy, all put together in his work without your noticing what's happening. That first experience of seeing his company was like finding a friend. It's very mysterious, I mean how is it that you find a book or a painting or any kind of art that you really like and go on liking, not just for that moment but something you like at the moment and go on liking over and over again and it doesn't seem monotonous to you? That capacity is something that's in people to start with and that is what criticism is about.

JH: I wasn't going to ask you about any of your many wonderful comments about dance, but I do remember that you have written "A tradition is a practical guide to an artist." How did you feel when you saw dance by the Judson choreographers who were as aggressively antimodern dance as modern dance had been antiballet?

ED: There was always something terribly interesting in it and something I didn't like at all. I was going only for myself, I wasn't writing then. I liked the atmosphere of the place but was very puzzled by much of the work and the first Happenings, too. Although by then, I had been through the years of abstract expressionism. By chance, Bill de Kooning lived right next door. When Rudy Burkhardt and I were first here, sharing this loft, there was somebody playing Spanish gypsy music and Mozart full blast at three in the morning. Three in the morning was a natural time for me to be up but I was surprised, because it would never have occurred to anybody who lived on this slum street to play that music. They were very good gypsy records and, of course, Mozart. They belonged to somebody who had an ear. So gradually I got to know this person and he was de Kooning. He had a lot of artist friends in this neighborhood and we all saw each other's work for several years. That has nothing directly to do with Judson but it was a question of not being in one particular world but in several. So I think the mixture of artists at Judson didn't bother me.

JH: Were you thought of by modern dancers as being in the ballet camp?

ED: I suppose so. I didn't know enough dancers personally to know. It was really writing for this musical magazine, I never did explain that, did I? The reason I took that position was that my friend said the only people who read it were composers. Because I had said I wasn't a critic. My friend said none of them knew anything about dance but many of their works and performances were done with dancers and they would be pleased to have them noticed. Otherwise, they wouldn't be reviewed at all. So no one would object to what I said.

JH: They would be an ideal audience for you, interested but in a nontechnical way. Was that the idea?

ED: They would be looking for their name. They'd be mentioned and that proved that they had written the piece and that it had been performed and that was what was important. So I started writing. Mina Letterman, who was running the magazine, was this brilliant woman who taught me how to express myself clearly. Of course, she was editing the communications from all these advanced musicians which were sometimes totally unintelligible, and she had to do something to make them intelligible. She trained some very good writers, like Elliot Carter and Virgil Thomson, who was very good, and Aaron Copland. She also tried to find the composers who could express themselves verbally and encourage them.

In the same way, she encouraged me. It was very difficult at first because my ideas and feelings and emotions were unintelligible, as they naturally are. I mean, when you look at dancing, how can you understand it? You can like it or dislike it, you can be excited or fall asleep, but what you feel is very mysterious. You put it into words and it evaporates. Mina went over my writing very carefully and said, Now this word I understand but this word I don't. And I would say, What do you mean? That's perfectly clear. And we would talk about it. She took the trouble to edit me closely and in a nice way until I realized, It's true, if I stand outside myself and look at this, it doesn't make sense. It may be poetry but it doesn't make sense from the outside. There's no reason I should write poetry about somebody else's dancing, that's not what poetry's meant for. It was thanks to her that I went on, and it was thanks to her that I kept the job on the *Tribune*. She telephoned me every week and talked to me, criticizing what I had written. Luckily, I was able to learn.

JH: Were you the only dance critic on the *Tribune*?

ED: Yes, and up until my time, they were always trained musicians. They evaluated dance from that point of view, which was what readers wanted I guess. I only got the job because two critics in succession joined the army. Then the editor in chief, who admired Virgil Thomson and had gotten him his job as music critic—a great journalistic coup because Virgil was always causing uproars—asked Virgil if he knew anyone who could fill the job. Virgil told him about me and showed him what I had written in *Modern Music*. I got the job for fifteen dollars a week as I remember.

The war had just begun and I had the choice between going into a factory and taking this job. I needed some money, and I thought how interesting it would be to work in a factory after reading Marx and all those social ideas for so many years, to actually be in one and see what it is that those people are talking about. This was my chance, because normally I wouldn't be accepted for a factory job, but in the war years they needed any kind of person to work there. At the same time, I got this other offer, and a friend of mine said he would give me another ten dollars or so, so that I could accept it, so I was persuaded to work for the *Tribune*.

And I was miserable because I wasn't used to writing right off the bat. I would go to a performance, then to the office, write about it, it would be printed, and that was that, it was gone. I was used to working for months on a poem. Luckily, I trained myself writing prose by writing a mystery story, I knew something about that part, but it was an entirely new thing to work like that and condense it to that point. Because of the war, you were given very little space. On the other hand, the technical problem did interest me, and no one from the newspaper criticized me.

It took me a while to learn within that form. Then, as the writing went on, it was obviously slanted toward ballet and toward Balanchine as being more interesting than Martha Graham was, more than any of the other four or five principal modern dancers. I liked Martha better than any of the others because I could understand it in the sense of sympathizing with it. That went back to my own training. I could understand someone who came up antiballet and went on from there, if they got somewhere where I could find a contact again.

JH: Was the acting quality of her pieces the contact for you?

ED: As an actress, she was wonderful. As a dancer, too, for that matter, and Merce, who was with her then, was always amazing on the stage as a personality, as an actor, and as a dancer. She knew how to use him wonderfully, she used everybody in her company well. Within their particular possibilities, she could make them interesting. I didn't know her very well personally because it influences you too much, you don't look at it in the same way. It's all right to be an outright partisan, but it's not all right not to see it in relation to the whole field. You can't help liking some things better than others.

JH: Do you have any ideas why the whole field of dance of every kind has attracted so much attention within the past few years?

ED: I suppose it's because people have more time and more money than they did in the thirties, that's easy enough. But as to why now compared to the fifties, I don't know. When City Ballet was at Fifty-fifth Street, they got bad reviews from practically everybody and the house was comparatively empty. There would be fifty or sixty ardent fans. We used to sneak in because we couldn't afford to go. We'd hang our coats in the bar across the street and go in at intermission. It was hard to hide in the small audience though, and once the house manager saw me and ran after me, chasing me up the stairs. But he was a little older than I and couldn't run as fast, so he lost me.

JH: Do you think this new large audience makes it harder for dancers?

ED: I think it's harder for dancers now because there's so many of them. You'd think the best ones would come out that way because there's more for a choreographer to choose from. But I don't know. I've gone to performances of the ballet at the Metropolitan that I thought were absolutely terrible, but the house was crowded and enthusiastic. Something's wrong there. Luckily, it doesn't matter. I don't care, because there are more things to do in New York that one likes to do and wants to do. The idea of having an absolute judgment has gotten further and further from anything I can see.

JH: What do you think about dance criticism now?

ED: There are half a dozen excellent dance critics in New York right now. They write very clearly, they describe exactly what they see in words you can understand and you can see it in your own mind as you read it, and they evaluate it. You may or may not agree with the evaluation but you at least see the point that they made. There are also half a dozen excellent dance critics who seem to like everything a great deal, who say something nice and attractive about things I know I don't like. It's often about things I don't see, so maybe I shouldn't say that, but that's my feeling. It's too vast an area now.

JH: What kind of new dance do you see?

ED: The very super avant-garde ones like Lucinda Childs' concert at the Kitchen, which is the most avant-garde I ever saw in my life. The actual range of movement was incredibly small and the control was enormous, vast and rich and fine, and it was only possible to get that control through twenty years of concentrated action and thought by the artist. That she then comes up with something that also takes, as far as I can see, twenty years of concentrated thought to appreciate is amazing. There was an audience there, it was crowded each of the two times I went, and the audience seemed to understand it.

JH: And that surprised you?

ED: Yes, because it took all my strength to experience it. I understood what she was doing and I enjoyed it, but to hold it in my mind, it took all of it. What the dance would have looked like without that kind of attention, I don't know. I thought the form I was looking at was too difficult for anyone to see. I was wrong, obviously it was completely within the possibilities of all those people who were there. It's true there weren't twenty thousand people there, or even two thousand. She was doing it in a small place for a small audience where one could see. And it was calculated for that, so that's nothing against it.

When she danced at the Metropolitan Opera in *Einstein on the Beach*, she had no trouble getting across to the audience or in filling the stage. The movement there was also small, those beautiful hand movements, but everybody saw them. I think it was Bob Wilson's genius as much as hers that everybody could see it. He knows about large space. I'm looking forward to her new big piece with which Bob is not involved to see what she does then.

JH: But of course you had been going to Cage concerts for years. So you must have been immune to surprise.

ED: Cage is an extraordinary man partly because he's done things all his life that his friends have disapproved of. I always went with the greatest pleasure to anything he put on because there was always a drama that I hadn't expected, some notion of something happening on the stage that I couldn't expect. He seemed to be able to think up something new every time he appeared. His sense of time is simply unbelievable and his pitch sense, too. That he can stand the music that is made amazes me very often.

JH: I saw you at Meg Harper's concert. What did you think of that?

ED: I enjoyed myself enormously, I thought it was fantastic. It was nothing like Merce and nothing like what she used to do with Merce. There was no form to follow, there was no structure, the music didn't help except as a diversion, I mean, it didn't support them, so I wondered, How can they remember it, how can they keep it so alive, how can they keep the speed right? For over an hour, they kept a wonderful kind of concentration and kept it perfectly. How she could invent a piece not in the style of Merce simply amazed me after her years of being absorbed in the company. It was full of very rich and unique movement. So I followed the dance with the greatest interest and enjoyment.

JH: Looking at dance today, whose work impresses you most?

ED: Oh yes. There's Douglas Dunn, who I think is the coming thing. His work is absolutely among the very best I've seen. Of course, Merce himself remains perfectly recognizable through all these years.

Bessie Schoenberg

BESSIE SCHOENBERG BEGAN HER CAREER as a dancer, appearing in works by Doris Humphrey and, especially, Martha Graham, with whom she trained in the thirties. Born in Hannover, Germany, she recalls growing up in Dresden and her passion for what she refers to as "rhythmic gymnastics" and the Jacques Dalcroze craze, before settling in America. At the University of Oregon, she met Martha Hill, whom she credits as her first serious teacher in dance; later they both moved to New York, where Schoenberg studied with Graham and took classes at the Neighborhood Playhouse.

Her appearance in classic Graham works such as *Primitive Mysteries* and *Ceremonials* would have assured her a successful career were it not for a torn cartilage that left her unable to dance. Subsequently, Schoenberg went on to teach dance at the Bennington School of Dance and, for over thirty years, at Sarah Lawrence, serving as the head of its Dance Department. At that institution, Schoenberg's many distinguished students included Meredith Monk and Lucinda Childs. The former Cunningham dancer Meg Eginton, who with John Howell questions her, had also been one of Schoenberg's students. Schoenberg's reputation as a teacher was legendary and in recognition of that fact, the "Bessies," the annual award ceremony of Dance Theatre Workshop for the best in contemporary dance, was named after her.

The pedagogical implications of teaching dance, with its emphasis not only on technique but on theories of movement and an insistence on choreography, is what distinguishes Schoenberg's approach: "The sharing of ideas in dance is an important lesson that no technique class gives you." A lifelong supporter of contemporary dance, she nonetheless concedes at the time of this interview that much of it is derivative and self-indulgent. She has equally harsh words to say about critics who have lowered their standards in reviewing new dance, and about funding agencies who give grants tied to projects instead of to the work process. In this, as in her observations on academic versus professional training, Schoenberg's remarks resonate to this very day and bear implications not only for dance but for all the arts.   GD

Conversation with Meg Eginton and John Howell, 1979

A Lifetime of Dance

John Howell: How did you first become interested in dance?

Bessie Schoenberg: I've always danced, that's all I remember. It seems that it was slightly an agony within the family that I was always dancing in a nondancing family. Mind you, it was a very musical family. Whether as a child I thought that I should dance in the way that one thinks of a dance profession I can't even remember. To me it was simply a way of being.

JH: Did you take lessons?

BS: We had some kind of rhythmic gymnastics at high school. I achieved something of a position for myself there because I remember that I was asked to make dances for what we now in America would call assembly programs.

JH: Where was this?

BS: In Dresden. I transferred from a private school into a public high school because it was of a better scholastic caliber. The wind blew quite differently in a public high school, it was a very modern institution, and I was, like very often in my life, at the right place at the right time. Just luck. The school decided that for the upper three years students would have a choice to be either in a group of Romance languages, natural sciences, or the arts or general studies. Of course there was no question as to what my choice was going to be. And there the visual arts and music were strongly emphasized, more than say theatre or dance, although some of that came into it, too. That is when my longing to study dance began.

JH: Was the dance you got in those schools an educational policy or was it influenced by any of the early modern dance that had been going on?

BS: This is a little bit earlier than Wigman. Both Wigman and Graham we consider as starting in the twenties. My school years were during the First World War.

Meg Eginton: So it was an outgrowth of the physical education program?

BS: Yes. You see, Swedish gymnastics and German exercise had a tremendous influence. You did climbing on things along the walls, and swinging from ropes. You also had a section of dance probably more rhythmic, that's why I say rhythmic gymnastics. I was always considered somewhat strange in what I came up with, probably because I was doing things that came from me rather than from any learning. There was a family discussion that I should go to the opera ballet school and then that was ruled out, strictly because young people who went to the ballet school were certainly lower-class and that was not to be considered.

JH: Was that true?

BS: Absolute rubbish. I'm sure it was nothing but sheer upper-class prejudice. So then along floated Dalcroze. And that was considered acceptable because it was such an outlandish thing, who would do it anyway? You see it was just a few crazy people and after all, it was under the aegis of music. So this is how I got my start, and of course I loved it. I couldn't go to Hellerau, that was too far to go, and so I went to Dalcroze classes in the city, which were done in the empty dining room of a vegetarian restaurant. And in my physical memory I always have these memories of cold cabbage connected with going one, two, three, four.

They were heavenly months, but alas, only months because in my enthusiasm I would take everything that I learned and carry this back to school. I would gather everybody around me at intermission and teach them what I had just learned. Until one day when I came home I had a letter from the principal saying, Something is distracting Elizabeth's attention and it must be removed. That was the end of Dalcroze.

ME: How young were you then?

BS: I was probably nine. Finally I had to put the Atlantic Ocean between me and all that in order to start dancing again.

JH: How were you able to come to the States?

BS: My mother was American. She had a voice and the family decided she had better go to Germany and study singing, which is what one did at that time. In the course of all that she met a young engineer who was German and that was my father. One day she became too red-haired and Irish and decided to go home for a while, and was prevented from coming back by the First World War. And their separation, which I think was in the making anyway, really took place because of the long separation during the war. Father was in the army. Finally, Mother came to Dresden to fetch me and I went to America ostensibly for one year of study on a student visa. By that time, Mother was singing and teaching at the music school at the University of Oregon in Eugene and we went there. This is where I met Martha Hill, which is the beginning of my serious dance study.

ME: She was in the Graham company with you.

BS: Yes. Then she taught at the Department of Physical Education. I started dancing with a very lovely and earnest lady who taught dance at Eugene named Miss Stupp, who was a student of Margaret H'Doubler's at Wisconsin, which was an educational and philosophical offshoot of Duncanesque thinking. We tossed around balloons and scarves and wore little tunics and I thought it was the most awful stuff, but anyway you could use your body and fly about like mad. Then Miss Stupp retired and I still had to do some physical education, even as a special student. So I thought somebody must be teaching dancing, and I went along the corridor to the dance office and saw somebody very pleasant sitting at a desk and that was Martha Hill.

ME: How did she end up there?

BS: She had been teaching in the East, and had studied with Graham. She came West because a very good friend of hers was in the Literature Department at Eugene and there was this job in dance and she needed money. So she came out there and revolutionized the whole teaching of dance, not entirely to the liking of the students who had liked very much what had been going on. They found that she stripped everybody down to a leotard and did movements that didn't mean anything but were just movements.

You can imagine who was having the time of her life. I took practically every class that she taught. After two years, Martha Hill decided to quit her job to go back East, primarily because she thought she needed to study with Graham and be where things were going on. You see, this was not only Graham's emancipation, but Humphrey and Weidman and Wigman were very important during that time. She went to New York to see what was going on and I went along.

ME: How?

BS: I didn't have any money, and was totally dependent. I had no way out of that so I marched myself down to the main street in Eugene and went into the First National Bank and asked to see the bank director. I said, I'm Bessie Schoenberg, I think I have talent and I need five hundred dollars to go to New York. And he gave it to me. So with those five hundred dollars I went to Martha Hill and said, I'm coming with you. And she fell off her chair because she could see all sorts of responsibilities. I was lucky, I still don't know why this man took this step or had this faith; he eventually found out what my credentials were and that they were good, but he was with me without any questions asked. I thought it was the way America was.

JH: What happened when you got to New York?

BS: Martha Hill and Mary Jo Shelly took me in hand. I don't know what would have happened without them. They were very practical and found the cheapest room International House had, which was very good thinking. I was out of Germany only three years and I qualified as a foreign student. Eventually I had a scholarship from the Neighborhood Playhouse, from Mrs. Morgenthau who was the director of the school, and from Martha Graham. This was all from the good graces of Martha Hill and Jo Shelly who made all the introductions. But I found study very difficult.

ME: Why?

BS: I was a very undisciplined person in many ways. I found everything hard to do, I found that everything hurt. The love of dancing that had been part of my life so far, I found there was little space for. All the things had to do with stretching, with pulling the body, and with moving slowly and hard. I was awfully good if one had to whip into the floor and get back up quickly, stuff like that. I had agonizing times in acting because Laura Elliot, the really remarkable woman who taught acting, was not the most sensitive psychologist. She would refer to people who think with their legs, meaning me. Actually she was annoyed that I made so much allowance for dance and gave so little time to acting.

JH: Was she someone dancers in particular went to?

BS: No, this was the Neighborhood Playhouse. At the time I studied with her, she was a coach of Katherine Cornell, Marlene Dietrich, Greta Garbo, and any number of foreign actresses, especially for diction.

ME: How did you get to study with her?

BS: You went to the Playhouse and took all the courses you were supposed to take as a scholarship student, and this was part of it. The Playhouse in that sense was very modern in its thinking. I was on a scholarship, which wasn't very much, fifteen dollars a week and you had to get rent out of it and food. It was a real student life . . . I think Graham had a lot to do with the fact that there were no transitions from study into doing. She preached that you should dance at every dogfight and any time anybody wanted me to dance in anything, I danced. It was a splendid way of learning about disciplines of the theatre.

ME: How did Graham teach her classes? Was her movement style fairly codified already?

BS: Yes, but codified is the wrong word to use for a very simple reason. These were Martha's formative years, and I am forever and eternally grateful to her as any young dancer who had the opportunity of studying with Graham during those years. She was one day further along in learning about herself every day you met her. When I came to her, her company had been by and large three girls. Then she added to that, taking Martha Hill and me into the company and others. I think we were about a dozen or so at that time. But you went to classes every day and I had classes with her in addition at the Playhouse, so I was doubly blessed.

What was fascinating about her, even though her classes might have been white agony, and most of them were, you'd go home and work on what you'd had and come the next day to be a little bit better and she'd say, "I've changed it." She had gone a step further in her own thinking. She was beginning to visualize what the body could do or should do on her terms. Of course, her own body, that of the young Graham, was such an amazing example to work with because it could do anything. That I should probably qualify, because she chose not to do certain things; perhaps deliberately, perhaps not. She was not interested in elevation. Surely she did some jumps, but the kind of things we might call soaring or ranging through the air was not part of what she was interested in doing then.

ME: What was the working process then?

BS: We had to work late at night or early in the morning. It became a habit to work and that stays with you the rest of your life. You took little jobs whenever you could. Graham expected us to be at rehearsals practically every night. We were in no way organized, so the hours were endless. Time and time again we went home in the gray hours of the morning, sewing our costumes on the subway. We made our own costumes as there was no other way to have any.

JH: What kind of pieces was Graham making around this time?

BS: The kind that had more social content: *Sketches of the People,* her own solos of *Steerage* and *Strike,* then *Frontier.* Her own growing awareness of America was very interesting to watch. Martha became very self-conscious in the late thirties and early forties, like everything else, like even the musicals, *Oklahoma!* and so forth. Martha and Louis Horst, her musical collaborator and friend, had made a trip to the Southwest together and that made a deep impression on her. It was a source and inspiration for a number of things, certainly *Primtive Mysteries* and *El Penitente.*

ME: What did you think about all that work?

BS: I think that I was very lucky. She was an absolute and total answer to all my questions and longings at that time. For that period of time, she was utterly right. I think to be a disciple and to feel this way is a remarkably good fortune. It never lasts, but while it lasts it's utter bliss. Remember, this was a time when Martha could dance maybe twice a year and one of them an afternoon at the Guild Theatre with a small audience. Once she did a piece called *Dance;* it was a statement, a credo. It was so sparse, so limited as to movement that someone said she stood on that little platform as if she dared anybody to ask her to lift her legs. She really made a statement of the movement of the torso, and of movement coming simply from the spine. It was very arrested, very sparse, and the curtain came down and there wasn't a hand in the house.

People simply didn't know what they were looking at. So we in the company would run back from our dressing rooms when we were done, and stand in the back of the house and shout "hooray" and "bravo." That kind of thing is now no problem at all but there was no audience for it then, there was no understanding. She got terrible reviews.

ME: You must have wondered at some point just what you were doing, or what was going to happen to you?

BS: I was not very philosophical about the future, or where I was headed, as long as I was going to do more of what I was doing at the time. To become better at what I was doing and to have more opportunities to do that was of the greatest importance. And I had enormous curiosity as to where Graham was headed. I couldn't wait from day to day to see what she was going to come up with next.

ME: It must have been an incredible experience to have danced in *Primitive Mysteries*. It's one of the pure ritual dances that works.

BS: It's beautifully conceived. I'm sure Graham herself thinks it's a period piece now. Certainly no one can dance it in the way it was meant anymore.

JH: It was a physical problem that kept you from continuing to dance with her, wasn't it?

BS: Yes. As Martha's technique developed, it ranged wider and made more and more demands on the body. I continued to push myself and I tore a cartilage in the knee. I eventually left the company because of that.

JH: And you began to teach?

BS: Again Martha Hill stepped in and said, Maybe you should look into teaching. Martha said it's what I had been doing all my life and she invited me to go to a graduate camp of NYU near the Catskills. This was in preparation for taking me with her up to Bennington as her assistant where she had just taken on a position as head of dance while she was also head of dance at NYU. This was typical of her. Now she's head of dance at Juilliard. What she had figured out was that she would spend half the week at Bennington, and I would carry on while she spent the other half at NYU. I was probably a complete failure as a teacher, because at the end of the year Martha and I had a walk in the woods in which she told me how bad I was; she really took me apart. Which wasn't news to me, I was still evidently wrestling with the idea that this was all transitional and that I was going to go back to dancing.

ME: Dancing or choreographing?

BS: Choreographing was very secondary. Primarily dancing and performing. I was thinking that all this was a nightmare and would go away and that things would heal, not knowing that these things don't heal. But certainly I couldn't embarrass Martha Hill, so I tightened the belt and became a teacher, and it was really fun because I meant to do what I was doing.

JH: Did Sarah Lawrence have a dance department before you came?

BS: Yes, in those days Sarah Lawrence and Bennington were practically the only institutions of higher learning that had autonomous dance departments, independent of physical education programs.

JH: What days were those?

BS: Around '33. After graduating from Bennington, I had gotten married and moved back to New York and I thought, Now what? I became a sort of traveling salesman of modern dance. I taught simultaneously at Greenwich and Stamford, Connecticut, Philadelphia, New York City, and Briarcliff Junior College. I was on the train so much I didn't know if I was coming or going or where from or where to. And then I added Sarah Lawrence to that as a part-time assistant to teach technique.

Meanwhile, with two other dancers who were very serious about dance, I started a dance school in New York. This was the beginning of the Dance League School, and some very good things took place there. Then Helen Tamiris became chairman of the American Dance Association and I became vice chairman, so I began to be interested in organizational work in dance. And it's in the school that I taught composition for the first time.

JH: Since you've taught at Sarah Lawrence so long, how did you deal with New York City's increasing attraction for dance students?

BS: This is not an entirely painless subject. It's a very interesting problem but a difficult one, too. It was obvious that as interest in dance grew, and New York became more and more the mecca where the great things in dance were going on practically next door to Bronxville, to compete with those attractions was pretty difficult. I saw a great danger in students wanting to go to New York.

ME: Didn't it have something to do with your theory of teaching, of how one learned to dance?

BS: That too. I've always felt that the more intensely you can work in limited areas at one time rather than gypsy around, the more you'll get out of it. I feel that the tendency of studying here and there gives you a kind of mixture of points of view, so that you have to spend a great deal of time sorting out your own values if you can do that. I think it's better to study with somebody for a considerable amount of time and see what you can glean there. But the other thing I found really difficult was that you couldn't count on students to be certain places you would like them to be within the program because they made other commitments in the city.

Finally, I developed what I called the Friday program. Ideally, I thought that having some one person for the entire Friday teaching load of the year would be marvelous. In the early days, José Limón would come for a year, Merce would come for some part of a year; all sorts of fascinating people took to our Friday program and taught there. So that we had the beginning of a very good balance for a student who might not like one thing but who might be able to do something else instead. I also thought harder and harder about how to depersonalize movement teaching, to teach theories of movement rather than a technique.

JH: How would you describe the difference?

BS: A theory of movement to my thinking is, How many ways can you fall or run or turn? To explore the principle of turning and all the variations. You might say Humphrey taught a technique of turning that was like this.

JH: And you think that's an advantage a college can offer?

BS: I've warned students who wanted a professional career not to go to college but to go to New York. At times, I have talked students out of their third year in college and told them to take a year in New York to find out what they wanted to do. What I found fascinating is that most of the students who left for the junior year came back for their last year. They were much more directed toward what they could get out of the particular program we had to offer and which they couldn't find in the city.

JH: But in the sixties it was not only a college and town conflict, but an aesthetic one as well, wasn't it?

BS: If you think of the dance world as we know it, some of the more controversial dancers came out of Sarah Lawrence. We became known as a school that emphasized choreography. I insisted on that because a viable college program had to depend on an evaluation of what the students did out of themselves, not the passive act of going to classes. We don't accept that somebody practices the piano, you accept how somebody finally plays a piece or possibly writes a piece. It wasn't my intention that everybody who studied dance was going to become a choreographer. But that is the vehicle which is open to us for the student to do something with all the movement material the body amasses. Here's an outlet to speak, to become articulate. And working back again, to become more articulate about dancing. Because not only do you become more knowledgeable about movement, you're beginning to use it. You choose and as you choose you do a movement that now speaks for you. You work on it very differently and you learn something you don't learn in classes.

The sharing of ideas in dance is an important lesson that no technique class gives you. To look at movement, not via a technique, but via a choice that a student has made by moving. This is kinesthetic thinking that has nothing much to do with the head, but has to do with going into a studio and making yourself move according to the limit of a certain assignment. This I think is viable material academically. To bring things down to a more basic thinking, to a more basic understanding seemed to me of more value to our students. If you arrive at New York studios and just see these trends, you are moving into an atmosphere that has tremendous limitations. These personalized techniques, which we know by these great names, are made on the bodies of certain people. The least personalized techniques that are taught in New York are the ballets, because three hundred years and thousands of bodies have gone into them.

JH: Do you think some techniques are more available to adaptations? Is that why Cunningham was so attractive to so many people in the sixties?

BS: Certainly. Merce's influence on this whole period is almost dangerous. The people who have soaked up what Merce has done and have arrived at themselves are still very few. You find that the various teachings of Merce are very much distorted. For instance, one of the most important things he has said is that any movement can be as good as any other movement. That's the credo by which an awful lot of young choreographers go.

ME: I think it's available too because it draws partly on other techniques. He has a Graham heritage and a ballet heritage.

BS: He's a hoofer, too.

JH: And that rhythmic thing that comes indirectly from tap.

BS: Yes, his base is much wider than most. He's never had quite the ritual that our other well-known techniques have. If you see a Graham class, the ritual begins maybe twenty or thirty minutes after the class begins in which every student knows what to do almost without the teacher talking. In contrast to this, at Sarah Lawrence I insisted that we would start every class differently so that no class was something that the student expected. This was sort of revolutionary, too.

What was beginning to happen in New York was that forms and techniques were beginning to jell and students began to demand—this was where I was in conflict—something to hang onto. I felt that what we needed to teach was, to borrow my good friend Ruth Lloyd's words, "to be happy with danger," to be comfortable with the unexpected, to be alert and alive now. And this is where I feel very much in sympathy with a Merce perhaps not of today but of an earlier day, where everything that he did was very immediate and was not yesterday or tomorrow but now. His classes, his dancing, his performing, and his way of doing practically everything was extremely present tense. This is very sympathetic to me.

JH: We've been talking about the sixties and present tense and we've got to remember that the seventies are almost over. What's different in the past few years?

BS: I find myself at odds at the moment with what is going on. I think our period of nondance has gone almost uncomfortably far. I think I never expected that I would not be acutely interested every moment I saw anything being done in the name of dance. I found myself being really bored with an awful lot of things I had seen in the past two years. Several things bother me, the degree of self-indulgence, the degree of exclusion of the viewer from the act of performance. Again and again, I find that what Meredith Monk does is one of the most fascinating things of our day. I feel that she is an extraordinary theatrical personality, and even though she hasn't apparently the vaguest idea of any kind of compromise to an audience, it can rivet you, totally absorb you in what she is doing. But we have very few Merediths.

JH: What part do you think a climate plays in this?

BS: I think the climate in New York has become very soft. I think everybody is very gentle, not only dancers to each other but the critics as well. I think there is too much support of nothingness. Fellow dancers tend not to say that this is nonsense or junk. I've arrived at this impression because of a feeling that I can no longer talk straight out to people who've been my students. If you read the press, there's an awful lot of letting down easily of people who should never be encouraged to start doing what they're doing. I do have certain friends among choreographers who treat me as another pair of eyes. I go to rehearsals and the agreement we have between us is to let me say anything that I feel about what I see. I think we have a proliferation of very great mediocrity in dance products.

JH: You've said in the past that from your experience on various grant panels you think young choreographers should be funded to work, not produce pieces.

ME: To have a long laboratory period without the pressure to produce a final product.

BS: This would be ideal, if people could get money to work, not just to produce. Now, you get funding if you have a new project. When you're a young dancer you need some guidance or you're simply going to be derivative of what you see. The Judson crowd for very good reasons was a group in which ideas fermented, and they did some very fascinating things. But people who came after them were only influenced by that period and they in turn influenced others and it got watered down without any graphic instruction or real exchange in there. So what we have now is so many young groups who become a company, get incorporated, and apply for grants. When you see them, you know who they've looked at.

JH: But it takes quite a bit of experience to develop a personal viewpoint, doesn't it, and dancers are by necessity young.

BS: Right. Dance has many strikes against it. One is its transitoriness. And you have to be young because you need your body at its best; it's essential. We used to think that dancers were through when they were thirty-five.

ME: But Graham was about thirty before she even left Denishawn to begin choreographing.

BS: Yes. I just think young choreographers should be a little more modest. Nobody would have anything against making a little piece here and there. To immediately become a company and incorporate and tie your audience down for an evening, that's something else again.

JH: Do you think audiences and money will keep supporting dance?

BS: Why not? The growth of popularity of dance is gratifying to see. In America we have several first-rate ballet companies that have large enthusiastic audiences, and we have a varied assortment of modern dance companies that have strong audience support. There is more funding. I am optimistic. Certainly we dance better in America today than anywhere else on earth.

Ellen Stewart

THE STORY OF ELLEN STEWART and the founding of La MaMa in the early sixties is like some kind of miracle. This theatre is now an institution and of such worldwide renown that it is difficult to imagine how rudimentary its beginnings actually were. A stage was any room or basement Stewart, who designed clothes to support her dream, could find for the young playwrights and directors who had gathered around her. She was harassed, issued summons, even jailed by police who thought she was a prostitute entertaining men in the subterranean quarters she called a theatre. In these bohemian times before the off-off-Broadway theatre scene, "downtown" was defining itself in Happenings, John Cage and Merce Cunningham collaborations, Beat culture, independent filmmaking, and the stirring of Judson activities in dance and theatre. Only Caffe Cino had preceded La MaMa as a regular site for the newest plays.

In the thirty-five years since La MaMa has been a force in non-mainstream theatre culture, the list of artists—as writer, director, performer, company, composer—who have worked there is incalculable: Shepard, van Itallie, Foster, Eyen, Shawn, O'Horgan, Gregory, Schechner, Sellars, Serban, Monk, Jesurun, Skipitares, Chong; Play-House of the Ridiculous, Open Theater, Mabou Mines, Ontological-Hysteric Theater, Talking Band; Peaslee, Glass, Swados, Moran. Those are just the Americans. From the beginning, La MaMa has been international, welcoming Kantor, Brook, Grotowski, Terayama, and, in more recent years, work from Estonia, Poland, Korea, the Philippines, Brazil, Venezuela, Israel. How ironic that in the period referred to in her exchanges with theatre critic Glenn Loney, the NEA had cut funds for La MaMa because there was too much "foreign" work. Stewart, who has received a MacArthur Award, was way ahead of the arts in her intercultural vision, and she would not make La MaMa a black theatre because she is a black woman. "I believe very much in the universality of man," she states unequivocally, which is why La MaMa is not a simply a house, but a home.   BGM

Conversation with Glenn Loney, 1982

La MaMa and the American Theatre

I came to New York in 1950. I came from Chicago to go to the Trapha-
gen Fashion Institute. Colored people couldn't go to a school like that in
Chicago. I was supposed to meet a friend who lived in New York. Two
Chicago friends had come along with me. We waited at Grand Central
"under the clock," but my friend never showed up. I had only sixty dollars. I didn't want to tell anyone in Chicago what had happened. My
friends left New York, but I was too proud to go back home. I had to find
a job. Like a miracle, I found one at Saks Fifth Avenue. While I was looking for a job, I got lost and went into St. Patrick's—I didn't know it was
St. Patrick's then. I lit a candle and asked for a job. Thirty minutes later, I
had one. I was to be a porter at Saks. Sundays, I'd get on the subway and
go anywhere, exploring the city wherever I got off the train. One Sunday,
I discovered Delancey Street and all those little shops with clothes and
fabric. I wanted to be a dress designer and here was all this wonderful
fabric!

You could *look* at anything you liked. You could try things on. No one
said anything to you. And this little man—my Papa Diamond—came out
of his shop. He was wearing a little black cap on his head. He tried to sell
me some fabric. I told him I had no money. He said, "Come inside. Maybe
you'll see something you like better?" Finally, he understood I really
hadn't a cent. Also, that I didn't have anybody, no family in New York.

It was love at first sight, my papa Abraham Diamond! He adopted me
on the spot. I became the Artist Daughter. Every Sunday, I'd come and
spend the day with the family. When I left, he'd give me a piece of fabric
in a package. I'd open it when I got home. I had a little sewing machine
in my room. Every week, I'd make a dress or an outfit and wear it next
Sunday. He'd show me all around the street—his daughter, the designer.

Now, at Saks Fifth Avenue, the colored had to wear blue smocks at
work. The whites didn't. So there I was, like Cinderella, under my smock.
It all happened very fast. I'd come to Saks in May. With the interest in my
little homemade clothes, by August I was one of the executive designers.
I did that for eight years—and I never got to design school at all. In the
meantime, my Papa Diamond told me that when he came to New York
from Romania at age eleven, he was the first to put out a pushcart in the
Delancey Street area.

He said I should have a pushcart, too. And, if I pushed the pushcart for other people, it would take me where I wanted to go! . . . I got very sick. I had many operations. I didn't know if I was going to live. I went to Morocco. A Dybbuk came to me and told me to get my pushcart. So I left Morocco to return to New York. I decided my pushcart would be a little theatre where my brother Fred Lights, and Paul Foster, could have their plays performed. That's exactly what I did. And that's why La MaMa is often referred to as a "pushcart."

My first little basement in 1962 wasn't as large as a small room, but it's where Harold Pinter had his first American production. We had some tables and chairs there, like a coffeehouse. There was to be a World's Fair, and Commissioner Robert Moses didn't like places like mine. He said we were providing "entertainment in a squalid little dump." He wanted to clean up New York for the Fair—and to make his own name look good.

Ed Koch was just beginning to make a political name for himself as well. So their cleaning-up was always me and La MaMa. They were always closing me up. Giving me summonses. I went to jail so many times. Under many names. I spent many a night at the old Womens' House of Detention. You see, if you got convicted of offering entertainments without a license, under Commissioner Moses, you got sent to jail. I can still remember Koch saying, "You will learn to live within the law—or suffer the consequences!"

Doing off-off-Broadway theatre was always a struggle with the law. In 1967, I had been convicted twice under my own name—not counting the times with aliases. In New York City, if you are convicted three times, you are branded a felon, and you are not allowed to do certain things anymore. It's a stigma. I was very worried about getting a third conviction.

Running away from this political persecution, each time I'd move, and each time La MaMa was larger. The first stage we had was the size of a table—about three feet by ten. But, with larger stages, the playwrights had to write larger plays. We had a bed. That was our one set and prop. Nobody was fornicating on it. Nothing like that! But the bed was always the center of our early plays. You got murdered in the bed. You had babies in that bed. You sat on it. You lay on it. You hid under it. You know the actress Shirley Stoller, the big girl who played Lolita's mama on Broadway? Well, our stage was a little shaky—and she had the floor go out from under her. That was her beginning in the theatre at La MaMa.

Today, people often ask me, "How do you develop plays?" Well, with La MaMa, it had to do with the kind of space we had. But the little plays we wrote then don't work anymore. I moved from 321 East Ninth Street—where neighbors tried to close me down because they thought I must have been "entertaining" a lot of white men, or why else would so many young men be going to see a colored woman in her basement—to 82 Second Avenue. From there, La MaMa moved to 122 Second Avenue. And from there to 9 St. Marks Place. And, finally, to where we are now, at 74 East Fourth Street. We had five moves in eight years, from 1961 to 1969. And the plays developed with the moves. Each space triggered the imagination a little more and a little more . . .

I paid for it. I'm very proud I was a good designer. I was the only American then invited to work in Christian Dior's atelier in Paris. I was the only American to have two gowns at Queen Elizabeth's Coronation Ball. I dressed two of the very few American women who were invited. So my creations were floating around. I made money, and with that money, I made La MaMa.

But I still made all the costumes for our plays myself. I paid the rent on the space. I paid for the utilities. And I paid the rent for a lot of people who worked with La MaMa. Rents weren't so much then. For some whose rent I didn't pay, I'd give them a dollar. Those who needed more, I'd give two dollars. In my little railroad flat, I lived with Tom O'Horgan, Paul Foster, and Jim Moore, who is still La MaMa's business manager. That way, it was only one rent to pay for four people. That's how we lived then. It was total sacrifice for those people. They didn't have any money to contribute—only their art. They worked when they could, but in those days, there wasn't much work.

I started touring La MaMa in 1965, and we were then in Germany. I dreaded what might happen when we came back to New York. In Munich, they volunteered to support me and Tom O'Horgan and the company for a year, until I could get back on my feet. I was thinking of moving to Germany.

I had to leave 122 Second Avenue or get another summons. Con Edison harassed me. They wouldn't give us any current unless I put in a special main for my second-floor premises. Where was I to get the money? Always this harassment. One day I came back from my design work, and the whole wall of La MaMa was gone—on the second floor! That was to get me out. So many ugly incidents. Today, you'd think they couldn't be true, but they were.

You can see why the German offer looked good. I knew no one was going to help us. That's the reason we started touring in 1965. Critics wouldn't come to see our shows. We had no real reviews. I thought our plays were good, but publishers didn't want to print them unless we had favorable reviews. Or, if some critics did come and write reviews, their papers wouldn't print them. So I thought we should go to Europe and get reviewed there.

We sailed on a student ship for $118 one way. Sixteen people sailed off with twenty-two plays. I split the company into two groups. One would play in Paris at the American Center, the other would play in Copenhagen at the Comedia Huset which I had rented. Tom O'Horgan headed one troupe; Ross Alexander, the other. They'd play in each city, then switch.

Robert Wilson—another early La MaMa child—had made the huge puppets for *America Hurrah*. Worn by actors, they destroy a motel room and write "Cock" and "Fuck" all over the walls—it's in the play. Well, when we did that in Paris, the director of the American Center said we'd disgraced it and we'd have to leave. We finished the play, but I had to take those dolls away. I got the French railroad to agree that I could ride in a freight car with those dolls, to get them to Denmark.

They didn't like us in Paris. We were doing Sam Shepard, Leonard Melfi, Jean-Claude van Itallie—all required reading now. We had a big success in Copenhagen. They thought we were terrible actors, but what the critics liked was our way of expressing the plays. Our energy. They said we were like lovable little puppies.

Some Yugoslavs were there and liked our puppy-energy. They invited us to Yugoslavia to the Student Drama Festival. We were the first American theatre group to be invited into an Eastern European country. We went in 1966. We were invited to Sweden. And to Nottingham, in England. So we now had definite invitations, and that's the way the La MaMa tours began. Now it's very common for American troupes to go to Europe on tour, but we pioneered it and opened all the doors. Peter Iden invited us to Frankfurt and *Experimenta*. Then, in 1967, we went to the Kammerspiele in Munich, where we were invited to stay.

I decided to go back to New York and try again. I would call all the foundations in New York. Someone told me who they were. I didn't know what you were supposed to do, or what you were supposed to ask for. So I just asked for someone to come down to see our work and see if they could help us.

One day the Ford Foundation called. So this man and his wife came. They asked if I'd like to talk after the performance. I took them to the Fifth Street Deli for hotdogs and sauerkraut. I explained what I was doing. If I had $25,000, I told them, I could put $10,000 down on a building on East Fourth Street, fix it up inside for $15,000, and I'd have my own legal premises. I wouldn't always be running.

The man nodded and said goodnight. About a week later, I got a call to come to the Ford Foundation. I went up and got an envelope. It had a check for $25,000 in it. The man was MacNeil Lowry. It was quite a while before I found out that this was *not* how you get grants . . .

Our building had only three walls. You could stand in it and look up at the sky. There was a dirt floor in the cellar. The Ford Foundation fixed it up for us. It cost a few hundred thousand, but they did it. And we had a home.

When we went to Yugoslavia I met the young director Andrei Serban. MacNeil Lowry gave him a Ford grant to come to America. That was in 1969. He developed his *Medea* in the cellar. That was his second piece for us. This we were invited to play in the ruins of the Temple of Baalbek in Lebanon. I'd heard of the Parthenon, but not of this incredible expanse of ruins. I asked why we'd never heard about it, and they said it's because the Greeks wrote the history books. So we played *Medea* outdoors, beginning in the ruins of the Palace of Dionysus, which has been sitting there for two thousand years. We played the whole expanse of the ruins—like ten city blocks square. Serban spread it out to every corner of the complex, the audience following the action around.

So, when we came back to New York, we just couldn't play *Medea* in the cellar anymore. We had to have a larger space. I went again to the Ford Foundation, and that's how we got the Annex, where Serban's *Trilogy—Medea, Electra, The Trojan Women*—was produced.

In 1980, I got a big cut in the money the NEA was giving me. I couldn't imagine why. I was in Europe at the time, but when I got back, I asked for an audience, and it was granted. I went down to Washington and asked Arthur Ballet [NEA Theatre Program director, 1979–80]—who disbursed the theatre grants then—why La MaMa was cut. This was before the Reagan cuts; the NEA still had plenty of money to dole out. He said the NEA Theatre Panel didn't think I was really American and that La MaMa was not American enough.

He said I was responsible for bringing more European artists to America. Not big companies like the Bolshoi, but individual artists— like Serban—who had so influenced the American theatre with European ideas that it made it too competitive here for American artists. The Theatre Panel wanted—or so he said—to support American stages doing American plays for American audiences.

This hurt me. La MaMa had taken new American plays, plays no one else would do, abroad many times. I've worked in at least fifty countries for La MaMa, helping develop theatre. Only when we played Herod's Palace in Tel Aviv were our trips paid for by the government. Many people assume when La MaMa goes abroad that the State Department pays our way. It does not.

Quite the contrary. Even a country as poor as Yugoslavia pays our way. The countries we have visited over the years have paid everything for us. And when their troupes come to La MaMa, they pay for that, too. I don't have any money for that. I have never used any NEA or other grant money to pay for a foreign troupe. I can show proof of that. I told Ballet that, and he said, That's all very well . . . but when the company comes, you let them keep the box-office receipts.

Well, if nobody comes to see the show, they aren't very much. And if you have a company of thirty-five people coming to New York for two or three weeks, it costs a lot to pay for hotels and eating. And the trip to New York costs a lot, too.

He told me: If you are making it possible for an American ticket buyer to see a foreign performance, you are making it possible for them to subsidize a foreign troupe. We want the American ticket buyer to buy tickets for American performances. If there are no foreign performances . . .

I brought Grotowski to this country. I visited him in 1965. Ted Hoffman of NYU helped me do this. Well, Ballet said they were watching me. If I didn't improve, I'd be cut again. And I was. He said it wasn't censorship. That the NEA gives money to what it likes, but it didn't like what I was doing.

Later that year, 1980, Peter Brook and his company came with *The Ik* and *The Conference of the Birds*. They stayed at La MaMa for seven weeks. Outside of his center in Paris, La MaMa is the only place he's stayed that long. And Brook made five trips to America to raise the money to play in my poor little theatre. He was offered Broadway theatres. Joe Papp offered him the Public Theater. Harvey Lichtenstein offered him BAM, where he'd been before. Alex Cohen helped—he was able to get $50,000 for Brook. And the New York State Council gave an extra $20,000 so his company could come.

I was feeling pretty good about this. I knew all year I'd programmed beautiful things. And they cut me again. A friend at the NEA had some advice for me. If I'd go to Los Angeles on a two-week residency, they could have Gordon Davidson teach me everything he was doing at the Mark Taper Forum. Then, I was told, I could come back to New York and make La MaMa into the Mark Taper Forum East. If I did that, she said,

I'd get all the money I needed, because, for the NEA, the Mark Taper Forum under Davidson was the epitome of excellence in U.S. theatre.

I told her I'd worked for eighteen years *not* to do what they are doing at the Mark Taper. And I wasn't going to start now.

One of the things I'm most proud of is the work we are doing with TWITAS—The Third World Institute of Theatre Arts Studies. This program is headed by Cecile Guidote, who had done some fine theatre work in the Philippines before coming to La MaMa. During the Year of the Child, we were able to bring individual folk artists from many countries to La MaMa, where they taught each other the songs, stories, plays, and dances of their native lands. One of them might be an expert dancer in his country. Another could be a well known puppeteer. But all of them were familiar with more than one kind of performance and were also well acquainted with the rituals and traditions of their lands.

This was a kind of Little United Nations. You could say that—and they also performed at the United Nations several times. Andrew Young was the U.S. Ambassador to the UN then, and his wife, Jean Young, was one of our most important sponsors. We had an artist from India and from Bangladesh. We had performers from Jordan and other Arab lands. We also had a wonderful director-performer from Israel, Rina Yerushalmi.

The first week she was in the program, the Arab artists were wary of her. They were critical. She was "the enemy." By the second week, she had become "our beautiful enemy." By the third week, everyone was working together, excited at the progress of a performance project. And she was now "our beautiful friend." When you bring real artists together and then give them the chance to get to know each other through their artistic gifts, you can do a lot to remove old prejudices.

One of the main ideas behind this Year of the Child work at La MaMa was to show teachers how to make classroom instruction about other countries more interesting—and accurate. By using storytelling, puppet-making, dancing, and singing, you can keep kids involved and still get the facts about history, geography, and culture across to them. Brooklyn College helped us in this by making arrangements for our visiting artists to work in an elementary school in the Bedford-Stuyvesant district.

We performed for schools in Manhattan, especially here on the Lower East Side. But we took our work to old people's homes, hospitals, and other places where they needed something to cheer them up. They also got an idea about artists from other countries, not from London or Paris, but from the Third World, which Americans know so little. After the project was over, the artists returned to their own countries, to share the things they had learned from other nations and from their stay in New York.

But our work with Third World artists continues. It's too expensive to bring a lot of individual artists together. Visas and permissions are difficult. Living costs in New York are worse. But when La MaMa can, she brings artists here to show others what they do and how they do it. It's nothing big, like it was for the Year of the Child, but it goes forward. The problem at La MaMa is that the government doesn't want to spend any money on foreign artists or productions. Even if American artists can learn from them. There are a lot of people out there in the Third World. Some of them are wonderful performers. We need to get to know them, and their cultures and countries.

In the office, I have a staff of one: Mr. Jim Moore, who's been with me for twenty-three years now. He takes care of the books. You know, a lot of people are disappointed in me—or what they think La MaMa should be. They write letters, and they don't get answers. Or there's nobody to talk to them on the telephone. They want to come to talk to me, and I don't have the time to see them.

That's what bothers me most. I don't have the money to answer letters. To take care of all the phone calls. To take time to talk with people. It's courtesy to do those things, but I don't have the time. For example: at 3:00 A.M. this morning, I was working with a Cuban cast. I was awakened at 6:00 A.M. by someone calling me from Italy. At 7:00 someone from Nigeria called me from Kennedy Airport. At 8:00 a Korean visitor arrived. At 8:30 a French guest came. Then Goethe House called for a talk. Then came a call from France. And one from Japan. From 3:00 to 10:00 this morning, I communicated with ten different countries. At La MaMa, that's a matter of daily course.

I believe very much in the universality of man. I still use that term: man. I think communication helps what I call universalization—and the theatre helps to communicate beyond one's own language.

At La MaMa, we do nothing without some kind of text, but I want our La MaMa playwrights, in creating, to think about play*making*, not about playwriting. So no matter what is spoken, the audience will *see* something onstage that also communicates. No matter what the audience, I want them to make a connection with what's happening on the stage. That's the kind of work I'm interested in. The other kind—where the playwright has a lot of words to say, but nothing to *show*, which is what most of American theatre is about—is not of interest to me . . .

Even if the work, the production, isn't remarkable, how will young people learn to do better if they don't have a chance to start? I want to let them have that chance. We have produced more than a thousand plays now at La MaMa, and most of them have been American. We have not been remiss in that. I think we have a better track record than any other theatre in America on that score. I also feel that music is integral to what happens in the theatre, so for me the composer is also a play-maker. We've counted some 340 original scores for La MaMa plays.

I feel very strongly that someday we will have to do more than just say hello to other people. There has to be a visceral understanding among men—not just a greeting. So I try to use La MaMa as a pushcart to help push us in this direction.

Joseph Chaikin

"ALL MY LIFE I imagined I was going to die . . . It gave me a kind of urgency," Joseph Chaikin reveals in this interview, which shows a very personal side of the actor, director, and founder of The Open Theater (1963–73), whose *The Mutation Show* and *Terminal* are considered avant-garde classics. Early in their careers the company was a workshop for Sam Shepard, Maria Irene Fornes, Jean-Claude van Itallie, and Megan Terry, who helped create a new "transformation" style of acting and thinking about plays. At the time of his conversation with Polish critic Andrzej Bonarski the company had disbanded and Chaikin was moving in the direction of The Winter Project. Distinguishing himself from the more anarchist views of The Living Theatre, which he had formerly joined as an actor, Chaikin proposes no grand vision of transforming the world, but seeks instead a more one-on-one relationship: to awaken those people who can be awakened. Extending many of the group ideals of his own theatre and of the sixties, he emphasizes the importance of being part of a real community of shared consciousness.

Chaikin's belief in the possibility of theatre to create models of the imagination underlies his search for a universal grammar in the "vocabulary of emotions that is common to the human character . . . subcultural." His research as an actor carried him deep into the life force to discover what it is that makes one "act" human. The actor, in his view, should give an example to the audience of the fullness of life by communicating values often ignored in society. He called his book *The Presence of the Actor.*

Unlike many artists who created theatre in the sixties and seventies, Chaikin never abandoned language as a tool of communication. As he explains, language should be reconstructed by poets, scholars, and all those who decry its erosion of meaning. His own work has always addressed matters of life and death, most recently in the contemporized (by Susan Yankowitz) and restaged (with members of the original cast) *Terminal,* now two decades and a half later, just as compelling.   BGM

Conversation with Andrzej Bonarski, 1977

The Search for a Universal Grammar

Andrzej Bonarski: What do you think we should talk about nowadays? What is worth talking about? What is not worth talking about at all? What should we be silent about?

Joseph Chaikin: First of all, what should we not talk about. I believe there is nothing we should not say. I think there is a natural wish to say everything, everything. But it seems clear that one can't say everything in all situations. Everything that can be, should be said, in whatever form possible, and to those who can understand. Breathing is freer and fuller where more can be talked about. Living is so intense. If we have to hold in what we experience, it's too isolating and we don't learn what's shared and what are the differences. I think that there are moments—I am imagining that everyone has them—when we look at human activity and it all looks like the same kind of driven motion, as if you see bees or if you see many ants. But it all has the same kind of futility; all of it looks like a lot of motion without any meaning, no matter how much conviction the person has. Still people have these moments when it's totally meaningless. And then one resupplies oneself with the meanings and proceeds to continue in one's own direction. In a way, I think that an awful lot of motion that people do isn't useless, and sometimes is even illuminating.

To me one of the very constant questions is: What can be affirmed? Well, to me this question is very, very difficult, because, for example, in my experience, I had been involved with different political people for a long time. People I knew spoke very well about ideals . . . and it was very good . . . and it took years before I observed that rhetoric and actions were rather unrelated and what they had been doing was refining rhetoric. So when I say what to affirm, I don't mean necessarily in slogans or in statements like one can "affirm family," one can "affirm love." I'll tell you something that is very important to me personally. What is very important to me is a community of people. And I don't mean that on a domestic scale. I come across people in different countries and different cities who share a kind of consciousness. I mean, for me it's very important that there is a recognition between people. There is this French expression—I don't remember what it is, but it goes something like "Save who you can save . . ."

I am very interested in people who try to reconstruct language. Many mystical people I come across are rejecting language and saying, "We can't speak, we meditate the silence, we can make sounds together, we can do different kinds of trips together, but when it comes to speaking, it destroys meaning." I don' think that way. I think it is for people involved with people, for poets, for scholarly people, for various kinds of people who are agitated by the erosion of language, to reconstruct it.

Things that I think are really not important to talk about? For example, "capitalism" is so manifestly, so evidently, corrupt that one doesn't have to argue with it anymore. "Communism" except on paper doesn't exist in any livable form. Personally, I find it inessential to talk about art. Whether art has value or doesn't have value. All the definitions of art serve only the people who have made those definitions. So Trotsky's whole book on what art is and Grotowski's convictions of anti-art are empty arguments to me. I mean, one could say, "There is no use for art" or "Art is the most valuable thing in the world," and they are equal.

Americans are driven by people in power who are businessmen — those are the people who run the country. They run it entirely on the basis of more and more business, and more and more and more money . . . and a kind of human enslavement happens from this process, which is supported on every level. It is very important for me to find ways to oppose this. I oppose it in aspects of my work, I oppose it in my consciousness . . . even though I also benefit from its privileges in some ways.

AB: The power of schismatics lies in their faith, their risk and weakness, and they are sometimes burnt. You are in the leadership of the theatrical schisma. Aren't you afraid?

JC: Yes, I've been afraid of that. Since I started to be a director and founded a theatre and made innovations instead of doing what I was taught to do, I made a very, very conscious strategy. For example, the first performance that I did, I refused critics. And thereafter made very particular choices as to which critics would be invited. That was one thing. The critics control the theatre of America; they control the destiny of the theatre. Some critics are businessmen who are hired to maintain the theatre as it is. Second, The Open Theater financially was never profitable to anyone, ever. Everyone made exactly the same amount of money, except those who had children made ten dollars a week more for each child. And this was very hard to maintain. With a group there is an ongoing struggle. The institutionalized theatre has mysterious disguises—people are taken over, or destroyed, or burned, or accepted in such a way as to render the very thing you're doing without value, without life. But the stopping of The Open Theater for me was a turning point.

AB: You've stopped making a certain kind of theatre. Are you dreaming of some other?

JC: Well, I feel it better than I can describe it. I'd like to see if there is some way to bring about forms where people can speak of experience—through word, through action, through gesture, through face, through song, through voice, through silence. When I start to work, the active idea often changes completely from the idea that it becomes. The new study that I will be working on is called "The Winter Project." The necessity and danger of the exploration has to be taken from the way that we *speak* and will very probably affect the way that we will come to speak. A test to see what can be shared of experience and what can't. Also I want to work with a group again. I want to perform sometimes . . . but it's not what I want to do always.

AB: Do you believe, as Chomsky does, that there is a universal grammar? Do you believe that there is some universal grammar of emotions and that we should look for it?

JC: When you ask what is my dream, that's it. Except that that's very immodest. I do think that there are many things that are universal in human character—a basic structural histrionic common map. When I think of bourgeois cultures like we have in America, and you also have in Poland, it makes me feel that the emotions are made banal, and the repertoire of sensations stifled and classified. But it doesn't mean we don't contain an infinite range of feeling. To me, the most ambitious thing . . . the thing I would most want to do . . . the guiding thing . . . is to try to find some part of that vocabulary of emotions that is common to the human character . . . subcultural.

AB: Don't you think that in all this world of rapid motors and all that, people are sleeping?

JC: I don't know about the world. At this moment, and maybe in three months, I'll consider it counterrevolutionary again and immoral to speak that way, but at this moment it's much more my interest to awaken those who can be awakened, than to try to do it with the world. At least I haven't any clue about the whole world. If I did, if I knew what to do . . . if I had this determination the way, for example, I think my friends from The Living Theatre have a determination to transform the world, I would start doing it with television. I would try to infiltrate TV. But, for one, television repels me and, two, I'm not certain that I wouldn't be changed by my involvement in TV. But I would start there because that's where the world is looking.

AB: It's not amazing for us when something living dies and something new is born and replaces it. What amazes us is that something like that happens in art, too. Should we really believe that works of art are eternal and unshakeable? Even in the most "fluid" sense of the word . . .

JC: I think that performing theatre is different from other arts in certain ways. One of the things in stage acting is to give a kind of example to the audience. The question is, What is it an example of? Another question is, to me, essentially related. It's the question of presence. I know that it's a catch term and one can say "presence" and go into mystifications about it, but I don't mean it that way. What I mean is a certain kind of vitality, a certain kind of lifeness that is now very undervalued and often unnoticed. So that when people go to the theatre, they say, "I'm watching a movie." That's the kind of consciousness that people often bring to the theatre. To me, there is something very wrong in it. The deepest part of this question is that I feel it's often the same in terms of interaction between people. A person may not know that the other person is alive. And the theatre partakes in this kind of perplexity. I think it's related to technology. I mean, there is a kind of acceleration of people as "things" onstage. There are very few ways to talk about it.

I think, no matter how one wants to get around it, theatre has a social function. Theatre traditionally tends to be about the crisis of the time. Much of the theatre I see is much more like the movies. Sometimes the contemporary theatre that reflects the numbness and technological emptiness of the time also reinforces it. I think there are certain things about creative work that are really not explainable, until afterwards . . . and afterwards one can make certain judgments about it. But while it's going on, it's something that is really not clear. There is a kind of confusion and a kind of "lostness" . . . and out of that disequilibrium comes very often something creative. Very rarely does it come from "Now I will do this," or "This is a good idea," or "This is a good thing to serve." I think especially in the experimental arts one is always replaced . . . no way out of it. It's fairly recent for me that I have so much appreciation for traditional material. It's not temperamentally in me to do it very much . . . to do the old plays I love. But I don't want to do one production after another. Still I feel my inclination is to experiment, so to speak . . . I want to go back and forth between inherited material and experiments of this time.

AB: I have some vague feeling that art—this "Truth Content"—is for you a kind of medicine for the evil of the totalitarian world. And that art eliminates the evil . . . that it's like a prayer for a believer.

JC: I don't think it's a measurable good. I don't think it's measurable the way people might campaign for abortion reform in Italy, for example. Then you can measure whether or not the reform happens. I mean, I don't think it's a measure in terms of the good of art. To me, it's a very, very profound kind of good. For example, the Greek tragedies are an expression of a certain kind of inevitability in human interrelationships. It's not saying it's a good thing. It's saying that we are brought together in a human family . . . in some way. In the theatre of Brecht and in other kinds of political theatre, it's to see in order to make change. Greek theatre is not to change the forces, it's to know them.

And music is different, of course, and in a way much more mysterious. I used to hear stories about the SS who would listen to Beethoven and Mozart on the radio while they were keeping guard on their prisoners. So in the sense of music being good, that is not certainly true on that level. One of the things that's so marvelous in Mozart is that music is a demonstration of human creativity. That's very affirming to me . . . marvelous. Not to be worshiped in a sense of praying to it. I think it's another dimension, not a mystical or religious dimension. I mean, people create things that are not measurable and often not even useful.

So many people now, for example, are going into religious directions. Some people become alcoholics and some people get involved with drugs and some people find a very obsessive sexual escape, and all of those things are an invitation to everybody. And now there are many, many invitations for religion. Particularly, transposed Eastern religions. I don't think of art in the same way. On the contrary, I think it doesn't permit one to escape. But I'm also very close to some aspects of the mystic choice, because I also think that there is something in it which the rational world doesn't provide for the most part. So often people reject the world. And escape from the world. But the cost of leaving the world, to transcend the world, is too big a cost. Still there is a basic human yearning to transcend what's given . . . I respect it in others and I experience it in myself.

AB: How are you living in this world where almost everything has been prostituted, where words like love, truth, art are either dead or commercial?

JC: Step by step. I have never been comfortable. Every once in a while I say to myself, "Since I have never been comfortable, why should I keep trying to be?" But discomfort is something one is constantly trying to overcome. And even when I can accept one kind of discomfort, it comes in a new form, so I'm again uncomfortable. Also I feel like an exile in the world. And there again I'm not alone. And I don't have—I had ten years ago—

I don't have enormous ambition, as I mentioned before, about changing the world . . . And I am sorry in a part of me . . . a little bit regretful that I don't have it . . . but I'm not reconciled to my life as it is, and I'm not reconciled to the status quo. I'm just reconciled to the fact that total world transformation is more likely not to happen in my lifetime. Sometimes when I feel a terrible despair, it's a very, very great struggle. And despair comes in such a way that it wipes out memory of former despair. So if one can remember the pattern that one despairs and then one overcomes it, then one again has strength and the restoration to go on.

I have many hungers that go on unsatisfied. And there, I think, I'm also like everyone else. I find most people almost impossibly boring, and I act like I don't . . . but I do . . . it's a relief to say that. One of the mysteries of living is that it's impossible almost all of the time to endure . . . but I look around at all kinds of other survivors. I have many pleasures: making love, music, to be by the sea, friendships, and that's very important to me now . . . because I used not to be able to have pleasures. If I had pleasure, I would feel a little bad about it. Pleasure brought with it also another feeling of pressure. There was something wrong in pleasure and it was a betrayal to other people, and to some very abstract idea of sin that I never really defined. I'm not worried at all about becoming unconscious . . . or blank . . . or without pain . . . or without other feelings as a result of that.

AB: Your origin makes you a somewhat dreaming type . . . utopian and sentimental. You have just a good Jewish heart.

JC: Sometimes I really have the experience that birth is very accidental . . . and that I could be born in Africa in a bush, and somebody else could be me, that in fact the life that I am given to live is in a certain strange, existential way, arbitrary. Other times I feel claimed by my particular existence, by circumstances of that existence. My family were refugees in New York and never became American. They're both dead, my parents. But they never, for one hour of their lives, adapted to America . . . they were always in Eastern Europe. I was ashamed of them as emigrants, because they were hopelessly poor and haunted by problems. My father worked in a factory, which he was taken out of when they didn't need him anymore. The factory made sweaters, and we never could afford a sweater. And I never knew whether I was more ashamed of the Jewish or of the refugee thing. When they would visit school I would try to make believe I had nothing to do with them . . . and I endorsed, very much my fantasy, which I've later learned is a fantasy of many, many children. In fact, it's a universal fantasy . . . that your parents aren't your real parents, and you're really born of some other people. Sometimes you even find qualities in people and you put them together and make this fantasy-parent.

But much later, I found it necessary to reclaim those things that I, as a child, rejected very strongly. I found it important to do so — it was in me anyway, in my moods, in my languages. I only noticed my mother and father at the end of their lives. Our lives passed each other, but we didn't register each other until the end, like people who pass on a street and notice the other after crossing.

I hated being Jewish . . . I hated it. I didn't choose it, so why did I have to continue this life? If one chooses it, it seems to me reasonable that one should bear the consequences of it. But I didn't choose it; I should then be able to abandon it. Now it's quite different. I don't feel ashamed of being Jewish. I enjoy aspects of it very much. I don't wish I were anything else. I don't wish I had been christened, I don't wish I were born atheist particularly, or anything else . . . maybe sometimes I have a fantasy I was born a Sufi, because maybe I would start life with a kind of wisdom. But maybe it would be just as dogmatic in another way . . . I don't know . . .

I also feel that I have a gift . . . I don't feel it's something mysterious. I think some people have a very good singing voice, and that it's not so mysterious. If I had a good singing voice I would sing very, very often. I feel I have a kind of gift and it's related to the theatre. And I find working in the theatre, as a context, absolutely no better than working in . . . I don't know . . . a shoe store. And I don't find theatre to be a place of any special enlightenment. I feel that it's possible within the theatre to create models of the imagination. And I cherish that.

AB: Art — death — immortality — emotions . . .

JC: All my life I imagined I was going to die. My imagination of dying was much more often than the actual possibility of it. And on many more occasions this gave me something. At the same time it took something away. It gave me a kind of urgency. Immortality, I am persuaded, is a deep yearning of everyone. I think a certain kind of competition that society provokes is an exploitation of that very deep, very invisible yearning. I mean this yearning for immortality is one of the basic yearnings which one can't admit to, and can't do anything about . . . unless you are religious and you think you can. One of the things about theatre is that it doesn't survive, it's also one of the things that is precious — its perishability. It's alive and it's finished . . . it's like eating. And in theatre it's the meeting that's so deep to me, potentially, but very rarely experienced. Everybody in the theatre now takes a film of every single work they do, which, I think, is not only for the universities, but I think it's for "immortality." This film is not usually very good, because the real experiences of the theatre can't be recorded . . . Mostly the theatre I care about deals with extremes. Theatre that attempts to explore the limits, the polarities. There is such an amazing tradition of theatre as ceremony and as play. At the borders of extreme living experience is not only the tragic, but the savage, the wonder, and the limitless imagination.

Lee Breuer

INTERCULTURALISM has been an issue in the arts debate for more than a decade. Writer-director Lee Breuer, one of the founding members in 1970 of the experimental theatre group Mabou Mines, was influenced by Japanese theatre early in his artistic career. In one of his most memorable pieces, *The Shaggy Dog Animation,* Rose, a dog who is a filmmaker, is also a Bunraku-style puppet. *The Warrior Ant,* a new work at the time of this discussion with theatre critic Gabrielle Cody, was rooted in the imagery and sounds of Asian, African, Latin, and European cultures. Well before cross-cultural experiments became prevalent in international theatre, Breuer, a recent MacArthur Award winner, had evolved an aesthetic that would draw on cultural traditions beyond the European model, his poignant comment here on the profound gesture toward nothing that links Bunraku and Beckett, offering an insight into his metaphysics of art practice.

Breuer is uneasy with the one-world approach to culture and just as anxious to move beyond the cry of cultural imperialism in East-West encounters. He suspects the political and economic motives of those who promote and fund intercultural exchanges. His own cultural position is scientific: "I am more and more interested in the idea of behavior as culture, in cultural biology rather than cultural politics." Breuer views culture as a form of mass behavior, the collective acts of genetic groups, and cultural icons as the "semiotics of societies."

His *Oedipus at Colonus* was structured as a black church service, resplendent with gospel music. An all-women *Lear,* combining his interests in race and gender, took place in the rural American South, with a black actress playing Gloucester. However, as Breuer explains, gender-blind or color-blind casting is not as challenging as conceptualizing an entire production along racial and gender lines. What really preoccupies him is the dream of creating an American classicism, free to explore its own roots in the cultures of the Americas.   BGM

Conversation with Gabrielle Cody, 1989

Interculturalism and Performance

Gabrielle Cody: Your theatre work has led you to deconstruct American culture in pieces like *Prelude to Death in Venice* and *The Shaggy Dog Animation*. It seems to develop an intercultural aesthetic, culminating in *The Warrior Ant* and *Lear*. I wonder if, at this point, you have a position on interculturalism. How would you define it? What motivates you to blend cultural traditions? And what might be the political implications of such work?

Lee Breuer: I am desperately trying to develop an overview of what it means to be working interculturally in the theatre. There are a lot of underviews. They fall in the pattern of either I love the world and the world loves me, let's all get together and party interculturally, or the notion of Western cultural imperialism—that we are ripping off every cultural icon we can get hold of, and then selling it. These underviews of intercultural work are deeply enmeshed in the given politics of the moment. I'm trying to see the picture in a larger sense. But I realize that different positions are satisfactory and proper for different levels of points of view.

For instance, it is useful in contemporary politics to view intercultural events from the point of view of who owns what, which culture owns what bid, whose song belongs to whom, what dance step came from where, and who's ripping who off. It is equally useful, politically, to view intercultural activity as an attempt to get to know each other and appreciate each other's culture. But both of these approaches are morally informed; they stem from a moral point of view about what's right and what's wrong, and that morality is itself culturally determined.

I am more and more interested in the idea of behavior as culture, in cultural biology rather than cultural politics. If behavior is deterministic, part of the genetic picture, then it is a reasonable assumption that culture is part of the genetic picture as well. I think that what constitutes the basis of the form that we perceive as culture is really mass behavior, the collective behavior of various genetic groups, not single individuals. Cultures are, in a sense, the behavioral phenotype of a genetic grouping that manifests itself in certain imagery and form. What I have been trying to look at are the various cultural movements over the face of the earth through theatre. And in the same way that life is ultimately deterministic in that it replicates itself through genes, theatre is how culture duplicates itself. The idea of being theatrical—of theatre, in the abstract sense—is in itself the idea of adding energy to an image so that it will cross over and reembed itself in another individual.

Theatre is the business of constructing cultural icons, and icons are the semiotics of societies. Now the problem is that there has been a tremendous usurpation of these icons. For instance, in the Western Hemisphere, there has been an intricate influx of what, in an interesting political coup, has been called "Hispanic imagery." But it's not Hispanic, it's Indian. There is nothing Hispanic about the entire Western territory from Guatemala on down. It's Indian. The Hispanic overlay is a European usurpation of pre-Colombian imagery and energy. Spain tried to usurp the Moorish culture too. But the idea of calling this Hispanic America is a double irony. Even in naming a Third World, we give it a European metaphor. The politics are fascinating.

There is no question that we are locked in a large-scale, profoundly Darwinian biological struggle for the advantage of certain cultures. I think each culture has to be perceived as a Darwinian competing agent, just like people competing for jobs or genes competing to be chosen. It's highly biological, particularly since European standards have so far determined world morality. But what's morally white is not morally black which isn't morally Asian. Our entire idea of what is right or wrong is culturally determined. There is no universal. What I am interested in doing is to put Europe in its place in American culture, because it is only about one-third of the whole story. I am trying to work against measuring everything by European rules. But right now, in funding circles and throughout the critical establishment, all Third World aesthetics are still being viewed through European aesthetics. Third World art is defined as good, depending on how it approximates European standards. Minimalism is recognized, is considered good because Europe happens to understand minimalist art in this decade. The only way of moving toward a universal understanding is the complete interrelationship of cultures.

GC: Yes, but I think there are some problems with that argument. You seem to be implying that culture is a strictly aesthetic notion. When a culture is introduced into another context, taken out of its own setting, isn't there a risk of depoliticizing it, of neutralizing it? What about the dangers of interculturalism?

LB: Even though there is a thrust toward interrelationship of cultures, each culture is struggling at the same time to keep its own sense while being usurped by larger and more powerful cultures. So what is absolutely imperative is to ask ourselves why this thrust toward the integration of cultures even exists. For whose benefit? To whose advantage? As a white man living in New York, is it to my advantage to suggest that we integrate Caucasian and African art? Would it be to the advantage of a Sengalese? Who is saying, "Let's integrate"? We've got to allow for some cynicism in looking at the ultimate purpose of interculturalism. But I also feel deeply involved with the side that says culture can be shared, without its power being taken away in the process of the exchange.

In fact, my interest is in seeing the resurgence of cultures that have been wiped out by the European imperative. Having just gotten back from the Yucatan, I have a strong sense of the Western world stretching across the bottom of Mexico, including Guatemala and beyond. That culture is turning radically to the left, disengaging from capitalist economics, from white European thinking and theology that has attempted to quash the enormous force of pre-Colombian beliefs, and has been unsuccessful.

GC: And do you think artists in the United States have to do the same thing?

LB: Yes. When I got back to the United States in 1970, after five years in Europe, I found that my real interest was in trying to define an American classicism that didn't exist. I was angry and disturbed at the critical establishment's unquestioned purchasing of British culture as American culture. I constantly questioned whether Shakespeare should really be the key to American cultural classicism. Is Racine the culture of Haiti? Is language culture? No, language is not culture, it is just one element of it. American culture today is becoming triangular. The influx of African, Caribbean, and Asian cultural ideas, along with European ideas are creating a new culture—no longer a strictly European one. This is the ultimate melting pot. A country's classicism is its statement. Molière, Corneille, and Racine say it for France. Shakespeare says it for England, but nobody was saying it for America or they were saying it in such a minimal way, a neo-European way, that I didn't think it was really an American statement. Is O'Neill really an American statement? No, he is another Irish playwright writing another Irish play.

GC: That's one reason you're doing a Southern *Lear*, taking an English cultural statement and making it American?

LB: The idea and the fundamental question in *Lear* is whether power has its own behavior or whether it is tied to sex or race. My position is that power has its own behavior. To me, it is interesting to see the violence associated with the manipulation of power in *Lear* as executed by women onstage. Their behavior becomes not only logical, but normal. They are shocking but not beyond the realm of imagination. We rarely see this onstage. I feel that since *Lear* is about power and the metaphor for power in bourgeois society is money, it becomes important to look at race and gender and what it can represent on stage.

GC: Doesn't gender-blind and color-blind casting homogenize race and gender rather than recognize them?

LB: I don't believe in color-blind and gender-blind casting. You can't say you don't see what you see. But I do believe in the idea of conceptualizing a particular production to allow for various races, actors, actresses to take part in this representation. Casting *Lear* in the contemporary South allows for roles to be taken by black actresses. Reverse gender casting is an attempt to perceive the behavior pattern of women in a way that represents the manipulation of power in the abstract. If dogs and cats had the same opportunities for territory and wealth as men and women do in terms of *Lear*, they would tear each other's eyes out. Anything alive will react the same way. It really is Darwinian. Of course it contradicts one opinion held, that the behavior of men and power are synonymous and that the behavior of women and power is not.

GC: And you think it is?

LB: It's a debatable point. It's a question, a discussion point. Since power is perceived in economic terms, it becomes logical that Gloucester might be Lear's servant and might have had an illegitimate child with a white man, and that therefore one of the two daughters passes for white. It is logical that Goneril would have a servant who is black. I feel that I am stretching things but always logically. When you cast Gloucester as a black rural woman and Lear as a white woman with the power, you see what the play is about.

GC: You also deal with questions of power in *The Warrior Ant*. There, you draw on the Japanese warrior institution to comment on American culture.

LB: The *Ant* is a piece about machismo—about sexual politics, about contemporary political movements of feeling between men and women in the United States. It is a piece about the women's movement but with a kind of different take on it than my earlier works. *The Shaggy Dog Animation* deals with many of the same elements but from a female point of view. *Ant* is a male look at these elements, but it is a mock point of view. Bushito—the samurai tradition—is the epitome of macho, to the point of absurdity, which is an important aspect of this work. The samurai warriors in Japan were barely five feet tall. It is a humorous look at the hero, at the maleness of heroism.

GC: What is it about the Bunraku tradition that expresses you beyond your own writing?

LB: Bunraku puppetry is perfect illusion. A head of wood and a bunch of cloth lying there . . . totally lifeless. It means nothing. It has no form. Then somebody puts his hand inside the puppet and suddenly it will drink, eat, make love, fight, and die. When the hand comes out, it collapses again. This is how life is: a hand, or force of energy inside a piece of material. And this is the great lesson of Buddhist puppetry. Life is an imitation, a mechanism that can cease at any point in time. This kind of puppetry is really a prayer, a form of meditation. Plus there are other ramifications in that you see the black figures hovering around the Bunraku puppet. They are part of the mystery of where this energy comes from. You have the feeling that the puppet is both manipulating the puppeteers and they are manipulating the puppet.

GC: Is one more present than the other? Who causes the other to exist?

LB: It constantly fluctuates. That's the final dialectic. I feel that this experience is almost unspeakably exciting and astute because you are constantly aware—and this is what Beckett is all about—that every gesture is against nothing. In Beckett, every word is against the void, against death. There is no guarantee that the next word is going to happen. In this form of puppetry you have the sense that there is no guarantee the next gesture is going to happen. So the metaphysical experience of illusion and theatricality is for me readily represented in classic terms in this kind of puppetry.

GC: Was the critical response to *The Warrior Ant* part of the Darwinian battle you were discussing earlier?

LB: Yes, it was absolutely part of this battle. But the split operates on an economic level, too. There's a Marxist base to it as well. A culture is composed of any group of people that identifies itself as a group—whether economic, racial, aesthetic, or of métiers—artists versus nonartists—any group. My particular division is economic. I'm a borderline petit bourgeois or working-class intellectual. The criticism from the upper middle class is a criticism that is politically determined.

I think that a whole cultural grouping of people had problems with the *Ant* because they perceived it as politically committed even though it's not finished and a lot was unclear . . . the sense they got was that it was committed politically and that its political commitment is to the left. It's a political commitment that views Broadway and capitalist America as a lie. And since Frank Rich has already defined his favorite piece of theatre as being *Eastern Standard*, it's not surprising to me that *Ant* had nothing to say to him. I do not accept his criteria. I cannot credit him with an intellectual response to my work; it would be playing his game and the party line of the cultural elite's to pretend that there is anything motivating their criticism except self-interest. Anything that in any way threatens their metaphysics, their politics, their sociology—their wing of culture—is threatening and must be eliminated.

I gave a showing of *Lear*, which is also a work in progress, at the Public Theater. It was supposed to go to Spoleto. But it was refused. I was told it was too politically hot, too feminist, too black, too integrated, and, basically, bad for funding. Money is doing the talking now. Deep right money. The only reason we got away with *Gospel* is because it fooled people. The music essentially is nonpolitical even though the event was highly political, and one of the things that actually made me uncomfortable is that I was getting support from people I didn't want support from. I don't need conservative support, I don't want it.

Politically, the country has moved too far to the right for me to have enough support for my kind of work. I've just had a long talk with Richard Foreman and he feels exactly the same way. He wants to go back to doing closet work in his loft. I'd just as soon write. But I don't want to do any more theatre. I'm tired of spending 90 percent of my time fundraising. I am retiring. *Lear* will be my last show.

Bruce D. Schwartz, Theodora Skipitares, Julie Taymor

PUPPETS HAVE LONG BEEN ASSOCIATED with modernist theatrical practices, from symbolist and futurist plays to cabaret performances between the
wars. In the American avant-garde theatre, they played a central role in Bread
and Puppet Theatre productions, Mabou Mines' *The Shaggy Dog Animation*,
and the exquisite creations of Winston Tong. In recent years, puppetry's ac-
knowledgment as an autonomous art form was assured by the success of the
New York International Puppet Festival, held annually in the fall.

The avant-garde's interest in puppetry came about, as confirmed by the
three artists interviewed here by theatre critic C. Lee Jenner, mainly to thwart
the excessive psychological realism on which traditional theatre is based,
allowing them to explore abstract ideas in art. This approach is particularly
true of Theodora Skipitares, a sculptor whose work combines performance
art and theatre in the use of puppets, cut-out figures, and shadow images to
construct complex narratives that deal with epochal issues, such as the history of invention or, more recently, the history of medicine.

In the modernist tradition of commingling high and low art forms, Bruce
D. Schwartz in his solo performance cycle, *The Rat of Huge Proportions and
Other Works*, pays homage to both puppetry's fairground ancestry and the refined techniques of Bunraku. "There is room within the context of puppetry
for everybody, including those who aspire to high art, those who want to
hold on to the crudeness and accessibility of the form, and those, like myself,
who want both sides," he explains. During the seventies, with multimedia
theatre in vogue, artists such as Julie Taymor, later best known for her production *Juan Darien*, began using puppets and masks together with live actors
to create compelling spectacles for the stage. Drawing on her knowledge of
Indonesian and Japanese staging devices, and relying on shifts in scale and an
eclectic array of theatrical techniques, she mounts productions that "help you
move through different levels of reality." Nowhere is this more evident than
in Disney's hugely successful Broadway production of *The Lion King*, which
she directed and whose masks and costumes she designed, creating a spectacular melding of avant-garde bravura and entertaining popular fare.   GD

Conversations with C. Lee Jenner, 1983

Working with Puppets

Bruce D. Schwartz

C. Lee Jenner: What drew you to puppets at such an early age?

Bruce D. Schwartz: It's my theory that puppets appealed to me as a child because I liked to do things by myself. I think it's temperamental. One of
the family stories is that I liked to go into the closet in my bedroom, turn
on the light, shut the door, and look at picture books. I think puppet theatre lends itself to that taste.

CLJ: As you were growing up, were there any puppeteers performing whom
you particularly liked?

BDS: Burr Tillstrom. I think he is the greatest living puppeteer in the world.
I suspect he will prove to have been the greatest puppeteer of the century.
He has the biggest soul. He's sort of the Rembrandt of puppet theatre.
He uses rags, the ugliest of puppets, but they're full blown and they get
to you, move you. I have tried to catch something of that spirit with my
Elizabethan glove puppets, which are nothing but tatters of cloth.

CLJ: How do you explain the renaissance in puppetry and other popular theatre art forms?

BDS: When off-off-Broadway started in the sixties, the movement led the
new generation to search out forms that had been neglected. People were
looking for something different from what Hollywood and Broadway
offered, alternatives to conventional plays. They took up pantomime,
commedia, and folk arts like puppetry, which had fallen by the wayside.
The whole climate in the arts changed. It doesn't have to be a painting
anymore, it can be a quilt; it doesn't have to be a realistic play, it can be
a puppet show. Our ideas of what is worthy of our attention have been
modified. The whole crafts movement is a major influence on my work.
Your word, "renaissance," is a good one, because it was through the Renaissance Pleasure Fairs on the West Coast in the early seventies that the
folk revival touched me. You could buy something from people who had
made it with their own hands and see others in raggle-taggle costumes
up there onstage doing *commedia* plays and singing madrigals. Puppetry
is about as handmade as theatre can get. I make everything to do with
my shows myself—story, characters, dialogue, puppets, scenery—everything, except I do use some taped music. Up to now I have also acted all

the parts myself, too. I think people appreciate that kind of giving and the handmade aspects.

I got a lot of my so-called street sense working the fairs, and met others of like mind. The idea was to take it all away from the merchants, Hollywood moguls, TV, and the legitimate stage, and do it yourself. The Renaissance Fair as a concept has become dated and has lost its original vitality, but some of the spirit lives on.

CLJ: You mentioned meeting "others of like mind" at the Fairs. Did any of them have an influence on your work?

BDS: I met the two puppeteers from whom I learned about rod puppetry, Craig Victory, a San Francisco puppeteer, and his then-partner, Winston Tong. Craig showed me that a puppet could move gracefully. Winston changed my ideas about what a puppet should look like. Up until I met them, I'd been doing glove puppets in a crude, scrap-bag style. Winston showed me that a puppet can be exquisitely beautiful. That was a real revelation. I have very little else in common with Winston. He always had an awareness of people looking at him, whereas I have never been that kind of performer. He used puppets to express himself as himself; I try to be as much in the background as possible. He became a performance artist, working with present-moment emotions. Basically, I have a backward glance, a historical perspective. I feel that a puppet as an object is a very effective means of evoking an atmosphere of the past. I want to re-create the feeling of something that has vanished.

CLJ: Yet, your work, at least the part of it that refers back to the bawdy, Elizabethan walking puppet stage, has a very contemporary feel.

BDS: Sure. That's the comic side of my work, the central device of which sets something up and then destroys it. I establish an Elizabethan atmosphere with glove puppets and recorder music. Then, through my character, Elinor, who is an Elizabethan actress, I destroy the illusion by undercutting it with the anachronism of a raunchy, California sensibility.

CLJ: The serious side of your work draws on Victorian and Japanese traditions.

BDS: I studied in Japan for a year. Puppetry is a revered art form there. Bunraku has an intensity and release that I think audiences can find liberating. The puppets, dolls, and masked figures of many primitive societies were mediums through which the gods spoke to men, often to cure. That involves the release of an emotion or exorcism of an illness seen as a foreign presence. Japan hasn't been a primitive society for centuries, but Bunraku is a sophisticated form that does, however, retain some of that original, ritual purpose. The puppet can express large emotions, display feeling publicly, that would be impermissible in daily life and embarrassing in a human actor. You see, puppets have no egos. They can become emblems of heightened or extreme emotional states: passion, rage, sorrow. The kind of release provided is the serious counterpart of the laughter produced by comedy. With puppets you can laugh about things or behavior that real actors could never get away with.

CLJ: Besides giving you the opportunity to hide and to control all aspects of your craft, why are you attracted to puppetry?

BDS: It's the transcendence of my existence as who I am. I basically think of myself as too boring and neutral a personality to be an effective actor. I could never successfully play a Japanese court lady by myself. Neither could I be a ballet dancer, nor an eighty-year-old woman, nor a Chinese ivory statue come to life. Still, I have the desire to create these characters. I want to be them so badly, and have the audience believe in them. I just couldn't do that by myself as an actor. So, we meet, the audience and I, in the abstract figure of the puppet.

CLJ: You are never completely hidden when you perform? Why is that?

BDS: It's a paradox. I keep the mechanics out in the open because I don't want people to pay attention to them. I don't want them to wonder, "What is going on that I can't see?" My theory is that watching me move the puppets with my hands will become dull after a little while. When it does, the puppets will be more interesting than I am, and audience attention will turn to them. Also, that I am visible stresses that the puppet is not alive. I'm asking people to come *into* my fantasies with me by cutting me *out*.

CLJ: How does traditional puppet theatre differ from what we see today?

BDS: Historically, puppetry in a particular culture will almost always have an unbroken tradition, centuries long, during which puppeteers do the same scenarios from generation to generation in the same way with the same kinds of puppets, expressing a popular system. It's like balladry: there is something about ballads that has no individual personality. They express the whole tenor of a culture, its ethos or mythos. Likewise, traditional puppet forms act as mouthpieces for something that is shared. While my work is not autobiographical, all the pieces I create come from things that I respond to internally. I think that is also true of Julie Taymor and other of my contemporaries who work with puppets. We sometimes draw on long traditions, but as a framework to say something more personal, more individual, about who we are and what our concerns are.

CLJ: Does treating puppetry as a more individual art sap any of its original folk energy?

BDS: It can, but it need not. I do think it's important to remember that there is something about puppet shows that is very comic book, sitcom, low. I like that element of it. Even though I do think of puppetry as an art, it would be sad if puppet theatre was deprived of its vulgarity, crudeness, and showy tawdriness. There is room within the context of puppetry for everybody, including those who aspire to high art, those who want to hold on to the crudeness and accessibility of the form, and those, like myself, who want both sides.

Theodora Skipitares

C. Lee Jenner: You began your career as a performance artist in galleries. How were you drawn from the galleries toward theatre and puppets?

Theodora Skipitares: I didn't make my first puppet until 1980. First I studied graduate set design at NYU. That was in 1969. I was then and still am a sculptor, so my approach to theatrical design remained very sculptural and turned out to be widely impractical. For instance, one of my costumes was made out of ninety pounds of glass. Actors couldn't move in what I designed. I turned to performance art, but at the same time, I was attracted as a spectator to theatre in a more general way, theatre that had a strong performance art aspect. Part of the reason I eventually left the galleries was practical. The art world became less and less supportive of performance. It suffered an economic crisis, because of which it had to push things that would sell as big investments.

Another part was artistic. My earlier work was autobiographical, intimate, in a way, made for a small audience. I grew restless with it a year or two ago. I felt I had reached the limit to which I could go in that direction. What I began to like about a small fringe of the theatre world, extremely visual theatre, was that it often had a bigger vision than one person's, that more people were involved in it, and it had an appeal to a larger audience, even though that is only in comparison with audiences for art world performance. You have to realize, I was always somebody who worked in a studio every day alone. For my first puppet piece, *Micropolis*, I worked with an assistant, Eli Langner. For the new piece, which is bigger, I worked with four additional assistants. I find I love it. I don't ever again want to have my private visions alone in the studio hour after hour.

CLJ: Who were some of the theatre people whose work attracted you?

TS: Grotowski was teaching at NYU, and the work of Mabou Mines, Richard Foreman, Robert Wilson, and The Wooster Group helped form my vision. All of Liz LeCompte's work, starting with the *Trilogy*, has been very influential, and the marriage of performance art and theatre happened for me when I saw Spalding Gray's first monologue. The two forms merged in such a complete way that the term "performance art" no longer has any meaning for me. What was wonderful about performance art while it lasted, and that Spalding retains, was the totally fresh, off-the-wall attempt to deal with live presence.

CLJ: How and why did you come to use puppets?

TS: My interest in sculptural figures eventually drew me to puppets. I had been making static pieces with objects, masks, a stainless steel apron on which I lit candles—all objects used in tableaux. Slowly the pace with which I wanted to move from one tableau to the next wanted some kind of animation. As I came to the end of my life as a solo performer telling stories of my life, I wanted, as I mentioned, to work with other people. Yet, I still didn't want to bring other performers into my work. So, what do you do to include other voices? Puppets, little humanoids.

CLJ: Describe the making of your first puppet.

TS: The first one is the figure that became Sylvia in *Micropolis*. I did a sculpture, about one-third life-size, which was a very carefully made self-portrait of my whole body. It just sat around my studio for the longest time. For *Micropolis*, I made a mold and I turned out these female forms. I used my face on the dinosaur in the last scene, too. Even the male puppets were adjusted Theodoras. My latest piece, still untitled, is dominated by men. My assistant and I took a female Theodora and we slightly changed her body and added male genitals; then we made a new mold, generating new, maleish Theodoras. I should add that my new piece is historical. It's about invention. Two of the puppets represent identifiable historical figures. That's a big change both in subject matter and in using a model other than myself.

CLJ: Interesting progression: first you include your real physical self in works of autobiographical performance art; next you step physically to the borders of your work and send in look-alike substitutes; now some of the puppets either are not based on your image at all, or that image undergoes such extensive plastic surgery that only you could spot the kinship.

TS: It's part of my movement away from pure performance art. Half naively I have stumbled in my own way, in my own time frame, into my own kind of theatre. My work is increasingly taking a theatrical direction. The puppets did that for me. The puppets *on their own* do that. I feel the need in these early eighties for didactic theatre that communicates through at least some popular elements. For me the puppet is one of those elements.

CLS: Had you seen any puppet theatre that influenced your work?

TS: I was really taken by Winston Tong's work when I first saw it. What I share with him is a unique way of mixing media. That was once a pretty clear characteristic of performance art. For instance, I would never call Winston a puppeteer. I don't even want to call myself a puppeteer, because that's just one of the things that I'm working with. Winston is a wonderful actor, there are incredibly interesting things going on in terms of the sound tape, there are rich visual things, *and* the puppets.

CLJ: Do you feel as if you are a part of a group of puppeteer/experimentalists?

TS: More and more. Besides Winston Tong's impression on me, there was Lee Breuer's *Shaggy Dog Animation*. When I first saw those puppets, I thought to myself, "This is the perfect way to translate Bunraku." He wasn't re-creating Bunraku characters and plays, but putting the characters into a contemporary story and dressing them in blue jeans. Breuer is another guy who dared to throw together the most disparate things, wild combinations. And then there's his strong connection to Brecht. Distancing devices always recall Brecht to me and *Shaggy Dog* was just full of them. My work, too, is beginning to be full of them. Puppetry itself is one. I'm now using different sizes of puppets juxtaposed: thirty-inch puppets next to five-foot puppets next to a live reader who reads the lines of the puppets. Maybe it's even Piscator, too. After all, he was the first multimedia maniac, wasn't he?

CLJ: What direction is your current work taking?

TS: I'm starting to be more and more interested in using the puppets for propaganda, a cross between sculpture and propaganda. I've discovered that you can put a puppet up there and you can do so many things that you would never be able to pull off with a human actor. Why that is I don't really know. Maybe the ego of the actor interferes at times, casting a competitive magnetic field.

CLJ: What is the connection between your own persona and that of the puppets you use?

TS: I remember being amazed by the look of caring, and love, and focus that the four or five people handling the puppets in *Shaggy Dog* would direct toward the figures. That must have stayed with me, because it's happening in my work now. In my latest piece I have five-foot puppets and several people manipulate each one. You glance occasionally at the performers, and on their faces there is this look of love, adoration. You see that in Bruce Schwartz's work, too. He always seems to go into a trance at times. He closes his eyes a lot, the better to focus inwardly. It's a tremendously intimate kind of thing. And then, I'm not an actor, but with puppets I think I've found a way for me to be one by extension. I'm on stage, in shadow, with my energy directed toward the puppet, who in turn directs toward the audience. That's comfortable for me.

CLJ: I'm surprised you have any discomfort at all with performing. After all, your earlier works were solo performances.

TS: Well, yes and no. Working against those big walls, I developed a notation system to tell a story. It was like reading a painting. I certainly was there physically, but I functioned as someone who got objects ready to tell the next phase of the story. I was a glorified stagehand, really, just as Japanese puppeteers are stagehands, sacred stagehands. I was a designer/technician, functioning in front of people and I still function in that way. I don't do autobiographical works anymore, but I'm present in the works, speaking and handling the puppets. I suspect that even though the autobiographical impulse has almost disappeared, I still want that to be in my work as much as possible.

Julie Taymor

C. Lee Jenner: Puppetry, magic, clowning, and other popular theatre arts have captured the imaginations of a number of innovative theatre people in the past decade or two. Why?

Julie Taymor: Because if theatre is going to survive, it has to do what it does best. What it does best is the nonliteral. Film and television have virtually coopted naturalism. To compete, theatre must be more theatrical.

CLJ: Puppets are naturally theatrical, aren't they?

JT: Exactly. If you want to create a big emotion, you can have a giant woman with one huge crystal tear. It's much more poetic and abstract. In *The Haggadah,* for example, I used a piece of flannel cloth split down the middle for the parting of the Red Sea. By abstraction, it became an image, a poetic metaphor. Same thing with the Seven Plagues. By using shadow puppets to symbolize them, I could present the essence of each one with artistic economy and in a stageworthy way. The beauty of puppetry is that it takes the everyday and puts it into another style so that you gain a new appreciation of it. The theatre gets boring when it's trying to do what the mechanical media do better. Magic doesn't work on television, where it could be an electronic trick. The skill of a Bill Irwin or a juggler or an acrobat or a puppeteer is very tangible, accessible. You know it's not produced by some kind of technology that you don't understand, so the magic of transforming a character or locale is doubly powerful. With puppetry, the third dimension, which is missing from camera art, is very important.

CLJ: Your work tends to be large-scale, doesn't it?

JT: Yes, and I couldn't do that if it weren't for puppets. I don't have to worry about finding enough money to pay for the hordes of actors needed for a battle scene. I will use a scroll with hundreds of people painted on it, but only two live people paid to manipulate that scroll. And if I want characters to be ambushed, I can use the scroll of painted soldiers to encircle them. I work something like a film director. Crowd scenes in the equivalent of long shot, using lots of small puppets. Then, say, for an interior monologue, I will empty the stage and pinspot a live actress. That's like close-up. If you want extreme close-up, you might have a huge, painted puppet face. I did that for *Savages* at the Center Stage. What is key here is mixture. I don't really consider myself a puppeteer. I am a theatre maker, a mixed-media artist. I just use puppets as one medium, even though I use them a lot. For example, *Tirai*, the play I created with my Indonesian company, uses masked actors and no puppets at all.

CLJ: So the scale and mixing are crucial to you?

JT: Very much so. The change of scale, the mixture of media—live actors, next to masked actors, next to puppets—helps you move through different levels of reality. You can go from a normal, naturalistic scene straight into fantasy or the grotesque just by switching from people to puppets.

CLJ: When did you start to use puppets?

JT: I played with marionettes when I was a child. Later, I was impressed by both the Bread and Puppet Theatre and the Chinese Shadow Puppets, which toured when I was an undergraduate at Oberlin. Then I went out to the Society for Eastern Arts in Seattle one summer to study Javanese shadow puppetry, woodcarving, and Japanese forms. I was intrigued with the techniques more than anything else. My first puppets were created for a campus production of Brecht's *The Elephant Calf*. About the same time I made up my own version of Bunraku for *Peer Gynt*. Designing an epic like that one with puppets really fascinated me, partly because I loved the idea of staging a huge, complex thing with grand ideas in a simple old medium.

CLJ: What did you learn from studying with Peter Schumann?

JT: I learned puppet construction mostly. Peter's primitive style doesn't come naturally to me. Therefore, it would be pretentious if I tried to emulate him. I think I can achieve my own kind of simplicity in a different way, by selecting my techniques. For instance, I used projections of IBM cards for a city building in *Way of Snow.* The means are simple, but not the visual style. My style is more complex and sophisticated than Peter's. One isn't better than the other, just different. Also, Peter has an identity, both stylistic and in terms of themes. I'm much more eclectic. I like to challenge myself, so I pick my medium and technique and adapt my style according to what I have to say. I work to develop new approaches each time.

CLJ: How have you made Javanese and Japanese theatre crafts your own?

JT: From the Japanese theatre I took the idea that there is first a form. To know the limitations of that form is the only way you can know how and if you can fill it. A form lets you know the end. You can see this principle in *Way of Snow.* The shaman costumes are very difficult to deal with, but they give a structure and a shape that helps define the work of the performer. You have to look at the essence of something if you are going to use puppets. The Woman Who Walked puppet in the same play could only walk. That's the strength of it. It goes to the extreme of what it should do. Beyond philosophic things, what I absorbed from Asian puppetry was, again, technique, not style.

CLJ: You majored in folklore and mythology at Oberlin. Did your study of shamanism and the ritual origins of theatre influence your vision of theatre?

JT: Yes. I was particularly interested in masks, I noticed right off that you could use them to break down the barriers between what is real and what isn't. You see, I'd been involved with experimental theatre since I was thirteen, when I joined the young people's division of Julie Portman's company in Boston. At Oberlin I was working with Herbert Blau. I already knew that theatre was based on cultural rituals, storytelling, and religion, so studying folklore and myth was an inspiration to me theatrically.

CLJ: How do you choose when to use a puppet and when to use a live person?

JT: As soon as you put a mask on, to me you're a puppet. Puppets are ideographs, emblems of either character, state of mind, or emotion. One puppet represents anger, another puppet represents power—they become archetypes, ideas. Schumann's Fatso has no personality; he represents all rich businessmen who run the world—he's the archetype. Take *Savages:* I was supposed to design costumes for Brazilian Indians, and Brazilian Indians don't wear anything. If you use nude people, it's distracting and it becomes extremely personalized.

CLJ: How about using puppets as a distancing device?

JT: That's part of what I've been talking about. They objectify. That's what Brecht was all about, and why his plays work so well in puppetry. Puppets automatically distance you. Some people think that's dehumanizing and antiemotional, but I find it more moving that way. You don't get caught up in the idiosyncracies of a performer and can focus on the essence of character or emotion.

CLJ: What else do you like to mix besides people and puppets?

JT: Scales and styles. *Tirai* had dance and mask and acting styles ranging from traditional Asian to realism. I do it really because it's fun. I'm serious about theatre but at the same time I want to entertain myself and audiences. The theatre I found in Indonesia had both those things. It didn't fall into little boxes. There is no children's theatre versus elite, intellectual theatre. It is all one theatre. I try to do that, too. That's why I use puppets and other visuals so heavily. If you don't get all the intellectualization, all the meaning behind something, you can still enjoy the raw story, the entertainment part.

Laurie Anderson

"HELLO. EXCUSE ME. Can you tell me where I am?" The friendly demeanor of Laurie Anderson's inquiry, echoing through *United States, Part II*, belies her darker opinions of big government, corporations, and nuclear missile sites masquerading as grain silos on Midwestern farms. Created by a thirty-three-year-old Anderson, as a work-in-progress that would grow to four parts three years later, *United States, Part II* premiered in 1980, as one of the most innovative musical works to be seen in New York since the 1976 Wilson–Glass opera, *Einstein on the Beach*.

Anderson, a performer of great charm and androgynous dimpled-looks, appeared in a black suit, trademark hair on end, accompanied by two other singers and five musicians, her voice famously altered through the use of vocoder and harmonizer. A highlight of the performance was her use of the tape-bow violin with its playback head in place of strings, Anderson's white wand of light cutting diagonals into the blackness onstage. *United States*, with its art world concerns and pop affinities, combined photography, drawings, film, slides, video, and electronic sound in an aesthetic openness comfortable with both minimalism and the cartoon strip. The cool, mediated style of this work was evident in the collage of texts and rhetorical textures through which a wired-up Anderson talked and told stories of Reagan's America and showed off her quirky humor and sophisticated wordplay, even quoting William Burroughs with her song, "Language Is a Virus."

"Is it performance or theatre?" the savvy John Howell who published a book on Anderson asks her, knowing well the New York art world's bias against theatre. But this issue was already fading by the early eighties, as theatricality and spectacle became more characteristic of the arts and of American culture itself. Anderson, who brought visual art and popular culture, the avant-garde and mass media, closer together in a special kind of American vernacular, is already expressing her feeling of constraint in the "downtown" culture, and longing for a wider audience. She was soon to have it.   BGM

Conversation with John Howell, 1980

United States

John Howell: How did this four-part *United States* performance begin?

Laurie Anderson: I did a birthday party concert for Horace Solomon at Carnegie Recital Hall in 1979. That was an early version of *Part I,* then called *Americans on the Move.* It was a sort of holiday for keyboards with six of us playing because I wanted a really massive sound. When I did other versions of that piece later by myself, I began to see what the important parts were and to weed out the musical lines that didn't need to be there. Then what happened was that I had to fill it up somehow and be more in the foreground myself. Then in a way, I felt more comfortable because I had more control.

JH: *Americans on the Move, Part I,* or as you now call it, *United States, Part I,* is a solo performance with a few supporting players. In *Part II* you worked with a large rock band. How did that affect your performance?

LA: The problem was how to keep my words foreground and still let the music cook. The rock solution is to use repetitive language, that's one choice. But a one-shot concert is not like a record, where you have a chance to pick it up after listening three or four times. You either hear the words and pay a lot of attention to them or you don't bother. So I tried to keep the instrumentation real simple by keeping the musical pitches within talking range. Then you can pay the same kind of attention to the voice as to the melody. But even then, with so many people coming in with their musical lines, I didn't feel quite free enough to put more of myself in. So I didn't feel that I was quite *there* in the Orpheum performance.

JH: Does *Part II* have a solo version?

LA: I just performed it solo for the first time and I liked it a lot better although I missed hearing the other musicians.

JH: Let's talk about *Part II*'s songs. The program note says the song "O Superman" is "for Massenet." How did that happen?

LA: I heard a concert by Charles Holland, an incredible singer who worked with Fletcher Henderson in the thirties. He couldn't get much work in the United States so he moved to Amsterdam. He and Dennis Russell-Davies did a concert in Berkeley that I heard in May. The guy was so nervous because he was coming home after thirty years of being a musical exile that he couldn't sing. He dropped his glasses, dropped the music, apologized after each song, saying, "I'm sorry, this is a beautiful song and I've ruined it." The audience was just dying for him. Then he began this

Massenet song which is really a kind of prayer: "O Souverain, O Juge, O Pere," then lyrics that say "All my dreams of glory are gone, your picture is in my soul, I submit to you, the light is dark, the soldiers march." I could only pick up fragments of the French. Suddenly he could sing because this song was an appeal for help. It was an amazing turnaround moment, the feeling in that room was very intense, and everyone was so relieved. I couldn't stop thinking about those first five notes of the melody—after that I couldn't remember how it went. So "O Superman" was made around those fragments.

JH: What about that counterpoint line behind the main theme? Sometimes it sounds like "Ha-ha-ha-Ha-ha-ha," like laughter, and other times it sounds like "Ah-ah-ah-Ah-ah-ah," like sighs.

LA: I thought of it as "ah." Rudolf Steiner thought that children should be taught the alphabet by getting them to believe that every sound has an emotion. So that when they pronounce "a," they should really let loose an "AH."

JH: Have you heard this technique in action? It sounds frightening.

LA: It is. I heard it in Bern at a special school.

JH: Did you think about *Part II* as being infantile?

LA: Sure. Babies is a kind of theme, this is a piece for a certain kind of baby. Someone said it was macrocephalic. You know those Dürer drawings of babies? That was the image. That would be frightening if adults had the proportions of babies.

JH: That image appeared several times. There's the mailman's nightmare—

LA: —who dreams that everyone in the world has a baby's proportions. People can't read or write and he sees them walking down the street. It's a dream that I had, part of a series in which I asked people who had a profession related to the dream to read them. In this case I chose a mailman because of the aspect of delivery.

JH: How did the idea of "baby" affect your language?

LA: I tried to keep words to one or two syllables. That was one goal, to do a very Anglo-Saxon language piece with as many nouns as possible, to be as concrete and basic as I could. Also, the percussive aspect of the electronics I was using, and especially the repeat mode on the harmonizer, tended to influence the music because a lot of the basic tracks came from them. I wanted to pair that sense of a digital beat to appropriate language: nothing too flowery. So the words tended to be short. The phrasing tended to be slogans or repetitive progressions, like "when love is gone there's always justice, when justice is gone there's always force."

JH: Then you go on to say "there's always Mom." Don't those responses that objected to feelings of helplessness come from those baby allusions, from coupling the loss of love and justice with Mom?

LA: You could make a case for that. The six times babyhood is pointed to powerlessness is present. But I was surprised when people told me that the piece was satanic.

JH: Referring to all the blackness?

LA: I think they meant dark, scary, evil. Well, I don't know about evil.

JH: There is a tradition that black or dark equals evil.

LA: It was not really intended to be so dark. We were trying some backlighting.

JH: Isn't that talk about color a way of talking about emotional tone, of apocalyptic content? Could we say that your earlier performances were more humorous and autobiographically anecdotal, and that *Part II* is straight eighties politics, and that's a grim picture?

LA: It was very odd for me to hear that this was a helpless, hopeless piece because I think you can talk about things without being them. My impression about performing is that I don't feel helpless, and I didn't feel that the work would encourage people to feel helpless. I was interested in infantilism but I don't feel infantile. I don't think you have to be what you talk about.

JH: When we talked about acting and nonacting in performance last year you spoke of not using "I" so much in your texts and attitudes.

LA: In *Part II* I tried as much as possible to be an observer more than a first-person commentator, and to try to stick to some kinds of factual information. There are several sections that begin with "I" or an implied "I" that's more like acting. That William F. Buckley song, for example, "Private Property," is an attempt to refer to his voice as well as talk about him. The flip side of that is that I didn't say "you" consciously in *Part II*. There was a floating idea of babyhood. Now I was not the baby. Who was? The viewer is not about to think, "I'm the baby." So babyhood just hovers around.

JH: You're not saying you don't take on any of the characteristics or moods of whatever you're talking about?

LA: Oh I do. Right now I feel helpless politically as I think a lot of people do. But that's not the extent of what I feel, it's one mood. One of the reasons that I want to do the whole *United States* as a four-part series is that there are other moods in other parts.

JH: There's a lot of frustration in *Part II:* The first few stories are "I can't speak French," "I can't see the traffic," "There's a newspaper strike on and everything's wrong on television," and so on. There's a repeated idea that things are going wrong in a very powerful and significant way. Don't you think that some of the audience projected those expressions as your feelings because they didn't want to admit to their own frustration or political helplessness?

LA: What resentment there was only reinforced my own ideas about how people do feel helpless. I don't see how it could be any other way after being able to feel your own political power in the sixties.

JH: The first group of stories ended with the image of gridlock, the ultimate irony of the highly technical, complexly organized society—of which New York is supposedly the epitome—frozen in complete paralysis.

LA: I don't blame people for not wanting to identify too heavily with that, it's not a beautiful picture. But I didn't see any reason to soften it or to come to terms with it, I just wanted to present it.

JH: Don't you occupy a politically ambiguous zone by only pointing to issues and refusing to specify solutions?

LA: I don't think of myself in any way as a warmonger, but if you start pointing to information like that, you have to take a clear position about your feelings. I tried to avoid taking a political position although I'm sure I did just that by the way things worked out.

JH: Do you think the piece itself has a politics?

LA: Let's say that it's political sense, a certain kind of attitude that I think people in the art world share. I didn't really say what I thought should be done. I'm not running for office. It's not my job and it's not what interested me in doing this work. Politics is about problem solving. I wasn't attempting to solve any problems, I was simply looking at problems and using them for my own purposes. One of my purposes was to see what kind of real, basic, down-home attitudes have to do with political attitudes. Another reason I chose to look at these issues is that I'm really bored with working with things that can only be judged in aesthetic terms. That's not enough anymore. I wanted to look at something more or less real, although the more I looked at these particular political issues, the more unbelievable they became.

JH: We could call them subjects of the larger world. The news seems very unreal these days.

LA: Someone wrote that *U.S. Part II* was a lot of in-group wordplay and asked, "What does it mean?" This person is, I believe, a dance critic. I'd never ask what a dance "means." In all of the work I've ever done, my whole intention was not to map out meanings but to make a field situation. I'm interested in facts, images, and theories that resonate against each other, not in offering solutions. And also *not* in stating my case in a way that is dogmatic. I don't think that means that the work is unclear or that it's just playing with words.

JH: So it's more an impression than an analysis —

LA: —like a thermometer —

JH: —taking the temperature of the subject rather than x-raying it. Most viewers found that *Part II*'s dark mood and so-called lack of answers was an accurate and moving picture.

LA: But those other reactions are the ones that interest me the most. It really bothers me that some people felt that it was upsetting, that it was frustrating.

JH: Was working on the piece frustrating for you?

LA: Yes, but it became my channel for saying something about that mood so maybe I was able to relieve myself.

JH: I know you feel that the work's refusal to present solutions doesn't imply any lack of meaning, but when you say you don't ask what something means . . .

LA: I take that back. By "mean" I meant to write a paragraph, to distill the whole experience so that you end up with "she's talking about frustation." That doesn't tell you anything. I certainly didn't mean that this piece meant nothing.

JH: You're saying that your meanings are not detachable from the complex of ways — text, music, visual image, media — in which you are presenting them.

LA: Exactly. This code is opaque. *Part II* was about a certain mood that *was* that mood. The song "Let X=X" was saying leave this code alone, this code is self-reflexive.

JH: Reducing or summarizing your statement is not your job.

LA: Right. I'm only interested in thinking that way when I see other people's work.

JH: In earlier performances, your texts were more about storytelling, narrative anecdotes in which the listener is mostly a passive receiver. Are you opening up that mode in *Part II?*

LA: These days I feel more comfortable with songs that are more disjunctive than linear. This piece is more about words than others but in another way. How can you say what's on your mind without letting it all out? People came down on that, too, saying I used language to say that it was impossible to use it.

JH: Do you plead guilty? What about the song for Burroughs, "Language Is a Virus"?

LA: One of Burroughs' main themes is that language is a kind of disease and that when you open your mouth, you should know it's communicable. If you interpret that statement in the Buddhist sense of getting rid of the split between the thing and the word, then the idea is "don't name it, let it exist." So I don't feel I was untrue to one sense of Burroughs' quote. I referred to things but didn't get carried away with their analysis. You can say a word, refer to that word in a discrete situation, then let it sit as a noun.

JH: You also referred to that original language-as-problem man, Wittgenstein.

LA: In Bern I met Jacqueline Burkhardt, a descendant of Jacob Burkhardt, one of my cultural heroes. She came to my solo performance of *Part II* and couldn't believe this translation of Wittgenstein's quote. She said it should be "If you can't talk about it, don't talk about it at all" instead of "If you can't talk about it, point to it." She also said she loved my translation because it was so mute and clear in itself.

JH: I think the last phrase is something like "be silent" in German. How was *Part II* received in Europe?

LA: Very well. Europeans didn't identify with it so directly so there wasn't that immediate problem with the politics. But it was not taken as political propaganda either; the reactions focused on the language issue. On the whole, the piece was more clearly perceived there than in New York.

JH: Did you feel like you were feeding Europe a black view of America that they like to have confirmed?

LA: I had some reservations about that but I can't rewrite a work for each audience.

JH: Were you surprised by how people took you to be or not be "you" in *Part II?*

LA: I was surprised nobody asked why I was in drag, a reaction I got when I first started using those clothes with those male voice filters.

JH: It's ambiguous because you're using several voices, filtering your voice through electronics to create voices that are part yours and part machine, part you and part that other voice.

LA: When I'm doing a song with that deep male voice, I completely disassociate myself from it. It seems so separate, it really is another voice coming out of a speaker over there. It's not me, it's the Voice of Authority, an attempt to create a corporate voice, a kind of "Newsweekese."

JH: How do you feel about your voice as an instrument?

LA: Captain Beefheart or Meredith Monk have voices that are really musical instruments. I have the voice I'm using now. I guess I could take voice lessons, but I'm not interested in that kind of virtuosity. If I can achieve the effect I want electronically, I will.

JH: Did the experience of performing at the Orpheum Theatre make you think about differences between performance and theatre?

LA: I've lost interest in that as a distinction.

JH: Are you saying the labels have no meaning?

LA: No, but I don't think about it. I don't think the work becomes more or less theatrical because of the space. I don't wonder whether I'm doing performance or theatre, and basically I don't care what it's called at this point. I used to be manic about the fact that I was not doing theatre. Maybe it's because I'm getting closer to theatre that I don't care, maybe it's a way of saying that it's okay to be theatre if that's what it is.

JH: Don't you think that question influences how people perceive what you're doing? You know there are mixed feelings in the art world about "theatre."

LA: Oh sure, but I like the idea of work entering the culture in a different way and that's what I'm trying to do. For years I've thought about a way to have something to do with the larger culture rather than just being part of a museum-gallery, downtown art culture, and to try to get away from being supported only by government funds. Radio is another way out.

JH: *Part III* will be about money, what about *Part IV?*

LA: Love. That's a solo.

JH: And you'll do the whole cycle at once when those parts are finished?

LA: I would like to do two parts a night, two three-hour shows on consecutive nights, which would show all four parts. I feel very strongly that there's a lot of consistency in these pieces and that they need to be done together even if just to avoid things like misunderstandings about the politics in *Part II.*

JH: Were you surprised by the large audience for this Orpheum show and the extensive publicity it attracted?

LA: I don't think of myself or my work in terms of fashion. I think of this as something I'm going to be doing for a long time. If my work appears fashionable, I think I'll survive that. Performance art was fashionable five years ago, it's out of fashion now.

JH: Fashion in art now is a certain kind of painting.

LA: Fashion—art: a snake that bites its own tail.

Richard Elovich, Karen Finley, Ishmael Houston-Jones, John Kelly

AT THE END OF THE EIGHTIES, the performance scene had vastly changed from the work of a decade earlier. Issues of race, gender, and identity had moved performance toward the linkage of the autobiographical and social and away from the formal and stylistic, from group to solo work, and, therefore, to the body, reflected in a turn to personal expression as the center of contemporary performance life. However, the contrapuntal voices of these artists, whose work has been supported by "downtown" spaces such as The Kitchen, P.S. 122, La MaMa, Dance Theatre Workshop, and Danspace, demonstrate in this series of remarks recorded by *PAJ* contributing editor Marc Robinson that performance is not easily categorizable or always moving in one direction. If both Karen Finley and Ishmael Houston-Jones emphasize the importance of the authentic self improvised from personal histories that aspire to universals, Richard Elovich and John Kelly draw their inspiration from the images and texts of other artworks. Houston-Jones sums up the ambitions of his era: "I am going back and searching for roots in some sense: performance roots, personal roots, historical roots."

One of the characteristics of the decade was a return to narrative and to an interest in biography and storytelling. In describing her way of connecting to an audience Finley says, "I try to point out that we all have a story." The talking pieces of Trisha Brown and the autobiographical works of Spalding Gray are cited as influential examples of the use of speech in performance, but also as approaches to breaking down the boundaries between audience and performer. Elovich notes his interest "in a kind of Cubism in performance," where the focus is on the activity of looking rather than on an art object. Kelly's views also express a visual arts perspective, but to a declaration that all his work is autobiographical he adds an interesting aesthetic touch: "the work is not so much about my life; it's more about my way of looking." The focus on the personal has favored artistic process over the work of art and challenged widely held notions of spectatorship and aesthetic experience, as these performers elaborate. BGM

Conversations with Marc Robinson, 1987

Performance Strategies

Ishmael Houston-Jones

I want to use performance as a way to equalize the power relationship between the audience and the performer. I'm concerned about how much control I have over an audience—and about the power I have as a performer to inflict my vision on them. So during my performances I try to make it clear that I am not extraordinarily different from a lot of people in the audience—that I'm a person, too; that I have a history and a life away from the stage. A lot of current work is very elitist, art made for artists, full of "in" jokes. It's usually very distant: behind the proscenium, in front of scenery, under lights, curtained. It's almost like TV. In fact, the performance could be on monitors, for it doesn't seem to matter that there are real people doing it. I hope my work never seems like that. It should be accessible and open for most people. I always want to remind the audience that they're watching a performance made by a human being.

If I use any technique to do this, it's improvisation. I don't like seeing an obviously trained, highly visible virtuosity in dance and performance work—a skill that sets the audience in opposition, or the performer in a position of superiority. So, I do movement that almost anyone my age, in reasonably good shape, could do. And I allow myself to be open enough to let things happen at the moment.

I write like I dance: it's automatic, unedited, improvised work. I approach the page in the same way as I approach the stage. I started using texts with my dance around the time I saw Trisha Brown do her talking piece, *Accumulation with Talking plus Watermotor*. That's not something I would ever do, but I like seeing her keep two stories and two dances going at the same time, switching back and forth. In my work, I was stuck in a storytelling mode. The work was really literal: it wasn't writing for performance. So I began to reduce the writing, until finally all my writing became lists. For *DEAD* I improvised a list of all the people I could remember who had died while I had been alive. The *f/i/s/s/i/o/n/i/n/g* program contains a list of twenty-three sentences. In *Relatives*, I list the names in a family history while I dance. This kind of improvisation, both with words and movement, seems like a less manipulative way of performing.

I was very influenced in all these choices by the early work of Steve

Paxton. I have very little technical training, unlike your average dancer working in New York, but I did do political theatre in college, some street work. In Philadelphia, I worked with the dancer Terry Fox and a musician, Jeff Cain, for two years—just jamming together, occasionally improvising a performance. Then I came to New York, where I've been working with several other improvisers—Daniel Lepkoff, Stephanie Skura, Yvonne Meier, Fred Holland, and the whole Open Movement project—for the past seven years.

Since coming to New York, some of my most memorable experiences have been leaving New York: I visited Nicaragua twice. The first time in 1983, to observe a theatre festival, then again in 1984. I was a guest of the government the first time, but I traveled there on my own for the second visit—just got on an airplane and went. I wound up teaching at a theatre school for a month.

I got really turned on by the place. Two Nicaraguan theatre people— Alan Bolt and Jeanette Jarquin (Jeanette was killed between my two visits)—shared with me their process of making practical, accessible work. They take their work out of the art context and bring it to the campesinos: they do it in fields, in factories, and on farms.

I find that way of working very scary—but really successful. I wish I did it more. I once performed at a senior citizen center in the Bronx, a lecture/demonstration to fulfill the community service requirement of my New York Foundation fellowship. That performance really opened me up to a lot of possibilities—especially the conversations with the senior citizens afterwards. I always ask myself why I'm afraid to do that more, to take my work into another context. It's very comfortable to perform for an informed audience, one that takes the form of the work as a given. But I need to break out of the downtown ghetto. I'd like to take my work to other cities, to get away from here for a while.

Those performances in the Bronx and the ones I learned about in Nicaragua lessened the distance between the performer and the spectator. In all my work, I'm still trying to do more of that. Sometimes, I'll describe how I made the piece while I perform it: that commentary becomes a leveling device. In *Cowboys, Dreams, and Ladders*, I described how Fred Holland and I researched the piece—going to the Lincoln Center library, looking at videotapes of Agnes de Mille ballets. In *Relatives* I describe the style of my dancing, explaining why, for instance, I am dancing in the dark. When I was first performing *f/i/s/s/i/o/n/i/n/g* I talked about my feelings about being a political artist and making a piece of political dance. All of this narration, this talking about myself, opens up the pieces, makes them less remote.

I use autobiography for the same reason. In *Them*, especially, I was working out parts of myself, working out fears of disease, violence, and death, trying to find a way of dealing with those issues for myself. That's how autobiography lets the audience in. I don't want to make hermetic work, but I don't know how to make political work that's not personal: I'm trying to show myself as a human being facing these big issues—and sometimes failing. In my life, as well, I sometimes fail to deal with these issues—but I'm not afraid to do that publicly.

Consequently, a lot of my work has to do with invisibility—hiding identity to survive artistically, or revealing identity to be subversive artistically. I try to subvert invisibility through performance—to bring what's invisible out into the open. As a black man in mostly white downtown performance, I became fascinated with the idea of invisibility. So, in *Adolfo und Maria*, I put a multiracial cast in blackface, then set it in Nazi Germany. In *Cowboys, Dreams, and Ladders* Fred and I looked at the invisibility of the black cowboy. Improvisation itself is almost an invisible form these days. I am making my life visible with my work—offering my view of what America is, or what my life in America is. I'm asking people not to accept certain conventions as either the norm or as an acceptable way of life. I am going back and searching for roots in some sense: performance roots, personal roots, historical roots. I try not to forget history, personal and global. I try to remember that we're on a continuum— that this is not an ending. What my mother said in *Relatives* is very true: "You've got to know where you've come from before you know where you're going."

It's difficult to figure out where performance is going next. I think that it's getting more Republican. I see people from my own generation whose work I thought was very interesting four or five years ago now becoming much more formal in a much less interesting way. I've nothing against someone's work becoming less slapdash and chaotic, but I'm disturbed by the "least-common-denominator"-ism of current work. There seem to be two trends. One is naive-but-fun nihilism: the mess girls— Dancenoise, Mimi Goese, Jo Andres. They are all exploring and working with chaos. On the other hand, there is a lot of more formal work—practically ballets. Work that doesn't show the mining, that doesn't go deeper into the structure and form. The first type of work seems to be made by women, mostly; the second type, by a lot of younger men.

My own work tends to change radically, because my interests change radically from piece to piece. *Adolfo und Maria* and *Them* were made in the same year. I think the press and the public don't know what to do with me. People don't know what the handle is. But my work does reflect my personality—my worldview, shaped by thirty-five years of living, being alive and being aware—letting stuff in and letting it flow out again: improvisation as a performance mode and as a way of life.

John Kelly

I was trained as a visual artist, so performing is a lot like drawing: it is about line, color, and shape—separate elements assembled into a composition. When I drew regularly, I would work in short bursts, ten or twenty minutes, and then stop. Later I would come back and start again. I worked to music. It was a highly concentrated and intense activity that would manifest itself in my body—a dramatic way of working. I loved the *doing* of painting more than the result. The result was important, but mostly as a record of what you just went through. Painting didn't need to look beautiful or pretty. If you went through something, it was going to be beautiful in itself, unlike anything else. When I started performing, I just translated that activity to the stage. I used the same process. Performance is visual art that remains process.

A lot of my work asks, "What is an artist?" Most of my characters are artists of one kind or another: that's a deliberate choice. In that way, all my work is autobiographical. However, the work is not so much about my life; it's more about my way of looking. I like how Robert Wilson's spirit permeates everything he puts onstage. I want to go after that: making the work that much your own, a reflection of yourself. That's what is fascinating about doing a body of work: it winds up looking like you. The quality of my work is the quality of my personality. All the stories and quotations from art history become part of that personality. When a work is good, it reeks of the person who made it.

At the same time, I deliberately try to obliterate myself onstage. I try to achieve a different state. It's an exaggerated form of traditional acting: immersing yourself in a world and a character. Sometimes, when I am so far inside my characters, I get outside them. I feel like I'm watching them.

If there's a way of manifesting a character or psyche of a character, it's probably by making him do crazy things onstage. He has to be externalized. If I ever did naturalistic work onstage, it would probably look funny or cynical. I think things need to be bold now, because we're competing with everything else—the media, for one. We have to make the work exciting. It can still be art, but it shouldn't be boring. The time for boring art has passed.

What I'm talking about has a lot to do with my experience in clubs, where the work had to be short, abbreviated, and to the point. That was good for me to go through. People at Sarah Lawrence should have to do things in clubs. When I started doing performance, I went into it like a banshee: I was in drag, screaming, and lip-synching. A lot of my work used these attention-getting devices. It's the showman in me. The club scene embraced the whole prewar Berlin myth: drag, drugs, debauchery. But, now, that's all out of my system. That was a time when "anything goes." I don't think that's enough now—so I'd like to take more time workshopping and developing pieces. But I still plan to transport my audiences.

I want to take the spectators somewhere else. I don't want to reiterate what we're seeing on the streets. I want to give them something that they haven't gotten before. There are only so many things that we can talk about, as artists. So it's the *way* that we talk about them that's important.

In the *Pass the Blutwurst, Bitte* piece, I wanted people to look at the way I put things together, the way I chose to tell a story that you knew from the start. Other pieces are also derived from familiar sources. That's a luxury we have right now: we can make art as we quote art. But I use that historical material to go somewhere I've never gone to before. I could easily use material from the present, but I don't want to. It's around us all the time. The first chance I get, I want to get away from it. Even if I were dealing with mundane, present-day things, I would still try to transform them into some other reality.

I haven't yet dealt with language or dialogue, but when I do, it will probably be as explosive or abstract as the other components. I'm not interested in naturalistic or conversational dialogue. If I were ever to use that style, I'd probably bracket it—put it in quotes: talk is cheap. You can talk all the time. You turn on the TV, people are talking. Unless you deal with language in a new and revelatory way, it's still just talking.

I think that politics can be a very strong part of a work, but that's not what I'm about. When I sing in a high voice, that's political. But, generally, politics breaks through a piece and brings it back to the present. And, when it comes to making art, I want to go somewhere else.

All the same, I love being in front of an audience and working with them. I put myself on the spot all the time. You get an enormous amount of energy from an audience. I try to fill the space with my own energy and life. It's an exchange. If I weren't interested in that exchange, I would still be making pictures—something private. I'm more interested in being in front of people. As long as they react in some way, that's all I need.

Karen Finley

All of my pieces are works-in-progress: each night I perform one I work on it more. Each time I try out certain things for myself. I don't rehearse my performances. My show may fail when I go up there. I don't know exactly how the words will come out. I don't know what I'm going to be doing. I don't plan out the order of the scenes. The only thing I do beforehand is write my script. I spend a long time doing that. But I can always get rid of the script. The piece may not have a center when I perform in this way—but that's what makes it performance: that gives the work an edge. It gives it a sense of real time. The biggest difference between performance and theatre is real time.

I came out of the California art scene—where performance art first broke out of the structure of theatrical time and formality. Chris Burden would do his thirty-second pieces—taking a plant and throwing it on the floor, then leaving. Acconci could do his stuff in galleries. The Kipper Kids were making their work then. An artist could even scale a fish in front of people and call that a performance. The art wasn't about writing proposals, or paying your dues, or waiting fifteen years to have a show someplace. I didn't have the patience for that. Instead, you could make your art *now;* you could do it *now;* anyone could do it.

I try to keep working that way even when I do something in a place like The Kitchen. (Did you know that The Kitchen actually had a line on their contract that said I had to perform for at least forty-five minutes? I refused to sign it. I refused to be a part of that. What does the *length* of my piece have to do with my piece?) Many people thought that the night you saw it *The Constant State of Desire* didn't go very well—but for that reason I thought it was the best night: people could see me as I am. I showed that a performance is really hard to do. I think it's my duty as a performer to be completely honest, to show what I'm going through. During a performance I try to let all the different voices going on inside my head be heard. I say what is usually left unspoken in a performance— what is on my mind at the moment. I don't censor myself. The world of my performances is this inner world—inside me, inside anyone.

That's why I deal with a lot of personal information in my pieces. When I started performing, I would talk a lot about autism and suicide. I wanted to use things that happened in or around my personal life. I think that the feminists were doing that a bit. I want to explore even more of that now. I plan to continue taking my senses, rage, and emotions into performance.

In other cultures, dreams and personal life have always been sources for art. But we think that there is something wrong with that. I've seen pieces in which artists are talking about something they know nothing about. I think that's even worse. If you're not working with personal material, the goal is to make it look personal. And if the work *is* personal, the goal is to make it seem universal.

So it's not important whether or not I actually have experienced what I talk about. That's not relevant to my performance. There is a more important reason to perform personal experience: if you were raped by your father, or molested by an uncle, or left for dead when you were five years old, you feel completely alone. You feel like you're the only one. I'm very concerned about people who have suffered a tragedy and carry it on their shoulders to their graves. They don't let it break. They keep it inside themselves. In my work, I try to point out that we all have a story.

I think my work is getting more political because of that. Right now, I'm interested in AIDS and AIDS victims—bad things happening to good people. I also try to show females in power, and to show different ways in which women have been abused. I use the fact that women are the ones who feel for both men and women—or at least they think that they should be. I use that as a strength, not as a weakness, and try to make my work very passionate, not conceptual. In my performances, I also try to dispel myths. I feel I have a responsibility to denounce the myths about women and psychology created by Freud and others like him. I have to talk about these things until people stop asking me whether or not I'm a feminist.

A lot of my work has to do with ideas of sanity and insanity. I was very affected when I read *The Madman and the Nun* by Witkiewicz. I like how he depicted insanity. Sanity for me is the ability to let yourself go—to release yourself—and then to pull yourself back in again. I try to show that progression in my pieces: the rhythm and beat of my performing is very important. It's like a heartbeat. I'm dependent on words for this; the audience has to create their own images from my words. So I use all my energy to speak them. It's almost like a trance—or something religious. Sometimes the tension gets very intense. That's when I snap off very quickly. I think I'm cruel to the audience that way. I sometimes break the tension by doing something with the food I have onstage. If, for instance, I'm talking about rape—you need something to relieve that intensity. I use food—something that allows me to be physical for a change. What's important in all of this is the rhythm—which I can change and experiment with in each performance. I'm looking for a new timing. I always have been, ever since I started performing in California.

Richard Elovich

I can safely close my eyes while watching a lot of current theatre and still know what is happening onstage. So I want to make puzzling performances that compel the audience to watch. The spectators will have to orient themselves; they will be making choices. There is no centralized intelligence telling them what to look at. Instead, I want to provide various routes for an audience to travel through a piece. My work, though narrative, should leave room for people to participate—to construct the piece by choosing how to watch it. Spalding Gray said that *Sakonnet Point* "allowed the mind of each audience member the chance to create its own text." I'm working with that process myself.

For this reason I'm interested in a kind of Cubism in performance. Cubist pictures are about the process of looking, rather than its object. I think Cubism is closer to how we actually see or experience. Most of the things that happen to me are fragmented—events in the day, relationships—and, in order to understand them, I have to first assemble the pieces: I have to re-collect them. I'm not sure that I find a linear piece convincing: it doesn't reflect that task. Instead, I'm interested in a kind of "exploded reality"—a flattened perspective of reality that reveals its structure.

I arrived at this way of thinking after watching a lot of dance. I grew up on theatre, but it really didn't contribute to my development. I went to Broadway as a kid. When I was older, I saw my first Jeff Weiss play, an early part of *And That's How the Rent Gets Paid*. But I didn't think, "This is something that I would like to make." I never felt a connection to it. I saw The Wooster Group's *Point Judith* in 1979. I saw a lot of Charles Ludlam. André Gregory's *Alice in Wonderland*. Nothing. The first connection came while seeing Merce Cunningham's dance: I was absolutely exhilarated with what I saw. I never once believed that his choreography was arbitrary or abstract, but I loved the fact that I could sit in the audience and make choices or follow different tracks. I knew Jim Self, then a member of the company, and could sit in on rehearsals. When watching Cunningham's dance, I would always want to try out some sort of text with it. Not a text that would limit, pull, and pin the dance down to the ground—but a text that would fly with the movement. I wanted to write like Cunningham choreographed.

Writing, for me, is about gathering. I'm accumulating source material all the time: writing things down, writing stories, something that might be happening to me, that I read, that I remember. When I sit down to write a script, I assemble all these fragments. It's all appropriated—even if I wrote some of it. That's how I redefine "originality": originality lies in assembling, not writing, a work. I believe the way that I'll assemble the found material will be original.

Rauschenberg used to refer to some of his works as "combines"—assemblages of many things. I'd love to use that term in relation to performance. Rauschenberg also made paintings comprised of various photographs. He used three types of photograph: a newspaper photo, a photo or reproduction of something famous—a Leonardo, for example—that is more well known than the original, and a photo of a famous person, someone known mostly by his or her face as reproduced in the media. Again, that's how I work. Instead of photographs, I appropriate well-known scenes from performance: *Bobby's Birthday Like That* is partly made up of scenes from *The Invisible Man, Midnight Cowboy,* and *A Man and A Woman.*

For that reason, I dissociate myself from playwrights. I'm not interested in writing a play. Nor am I interested in reading plays or seeing plays performed. It's already a fixed form. It's more interesting to me to create a form, to grapple with something for which a form has not yet crystallized. With plays, I get overwhelmed by the dominance of established craft: ideas are reduced by formulas. I prefer to fight my way out of a paper bag, to make the rules. The rules will come from my own experience, not some playwriting workshop.

When I stage my work, I try to treat my own texts as someone else's. I don't think that I could completely divorce the writer and director in me; but I would like to get a bit detached from my text. Complete the text, know the text is there—and then pull away from it. I know that I couldn't work successfully as a director if as a writer I felt I had created a finished manuscript. A finished script is too prescriptive. For me, a script is unsized material that's meant to be cut, sized, and sewn together in the rehearsal period. The writing is continued as staging. Scripts, like videotapes, are documentations.

I read recently about Liz LeCompte directing Spalding Gray in the *Rhode Island* trilogy. As Gray would go through his autobiographical text, LeCompte would take notes about what she liked and didn't like. She would direct by selection. I wonder if that is something I can do by myself. I try to remove myself from my autobiography when I write my pieces. To do this, I write my autobiography as biography: I borrow and stage fragments of other biographies as a way of getting at mine.

Four biographies have recently had a large impact on me: the biographies of Giacometti, Frida Kahlo, Diane Arbus, and an autobiography called *The Words to Say It* by Marie Cardinal—about her recovery from mental illness. I find something of myself in each of these stories: by being very selective, I find something in them that I can wear. Like a mask, biography conceals my face, but reveals a personal truth. It is akin to a screen.

I think about screens in terms of painters. Chaim Soutine grew up in a Russian village that prohibited the direct perception of certain things: it was an orthodox Jewish taboo. If a hoary-looking stranger came through the town and a pregnant woman looked at him, it could affect her unborn baby. Soutine was fascinated by this. As a child, he once made a drawing of a rich townsman, and consequently, was beaten. When he moved to Paris—and finally had the freedom to paint the naked object—he still put up a screen: it was called expressionism.

Another example is the Walt Disney of surrealism, Chagall. Chagall always painted through the screen of fantasy. Also, there is Mark Rothko. Rothko's early work is very surreal. Later, Rothko was painting the screen itself. His screens had the resonance of life behind them. I wonder if I can't do something similar with the biographies, the quotations from films and other sources. I can't find the words to say something directly, so I have to use a lot of other material to talk about something very simple and private.

Many of my pieces are about this problem of telling. My work is full of stories, yet I want to draw attention to the storytelling: I don't want to illustrate. My performances go back and forth between the story and the telling. The stories in my work may be borrowed or made up, ordinary or idiosyncratic, transparent or opaque—yet I hope that the method of storytelling will betray the truth of experience. It's not a talking cure. There's nothing therapeutic about this. But it's only by witnessing someone else telling my story that I find out what it is about.

That's why I'm not interested in solo performance. The first test of material, before you take it to an audience, is to get other people engaged with it. If the material is too private or solipsistic, then it probably won't interest other artists, other performers. It doesn't surprise me when someone says that all my characters sound the same—because I think they do: they're all coming from me. But even though a lot of my work is autobiographical, it's often unrecognizable to me after I finish rehearsing it. After I assemble fragments of biographies, put stories into the mouths of characters, and give it all over to performers, I think the material fascinates me less: it becomes less self-absorbed and narcissistic. It becomes a dwelling that other people can live in—that other people can perform in and contribute something to. It becomes a shared work, rather than a personal ritual.

That collaboration is also a first step to effective political theatre. I think we can find an enormous power in working together, in collective behavior. Organizing is very important—feeling connected to the people you're working with. Our lives are bound by a lack of sharing. We're wrapped up in ourselves, on treadmills, caught in what Burroughs called "the algebra of need." Sometimes I think my life is so small, unambitious, and impoverished. But in performance, I can learn how to conceive something larger, and then learn how to share it—without feeling that I've lost something. The first thing to do is to find your own way and make your own rules. That's where we are now—in performance, in life: you've got to find your own place to start. You're able to learn something then.

Charles Atlas

Now that video has generated some of the most striking recent exhibits in museums and galleries, it challenges the imagination to think that the art form is only three decades old. Charles Atlas, a pioneering force in video dance, comments on its early development in his discussion with Matthew Yokobosky, associate curator of film and video at the Whitney Museum of American Art, which exhibited Atlas's 1997 video installation *The Hanged One*. Atlas, who is also a performer, directed many of the video dances of Merce Cunningham, including the solo *Blue Studio*, and the ensemble works *Locale*, *Torse*, and *Channels/Inserts*, for which he created traveling mattes to represent the simultaneity of dances in multiple spaces. Earlier painstaking processes of editing on paper or on video equipment, which Atlas describes, have by now given way to computer editing, a technology more tuned to his emphasis on spatial detail and frame accuracy. The dynamic interplay of time and space conceived by Atlas points up the difference between dance as event and dance as document. Whether live performance or electronic media, Atlas explains: "I view all of my work as negotiating time. I really think about time as a medium."

Atlas, who recognizes the distinctions among video dance, film dance, and dance for television, is an admirer of the Hollywood musical and popular dance, while also regarding as an early influence the split screen of Andy Warhol's *The Chelsea Girls*. His videos, and set, costume, and lighting designs for artists as diverse as Cunningham, Karole Armitage, Michael Clark, Marina Abramovic, and such companies as the Joffrey Ballet, Paris Opera Ballet, and Deutsche Oper Berlin, reflect an openness to many tastes and styles and to theatrical elements. Of *The Hanged One*, Atlas contrasts its outfront sexual content, incorporating fetishism and drag, with the more circumspect demeanor of his Cunningham/Cage roots, whose aesthetics of chance he now views, provocatively, as a strategy for avoidance of any declaration of identity. The contemporary proliferation of video and installation work reflects the focus on personal imagery and the body, and issues of public space and spectatorship, that increasingly occupy American culture in its address of technology and human presence as persistent motif.   BGM

Conversation with Matthew Yokobosky, 1997

The Real Charles Atlas

Matthew Yokobosky: The Hanged One (1997) seems to be a culmination of your work in several media—video, set design, lighting. What was the process that you used to fully realize and integrate these media, because in other situations you're asked to work on a video or you're asked to design a set or lighting, but *The Hanged One* is an example of a situation in which you are creating all of the elements.

Charles Atlas: Well, partly the creation of *The Hanged One* was a culmination of a process that began many years earlier, when I created the video installation *Times Five: For Merce* (1983). And it was also a result of my artistic choices—visually, aesthetically, and thematically. *Times Five* was a five-channel video installation, which utilized material that I had created during the years I worked with Merce Cunningham. I think at that point, 1983, we had been working together for about ten years. I was trying to combine the work we had done in film and video dance [including *Blue Studio: Five Segments,* 1975–76] with Super-8 footage that I had casually shot on tour, in addition to some historical material from the Cunningham archive.

MY: So it was a ten-year piece.

CA: Yes. A memory piece. It was done at a time before computer editing and the way I planned the editing was on graph paper. Before I began the physical editing of the videotape, I laid down the same base material on all five tapes. It consisted of twenty-second color fields, alternating with ten-second countdowns—10, 9, 8, 7, 6, 5, 4, 3, 2—and then I'd go to a color field again. Then I went back to this big chart (graph paper), and certain things would be edited out of synch and others would be in synch across the five channels. It had a kind of a musical feeling. This work was created at a time before the advent of synch boxes. So the synch was: say "go," press play on all five videotape players at once, cross your fingers, and hope that they all ran in synch. The result was this piece where numbers were popping, colors were sometimes happening, and sometimes the dance material, the Super-8 footage, or the historical footage was on the monitors.

MY: Did it have sound?

CA: It had sound. It had the audio from the various dance pieces, but sometimes I kept it silent, depending on what else was happening visually. *Times Five* was my first real installation experience; later, I did a version

493

of it at the Centre Georges Pompidou, Paris. There it became a twenty-monitor installation that was very mixed up, very Cunninghamesque.

MY: And how were the monitors arranged?

CA: On one side about twenty monitors were scattered and inset into the walls; and on the other side of the room, there were five free-standing monitors in a row displaying all five channels of the piece. Images moving side by side was of interest to me because it was an outgrowth of the two-channel pieces [*Torse* (1977); *More Men* (1980–82)] that I did both in film and in video earlier on. One of the films that had influenced me at that time was Andy Warhol's double-screen film *The Chelsea Girls* (1966). It was just something I always liked: two at once. That's the part that developed into installation for me. I didn't do any other installation work until I did an earlier version of *The Hanged One*, which was titled *The Laugh of Number 12* (1994) at the nineteenth-century Fort Asperen, The Netherlands. My installation was one of three parts of a larger exhibition conceived by Anna Tilroe. The other two parts were by Tony Oursler and Irene Grundel. We each had a floor of the Fort; my floor had fifteen rooms. Each section of my installation was in a different room or alcove, but in a consecutive sequence. So I was able to control how people encountered the work; they could only walk one way. It was both an ordered experience and an amusement park ride, or maybe more like a haunted house at a midwestern carnival.

MY: In a theatre situation, you have to sit and the imagery moves in front of you. In a museum installation, you have to walk from room to room in order for the images to change.

CA: Yes. Basically, I view all of my works as negotiating time. I really think about time as a medium. Part of my sense, though, of how to create an engaging installation has to do with my response to having seen other installations that quite frankly were boring. I remember though one video installation that I thought, "Oh, maybe there's something a little bit more complex going on here." It was a work by Raul Ruiz in Paris. The video wasn't that complicated, but it was really an interesting installation. It was about an image and it was about a feeling. I wish people would create more works that reach the complexity of live performance. As I remember the work, it was two rooms side by side. One was the inverse of the other and there was a television in both rooms that had images, but it just felt like memory. It really had a visceral feeling. You could look and find other layers of meaning in the images, and how they were arranged in the rooms. It wasn't presentational like many installations, where you know nothing's going to change more or less—you understand the concept and then you just wait for it to happen.

So one of my impulses in creating *The Hanged One* was to make an installation that I would like to see, where you weren't sure what was going to happen next; things would change, it would have a sense of sequence, it wouldn't be predictable. In order to accomplish this, I wanted to use all of the resources available, and utilize the video within the design of the space, sound, and lighting—something I rarely have seen. Also, theatrical lighting is not something that's normally done in an installation, and I realize how important that is in the overall feeling of a work, from my experience in lighting design for the stage. So I wanted to include lighting as a means to define the space. You see, I've never really made objects for sale, and so it's not like lighting to highlight objects. For me, the lighting is an essential part of the whole, as a means to indicate a sense of change and a sense of mood.

MY: You created a very active space in *The Hanged One*. It's not just looking at one monitor or one image. A motorized sculpture vibrates unexpectedly every few seconds or an image suddenly bursts onto a screen. You maintain the element of surprise throughout the entire experience.

CA: Thanks. I do feel that surprise is a necessity in order to grab a person's attention in a world soaked by the media. Someone like Andy Warhol was very good at grabbing your attention. But after you grab their attention, there has to be something else that will keep them interested—something that will repay the viewer for staying with it. And that is where having worked in performance has been an asset. A presentation these days has to be entertaining in some way; other matters can be included, but if you don't have the audience's attention . . . I have always had a taste for pop culture and media things anyway, or from the lower art world, I should say.

MY: One of the aspects that has always been striking to me about *The Chelsea Girls* is the mix of formal elements, black-and-white and color film stocks, and its being a dual projection—two films projected side by side. But also many of Warhol's works are very sexually charged. When you look at attendance records from the sixties for avant-garde films, it was the films that dealt with sexuality that were the most popularly attended: Kenneth Anger's *Scorpio Rising* (1963), Jack Smith's *Flaming Creatures* (1963), and Warhol's films, some of which were actually shown on Forty-Second Street. Those were the highest attended films. Not Stan Brakhage. And so I felt that you were dealing with subject matter in this video installation that most artists creating video installations tend not to address. Your work strongly explores varieties of sexual expression: exhibitionism, fetishism, drag, which are all highly aesthetic sexual cultures. It was the same with Anger and Smith and Warhol.

CA: I try to do things, first of all, that I haven't seen. Yet they have to be part of my experience. So I have found that if I present aspects of my normal experience in the arena of the general culture, it seems pretty extreme to some people. It's been a quality that my work has had, but how consciously I incorporated those elements into my work is difficult to know. When I was working more in dance, I was bringing elements that were parts of my life into that arena. And it wasn't that they were *such* shocking elements, but in the context of the dance world, some people felt that it cheapened the dance experience.

MY: As if modern dance was devoid of pop culture, pop sexuality.

CA: I grew up in the school of Cunningham/Cage. At a certain point though, I realized that if you were very tuned into their style, you could see that there were personal expressions there, but it was very oblique and covert—coming from a time really formed in the forties and fifties when people's sexuality, especially gay sexuality, wasn't acceptable even in the art world. Artists were released when they could do work that wasn't about who they were.

MY: They could still be dancers, but they didn't have to be sexual.

CA: They didn't have to do a tango with two men or they didn't even have to express their sexuality at all. If you take that to a further point, you didn't really have to express anything of who you were. It became a chance world; there was no way of connecting it with your intention. At a certain point, I saw that as well, though it's not what I wanted to find. It was a cover-up, and I have an impulse which is very much to tell it like it is; I want to see things that have credibility. And, yes, I have found that really absent from a lot of work in a lot of areas.

As far as the sexuality or many other aspects that I'm dealing with . . . a big influence on my work has always been the films of Samuel Fuller, especially *The Naked Kiss* (1964). You go for the obvious. It's not like you're going for the *obvious*, but that you don't want to be afraid to confront something head on. You don't want to talk about it around the corner. My favorite painter is the same way, Manet. His work is very flat. Confrontational yet absent. He gives a kind of ambiguity of surface, and that's my favorite kind of thing. Warhol had that too. Absolute directness and yet by the choice of image, it resonates. I don't know if that's the right way to say it, but I think that my work resonates. And each work explores very different areas . . . I work with different ideas in different kinds of projects. Some people have said, "Oh, he's a chameleon. He doesn't really do any one thing." But—

MY: —your whole body of work does have common threads running through it.

CA: Some projects, since a lot of my work has been collaborative, are really the results of a collaboration . . . but I have always had a very strong, formal input.

MY: Obviously a collaboration can happen when someone is approaching you or you're approaching someone else. But if it's your project, how do you choose the collaborators that you are going to work with?

CA: Love. When someone asks me, Why are you working with Michael Clark, and not working with people who are older and more famous? I have always said, "I just love his work, and that was it." I loved it and that was my impulse. Of course, that was a major collaboration for me that lasted for many years in many, many different formats. I have been a little slower to take on new collaborations, knowing that even if you love something or someone, there has to be personal chemistry. There are a lot of artists. I've worked with some other artists who were very difficult and picky, but that goes with the territory if you do the kind of work that I like. And sometimes I felt, "Well, it's worth it." And sometimes I felt, Well, I love the work, but I really shouldn't be working with this person. I learned collaboration from the master of collaboration, Merce Cunningham. And he had John Cage. Two very strong people. They both had to figure out a way to work together and not impinge on each other. And they figured out something that worked for them. Merce then had the great fortune of working with some other really incredible artists.

MY: It almost appears as if the collaborative part really was also a chance operation.

CA: But not really. I felt that the collaborative part was temperamental. In the overall scheme, if you have artists like Bob Rauschenberg, who has very strong, attention-getting ideas . . . you wouldn't cast him as your designer if you didn't want his work to either fit into a piece or to go against it. Whereas Jasper Johns is a different kind of artist. His work blends in a different way. It's not so interruptive.

MY: So that's how you choose somebody that you want to collaborate with . . .

CA: I have also found that, especially when I started working with Michael Clark, that it was really fun because he was very young at the time. He was like twenty, twenty-one. For some reason I always prefer work that's a little bit rougher than the more finished work. And as a collaborator, it certainly gives you more space to work within . . . if you respect the other artist's work. Michael had such a clear voice. I figured out many ways to work with him. There was room for me if I wanted to put my imprint; but, I don't want to cover up something that a dancer is doing if it's beautiful.

MY: That brings up a very good point. "Video dance" has gotten a bad reputation because it often ends up being a document of a dance rather than being a videotape. You've been able to negotiate that territory in your works that are video, not a document. How do you negotiate that?

CA: It's a question of casting really. I have had arranged marriages, a couple, and other times I've had collaborations that don't work in the best way. But I don't feel that I've ever had one that I've regretted or that I didn't learn something from. I see what happens in the process with people and the ego conflicts. It's really luck as to whether a collaboration works or not. Not totally luck.

MY: Your works though don't appear as if they are staged or performed, and then simply videotaped. It's also the way you edit the material together. When I look at a scene such as the one in *Because We Must* (1989), where Michael Clark is wearing the dragon tail, and you continually have images roll in from the top of the screen down. It's going against a type of seamless editing. It's more of a rhythmic editing. You're not just recording. You're also adding editing into the formula of collaboration.

CA: I think it goes back to what kinds of things I like to see. I am a big movie buff and I have always loved movie musicals. Dance film at its most developed is still shocking in its accomplishment; that those Hollywood filmmakers, cameramen, actors, designers, et cetera, were all able to figure out how to accomplish those difficult setups before the age of video. Now you can have feedback on video, and more precisely choreograph elaborate shots. There must have been a lot of notation on paper. Those films were a big influence on me, and that's how I like to see performers. When I went into the more serious, the fine art side of dance, I always wanted to bring in things that made for an experience that I would want to share with someone.

MY: So when you did your three-hour history of dance in film for Dutch television, *Television Dance Atlas* (1993), were you choosing works that influenced you, or were you really trying to tell a history of dance? You included works and sequences that perhaps wouldn't be included in a volume of *That's Entertainment!* (Jack Haley Jr., 1974). You included Mary Wigman, ice dancing . . .

CA: The thing that I felt that I was really trying to address in that piece was not video dance, not film dance, but dance for television. In other words, television being something that you watch in your house. I wanted to try to hold an audience. I was given the whole evening to program: three and a half hours. So I had a two-and-a-half-hour section and then a break and then they had news and commercials and then they showed my collaboration with Michael Clark, *Because We Must,* for an hour at the end. I really went through my work and the work of others. I really didn't include any shot that I didn't think was good. If I couldn't edit something, I didn't use it. Every shot had a logic for me and that was a real pleasure to just put in sequences that I thought were excellent, and made sense and were really television dance. There was competitive ice skating, which I discovered after looking at more performancey ice skating on video. The best ones were the ones where there was full light, with signs in the background and a commentator. That's all a part of the form. Then I tried to organize it by themes. I never ever saw the whole thing from beginning to end before it was broadcast, because there was no time to play back such length and see what I had done. I just had to figure it out on paper.

MY: Well, it was really just terrific. I watched it twice.

CA: Oh really? Thanks. Now when I watch it, there are aspects of the work that I would change—little things. Mainly moments of repetition, but every moment in the videotape contains work that I really felt was something I would want to see, exploring the many different definitions of what dance is, specifically on television.

MY: The editing style that you used for *Television Dance Atlas* and your earlier descriptions about editing on paper—working out all the timings/editing decisions on paper—indicate how you were working with a time-based media; how you were working with a medium that has time codes. Now you are working with computers and new technologies. How have these advancements expanded your editing vocabulary?

CA: In terms of editing, I feel fortunate that I came of age in the age of film because editing film is very precise—frame-accurate. I always felt in the early moments of video art history, the editing was very poor, mainly because it was so approximate due to the equipment's lack of precision. When I got involved with dance, I became frame-obsessed. There was one frame that was the right frame to edit on and one frame that wasn't the right frame. And so all through my video editing—it's more common nowadays—I was always striving for frame-accurate editing, knowing what kind of rhythm I wanted to create. I would, and still do, watch footage over and over again and then edit a piece. Now I can look back and point out which edits took me forever. When I was doing that early editing, I learned a lot. And my learning curve went way up in terms of understanding dance when I started editing Merce's work: the discussions I had with him about what were good performances and bad. I really learned about phrasing too.

MY: Clearly, the majority of your work has been with dance and performance. How did you make the choice between becoming a video artist as opposed to becoming a choreographer since now you're putting the elements of choreography onto other media—motorized sculptures, movement through editing, et cetera?

CA: From my childhood I wanted to make films. I used to go to films every Saturday in St. Louis. I was a film nut. So, when I went to college, I went to see everything: European films, American films, old Hollywood films. About the time that I began making film, I met Merce and I realized that I had a feeling for movement and dance, though I was never a dancer. I never had thought about it.

MY: Not a dancer, a choreographer.

CA: But there is no one who ever became a choreographer in the modern dance movement who wasn't a dancer first; it was not like in ballet. But even in ballet, you had to have a lot of dance training though you didn't have to be a star dancer to be a choreographer. In modern dance, the whole tradition had been to become a dancer: dance with a company, find your own style, do your own choreography based on your own individual body—your body's own idiosyncratic movement. And so it never even occurred to me. It's only later in the middle of my working when I was taking phrases of dance on videotape and altering them so radically through the editing that I felt like I was in a sense choreographing.

MY: When you edit, do you review and judge your footage in the same way that you did for *Television Dance Atlas*, only using the pieces that you feel are absolutely the best? The videotapes in *The Hanged One* are seamlessly edited; very specific pieces of footage were chosen.

CA: The question for me is usually how to get the material down to a manageable, workable size. I am really very strict with what I allow myself to use . . . sometimes I like to be messy, but on purpose.

MY: Has editing on a computer allowed you to be more precise? For example, the images of Nicola Bateman Bowery swinging in *The Hanged One*. You've altered the speed at which she swings.

CA: It has, to a point. But I've always pushed the limit of the technology that I was working with at the time. Over time, though, technology catches up and it's easy to do. I think of *Channels/Inserts*, the film I did with

Merce; some of the transitions were animated frame by frame. It took six months to do, because we were very, very into cuts. We never did a dissolve because it was not precise enough. It was like a failure of precision.

MY: You never use dissolves.

CA: I use them now, but only as an effect, for fun. But even when it was easy to do dissolves later with advanced videotape editing equipment, I always felt I had to make the choice. Because there is a *choice*. There is a right place to edit. I didn't like work that was approximate. So in *Channels/Inserts* I wanted to do the traveling animation as a way of changing an image, but not in a one-count, which is what a cut or edit is. I had these things that changed in relation to the image, these strange patterns. That was a six-month process, drawing and painting the mattes, pencil testing, et cetera. It was just ridiculous. And it's the same thing with computer editing. I did that five-channel piece [*Times Five: For Merce*] completely like you would now do with computer editing, but then we did it without a computer.

Every time I would go into an editing studio, I had to brace myself. The editors in general wouldn't care whether it was two frames after the blink or one frame, but it did matter to me. I would draft my notes and I would say, "Edit two frames" instead of a number because there were no time codes. I was essentially doing computer editing in a sense before there really was computer editing. So I was relieved when it became possible. It is a big improvement for me to have a computer. It drove me crazy to do editing on video equipment, when you couldn't be frame-accurate. Frame accuracy especially makes a difference when you're editing to music. It's also possible to take two frames and repeat and repeat and repeat and repeat them. Whereas if you were going into an online edit in the mid-seventies and told the editor, "Now edit these two frames and then these two, and repeat," they basically did not want to do it.

MY: You talked a bit about how difficult it was to edit the music then. It seems that the role of music in your pieces has changed over the years. Meaning, it seems that at the beginning of your career with Merce you were working with music and chance associations. The music could be added after the editing. Then with Michael Clark, it's been more on the music itself. In the installation, it's more ambient; it's more afterward. How do you decide how the music will interact with the imagery?

CA: It's really project by project. I don't have total control over every project I do. The issue really is music and not music. It was a huge advantage for me as filmmaker to start my work in dance within silence, because I happen to be more of a visual person than an audio person. So I've never been as sensitive to sound as I've been to visuals, but also I was trained to make things work visually and kinesthetically. The music was added on however it went with the dance, which was something that I accepted early on as a part of Merce's work. Then I found that I did have some control within that area of chance. I remember *Channels/Inserts*. It had audio by David Tudor, and I was just given the music to put onto the videotape, but I did have a choice of having it two seconds earlier or two seconds later to start. That was the only choice I had. I had a range, which it would have been okay to use, so I could have just done it by chance and let it be, but, of course, I had to play it every possible way to see which one worked best. And there was one which I felt was the best, and that's what I did. It didn't influence the editing; it influenced the way I put the music on.

The first music piece I did where the image and the music were together was *Parafango* (1983–84). The music was by David Linton, and there were some sections where Karole Armitage's choreography was not really set. In some sections the music was very percussive, where I edited both to and against the music. The amount of extra time and complexity was worth it for me because I loved the music, but it really was an astonishing experience and a new thing. Before that I did a piece called *Secret of the Waterfall* (1982–83), where instead of music, we used poetry and it was very much like working with music. It was with Anne Waldman, Reed Bye, and Douglas Dunn. So that was about using the sound and the rhythm of the words, and then also it was so instructive about how movement and sound could work together. I've always been concerned about legibility, that things can be heard together, that you can see something and hear something, so that you can experience the totality of the work. That's been a guiding principle. With Michael Clark's work, again, he used music in a much more traditional way even though it was non-traditional music, on the beat.

MY: He was trained in classical ballet.

CA: He was trained in classical ballet, but he really liked punk music as well as many other different kinds of music. One thing that I learned from doing *The Hanged One* is how—and this was an ambitious piece, fifteen channels—several sounds could be controlled and distinct within one common space.

MY: In a lot of what you have said, you've talked about how you've tried to push the technology, the editing. Your choice of subject matter for *The Hanged One* definitely pushed the boundaries of various themes: hanging, bondage, foot fetishism. Do you feel that your choice of subject matter is an attempt to push the audience as much as you're pushing yourself?

CA: It's strange. I've always liked work and done work that has pushed. Working in television, subject matter was always an issue. But it's really not a question of pushing the boundaries, as much as it's a question of the culture getting more restrictive.

MY: The culture(s) you experience are much more free than the general culture. You go out to drag clubs for an evening, or you go to some other environment with colored lights, lots of ambience, sound. But it's also people in more dramatic styles of dress. Those are things that you then bring into your work, because those are the things that fascinate you. The people coming to see this work during the daytime are not the same people that are out at midnight until 3:00 A.M. You are bringing a kind of nighttime culture into the daytime and that's a real transfer of aesthetic.

CA: These are the arenas of freedom these days. The more underground, smaller venues. When I look at my own history and the people I've worked with, I've always been attracted to the extreme fringe—the creativity of those cultures. When I was working with Merce Cunningham and then with Karole Armitage, who was a kind of punk breakaway at the time, and then Michael Clark, who was even more extreme, then with Leigh Bowery . . . this is where my interest and attention goes. I tend to like younger work, work that's more open and explorative and not quite formed, because I find it more expressive. I know it even in my own work. I know when I'm doing something as to whether it resonates for me, and even then I will still try to be open to something else.

I remember being in London working with Michael Clark, and I had some crazy friends who used to make scratch videos for screenings in clubs. I showed them an early version of *Hail the New Puritan* (1985–86), a piece that I had just finished with Michael. One of the guys said, "Oh, you should have more fun with it." And that's something I've always thought. He was absolutely right. There's no reason that I can't have fun.